Fifth Edition

Thinking About Women

Sociological Perspectives on Sex and Gender

Margaret L. Andersen
University of Delaware, Newark

Allyn and Bacon
Boston • London • Toronto • Sydney • Tokyo • Singapore

Series Editor: Sarah L. Kelbaugh
Editor in Chief, Social Sciences: Karen Hanson
Editorial Assistant: Jennifer DiDomenico
Marketing Manager: Brooke Stoner
Editorial-Production Administrator: Annette Joseph
Editorial-Production Coordinator: Susan Freese
Editorial-Production Service: TKM Productions
Electronic Composition: WordCrafters Editorial Services, Inc.
Composition Buyer: Linda Cox
Manufacturing Buyer: Julie McNeill
Cover Administrator: Linda Knowles

Copyright © 2000, 1997, 1993, 1988, 1983 by Allyn & Bacon
A Pearson Education Company
160 Gould Street
Needham Heights, MA 02494
Internet: www.abacon.com

Between the time website information is gathered and then published, it is not unusual
for some sites to have closed. Also, the transcription of URLs can result in unintended
typographical errors. The publisher would appreciate being notified of any problems
with URLs so that they may be corrected in subsequent editions. Thank you.

Library of Congress Cataloging-in-Publication Data
Andersen, Margaret L.
    Thinking about women : sociological perspectives on sex and gender
/ Margaret L. Andersen. — 5th ed.
      p. cm.
    Includes bibliographical references.
    ISBN 0-205-30226-2
    1. Women—United States—Social conditions. 2. Feminism—United
States. 3. Social institutions—United States. 4. Social change.
5. Feminist theory. I. Title.
HQ1426.A6825   1999
305.42'0973—dc21
                                          99-26314
                                            CIP

Printed in the United States of America

10 9 8 7 6 5 4 3 2 1   04 03 02 01 00 99

For my grandmother,
Sybil R. Wangberg
(1895–1995)

*A woman who always said she was just ordinary
but who was very special to those of us who loved her*

❧ Contents

Preface   ix

About the Author   xiv

PART I   *Introduction*

1 Studying Women: Feminist Perspectives   1
The Sociological Imagination   4
Defining Feminism   7
Women's Studies and the Inclusion of Women   10
The Sociological Framework for Thinking About Women   16
Summary   16
Key Terms   17
Discussion Questions/Projects for Thought   18
Suggested Readings   18

PART II   *Gender, Sex, and Culture*

2 The Social Construction of Gender   19
Sex, Gender, and Sexuality   20
The Institutional Basis of Gender   22
Sex Differences: Biology and Gender   24
Socialization and the Formation of Gender Identity   30
Socialization across the Life Course   35
Theoretical Perspectives on the Formation of Gender   41
Limitations of the Socialization Perspective   46
Summary   48
Key Terms   48
Discussion Questions/Projects for Thought   49
Suggested Readings   49

**3 Gender and Culture: The Social Construction
of Knowledge   51**
Gender, Language, and Popular Culture   53
Gendered Images in the Media   56
The Sociology of Knowledge   65

Women and Educational Thought   69
Gender, Science, and Society   74
Summary   78
Key Terms   78
Discussion Questions/Projects for Thought   78
Suggested Readings   79

4   Sexuality and Intimate Relationships   80
The Social Construction of Sexuality   80
The History of Sexuality in the United States   81
Contemporary Sexual Attitudes and Behavior   83
Race, Sexuality, and Power   87
Sexual Development over the Life Cycle   88
Love and Intimate Relationships   92
Friendship   96
Lesbian, Gay, and Bisexual Experiences   97
Summary   102
Key Terms   103
Discussion Questions/Projects for Thought   103
Suggested Readings   104

PART III   *Gender and Social Institutions*

5   Women, Work, and the Economy   105
Historical Perspectives on Women's Work   106
What Is Work?   114
Gender and Class Stratification   115
The Contemporary Status of Women   117
Poverty and Welfare   136
Work Environments for Women   139
Intersections of Family and Work   143
Policies for Gender Equity   148
Summary   150
Key Terms   151
Discussion Questions/Projects for Thought   151
Suggested Readings   151

6   Women and Families   153
Historical Perspectives on Modern Families   154
Feminist Perspectives on Families   158
Portraits of Contemporary Households   163
Race, Gender, and Families   174
Families and Social Problems   181
Summary   192
Key Terms   193
Discussion Questions/Projects for Thought   193
Suggested Readings   193

7   Women, Health, and Reproduction   195
The Social Structure of Health   196
Race, Class, and Health   198
Women, Work, and Health   200
Gender, Health, and Social Problems   204
The Politics of Reproduction: Birth Control, Abortion, and Childbirth   210
Women and the Health Care System   224
Summary   227
Key Terms   228
Discussion Questions/Projects for Thought   228
Suggested Readings   229

8   Women and Religion   231
Sociological Perspectives on Religion   232
Religion and Social Control   234
Religion and the Emergence of Feminism in the United States   236
Women and Religiosity   238
Women's Status in Religious Institutions   243
Religion, Racism, and Social Change   247
Religion as a Basis for Antifeminism   249
Faith, Feminism, and Spirituality   252
Summary   255
Key Terms   257
Discussion Questions/Projects for Thought   257
Suggested Readings   257

9   Women, Crime, and Deviance   259
Origins of Deviance Theory   261
Sociological Perspectives on Crime and Deviance   263
Women as Criminals   269
Women as Victims of Crime   274
Women in the Criminal Justice System   282
Summary   287
Key Terms   288
Discussion Questions/Projects for Thought   288
Suggested Readings   288

10   Women, Power, and Politics   290
Defining Power   291
Women and the State   293
Women and the Law   295
Women in Government   297
Women and the Military   303
Rethinking the Political   308
The Women's Movement   310
Summary   320
Key Terms   321

Discussion Questions/Projects for Thought   321
Suggested Readings   322

PART IV   *Feminist Theory and Social Change*

11   Women and Social Reform: Liberal Feminism   323
Frameworks of Feminist Theory   324
The Liberal Basis of Modern Feminism   326
Liberalism as a Mode of Social Thought   327
An Enlightenment for Women?   330
Mary Wollstonecraft   331
Harriet Martineau   333
John Stuart Mill and Harriet Taylor Mill   335
The Critique of Liberalism   343
Summary   344
Key Terms   345
Discussion Questions/Projects for Thought   345
Suggested Readings   346

12   Radical Alternatives: Socialist and Radical Feminism   347
The Political Context of Radical Feminism   348
The Marxist Perspective   350
Socialist Feminism   357
Family and Economy in Capitalist Society   358
Radical Feminism   362
Intersections of Capitalism and Patriarchy   365
Comparing Liberal and Radical Feminism   371
Summary   373
Key Terms   374
Discussion Questions/Projects for Thought   374
Suggested Readings   374

13   Conclusion: New Directions in Feminist Theory   376
Feminist Epistemology   377
Feminism and Postmodernism   380
Feminism and the Analysis of Race, Class, and Gender   385
Key Terms   387
Discussion Questions/Projects for Thought   387
Suggested Readings   387

Glossary   389

Bibliography   393

Name Index   421

Subject Index   429

❧ *Preface*

Thinking About Women, Fifth Edition, introduces students to understanding women's experiences in society from a sociological perspective. The book provides a comprehensive review of feminist scholarship in the social sciences and is interdisciplinary in scope, although it is grounded in sociological theory and research. The sociological perspective is particularly important to women's studies because it situates individual experience in the context of social institutions. *Thinking About Women* is not intended to help students find personal solutions to collective problems, but it does show how the experiences of women and men are created through social institutions and can therefore be transformed through institutional change.

Although the primary focus here is on women, one cannot study gender without reexamining the social structure of men's lives, as well. Gender patterns the experiences of both women and men in society through the construction of identity and consciousness, the development of belief systems, and the distribution of power and economic resources. *Thinking About Women* reviews each of these dimensions of women's experiences in society. It does so through reviewing the current research on the social construction of gender and gender stratification in contemporary social institutions.

Since the publication of the first edition of *Thinking About Women* in 1983, feminist scholarship has flourished in all disciplines. Within sociology, the sociology of sex and gender is now the largest research section; women's studies programs across the United States and, indeed, around the world have continued to grow. Early in my academic career, I could read every piece of feminist scholarship written; now, it is barely possible to keep up with developments in my own field, much less the other disciplines. Such excitement makes working on a book such as this both thrilling and daunting. One book cannot possibly reflect the breadth and depth of feminist writing, but it can excite readers about the possibilities for the new thought, research, and action that feminist scholarship brings.

The fifth edition of *Thinking About Women* represents some of the transformations that have been made in the scholarship on women in the last two decades. In this edition, I did not find it as necessary to provide an ongoing critique of existing sociological work so much as to integrate new research and scholarship on women and gender into the subjects covered in previous editions. Reviewers of the previous editions also indicated that contemporary students were extraordinarily diverse in their reactions to feminism and in their own feminist beliefs. Some students (women and men) are strong feminists in their own right, com-

ix

mitted to multiculturalism, and sophisticated in their understanding of the significance of gender in everyday life. Others are more conservative; reviewers indicated they needed an approach that would make feminist thought accessible to those who were initially put off by it. The introductory chapter will capture the attention of students who think there is no longer a need for feminism. I hope this new edition continues to educate students of diverse backgrounds and perspectives in the continuing necessity for feminist analysis and action.

Like the earlier editions, this new edition of *Thinking About Women* integrates scholarship on race, class, and gender throughout. Just as traditional scholarship has been flawed by excluding women, so is feminist scholarship flawed whenever it excludes women of color. Feminist studies are not meant to construct abstract analyses that have no relevance to human lives. Although one purpose of feminist scholarship is to develop more accurate accounts of social life, its purpose also is to provide the knowledge that will enable the creation of a society that works for all women. Feminist studies are flawed whenever they reflect only the experience of White, middle-class women. Throughout this book, readers should ask, "Is this true for women of color?" Because feminist analysis seeks to understand the commonalities and differences in women's experiences, sound feminist scholarship should reveal the interconnections of race, class, and gender in all social relations.

Similarly, feminist theory has provided rich analyses of the structure of heterosexual institutions and social construction of sexual identities. This edition incorporates these analyses, both in the chapter on sexuality (Chapter 4) and in other discussions throughout. Data and research have been updated to keep the book as current as possible, although the organization of the book is much the same as in earlier editions. This new edition includes current material on welfare reform, teen pregnancy, and poverty among women. It also includes a new section on language, gender, and popular culture, added in response to suggestions from reviewers. More research on bisexuality and transgendered identities is presented and the discussion of the sex-gender continuum has been strengthened. Tables, figures, and data have been updated throughout to reflect the most recent material available.

Part I introduces students to feminist perspectives in women's studies, and Part II studies the significance of gender in everyday life, including the social construction of gender (Chapter 2); the gendered character of knowledge, including in popular culture, the media, and education (Chapter 3); and the importance of gender in sexual and interpersonal relationships (Chapter 4).

Part III examines gender in the context of contemporary social institutions, including work, family, health, religion, crime, and politics. These chapters (5–10) show how gender is experienced and structured within institutions and include reviews of empirical literature in these diverse subject areas.

Part IV reviews theoretical perspectives in feminist thought and the origins of the women's movement. These chapters (11–12) are organized according to the dialogue that exists among liberal, socialist, and radical perspectives in feminist theory. Chapter 13 examines new developments in feminist theory, particularly new questions in feminist epistemology, feminism among women of color, and postmodernist theory.

Throughout the book, research findings are integrated with concepts and theory. The book's basic premise is that empirical research makes sense only in the context of theoretical analysis; thus, attention is given to the frameworks of feminist analysis and what they reveal about observed social facts in regard to gender and women's experiences.

A Note on Language

Transforming thought to be more inclusive of gender, race, and class also involves a process of transforming language. As the civil rights and women's movements have taught us, the language we use to describe different groups is deeply social and political in nature. It can belittle, trivialize, marginalize, and ignore the experiences of different groups.

In this book, I have capitalized *Black* because of the specific historical experience of African Americans in the United States and because, increasingly, this practice represents the self-identity of African American people in this country. For consistency, I have also capitalized *White*. The experience of being White has not historically been associated with a group identity in the same sense that being Black has signified a racial identity; yet new scholarship is emerging that now shows how the term *White* has been socially and historically constructed. Categories like *Black* and *White* are fraught with social meaning, with implications far beyond seemingly simple matters of writing style. Although not all readers will agree with my stylistic decisions about capitalizing these contested terms, I hope it will challenge them to probe the sociological meanings of these labels. The terms *African American* and *Black American* are used interchangeably throughout the text. I have also used *Native American* and *American Indian* interchangeably.

When referring to Latinos, I use *Latino* in the most generic sense—to refer to all groups of Spanish descent in the United States. I use the feminine form, *Latina*, where appropriate. *Latino* and *Hispanic* are sometimes used interchangeably. I use *Chicana/Chicano* to refer specifically to those of Mexican descent born in the United States. I have used *Hispanic* when that is the label used in the research being cited. These distinctions are particularly problematic in citing government data. In most reports, the U.S. Census Bureau groups Puerto Ricans, Cubans, and Mexican Americans together. Even worse, in many of these reports, Hispanics are included in the category "Black," as well as "White."

I realize that these general categories homogenize the experiences of groups with diverse social, cultural, and historical backgrounds. The same is true of the phrase *women of color*. These categorical labels also reflect common experiences held across groups and, as such, are sociologically useful despite their limitations. Likewise, "Asian American" is a category incorporating highly diverse group experiences. Many of the data sources used here do not report on Asian Americans; thus, some of the empirical work here is limited in its ability to capture these diverse experiences.

My choices about language and style are not perfect, but language and style reflect ongoing social and political, as well as linguistic, problems. Readers should be aware of the significance of language in discussing the many topics that are part of this book. New scholarship on gender and different racial and ethnic groups also promises to add to our knowledge in years to come.

Pedagogical Features

The fifth edition of *Thinking About Women* retains the pedagogical features of the fourth edition. Graphics, where appropriate, illustrate the empirical data discussed and break up the visual presentation of text to capture students' attention. At the end of each chapter is a list of Key Terms to highlight major concepts. A glossary of all key terms, with brief definitions, is included at the end of the book.

There is also a list of Suggested Readings at the end of each chapter, with annotations to catch students' interest. The books included were selected particularly for their significance in the literature and for their accessibility to undergraduate readers. These lists of readings are intended to provide students with materials that can be useful in class projects or research papers or to simply give them additional readings on subjects they find fascinating.

Finally, I have included several Discussion Questions/Projects for Thought at the conclusion of each chapter to stimulate student interest and provide the basis for classroom projects, exercises, or group discussions. The questions and projects synthesize and highlight major topics from each chapter.

Acknowledgments

I am fortunate to work in a community of scholars who take seriously the study of gender and its relationship to race and class. Over the years, my work has been enriched by collaborating with many faculty in colleges and universities across the United States who are working to incorporate more on gender, race, and class into their teaching and thinking. There are many people to thank for sharing ideas, research literature, teaching practices, and citations with me. I especially thank Maxine Baca Zinn, Anne Bowler, Patricia Hill Collins, Ken Haas, Valerie Hans, Sandra Harding, Elizabeth Higginbotham, Lionel Maldonado, Carole Marks, Patricia Yancey Martin, Joanne Nigg, Harry Shipman, Ronnie Steinberg, Howard Taylor, and Lynn Weber for their friendship and support. Discussions with them have helped me think about many of the questions this book raises.

I also wish to acknowledge those individuals who reviewed the fourth edition of this book for Allyn and Bacon and provided useful comments: Pearl Green, University of Southern Colorado; Lin Huff-Corzine, University of Central Florida; Ricki Ann Kaplan, East Tennessee State University; Amy Lee Oliver, Bluefield State College; and Susan Ostrander, Tufts University. In addition, I would like to acknowledge those individuals who reviewed earlier editions: Nancy R. Kelley, Fitchburg State College; Nancy L. Meymand, Bridgewater State College; Brent S. Steel, Washington State University at Vancouver; and Anne Szopa, Indiana University East.

I also thank the students at the University of Delaware who have discussed this book with me in a variety of contexts—both in and out of classrooms; their curiosity and willingness to learn more makes writing this book for them a real pleasure. I thank especially Wei Chen and Cathleen Brooks for the work they have done as my assistants. Thanks, too, to Sarah Kelbaugh, Series Editor, and the editorial staff at Allyn and Bacon for the work they have done to help produce this project.

I have completed this edition of *Thinking About Women* while serving in an administrative post at the University of Delaware, which has made finding the time to write (indeed, the time to think!) a serious challenge. I would find my administrative work far less satisfying, however, if I had not found a way to keep working as a scholar/teacher, too. All this would be impossible to do alone, even though managing a full-time administrative job and several writing projects means I spend many weekends and early morning hours alone in my study. I could not have accomplished all this without the help of those who support my work. I thank Melvyn D. Schiavelli, Provost at the University of Delaware, for helping me keep my work as a sociologist going while I work as an academic administrator. My very special thanks go to Ann Draper, Lisa Huber, Jeffrey Quirico, Donna Goldman, and Cindy Sterling for all they do to support my work; I simply could not have done this without their help.

My gratitude also goes to Richard Rosenfeld for understanding and supporting my work—now through five editions and numerous other projects. His love and the extra care he provides marshal my energy and keep me on an even keel.

M. L. A.

About the Author

Margaret L. Andersen (B.A., Georgia State University; M.A., Ph.D., University of Massachusetts, Amherst) is Professor of Sociology and Women's Studies at the University of Delaware, where she has also served as Dean of the College of Arts and Science and Vice Provost for Academic Affairs. In addition to the sociology of gender, her research and teaching interests include race and ethnic relations; she has consulted nationally on the integration of race, class, and gender studies into educational curricula. She has served as editor of *Gender & Society* and is the author of *Race, Class, and Gender: An Anthology* (Wadsworth, 1998; coedited with Patricia Hill Collins), *Social Problems* (Addison Wesley Longman, 1997; coauthored with Frank R. Scarpitti and Laura L. O'Toole), and *Sociology: Understanding a Diverse Society* (Wadsworth, 2000; co-authored with Howard F. Taylor). Andersen is a recipient of the University of Delaware's Excellence-in-Teaching Award and is former president of the Eastern Sociological Society.

❧ Chapter 1
Studying Women
Feminist Perspectives

Why think about women? According to much popular thinking, equity for women has been achieved. Formal barriers to discrimination have been removed. Women have moved into many of the top professional positions, are now the majority of college graduates, and are more visible in positions of power than at any other time in the nation's history. Over the past 25 years (the full life span of many of you reading this book), the position of women in U.S. society has changed dramatically. The majority of women are employed, and they now number close to half of those in the workplace.

Attitudes have changed, too. The majority of young women now say they would prefer to combine marriage, children, and a career. Men have also changed. In the early 1970s, nearly half of all men thought that a traditional marriage—in which the husband provided for the family and the wife ran the house and cared for the children—would be the most satisfying life-style. Now, half of all men say the most satisfying life-style would be a marriage in which the husband and wife share responsibilities—work, housekeeping, and child care (Roper Organization, 1995). The majority of Americans also favor continued efforts to strengthen women's status (see Figure 1.1).

These changes have led many to conclude that women now have it made, that as long as women and men choose a satisfying life-style, no further change is needed. Consider the following facts, however:

- In the 1990s, women college graduates who worked full time earned, on average, 70 percent of what men college graduates earned working full time (U.S. Census Bureau, 1998a).
- Despite three decades of policy change to address gender inequality at work, women and minorities are still substantially blocked from senior management positions in most U.S. companies (Glass Ceiling Commission, 1995).

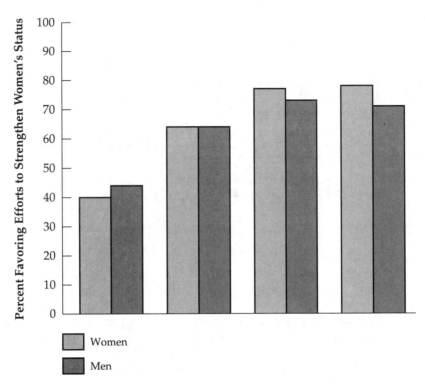

FIGURE 1.1   Changing Attitudes: 1970–1995

Source: Data from Roper Organization. 1995. *The 1995 Virginia Slims Opinion Poll.*
Storrs, CT: Roper Search Worldwide.

- One-third of all households headed by women are poor; the rates are higher for African American women, Latinas, and Native American women (U.S. Census Bureau, 1996).
- Each year, 5 million women experience some form of violence, two-thirds of it committed by someone they know (Craven, 1997).
- Despite the fact that they are the most likely to be employed, women of color are concentrated in the least-paid, lowest-status jobs in the labor market (U.S. Department of Labor, 1998).
- Employed women work, on average, an additional 33 hours per week on household tasks, not including child care; the average for employed men is 20 hours (Shelton, 1992).

These facts indicate that although women may have come a long way, there is still a long way to go. Look around, and you will see many signs of the status of women in society. In the grocery store, for example, women are clustered in those departments (deli and bakery) that are least likely to lead to promotion; men, on the other hand, predominate in departments such as produce and groceries, where the majority of store managers begin (Reskin and Padavic, 1994). In schools, women constitute a large majority of elementary school teachers, but through the higher grades and into college, women become a smaller proportion of the faculty. Despite the recent movement of more women into political office, the vast majority of those who make and enforce laws are men, particularly among those holding the most influential positions. Women can now be ordained in some religious faiths, but many religions still hold that women's proper place is in the home, reproducing and rearing children.

Even in interpersonal interaction, the difference in status between women and men can be observed. Watch the behavior of men and women around you—how they act with each other and with those of the same sex. In public places, men touch women more often than women touch men. Men also touch women in more places on the body than women touch men. Despite stereotypes to the contrary, men also talk more than women and interrupt women more than women interrupt men or men interrupt each other. Women are more likely than men to smile when interacting with others (especially with men), even when they are not necessarily happy. Men, in general, are less restricted in their demeanor than women and use more personal space. Although these patterns do not hold for all men and all women, nor necessarily for people from different cultural backgrounds, in general, they reflect the different ways that women and men have learned to interact (Basow, 1992).

Many current social problems also call attention to the status of women in society. Violence against women—in the form of rape, sexual harassment, incest, and wife beating—is common. Changes in U.S. families mean that more families are headed by women. Although there is nothing inherently wrong with such arrangements, the low wages of many women mean that female-headed households have an increased chance of being poor. As a consequence, the rate of poverty among children in such households has increased dramatically in recent years. As a final example, the national controversy over health care also has particular implications for women. Although women live longer than men, they report more ill health than men do, spend their later years with more disabling conditions, and tend to take primary responsibility for the health of others in their families (Horton, 1995).

Thinking about women helps us understand why these things occur. For many years, very few people thought seriously about women. Patterns affecting the lives of women were taken for granted as natural or to be expected. Few people questioned the status of women in society, presuming instead that studying women was trivial, something done only by a radical fringe or by frivolous thinkers. Even now, studying women is often ridiculed or treated with contempt. For example, conservative talk-show hosts portray feminism as "leftist extremism," "out of touch with the mainstream," and "an attempt to transport unpopular liberalism into the mainstream society" (Limbaugh, 1992:186–187). Attacks on new multicultural studies, of which women's studies has been a strong part, have accused such studies of only striving for "political correctness" and weakening the traditional "standards" of higher education. Despite these claims, women's studies has opened new areas for questioning, has corrected many of the omissions and distortions of the past, and has generated new knowledge—much of which has important implications for social policy.

Women's studies, as a field of study, is relatively new, having been established in the late 1960s and early 1970s to correct the inattention given to women in most academic fields. Because of the influence of the feminist movement, scholars in most fields have begun thinking seriously about women. Whereas 25 years ago the study of women's lives and gender relations had barely begun, now women's studies is a thriving field of study. It has grown as scholars have thought seriously about women's lives and, in so doing, have reconsidered their understanding of men, too. This process has often required challenging some of the basic assumptions in existing knowledge—both in popular conceptions and in academic studies. Scholars have found that thinking about women changes how we think about human history and society, and it revises how social institutions are understood. Thinking about women also reveals deep patterns of gender relations in contemporary society. Much of the time, these patterns go unnoticed, but they influence us nonetheless. Often, we take these patterns of everyday life for granted. They are part of the social world that surrounds us and that influences who we are, what we think, and which opportunities are available to us. Women's studies scholarship is transformative; it informs our understanding of women's experiences and changes our thinking about society and the assumptions that different academic fields use to understand the social and cultural world.

The purpose of this book is twofold: to show how the sociological perspective explains women's lives and to show how sociology itself has been transformed through thinking about women. A single book cannot discuss all of the research and theory that has been developed to understand women's experiences, but it can show how knowledge has been reconceptualized as the result of thinking seriously about women's lives. This chapter introduces you to some of the basic premises of sociology and how it has been informed by feminist scholarship. The feminist movement has been the basis for the emergent field of women's studies and, as such, it has influenced how scholars in all fields think about women. Feminist scholars within sociology, like their counterparts in other disciplines, have asked how gender is constructed, how it is organized in social institutions, and how social change is possible. The influence of feminism on sociological thinking has been considerable, as you will see.

❧ *The Sociological Imagination*

As already noted, patterns in gender relations are found throughout society, although much of the time these patterns remain invisible to us. At some point, however, you may start to notice them. Perhaps at school you see that most of the professors are men and that, among students, men tend to be more outspoken in class, or perhaps at work you notice that women are concentrated in the lowest-level jobs and are sometimes treated as if they were not even there. It may occur to you one night as you are walking through city streets that the bright lights shining in the night skyline represent the thousands of women—many of them African American, Latina, or Asian American—who clean the corporate suites and offices for organizations that are dominated by White men.

Recognizing these events as indications of the status of women helps you see inequities in the experiences of men and women in society. Once you begin to recognize these patterns, you may be astounded at how pervasive they are. As the unequal status of women becomes more apparent, you might feel overwhelmed by the vast extent of a problem most people have never acknowledged. What you see might become troubling, and you may find it difficult to imagine how these long-standing inequities can be changed, but once you start to question the position of women in society, you will want to know more and will begin to ask questions such as: What is the status of women in society? How did things become this way? How does learning about women's experiences change one's thinking about men? How can we change the inequalities that women experience?

Adrienne Rich (1976), a feminist poet, suggests that simply asking "What is life like for women?" will create a new awareness of the situation of women in society and history. This questioning, in part, is what the feminist movement has encouraged in most of the academic disciplines. With whatever question we begin—whether it is "Why is there so much violence against women?" or "Why is it that women clean the offices and men manage them?"—by virtue of asking, we are creating new questions and new issues for investigation. These questions form the basis for feminist theory, and it is this process of questioning that gives birth to a sociological and a feminist imagination.

The **sociological imagination** was first described by C. Wright Mills (1916–1962), an eminent sociologist and radical in his time. Mills's radicalism was founded, in part, on his passionate belief that the task of sociology is to understand the relations between individuals and the society in which they live. He argued that sociological understanding must be used in the reconstruction of more just social institutions. Except for the masculine references in his language, his words still provide a compelling argument that sociology must make sense of the experiences of women and men as they exist in contemporary society. He writes:

> *Nowadays men often feel that their private lives are a series of traps. They sense that within their everyday world, they cannot overcome their troubles, and, in this feeling, they are often quite correct. What ordinary men are directly aware of and what they try to do are bounded by the private orbits in which they live. . . . The sociological imagination enables its possessor to understand the larger historical scene in terms of its meaning for the inner life and external career of a variety of individuals. . . . The first fruit of this imagination—and the first lesson of the social science that embodies it—is the idea that the individual can understand his experience and gauge his fate only by locating himself within his period, that he can know his chances in life only by becoming aware of those of all individuals in his circumstances. (Mills, 1959:3–5)*

Mills's ideas are strikingly parallel to the feminist argument that women can see how their private experiences are rooted in social conditions by discovering their shared experience with other women. In fact, Mills professes that the central task of sociology is to understand personal biography and social structure and the relations between the two. His argument is best illustrated in the distinction he makes between personal troubles and social issues.

Personal troubles are part of the personal experience of an individual. They are privately felt, and they involve only those persons and events in an individual's immediate surroundings. **Public issues** are events that originate beyond one's immediate experience, even though they are still felt there. Public issues involve the structure of social institutions and their historical development. Mills's own example is that of marriage. He says, "Inside a marriage a man and a woman may experience personal troubles, but when the divorce rate during the first four years of marriage is 250 out of every 1,000 attempts, this is an indication of a structural issue having to do with the institutions of marriage and the family and other institutions that bear upon them" (1959:9). Mills's point is that events felt as personal troubles often have their origins in the public issues that emerge from specific historical and social conditions.

Another example is that of a woman who is beaten by her husband. She experiences deep personal trouble, and perhaps her situation appears to her as unique or as only a private problem between herself and her husband. When others in the society have the same experience, then a public issue is found. Common patterns in the experiences of battered wives reveal that wife beating is more than just a private matter. It has its origins in complex social institutions that define women's place as in the home, as subordinate to their husbands, and as dependent on men. In this sense, wife beating is both a personal trouble and a public issue. As Mills would conclude, it is then a subject for sociological study. For feminists, this junction between personal experience and the social organization of gender roles is also a starting point for analysis.

The relationship between personal troubles and public issues reveals an essential premise of the sociological perspective—that individual life is situated in specific social and historical environments. These environments condition not only what our experience is but also how we think about it. Thinking about women from a sociological perspective asks us to look beyond taken-for-granted ways of seeing the world and, instead, to ask how social structures generate the patterns that we see around us in everyday life.

The concept of social structure is central to sociology. **Social structure** refers to the organization of society that shapes social behavior. This is a broad and abstract concept, one that emphasizes the collective and social basis for behavior, not individual motivations and actions. Of course, abstract realities like social structure ultimately have their origins in how individuals behave, but it is the collective and persistent results of that behavior that make social structures; moreover, social structures exist above and beyond individuals in society. Social structures shape individual and group choices, opportunities, and experiences. People can feel the effects of social structures in most of what they do. It is the observation of social structure that is the basis for sociological inquiries.

The concept of social structure is aptly described in the feminist philosopher Marilyn Frye's discussion of oppression. Using the metaphor of a bird cage and supposing that you are looking at the cage from the perspective of the bird, Frye observes that if you look only at one wire, you cannot see the other wires; you miss seeing the whole, because you are focusing only on one part. Even if you look at each wire, discovering all of its properties, you will still not see the whole. Only when you step back from the cage and look at its structure as a whole—seeing all of the parts in relationship to each other—can you understand why the bird cannot escape the cage. As Frye writes, it is then

> *perfectly obvious that the bird is surrounded by a network of systematically related barriers, no one of which would be the least hindrance to its flight, but all of which, by their relations to each other, are as confining as the solid walls of a dungeon. It is now possible to see and recognize: One can study the elements of an oppressive structure with great care and some good will without seeing or being able to understand that one is looking at a cage and that there are people there who are caged, whose motion and mobility are restricted, whose lives are shaped and reduced. (1983:4–5)*

Oppression and social structure are not the same thing. Some social structures are clearly beneficial to some groups. Frye's metaphor, however, helps us understand the meaning of social structure and, in studying oppressed groups, helps us see the social structural basis for group oppression.

As you will see throughout this book, gender is one element of social structure that, along with class and race, shapes the experience of all groups in society. The sociological perspective is fundamentally structural; that is, sociology helps us see the structural origins of individual and group experiences in society. For this reason, it is a critical component of thinking about women.

The study of women requires more than a sociological perspective, however. Much of the current scholarship on women is interdisciplinary. This means that the perspectives of multiple disciplines—whether history, anthropology, psychology, economics, or the humanities—contribute to our understanding of the position of women in society. Although the primary focus of this book is sociological, much of the research on which the book is based is interdisciplinary in character. In addition, contemporary scholarship has been much informed by the women's movement. Feminist thought has stimulated and enriched our understanding of women's lives in society. Feminism shares certain premises with sociology—namely, in understanding that the origins of women's experiences lie beyond individual realities, as Frye's work shows. Feminism, like sociology, points us to understanding the social basis of women's experiences. At the same time, feminism is based on a philosophy of change, particularly that we can build a more just society for women if we consciously understand and seek to transform the social behaviors and institutions that are the basis for women's experiences.

❧ Defining Feminism

Feminism is not easy to define because it includes a variety of political perspectives and ideas. As this book will show, there is no single feminist perspective, and feminist theories and programs for social change sometimes differ quite substantially from one another. Still, there are certain common assumptions within feminism.

Feminism begins with the premise that women's and men's positions in society are the result of social, not natural or biological, factors. Although different varieties of feminist thought have developed, feminists generally see social institutions and social attitudes as the basis for women's position in society. Because in sexist societies these institutions have created structured inequities between women and men, feminists believe in transforming institutions to generate liberating social changes on behalf of women; thus, feminism takes women's interests and perspectives seriously, believing that women are not inferior to men. Feminism is a way of both thinking and acting; in fact, the union of action and thought is central to feminist programs for social change. Although feminists do not believe that women should be like men, they do believe that women's experiences, concerns, and ideas are as valuable as those of men and should be treated with equal seriousness and respect. As a result, feminism makes women's interests central in movements for social change.

Public opinion polls indicate that the majority of women in the United States support feminist issues such as equal pay for equal work; improved child care policies; reduced violence against women; and greater opportunities for women regardless of their race, class, or sexual orientation. Why, then, is the label "feminist" so problematic? The word *feminism* conjures up different images to different people. As a result, many who might even agree with feminist ideas and programs for change find it difficult to call themselves feminists. Sometimes not calling oneself a feminist reflects actual disagreement with feminist policies and perspectives, as will be seen in the discussion of antifeminist movements in Chapter 8. Often, people are reluctant to call themselves feminists because of misunderstandings about what feminism means. Feminism is often equated with being a lesbian, which, in turn, is equated with man hating; thus, for many, rejection of feminism is linked to fears and stereotypes about lesbians. Others feel it is risky to become a feminist, fearing that friends and lovers might reject or tease them. These reactions show how threatened people can be by a movement that advocates change in women's lives. Some have come to think that feminism is no longer necessary, assuming that discrimination has been eliminated by recent reforms and that women and men now stand on relatively equal terms. This book will examine these assumptions, but the point is that many hesitate to call themselves feminists, even when they agree with the ideas of feminism.

The fact is that feminism is threatening to those who want to protect the status quo. This was vividly pointed out in an international context in 1994 when feminist Taslima Nasrin of Bangladesh was threatened with death by Muslim fundamentalists in her home country. Nasrin is a novelist and poet who, in her writing, has challenged Islamic decrees on the role of women, as well as Islam's taboos on female sexuality. When religious leaders called for the writer's death, the Bangladesh government sought to arrest her. With permission of the court to travel outside the country, Nasrin fled to Sweden, although in 1998 she returned to

Bangladesh, where Islamic radicals have revewed their death threat and offered a $5,000 reward to anyone who kills her. This may seem like an extreme case because of the strict control of women, but it demonstrates the challenge that feminism poses to the existing status of women throughout the world. In the United States, resistance to feminism is not so extreme, but it is threatening to many, nonetheless, because it makes people question relationships and social systems that they may have previously taken for granted.

Why is being a feminist so stigmatized? For some, feminism conjures up images of man-hating and aggressive fanatics, as if to be feminist means one cannot be gentle and kind, be reasonable, or have good relationships with men. This is simply not true, as any careful look at the diverse women and men who are feminists would show. Others will say, "I'm not a feminist; I'm a humanist," reflecting their belief in the betterment of life for all persons—men and women alike—but such a view does not preclude being a feminist. In fact, if one really is in favor of the betterment of all human beings, then it is logical to call oneself a humanist, antiracist, *and* feminist. The fact that the label "feminist" carries a stigma to some reflects the deep and continuing devaluation of women throughout U.S. society. Popular stereotypes of feminists as angry, radical, man-hating women encourage this kind of thinking. Some feminists are, indeed, angry—angry about the injustices women face in the workplace, angry about the violence perpetrated against women, angry about persecution of gays and lesbians, and angry about the persistent denigration of women in popular culture. Many feminists are also radical thinkers, particularly if we take *radical* to mean looking at the roots of women's status in society. Feminism includes a wide range of feeling, thought, and ways of being, none of which are so narrow and ugly as the popular stereotype of feminists suggests.

Finally, many feminists are men, although men may find calling themselves feminists especially difficult. Adopting a pro-woman attitude puts men and women at odds with the dominant culture. Men may think that by calling themselves feminists, they will be thought of as gay, itself a stigmatized identity in the dominant culture. As you will see in Chapter 4 on sexuality, this labeling, rooted in the homophobic attitudes of our culture, is a form of social control. It is culture's way of trying to force men and women into narrowly proscribed roles as feminine and masculine heterosexuals. Men who call themselves feminists—some of whom are gay, others of whom are not—are men who support women's rights, who do not believe men are superior to women, and who are willing to work for liberating social changes for women and men. This shows another point about feminism—that men are subjected to cultural expectations about masculinity that affect their emotions, identities, and social roles.

Although not everyone who reads this book will be or become a feminist, each person should at least be willing to examine the questions that feminism raises in order to learn what constitutes feminist thinking, to be able to describe and understand the situation for women and men in contemporary social institutions, and to make informed judgments about thinking about women and diverse feminist perspectives.

❧ *Women's Studies and the Inclusion of Women*

The development of women's studies as a discipline stems from criticism of other disciplines that have excluded or distorted women's lives. Traditional systems of knowledge have ignored women altogether or frequently portrayed them in stereotypical and demeaning ways. Women's studies—such as African American studies, Latino studies, Asian American studies, gay and lesbian studies, and Jewish studies—teaches about the history, culture, and contemporary experiences of those who have been excluded from traditional academic fields. In doing so, these fields have transformed scholarship across the disciplines by bringing more complete and inclusive analyses to the study of diverse human groups.

Women's studies, with its origins in the women's movement, is grounded in research and theory and in political commitments to improve and transform the status of women in society. Feminist scholars see that educational curricula are nested within the traditional culture and therefore reflect the same sexist, racist, cultural, and class biases that are found in the dominant culture. Women's studies rests on the premise that changing what we know about women will change women's and men's lives; consequently, developing women's studies as an academic field is seen as part of the process of transforming women's situation in society.

Not only do feminist scholars believe that academic inquiry must be tied to social change, but their critique of traditional scholarship is focused on problems in the content and method of traditional scholarly work. They assert that what is known by scholarly study must make sense of women's experiences. Traditional social thought and scholarship, based largely on the lives of men, have not provided such an account. As a result, feminist scholarship is transforming academic knowledge and the theories and research on which it rests.

Since the resurgence of feminism in the 1960s, women's studies has produced a dramatic outpouring of studies and theories about women in society. These studies have questioned the assumptions and biases of existing work in almost every field, including science, the humanities, and the social sciences. Women working in different fields have discovered that much of what stood for knowledge in their disciplines either was overtly sexist or ignored women altogether. Often, academic women found that they had more in common with each other than they did with the men in their disciplines. As they began to study what their disciplines said about women, they forged new ideas that were critical of preestablished thinking in traditional disciplines. Feminist reconstructions of academic scholarship have now touched every discipline and have resulted in major changes in the assumptions, theoretical frameworks, and research data on which the disciplines rest.

Phases of Curriculum Change

The development of women's studies has evolved through a variety of phases, beginning with the exclusion of women from academic studies. This is what people have labeled the "womanless, all-white curriculum" (McIntosh, 1983; Andersen, 1987). Historically, most academic studies have excluded women altogether. Likewise, most studies have ignored the experiences of Latino, Native American, African American, and Asian American people, or when these groups have been included, their experiences have been shown only through the eyes of dominant groups. Even now, it is common for academic courses to ignore or minimize these groups; the development of multicultural studies in recent years is an attempt to educate people about diverse cultural experiences. Resistance to these more inclusive studies has been fierce and indicates the extent to which new knowledge from women's studies and the different racial-ethnic studies programs challenges existing ways of thought.

As teachers and students have recognized the exclusion of different groups from the curriculum, they have typically moved to a second phase of thinking: the study of women in society, or what has been called the "add-women-and-stir" approach (Bunch, 1987). In this phase, notable women, notable members of racial-ethnic minority groups, or notable gay and lesbian heroes and heroines are added to courses of study. This phase has the advantage of showing the diverse and important contributions made by people who have been ignored; in this sense, it is an important part of reclaiming group history and accomplishments. For example, noting that Dr. Pearl Luella Kendrick invented the first standard DPT vaccine used to protect against diphtheria, whooping cough, and tetanus or that an African American woman, Alicia Paige, was the first to suggest that librarians could use computers to search for books by author, title, or subject (Stanley, 1993) provides important models for achievement and sets the record straight in bringing the contributions of diverse groups to people's awareness.

This "add-and-stir" approach is valuable for unearthing the experiences and contributions of forgotten groups. Often, however, such studies only try to fit women and racial-ethnic groups into preestablished modes of thinking, still taking the White, male-centered experience as the standard through which other experiences are seen. The experiences of women and people of color are not the same as those of White men, however. As feminist scholars have shown, theories of social life centered in White men's experiences are unable to explain the experiences of women and people of color; therefore, new ideas and new ways of looking at the world have been formulated through looking at the experiences of previously excluded groups.

The third phase in curriculum change is one in which women are conceptualized as a subordinate group and their experience is defined as problematic. In this phase, scholars have documented the barriers that women and minorities have experienced in society and history. This phase shows how pervasive and systematic discrimination is in women's experiences, but it also is a phase of scholarship that conceptualizes women primarily as victims. For students, this can be a depressing phase of learning, although it is important in comprehending the conditions that women and minorities have faced in society and history.

None of these phases takes women's experiences as the primary lens through which we see society, culture, and history. In the fourth phase, unlike the previous phases, women are seen in their own terms—not as deviants, exceptions, or problems. Scholarship in this phase values the world of women that has been overlooked and trivialized by studies that take only the dominant-group perspective to be the norm. As a result, scholars working from this perspective have discovered a richness and vitality in women's experiences and cultures, and they have shown how traditional concepts and theories are revised when centered in the experience of previously excluded groups.

One of the best examples of this phase comes from considering housework. Although feminists have encouraged us to think of housework as work, it does not fit neatly into the frameworks typically used to study work. For example, one's occupation usually provides a good measure of one's social status, but because status is also derived from income and because housework is unpaid labor, the status of housewives is difficult to evaluate; moreover, sociologists usually distinguish work from leisure, although this distinction is not so clear in the case of housework. Would we, for example, consider mothering a child to be work or leisure? Child care certainly contains many of the features of work—including a schedule, routinization of tasks, and physical exertion—but it also includes elements of leisure, such as reading a story or walking to a park. It would be difficult to compare the emotional commitment of a mother with that involved in other forms of labor. This example shows that were the study of work to have been generated from women's lives, perhaps different concepts would have emerged to frame our understanding of the work experience.

Asking sociological questions from a woman-centered perspective transforms traditional models of inquiry. Examples from many disciplines show that when women's experiences are taken seriously, new methods and perspectives must be established. For example, in history, feminist scholars have criticized the "women worthies" approach for recognizing only women who meet the male standards for eminence in history. Although it is important to recognize the contributions of prominent women in history, these women stand out because they are exceptional. They do not represent the experience of the majority of women in their time. In their transformations of historical scholarship, feminist historians have shown how even the periods used to define time frameworks in history are based on men's achievements and men's activities (Lerner, 1976). The Renaissance, for example, is typically depicted as a progressive age that encouraged humanism and creativity; yet for women the Renaissance was a time of increased domestication of bourgeois wives and intensified persecution of witches—most of whom were single peasant women. To see the Renaissance from a woman-centered perspective is to see that this was a period marked by increased restriction of the powers of women (Kelly-Gadol, 1976), not the era of creativity and humanism that male-based studies have defined.

Similarly, in the area of psychological development, feminists have revised models of development that have been based on male experience. Gilligan's (1982) classic work on moral development shows how theories of moral development have taken the male experience as the norm and then measured the female experience against it. In fact, as Gilligan shows, women's moral development follows a different plan from men's, with women's orientation toward morality being more contextual than that of men. In other words, women make moral judgments based on their assessments of conflicting responsibilities in a given situation, whereas men are more likely to make moral decisions based on their judgments of competing rights and abstract principles. Gilligan's point is to show not only that men and women have different conceptions of morality but also that men's experiences have been taken by psychologists to be a universal standard by which both men and women are evaluated.

A woman-centered phase in the development of scholarship shows how ideas and theories have been derived from the particular experiences of some men and then have been used as the universal standards against which all others have been seen and judged. In any field, whenever men's experience is the standard, women and other subordinated groups (including many men) can only appear incomplete, inadequate, or invisible.

One objective of women's studies scholarship is to see all groups in relationship to one another and to include multiple human groups in the concepts, theories, and content of human knowledge. Including women and people of color in our studies reveals hidden assumptions in what we have learned from more exclusionary studies. This would be a fifth phase of curriculum development and thought: inclusive thinking—that in which women's and men's experiences are seen in relationship to the other and in which multiple human groups are included in the concepts, theories, and content of human knowledge. These different phases are important descriptions of the academic curriculum, not so much because they measure one type of thinking against another, but because they help us identify hidden assumptions in our thinking. Revealing the assumptions embedded in ideas or knowledge helps us envision the process by which knowledge can become genuinely inclusive and take gender, race, and class together as part of the complexity of human experience.

The Significance of Gender, Race, and Class

The transformation of knowledge through women's studies has shown the inadequacy of generalizing from studies of men to thinking about women. **Faulty generalization** takes knowledge from one experience and incorrectly extends that knowledge to another (Minnich, 1990). Women's studies has shown how not to generalize from the experience of men to the experience of women. Similarly, studies by and about women of color have shown the importance of not generalizing from the experiences of White, middle-class women to all women. Doing so only replaces one false universal (White men) with another (White women).

Developing inclusive thinking reminds us that women's experiences vary by race, class, age, and other social factors. Although women as a group share many common experiences, recognizing and understanding the diversity of those experiences are equally important in the construction of descriptions and theories about women's lives.

For example, again using the example of housework, although much is now being said about the "double day" women experience whenever they are employed and also do most of the housework in their own homes, this situation is not a new development for women of color, who, since slavery, have worked in the homes and raised the children of White women while also caring for their own families. Analyses of domestic work that ignore the domestic labor of women of color, including the relations with White women such a labor system creates, are faulty and incomplete. One of the major challenges for feminist studies is to create knowledge that penetrates the complex dynamics of race, class, and gender relations in shaping the experience of all persons.

Gender, race, and class are overlapping categories of experience that shape the experiences of all people in the United States. This means that race relations shape the experiences of White people and shape the experiences of people of color but in different ways. In the same vein, gender shapes the experiences of women and shapes the experiences of men; furthermore, class relations affect not just the poor and working class but also the experiences of elites and the middle class.

Each of these categories also overlaps with others. This results in distinct experiences for members of different race, gender, and class groups. Individuals may feel the salience of one or another category at a given time, but their life experiences are shaped by the confluence of all three. As an example, an Asian American woman who hears a derogatory remark about Asian Americans experiences racism, but she may also be stereotyped as a woman. That stereotype, however, is likely to be unique to Asian American women (e.g., that they are submissive and passive), whereas a gender stereotype about another racial group of women may manifest itself differently (e.g., that all blondes are dumb). An Asian American woman's experience will depend not only on her gender and race but also on her class. Her identity at any given time may be centered in any one or more of these experiences, but the point is that her position in society (including the opportunities available to her and what people think of her) is conditioned by her race, class, *and* gender position.

This perspective on the simultaneity of gender, race, and class is different from the additive model that has characterized some thinking about women of color. The term *double jeopardy,* for example, has been used to describe the disadvantage that women of color experience because of their race and their gender. This phrase, however, conjures up images of race and gender as separate experiences, whereas they are integrally related in the experiences of different groups. Race, class, and gender form a **matrix of domination**, meaning that the particular configuration of race, class, and gender relations in society is such that together they establish an interlocking system of domination; no one of them can really be understood without understanding the others, as well (Collins, 1990; Andersen and Collins, 1998).

Consider the following: White women may be privileged by their race but disadvantaged by their gender and class. Likewise, African American men may be privileged by their gender, but in the context of race and class oppression, this means something different from saying that White men are privileged by their gender. In fact, thinking about race and class oppression in the lives of African American, Native American, and Latino men makes a word like *privilege* even seem out of place. Analyses that are inclusive of race, class, and gender also do not see White men as a monolithic group. Although White men have historically benefited from their gender and race position, class differences among them, not to mention differences in White men's behavior and beliefs, make universal statements about men inaccurate, just as it is incorrect to generalize to all women based on the experiences of some. As you will see throughout this book, studying women requires an understanding of race and class, too. Scholarship about women of color is newly emerging and is an important dimension of women's studies.

The Growth of Men's Studies

The development of more inclusive work on women has spawned the development of another new field: **men's studies**. As scholars have revised their thinking about women, they have likewise reconsidered the lives of men (Brod and Kaufman, 1994; Kimmel and Messner, 1998; Messner, 1998). The field of men's studies is different from just studying men. Men's studies specifically challenges the patriarchal bias in traditional scholarship, which has tended to take men as the given universal standard against which others are judged. The debates about using the pronoun *he* as a universal term illustrate this well. Research has now found that when *he* is used in the universal sense, those who hear it do tend to presume they are hearing only about men (Henley, 1989). Although use of the word *he* may be intended universally, it has a particular effect and that effect is exclusionary. That is, women become invisible and men emerge as a universal standard. Men's studies challenges this kind of thinking.

Men's studies is also explicitly feminist. In fact, men's studies emerged from the women's movement as men, too, began to see how gender and sexism shaped their lives. Men's studies challenges existing sexist norms and, like women's studies, has an activist stance. As a result, it is not just knowing about men that is important, but men's studies encourages using that knowledge to create a more just world.

Like women's studies, men's studies takes gender as a central feature of social life, seeing how gender shapes men's ideas and opportunities; thus, men's studies is not just about men but sees men as gendered beings. Without men's studies, there is a tendency to presume that only women are gendered, as if gender only affects one group. We know, however, that gender affects the experiences of us all, although in different ways, as we have already seen in the earlier discussion of race, class, and gender. Because of this, men's studies also sees variety among men as important to understanding men's lives. Not all men are sexist in their attitudes and beliefs, although as a group, men benefit from gender privilege; again, however, this varies by social class and race.

Men's studies, like women's studies, also recognizes the importance of sexuality within the matrix of gender, race, and class domination. Heterosexuality is a privileged form of sexual identity; consequently, gays and lesbians suffer oppression because of their sexual orientation. Together, men's studies and women's studies have analyzed the social structures that generate heterosexual privilege, now leading to new areas of inquiry within gay and lesbian studies. Some of this work is examined further in Chapter 4.

❧ *The Sociological Framework for Thinking about Women*

The framework for this book is distinctly sociological. Although much of the research within it comes from other fields or from interdisciplinary work, a sociological perspective forms the core of the book. As you have already seen, the social structural analysis provided by sociological thought is essential to comprehending the situation for women in society. In addition, sociology is an empirical discipline, meaning that its method of study is the observation of events in the social world. Sociologists observe social events, discover their patterns, and formulate concepts and theories that interpret relationships among them. An important point about empirical studies is that when the theories that explain observed events no longer make sense of what is observed or when one's observations change, then revisions are necessary. A central point in feminist criticism of sociological work is that conventional theories have not always made sense of women's experiences and therefore must be revised.

Sociology is also a discipline that claims social improvement as part of its goal. Most sociologists believe that sociology should contribute to the improvement of social life. They differ in how to produce this change—some emphasizing gradual improvement through existing governmental and political channels and others believing that only radical social change can solve contemporary social problems. Regardless of their differences, sociologists believe that the purpose of sociological investigation is to generate improved social policies and consequently to generate social change. Sociologists share with feminists the idea that knowledge should provide the basis for improving the lives of women in society.

In sum, sociology is a discipline that purports to give accurate accounts of the social world and its social problems, with the purpose of suggesting policies and possibilities for humanitarian social change. Feminists have argued, however, that sociology has not always made good on its claims. The purpose of feminist scholarship in sociology, as in other fields, is to use the perspective that the discipline offers to develop more complete and accurate understanding of women's and men's lives.

❧ *Summary*

Although some obstacles to women's equity have been removed, gender inequality can still be easily observed. Despite the fact that many believe equity for women has been achieved, studying the historical experience of women reveals the structures in society that shape gender relations and opportunities for different groups. Learning about women is one way to understand how social structures influence the lives of women and men.

Women's studies is a relatively new field that has often challenged existing modes of thought in most academic fields. A sociological perspective can be used to understand patterns of gender relationships in society. Feminist studies also recognize the experiences of African American, Latino, Native American, White, and Asian American women as unique. Grounded in an analysis of gender, race, and class, these studies have us consider the variety of women's experiences in society and think about how to improve their lives. Feminist perspectives also change how we see men and have led to the development of another new field, men's studies.

Feminist scholars argue that by providing new insights, we are improving social thought, because we are more aware of observations and ideas that have previously gone unnoticed. Early on, two sociologists, Marcia Millman and Rosabeth Moss Kanter, described this process of awareness, drawing from a classic parable:

> *Everyone knows the story about the Emperor and his fine clothes: although the townspeople persuaded themselves that the Emperor was elegantly costumed, a child, possessing an unspoiled vision, showed the citizenry that the Emperor was really naked. The story instructs us about one of our basic sociological premises: that reality is subjective, or, rather, subject to social definition. The story also reminds us that collective delusions can be undone by introducing fresh perspectives. Movements of social liberation are like the story in this respect: they make it possible for people to see the world in an enlarged perspective because they remove the covers and blinders that obscure knowledge and observation. In the last decade no social movement has had a more startling or consequential impact on the way people see and act in the world than the women's movement. Like the onlookers in the Emperor's parade, we can see and plainly speak about things that have always been there, but that formerly were unacknowledged. Indeed, today it is impossible to escape noticing features of social life that were invisible only ten years ago. (1975:vii)*

Seeing without the blinders of earlier perspectives will not reveal ultimate truths about social life any more than will other forms of social thought. Women's studies does not offer final solutions to the problems experienced by women or men in contemporary society, but it has dramatically shown how little we know and what distorted information we have about at least one-half of the human population. Feminist critiques emphasize that much of what we know is tied to the perspectives and interests of dominant groups. The insights feminist thought provides and the self-criticism it encourages have created a new challenge for scholars who are committed to new visions of the future.

❧ Key Terms

faulty generalization	men's studies	social structure
feminism	personal troubles	sociological imagination
matrix of domination	public issues	women's studies

❧ Discussion Questions/Projects for Thought

1. Think about one of the other courses you are currently taking. How are women depicted in this course? If you were to use the phases of curriculum change discussed in this chapter to analyze the presentation of women in this other course, what would you say?

2. Interview your friends and/or family about what feminism means to them. What assumptions do they make about those who call themselves feminists? What does this reveal to you about how feminism is popularly defined?

3. Put yourself in a familiar situation—perhaps at a party or in a classroom or an office. Ask yourself the question similar to what Adrienne Rich has posed: What is life like for women in this situation? What new questions might you ask that would reveal more about women's experiences in this setting than what might be immediately apparent?

❧ Suggested Readings

Baca, Zinn, Maxine, Pierrette Hondagneu-Sotelo, and Michael A. Messner, eds. 1997. *Through the Prism of Difference: Readings on Sex and Gender.* Boston: Allyn and Bacon.
This anthology explores the race, class, and sexual diversity among women and men, both in the United States and in international settings. Through comprehensively examining differences, the editors show how gender is structured in relationship to other social facts.

Brod, Harry, and Michael Kaufman. 1994. *Theorizing Masculinities.* Thousand Oaks, CA: Sage.
A collection of articles articulating the basic concepts and ideas of men's studies, this anthology provides an excellent overview of how feminist thinking is influencing studies about men.

Goetting, Ann, and Sarah Fenstermaker. 1995. *Individual Voices, Collective Visions: Fifty Years of Women in Sociology.* Philadelphia: Temple University Press.
This biographical collection of essays by women sociologists explores their diverse lives and shows how individuals' experiences have led to sociological perspectives on women and society.

Lorber, Judith. 1994. *Paradoxes of Gender.* New Haven, CT: Yale University Press.
This book develops an institutional analysis of gender, showing how it is constructed in society and its significance in all aspects of women's lives.

Minnich, Elizabeth Kamarck. 1990. *Transforming Knowledge.* Philadelphia: Temple University Press.
Minnich's book shows the transformative power of thinking about women, discussing the common errors in thinking that stem from excluding women.

Smith, Dorothy E. 1987. *The Everyday World As Problematic: A Feminist Sociology.* Boston: Northeastern University Press.
As one of the foremost feminist sociologists, Smith provides a critique of traditional sociological thought and new directions for feminist sociological scholarship.

Walker, Rebecca. 1995. *To Be Real: Telling the Truth and Changing the Face of Feminism.* New York: Anchor.
This anthology of writings is directed at young women who are examining the meanings of feminism in their own lives. As experiential and analytical essays, these papers help young women understand the multiple currents of identity in their lives.

Chapter 2
The Social Construction of Gender

To understand what sociologists mean by the phrase *the social construction of gender*, watch people when they are with young children. "Oh, he's such a boy!" someone might say as he or she watches a 2-year-old child run around a room or shoot various kinds of play guns. "She's so sweet," someone might say while watching a little girl play with her toys. You can also see the social construction of gender by listening to children themselves or watching them play with each other. Boys are more likely to brag and insult other boys (often in joking ways) than are girls; when conflicts arise during children's play, girls are more likely than boys to take action to diffuse the conflict (McCloskey and Coleman, 1992; Miller, Danaber, and Forbes, 1986).

To see the social construction of gender in another way, try to buy a gender-neutral present for a child—that is, one not specifically designed with either boys or girls in mind. You may be surprised how hard this is, since the aisles in toy stores are highly stereotyped by concepts of what boys and girls do and like. Even products such as diapers, kids' shampoos, and bicycles are gender stereotyped. Diapers for boys are packaged in blue boxes; girls' diapers are packaged in pink. Boys wear diapers with blue borders and little animals on them; girls wear diapers with pink borders with flowers. You can continue your observations by thinking about how we describe children's toys. Girls are said to play with dolls; boys play with action figures!

When sociologists refer to the **social construction of gender**, they are referring to the many different processes by which the expectations associated with being a boy (and later a man) or being a girl (later a woman) are passed on through society. This process pervades society, and it begins the minute a child is born. The exclamation "It's a boy!" or "It's a girl!" in the delivery room sets a course that from that moment on influences multiple facets of a person's life. Indeed, with the modern technologies now used during pregnancy, the social construction of gender can begin even before one is born. Parents or grandparents may buy expected children gifts that reflect different images, depending on whether the child will be a boy or a girl. They may choose names that embed gendered meanings or talk about the expected child in ways that are based on different social stereotypes about how boys and girls behave and what they will become. All of these expectations—communicated through parents, peers, the media, schools, religious organizations, and numerous other facets of society—create a concept of what it means to be a "woman" or be a "man." They deeply influence who we become, what others think of us, and the opportunities and choices available to us. The idea of the social construction of gender sees society, not biological sex differences, as the basis for gender identity. To understand this fully, we first need to understand some of the basic concepts associated with the social construction of gender and review some information about biological sex differences.

✎ Sex, Gender, and Sexuality

The terms *sex, gender,* and *sexuality* have related, but distinct, meanings within the scholarship on women. **Sex** refers to the biological identity and is meant to signify the fact that one is either male or female. One's biological sex usually establishes a pattern of gendered expectations, although, as you will soon learn, biological sex identity is not always the same as gender identity; nor is biological identity always as clear as this definition implies.

Gender is a social, not biological, concept, referring to the entire array of social patterns that we associate with women and men in society. Being "female" and "male" are biological facts; being a woman or a man is a social and cultural process—one that is constructed through the whole array of social, political, economic, and cultural experiences in a given society. Like race and class, gender is a social construct that establishes, in large measure, one's life chances and directs social relations with others. Sociologists typically distinguish sex and gender to emphasize the social and cultural basis of gender, although this distinction is not always so clear as one might imagine, since gender can even construct our concepts of biological sex identity.

Making this picture even more complex, **sexuality** refers to whole constellation of sexual behaviors, identities, meaning systems, and institutional practices that constitute sexual experience within society. This is not so simple a concept as it might appear, since sexuality is neither fixed nor unidimensional in the social experience of diverse groups. Furthermore, sexuality is deeply linked to gender relations in society, as you will see in Chapter 4. Here, it is important to understand that sexuality, sex, and gender are intricately linked social and cultural processes that overlap in establishing women's and men's experiences in society.

Fundamental to each of these concepts is understanding the significance of culture. Sociologists and anthropologists define **culture** as "the set of definitions of reality held in common by people who share a distinctive way of life" (Kluckhohn, 1962:52). Culture is, in essence, a pattern of expectations about what are appropriate behaviors and beliefs for the members of the society; thus, culture provides prescriptions for social behavior. Culture tells us what we ought to do, what we ought to think, who we ought to be, and what we ought to expect of others.

The concept of culture explains a great deal to us about variation in human life-styles and human societies. Cultural norms (the expectations that culture provides) vary tremendously from one society to another and, within any given society, from one historical setting to another and among different groups in the society. Cross-cultural studies reveal an immense diversity in human social relations, because human creativity and cultural adaptations to different circumstances create a rich and complex mosaic of the different possibilities for human life. As a result of the cultural basis for gender, what it means to be a woman or a man varies across cultures.

In every known culture, gender is a major category for the organization of cultural and social relations, although specific cultural expectations vary from society to society. One feature of a culture is that its members come to take cultural patterns for granted; thus, culture provides its members with tacit knowledge, and much of what members believe as true or what they perceive as real is learned to the point where it is no longer questioned. Culture provides assumptions that often go unexamined but that, nonetheless, fundamentally guide our behavior and our beliefs.

The cultural basis of gender is apparent especially when we look at different cultural contexts. In most Western cultures, people think of *man* and *woman* as dichotomous categories—that is, separate and opposite, with no overlap between the two. Looking at gender from different cultural viewpoints challenges this assumption, however. Many cultures consider there to be three genders, or even more. Consider the Navaho Indians. In traditional Navaho society, the *berdaches* were those who were anatomically normal men but who were defined as a third gender and were considered to be intersexed. Berdaches married other men. The men they married were not themselves considered to be berdaches; they were defined as ordinary men. Nor were the berdaches or the men they married considered to be homosexuals, as they would be judged by contemporary Western culture. Similarly, in some African and American Indian societies, there are those who are biological females living as men, known as *manly hearted women*. They are considered "female men," but they do not have to dress or act like men; they only have to have enough money to buy wives (Lorber, 1994; Nanda, 1990; Amadiume, 1987; Blackwood, 1984).

Another good example for understanding the cultural basis of gender is the *hijras* of India. Hijras are a religious community of men in India who are born as males, but they come to think of themselves as neither men nor women. Like berdaches, they are considered a third gender. Hijras dress as women and may marry other men; typically, they live within a communal subculture. An important thing to note is that hijras are not born so; they choose this way of life. As male adolescents, they have their penises and testicles cut off in an elaborate and prolonged cultural ritual—a rite of passage marking the transition to becoming a hijra.

Hijras occupy a special place within Indian culture and society, a situation stemming from Hindu religion which, different from Western culture, values the ambiguity of in-between sexual categories. Hinduism holds that all persons contain both male and female principles within themselves, and Hindu gods are commonly seen as sexually ambiguous. Hijras are believed to represent the power of man and woman combined, although they are impotent themselves. Hijras perceive sexual desire to result in the loss of spiritual energy; their emasculation is seen as proof that they experience no sexual desire. Their special place within Indian society is evidenced at Indian weddings, where hijras often perform rituals to bless the newly married couple's fertility. They also commonly perform at celebrations following the birth of a male child—an event much cherished in Indian society and the cause for much celebration (Nanda, 1998).

These examples are good illustrations of the cultural basis of gender. Even within contemporary U.S. society, so-called "gender bending" shows how the dichotomous thinking that defines men and women as "either/or" can be transformed. Cross-dressers, transvestites, and transsexuals illustrate how fluid gender can be and, if one is willing to challenge social convention, how easily gender can be altered. The cultural expectations associated with gender, however, are strong, as one may witness by people's reactions to those who deviate from presumed gender roles.

Gender expectations in a culture are sometimes expressed subtly in social interaction, as, for example, in U.S. culture, where men interrupt women more frequently than women interrupt men, where women smile more than do men, and where women have more frequent eye contact with others (Basow, 1992). At other times, gender expectations are not so subtle, as in the cultural practices of Chinese foot binding, Indian suttee, European witch-hunts, and the genital mutilation of women documented in some African countries (Blake, 1994; Hosken, 1979; Jacobson, 1974; Stein, 1978; Wong, 1974). Within U.S. culture, extreme physical practices are also evidenced in the sadistic treatment of women in pornography and in the common surgical practices of face-lifts and silicone implants.

In different ways and for a variety of reasons, all cultures use gender as a primary category of social relations. The differences we observe between men and women can be attributed largely to these cultural patterns.

⮞ *The Institutional Basis of Gender*

Understanding the cultural basis for gender requires putting gender into a sociological context. From a sociological perspective, gender is systematically structured in social institutions, meaning that it is deeply embedded in the social structure of society. Gender is created, not just within family or interpersonal relationships (although these are important sources of gender relations), but also within the structure of all major social institutions, including schools, religion, the economy, and the state (i.e., government and other organized systems of authority such as the police and the military). These institutions shape and mold the experiences of us all.

Sociologists define **institutions** as established patterns of behavior with a particular and recognized purpose; institutions include specific participants who share expectations and act in specific roles, with rights and duties attached to them. Institutions define reality for us insofar as they exist as objective entities in our experience. They are "experienced as existing over and beyond the individuals who 'happen' to embody them at the moment. In other words, the institutions are experienced as a reality of their own, a reality that confronts the individual as an external and coercive fact" (Berger and Luckmann, 1966:58). Institutions

> *are not only here-and-now, given, and self-evident, but also arise within particular and historic environments, and in response to certain felt interests and needs; and as these interests are served, and needs are met and continue to be met in certain typical ways, actions are repeated, grow into patterns, and become firmly entrenched in practice and consciousness. It is just at this stage, when practice and habits pass over into highly organized forms, that we begin to speak of "institutions" as opposed to mere custom or habitual activity. (Payer, 1977:30)*

Understanding gender in an institutional context means that gender is not just an attribute of individuals; instead, institutions themselves are *gendered*. To say that an institution is gendered means that the whole institution is patterned on specific gendered relationships. That is, gender is "present in the processes, practices, images and ideologies, and distribution of power in the various sectors of social life" (Acker, 1992:567). The concept of a gendered institution was introduced by Joan Acker, a feminist sociologist. Acker uses this concept to explain not just that gender expectations are passed to men and women within institutions, but that the institutions themselves are structured along gendered lines. **Gendered institutions** are the total pattern of gender relations—stereotypical expectations, interpersonal relationships, and men's and women's different placements in social, economic, and political hierarchies. This is what interests sociologists, and it is what they mean by the social structure of gender relations in society.

Conceptualizing gender in this way is somewhat different from the related concept of gender roles. Sociologists use the concept of social roles to refer to culturally prescribed expectations, duties, and rights that define the relationship between a person in a particular position and the other people with whom she or he interacts. For example, to be a mother is a specific social role with a definable set of expectations, rights, and duties. Persons occupy multiple roles in society; we can think of social roles as linking individuals to social structures. It is through social roles that cultural norms are patterned and learned. **Gender roles** are the expectations for behavior and attitudes that the culture defines as appropriate for women and men.

The concept of gender is broader than the concept of gender roles. *Gender* refers to the complex social, political, economic, and psychological relations between women and men in society. Gender is part of the social structure—in other words, it is institutionalized in society. *Gender roles* are the patterns through which gender relations are expressed, but our understanding of gender in society cannot be reduced to roles and learned expectations.

The distinction between gender as institutionalized and gender roles is perhaps most clear in thinking about analogous cases—specifically, race and class. Race relations in society are seldom, if ever, thought of in terms of "race roles." Likewise, class inequality is not discussed in terms of "class roles." Doing so would make race and class inequality seem like matters of interpersonal interaction. Although race, class, and gender inequalities are experienced within interpersonal interactions, limiting the analysis of race, class, or gender relations to this level of social interaction individualizes more complex systems of inequality; moreover, restricting the analysis of race, class, or gender to social roles hides the power relations that are embedded in race, class, and gender inequality (Lopata and Thorne, 1978).

Understanding the institutional basis of gender also underscores the interrelationships of gender, race, and class, since all three are part of the institutional framework of society. As a social category, gender intersects with class and race; thus, gender is manifested in different ways, depending on one's location in the race and class system. For example, African American women are more likely than White women to reject gender stereotypes for women, although they are more accepting than White women of stereotypical gender roles for children. Although this seems contradictory, it can be explained by understanding that African American women may reject the dominant culture's view while also hoping their children can attain some of the privileges of the dominant group (Dugger, 1988).

Institutional analyses of gender emphasize that gender, like race and class, is a part of the social experience of us all—not just of women. Gender is just as important in the formation of men's experiences as it is in women's (Messner, 1998). From a sociological perspective, class, race, and gender relations are systemically structured in social institutions, meaning that class, race, and gender relations shape the experiences of all. Sociologists do not see gender simply as a psychological attribute, although that is one dimension of gender relations in society. In addition to the psychological significance of gender, gender relations are part of the institutionalized patterns in society. Understanding gender, as well as class and race, is central to the study of any social institution or situation. Understanding gender in terms of social structure indicates that social change is not just a matter of individual will—that if we changed our minds, gender would disappear. Transformation of gender inequality requires change both in consciousness and in social institutions.

❧ Sex Differences: Biology and Gender

Understanding the social basis of gender raises interesting questions about the significance of biological sex differences. If gender is a social construction, does biology matter? If differences between women and men were determined by biological factors alone, we would not find the vast diversity that exists in gender relations from society to society; moreover, if sex differences were universal in content, what it means to be a man or a woman would not vary from one culture to another. There is, nonetheless, a biological basis for human life. What significance does biology have in shaping the different experiences of women and men in society?

Biological explanations of gender differences are commonplace and popular. It used to be said that women's status in society was somehow "natural," stemming from the fact that women bear children. Although this is believed less now than in the past, how often have you heard people, perhaps even feminists, say, "Oh, he's just behaving that way because of too much testosterone (the male hormone)," or, referring to some observed difference between women and men, "That's just the way women are." Biological explanations of gender patterns in society have a deep hold in people's thinking, but, as you will see, there is not necessarily a fixed relationship between biological features of human life and the social creatures we become. The link between biology and human life is highly mediated by social and cultural influences.

The Biological Basis of Sex Identity

The biological sex of a person is established at the moment of conception and is elaborated during the period of fetal development in the womb. During conception, each parent contributes 23 chromosomes to the fertilized egg, for a total of 46 (or 23 chromosomal pairs). One of these pairs determines the sex of the offspring; they are called the **sex chromosomes**. Under normal conditions, the sex chromosomes consist of an X from the mother's egg and an X or a Y from the father's sperm. The 23 paternal chromosomes (including the X or Y sex chromosome) are selected randomly when the sperm is formed (Hoyenga and Hoyenga, 1979). Genetically normal girls have a pair of X chromosomes (designated 46, XX), and normal boys have the chromosomal pair XY (designated 46, XY). Because the sex chromosome from the ovum is always an X, the chromosome carried by the father's sperm (either an X or a Y) determines the sex of the child. Despite popular belief, there is no evidence that Y chromosomes are stronger than Xs. In fact, the XY male chromosome pair forms a link that is less viable in genetic coding than is the XX female pair. This fact accounts, in part, for the greater vulnerability of male fetuses in the womb and may contribute to higher prenatal and early childhood mortality rates for males (Harrison, 1978).

Following fertilization of the egg, a complex process of **fetal sex differentiation** begins. Before the sixth week of development, the XX and XY embryos are identical; the external genitalia of the embryo remain identical until the eighth week of development. Scientific reports of the process of sexual differentiation of the fetus, however, have been clouded by pervasive images of the passivity of females. The process of sexual differentiation has, as a consequence, routinely been reported in scientific work as determined primarily by the presence or absence of the Y chromosome, leaving the impression that females develop as incomplete or deficient males.

In fact, during the sixth week of fetal development, the Y chromosome stimulates the production of proteins that assist in the development of fetal gonads (Hoyenga and Hoyenga, 1979). Sexual differentiation also involves complex genetic messages encoded on the Y chromosome, the X chromosome, and the non-sex chromosomes; therefore, the Y chromosome, although involved in the process, is not solely responsible for the process of sexual differentiation. Recent research suggests that the XX gonad may synthesize large amounts of estrogen at about the same time that the XY gonad begins synthesizing testosterone, making it appear that ovarian hormones are just as involved in the development of female genitalia as androgens are involved in the development of male genitalia (Fausto-Sterling, 1992).

Ambiguous Sexual Identities

Under normal circumstances, the process of fetal sex differentiation results in unambiguous sex characteristics; however, cases of chromosomal abnormalities sometimes occur, resulting in biologically mixed or incomplete sex characteristics. Studies of such cases reveal the complex relationship between biological sex and the social construction of gender.

Hermaphroditism is "a condition of prenatal origin in which embryonic and/or fetal differentiation of the reproductive system fails to reach completion as either entirely female or entirely male" (Money and Ehrhardt, 1972:5). Normally, during fetal development, fetal gonads would produce sex hormones that, in turn, produce the internal and external sex organs (Hoyenga and Hoyenga, 1979). In cases of hermaphroditism, babies are born with their sexual anatomy improperly differentiated; thus, they may be born with both testes and ovaries or will appear ambiguous or incomplete.

Such cases add an important dimension to discussing the relationship between genetic sex, biological appearance, and sex of rearing. True hermaphrodites typically possess the chromosomal patterns characteristic of normal females or normal males. For example, a genetic female who is prenatally androgenized may be born looking like a boy—that is, with a penis (although sometimes incomplete) and no clitoris. On the other hand, a genetic male may be born with the genital appearance of a normal female. Other cases of hermaphroditism may involve mixed genital appearance. Because we typically assign sex according to the appearance of the external genitalia at birth, cases of hermaphroditism allow us to look carefully at the role of biology and culture in the development of gender identity.

Studies of hermaphroditism reveal the complex interaction of genetic, biological, and cultural factors in the development of a social gender identity. In one case, a genetic male was born with a tiny penis (1 centimeter long) and no urinary canal. At age 17 months, the child was reclassified as a girl. She was given a new name, hairdo, and clothing. Shortly after the sex reassignment, the parents noticed a change in the older brother's treatment of her. Before the sex reassignment, he had treated his "brother" roughly; now he was very protective and gentle toward his new "sister." By age 3, the daughter had developed clearly feminine interests. "For Christmas, she wanted glass slippers, so that she could go to the ball like Cinderella, and a doll. The parents were delighted. The girl continued to receive typically girlish toys from her parents. She continued more and more to show feminine interests, as in helping her mother" (Money and Ehrhardt, 1972:125).

In another well-known case of sex reassignment, the reassignment did not follow from hermaphroditism, but from accidental mutilation when a biologically normal male, age 7 months, had his penis burned off during a routine circumcision. The boy was recreated as a girl, using surgical and hormonal treatment. This child had difficulty adjusting to her identity and at age 14 chose to live as a man, undergoing extensive surgery to partially restore his penis and having a mastectomy. At age 25, he married a women and adopted her children. Some have concluded that his case reveals that one's sense of sex identity is innate, but there is another side to this argument. When the child was growing up as a girl, her peers teased her mercilessly and refused to play with her; she also spent much time having her genitals scrutinized by doctors. By the time the child was a teenager, she was miserable, contemplated suicide, and was then told of what had happened earlier in life (Diamond and Sigmundson, 1997). Although biological identity may have played some role in the child's difficulties, it is also clear that social factors (such as peer ridicule) strongly contributed to the child's difficult adjustment. Thus, the case is evidence for the strong interplay of culture and biology.

These cases demonstrate that biological sex alone does not determine gender identity. In fact, one's gender identity can be different from one's genetic sex. Research shows that sex of rearing is the key factor in determining gender identity, even though prenatal hormones can have some effect on behavior (Money and Ehrhardt, 1972). In other words, gender identity cannot be reduced to biological categories alone.

Nature/Nurture and Sexually Dimorphic Traits

Controversies about the relative effects of nature versus nurture on human social behavior have for years been plentiful in the scientific and social-scientific literature. Although the nature/nurture debate has been posed as an either/or question, it is reasonable to conclude that individual and group characteristics emerge from the complex interdependence of biological factors and social systems. Indeed, any given behavior—including those seeming to be mostly biological events, such as body size and strength, hormone levels, and brain development—can be affected considerably through environmental influences. Body size provides a good example. Although men are, on the average, larger than women, body size is known to be influenced by diet and physical activity, which, in turn, are influenced by class, race, and gender inequality. Explanations of sex differences that ignore these sociological factors are incomplete and misleading. Genetic research itself shows the strong effect of culture on the expression of genetic traits.

Geneticists use the term *genotype* to refer to inherited genetic characteristics; the *phenotype* is the observed expression of the genes as they interact with each other and with the environment in which they appear. This is no simple process, although popular conceptions of genes imagine them as mechanical things that exert a direct influence on human behavior. The expression of genetic codes is, in fact, a complex process, involving the molecular structure of DNA and protein synthesis (Fausto-Sterling, 1992). Even the most simple traits involve complex processes of genetic expression. Explaining these traits requires an elaborate and multidimensional analysis. Simple assertions claiming a direct association between genetic structure and social behavior do not match the intricacy of this process.

Sex differences that do appear between males and females are known as **sexually dimorphic traits**. These include physical as well as social and cultural differences; they are traits that occur in different frequencies among male and female populations. For example, color blindness is a sexually dimorphic trait that is found more often in men than in women. Most sexually dimorphic traits are distributed widely throughout both male and female populations. They are dimorphic usually because there is a significant difference in their distribution between the two populations, not usually because a sexually dimorphic trait appears only in one sex.

Statistical measures of the variation of a trait within a given population represent the degree to which the population deviates from the typical case. Most sex differences are distributed widely throughout the population, leaving a wide range of variation on any given trait appearing among men or among women. Body weight provides a good example. On the average, men weigh more than women, but weight differences among women and among men far exceed the average weight difference between men and women as populations. A sex difference may be found when comparing male and female populations as a whole, but it may not be found when comparing any given male-female pair.

The point is that the variability within gender is usually larger than the mean difference between genders. Sexually dimorphic traits are so labeled because they are found in different frequencies in men and women. For any given trait, there may be a substantial degree of overlap between the two populations. Usually, sexually dimorphic traits represent quantitative, not qualitative, differences between the sexes.

Research has found very few consistent sex differences, although discussions of male-female traits almost always emphasize traits that are different instead of similar in men and women. Simply put, the vast majority of human traits are shared by both men and women. Because knowing a person's biological sex does not even provide a very accurate prediction of his or her physical characteristics, we have to wonder why biological differences are so often claimed as explaining inequality between the sexes.

Biological Determinism

Although there may be a general biological basis for human societies, human biology sets extremely broad limits for behavior. Most of us vastly underuse our biological capacities, including both motor skills and cognitive ability; yet differences between the sexes have often been attributed to biological origins, thereby giving the impression that nature is more significant than nurture in determining our social identities and social positions. An argument that reduces a complex event or process (such as social identity) to a single monolithic cause (such as the form of one's genitals) is called **biological reductionism**. A related form of argument is known as **biological determinism**. Determinist arguments are those that assume that a given condition (such as the presence of a penis) inevitably determines a particular event (such as male aggression). Arguments about the biological inferiority of women are usually both reductionist and determinist in that they explain gender differences in the social world as the natural and inevitable consequence of the singular fact of women's biological nature.

Determinist and reductionist arguments are closely related and can be made in any number of forms, including psychological, economic, and cultural contexts. Biological determinism and reductionism have been especially rampant in the discussion of gender and race differences, and they have been the basis for conservative views about the proper role for women and racial-ethnic groups in society.

Biologically determinist arguments often assume that hormonal differences between women and men explain presumed differences in aggressive behavior. This argument should be examined carefully. To begin with, both males and females have measurable quantities of the three major sex hormones—estrogen, progestin, and testosterone. Hormonal sex differences are caused by differences in the levels of production and concentration of each, not in their presence or absence per se. The greater production of testosterone in males is because of stimulation by the testes, whereas in females the ovaries secrete additional estrogens and progestins. Before puberty, however, there are few or no sex differences in the quantity of sex hormones in each sex; at this time, all of the sex hormones are at very low levels. If high levels of testosterone were needed to produce aggression, then we would expect to see little difference in aggressive behavior between prepubescent boys and girls. Much research, however, shows that boys are more aggressive at an early age, thereby contradicting the implications of biologically determinist arguments.

Similarly, following menopause, women actually have lower levels of estradol (the major estrogen) and progesterone (the major progestin) than do men of the same age (Hawkins and Oakey, 1974; Hoyenga and Hoyenga, 1979; Tea et al., 1975). Because there is no empirical evidence that older men are more feminine than older women, we must doubt the conclusion that hormonal differences explain differences in the behavior of the sexes.

Research on human males shows that changes in testosterone levels do not consistently predict changes in aggressive behavior (Hoyenga and Hoyenga, 1979). Studies of "chemical castration" show that the procedure is not very effective in reducing violent or aggressive behavior in men; similarly, studies of castrated rhesus monkeys show no straightforward relationship between castration and the lessening of aggression (Fausto-Sterling, 1992).

Some studies find small correlations between the level of testosterone and aggressive behavior, but correlations show only association, not cause. Although there may be a slight tendency for aggression and testosterone to vary together, "this does not mean that testosterone caused aggression or dominance; the reverse could just as well be true" (Hoyenga and Hoyenga, 1979:139). In fact, much of the research on hormones and aggression shows that experiential factors (such as stress, fatigue, or fear) may have a greater effect on hormonal production than hormones have on behavior (Hoyenga and Hoyenga, 1979).

A study of testosterone levels found among different occupational groups of women workers provides a case in point. The study found somewhat higher levels of testosterone among students and professional and managerial women than among women clerical and service workers and housewives (Purifoy and Koopmans, 1980). Although at first glance this may make it seem that "male hormones" encourage women to move into "male" occupations, the researchers found support for a very different conclusion. Because stress is known to lower testosterone levels, the greater stress experienced by clerical and service workers and housewives resulted in a lowering of their testosterone levels, compared with other women in the sample (Fausto-Sterling, 1992; Purifoy and Koopmans, 1980).

In sum, reductionist arguments do not account for the complexities of patterns of human aggression or for the wide variation in patterns of aggression among and between men and women. No single hormonal state is a good predictor of any form of social behavior. Studies of the relationship between hormones and aggression typically confuse biological and social facts anyhow, because measuring and defining aggression is itself a matter of interpretation.

Biologically reductionist arguments rest on the assumption that differences between the sexes are "natural"; yet, in fact, it is quite difficult, if not impossible, to distinguish so-called natural and social events. Cultural attitudes influence what we think of as natural, since what is deemed natural is typically only that which we believe is unchangeable. Biology itself is neither fixed nor immutable, since biological processes themselves can be modified through cultural conditions (Lowe, 1983).

❧ Socialization and the Formation of Gender Identity

The fact that gender is a social, not a natural, phenomenon means that it is learned. Although rooted in institutions, gender is passed on through social learning and is enacted through what sociologists call gender roles. Gender roles are the patterns of behavior in which women and men engage, based on the cultural expectations associated with their gender. Gender roles are learned through the process of socialization. It is through the socialization process that individuals acquire an identity based on gender. **Gender identity** is an individual's specific definition of self, based on that person's understanding of what it means to be a man or a woman. In other words, it is through the socialization process that gender is socially constructed.

Sanctions and Expectations

Through gender socialization, different behaviors and attitudes are encouraged and discouraged in men and women. That is, social expectations about what is properly masculine and feminine are communicated to us through the socialization process. Our family, peers, and teachers, as well as the media and religious groups, act as agents of the socialization process. Although probably none of us becomes exactly what the cultural ideal prescribes, our roles in social institutions are conditioned by the gender relations we learn in our social development.

Some persons become more perfectly socialized than others, and sociologists have warned against the idea of seeing humans as totally passive, overly socialized creatures (Wrong, 1961). To some extent, we probably all resist the expectations society has of us. Our uniqueness as individuals stems in part from this resistance, as well as from variations in the social experiences we have. Studying patterns of gender socialization does not deny individual differences, but it does point to the common experiences shared by girls as they become women and boys as they become men. However much we may believe that we were raised in a gender-neutral environment, research and careful observation show how pervasive and generally effective the process of gender-role socialization is. Although some of us conform more than others, socialization acts as a powerful system of social control.

Peter Berger (1963) describes social control as something like a series of concentric circles. At the center is the individual, who is surrounded by different levels of control, ranging from the subtle (such as learned roles, peer pressure, and ridicule) to the overt (such as violence, physical threat, and imprisonment). According to Berger, it is usually not necessary for powerful agents in the society to resort to extreme sanctions, because what we think and believe about ourselves usually keeps us in line. In this sense, socialization acts as a powerful system of social control.

The conflicts we encounter when we try to cross or deny the boundaries between the sexes are good evidence of the strength of gendered expectations in our culture. Although most of us resist the idea that we are controlled, because we like to think we are individuals, the effects of social expectations are easily seen in some simple experiments. Think of what you would have to change about yourself if you were to act and appear to be a member of the other sex. First, you would likely have to change some of your physical appearance: your hairstyle, your clothes, and perhaps even how you talk, walk, and sit. You would also have to change your behavior—perhaps smiling less (or more), being more or less assertive, and becoming more or less deferential to others. If you were able to carry this off and play a convincing role, you would also likely find people responding differently to you—that is, if you could bring yourself to do this. Most would find this hard to do—not because they cannot change their behavior, but because they would find it awkward and embarrassing to do so. Interestingly, researchers have found that women are given more latitude than men in deviating from expected gender roles (McCreary, 1994). This is probably because men who do so are presumed to be gay, which is indicative of the link between gender socialization and expectations about sexual identity, something that will be discussed further.

The pressure to adopt gender-appropriate behavior is evidence that the socialization process controls us in several ways: (1) it gives us a definition of our-

[handwritten margin note: Are lesbians more acceptable then?]

selves, (2) it defines the external world and our place within it, (3) it provides our definition of others and our relationships with them and (4) the socialization process encourages and discourages the acquisition of certain skills by gender.

Gender socialization is a powerful process involving our individualism, as well as the multiple forms that gender roles can take. *Gender expectations* confront us everywhere and shape our identities and relationships with others, perhaps even at times when we might wish they did not. Some argue that the pressures of gender socialization are even more restrictive of boys, at least at the early ages, than of girls. Men's roles are more rigidly defined, as witnessed in the more severe social sanctions brought against boys not to be sissies, compared with girls who are thought of as tomboys. For girls, being a tomboy may be a source of mild ridicule, but it appears to be more acceptable (at least until puberty) than being a sissy is for boys.

Some researchers explain this finding as the result of **homophobia**, defined as the fear and hatred of homosexuals (Pharr, 1988). Homophobia acts as a system of social control because it encourages boys and men to act more masculine, as a way of indicating that they are not gay. Homophobia further separates the cultural roles of masculinity and femininity by discouraging men from showing so-called feminine traits such as caring, nurturing, emotional expression, and gentleness.

Researchers conclude that "homophobia thus appears to be functional in the dynamics of maintaining the traditional male role. The fear of being labeled homosexual serves to keep men within the confines of what the culture defines as sex-appropriate behavior, and it interferes with the development of intimacy between men" (Morin and Garfinkle, 1978:41). Men who endorse the norms of traditional male roles are also more homophobic, as are men who hold strong beliefs in the moral value of sports—as if athletic prowess is the mark of a "real" man (Thompson, Grisanti, and Pleck, 1985; Harry, 1995).

Conformity to traditional roles takes its toll on both men and women, and research shows that those who conform most fully to gender-role expectations experience a range of negative consequences. For example, higher male mortality rates can be attributed to the stress in masculine roles; women who score as very feminine on personality tests also tend to be dissatisfied, be anxious, and have lower self-esteem than do less traditionally feminine women (Thornton and Leo, 1992). Research also indicates that depression is related to traditional gender roles. Generally, women have higher rates of depression than men, although men who most conform to traditional masculine roles tend to be more lonely, even though they are reluctant to admit so (Silverstein and Lynch, 1998). The higher rates of depression among women are related to women's adherence to traditional feminine ideals. Women who score as very feminine on personality tests exhibit more depressive feelings and report feeling less in control of their lives (Sayers, Baucom, and Tierney, 1993; Sprock and Yoder, 1997).

These patterns in mental health reflect not only adherence to traditional ideals but also a response to the different external conditions that women and men experience. It is generally acknowledged that women have more social support systems than men, but ironically, these systems can also generate stress, which, in turn, can produce depression. Thus, researchers have found that women with extensive family support networks, but who are not employed, are overloaded by the expectations to support others, such that the family network itself can reinforce depression (Veiel, 1993). At the same time, most research finds that maintaining multiple roles results in positive self-esteem, better mental health, and more security for women (Gerson, 1985; Sprock and Yoder, 1997).

All of these patterns are confounded by race, class, and sexual orientation. Poor women, regardless of their race, have nearly twice the rate of depression as middle-class women; most researchers associate differences in depression by race to the influence of social class. Lesbian women also face unique problems of mental health, although there is no evidence that they have rates of depression different from heterosexual women. Lesbians face discrimination and homophobic attitudes, contributing to stress; in addition, they have higher rates of poverty and barriers to health care access—both of which contribute to problems with mental health (Bradford, Ryan, and Rothblum, 1994; Greene, 1994).

Figure 2.1 reports the sources of the changing stress patterns that men and women experience. Note that in the brief five-year period between 1990 and 1995 (the time of the two surveys), the percentage of women and men reporting certain sources of stress nearly converged—especially stress associated with money and the amount of work in a day. Still, in other areas, women still experience significantly more stress than men—namely, stress from children, spouses, parents, and the chores of shopping and driving people around (Roper Organization, 1995). These data suggest that not only is gender an internalized role but it is also a pattern of behaviors and expectations that shapes the daily experience of women and men in different ways.

Race and Gender Identity

Gender socialization does not occur in a vacuum—apart from the other features of our lives that also shape our experiences. As one would expect, given the intersections of gender and race, gender identity is also mediated by the racial identities we acquire. Most studies of gender socialization have been based on studies of White, middle-class women and men (or girls and boys), although that is beginning to change. As a result, many of the conclusions in this literature may not be generalizable to other populations. For example, many of the characteristics associated with feminine stereotypes—for example, that women are dependent on men or that women are weak and more helpless than men—are simply not typical of many women of color. For that matter, research, for reasons you will see later, may also have exaggerated these differences among White men and women. African American women, for example, like White women, are socialized to place primary emphasis on nurturing their loved ones, but they are also socialized to be self-sufficient, to aspire to an education, to regard employment as part of the role of women, and to be more independent than White women (Carrington, 1980; Collins, 1987; Ladner, 1995).

This does not mean that women and men of color are unaffected by gender socialization. It is only to say that gender is manifested differently among different groups. In other words, gender identities intersect with racial identities. Asian

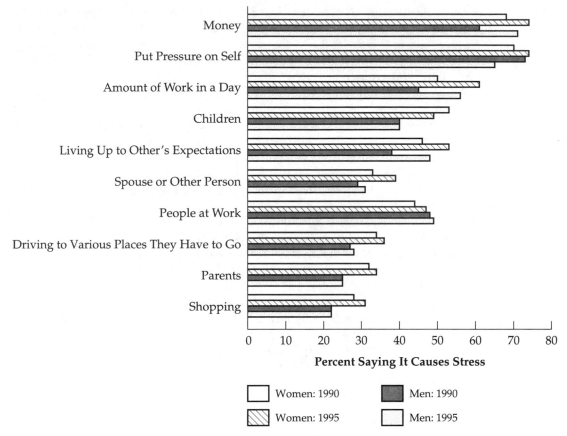

FIGURE 2.1   Gender: The Toll It Takes

Source: Data from Roper Organization. 1995. *The 1995 Virginia Slims Opinion Poll.* Storrs, CT: Roper Search Worldwide, p. 84.

American women, for example, have a strong degree of gender consciousness, based in part on their socialization in traditional cultures with restricted definitions of gender roles, the maintenance of gender stereotyping, and devalued and subordinated roles for women. Like other minority women, their gender consciousness intersects with their consciousness of their racial and class status in U.S. society (Chow, 1987). Similarly, in Chicano communities, women's roles are adaptations to the conditions of exclusion, marginality, and hostility that have characterized the relations of Chicanas to U.S. society (Baca Zinn, 1982b).

Gender expectations also change as the result of new experiences. In a study of Mexican immigrants to the United States, Hondagneu-Sotelo found that men's expectations about their roles changed as the result of the migration experience. Because families are often separated during the early phases of migration, men may live in bachelor communities when they first migrate. They learn to cook and clean for themselves. Once the family is reunited, the men do not necessarily discard these newly learned roles (Hondagneu-Sotelo, 1992; 1994). Likewise, Chinese women who migrated to the United States found they had to find employment to help support their families. Their earlier-held cultural norms about the desirability of women's employment changed as a result (Geschwender, 1992).

Clearly, generalizations about gender-role socialization need to be carefully examined in the context of the experiences of different groups. This is often difficult to do because authors do not always report the racial composition of groups on which they have based their conclusions. As you read the results of studies, including those related here, you should ask yourself if the same conclusions would be reached were the studies based on the experiences of women and men of color.

These cautions are not meant to deny the significance of gender expectations in the experience of women of color, nor the significance of this body of research. Gender is an important part of the experience of all women and men in this society. It also may be true, however, that the further one moves into the social system, such as in joining a corporation or moving into a position of power, the more rigid gender expectations become. Because success in the dominant world tends to demand conformity, it is likely that those who benefit the most from sexist and racist institutions are those most likely to uphold the attitudes, beliefs, and behaviors on which such institutions rest.

Socialization across the Life Course

Socialization begins at birth, and it continues throughout adulthood, even though gender roles are established very early. When we encounter new social experiences, we are socialized to adopt new roles through the expectations others have of us. Socialization patterns can be observed in many individual and group experiences and in the context of all of the institutions of society. This section examines the processes and consequences of gender socialization as it occurs throughout the life course.

Infancy

Beginning in infancy, boys and girls are treated differently. Research on infant socialization shows, in fact, how quickly gender expectations become part of our experience. One innovative study asked first-time parents to describe their babies only 24 hours after birth. Although physical examination revealed no objective differences between male and female infants, the parents of girls reported their babies to be softer, smaller, and less attentive than did the parents of boys. More than mothers did, fathers described their sons as larger, better coordinated, more alert, and stronger than girls; also more than did mothers, fathers described their daughters as delicate, weak, and inattentive (Rubin, Provenzano, and Hull, 1974). In an interesting twist of this classic study, researchers have found that young children describe infants in more gender-stereotyped ways than do adults (Stern and Karraker, 1989). Parents have also rated their male children as more intelligent than female children (Furnham and Gasson, 1998).

Research continues to show that parents treat their infants differently, depending on the infant's sex. How parents act may even be unintentional or subtle, but it has an effect on later life, nonetheless. In one fascinating series of studies, researchers observed fathers and mothers (in couples) walking young children through public places. Both fathers and mothers were more likely to let boy toddlers walk alone than they were to allow girls to do so. These same observers found that even when the child was out of the stroller, mothers were far more likely to push the empty stroller than were the fathers, demonstrating the attachment of mothers to child care roles (Mitchell et al., 1992). Despite the fact that mothers are much more likely than fathers to engage in and manage child care, research also finds that fathers are more likely to gender-type their children (Mitchell et al., 1992). Parents living in nontraditional households, however, do tend to gender-stereotype their children less than parents do in traditional families (Weisner, Garnier, and Loucky, 1994).

Parents are not the only agents of gender socialization, however. Other children have just as important an impact on learning gender roles. Children of all ages notice the sex of infants and use it as a basis for responding to the child. Preschool girls also show more interest in interacting with babies than do preschool boys, a pattern that is most pronounced among children whose parents hold gender stereotyped attitudes (Blakemore, 1998). As children grow, their engagement in gender stereotyping also increases, especially between the ages of 3 and 14 (Vogel et al., 1991). Peers develop expectations and definitions of gender-appropriate behaviors and use those expectations as the basis for their interaction with others.

Childhood Play and Games

Research in child development emphasizes the importance of play and games in the maturation of children. Through play, children learn the skills of social interaction, develop cognitive and analytical abilities, and are taught the values and attitudes of their culture. The games that children play have great significance for the children's intellectual, moral, personal, and social development—and for their gender identity.

George Herbert Mead, a social psychologist and major sociological theorist in the early twentieth century, described three stages in which socialization occurs: imitation, play, and game. In the *imitation* stage, an infant simply copies the behavior of significant persons in his or her environment. In the *play* stage, the child begins "taking the role of the other"—seeing himself or herself from the perspective of another person. Mead argues that taking the role of the other is a cognitive process that permits the child to develop a self-concept. Self-concepts emerge through interacting with other people and from learning to perceive how others see us. The other people most emotionally important to the child (e.g., parents, siblings, or other primary caregivers) are, in Mead's term, significant others. In the play stage, children learn to take the role of significant others, primarily by practicing others' social roles—for example, "playing Mommy" or "playing Daddy."

In the *game* stage, children are able to do more. Rather than seeing themselves from the perspective of only one significant other at a time, they can play games requiring them to understand how several other people (including more than just significant others) view them simultaneously. Playing baseball, to use Mead's example, involves the roles and expectations of many more people than does "playing Mommy." Eventually, children in the game stage learn to orient themselves not just to significant others but to a generalized other, as well. The generalized other represents the cultural expectations of the whole social community.

Mead's analysis of the emergence of the self emphasizes the importance of interpretative behavior in the way the child relates to others in the social environment. Early activity, especially through play, places children's experiences in a social environment; therefore, meanings communicated through play help the child organize personal experience into an emerging self. Children's play, then, is a very significant part of the socialization process.

Research reveals the pervasiveness of gender stereotyping as it is learned in early childhood play. The toys and play activities that parents select for children are a significant source of gender socialization. Researchers have found that parents perceive gender-neutral toys as the most acceptable (i.e., those that are not stereotyped as presumed for one gender). Interestingly, observations of parents interacting with children playing with masculine-typed, feminine-typed, and neutral toys find that parents spend the least time interacting with children when the children are playing with feminine-typed toys (Idle, Wood, and Desmarais, 1993).

Clearly, parents' values influence the gender play of children. One study videotaped preschool boys in a playroom where they could play with tools or a dish set. The researchers found that boys who think their fathers see cross-gender toy play as "bad" (i.e., boys playing with dishes) were far less likely to play with the dish set (Raag and Rackliff, 1998). Other studies find that parents, especially fathers, are more likely to be involved in physical play with boys than with girls; not surprisingly, then, boys are more likely to play physically than girls, whereas girls engage in more fantasy or "pretense" play (Lindsey, Mize, and Pettit, 1997).

These patterns are not fixed, however, since changing attitudes among parents are reflected in the values their children learn. Compared to 20 years ago, young girls now express a greater number of occupational aspirations—more so than young boys (Helwig, 1998). Mothers' education and employment also have a significant impact on the gender attitudes of their daughters and sons; in general, there has been some shift in attitudes toward more egalitarian roles—a fact that will influence the gender attitudes of future generations (Harris and Firestone, 1998; Helwig, 1998; Ex and Janssens, 1998).

Even with these changes, however, the world children encounter is laden with gender-stereotypic expectations. Children's literature, video games, and television bombard young people with images that influence the development of their gender identity and gender attitudes. In children's literature, female characters are more likely to be depicted using household objects, whereas male characters use nondomestic objects (Crabb and Bielawski, 1994). Although there has been improvement in the inclusion of women in children's literature, girls and women are still depicted as less adventurous and more domestic than boys. One study comparing nonsexist picture books with conventional children's books found that females are shown as more independent and men as less aggressive in the nonsexist books; however, females in the nonsexist books are also shown as more nurturing, more emotional, and less physically active than they are in the conventional books (Davis, 1984; Purcell and Stewart, 1990). In general, there are still more males than females in children's picture books and males are shown as more potent and active, although, interestingly, more positive adjectives are used to describe female characters (Turner-Bowker, 1996). Books written by African Americans are more likely to show girls and women as less dependent and more competitive, but they also show them as more nurturing than do books written by White authors (Clark, Lennon, and Morris, 1993).

In television cartoons, boys are depicted as more violent, girls as more domestic; furthermore, children who watched such cartoons subsequently express more traditional job expectations for themselves and others (Thompson and Zerbinos, 1997). Even the Sunday comics communicate these expectations, with researchers finding that, although some stereotypical images have diminished over the last 20 years, there is now a return to earlier levels of stereotyping (Brabant and Mooney, 1997). In video games—one of the major outlets for children's play—traditional gender roles and violence are central themes. Using a sample of Nintendo and Sega Genesis Games, researchers found that 41 percent of the games had no female characters at all, 28 percent portrayed women as sex objects, and 80 percent included aggression or violence as the strategy. Half the games included violence directed at others; the other half depicted violence toward women (Dietz, 1998). All told, these sources of socialization send powerful messages to young boys and girls. The numerous examples that can be found in children's play, literature, and other cultural systems demonstrate how gender is socially constructed.

Socialization and the Schools

Although we tend to think of the family as the primary source of social values and identity, peers, teachers, the media, and other significant others are important agents of the socialization process. Schools, in particular, exercise much influence on the creation of gendered attitudes and behavior, so much so that some researchers call learning gender the "second curriculum" in the schools (Best, 1983). In the schools, curriculum materials, teachers' expectations, educational tracking, and peer relations encourage girls and boys to learn gender-related skills and self-concepts.

Within schools, teachers and older children display expectations that encourage children to behave and think in particular ways; moreover, these expectations are strongly influenced by gender. Teachers, for example, respond more often to boys in the classroom. Even when they do so in response to boys' misbehaving, they are calling more attention to the boys (Sadker and Sadker, 1994). Differences between boys and girls become exaggerated through practices that divide them into two distinct human groups (Thorne, 1993). In schools, children are often seated in separate gender groups or sorted into play groups based on gender; these practices heighten gender differences, making them even more significant in the children's interactions. In school, boys tend to be the center of attention, even when they are getting attention for disruptive behavior; girls are, in general, less visible and more typically praised for passive and acquiescent behavior (Sadker and Sadker, 1994; American Association of University Women Educational Foundation, 1992).

These gender-typical behaviors have consequences for what boys and girls learn in school. Although boys and girls enter schools with roughly equal abilities, and although overall gender differences in such important areas as math and science are no longer pronounced, girls report liking these subjects less than boys and they express little confidence in their math and science abilities. Those who report liking math and science have higher self-esteem and have higher career aspirations than other girls (American Association of University Women Educational Foundation, 1992; Phillips, 1998). The influences that young girls experience in their early years at school can thus have profound effects on the extent of their gender segregation in the labor market in their adult years.

Families and schools are not the only sources of gender socialization. One of the reasons that gender is so extensive in its influence on our lives is that it is so pervasive throughout all social institutions. Gender expectations are also visible at work, in voluntary organizations, in health care organizations, and in athletics. Religion, as you will see in Chapter 8, also has a significant effect on our concepts of who we are and our consciousness of gender. Families and schools are primary sources for some of the earliest influences of gender socialization, but the process of learning and enacting gender goes on throughout people's lifetimes.

Adult Socialization and the Aging Process

As we encounter new experiences throughout our lives, we learn the role expectations associated with our new statuses. Although our gender identities are established relatively early in life, changes in our status in society—for example, graduation, marriage, or a new job—bring new expectations for our behavior and beliefs.

Aging is perhaps the one thing about our lives that is inevitable; yet, as a social experience, it has different consequences for men and women. Cross-cultural evidence shows that aging is less stressful for women in societies where there is a strong tie to family and kin, not just to a husband; where there are extended, not nuclear, family systems; where there is a positive role for mothers-in-law (rather than the degrading status attached to it in our society); and where there are strong mother-child relationships throughout life. Even within our own society, racial and ethnic groups attach more value to older persons, thereby easing the transition to later life. Although the elderly in African American and Latino communities experience even greater difficulties with poverty and health than do the White elderly (Atchley, 1997), their valued role in the extended family seems to alleviate some of the stress associated with growing old.

does she feel this?

Gender differences in the social process of aging can be attributed greatly to the emphasis on youth found in this culture and, in particular, to the association of youth and sexuality in women. Cultural stereotypes portray older men as distinguished, older women as barren. As a woman ages, unlike a man, she will generally experience a loss of prestige; men gain prestige as they become more established in their careers.

The effects of aging for women and men are, however, strongly influenced by factors such as one's class, race, and so on. For example, although there is a strong belief that retirement negatively affects the mental health of men, sociologists find little support for this idea. The greatest source of stress for both women and men during retirement is the death of one's spouse (Atchley, 1997). The other major influence on satisfaction during retirement—for both women and men—is health status. Except for those who retired for reasons of poor health, studies of retired men show that they actually score higher on measures of mental health than men who are still employed (Crowley, 1983; Atchley, 1997).

Financial stress, however, for both women and men, is one of the most significant factors influencing patterns of stress during retirement. Race, gender, and class therefore make certain groups, especially African American women more vulnerable to stress during retirement because of financial problems (Logue, 1991). One result is that African American and Hispanic women and men, as well as White working-class men and women, are more likely to continue intermittent patterns of employment well into their retirement years. This is especially true for those who have had work histories marked by unemployment, intermittent or part-time jobs, or jobs with few retirement benefits—patterns of employment most common among women and racial minorities (Calasanti, 1992; Zsembik and Singer, 1990).

At the same time, however, aging relaxes some of the social pressure experienced by younger people. Many women report more satisfaction and personal freedom in their later years than they felt during their earlier lives (Hess and Markson, 1991). How positively one experiences the aging process depends to a large extent on the economic and cultural resources one has available, as well as the social supports received from family and friends. One study of retired African American professional women has documented, for example, the satisfaction that these women experience from their achievements, especially in regard to the social supports they both create and rely on over a lifetime of confronting racism (Slevin and Wingrove, 1998).

There is little doubt that women experience significant disadvantage during the aging process. At the same time, however, the capacities and strengths that women acquire over their lifetimes also give them certain advantages as they grow old. Older women report higher levels of emotional support than do older men, and they tend to have more extensive social contacts and friendships. In general, the fact that women work throughout their lives to maintain social and emotional networks helps them maintain this connection in their older years, whereas men may experience greater social isolation. Better social support also has a known positive effect on people's ability to withstand stressful life events; thus, this learned ability among women helps them face the difficult problems of death, loss, and, perhaps, poor health in their elder years (Gibson, 1996; Stoller and Gibson, 1997).

⁊⁍ *Theoretical Perspectives on the Formation of Gender*

Social scientists use different theoretical perspectives to explain gender socialization and the formation of gender. Each carries different assumptions, but all contribute to our understanding of the social construction of gender identity.

Identification Theory

Identification theory interprets children as learning gender-appropriate behaviors by identifying with their same-sex parent. This explanation is based on a Freudian psychoanalytic perspective that assumes that children unconsciously model their identities on the behavior of their parents. Identification theory posits that children learn behaviors, feelings, and attitudes unconsciously; through unconscious learning, children develop motivational systems. The child's identification with the same-sex parent, coupled with the powerful emotion associated with the parent-child relationship, results in an unconscious psychosexual bond that shapes the child's sex-role identity.

Empirical evidence to support the perspective of identification theory is, at best, shaky. Because the focus of this theory is on unconscious states of mind, it is impossible to measure directly the internal motivation of the child. Instead, researchers study motives indirectly by examining characteristics of the parents and associating those characteristics with behaviors and attitudes of the child. Such associations do not show a causal relationship between the parents' characteristics and the personality tendencies of their child. Because there is no direct way to observe the process of identification, this theory remains largely speculative; moreover, evidence that children are oriented to same-sex models is inconclusive, casting further doubt on the validity of identification theory.

Chodorow's (1978) theory of gender identity is related to the perspective of identification theory. Chodorow argues that modern nuclear families are characterized by an "asymmetrical structure of parenting," meaning that parenting is characterized by a division of labor in which women "mother" and men do not and in which women's work is devalued. This creates a dynamic of identification in which only girls adopt the personality characteristics associated with mothering. In Chodorow's theory, called **object relations theory**, as boys and girls develop their own identities, they must become psychologically separate from their parents. Boys, who gender-identify with their fathers, form personalities that are more detached from others, because family structures in this society are based largely on the father's absence. Girls, who gender-identify with their mothers, become less detached because the mother's role in the family is one of close attachment to others. Girls' personalities, then, are more focused on attachment behaviors and on orientation to others. Boys, on the other hand, have personalities characterized by repression of their emotional needs and their commitments to others. Chodorow's work maintains some of the orientation of identification theory in its emphasis on unconscious psychic processes. It is distinguished, though, from traditional psychoanalytic theory by its placing of gender identity clearly in the context of the division of labor by gender in work and in the family.

Because the family form Chodorow analyzes is not universal, critics have questioned whether it holds only for White, middle-class nuclear families. Would this theory, for example, hold in families marked by different cultural traditions and a different family structure? This has been examined in the context of Chicano families (Segura and Pierce, 1993). Chicano families are characterized by *familism*—a concept describing the generally large size of Chicano families, the existence of multigenerational households, the value placed on family unity, and the high level of interaction between family and kin (Baca Zinn and Eitzen, 1999). Segura and Pierce found that Chodorow's analysis is useful in describing the experiences of Chicana mothers and their daughters. Chicana mothers' identity tends to revolve around family and home, and they tend to identify more with their daughters than their sons; however, Chicanas do not practice exclusive mothering. Mothering figures include other women, such as grandmothers, aunts, or godmothers, just as African American communities often involve the extensive engagement of "othermothers" (Collins, 1990) in the care of children and kin. As a result, young Chicanas identify not only with the mother but also with other women in the family system. Segura and Pierce conclude that, especially considering the cultural representation of women within Chicano culture as sacred and self-sacrificing, Chodorow's point about gender identification and attachment is particularly salient for Chicanas.

Chodorow's analysis of families sees them in relationship to particular cultural ideals and social forms. The importance of her work lies in the connection it makes between gender identity and family structure. Her theory also suggests that transformation in family structures is a necessary prerequisite toward creating more gender-balanced personalities.

Social Learning Theory

A second theoretical perspective is **social learning theory**. Whereas identification theory rests on the idea of unconscious learning, social learning theory emphasizes the significance of the environment in explaining gender socialization. Social learning theory is a behaviorist orientation, meaning that it sees social behavior as explained in terms of human responses to the environment. According to behaviorists, appropriate social responses are positively rewarded, whereas inappropriate responses are punished. Social learning, then, occurs through an ongoing process of reinforcement from other people (Frieze et al., 1978). Like identification theorists, many social learning theorists believe that children model themselves on the behaviors and attitudes of same-sex parents. From a social learning perspective, behavior is not fixed according to early established patterns; rather, behavior and attitudes change as the situations and expectations in the environment change. Learning gender roles, although very significant in childhood, continues throughout life. As a consequence, one's gender identity is not fixed or permanent except when the social environment continues to reinforce it.

Like identification theory, social learning theory rests on the assumption that children model their behavior according to the roles of same-sex significant others, but social learning theorists point out that parents are not the only significant role models. A wide array of images and expectations in the culture serve as reinforcement for gender identity. Empirical evidence to support social learning theory comes from the vast amount of research on variations in parental expectations for children of different sexes, stereotypic responses from teachers and peers, and the influence of institutional practices that reinforce gender stereotypes. One implication of social learning theory is the view expressed by some feminists that women need women as role models in positions of leadership and authority to compensate for the learned sense of self that they acquire through traditional socialization practices.

true

Cognitive-Developmental Theory

The third theoretical framework used to explain gender-role learning is **cognitive-developmental theory**. This theory is based largely on the work of Swiss psychologist Jean Piaget and, more recently, psychologist Lawrence Kohlberg (1966). Piaget suggested that children create *schemata*—mental categories that emerge through interactions with the social world. These schemata, in turn, are used in the child's subsequent encounters with his or her environment; thus, the child accommodates and assimilates new information into this existing stock of knowledge. According to Piaget, all children experience distinct stages of cognitive development, so that the developmental process is marked by alternate states of equilibrium and disequilibrium. In other words, as the developing child discovers new information or experiences in the world, he or she must adjust previously existing schemata to fit these new observations. At various points in cognitive development, the child reaches equilibrium because the child's reasoning ability is limited. Most importantly, cognitive-developmental theory emphasizes that the process of social development is one in which the child interacts with the social world through the mediation and active involvement of his or her cognitive abilities.

Kohlberg uses Piaget's perspective to explain the emergence of children's gender identities. According to Kohlberg, children discover early that people are divided into two sexes. They come to know their own sex, and they categorize others as either male or female. As their own gender identity stabilizes, they also begin to categorize behaviors and objects in the social world as appropriate for one sex or the other. At this point, gender has become an organizing scheme for the developing child, and the child attributes value to the traits and attitudes associated with his or her own sex. Children also begin to believe that gender is an unchanging category. As a result, they model their own behavior on the behaviors of those of the same sex, and they develop a strong emotional attachment to the same-sex parent.

Symbolic Interaction and "Doing Gender"

The previous three theoretical perspectives have been developed primarily by psychologists. Both the cognitive-developmental perspective and social learning theory are related to a perspective in sociology called **symbolic interaction**. According to symbolic interaction theory, people act toward things (including objects, abstract ideas, and other people) based on the meaning those things have for them. That meaning evolves from culture. From this perspective, the socialization process develops as people (initially, young children) take on the roles of others around them. In this sense, the concept of role models, as in social learning theory, is an important one. Critical to the symbolic interactionist perspective, however, is the idea that people reflect on how others see them and through this reflection form their self-concepts. From this point of view, the self is established as one becomes an object to oneself—something upon which people reflect. Symbolic interaction also emphasizes the ability of humans to form and understand symbols; it is through *symbolic* interpretation that consciousness and, therefore, the self are formed.

Evolving from symbolic interaction is a new way of conceptualizing how gender is formed. This is called the "**doing gender**" perspective. This perspective sees gender as an accomplished activity—accomplished through the interactions one has with others (West and Zimmerman, 1987; West and Fenstermaker, 1995). Stated another way, this perspective analyzes gender not as something essential to men and women nor fixed in biological status or social roles. Instead, it sees people as constantly re-creating gender meanings and gendered social structures whenever they act in gender-typical ways. From this point of view, gender is routinely reproduced in everyday interaction. It is not an individual trait; rather, it is created through social interaction.

From the perspective of "doing gender," whenever someone interacts with another in a way that displays a particular configuration of gender, gender is "done." This perspective conceptualizes social structure as existing only insofar as actors continue to act in ways that reproduce gender relations. Gender is thus constituted through routine social interaction, as individuals (consciously and unconsciously) engage in behaviors identified with specific gender meanings. The woman who smiles at a man (even though she may not like him), the man who opens doors routinely for women (regardless of who is more conveniently able to do so), the woman who dresses in feminine clothes, or the man who takes the lead in dancing are all "doing gender." Harmless though their behavior may seem, it contributes to the social reproduction of gender relations in society.

The perspective of "doing gender" emphasizes the fluid character of gender identity. Rather than seeing gender as a fixed or learned set of roles, this framework interprets gender as an ongoing and fluctuating series of behaviors that is created through social interaction.

A good way to illustrate this is the case of Billy Tipton, a famous jazz musician who died in 1989 at age 74. Tipton married five times and had three adopted sons. Not until the day he died did many learn that the man whom everyone thought was such a fabulous musician and loving husband and father was really a woman! Few knew of how he had "done gender." Tipton began his identity as a woman in the 1930s, when he was relatively young—a time when an unwritten code in the jazz world kept women from being hired. One cannot help but marvel at the effort it took to maintain this social identity and to imagine how his life would have been different, including what his career would have been, had it been known that "he" was a woman (D. Smith, 1998; Middlebrook, 1998).

This is a highly unusual example of "doing gender," but understanding gender as an accomplished act helps one see how people create the gender categories that constitute being a man and being a woman. Whether putting on makeup (Dellinger and Williams, 1997), asserting oneself in a group, or exercising power in an organization, one may be "doing gender" in a way that continually re-creates, but also can change, the social definition of gender.

Comparing Theoretical Perspectives

There are important differences between these four perspectives. Identification theorists assume that imitation of same-sex persons is motivated by fear—the fear of separation from a psychosexual love object. Cognitive-developmental theorists assume a more positive motivational basis for learning—namely, mastery. In the cognitive-developmental framework, children are actively involved in the construction of the social world. In contrast, both social learning and identification theories assume a more passive view of the child's development. That is, "in contrast to both identification and social-learning theories, cognitive developmentalists assume that the initial emergence of gender as an important social category is the result of the child's cognitive system rather than the result of either psychosexual dynamics or the impact of external models and rewards" (Frieze et al., 1978:120).

Both the social learning and cognitive-developmental perspectives emphasize the role of culture in shaping gender identity. Social learning theorists have a more deterministic view, however, in that they see culture as a model and reinforcer for what the child becomes. In the cognitive-developmental framework, the child does more than simply react to the culture. He or she searches for patterns in the culture and actively seeks to structure and organize the concepts of the world that the culture provides. The perspective of "doing gender" takes a completely interactionist point of view—that is, seeing gender as real only insofar as people continue to do it. This perspective has been criticized for understating the significance of institutional arrangements in shaping gender relations. It tends to make power differences between men and women less visible and understates the significant economic and political advantages that existing social arrangements give to men. Like the other perspectives, however, it helps us see how gender is constantly reproduced through the behaviors of women and men. Each of these theories shows us how central gender is to the formation of our gender identity. From the day we are born to the day we die, social expectations about our gender confront us in the everyday world. These external social expectations become internalized in our self-concepts, and they become identities through which we experience the social world.

❧ *Limitations of the Socialization Perspective*

Questions about gender identity and socialization as an origin for gender differences are more than academic matters. Whether women hold the status they do because they choose their positions or whether there are structural obstacles to their well-being lies at the heart of many public policy discussions about the status of women. Of course, socialization and structure are highly interrelated; as this chapter has shown, gender socialization originates in gendered institutions. If men and women become different from each other as the result of socialization and social structures, should social policies treat them differently or the same? This question is the focus of many current debates—affirmative action being one example. The framework of U.S. law, based on the principle of equality, theoretically means that all groups should be treated the same. If men and women are different as the result of their social experiences, should we expect that treating women like men will result in fairness and justice for them? If we develop gender-blind policies, will they assist only women who make choices as men would make them? In a world where policy values sameness, not difference, how do we recognize, value, and support the lives of women and men, regardless of the gender roles they take on? Should women have to become like men to be accorded the privileges men hold?

These questions are well illustrated by an important court case involving Sears, Roebuck and Co. In 1979, the Equal Employment Opportunity Commission (EEOC) brought a sex discrimination suit against Sears, Roebuck and Co. The EEOC alleged that Sears had engaged in sex discriminatory practices by failing to hire female job applicants for commission sales positions on the same basis as male applicants, by failing to promote female noncommission salespersons to commission sales positions on the same basis as males, and by paying women in certain management jobs less than similarly placed men. The EEOC presented extensive statistical and qualitative evidence of the disparities at Sears between women and men in commission sales; Sears did not deny these data. Sears's defense, however, was that there were fundamental differences between men's and women's qualifications and preferences for such work. Sears argued that men were more interested in and willing to accept commission sales jobs, in part because they were willing to take more risks. According to Sears, women's underrepresentation in commission sales was not a result of discrimination, but of women's own job preferences. The plaintiff (EEOC) argued that "what appear to be women's choices . . . are, in fact, heavily influenced by the opportunities for work made available to them" (Milkman, 1986:376). The case was tried in 1984 and 1985; in 1986, a U.S. district court ruled in favor of Sears.

At issue in this case was whether women chose the positions they were in or whether there were structural obstacles to their success. The question of separate spheres lies at the heart of this discussion. Do differences between men and women exist and, if so, are they actually learned preferences or do they only reflect institutionalized practices of gender discrimination? The answer, of course, lies in both, although, in the context of public policy, there is little room for such nuance. The complexity of these questions and their seriousness for social policy bring urgency to our discussion of gender relations. Socialization does not occur in a vacuum. It is a process by which human beings adapt to their environment, and in this culture that environment is one structured on gender inequality. Socialization does explain the origins of inequality, but it is a very effective way of explaining how that inequality is reproduced. If we limit ourselves, however, to thinking of gender differences as only a matter of learned choice, we overlook the patterns of institutionalized gender inequality that pervade this society.

Individual experience reflects the larger society; reexamining the events in our lives that created our gender identity is a fundamental step in recognizing how we came to be who we are and how we can change. There are, though, limitations in seeing gender relations as emerging primarily through socialization. Although the socialization process shows how individuals become gendered persons, it does not explain the social structural origins of gender inequality. Understanding socialization helps us see that gender expectations have their origins outside the individual, but socialization theories do not explain the institutional bases of those origins, and therefore they are not causal theories of women's status in society.

People are not mere receptacles for social life; rather, they actively participate in and create social change. Role-centered perspectives may exaggerate the extent to which we become socialized, leading to an oversocialized view of human life. Focusing on gender roles also tends to exaggerate the differences between the sexes because, by definition, its emphasis tends to be on differences, not similarities. In gender-role research, gender differences are typically built into research designs. The items on questionnaires, for example, or the factors selected for manipulation in experimental studies necessarily reflect the differences that a researcher wants to test. The end result may be that the research literature on gender roles exaggerates and polarizes masculine and feminine differences.

Additionally, it has been found that the gender of the researcher is a good predictor of whether gender differences will be found in research studies. Men are more likely to find gender differences than are women; thus, research conclusions may subtly reflect the gender biases of the researcher (Eagly and Carli, 1981). In other words, if a researcher expects to find differences, chances are that the research will reveal that finding.

Not all girls and boys grow up in the gender-stereotyped way that the research literature sometimes suggests; nevertheless, research on childhood learning underscores the point that gender socialization is situated within social institutions that tend to value masculine, not feminine, traits. Were values associated with women—such as flexibility, orientation toward others, and cooperation—to be incorporated into dominant social institutions, then we might well produce more gender-balanced boys and girls. As it is, the process of socialization throughout life separates men and women and creates gender differences among children and adults.

❧ Summary

The social construction of gender refers to the different processes by which expectations associated with being male or female are passed on through society. This process pervades society and its social institutions. Sociologists use the term *gender* to refer to socially learned behaviors and expectations associated with men and women; *sex* refers to one's biological identity as male or female.

Controversies about nature versus nurture are longstanding in the social sciences, but even traits that have a genetic or biological basis are influenced by the social environment. It is misleading to argue that sex differences are rooted in the biology of males and females. Arguments that explain gender differences solely in terms of biological differences are known as biological determinism or biological reductionism. Biological determinism has tended to flourish particularly in times of social upheaval. The theory consists of conservative arguments that attempt to explain gender and race differences as inevitable. Many scientific studies, including those of hermaphrodites, show that human biology and culture are complexly interrelated.

The concept of gendered institutions has been developed to explain the total pattern of gender relations that exist in all social institutions. Gender, like race and class, is embedded in social structures and social institutions. As such, change in gender relations in society requires change both in human consciousness and in social institutions.

Gender socialization is the process through which gender expectations in the society are learned—by both women and men. Gender identity is also shaped by the realities of an individual's location in the race and class system. Homophobia, the fear of homosexuals, works as a system of social control that discourages men and women from identifying with members of the same sex. The process of gender socialization is ongoing and occurs across the life course from infancy to death. Cultural systems such as childhood play and games, the social structure of schools, and the cultural expectations surrounding aging all create different life experiences for women and men.

Four different theories are used to describe how gender develops: identification theory, social learning theory, cognitive-developmental theory, and "doing gender." Each reveals how central gender is to social interaction and social identity. Studies of socialization are, however, limited in explaining the origins of gender inequality.

❧ Key Terms

biological determinism	gender roles	sex chromosomes
biological reductionism	gendered institution	sexuality
cognitive-developmental theory	hermaphroditism	sexually dimorphic traits
culture	homophobia	social construction of gender
"doing gender"	identification theory	social learning theory
fetal sex differentiation	institution	socialization
gender	object relations theory	symbolic interaction
gender identity	sex	

🄳 *Discussion Questions/Projects for Thought*

1. Describe the play you remember from your childhood. Who did you play with? What did these games communicate about gender? How have they affected your current interests, skills, and aspirations? It would be good to discuss this question in mixed-gender groups.

2. Identify some of the research studies described in this chapter, and develop some experimental observations that let you replicate these studies. You could do this in the same setting as the original research or introduce new conditions or research subjects that let you develop further questions raised by the subject. For example, take a walk through some place where you are likely to see men and women with baby strollers. Who pushes the stroller when the baby is in it or when the stroller is empty? Observe places where you are likely to see toddlers and their mothers and/or fathers. Is there a difference in whether boy toddlers and girl toddlers are allowed to walk on their own? How much distance do the parents let each sex roam before going to get them? Does this vary depending on the sex of the parent?

3. Interview a racially diverse group of men and women, asking them to define what *womanhood* and *manhood* means to them. What do their answers tell you about the interplay of race and gender in the construction of people's identities?

🄳 *Suggested Readings*

Abbott, Franklin, ed. 1998. *Boyhood, Growing Up Male: A Multicultural Anthology*, 2nd ed. Madison: University of Wisconsin Press.
Using autobiographical accounts, this anthology shows the influence of gender—along with ethnicity, race, class, and sexuality—in shaping men's socialization.

Chodorow, Nancy. 1978. *The Reproduction of Mothering*. Berkeley: University of California Press.
This is a classic theoretical analysis, from a psychoanalytic perspective, of the formation of gender identity. Chodorow links the establishment of gendered identity among women to the unequal participation of men in child care.

Due, Linnea. 1995. *Joining the Tribe: Growing up Gay and Lesbian in the '90s*. New York: Doubleday.
Due's work explores, using personal accounts, the experience of growing up lesbian and gay. The book pays particular attention to the interaction of sexuality and gender.

Fausto-Sterling, Anne. 1992. *Myths of Gender*, 2nd ed. New York: Basic Books.
In a review of the research on biology and gender, Fausto-Sterling challenges many of the popular myths about the biological basis of gender.

Findlen, Barbara, ed. 1995. *Listen Up: Voices from the Next Feminist Generation*. Seattle: Seal Press.
Based on the accounts of young women, this collection explores many of the feminist issues facing the current generation.

Nanda, Serena. 1998. *Neither Man nor Woman: The Hijras of India*. Belmont, CA: Wadsworth.
This fascinating account of the hijras of India, a group of men with mixed gender/sex identity, probes the meaning of gender in different cultural contexts.

Slevin, Kathryn F., and C. Ray Wingrove. 1998. *From Stumbling Blocks to Stepping Stones: The Life Experiences of Fifty Professional African American Women*. New York: New York University Press.
Based on oral histories of retired African American professional women, Slevin and

Wingrove examine the satisfaction that these accomplished women experience during retirement, even in the face of racial and gender oppression.

Stoller, Eleanor Palo, and Rose Campbell Gibson, eds. 1997. *Worlds of Difference: Inequality in the Aging Experience*. Thousand Oaks, CA: Pine Forge Press.
Combining social science research with personal narratives, this anthology explores the experience of aging, by examining the diverse experiences of women of different class, ethnic, and racial backgrounds.

Thompson, Becky, and Sangeeta Tyagi. 1996. *Names We Call Home: Autobiography on Racial Identity*. New York: Routledge.

These autobiographical essays examine the complex connections between gender, racial identity, sexuality, and other dimensions of identity.

Thorne, Barrie. 1993. *Gender Play*. New Brunswick, NJ: Rutgers University Press.
Thorne examines how gender is constructed in schools, based on observations of boys and girls in school settings. By showing the socially constructed basis of gender, she also makes recommendations for teachers interested in producing greater equity within schools.

Chapter 3
Gender and Culture
The Social Construction of Knowledge

It is said beauty is in the eyes of the beholder. A new team of scientists has just concluded that beauty can be scientifically determined—or so the headlines promise. Women who have been wondering whether they are sexually attractive can now determine how they measure up against a scientific standard that purports to be the perfect measurement for a woman's body: weight in pounds, divided by 2.205 (to convert to kilograms), multiplied by height in inches times 0.0254 (to get meters), then that number times itself and divided into the weight. Does this sound like a hoax? Not if you think that a sound source of information is one of the world's leading medical journals, *Lancet*. In 1998, a group of scientists from England conducted a study in which they asked a group of 40 male undergraduates to observe pictures from magazines such as *Playboy* and rate the sexiness of 50 naked women of various shapes and sizes, but without faces. The results—that the men's judgments matched the body-mass index described above—were published in *Lancet* and reported throughout the world (Tovée et al., 1998; Tovée et al., 1997; Browne, 1998).

Cultural images of women's beauty—and implicit ratings of their bodies—are replete throughout the culture. One only has to glance at a magazine stand or skim through advertisements to see that we are bombarded with specific ideals for women's appearance—ideals that rarely match what real women actually look like. With scientific experts telling women that to be sexy they should measure up to the norms of 40 male undergraduates in one specific culture, one has to wonder why so much effort is put into establishing such expectations.

Think of the advertisements you have seen—for example, "Defend yourself" and "The protection you need" (*Cosmopolitan*, September, 1998). What is being sold here? Pepper spray? Alarm systems? No, shampoo and nail polish. Why should a woman need protection from her hair or fingernails? These and countless other advertisements convey the message that women should be afraid—afraid of aging, afraid of food, afraid of being alone. Other advertisements evoke images of women as beguiling and seductive; still others intimidate with fears of looking bad, growing old, or being overweight.

Advertisements are only one source for the ideas generated about women in the mass media and popular culture. Popular music, advice columns, television shows, and other cultural materials all carry explicit and implicit suggestions about gender. In computer trade magazines, for example, men appear in the illustrations twice as often as do women. In the same magazines, women are overrepresented as clerical workers and sex objects, whereas men are overrepresented as managers, experts, and repair technicians. Men are shown primarily in positions of authority, and only women are shown as rejecting computers (Ware and Stuck, 1985). Even the naming of commercial products reflects sexist assumptions, as in the example of the condom developed for use by women called the "bikini condom"!

The sexism found in popular culture, although transformed over time, has not necessarily declined, although its form has changed. For example, in popular music, images of women as needing a man were more common in the 1940s and 1950s; images of women as sex objects and possessions of men have endured over time. Mention of women's physical characteristics in popular songs has increased over time, and images of women as evil increased during the 1970s. Moreover, depictions of women as supernatural increased during the 1960s and 1970s (Cooper, 1985). Rock videos of the 1980s and 1990s have more often depicted White men as the center of attention and power; White women are usually shown in passive or solitary activity or as trying to get the attention of men. Music videos also emphasize women's physical appearance. African Americans are more likely than Whites to be seen singing and dancing; however, more than three-fourths of all MTV videos feature White male singers or bands led by White men (Brown and Campbell, 1986; Gow, 1996).

The ideas and images presented to us, whether through advertisements or other cultural media, exert a powerful influence over our lives. Each of us sees an average of 1,600 advertisements per day and notices 1,200 of them, although we respond, positively or negatively, to only 12 (Draper, 1986). Advertisements not only sell the products we use but they also convey images of how we are to define ourselves, our relationships, and our needs.

If men were shown in advertisements as women routinely are, people would probably find it laughable. How often are women displayed in ads in their underwear or lying on beds? Do you see men in such poses? Although the use of men as sex objects in advertisements has increased, it is not nearly so frequent as for women. The demeanor of women in advertising—in the background, on the ground, or looking dreamily into space—makes them appear subordinate and available to men.

Advertisements also portray stereotyped racial images of men and women. Aunt Jemima is a caricature of the Black mammy—overweight, smiling, and always waiting to serve; the Native American princess on packages of butter is a gender and race stereotype (Churchill, 1993). These images merge racial and gender stereotypes, as if Latin men were all rogues, African American women were docile and servile, and Native American women all beguiling. Whites do not escape such stereotyping either. Stereotypes about blonde women as being sexy, but dumb, are common in the dominant culture. Although blondes are only one-quarter of the White population, they are one-third of those shown in women's magazines and half of those depicted in *Playboy*. In fact, the number of blondes in *Playboy* has actually increased substantially since the 1950s (Rich and Cash, 1993). Studies of magazine ads find that the number of Black models has increased in the 1990s, but Latinos and Asians are still very underrepresented. Black men are still most typically depicted as athletes and musicians (Bowen and Schmid, 1997).

The ideas about women and men that these cultural objects portray greatly influence our thinking about gender. They convey an impression about the proper roles of women and men, their sexual and gender identities, and their self-concepts. The ideas we hold about women and men, whether overtly sexist or more subtle in their expression, create social definitions that we use to understand ourselves and the society we live in. The ideas that people have of one another guide their behavior, even though there is no direct fit between what people believe and say and what they actually do (Deutscher, 1973). What is known or believed about women and gender relations, even when it is based on distortions of social realities, influences our mental experiences. These experiences, in turn, become part of the basis for sexist social arrangements.

Ideas, although based in the interpretive realm of thought and subjectivity, direct our behavior and constrain the ways in which we see each other and others see us. Ideas also have a political reality because they affect how society works, who gets rewarded, and how things should and should not be. For example, if we believe that women's proper place is in the home, we are not likely to object to the sexist practices of employer discrimination. If we believe that women are as capable as men, however, we are likely to support policies and changes that would make more opportunities available to them.

This chapter studies the social construction of knowledge about gender. Popular culture, the media, even the language we use exert a powerful influence on how we define reality and men's and women's roles within it. Images of women conveyed by the dominant culture have been based on distortions and stereotypes that legitimate the status quo at the same time that they falsely represent the actual experience of women in the society. As a result, the ideas we acquire regarding gender relations poorly prepare us for the realities we will face.

೩⚬ *Gender, Language, and Popular Culture*

One of the first ways we see the influence of culture in the construction of gender is in how we speak. As the system by which we generally communicate with each other, language both reflects and reinforces the cultural systems in which it is used. Note that this is a two-way process in that language reflects the values of the dominant culture, and therefore can be one means by which stereotypes are communicated and reproduced. However, language can also produce changes in society, since, by changing how we think and speak, we can communicate new meaning systems to others.

Although it may seem trivial to insist on nonsexist language (e.g., calling women *women* instead of *girls*), changes in what we say can influence what we think and language can be used to break social stereotypes. For example, it is now commonplace to address women as *Ms.*, but not that many years ago all women were referred to as either *Miss* or *Mrs.*—as if the single-most important feature of a woman's identity was her marital status. Similarly, the practice of using the word *man* to refer generically to all people makes women invisible; the contemporary practice of being more sensitive to the specific inclusion of women has transformed language use throughout society.

These are not trivial issues, since language reflects the social value that is placed on different groups in society. Language also reflects the power dynamics that are embedded in systems of gender, race, and class inequality. Racial epithets provide a good example, since the numerous negative terms that have been used to label racial-ethnic groups hold very negative connotations. Likewise, feminists have pointed out that terms such as *chicks, gals, foxes,* and *babes* demean women by associating them with animals or little girls.

It is important to point out that language is contextual—that is, what something means can vary depending on the situation in which it is expressed. Thus, women who are good friends might refer to each other as "girl" or "girlfriend" and this can be affirming, not demeaning. On the other hand, a man who refers to his secretary as his "girl," given the power differences in that relationship, is trivializing her status and reaffirming the power relationship that exists between them. Similarly, lesbian women may affectionately refer to each other as "dykes"—as a way of reclaiming a stigmatized status—but this approbation has a highly negative and hateful meaning when used by homophobic persons who use it to demean or insult.

The gendered nature of language is not only a matter of content but also of *how* people communicate. Much research has been done on this subject and there is no simple way to summarize it, but one of the basic questions has been whether women and men use language in different ways and what this means in terms of power relationships between them (Cameron, 1998). Studies have shown, for example, that despite the stereotype of women as talkative, in a variety of settings (including classrooms, meetings, and other social interactions), men take more than their "share" of talk time (Crawford and MacLeod, 1990; Sadker and Sadker, 1994; Spender, 1989). In addition, men are more likely to interrupt women in conversation, whereas women are more likely to use hesitancy in speaking—perhaps deferring to others, speaking more softly, laughing, or just being silent in group discussion. Again, context matters, since scholars have also shown that, even though women talk less than men, men also use silence as a way to assert their power. Silence can control interaction by expressing little interest in the other or withholding information. Someone who does not respond may dominate interaction by controlling topic development in conversation or refusing to recognize others' contributions (Crawford, 1995; DeFrancisco, 1991; Sattel, 1983).

Studies of gender and language have generally focused on questions of difference between women and men, leading to debate about how significant such differences are. Popular stereotypes suggest that the differences are large and real, such as in the best-seller, *Men Are from Mars, Women Are from Venus* (Gray, 1994)—a practical guide for improving communication in marriage, premised on the idea that women and men communicate differently. The popularity of work by sociolinguistic scholar Deborah Tannen, author of *You Just Don't Understand: Men and Women in Conversation* (1990), *That's Not What I Meant* (1992), and *The Argument Culture* (1998) suggests that the perception of strong sex difference in conversational patterns and in communication systems touches a nerve among the general public.

There are two ways to think about gender differences in communication. One, referred to as **essentialism,** is the argument that men and women are basically different and that this shows up in bipolar patterns of language use, among other social behaviors. The other is the **social constructionist approach,** which sees people as constructing gender through their ongoing interaction with others. In this framework, gender is a system of meanings that people enact; moreover, even when "doing gender," people may not internalize what they do. This does not mean that stereotypes and patterns of behavior associated with one gender or the other do not exist, only that gender is a fluid category, one constantly changing and evolving through human interaction. The social constructionist approach, as you saw in the previous chapter, is a less simplistic approach to the study of gender in society than the essentialist framework, which sees gender as more fixed, even if by culture and society. More than seeing gender as a matter of differences, social constructionists see people as having human agency—that is, as actively creating their lives, even if within the context of social structures that supersede them. From this point of view, even when people conform to social stereotypes, they may do so without internalizing a belief in them. Furthermore, enacting gender may even be a form of resistance to traditional gender roles, as when people act "superstereotypically" as a way of mocking dominant expectations.

The focus on differences between men and women, not just in studies of language but in studies of all forms of social behavior, has been so strong that at times it seems the only alternative way of thinking is to deny the significance of gender differences altogether (Crawford, 1995). Certainly gender differences do exist and they are reported throughout this book, but it is important to understand that gender is a changing social construct and one that reflects complex patterns of social behavior and social change. At the same time, even in recognizing differences between men and women as a whole, we should also be careful not to overgeneralize about women. On all matters of social behavior, language included, there is significant variation *within* gender—by race, class, ethnicity, as well as social context.

Language is yet one dimension of what can broadly be referred to as **popular culture**—the beliefs, practices, and objects that are part of everyday traditions. Popular culture includes popular music, film, magazines, television, and some forms of the arts that are widely accessible to the public. Popular culture has an enormous influence on the cultural values of a society and is one of the dimensions of life that has been widely examined by feminists because of its significance in the social construction of gender. Take, for example, romance novels—a subject carefully studied by feminist scholars because of its influence on the fantasy lives of millions of women. Such novels portray women as dependent on men and desperate for their attention, although feminist critics also point out that women read such novels as an escape from the domestic demands of others (Radway,1984). At the same time, popular culture can provide for millions of women (and men) alternative images—such as in the growing popularity of feminist murder mysteries where independent, savvy, strong, and sometimes armed women work as private investigators, prosecutors, or sleuths of other kinds.

Images from popular culture reveal numerous contradictions with regard to gender. On the one hand, much of popular culture is deeply stereotyped by gender. A quick perusal of a greeting card rack will show you this. Women are ridiculed for aging (as are men, but in different ways), whereas cards presumably for men commonly promise them voluptuous, full-breasted women to make their day! Simultaneously, popular culture can be transformative, as exemplified by some contemporary performance art involving the portrayal of transgendered selves. As you begin to examine one of the most influential sites of popular culture—the media—you should keep in mind that culture is an ever-changing and dynamic process that is not an abstract thing, devoid of people's ability to interpret, resist, and change.

❧ Gendered Images in the Media

Even a cursory review of the image of gender roles in the mass media shows that women and men are portrayed in stereotypical ways. Not only are they cast in stereotypical roles but both men and women are also omitted from roles that portray them in a variety of social contexts. Women tend to be portrayed in roles in which they are trivialized, condemned, or narrowly defined, resulting in the *symbolic annihilation* of women by the media (Tuchman, Daniels, and Benét, 1978). Men, on the other hand, are usually depicted in high-status roles in which they dominate women.

The research method most often used to study media images is called **content analysis**. This method is a descriptive one whereby researchers systematically analyze the actual content of documents or other artifacts. By counting particular items within a defined category, researchers are able to systematize their observations of the content of the media.

Some might say that images of women on television and in other media have improved in recent years. To a limited extent this is true, because in some serials, women do play strong and intelligent roles. In most shows, however, men are still the major characters and women are cast as glamourous objects, scheming villains, or servants, and, for every contemporary show that includes more positive images of women, there are numerous others in which women are shown as either sidekicks to men, sexual objects, or helpless imbeciles.

Content analyses of television show that, during prime-time hours, men are the majority of prime-time television characters (Davis, 1990). Women prime-time characters are found primarily in comedies, and men, in dramas, giving the impression that men are to be taken seriously and women are not. On soap operas, strong, successful women are depicted as villains, and "good" women are seen as vulnerable and naive (Benokraitis and Feagin, 1995). Men on television are more likely depicted in high-status occupations than are women, and women are more likely depicted in family roles than work roles. One early study found that 75 percent of all television ads using women are for products found in the kitchen or the bathroom (Tuchman, Daniels, and Benét, 1978)! More recent research finds that women are more often depicted in commercials in service and clerical work than in professional roles (Coltrane and Adams, 1997). Popular television heroines, such as Ally McBeal, depict characters who, despite their professional accomplishments, feel empty without a man, seem fragile in relationships, and are constantly worried about their appearance. Critics have suggested that Ally McBeal's popularity stems from the real tensions young women feel between "wanting it all" and still grappling with traditional ideas about gender (Heywood, 1998).

Images of men and women on television reinforce not only gender stereotypes but also those of class and race. Studies of dominance in television programs find that both men and women of high occupational status are more likely found in dramas than in comedies. Working-class characters are more frequently depicted in comedies, where they are presented in class stereotypical roles. *Dominance* is defined as behavior that influences, controls, persuades, prohibits, dictates, leads, directs, restrains, or organizes the behavior of others. White men and women far outnumber people of color on television, even with a number of new shows featuring African Americans, Latinos, and some Asians. Although estimates are that African Americans and Latinos watch television more than Whites do, they are a small proportion of the characters seen. With few exceptions, there are limited positive images of people of color on television and they appear in a narrow range of character types. When Black women are portrayed, they usually appear in stereotypical roles as maids, comics, or support staff. Black men fare no better, typically seen as athletes, criminals, or entertainers. Rarely are Blacks and Hispanics portrayed as loving, intelligent people (Douglas, 1984; Dines and Humez, 1995).

Even today, Asian Americans, Hispanics, and Native Americans are virtually absent from television programming except as occasional diversions, exotic objects, or marginal and invisible characters. The invisibility of minority groups on television is also noticeable in the "disappearing" roles that Blacks, Hispanics, and Asian Americans often play in television dramas. For example, in soap operas, minority women and men silently appear in backgrounds to cater to the needs of dominant households or individuals. In popular shows, minority persons also frequently portray assistants to leading White male actors. In their interactions, the minority characters are deferential, respectful, and dutiful to their dominant partners (Graves, 1996; Rodrigues, 1997).

Other distortions of race and gender also appear. Nine of ten racial minority characters appear as wealthy or middle class; very few are shown as working class or poor. Only a few episodes in television drama take racial injustice as a theme, and, when they do, it is usually depicted as the result of individual conflicts, not oppressive social structures. Televised portrayals of the workplace also show no hint of bias, even though Whites are always seen as in charge (Steenland, 1989), and most people are shown as happy in their jobs.

In a slightly different vein, African American women in situation comedies dominate more than any other characters. In crime dramas, although African American and White men are more dominant than either African American or White women, African American women are shown as more dominant than White women. Such depictions reproduce racist stereotypes of the mythical Black matriarch by casting African American women in the role of humorous but dominating characters. In this example, as well as others, television acts as a system of social control, narrowing our understanding of people's experiences, discrediting and ridiculing serious subjects such as racism and sexism, and undercutting any resistance that the public might generate against dominant social institutions (Gerbner, 1978).

In children's television programming, gender and race stereotypes are probably at their worst—a particularly disturbing fact, considering the number of hours children spend watching television. Television acts as a powerful agent of socialization for young children. Ninety-eight percent of U.S. homes are equipped with at least one television, and these sets are turned on an average of six hours per day. By the time a child in the United States is 15 years old, he or she will have spent more hours watching television than attending school.

Television cultivates gender stereotypes for children. Numerous studies find that children's attitudes about gender roles are influenced by the amount of television they watch. Children report that they want to be like television characters when they grow up. One study, for example, found that whether young children (sixth- through eighth-graders) believed "women are happiest at home raising children" and "men are born with more ambition than women" was associated with television viewing (Morgan, 1987). Even in educational programming for children, where one might expect more progressive views, twice as many male characters are depicted as scientists than is true for female characters; women and girls are more likely seen as pupils and apprentices (Steinke and Long, 1996). These images matter, since children who watch the most television are those who also hold the most stereotypic, gender-typed values; furthermore, this seems to hold for adults, as well (Signorielli, 1989, 1991).

The mass media carry a certain authority, particularly because they provide a common basis for social interaction. The nature of printed and electronic media is such that, once an image is represented, it loses the more fluid character it would have in reality. Ideas and characters appear fixed, giving a singular impression of reality. Rarely does the public get a glimpse of how these images are actually produced; instead, they appear as objective facts.

Even the news, something supposed to be taken seriously and as objective, reporting of world events is loaded with gendered presentations. Consider those who bring you the news—especially the news that is supposed to be taken most seriously. Women represent only 15 percent of network news reporters, and 20 percent of print journalists, although they are 68 percent of journalism school graduates (Marzolf, 1993). Less than 10 percent of editors in chief, news publishers, and deans or directors of journalism programs are women. Men write two-thirds of the front page stories in newspapers and provide 85 percent of television reporting. Women of color provide only 2 percent of broadcast media stories. Men provide 90 percent of the voice-overs in television commercials and 90 percent of televised sporting events (Rhode, 1995). Men are also considered the experts on the news; they provide 85 percent of quotes or references, 75 percent of those interviewed on TV, and 90 percent of the most recently cited pundits—even on issues that involve women (Rhode, 1995). Despite the high visibility of a select few women reporters and analysts—such as Barbara Walters, Katie Couric, and Cokie Roberts—these women remain the exception.

Little attention is given to women's issues in major news reporting, and seldom are the implications of world events for women considered. When news about women does appear, it typically casts women in traditional gender roles. If you doubt this, study how Hillary Rodham Clinton has been depicted in the media. When portrayed as an independent thinker and professional woman, she has been ridiculed and denigrated; thus, not long into Clinton's presidency, she was "repackaged" to emphasize a more traditional role for first ladies. Think, too, of how and where women of color appear as news reporters. Although a few become news anchors, most often they report on "soft news" or human-interest stories that are broadcast late in the newscast. When they do appear as anchors, it is usually in late night hours, weekends, or holidays, when the "senior" staff has time off.

The significance of gendered and racial images on television is so enormous that some suggest that television acts as a national religion in contemporary U.S. society because it establishes a common culture and is resistant to cultural change. Gerbner writes:

> [Television] is used by practically all the people and is used practically all the time. It collects the most heterogeneous public of groups, classes, races, and sexes, and nationalities in history into a national audience that has nothing in common except television or shared messages. Television thereby becomes the common basis for social interaction among a very widely dispersed and diverse national community. As such, it can only be compared, in terms of its functions, not to any other medium but to the preindustrial notion of religion. (1978:47)

If television provides for the maintenance of culture, then it must resist social movements that challenge the culture and seek to transform social institutions. The media do not fully resist such changes; rather, they defend the traditional system by coopting new images that social movements generate. Consequently, we now see "liberated" images of women in the media, but ones that still carry stereotypic gender assumptions. For example, women may now be shown as working, but these women are all beautiful, young, rich, and thin.

Several approaches have been developed to explain the depiction of women by the media. These include the reflection hypotheses, role-learning theory, organizational theories of gender inequality, economic explanations of media organization (Tuchman, 1979), and, most recently, postmodernist theory. Each of these approaches has its own strengths and weaknesses, which are discussed here.

The Reflection Hypothesis

The first and theoretically the most simple explanation of the depiction of women by the media is called the **reflection hypothesis** (Tuchman, 1979; Tuchman, Daniels, and Benét, 1978). This hypothesis assumes that the mass media reflect the values of the general population. Images in the media are seen as representing dominant ideals within the population, particularly because the capitalistic structure of the media is dependent on appealing to the largest consumer audience. According to Gerbner (1978), the ideals of the population are incorporated into symbolic representations in the media. The reflection hypothesis asserts that, although media images are make-believe, they do symbolize dominant social beliefs and images.

The volumes of data produced by marketing researchers and ratings scales indicate that popular appeal is significant in decisions about programming content. Observations of shows such as soap operas also reveal that television attempts to incorporate into its programming social issues that reflect, even if in an overblown way, the experiences (or, at least, the wishes) of its viewers. Although viewers may escape into soap operas as a relief from daily life, the fact that they can do so rests on some form of identification (even if fanciful) with the characters and the situations portrayed (Modleski, 1980).

The reflection hypothesis leaves several questions unanswered. To begin with, as content analysis studies have shown, much if not most of what the media depict is not synchronized with real conditions in people's lives. In part, this phenomenon is explainable by a time lag between cultural changes and changes in the media (Tuchman, Daniels, and Benét, 1978). It is also explainable by the fact that the media portray ideals, not truths; furthermore, people may not actually believe what they see in the media, and, if they do, it may be because the media create, not reflect, viewers' beliefs. A causal question is asked in theoretical explanations of media images: Do the media reflect—or create—popular values? The reflection hypothesis makes the first assumption; other explanations begin with the second.

Role-Learning Theory

The values and images of women and men in the media represent some of the most conservative views of women and men. **Role-learning theory** hypothesizes that sexist and racist images in the media (and the absence thereof) encourage role modeling. That is to say, "the media's deleterious role models, when internalized, prevent and impede female accomplishments. They also encourage both women and men to define women in terms of men (as sex objects) or in the context of the family" (Tuchman, 1979). The assumption that the media encourage role model-ing is the basis for feminist criticisms of the media's depiction of women.

The role-modeling argument assumes that the media should truthfully reproduce social life and that there is some causal connection between the con-tent of the media and its social effects (Tuchman, 1979). In other words, the role-modeling argument assumes that media images produce stimuli that have pre-dictable responses from the public. This is an argument that sees human beings as passive receptacles for whatever media inputs are poured into them. People may, in fact, view media images much more critically or even with cynicism, making it unlikely that they would modify their behavior in accordance with the images. This possibility does not deny the fact that people, especially children, do learn from the media; rather, a criticism of role-modeling theory suggests that it is an oversimplified perspective. As you will see in examining postmodernist theory, many recent feminist theorists see role-learning theory as too one-dimen-sional and simplistic in assuming that images in the media are internalized by viewers.

Organizational Theories of Gender Inequality

Although both the reflection hypothesis and the role-modeling argument alert us to the fit between images and reality, neither adequately explains the reasons for sexism in the media. Other scholars have attempted to explain sexism in media content by studying gender inequality within media organizations. This perspec-tive assumes that the subordinate position of women and people of color in the media influences the ideas produced about them. If women and people of color are absent from the power positions where ideas and images are produced, then their world views and experiences will not be reflected in the images those orga-nizations produce. In addition, because those who occupy power positions come to share a common world view, the ideas they produce tend to reflect the values of the ruling elite.

Since the 1960s, White women and people of color have made many inroads into media careers, but they are still a distinct minority; in fact, recent data show that earlier progress has been stalled. The percentage of women in news broad-casting has stopped increasing, as it had through the mid-1990s, and the number of women who are news directors is actually declining, as is the percentage of minority news directors (Gibbons, 1998; Stone, 1998). This is likely the result of the courts striking down the Federal Communications Commission (FCC) rules mandating the hiring of women and minorities. African Americans, Asian Americans, Latinos, and Native Americans are 18 percent of the news work force, but less than 10 percent of those who direct the news, with little sign of increase. Interestingly, racial-ethnic groups are a larger share of the work force in the largest TV markets (Stone, 1998; see also Figure 3.1). To the casual observer, it may seem that women are an increasing presence in the media, since they do represent a large share of news anchors on the major networks (36 percent of news anchors on CNN, 42 percent on NCB, 43 percent on CBS, and 50 percent on NBC; Gibbons, 1992). Behind the scenes, however, these appearances are deceiving, when you

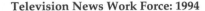

Television News Work Force: 1994

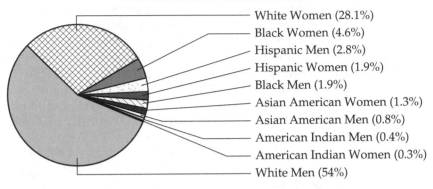

White Women (28.1%)
Black Women (4.6%)
Hispanic Men (2.8%)
Hispanic Women (1.9%)
Black Men (1.9%)
Asian American Women (1.3%)
Asian American Men (0.8%)
American Indian Men (0.4%)
American Indian Women (0.3%)
White Men (54%)

Television News Directors: 1994

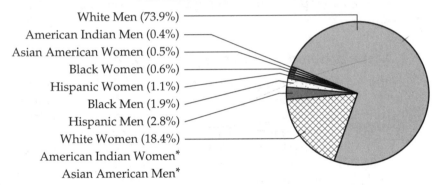

White Men (73.9%)
American Indian Men (0.4%)
Asian American Women (0.5%)
Black Women (0.6%)
Hispanic Women (1.1%)
Black Men (1.9%)
Hispanic Men (2.8%)
White Women (18.4%)
American Indian Women*
Asian American Men*

*Indicates too few to calculate a percentage

**FIGURE 3.1   Race-Ethnicity and Gender in Television:
Who's in Charge?**

Source: Data from Vernon Stone. 1998. "Minorities and Women in Television News."
Website: <www.missouri.edu/~jourvs/gvtminw.html>

consider the overall representation of women and the gender inequities that remain in salaries, as depicted in Table 3.1.

Do the numbers of women and minorities in the media matter, as far as explaining the images of women and racial-ethnic groups that appear? The argument that increasing the number of women and minorities employed by the media will transform the images portrayed of them presumes that men and women and Whites and people of color hold different values; this belief has not been consistently demonstrated in research. Persons who work in an organization become socialized to accept the organization's values. Those who do not conform are less likely to build successful careers; hence, organizational workers more often than not adopt the values of the organizations in which they are employed. Within the media, professional attitudes discourage workers from offending the networks. Professionalism encourages workers to conform to the bureaucratic

TABLE 3.1   Salary Averages across Media Industries

	Percent Women	Women's Median Salary	Men's Median Salary
Daily papers	39.0	$30,887	$36,959
Weekly papers	44.1	17,917	23,750
Television	33.7	25,000	25,961
Radio	32.4	18,611	21,176
Newsmagazines	45.9	58,750	68,333
Wire services	25.9	41,071	44,844

Source: Data from Sheila Gibbons. 1992. *Media Report to Women*, Vol. 20, Fall, p. 88.

and capitalist values of their organization (Tuchman, 1979). This influence affects how all workers portray gender and racial issues in the media because the organizational culture discourages controversy. That men and women working in the media adopt similar values to each other tells us not so much that men and women think alike, but that all workers' behaviors and attitudes are shaped by the organizations in which they are employed.

Capitalism and the Media

A fourth perspective used to explain sexism in the media attributes sexism to the capitalist structure of media organizations. According to this approach, it is in the interests of sponsors to foster images that are consistent with the products they sell. Many of these products encourage particular values; for example, promoting obsessive cleanliness is necessary to sell the numerous household cleaning products placed on the market.

This perspective also claims that it is in the interests of a capitalist power elite to discourage images of reality that would foster discontent. Not only will sponsors promote any values that will sell but they will also encourage traditional views that uphold the status quo, while discouraging and stereotyping those that challenge it. When the media respond to social criticism, they do so within the limits of existing institutions. For example, following the civil rights movement, when pressure was generated to increase the number of Black Americans in the media, more Black Americans appeared in advertisements and on television programs, but they were and continue to be primarily depicted in middle-class settings where they hold middle-class value systems and are not critical of U.S. society. Likewise, as noted previously, the feminist movement was depicted by the media as radical, trivial, and extremist. As the women's movement gained public support, the media selected its more moderate programs and leaders for public display.

An economic perspective of the media reminds us that the media are owned and controlled by the major corporations of U.S. society. From this perspective, Marx's idea is true that those who control economic production also control the manufacture and dissemination of ideas. The economic structure of the media explains much about how women are exploited through commercialism. This perspective has frequently been cited by feminists as the reason that women are portrayed either as sex objects or as household caretakers. These values, they point out, are consistent with capitalist needs to maintain women's services in the home and to make commercial objects out of everything, including sexuality.

In itself, this explanation encourages a somewhat conspiratorial view of media owners and management who, although they are motivated by economic profit, may not have the specific intent of exploiting women. This perspective, along with the gender-inequality approach, gives us, however, a more complete understanding of sexism in the media. Observing the economic and social organization of the media causes us to ask who produces media images and how these images define legitimate forms of social reality.

Depictions in the media can also be seen as social myths by which the meaning of gender in society is established. Anthropologists study social myths to gain an insight into the culture and social organization of a people. Myths provide an interpretation of social truths, beliefs, and relationships that guide a society in its vision of the past, present, and future. They establish a "universe of discourse" that integrates and controls its members; gives them a common reality; and creates structures for what is said, done, and believed (Tuchman, 1979). By creating a universe of discourse among their audience, the media act as powerful agents of social control. They engage people in passive fantasies, encourage dreams and visions that are consistent with the social structure, and establish a common basis for social interaction. In a fundamental way, the depiction of women, as well as men, in the media infiltrates our social consciousness and embeds itself in our imagination. Postmodernist theorists further explore this process.

Postmodernist Feminist Theory, the Media, and Popular Culture

Each of the preceding perspectives implicity assumes that the influences of the media is unidirectional—that is, there is little indication of how viewers (or readers) actually respond to these images. Also, these perspectives assume that, whatever the source of media images, they have a deleterious effect on those who watch or read them. This assumption is challenged by the arguments of postmodernist feminist theory—a theoretical perspective that assumes a more active perspective on the response of viewers to images perceived in various media outlets. **Postmodernism** views society as fully constructed through social meaning systems, which are highly fluid and changeable (see Chapter 13). From this perspective, symbols and representations are especially important to study because they reveal the meaning systems that shape society at any point in time. Postmodernist theory, which will be explored further in Chapter 13, thus places much emphasis on cultural studies, since it is through culture that one sees the various representations that define modern life. Unlike traditional analyses of things like media images, however, from a postmodernist perspective, social structures are not determinist in shaping gender identity, nor other forms of identity. Rather, the self is generated not just through the domination of cultural forms (such as media images), but also through the subjective understandings that people themselves bring to their reading of "social texts" (i.e., cultural images) (Currie, 1997; Walters, 1995).

Postmodernist theory tends to be highly abstract and has been criticized by some feminists for being so, since it is almost impossible for anyone but those trained in elite humanities programs to understand it. But, an important point derived from postmodernist theory is that social actors are creative in determining their identity, or, specifically, in the case of gender, what it means to be a woman or man.

In a concrete example of the study of cultural images from a postmodernist perspective, Dawn Currie (1997) has examined teen magazines and asked how young girls read them and the images of femininity they convey. Currie designed a study utilizing small *focus groups* (i.e., discussion groups whose conversation is observed and recorded by the researcher). The focus groups of teen girls observed images taken from *Seventeen* magazine and discussed what they had seen. Currie found that the girls did not just passively accept the images as ideals; instead they selectively choose ads that they enjoyed and rejected the images conveyed in others. She argues that these young readers distinguished between fantasy and reality and were often quite critical of ads that they saw as making no sense or posing unrealistic images. Indeed, the girls were quick to reject images that they saw as inconsistent with their own identity.

This does not mean that the images in the magazines were completely without influence. In fact, when asked whom they most wanted to be like, many of the girls chose celebrities who had just been featured in *Seventeen*. Currie suggests that the formation of gender identity, as influenced by the media, is not as simple as one might think. She shows that young women actively mediate what they see and what they think, thus emphasizing the role of human creativity in the formation of self, instead of seeing people as passive objects into whom cultural images are inserted.

We can see that postmodernist explanations of gender and culture go beyond theories of learned gender roles and gender differences by insisting on seeing agency in human behavior. This does not mean that domination by highly influential media industries is insignificant, nor does it mean that we should view the sexist images of gender in the media uncritically. Rather, postmodernism suggests that women and men view these images with an ability to shape the meanings of what they see, without necessarily completely internalizing such cultural ideals. Thus, postmodernist theory adds a strong social constructionist dimension to understanding how knowledge is created in society—a subject long studied in a field known as the sociology of knowledge.

❧ The Sociology of Knowledge

The preceding discussion underscores three essential sociological points: that knowledge in society is socially constructed, that knowledge emerges from the conditions of people's lives, and that knowledge is embedded in ideological systems—that is, knowledge is not pure. Rather, knowledge is often generated from and tends to reinforce belief systems that support existing social arrangements (i.e., the *status quo*). Whether reflected in language, the media, popular culture, or the arts, knowledge of gender is a powerful social construction.

In sociology, the study of the social construction of ideas is called the **sociology of knowledge**. The sociology of knowledge begins with the premise that ideas emerge from particular social and historical settings and that this social structural context shapes, although it does not determine, human consciousness and interpretations of reality. Studies in the sociology of knowledge relate ideas and consciousness to social structure and human culture. Intellectually, this perspective originates primarily in the works of Karl Marx and Karl Mannheim, both of whom, in distinct ways, grappled with the relationship between human knowledge and human existence. It was Mannheim who, in the early twentieth century, labeled the study of the sociology of knowledge and delineated its specific program, but Marx's study of ideology and consciousness is the intellectual precursor of Mannheim's endeavor.

Marx and the Social Construction of Knowledge

Karl Marx (1818–1883) based his study of human ideas on the premise that the existence of living human beings—that is, their actual activities and material conditions—forms the basis for human history and the ideas generated in this history. Although Marx recognized that human beings live within particular physical settings (including climatic, geographical, and geological conditions), it is the social relationships formed in these settings that make up human society. In other words, human beings transform their environmental conditions through the activities in which they engage. Human society and history emerge as people use their labor to create their social environment. Marx argued that human beings are distinguished from animals by the fact of their consciousness. Although we now know that other animal species have linguistic ability and rudimentary systems of social organization, no other species has the capacity of humans for the elaboration of culture.

Marx's theory of ideas originates with his argument that ideas follow from human behavior. In other words, thinking and the products of thinking are derived from the actual activity in which human beings engage. Marx discards the philosophical view that what humans think, imagine, or conceive precedes their actual life experiences. Within Marx's framework, it is not the consciousness of persons that forms the bonds (and chains) of human society; rather, specific relationships among people shape human society and therefore the ideas of its people.

Marx is not denying that social relations involve an interpretive dimension. He is arguing, however, that ideas emerge from our material reality. This theory has important consequences for social change, for it implies that changes in consciousness alone do not constitute the social changes necessary for the liberation of people. Instead, the material conditions of society must be changed if we are to liberate people from oppression.

Marx goes one step further by arguing that within society, the dominant ideas of any period are the ideas of the ruling class. It is they who have the power to influence the intellectual production and distribution of ideas. Consequently, although persons ordinarily form their ideas within the context of their practical experience, ideas produced within powerful institutions take on an objective form that extends beyond us and acts as a system of social control. In fact, Marx goes on to say that in societies having a complex division of labor, a split develops between mental and material labor. Those who work with their hands are not those who produce the society's dominant ideas. Especially for persons who are not in the ruling class, the dominant ideas of a society stand in contradiction to their experience.

A Marxist perspective relates ideas directly to the societal conditions in which they are produced. This view is summed up by Marx's statement that "it is not the consciousness of men [sic] that determines their being, but, on the contrary, their social being that determines their consciousness" (Tucker, 1972:4). In capitalist societies, those who own the means of production also determine the ruling ideas of the period. As Marx writes,

> *The ideas of the ruling class are in every epoch the ruling ideas: i.e., the class which is the ruling material force of society, is at the same time its ruling intellectual force. The class which has the means of material production at its disposal, has control at the same time over the means of mental production, so that thereby, generally speaking, the ideas of those who lack the means of mental production are subject to it.* (The German Ideology, *in Tucker, 1972:136)*

From a Marxist perspective, under capitalism, consciousness is determined by class relations, for even though persons will normally try to identify what is in their best interest, under capitalism the ruling class controls the production of ideas. Even though humans create practical ideas from experience, most of our experience is determined by capitalist relations of production; thus, the ideas that are disseminated through communications systems, including the media, language, and other cultural institutions, authorize a reality that the ruling class would like us to believe. According to Marx, when subordinate groups accept the world view of dominant groups, they are engaged in **false consciousness.**

Marx's ideas have been modified by feminist scholars who see class relations alone as inadequate in explaining the evolution and persistence of sexism. Feminists add to Marx's perspective on the social construction of ideas, proposing that it is men who own the means of production and therefore determine the ruling ideas of any given time. Sexist ideas justify the power of men over women and sanction male domination, just as racist ideas attempt to justify White supremacy. From a feminist perspective, ideas serve not only capitalist interests but also men's interests; moreover, men's ideas stem from their particular relationship to the gender division of labor, as explained by Canadian scholar Dorothy Smith.

According to Smith (1990), in patriarchal societies there is a gender-based division of labor in which men typically do not do the work that meets the physical and emotional needs of society's members. As a result, men's ideas (especially of those who engage primarily in intellectual work) assume a split, or bifurcation, between mind and body, and rational thought is accorded the highest value. This belief in the bifurcation of mind and body is made possible only because the labor of women provides for men's physical needs, mediates their social relations, and allows them to ignore bodily and emotional experience as an integral dimension of life.

In racially stratified societies, the gender-based division of labor also intersects with the racial division of labor. The ideas of White people, particularly those having the most privilege, are likely to take the labor of racial groups for granted, making it appear invisible or unimportant. Oddly enough, the ideology that supports racial inequality tends to define racial groups as "lazy" and "unwilling to work." This ideological belief does not reflect reality, but rather distorts the experiences of racial groups whose actual work affords certain Whites the privilege of not having to do menial labor. In addition, in societies structured by both race and gender privilege, the ideologies of sexism and racism intersect. Think, for example, of dominant cultural images of women on welfare (usually presumed to be women of color). The idea that they do not want to work pervades popular thinking, as if raising children on a meager income is not work.

Sexism as Ideology

Karl Mannheim (1893–1947) further developed the sociology of knowledge. Mannheim's sociology of knowledge seeks to discover the historical circumstances of knowledge by relating ideas to the conditions under which they are produced. His work also provides a foundation for feminist scholarship because he develops the thought that ideas grow out of the relationship of knowledge to social structure.

Feminists (as discussed in Chapter 1) suggest that what has been taken as knowledge reflects the system of male domination in which it is produced. This insight stems from the work of Mannheim, who relates what is known to the social existence of the knower. Mannheim and feminist scholars who have followed him challenge the idea that objectivity is based on the detachment of the knower from the surrounding environment. Instead, Mannheim suggests that the individual does not think alone. Not only do persons participate in what others have thought prior to the individual's existence, but even more fundamentally, all social thought involves a "community of knowing" (1936:31). Ideas expressed by a person are therefore a function of the person's experience as well as his or her social and historical milieu.

The task of the sociology of knowledge is to discover the relational character of thought, meaning to study how ideas are embedded in the social experience of their producers and the social-historical milieu within which ideas are formed. Intellectual change must likewise be seen in the context of social change, and all ideas must be evaluated within the context of their social making. This view is true not only for the grand ideas of intellectual history but also for the consciousness of human beings in their ordinary experience (Berger and Luckmann, 1966).

Mannheim suggests that new ideas are most likely generated during periods of rapid social change. He explains this belief by suggesting that as long as group traditions remain stable, then traditional world views remain intact. New ideas appear when old traditions are breaking up, although the persistence of customary ways of thinking is also likely to make new ideas appear to be "curiosities, errors, ambiguities, or heresies" (1936:7).

Mannheim is best known for his study of ideology. **Ideology** refers to a system of beliefs about the world that involves distortions of reality at the same time it provides justification for the status quo. Following from Marx, Mannheim sees ideology as serving the interests of groups in the society who justify their position by distorting social definitions of reality. Ideologies serve the powerful by presenting us with a definition of reality that is false and yet orders our comprehension of the surrounding world. When ideas emerge from ideology, they operate as a form of social control by defining the status quo to be the proper state of affairs.

From Mannheim's work, we can understand **sexism** as an ideology that defends the traditional status of women in society. Although, as Mannheim says, no single idea constitutes an ideological belief system, the collective totality of an ideology (such as sexism) permeates our consciousness and our comprehension of the world in which we live. It is here that the sociology of knowledge merges with the political goals of feminism because in debunking sexist ideology, the social-historical origins of sexist thought are found and new definitions of reality can be forged. Although Mannheim is careful to distinguish political argument from academic thought, he recognizes that the unmasking of ideological systems is a function of sociological theory.

For feminists, the sociology of knowledge creates the theoretical framework in which sexism and the generation of ideas about women can be understood. The theoretical perspectives of both Marx and Mannheim underlie the analysis of sexism and knowledge that feminists have offered. The sociology of knowledge helps us understand how ideas reproduce our definitions of social reality; who produces ideas; under what conditions ideas are made; and the consequences of ideas and beliefs that, in the case of sexism, systematically define women and men in stereotypical and distorted terms. The abstract theory of the sociology of knowledge is well illustrated by examining women and the gendered production of knowledge in two of the major institutions (other than the popular media) where knowledge is produced: higher education and science.

❧ Women and Educational Thought

The pursuit of knowledge has historically been considered the work of men. In the history of education, women have been outsiders. Either they were excluded by formal admissions policies or they were tracked into gender-typed fields and specialties. In the early history of higher education in this country, women's education was restricted by ideologies that depicted their minds as directed and limited by their bodies. Especially in the post–Civil War period, when major transformations were occurring in the traditional gender roles, leading educational reformers claimed that women's wombs dominated their mental life and thus they should not study or work vigorously!

One such reformer, Dr. Edward Clarke, was a member of the Harvard Board of Overseers and a member of its medical faculty. He published several popular books in the late nineteenth century, warning of the dangers that education and study posed for women. Clarke wrote, "A girl upon whom Nature, for a limited period and for a definite purpose, imposes so great a physiological task, will not have as much power left for the tasks of school, as the boy of whom Nature requires less at the corresponding epoch" (Clarke, 1873:54, cited in Rosenberg, 1982:10). Accordingly, he advised young women to study one-third as much as young men and not to study at all during menstruation!

Others also agreed. Professor Charles Meigs admonished his class at Jefferson Medical College to think of the womb as a "great power and ask your own judgments whether such an organ can be of little influence on the constitution and how much!" (Meigs, 1847:18, cited in Rosenberg, 1982:6). The prominent gynecologist Thomas Emmet argued:

> *To reach the highest point of physical development the young girl in the between classes of society should pass the year before puberty and some two years afterwards free from all exciting influences. She should be kept as a child as long as possible, and made to associate with children. . . . Her mind should be occupied by a very moderate amount of study, with frequent intervals of a few moments each, passed when possible in the recumbent position, until her system becomes accustomed to the new order of life. (Emmet, 1879:21, cited in Rosenberg, 1982:10)*

These admonitions reflect class biases of the time and also are consistent with racist arguments that defined Black Americans as biologically unfit for the same privileges accorded Whites. Such biological explanations of inequality are often used to justify oppression by race, class, and gender. Biological explanations of inequality seem to become especially popular during periods of rapid social change in class, race, and gender relations, because such beliefs develop as justifications for maintaining the status quo—a classic case of dominant group ideology.

Women are no longer formally excluded from higher education. In fact, women are now a majority of college students, but, as the educational pyramid represented in Figure 3.2 shows, the percentage of women in higher education declines, moving up the educational hierarchy. Women begin as a majority of entering college students and recipients of bachelor's and master's degrees. They are gaining as a percentage of those receiving doctorates and are predicted to be 80 percent of all Ph.D.s by the year 2005 (*The Chronicle of Higher Education Almanac,* 1998).

As faculty, however, women are concentrated in the lower ranks. Although women are 35 percent of all faculty, they are clustered in the lowest-status and

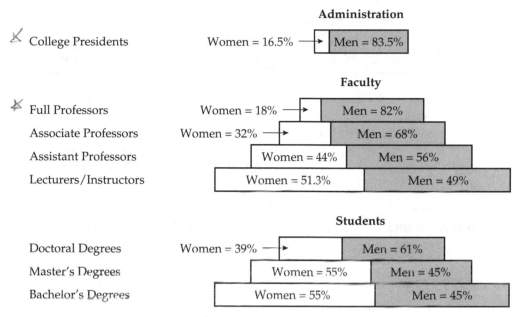

FIGURE 3.2   The Educational Pyramid: 1995

Sources: Data from Deborah J. Wilds and Reginald Wilson. 1998. *Minorities in Higher Education.* Washington, DC: American Council on Education, pp. 103 104; *The Chronicle of Higher Education Almanac,* Vol. 45. August 28, 1998, p. 26.

lowest-paid faculty positions, as instructors and lecturers. Women of color, like men of color, are an even smaller portion of college faculty, as Table 3.2 shows.

Women's status in educational institutions has important ramifications for how academic knowledge is constructed and how women are defined within it. Academic knowledge is created within specific institutional structures. Because the production of research and scholarship is tied to the setting in which it develops, the noticeable absence or invisibility of women in these settings has contributed to the invisibility of women and their distortion in research.

Women's status in academia has several consequences both for the personal experiences of women faculty and for the state of knowledge in general. At the personal level, women may find that their personalities (formed as they are through cultural expectations of femininity) are at odds with the values and behaviors surrounding them. This dilemma was expressed by Alice Rossi in 1970 and is still common today. Rossi wrote:

Women who are intellectually or politically brilliant are more readily accepted by men if they are also properly feminine in their style and deportment with men. This helps to assure that there will be few women of achievement for men to "exempt" from the general category of women, since the traits associated with traditional femininity —

TABLE 3.2   Who's on the Faculty?

	White, Non-Hispanic	Black	Hispanic	Asian American/ Pacific Islander	American Indian
Men					
(percent of all faculty)	**55.8%**	**2.5%**	**1.4%**	**3.7%**	**0.2%**
Percent of total at rank:					
Professor	74.6	2.0	1.2	4.2	0.2
Associate Professor	60.0	2.6	1.4	3.9	0.2
Assistant Professor	46.2	3.1	1.7	4.6	0.2
Lecturer/Instructor	41.2	3.2	2.0	1.9	0.4
Other	48.1	2.1	1.2	2.9	0.2
Women					
(percent of all faculty)	**29.2%**	**2.4%**	**0.9%**	**1.3%**	**0.2%**
Percent of total at rank:					
Professor	15.8	1.1	0.4	0.6	0.05
Associate Professor	28.1	2.0	0.7	1.0	0.1
Assistant Professor	37.2	3.3	1.3	2.2	0.2
Lecturers/Instructor	43.3	4.0	1.8	1.8	0.3
Other	39.3	3.0	1.0	1.7	0.3

Sources: Data from Deborah J. Wilds and Reginald Wilson. 1998. *Minorities in Higher Education.* Washington, DC: American Council on Education; *The Chronicle of Higher Education Almanac*, Vol. 45. August 28, 1998, p. 30.

softness, compliance, sweetness—are rarely found together with the contradictory qualities of a vigorous and questioning intellect, and a willingness to persist on a problem against conventional assumptions. (p. 36)

Women's status in academic life (as in other organizations) creates a feeling of standing out, if only because women are different from men—long the majority (Kanter, 1977). Moreover, women may find that their experience is translated into the concepts and categories that have been used to describe men's experience.

For students, the secondary status of women in education can also seriously affect their learning. Sexist attitudes about women students can discourage them from classroom participation or may even steer them away from particular courses and departments. Professors who fill their classes with sexist, racist, or homophobic comments can fill students with such anger that it is impossible for them to learn in that environment. Male students, too, are affected by such an environment because such an environment makes it difficult for men to see women as full peers and hampers men's ability to relate to women as equals in the worlds of work and families. For men with negative views about women, negative attitudes about women and sexist behavior in the classroom reinforce these views because these attitudes are confirmed by people with knowledge and high status (Hall, 1982).

The personal consequences of women's status in academia are troubling and can result in the demise of many women's careers. As you saw in Chapter 1, women's status in the academic disciplines has influenced what is known about them. Male domination of academic institutions influences the social production of knowledge because the existing schemes of understanding have been created within a particular setting, one in which men have authority over women. In sociology, for example, "how sociology is thought—its methods, conceptual schemes and theories—have been based on and built up within the male social universe, even when women have participated in its doing" (Smith, 1974:7). Because the male-constituted world stands in authority over women (both inside and outside the academy), sociologists "impose the concepts and terms in which the world of men is thought as the concepts and terms in which women must think about their world" (Smith, 1974:7). Women then become *outsiders*, not only because their status in universities is less than that of men but also because they are estranged from the dominant world view surrounding them in academic life.

Sociological theory provides insight in understanding how the status of outsiders influences their perspectives. Georg Simmel (1858–1918) described a stranger as one who is "fixed within a particular spatial group whose boundaries are similar to spatial boundaries. But his [sic] position in this group is determined, essentially, by the fact that he has not belonged to it from the beginning, that he imports qualities into it which do not and cannot stem from the group itself" (cited in Wolff, 1950:402). The stranger (or the outsider) is both close to and distant from the group and its beliefs. The outsider is both involved with and indifferent to the shared perspectives of the group as a whole. This detachment creates critical distance, so that what is taken for granted by group members may be held in doubt by outsiders. As feminists have put it, "The outsider is denied the filtered vision that allows men to live without too troubling an insight (Gornick, 1971:126).

Feminist criticism of the social sciences also describes the vision that women as outsiders bring to intellectual life. Feminist sociologist Marcia Westkott writes:

> *When women realize that we are simultaneously immersed in and estranged from both our own particular discipline and the Western intellectual tradition generally, a personal tension develops that informs the critical dialogue. This tension, rooted in the contradiction of women's belonging and not belonging, provides the basis for knowing deeply and personally that which we criticize. A personally experienced, culturally-based contradiction means that in some fundamental way we as critics also oppose ourselves, or, at least, that part of us continues to sustain the very basis of our own estrangement. Hence, the personal struggle of being both an insider and outsider is not only a source of knowledge and insight, but also a source of self-criticism. (1979:422)*

In the history of sociological thought, marginality and alienation, especially during periods of rapid social change, have produced many valuable insights. Scientific thinking, including sociological thinking, has flourished in periods of uncertainty because doubt and transformation foster the development of personal and collective creative thought. As C. Wright Mills suggests, personal and societal troubles that destroy the façades of conventional wisdom also form the scientific basis of the sociological and feminist imagination.

For outsiders, their paradoxical closeness to and remoteness from social groups may result in new perspectives on knowledge. It is the outsider who suspends belief in the taken-for-granted attitudes of institutions. As a result, the status of women as outsiders in intellectual life results in new methodologies and new perspectives in social and political thought.

Women of color within the academy also stand as outsiders, or as what Patricia Hill Collins (1986, 1998) calls "outsiders within." Marginalized by both their race and gender, women of color have a unique standpoint in the academy and can therefore provide distinct and revealing analyses of race, class, and gender. Insiders to any group develop similar world views; as a result, it often takes the perspective of outsiders to challenge these taken-for-granted views. As outsiders within the academy, women of color are in a unique position to generate new knowledge. They are trained in the methods and theories of their disciplines but do not necessarily share the privileges, patterns of belief, or historical experiences of insiders. Because they are outsiders within, women of color can generate new forms of insight and make visible those structures of oppression that are less apparent to members of more privileged groups.

❧ Gender, Science, and Society

Scientific knowledge in our society is seen as a source of great authority. Scientific careers carry much prestige, and scientists have a great deal of power to influence the everyday experiences of our lives. Scientific explanations are generally thought to be objective accounts that are uninfluenced by the values and interests of scientific thinkers. Science thus has the image of being value neutral and true to the facts. Objectivity in science is depicted as stemming from the calculated distance between the observer and the observed. In the scientific framework, personal characteristics of scientific observers are not expected to influence their results.

Despite the strong claims of neutrality and objectivity by scientists, the fact is that science is closely tied to the centers of power in this society and interwoven with capitalist and patriarchal institutions. This has many implications for understanding the social structure of science as well as for understanding how the social structure of science influences the production of scientific knowledge. As you have already seen in the previous chapter, allegedly scientific claims are often used to support sexist and racist beliefs. One could argue that such claims are simply a case of bad science, but feminist critiques of scientific knowledge go deeper, asking how the social structure of scientific professions is related to the scientific views and conclusions scientists make.

Science bears the imprint of the fact that scientists have been men, as many have documented the small proportion of women in virtually every scientific field. Women are not, of course, absent from science; they constitute a large proportion of the technical, clerical, domestic, teaching, and plant maintenance staffs required to do scientific work. Still, women, and especially women of color, appear as objects and "others" in science; they are exploited as research subjects, and their labor in the production of science remains invisible to the scientific elite. The decision makers in science—those who define scientific problems, set scientific agendas, fund scientific projects, and relate science to public policy—are overwhelmingly men.

Science is produced and applied within a distinctively masculine framework—one that values objective separation from the objects of research and, yet, is nonetheless gendered in the descriptions and explanations it offers of the natural and social worlds. Evelyn Fox Keller calls this a "science/gender" system—a network of associations between our concepts of masculinity and femininity and the construction of science. She argues that to examine the roots, dynamics, and consequences of the science/gender system, it is necessary to understand how ideologies of gender and science inform each other and how this affects social arrangements between men and women, science and nature (Keller, 1985).

Asking how and why women have been excluded from the practice of science is one way to reveal deeply embedded gender, race, and class patterns in the structure of scientific professions and consequently in the character of scientific thought. Rossiter's (1982) work on the history of women in science shows that the concept of a woman scientist is perceived as a contradiction in terms, since scientists are supposed to be tough, rigorous, rational, impersonal, unemotional, and competitive, while women are not. Often, when women make major contributions to science, their work is ignored, belittled, or claimed by men. A classic example is the discovery of DNA. James Watson, one of the scientists who discovered DNA, tells the story of his and Francis Crick's (a man) discovery in a famous book, *The Double Helix* (1968). The book reviles a woman colleague, Rosalind Franklin, who, it is clear from other accounts, should have shared Watson and Crick's credit (Sayre, 1975).

Sometimes women's exclusion from science is not only as scientists but also as subjects of scientific research. In the early 1990s, for example, several reports published in medical journals and reported in the national press documented the exclusion of women from major national health studies of heart disease, lung cancer, and kidney disease. Extrapolating from studies of men to the treatment of women leads to potentially faulty treatment. For example, although women suffer from depression more than do men, research on antidepressant drugs has involved only male research subjects. Other evidence has revealed that some antidepressant drugs have different effects when used during women's menstrual cycles; thus, medical researchers have warned that treating women based on the results of research from all male samples is risky (*New York Times*, September 9, 1991, p. A14).

Medical reports have also disclosed that doctors treat women with heart disease less aggressively than they treat men with heart disease. Although the effect of this differential treatment is unknown, women are less likely to undergo heart bypass surgery and balloon angioplasty than are men, even though women in the studies noting this pattern had more advanced heart disease than men (Kolata, 1991). Because of the inadequacy of prior research about women's health, in the wake of these reports, the National Institutes of Health has created a new research division, the Office of Research on Women's Health (Hilts, 1990).

Many argue (Fee, 1983; Harding, 1986, 1991, 1993) that gender identity is at the very heart of the definition of science because scientific norms of detachment, distance, and rationality match those of masculine culture. Feminist critiques of science also reveal that scientific thought often reflects the patriarchal ideology of the culture. One way this happens is through the projection of patriarchal values onto scientific descriptions of the physical world. For example, kingdoms and orders are not intrinsic to the nature of organisms but have evolved in a patriarchal world that values hierarchy and patrilineage (Hubbard, 1984). Note, also, the description of the experimental scientific method offered by Francis Bacon, one of the sixteenth-century founders of modern scientific thought:

> *For you have but to follow and as it were hound nature in her wanderings, and you will be able when you like to lead and drive her afterward to the same place again. . . . Neither ought a man to make scruple of entering and penetrating into those holes and corners, when the inquisition of truth is his whole object. (cited in Harding, 1986:116)*

The emergence of modern science is founded on an image of rational man as conquering the passions of nature, which is depicted as female. Consider Machiavelli's famed quotation regarding fortune:

> *Fortune is a woman and it is necessary if you wish to master her to conquer her by force; and it can be seen that she lets herself be overcome by the bold rather than by those who proceed coldly, and therefore like a woman, she is always a friend to the young because they are less cautious, fiercer, and master her with greater audacity. (from* The Prince; *cited in Harding, 1986:115)*

Such depictions of science and nature might be dismissed as old-fashioned ramblings of patriarchal days gone by, except for the fact that gendered descriptions of biological phenomena still influence the way we imagine physical events. Think, for example, of sperm, popularly depicted as lively and aggressive swimmers, rigorously pursuing the waiting egg. Alice Rossi describes this as a fantasy of male sexual power. She writes:

> *Ever since Leewenhoek first saw sperm under the microscope, great significance has been attached to the fact that sperm are equipped with motile flagella, and it was assumed that the locomotive ability of the sperm fully explained their journey from*

the vagina through the cervix and uterus to the oviduct for the encounter with the ovum. . . . Rorvik (1971) describes the seven-inch journey through the birth canal and womb to the waiting egg as equivalent to a 500-mile upstream swim for a salmon and comments with admiration that they often make the hazardous journey in under an hour, "more than earning their title as the most powerful and rapid living creatures on earth." The image is clear: powerful active sperm and a passive ovum awaiting its arrival and penetration, male sexual imagery structuring the very act of conception. (1977:16–17)

In fact, as Rossi points out, uterine contractions, stimulated by the release of the hormone oxytocin, propel the sperm through the female system so that "completely inert substances such as dead sperm and even particles of India ink reach the oviducts as rapidly as live sperm do" (Rossi, 1977:17).

In her study analyzing the images of reproduction in contemporary biology textbooks, Emily Martin, an anthropologist, has found that sperm are still described as active, aggressive agents, while eggs are portrayed in passive terms. According to Martin, the texts stress that sperm are actively produced, while female ova "merely sit on the shelf, slowly degenerating and aging like an overstocked inventory" (1991:487). Citing text authors, Martin writes that texts

liken the egg's role to that of Sleeping Beauty: "a dormant bride awaiting her mate's magic kiss, which instills the spirit that brings her to life." Sperm, by contrast, have a "mission," which is to "move through the female genital tract in quest of the ovum." One popular account has it that the sperm carry out a "perilous journey" into the "warm darkness," where some fall away "exhausted." "Survivors" "assault" the egg, the successful candidates "surrounding the prize." (1991:490)

The fact is, sperm do not merely penetrate a passive egg; rather, the sperm and egg stick together because of adhesive molecules on the surface of each. Nor are sperm as mobile as their descriptions suggest. Despite knowledge to the contrary, metaphorical descriptions of the biological reproductive process make the event seem like a contemporary soap opera or moral fable. As Martin illustrates, the descriptions used by scientists have prevented them from seeing how eggs and sperm actually interact. Thus, cultural values influence the discovery of scientific facts.

The point is not to abandon science, but to understand that within scientific studies, bias can enter the scientist's choice of topic, choice of research subjects, definitions of concepts, method of observation, analysis and interpretation of data, and manner of reporting (Longino and Doell, 1983; Messing, 1983). Gendered assumptions infiltrate the scientific record; many of the "truths" alleged by scientific studies merely reflect the interests of a male-dominated society. Feminist revisions of science call for a more inclusive and reflective perspective by recognizing the interplay between scientific knowledge and the social systems in which science is produced. Feminist revisions of science also seek a more humanistic science—one in which science is used for human liberation from race, class, and gender oppression.

🕊 *Summary*

Images of women throughout popular culture have historically rested on distorted views of women and men. Language reflects deeply gendered patterns of social life. Images of women in the media depict women primarily as sex objects, in domestic roles, or in less active postures than men. Although distorted and false, these images deeply influence our understanding of ourselves and the society in which we live. The sociology of knowledge explains how these images emerge from the particular social and historical settings and organizations in which they are created; it also explains how such images shape our interpretations of reality. Feminist scholars see negative images of women in the media, in the academy, and in scientific knowledge also as the result of male domination, because these images try to legitimate women's unequal status.

The concept of ideology is central to this analysis. Ideology is a system of beliefs that distorts reality at the same time that it seeks to justify the status quo. Sexism is an ideology that attempts to explain and justify institutionalized inequality of women. Likewise, racism is an ideology that attempts to justify white supremacy. Racist and sexist ideology has been deeply embedded in popular culture, as well as in academic knowledge, including science.

The women's movement challenges sexism and racism by teaching us to recognize negative images as they are found in the media and in the academy; feminist ideas can also help us imagine ways of constructing knowledge that are no longer bound by sexist and racist assumptions.

🕊 *Key Terms*

content analysis	popular culture	sexism
essentialism	postmodernism	social constructionist theory
false consciousness	reflection hypothesis	sociology of knowledge
ideology	role-learning theory	

🕊 *Discussion Questions/Projects for Thought*

1. Identify some aspect of popular culture (i.e., MTV videos, current children's films, television sitcoms) and develop a systematic way to observe the gender images portrayed. What do these images convey to the audience? Using the theoretical frameworks used to explain the depiction of women in the mass media, how would you explain the presence of these images? What do you suppose their effect is?

2. Find out what percentage of men and women are majoring in different subjects in your college. Are the majors segregated by gender? How will women's and men's choices of major affect their future work opportunities and earning ability? You may want to supplement your discussion by interviewing students about their chosen majors. What factors resulted in the gender patterns that you have observed?

3. As a way of exploring the difference in essentialist and social constructionist theory, ask a group of women to observe advertisements in a women's magazine and talk about what they see in the images. Based on what they say, would you say that these women have internalized the ideal that these images suggest, do they resist it, or something in between? What does this tell you about social constructionist theory and essentialism?

❧ Suggested Readings

Barthel, Diane. 1988. *Putting on Appearances: Gender and Advertising*. Philadelphia: Temple University Press.
Barthel's sociological analysis of gender and advertising shows how images of gender are constructed in advertising. Her sociological perspective shows these ads in the social production and reveals the social effects that they have.

Collins, Patricia Hill. 1990. *Black Feminist Thought: Knowledge, Consciousness, and the Politics of Empowerment*. Boston: Unwin Hyman.
This important book connects race and gender in the sociology of knowledge, by developing a framework for Black feminist thought. Collins uses this perspective to examine the controlling images that the dominant culture produces about Black women.

Crawford, Mary. 1995. *Gender and Language*. Thousand Oaks, CA: Sage.
This basic text is a good review of the gendered character of language. The author places her analysis in the context of theoretical debates about sex differences, their origins, and their significance.

Dines, Gail, and Jean M. Humez, eds. 1995. *Gender, Race, and Class in Media*. Thousand Oaks, CA: Sage.
This anthology explores the race, class, and gender images produced in the media, linking them to the perpetuation of cultural stereotypes. Some articles also explore the representation of gays and lesbians in the media, linking sexual stereotypes to other forms of cultural oppression.

Harding, Sandra. 1991. *Whose Science? Whose Knowledge: Thinking from Women's Lives*. Ithaca, NY: Cornell University Press.
Harding's work examines how scientific thinking has embedded gendered assumptions and how a feminist perspective can be used to enhance scientific objectivity.

hooks, bell. 1991. *Black Looks: Race and Representation*. Boston: South End Press.
A noted Black feminist scholar, hooks writes about the portrayal of African Americans in popular culture and the connection of these images to Black identity. Her powerful writing also discusses political resistance to racial and gender systems of domination.

Roderiquez, Clara E. 1997. *Latin Looks: Images of Latinas and Latinos in the U.S. Media*. Boulder, CO: Westview Press.
The articles in this anthology explore how Latinas and Latinos are depicted in the media, with a critical eye to changing cultural stereotypes.

Simonds, Wendy. 1992. *Women and Self-Help Culture: Reading between the Lines*. New Brunswick, NJ: Rutgers University Press.
Simonds develops a sociological perspective on popular culture, based on a content analysis of popular self-help books, and shows the significance of self-help culture in forming women's identities as how a generalized culture influences individual lives.

Walters, Suzanna. 1995. *Material Girls: Making Sense of Feminist Cultural Theory*. Berkeley: University of California Press.
Using postmodernist feminist theory, Walters explains that it is simplistic to see media images as solely negative in their impact on women, since such a view negates that women interpret and react to such images.

Chapter 4

Sexuality and Intimate Relationships

The Social Construction of Sexuality

Sexuality is an essential part of our identity and our relationship to others. It involves deep emotional feeling as well as issues of power and vulnerability in relationships. Human sexual expression takes a variety of forms, although the expression of sexual behavior is influenced and constrained more by cultural definitions and prohibitions than by the physical possibilities for sexual arousal. In fact, what distinguishes human sexuality from sexual behavior among animals is that "human sexuality [is] uniquely characterized by its overwhelmingly symbolic, culturally constructed, non-procreative plasticity" (Caulfield, 1985:344). Much of what we assume about sexuality, however, is distorted by assuming that sexuality is a "natural drive" or an internal state that is acted out or released in sexually exciting situations. Anthropologists have pointed out that "the culturalization of sex, the social production and reproduction of our sexual beings, is precisely that which is 'natural' about human sexuality" (Caulfield, 1985:356). In other words, how sexuality is expressed and felt varies according to the cultural context.

Information about sexuality is transmitted across generations and through the institutions of society (Vance, 1984). Thorne and Luria's (1986) research among fourth- and fifth-grade children shows, for example, that through gender segregation in play and in classrooms, children learn heterosexist and homophobic meaning systems and behaviors that are the basis for the later sexual scripts of adolescence and adulthood.

Even though people like to think of sexuality as a private matter, social institutions direct and control sexuality. Some forms of sexual expression are seen and treated as more legitimate than others. Heterosexuality is a more privileged status in society than is homosexuality. Because of this, heterosexuals (or at least those presumed to be so) have more institutional privileges than do those defined as homosexual; thus, married heterosexual couples may get employee health care benefits or can file joint tax returns. In general, gay men and lesbian women are also more directly controlled by laws and institutional policies than are hetero-sexuals. That heterosexuality is institutional can be seen by the many laws, religious doctrines, and family and employment policies that explicitly and implicitly promote heterosexism.

One of the ironies of our society is the fact that it is so sex conscious, yet, at the same time, it represses sexuality. Traditional definitions of sexuality see sex for women as passive and sex for men as performance and action oriented. Cultural proscriptions have also traditionally defined sex primarily in terms of heterosexual monogamy; consequently, our understanding of sexuality has fused sexuality, reproduction, and gender (Freedman and Thorne, 1984). More recently, the separation of sexuality from procreation, through the widespread availability of birth control, has revolutionized sexual behavior in contemporary society. Many feminists argue, though, that the so-called sexual revolution has not liberated women from oppressive sexual practices, because the sexual revolution has simply made sex a new commodity—something to be bought and sold and that uses women as sexual objects in a new, although still demeaning, manner (Mitchell, 1971).

Across cultures and within our own, human sexual expression includes a wide range of behaviors and attitudes. Although we tend to think of our sexuality as internally situated, it involves a learned relationship to the world. The feminist movement has inspired among us a new openness about women's and men's sexuality and has helped free women's sexual behavior from its traditional constraints (Bleier, 1984); yet, the persistent belief that heterosexuality is the only natural way of expressing sexual feeling continues to blind most people to other possibilities for human sexual feeling and practice. As we discard the notion that there is some single and unchanging way of expressing sexual feeling, we are much more likely to understand human sexuality and intimacy in all their variety and forms.

?• *The History of Sexuality in the United States*

It is commonly thought that over time sexual behavior and attitudes have become less restrained and more uninhibited. Most people believe that sexuality was largely repressed in the past and that only recently have sexual ideas and practice become more liberated. Such a reading disregards the variability and change in sexual attitudes and behaviors and the differing historical ways in which sexuality has or has not been regulated. The history of sexuality is not a simple story of movement from repression to liberation or ignorance to wisdom. Sexuality is constantly reshaped through cultural, economic, familial, and political relations, all of which are also conditioned through the prevailing social organization of gender, race, and class relationships at given points in time.

Historians of sexuality have argued that the dominant meaning and practice of sexuality have changed from their primary association with reproduction within families in the colonial period to their current association with relationships of emotional intimacy and physical pleasure for individuals (D'Emilio and Freedman, 1988). Additionally, sexuality has become more commercialized, and the tie between sexuality and reproduction has been loosened. Groups within society experience these broad-scale transformations in sexuality in different ways, however. For example, sexuality for women is still more closely linked to reproduction than it is for men; working-class and poor women are more likely to have to "sell" their sexuality in the open market than are middle-class or elite women. Gay men's and lesbian women's sexuality is more directly controlled by the state, and they are more subjected to continuing repressive attitudes than are heterosexual women and men.

Similarly, those who produce historical accounts must take care not to over-generalize about sexual experience from the experience of dominant groups. To say that sexuality in the colonial period and early nineteenth century was a family-centered, reproductive sexual system grossly distorts the sexual experiences of enslaved African American men and women. For them, family systems were neither recognized by the state nor respected by the dominant culture; sexual reproduction was often forced, not for purposes of a family-centered life, but for purposes of economic exploitation. Indeed, as is discussed later in the text, sexual exploitation was an integral part of the system of slavery. The images of African American men and women that emerged during that period to justify sexual exploitation continue to influence contemporary sexual stereotypes of African American women and men.

Three patterns recur in the history of sexuality (D'Emilio and Freedman, 1988). First, political movements that attempt to change sexual ideas and practices thrive at times when an older system is undergoing rapid change and disintegration. For example, the movements of sexual liberation that emerged in the 1960s occurred while there were great transformations taking place in women's and men's roles, the definition and shape of family relationships, and the social behavior of young people. Even technological change played a part as the easy availability of birth control made possible the separation of sexuality and reproduction. In the 1990s, further transformations in broad-based gender relations (including women's increased labor force activity and their later marriage and increased likelihood of divorce) created a context in which movements for increased sexual tolerance and diverse forms of expression flourish.

A second recurring pattern is the fact that sexual politics is integrally tied to the politics of race, class, and gender. Class and race hierarchies are often supported through claims that working-class people and people of color are sexually promiscuous and uncontrolled. These false images are then used to justify systems of social control; furthermore, gender inequality is maintained through controlling sexual images of women and men. The idea in the early twentieth century that professional women were "sexually inverted" (a veiled way of calling them lesbians) is a good illustration of how gender inequality is supported through manipulation of sexual ideas. Likewise, the contemporary belief that women who are raped must have "asked for it" maintains a fundamental injustice in the balance of power between men and women in the eyes of the state.

A third historical pattern is that the politics of sexuality is often linked to other social concerns, especially social movements and moral campaigns in which images of impurity and vice are used to stir public concern. For example, in the early twentieth century, nativist fears of immigration were often fueled by claims that immigrant women were wanton prostitutes. Rather than examining the economic needs of women immigrants, opponents incited moral outrage to further restrict immigration. In contemporary politics, those who have resisted programs on AIDS education in the public schools have based their position on the claim that distributing condoms will encourage promiscuous behavior.

The history of sexual attitudes and behaviors reveals much interconnection between sexual politics and other dimensions of race, class, and gender relations. Historically, systems of sexual regulation are highly correlated with other forms of social regulation. At the same time, historical analysis reveals the ever-changing nature of sexual meaning systems and sexual mores. Thus, reflection on the history of sexuality is a good way to see how sexuality is socially constructed and how it intersects with other features of the social structure.

(handwritten margin note: what are some systems of sexual regulation in effect today?)

ᘐ *Contemporary Sexual Attitudes and Behavior*

In this culture, male and female sexuality have been patterned by cultural definitions of masculinity and femininity. *Female sexuality* is defined as more passive and inhibited, whereas *male sexuality* is defined in terms of performance and achievement. As a result, for men, performance anxieties about sexuality are a primary source of sexual impotence. In fact, the use of the word *impotence* to describe the absence of male sexual arousal indicates how our concepts of male sexuality are rooted in the context of male power (Julty, 1974). Female sexuality, on the other hand, is seen as something to be contained and controlled, as we see in the traditional dichotomy of labeling women either as virgins or as whores. Such labels depict female sexuality as evil and dangerous if not constrained and imply that "good girls" repress their sexual feelings.

Women's sexuality in this culture has also been defined as male centered, as female sexual response has been seen primarily in relationship to phallic intercourse. **Phallocentric thinking** is that which assumes women need men for sexual arousal and satisfaction—in other words, thinking that is centered on the significance of the penis. In phallocentric thinking, *sex* is primarily defined as intercourse between a man and a woman, with penetration by the penis defining sex. This kind of thinking was readily apparent during the scandal involving President Clinton's affair with Monica Lewinsky, when he argued that, despite their sexual conduct, they did not have "sexual relations" because they did not have vaginal-penile intercourse. A significant portion of the public seems to agree with him, since surveys found that 20 percent of Americans also think that only actual intercourse is "sexual relations" (Gallup Poll, 1998).

Phallocentric thinking is also historically revealed by Sigmund Freud's theory of the double orgasm, a sexual myth that long distorted the understanding of female sexuality. Freud's argument, and one that was widely believed until very recently, was that women have two kinds of orgasms—clitoral and vaginal. Clitoral orgasm, in Freud's view, was less "mature." He maintained that adult women should transfer their center of orgasm to the vagina, where male penetration made their sexual response complete. Freud's theory of the double orgasm has no basis in fact. The center of female sexuality is the clitoris; female orgasm is achieved through stimulation of the clitoris, whether or not accompanied by vaginal penetration (Masters and Johnson, 1966). For nearly a century, the myth of the double orgasm led women to believe that they were frigid—unable to produce a mature sexual response. During this period, psychiatrists (most of whom were men) reported frigidity as the single-most common reason for women to seek clinical therapy (Chesler, 1972). In fact, the emphasis on male penetration meant that most women were not sexually satisfied in heterosexual relations because sexual intercourse and the ideology that buttressed it served only men's interests. This fact, in turn, supported the attitude that women needed men for sexually mature relationships, even though women have higher rates of orgasm when they masturbate, have sex with another woman, or engage in cunnilingus (English, 1980).

Phallocentric thinking continues to appear in the assumption that women's primary sexual orientation is naturally directed toward men. If one is heterosexual, one may never question that claim, but if one views the claim from the perspective of a lesbian woman's experiences, one is likely to think otherwise. The belief that heterosexuality is the only natural form of sexual expression is rooted in a cultural framework that defines heterosexuality as compulsory and homosexuality as deviant or pathological (Rich, 1980). **Compulsory heterosexuality** refers to the institutionalized practices that presume that women are innately sexually oriented toward men. In a social system structured on compulsory heterosexuality, women's sexual relationships with other women are not seen as a choice, but only as deviance from the social norm, unless they are eroticized in pornography for men. Although it may at first seem odd to think of heterosexuality as a compulsory institution, the social sanctions brought against women who are not identified as attached to men show how heterosexuality is maintained through social control. Even if women remain single and couple with no one, they are ridiculed and ostracized. If they love other women, they are seen as deviant or sexually pathological. In addition, lesbian women and gay men are subjected to legal sanctions that deny their basic civil rights, and they are often subjected to overt acts of violence and personal harm. The concept of compulsory heterosexuality indicates the degree to which sexual choices, relationships, and privileges are structured by social institutions. The belief that women need men to achieve a mature sexual response reflects the assumption that women are dependent on men for their sexual, emotional, social, and economic well-being. This assumption not only legitimates "compulsory heterosexuality" as an institution (Rich, 1980) but it also denigrates women's relationships with other women and subjects them to continued domination by men.

Cultural attitudes toward sexuality are strongly influenced by assumptions about gender. Men are stereotyped as having a stronger sex drive than women; women, as needing a penis for sexual arousal and orgasm. Men are stereotyped as helplessly driven by their sexual impulses; women, as having little sexual feeling. At the same time, women are cast into dichotomous roles, seen either as madonnas or whores (Lips, 1988). When sexually abused, women are often blamed for their own victimization. Unanalyzed for their underlying structure of

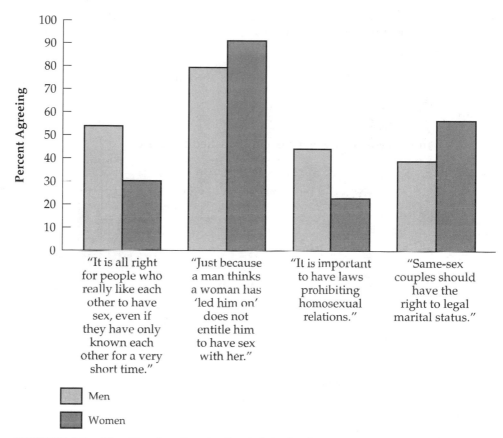

Men

Women

FIGURE 4.1   The Gender Gap in Sexual Attitudes

Source: American Council on Education and University of California at Los Angeles Higher Education Research Institute, 1997. "The American Freshman: National Norms for Fall 1997." Reprinted by permission.

what are the myths today?

Media images

gender relations and the assumptions on which they rest, these beliefs carry great force as cultural myths and reproduce the gender inequality on which they are based.

Contemporary sexual attitudes represent some loosening of rigid judgments about sexual behavior, but, predictably, these attitudes, too, are shaped by gender. For example, note the gender gap in sexual attitudes among entering college freshmen (1997) represented in Figure 4.1. More than half of the men (55 percent) agree that "it is all right for people who really like each other to have sex, even if they have only known each other a very short time"; only 31 percent of women think so. Perhaps the gap, then, in the numbers of men and women who think a man is entitled to sex with a woman he perceives to have "led him on" is not surprising (see Figure 4.1). Such differences can lead to significant conflict between men and women, as shown in Figure 4.2.

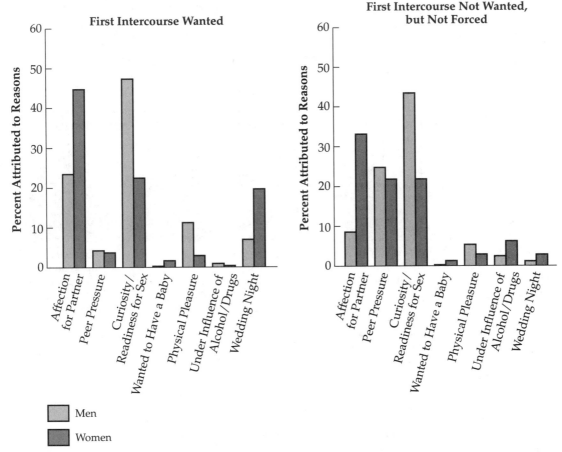

FIGURE 4.2   Reasons for Having First Sexual Intercourse

Source: Data from Robert T. Michael, John H. Gagnon, Edward D. Laumann, and Gina Kolata. 1994. *Sex in America: A Definitive Survey.* Boston: Little, Brown, p. 93.

Although only 48 percent of the public think that homosexual relations should be legal, women are more likely to think so than men; Whites are slightly more likely to think so than Blacks and Latinos, although the difference is not great. People are also more likely to hold antigay attitudes if they are politically conservative, religious, older, less educated, married or widowed, or from the South, although the effect of religion does not hold as well for African Americans (Seltzer, 1992). Women are more likely than men to think that premarital sex is wrong (53 versus 39 percent); older people are also more likely than the young to think premarital sex is wrong (Hugick and Leonard, 1991).

These data give only a glimpse into public opinion about sexuality, but they indicate some of the social conditions that influence sexual attitudes. Such variation in opinion also generates dissension and conflict over the many social issues and problems that involve sexual values. In contemporary politics, problems such as AIDS, teenage pregnancy, and child care are thus debated with intensity because they tap sexual value systems that are contested areas of public opinion.

These debates also show the extent to which sexual meaning systems are socially constructed; they are not merely inherent in human nature. Although it is experienced as physical pleasure, sexuality is as much a social construction as other features of identity are. As such, the character of sexual relationships and opinions must be interpreted in the context of other social-cultural systems and values.

defining "sexual relations" Clinton scandal

≈ Race, Sexuality, and Power

Although most people think of sexuality only in personal or individualistic terms, feminist perspectives examine sexuality within the context of power relationships. The term **sexual politics** refers to the link between sexuality and power (Collins, 1990). Sexuality and power are linked through the intersections of race, class, and gender oppression. Within this system, sexual politics are marked by the domination and social control of White women and women and men of color. The particular forms of sexual oppression experienced by each group depend on the group's specific location in the race, class, and gender system.

Under a system of race, class, and gender oppression, sexuality is restricted and repressed. Sexual politics support and maintain oppression by race, as well as by class, which can be seen in the controlling images of subordinated groups and the degree of protection afforded dominant groups who engage in sexual deviance and crime. For example, Black men and women have been defined as sexually deviant and threatening; the working class and poor are defined as promiscuous and indiscriminate in their choice of sexual partners. At the same time, dominant groups are less likely to be stereotyped as sexually violent.

The sexual politics of race, class, and gender oppression are also apparent in the perpetration of sexual violence against African American women. Sexual violence has been a means of controlling and exploiting African American women (Collins, 1990). During slavery, for example, African American women were used as sexual objects for the pleasure and economic benefit of White men. Marriage between African American women and men was not recognized. The rape of African American women by White slave owners both made African American women sexual objects for White men and added to the population of slave labor.

Both African American women and African American men are subjected to sexual violence, although the forms of sexual violence they have experienced are gender specific (Collins, 1990). Rape, pornography, and prostitution have been forms of sexual violence used to dominate and control Black women. Historically, lynching was a form of sexual violence used to control Black men. As Angela Davis (1981) argues, the myth of the Black rapist is one that was conjured up to justify the violence Whites directed against African American communities. Defining Black men and women as uncontrollably lustful and sexually uninhibited is a way of claiming the moral superiority of Whites and ideologically justifying social control and sexual violence (Collins, 1990).

The sexual politics of race, class, and gender oppression are revealed not only in history but also in the current period. The same controlling images that were developed during slavery continue to permeate dominant images of Black men's and women's sexuality. Dominant images of Black men still depict them as sexually threatening and uncontrolled. Black women in pornography are depicted as sexual objects, frequently in bondage, wrapped in chains and ropes—reminding us of slavery and creating cultural images that continue to oppress Black women (Collins, 1990; Tuan, 1984). Frequently, images of Black women (both in pornography and in advertisements) sexualize them in the context of nature, as if to say that Black women are wild, uncontrolled, and animalistic. As Tuan argues, depicting human beings as animals encourages their exploitation by implying that they can be bought and sold and need taming; even if seen with affection, they are treated condescendingly as pets. Either way, the image of Black women as associated with nature constrains and exploits their sexuality.

The intersections of race, class, and gender oppression are similarly revealed in the sexual politics shaping the experiences of all women of color. Asian American women, for example, are stereotyped as passive and subservient, willing to please and serve White men. The extensive use of Asian women as mail-order brides is evidence of this stereotype. In general, the stereotype of exotic Asian sexuality, centered on the pleasure of White westerners, permeates notions of Asian American sexualities—both homosexuality and heterosexuality (Leong, 1996). Native American women are often depicted in pornography as being tortured. Cultural myths also portray Native American women as sexually free and as using their charms to negotiate treaties between White men and Native populations (Tuan, 1984). Dominant-group stereotypes of Latinas define them as virgins or whores, a dichotomy that restricts their sexual identity and expression. These stereotypes of Latinas are accentuated by the significance given to virginity within Latino communities. Not only is virginity revered within the Catholic Church, but, in addition, within Latino families honor is strongly tied to the sexual purity of women (Espin, 1984).

All of these images distort the actuality of women's sexual experiences and mask the extent to which power relationships shape the intersections of race, class, gender, and sexuality. Although sexuality is thought to be purely personal and private, examining it in the context of race, class, and gender relationships reveals the extent to which structural power relationships influence the experience of all groups of women and men.

❧ *Sexual Development over the Life Cycle*

Sexuality is not a fixed, biological event. Once we understand this, we can better understand how sexual identity is an emergent process—one that evolves both through history and in the course of individual development. Understanding that sexuality is socially constructed need not, however, ignore the influence of biological processes. Sociological analysis of sexuality includes discussion of the relationship between biology and culture, as already discussed in Chapter 2. Feminists add to this discussion the recognition that the understanding of biological processes has been distorted by the sexist assumptions permeating scientific discourse, a discussion also addressed previously in Chapter 3.

Menstruation and menopause—two aspects of women's experience that are both social and biological in nature—can be used as an example. Both are defined as key to women's sexual development, although their significance may well be overstated. For example, sexist myths define postmenopausal women as asexual, an assumption disproven by women's own accounts of their experiences. Likewise, menstruation has been depicted as disabling women, making them "unfit" for men's work, even though there is no supporting evidence for such a claim. How has feminist scholarship recast what is known about menopause and menstruation?

Menstruation

Menstruation is a universal phenomenon, yet, like menopause, it is one that takes on different meanings in different cultures. In many cultures, menstruation is symbolic of the strength of women, and elaborate rituals and rites of passage symbolize that power (Powers, 1980). In other cultures, menstruation is seen as symbolic of defilement, and elaborate practices may be developed to isolate and restrict menstruating women. In the nineteenth century, for example, Southeast Asian women could not be employed in the opium industry, for it was believed that if a menstruating woman was nearby, the opium would turn bitter (Delaney, Lupton, and Toth, 1988). In contemporary U.S. culture, menstruation is depicted as secretive and invisible, as best seen in the advertising industry, which advises menstruating women to keep their "secret" protected, yet to feel confident, secure, and free.

As with menopause, most studies of menstruation define it as a disease. Exaggeration and alarm run throughout discussions of menstruation, probably showing more our culture's fear of women's reproductive processes than a genuine understanding of the menstrual cycle. Consider, for example, the apprehension generated by the so-called dangers of premenstrual syndrome (PMS). According to news tabloids, PMS is responsible for a wide range of deviant behaviors, including insanity, murder, and other criminal acts. When scientists declare that 25 to 100 percent of women experience PMS, what does that mean? It may simply mean that most women recognize bodily signs of oncoming menstruation, although it is possible that a small proportion of women do find the physical changes associated with menstruation to be incapacitating (Fausto-Sterling, 1992).

Most certainly, many women do experience premenstrual tension, but the definition of PMS as a medical problem gives the medical profession, not women themselves, the authority to interpret and "treat" PMS (Markens, 1996). The social construction of PMS as a disease or syndrome also means that any positive feelings and experiences associated with premenstrual cycles—such as enhanced feelings of sensuality, high energy states, or feelings of general well-being—are also ignored, since PMS becomes defined by medical authorities as a problem to be treated by them. Public attention to PMS also presumes that only women, not men, are regulated by bodily phenomena—reminiscent of traditional arguments of biological determinism.

These cultural attitudes can shape how young women experience menstruation. Studies show that most premenstrual girls (and boys of the same age) believe that menstruation is a physically and emotionally disruptive event. This can become a self-fulfilling prophecy. Also, 85 percent of girls believe that it is inappropriate to discuss menstruation with boys (Golub, 1983). Associating menstruation with fear and repulsion encourages feelings of shame and can discourage young girls from discussing menstruation with each other, which would potentially provide them more information and support. Menstruation symbolizes the reproductive and sexual potential of women, and its onset occurs at the same time that young girls are developing their sexual identities. The meanings given to this experience are contextualized by a society that both devalues and trivializes women, by defining them as sexual objects. This is bound to affect women's experiences with menstruation and, in particular, to affect how young girls see their developing sexual selves (J. Lee, 1994).

From a sociological point of view, menstruation is not just a physical process; it is laden with social and cultural meaning. An early study by two sociologists, Alice and Peter Rossi (1977), demonstrates this well. The Rossis asked college-aged women and men to rate their daily moods over a 40-day period. Women in the sample also noted their first day of menstruation as it occurred during the rating cycle. The Rossis then compared mood ratings as clocked by biological time (measured by phases in the menstrual cycle) and by calendar (or social) time. Surprisingly, the results showed that men marked more days per month when they felt "achy," "crampy," and "sick" than did women. More to the point, the Rossis' results showed that the most significant changes in moods occurred for women according to changes in the calendar week, not their menstrual cycles. Women were more likely to feel "happy," "loving," and "healthy" on weekends and "depressed," "unhappy," and "sick" on "blue Wednesday."

The Rossis' research also found no significant elevation of negative moods in the premenstrual phase for women; there was, however, an elevation of positive moods in the ovulatory phase of menstruation and an elevation of negative moods in the luteal phase (days 17–24 in a 28-day menstrual cycle). More important than the independent effects of biological and social time, this research found that moods (especially positive moods) were most strongly affected when biological and social cycles were synchronized (e.g., when ovulation occurred on a weekend).

This research indicates the interdependent relationship of human biology and social conditions. Physiological conditions such as menstruation cannot be understood entirely without a consideration of the social context in which they occur. This can be seen as well with regard to the process of aging and menopause.

Menopause

The biological process of aging is clearly one that is universal, inevitable, and based on human physiology. How long one lives is strongly influenced by one's gender. Life expectancy is shorter for men (73 years in 2000) than for women (80 years), and males have higher accidental death rates (in both childhood and adulthood) than do females (U.S. Census Bureau, 1997:88). Men also have higher suicide and homicide rates than do women (Horton, 1995). Some research has shown that men with personalities marked by ambition, single-mindedness, and devotion to work are more prone to heart attacks than others (Friedman and Rosenman, 1974). In fact, the risks associated with traditionally masculine roles are so great that one psychologist has called masculinity a "lethal role" (Jourard, 1974).

The physiological changes associated with aging are greatly affected by the social context in which aging occurs. Nutrition, for example, affects the biological health of aging persons, but social factors such as living alone or in an institution are known to affect dietary habits, as are factors such as income, cultural preferences for food, and exercise. Aging is also aggravated by stress—a condition generated by a variety of social and psychological difficulties.

For women, the aging process has its own strains. In a society in which women are valued for their youth and beauty, aging becomes a difficult social and psychological experience. Birthday cards that joke about women deteriorating after age 29 and commercials for creams that "hide your age spots" tell women in the United States that they should be ashamed of growing old. It should be no surprise, then, that a biological process such as menopause can become a difficult psychological experience. Research shows that menopause produces more anxiety and more depression in cultures that are less supportive of women as they age (Bart, 1979; Clay, 1977; Hess and Markson, 1991; Reitz, 1977).

Cultural beliefs about biological events imbue these with significance and a character different from that produced by the physiology alone. In the case of menopause, the scientific and popular literature is replete with the metaphor of menopause as a disease—a fact that has severely biased both the scientific and popular understanding of menopause.

The social context in which middle-aged women live, including their life histories and family relationships, is a more important predictor of emotional response to menopause than are the actual hormonal changes associated with menopause. Most women do not report menopause as a time of crisis, and there is no research to support the usually assumed association between menopause and serious depression (Fausto-Sterling, 1992). Postmenopausal women who do experience psychosis are women who have had a prior history of psychotic episodes (Winokur and Cadoret, 1975), a finding that suggests that depression and mental illness among menopausal women are a function of other factors in their experience, not menopause per se.

Research on menopausal women, conducted by researchers who do not see menopause as a set of disease symptoms, finds that menopausal women report no greater frequency of physical symptoms or concerns about those symptoms than do pre- or postmenopausal women (Frey, 1981). These investigations find that only 28 percent of postmenopausal Caucasian women and 24 percent of postmenopausal Japanese women report experiencing hot flashes and sweats during menopause. Restated, this means that the overwhelming majority of menopausal women report none of the stereotypical menopausal symptoms (Fausto-Sterling, 1992). Remarkably, 16 percent of the nonmenopausal Caucasian women and 10 percent of the nonmenopausal Japanese women in the study also report these menopausal symptoms (Goodman, 1980).

Physiologically, the process of aging is similar for both sexes, with the exception of menopause, but social myths surrounding menopause have made it a more difficult process than its physiology alone creates. Physiologically, at menopause the ovaries stop producing 90 percent of their hormones, and following menopause, women become infertile. Women may be as sexually active as they were before, however, and many women report an even more satisfying sex life once they are relieved from the connection between sexuality and childbearing.

Still, social myths portray the menopausal woman as prone to depression and anxiety, lacking sexual interest, and emotionally volatile; however, research indicates that when these problems exist, they stem from the social devaluation of aging women, not from the physiological process of aging itself (Clay, 1977; Livson, 1977; Reitz, 1977). If society valued all women, not just those who are young, White, and middle class, the aging process would likely not be filled with the emotional and social difficulties some women experience (Stoller and Gibson, 1997).

?? Love and Intimate Relationships

Intimate relationships are an important context in which gender identity is created, re-created, and understood. Such relationships are an important source of love and caring; they provide many forms of social support and are critical to our social identity. Within intimate relationships, gender identity is continually reproduced, an idea that is basic to sociological perspectives on gender and intimacy. Sociologists do not see gender as a fixed individual trait; rather, they see gender as constantly reenacted and reinterpreted in the context of interpersonal relationships. This idea distinguishes sociological perspectives from individual perspectives on gender and interpersonal relationships.

To explain further, people tend to think of love and intimacy as individual choices. Intimate relationships do provide psychological support, and the psychological dynamics within intimate relationships are of interest to sociologists. Intimate relationships, like other social relationships, are conditioned by the cultural context, historical period, and institutional structures in which they occur.

Intimate relationships take many forms, each revealing different sociological dynamics. Intimate relationships may include a sexual relationship or may be based only on emotional intimacy, such as in close friendships. The sexual orientation of partners in an intimate relationship is important, however, because it locates the relationship in an institutional system that differently values and rewards intimacy based on heterosexual versus homosexual bonds. Understanding this helps us see how society structures and creates sexuality and intimacy.

Most people believe that relationships are formed simply because people like or are attracted to each other. But there is another sociological dimension to all relationships, including friendships, heterosexual love, and gay, lesbian, and bisexual relationships. All forms of these relationships are situated within relationships of power, social institutional structures, and systems of inequality based on the intersections of gender, race, and class. Although intimate relationships—whether sexual or not—are formed, in part, by the individual attitudes and attributes of those within them, they are significantly shaped by the institutional and historical context in which they develop. Thus, patriarchy, heterosexist institutions, the class structure, and racism all have a strong influence on the formation of intimacy. whether sexual or not. How do we see this?

First consider the dimension of power. **Power** is defined by sociologists as an individual's or a group's ability to influence another person or group. The exercise of power can take many forms, ranging from persuasion to physical force. Power is institutionalized in society—meaning that social institutions are structured in ways that give more power to some than to others. In a patriarchal society, men as a group have more power than do women. This institutionalized power, structured at the societal level, also influences the interpersonal and intimate relationships between women and men. To begin with, those with more resources typically have more power than those with fewer. Men's greater control of resources thus influences their power in relationships with women. For example, a significant body of research shows that the greater a woman's contribution to household income is, the more power she exercises in family decision making (Spitze, 1988; Piotrkowski and Repetti, 1984).

At the institutional level, power is manifested in **patriarchal institutions**—the system that gives men systematic advantages over women. This can perhaps be most easily seen by looking at what happens when intimate relationships end, such as in divorce. What appears to be a private matter between two people terminating a marriage soon enters into a system of institutional advantage and disadvantage that overwhelmingly favors men. How can this be, when, theoretically at least, institutions are supposed to be based on equality before the law? Even without overt legal expressions of men's privilege, the law continues to operate in ways that advantage men. First, men typically have access to more financial resources than do women. Thus, men can afford better legal representation when filing for divorce—a fact that provides a clear advantage. Second, seemingly gender-neutral laws, such as no-fault divorce, have been shown to disadvantage women, who end up worse off financially after marriage than do men (Weitzman, 1985, 1996; Peterson, 1996a, 1996b). In addition, without counting the value of child care and housework in the assets of a marriage, most women rarely see what they have contributed to a marriage actually valued in the division of marital property and assets. These illustrations show that institutions can still be patriarchal even when they are not explicitly identified as such.

Heterosexual institutions also structure intimate relationships. **Heterosexism** is the institutionalized set of behaviors and beliefs that presume heterosexuality to be the only acceptable form of sexual expression; a heterosexist system negatively sanctions those who act or are presumed to act otherwise. This context provides structural privileges for those in heterosexual relationships, while denying privileges and rights to those who do not assume a heterosexual identity. For example, although they may be in long-term, loving, and committed relationships, gays and lesbians do not receive the same insurance benefits that married couples might. Because gay partners are not considered a part of the immediate family, they might also be denied visiting rights if a partner is hospitalized and under critical care.

Heterosexism can also discourage the formation of relationships, particularly as heterosexism is manifested in homophobia. **Homophobia** is defined as the fear and hatred of homosexuality. Homophobia can discourage intimacy between same-sex friends if it makes them fear being labeled as gay or lesbian. Thus, homophobia works as a system of social control. This is especially, but not exclusively, apparent in relationships among men where homophobia establishes boundaries of intimacy between men. Despite cultural strictures that discourage gay relationships between men, much of men's interaction is in homosocial settings (i.e., segregated settings that include only men). Studies of interaction between men in such settings find that their interaction is based on emotional detachment, competitiveness, and the sexual objectification of women. Through these forms of interaction, social concepts of masculinity are re-created and reinforced, with boundaries created between men that separate them from identification with homosexuality even in these homosocial environments. At the same time, the men interact in ways that lead them to devalue qualities that are associated with women (Bird, 1996b); thus, homophobia not only limits the character of intimacy among men but it also reinforces sexist attitudes toward women.

Although most people think of homophobia as having a negative impact on gays and lesbians, this argument shows how damaging homophobia is to all kinds of relationships. By ridiculing and punishing affection between members of the same sex, homophobia shapes the expectations and expression of intimacy. Thus, heterosexual friends of gays and lesbians may find themselves "suspect" in the eyes of others, or heterosexual women who display intimacy in public may be ridiculed and accused of being lesbians. Heterosexual family members who accept and cherish relationships with gay and lesbian siblings may be chastised by other members of the family who do not. In these and other ways, homophobia and heterosexist institutions frame and shape the intimate relationships of many.

It is useful to think of heterosexism and homophobia in terms of the system of social control developed in Chapter 2. There is a continuum of social control mechanisms, ranging from peer pressure (such as ridicule and joking) through institutional mechanisms (manifested in law and social policy) to terrorism and violence (as in hate crimes) that punish homosexual behavior and distribute societal privileges based on the presumption of heterosexuality.

Intimate relationships are also formed in a system of class and race inequality. Thus, research on friendship finds that working-class friendships have a high degree of reciprocity and interdependence with regard to material goods and services; middle-class friendships, on the other hand, tend to emphasize shared leisure, focus on networks of interesting friends, and place a high value on individualism (Walker, 1995). Class and race also shape such basic facts as what relationships are formed, as data on the small number of racial intermarriages clearly show. Historically, racial intermarriage was prohibited by law. For example, California state law in 1880 prohibited Chinese Americans and White Americans from marrying. Later, California laws were written to prohibit marriage between Whites and Filipinos, Japanese, Hindus, American Indians, and Malaysians (Takaki, 1989). Not until 1967 were such state laws, including those in the South prohibiting marriage between Whites and those defined as "Blacks," declared unconstitutional by the U.S. Supreme Court. Even now, intermarriage, although increasing, is still rare, with only 2 percent of all marriages being interracial (U.S. Census Bureau, 1997).

In sum, systems of class, race, and gender shape all intimate relationships, whether they are platonic friendships (as you will see in the section below) or sexual relationships. Even something as abstract as the concept of love illustrates the significance of historical context in shaping intimacy. Popular images of love see it as unpredictable, uncontrollable, and never ending, yet, the specific meaning of love is one that has evolved over time. In ancient Greek society, for example, social norms defined love for elite Greek men as occurring between them and boys. With the ascendance of the Catholic Church in medieval Europe, love was defined as occurring only within marriage; sex was defined as sinful if it occurred outside the marital relationship. In the nineteenth century, during the Victorian period, strict moral codes regulating sexual behavior were established. Many have linked those strict moral codes to the evolving manufacturing system. The industrial revolution moved work from the home to the factory, requiring new forms of social control to encourage discipline among workers. Strict control of the emotions and sexuality was one way to enforce such discipline. At the same time, the move to a capitalist society in the West created new concepts of love.

The transition to a capitalist society polarized men's and women's roles and created new concepts of individualism. The separation of family from economic production (see Chapter 6) created separate spheres of activity in the home and in the factory. Relationships at work became more impersonal, while the family was increasingly defined as the place for intimacy and caring. The ideal woman was then one who devoted her life to her husband and children; men, on the other hand, were to be independent, disciplined, and emotionally restrained (Cancian, 1987).

These transformations continue to influence our concepts of love and intimacy. Contemporary society emphasizes the significance of intimate bonds, even while human relationships are easily broken through workings of the economy. Intimacy is defined differently for men and for women; women are still defined as more other oriented and responsible for emotional ties, and men are defined as more isolated and individualistic.

In sum, intimate relationships are shaped by the same forces that structure gender relationships. In fact, intimate relationships are one of the primary arenas where gender relationships are played out. Within intimate relationships, men and women create their identities and develop beliefs about appropriate gender roles. Gender is continually reenacted through and within intimate relationships. From a sociological perspective, understanding gender and intimacy requires the same analysis of social structures and institutionalized beliefs and behaviors that would be used to examine less personal social behavior.

[handwritten margin notes: more platonic friendships between men/women]

❧ Friendship *[handwritten: sexual tension]*

Gender plays an important role in structuring the intimate relationships between people—whether in same-sex relationships or relationships between women and men. This has been shown to be true in friendships as well as in relationships that include a sexual partnership. Research shows, for example, that men are more likely to be intimate with women than they are with other men, even though they report more same-sex friendships than do women. Within friendships, men tend to focus on shared activities, whereas women are more likely to emphasize talking and emotional sharing as the basis for friendship (Floyd and Parks, 1995).

However differently expressed, friendship is clearly important to both men and women. Despite long-held assumptions that women's primary identity was attached to men, research now shows the important role that friendships between women have, including women who live within stable heterosexual relationships. Studies of friendship indicate that friendships do not happen automatically, nor are they simply extensions of presumed natural capacities between the sexes. Making and keeping friends are complex processes, not just a matching of people with similar attitudes and social backgrounds (Gouldner and Strong, 1987). How one makes and keeps friends is intricately connected to the gender, race, and class relationships in which one lives. For example, professional women put great financial resources (in the form of travel, long-distance phone bills, dinners, and the like) into the making and keeping of good friends (Gouldner and Strong, 1987). Less research has been done of friendships among working-class and poor women and among women of color; however, research done indicates the extent to which support from other women is a necessary part of women's ability to cope with the stress generated from class and race oppression (Sanchez-Ayendez, 1986). Women's skills in keeping close ties with other women also help them in old age by giving them a sense of control over their lives (Powers, 1996).

Comparing men and women, research finds that men and women place the same value on intimacy, but they have different ways of assessing it. Among young adults, men tend to be more goal oriented in their friendships; women tend to be more expressive (Fox, Gibbs, and Auerbach, 1985). Women are more likely than men to speak of the importance of being able to reveal themselves and be intimate in friendships. As they get older, men become more attentive to friendships, but they are still most likely to emphasize the significance of concrete helping as central to friendship, whereas women emphasize talking, sharing, and comforting each other (Lips, 1988). Other studies of friendship find that friendships involving at least one woman tend to be more satisfying than those that do not. For example, men report their friendships with women as more satisfying than their friendships with other men; women, on the other hand, find their friendships with other women and with men to be equally satisfying. Additionally, when men and women are asked to describe their standards for ideal friendships, they describe friendships between two men as the least ideal (Elkins and Peterson, 1993).

Intimacy between men is strongly influenced by the restrictive sanctions generated by homophobia. Fear of being called gay may make men distance themselves from one another. Friendships between men are also influenced by the social settings in which the men work. As men grow older (for example, after their college years), the structures in which men find themselves become less conducive to friendship. Competition in the workplace, as well as time spent with family commitments, may discourage closer interaction with other men. One consequence is that men may be robbed of the emotional support systems that intimate friendships can provide.

Cross-sex friendships are more common among younger people than among middle-aged and older adults. Except for friendships between couples, the norms of monogamous marriage seem to discourage friendships between men and women outside of marriage. Among middle-aged people, employed women have more cross-sex friendships than do women who work in the home only. Employment is not related to cross-sex friendships among men (Dickens and Perlman, 1981).

In sum, research on friendship shows the significance of sociological factors in what friendships are formed, what they mean, and how they are experienced. Although friendship is idealized as what happens when two people "click," in actuality, friendship, like love, is culturally mediated.

❧ Lesbian, Gay, and Bisexual Experiences

Sociological and popular understanding of gay and lesbian relationships has been greatly distorted by the false presumption that only heterosexual relationships are normal ways of expressing sexual intimacy and love. We live in a culture that tends to categorize people into polar opposites: men and women, Black and White, gay and straight. On the subject of sexual desire, however, researchers conclude that such bipolar categories of sexual desire do not exist for most people (Schwartz and Rutter, 1998). Rather, sexual desire is produced in the context of social relationships and identities; thus, "desire is created by its cultural context" (Blumstein and Schwartz, 1983:122). In addition, culture creates understandings about how people are sexual; people adapt definitions of their own sexual identities depending on their experiences over the course of a lifetime.

It is not surprising that a majority of people assume the sexual identity prescribed by the dominant culture, but this fact should not be taken as evidence of normal or biological drive. For example, heterosexual identity is the result of scripts that boys and girls learn early in life, including the belief that men have an overpowering sex drive and that women link love, sex, and attachment. One result is that what is erotic to a woman may differ from what is erotic to a man, because men are taught to view women's passivity as erotic and stimulating.

Sociological views of sexuality examine the social and historical circumstances that create possibilities for sexual behavior. The explanation of sexual behaviors and identities is then based on social conditions, not fixed biological or cultural categories. Understanding the social organization of gender, both in personal life and in social institutions, is critical to understanding sexuality.

There is a long-standing assumption that sexual orientation is an "either/or" identity—that is, a person is either gay or straight. Recent scholarship on sexual identity, however, challenges this dichotomy. First, many argue that, by their nature, human beings are capable of bisexual attraction. John Money, one of the nation's foremost experts on sexual identity, argues that human beings are "psychosexually neutral" at birth (Money, 1995). Throughout life, cultural proscriptions try to direct and channel people into socially legitimate sexual identities. Think, for example, of your childhood and teen experiences and the explicit and implicit messages you got to be heterosexual. Children's movies embed scripts about love between men and women; popular music extols the thrills of heterosexual love; adolescent jokes deride gays and lesbians. These and a myriad of other influences make it not surprising that most people become heterosexual, whatever their biological inclinations.

Second, studying the history of sexuality reveals that the categories of "homosexual," "gay," and "lesbian" have been created at specific historical points in time. As much as people revile *homosexuality* and think of it as biologically based, the term was not invented until the nineteen century by Havelock Ellis, an early sexologist, who saw it as sexual inversion. Not until the early twentieth century, however, were the terms *homosexuality* and *heterosexuality* widely publicized—as the public became increasingly fascinated with the scientific study of sex. The contemporary meaning of the term *gay* is even more recent. Used in the first half of the twentieth century primarily as self-satirizing and flippant adjective, in the 1960s, *gay* came to be used in a positive light to celebrate a community with a shared life-style. Specifically, *gay* was meant to shed the stigma that had come from the medicalization and criminalization of gay people (Money, 1998). Associated with gay liberation, the term *gay* took on a positive and self-affirming meaning—the result of political activism.

Third, recent scholarship on transgender identities and bisexuality challenges the binary (i.e., "one way or the other") or dualistic thinking that is represented by the assumption that a person is either heterosexual or gay. The emergence of **queer theory** has underscored the idea that all sexual identities are socially constructed and that the categories of sexuality that we presume to be fixed can be disrupted and changed (Gamson, 1995). Queer theory posits that institutional practices create sexual identities and that the boundaries that distinguish legitimate and illegitimate sex are politically constructed. Without questioning how sexual categories are constructed, theorists perpetuate the idea that only one form of sexuality is normal and all others are deviant, immoral, and wrong (Seidman, 1994). Queer theory emerged from a criticism of gay and lesbian studies that these terms are not inclusive enough (Stein and Plummer, 1994). That is, such studies do not incorporate the multiple sexual identities that people can assume, and in so doing, new light has been shed on studies of bisexuality, transgendered people, and gay and lesbian politics (Rust, 1995; Firestein, 1996; Califia, 1997).

Thus, from a social constructionist view, as noted in the chapter opening, all forms of sexuality are socially constructed. Even if there is some biological basis to sexual orientation, what people become in their sexual identity and how they express it is as much the result of social experiences as it is a fixed biological fact. Cultural proscriptions, stigmas, and practices influence the construction of all people's sexual identities; moreover, sexual orientation is an ongoing process that occurs over the development of the life course. Gay and lesbian identities, like heterosexual identities, are constructed through an ongoing series of events and meaning systems. For example, the *coming out* process rarely involves a single incident. Instead, someone in the process of coming out begins to see himself or herself in new ways and may develop new social contacts and reinterpret earlier experiences in a way that enables a new definition of self to emerge. Likewise, those who develop heterosexual identities are likely to support that identity through a system of consistent social supports and meaning systems that may even include denial or reinterpretation of experiences of being attracted to members of the same sex.

Current research shows that the development of sexual identity is not necessarily a linear or unidirectional process, with persons moving through a defined sequence of steps or phases. People do not move predictably through certain sequences in developing a sexual identity. While they may experience certain "milestones" in their identity development, many people move back and forth over a period of time between lesbian or gay identities and heterosexual identities. Some experience periods of ambivalence about their identities and may switch back and forth between a lesbian, heterosexual, and bisexual identity over a period of time. Studies of lesbian and bisexual women also find that some continue alternative identities even after defining themselves as lesbians; thus, some people defining themselves as gay may not necessarily keep that identity (Rust, 1993). Some people may engage in lesbian or gay behavior but not adopt a formal definition of themselves as such. Certainly many gays and lesbians never adopt a public definition of themselves as gay or lesbian, instead remaining "closeted" for long periods of time, if not entire lifetimes.

This research shows the socially constructed basis of sexual identity and how sensitive sexual identity is to its societal context. Changing social contexts (including dominant group attitudes, laws, and systems of social control), relationships with others, and even changes in the language used to describe different sexual identities all affect people's self-definitions. As an example, political movements can encourage people to adopt a sexual identity that they previously had no context to understand, but there can be negative consequences to assuming a publicly gay identity. In just one example, a study of gay-and-lesbian–activist academics found that there were negative consequences for them in terms of discrimination in hiring, bias in promotion decisions, exclusion from professional networks, harassment, and devaluation of their work on gay and lesbian subjects (Taylor and Raeburn, 1995). This context, where the stigma attached to gay identities is played out in power relations between dominant and subordinate groups, affects people's willingness to publicly claim a gay or lesbian identity.

Although sexual identity is socially constructed, individuals experience their sexual identities as stable. They perceive changes in their identities as part of the process of discovering their sexuality, often reinterpreting earlier life events as indications of some preexisting identity. From a sociological point of view, changing one's sexual identity is not a sign of immaturity, as if someone has missed a so-called normal phase of development; change is a normal outcome of the process of identity formation (Rust, 1993).

Understanding the socially constructed basis of sexual identity is in stark contrast to ideas that sexual orientation is biologically determined. Such ideas are popular, not only among those who promote heterosexual orientation as "normal" but also among many lesbians and gays. What is the biological basis for homosexuality? Periodic reports appear in the media claiming to have found a "gay gene" or other scientific evidence for the biological basis of homosexuality. On close examination, however, such studies are typically based on very small research samples, without the scientific controls needed to prove a genetic or biological basis to homosexuality (Gagnon, 1995; Hamer et al., 1993; Rist, 1992). Although there may be some basis to such claims, a biological basis for sexual orientation has not been soundly established. There is far more evidence of social and cultural influences on sexual identity—studies that are rarely reported in the media. Even if there is some biological influence on sexual identity, we know that environmental influences interact with biological predisposition; therefore, trying to explain sexual orientation as a matter of biology alone is poor reasoning. The fact is that public belief in the biological basis of homosexuality, including among lesbians and gays, is stronger than the scientific evidence supports.

How extensive is the lesbian and gay experience? Here again is a matter for debate. Many claim that as much as 10 percent of the population is gay or lesbian (Janus and Janus, 1993); others say the number is more like 4 percent (Laumann et al., 1994). In part, it depends on how this is measured (i.e., how the question is asked). The Kinsey Report of the 1940s first reported that a substantial number of people have some homosexual experience in their lifetimes. (Current surveys find that 22 percent of men and 17 percent of women do.) But this figure could refer to a single experience, not necessarily the adoption of a gay, lesbian, or bisexual identity. Surveys find that more men and women report having experienced desire for those of the same sex than will report being gay or lesbian (Laumann et al., 1994)—a fact that probably reflects the stigma associated with gay and lesbian identities.

Whatever the actual extent of gay, lesbian, and bisexual experience, the fact is that various social myths permeate our understanding of this experience. First among them is the idea that gays and lesbians are sexually perverted stems from reasoning similar to the previous argument. For example, fears that gays and lesbians are dangerous because they might make sexual advances toward strangers is a distortion of fact. Research consistently finds that it is heterosexual men who are the most frequent perpetrators of sexual abuse and other sexual crimes. Fears that gay and lesbian parents will have deleterious effects on their children are also unsupported by research. Children of homosexual parents more often than not grow up with heterosexual identities (Lewin, 1984); moreover, as in heterosexual households, it is the degree to which parents are able to develop good relationships with their children, not the parents' sexual identities per se, that has the greatest influence on the children's well-being (Joseph, 1984).

Another social myth that is especially associated with gay men is that they are all rich and leading expensive life-styles. Yet, studies find that workplace discrimination against lesbians, gay men, and bisexuals is extensive (Gluckman and Reed, 1997). Data from national surveys report that gay and bisexual men earn 11 to 27 percent less than heterosexual men with the same experience, education, occupation, and region of residence. There is some evidence that lesbian and bisexual workers earn less than heterosexual women, but the difference is not so strong, probably because of the general depression of all women's wages (Badgett, 1995). Many gays and lesbians remain closeted in the workplace to avoid the discrimination that comes from being "out" (Croteau, 1996). There are well-documented risks to being "out" in the workplace, including discrimination in hiring, exclusion from social and professional networks, harassment and intimidation, and, for those doing research on gay and lesbian issues, a devaluation of their work (Taylor and Raeburn, 1995).

The greatest difficulty that lesbian women and gay men face stems from the homophobia within society. Hateful harassment, physical violence, and insensitivity mar the everyday experience of lesbians and gays. Were as much time and energy invested in providing supportive social environments for all people, regardless of their sexual identities, as in telling homophobic jokes, bashing gays, and engaging in hate crimes, we would likely build a more caring society that embraced and sustained a diversity of loving relationships.

Gay and lesbian relationships lack the institutional support heterosexual relationships have. Gay and lesbian partners have no inheritance rights or tax subsidies, as do heterosexual married couples. Gay and lesbian relationships are not typically sanctioned by the legal community or the church, although in some places this is changing. Because of the absence of institutionalized support for gay men and lesbian women, they have to create their own forms of support and meaning within relationships and communities. As a result, researchers find that the maintenance of relationships among gays and lesbians is more dependent on the quality of the interpersonal relationship than on the institutional support the relationship receives (Meyer, 1990).

Still, the majority of people support equal rights for gays and lesbians in the workplace (Roper Organization, 1996) and a growing number of corporations are developing nondiscriminatory policies, including adding sexual orientation to diversity training and extending employee benefits to domestic partners. Gays and lesbians also won a major victory in 1996 when the U.S. Supreme Court (in

Romer vs. *Evans*) ruled that they cannot be denied equal protection of the law. This ordinance overturned local ordinances denying civil rights protections to gays and lesbians. Change is slow, however, and sometimes contradictory, as evidenced by the Defense of Marriage Act passed by the U.S. Congress. This law allows states not to recognize same-sex marriages that might be legally legitimate in those states that have extended this right to same-sex partners (such as Hawaii).

In recent years, political activism has resulted in greater visibility and more acceptance of gays and lesbians, but homophobia and hate crimes are still rampant, as cruelly exemplified by the murder of Matthew Shepard, a young student in Wyoming who was beaten to death by two young men in 1998 and left to die in a remote field. After beating him and leaving him to die, the young men who killed him also beat up two Hispanic young men, yelling racial epithets at them as they did. This horrid incident shows how homophobia is linked to hatred stemming from racial prejudice and violence. It should teach us about the connections between forms of sexual, racial, and gender oppression (Smith, 1997; Leong, 1996; Takagi, 1996).

ᘓ Summary

This chapter has emphasized that human sexuality is a socially constructed experience. The formation of a sexual identity is a complex process; sexual identity for any individual emerges over the course of a lifetime and is shaped by social and historical contexts. Feminist perspectives on sexuality have linked the study of sexuality to an analysis of power. Although sexuality is popularly believed to be a private, intimate, and individual matter, feminist scholarship has studied sexuality in the context of not only gender differences, but also the social construction of race, class, and gender oppression.

The history of sexuality shows that sexuality is shaped through cultural, economic, and political relations and is also conditioned by prevailing class, race, and gender relations. Contemporary sexual attitudes are shaped by phallocentric thinking—that which sees men as powerful and women as weak. They are also shaped by other social factors such as age, religious preference, and education.

Compulsory heterosexuality is defined as institutionalized practices and beliefs that presume women are always sexually oriented toward men. Compulsory heterosexuality shapes our understanding of gay and lesbian experience, as well as that of heterosexuals; it supports many of the myths in the culture that make life oppressive for lesbians and gays.

Sexual politics intersect with systems of racial oppression; thus, women and men of color are subjected to social control through sexual stereotypes and extreme violence. Although particular experiences vary, depending on the history of a given racial-ethnic group, study of the intersections between racism and sexuality reveal the extent to which sexuality is embedded in structural systems of power.

Studying sexuality in the context of the life cycle shows that sexual identity is socially constructed. This approach reveals that biological events like menstruation and menopause are also shaped by social conventions and beliefs. It is the social context, not the biological processes per se, that shapes women's experiences with these life course events.

Gender identity is created and reproduced through intimate relationships. These intimate relationships are themselves maintained through institutional and historical patterns. Male-female relationships, for example, have to be understood in the context of power relationships that stem from men's institutionalized power over women. Likewise, gay and lesbian experiences must be understood in the context of heterosexist systems that give greater power and privileges to those with presumed heterosexual identities. Heterosexist systems also encourage the development of homophobia.

Friendship is also a relationship shaped by gender relations. Research finds different patterns of friendship for men and women, but reveals that intimacy is important to both. In sum, all forms of interpersonal relationships are shaped by the race, class, and gender systems in which they are found. Social supports for interpersonal relationships have primarily been those encouraged by heterosexist institutions. As a result, people in other kinds of relationships have often had to generate their own support mechanisms. In doing so, they have created new models for the development of intimacy and caring among diverse groups.

❧ Key Terms

compulsory heterosexuality	patriarchy	queer theory
heterosexism	phallocentric thinking	sexual politics
homophobia	power	

❧ Discussion Questions/Projects for Thought

1. How would you describe the sexual norms on your campus? How are people's sexual attitudes and behaviors linked to gender in this setting?

2. Over a period of one week, keep a written log of the homophobic comments and incidents that you observe. At the end of the week, review what you have seen and discuss what it means to say that compulsory heterosexuality is enforced through the social norms of everyday life. As you do this exercise, be aware that what you hear will be hurtful to many. You should keep this sensitivity in mind when discussing this project. How would you feel if such comments were directed toward someone you love?

3. Pick an area of popular culture (a TV series, greeting cards, popular songs, children's cartoons, etc.) and do a content analysis of the images of love depicted therein. Pay attention in your observations to how these images are linked to gender. How do your observations support the idea that images of love are constructed in the context of sexual politics?

❧ *Suggested Readings*

Connell, R. W., and G. W. Dowsett. 1992.
Rethinking Sex: Social Theory and Sexuality Research. Philadelphia: Temple University Press.
This theoretical discussion of new scholarship on sexuality looks at the implications of this work for sociological theory and connects sociology to theories of gender.

D'Emilio, John, and Estelle B. Friedman. 1988.
Intimate Matters: A History of Sexuality in America. New York: Harper and Row.
An excellent history of sexuality in the United States, this book is also noted for its inclusion of the connections between sexuality, gender, race, and class.

Due, Linnea. 1995. *Joining the Tribe: Growing Up Gay & Lesbian in the '90s.* New York: Doubleday.
Written for a popular audience and based on many personal narratives, this book examines the sociological dimensions of growing up lesbian or gay.

Gluckman, Amy, and Betsy Reed. 1997. *Homo Economics: Capitalism, Community, and Lesbian and Gay Life*. New York: Routledge.
This collection of essays examines the economic status of gays and lesbians, including research challenging myths about the relatively high status of gay men. The anthology explores connections between oppression because of sexual orientation and race, class, and gender inequality.

Irvine, Janice M. 1990. *Disorders of Desire: Sex and Gender in Modern American Sexology*. Philadelphia: Temple University Press.

This discussion of the social context of sex research offers a sociological account of changing attitudes about sexuality and the social-historical context of sexual behavior.

Michael, Robert T., John H. Gagnon, Edward O. Laumann, and Gina Kolata. 1994. *Sex in America: A Definitive Survey*. Boston: Little, Brown.
Based on sociological surveys of sexual practices, this book provides an overview of sexual behavior in the 1990s.

Nardi, Peter M., and Beth Schneider. 1997. *Social Perspectives on Lesbian and Gay Studies*. New York: Routledge.
This collection of articles provides a sociological perspective on new research on gay and lesbian issues. It includes classic readings with the work of young scholars who are redefining questions about sexual identity, community, and social change.

Rubin, Lillian B. 1990. *Erotic Wars: What Happened to the Sexual Revolution?* New York: Farrar, Straus, and Giroux.
Rubin examines the presumed shift to more conservative sexual beliefs and the sexual mood of the U.S. public today. She explores the development of sexuality in people's lives and the meaning it has for them as it is shaped by social trends.

Schwartz, Pepper, and Virginia Rutter. 1998. *The Gender of Sexuality*. Thousand Oaks, CA: Pine Forge Press.
This review of sociological perspectives on sexuality links the study of gender roles to sexuality.

⮞ *C h a p t e r* 5
Women, Work, and the Economy

In 1997, women employed year round and full time earned $26,029; men employed year round and full time earned $35,248. Even after the women's movement has drawn attention to the earning gaps between women and men and, following almost 30 years of reforms intended to reduce discrimination, employed women still earn only 74 percent of men's earnings. Only 30 percent of employed women earn more than $35,000 a year, compared with 51 percent of employed men. Again, counting only year-round, full-time workers, women college graduates, on the average, earn less than men with some college and only slightly more than men with only a high school education ($35,378, women with bachelor's degrees; $35,945, men with only some college; $31,215, men with high school diplomas; U.S. Census Bureau, 1998).

These data are telling, but they do not reveal the variation among women in earnings, labor force participation, and occupational location, nor do they reveal the dynamics of the workplace that affect the everyday experiences of women at work. Although gender shapes the experiences of all women, exactly how this happens is also a matter of race, ethnicity, social class, age, and sexual orientation, among other things. Thus, the experiences of a top woman executive can be revealed by gender but also necessitate an analysis of class and race. How gender shapes her experience will be very different from how gender shapes the experience of a hotel maid, even though gender is highly significant in the lives of both workers. Sociological analyses of gender and work take all of these factors into account, thus revealing how social structure shapes the experiences of diverse groups of women and men in the workplace.

Without such analyses, women's role in economic life is obscured by various social myths, including that women are taking jobs away from men because of affirmative action, that women are achieving economic parity with men, that women's work is less valuable than men's, and that women who are at home with children are not working—the last myth being central in contemporary welfare politics. These points are examined throughout this chapter.

❧ *Historical Perspectives on Women's Work*

The history of women's work shows the societal developments that result in women's economic inequality and the devaluation of women's labor both inside and outside the home. As this section shows, the history of gender inequality in the Western world is intertwined with the history of racial and class subordination. A full analysis of the history of women's work would examine the work experience of women of color and working-class women as an integral part of the history of women's labor; moreover, studying race, class, and gender inequality simultaneously furthers our understanding of women's work in the contemporary world—both in domestic and global terms.

A brief history of women's labor cannot possibly capture the diverse experiences of different groups of women, but it can reveal the broad patterns in the evolution of women's work and thereby elucidate the social organization of gender and work in the United States. Any single group, however, has a unique historical experience, one that is distorted by lumping different groups together under single labels, such as Hispanic or Asian American. Asian American women's history of work varies considerably, for example, among Chinese Americans, Japanese Americans, and Korean Americans. Moreover, the work experiences of contemporary Asian American immigrants is substantially different from that of Asian groups migrating to the United States earlier in the century and, indeed, is significantly different even among diverse Asian immigrants today. Similarly, Puerto Rican women have a more recent historical experience than Chicanas, whose families may predate many White settlers in the U.S. Southwest. Luckily, many new histories are beginning to document carefully the work experiences of these different groups (Amott and Matthaei, 1996; Takaki, 1989, 1993; de la Torre and Pesquera, 1993; Acuña, 1988).

At the broadest level, however, the historical transformation of women's work can best be described as falling in three basic periods: the family-based economy, the family-wage economy, and the family-consumer economy (Tilly and Scott, 1978). Although these periods have been derived from studies of White European women's history, they do help organize the complex changes marking the development of the work system in the United States and the place of multiple groups of women within it.

The Family-Based Economy

The first period, the **family-based economy**, dates roughly from the seventeenth century to the early eighteenth century, although the time period shifts, depending on which group one considers. The family-based form of economic production was one where the household was the basic unit of the economy, since economic production was largely based on households, including small farms, large plantations, and haciendas. Although the specific form of different households would vary under this economic system, and different racial-ethnic groups were involved in different dimensions of this economy, the defining characteristic of this economic period was the household as the basic unit of production.

There would be little distinction during this period between economic and domestic life, since all household members (including nonblood kin, children, slaves, and other laborers) were all responsible for production. The typical household unit would largely have been agricultural, although, as cities developed, so did retailing; artisans' wives would also engage in household labor. In both rural and urban settings, the work of women and men was interdependent. Although the specific tasks done by each might vary, both women and men would be seen as contributing to the productivity of the whole.

White women's labor during this period was highly dependent on their class position and their marital status. Single women (unwed and widowed) might work in others' households doing traditional tasks such as spinning, weaving, and sewing (Kessler-Harris, 1982). Women in these households would supervise much of the household work, especially the labor of children; White women might also supervise the labor of slaves. White women were also engaged in agricultural labor and the production of cloth and food, although elite women would not likely engage in such labor.

African American women in the family-based economy labored as slaves, although in many states, African American men and women worked as free laborers, doing a variety of jobs as skilled craft workers, farm laborers, and domestics. African Americans were forcibly brought to the United States by the slave trade, beginning in the early seventeenth century and persisting at least until 1807, when England and the United States agreed, at least in law, to prohibit the trade (Meier and Rudwick, 1966). It is estimated that over 9.5 million Africans were transported to the United States, the Caribbean, and Brazil during this time, not counting the probably 20 million who died in passage (Genovese, 1972; Meier and Rudwick, 1966).

Black women in slavery did most of the same jobs as men, although in addition, they worked in the masters' homes and on behalf of their own families (Jones, 1985). The plantation economy functioned somewhat like the domestic economy because the plantation, like a household, functioned as the major unit of production. In the U.S. South, one-quarter of White families held slaves, although half of the slaves lived on farms with fewer than 20 slaves and three-quarters lived on farms with fewer than 50 slaves (Genovese, 1972).

Under slavery, slaves provided most, if not all, of the productive labor, while White slave owners had total control and ownership of slave labor and the profits it generated. The plantation economy represented a transition between an agriculturally based society and an industrialized one because the population of slaves worked as a cheap and fully controlled labor force. After the abolition of slavery, African American women and men entered the labor market as free laborers, but even then, they could not compete equally for the same jobs available to White women and men.

The early history of Chicana labor was also influenced by a family-based economy. The United States annexed Mexican territory in the Southwest following the Mexican-American War in 1848. Before U.S. conquest, Mexican families in the Southwest worked primarily as agricultural units. A strong gender division of labor was maintained, with women's work located primarily in the home but contributing directly to the family-based production. As you will see in the following section, the transition to a wage-based economy upset existing patterns of Chicana labor and family life (Baca Zinn and Eitzen, 1999).

Similarly, labor patterns for Native American women were disrupted by U.S. conquest of Native American lands. Although particular forms of labor, its meaning, and its relationship to other social systems varied across Native American societies, in general Native American societies accorded great respect to women, even when there was a marked division of labor between women and men. Colonization by Whites radically disrupted this way of life, while also imposing external institutions onto Native American societies (Allen, 1986; Amott and Matthaei, 1996).

The Family-Wage Economy

In the second period of the transformation to advanced capitalism, called the **family-wage economy**, the center of labor moved out of the household and into the factory system. This shift was the result of industrialization that began in England in the mid-eighteenth century, followed in France and the United States somewhat later. In the family-wage economy, workers earned their living outside the home and the household became dependent on wages that the workers brought home. The shift to wage labor and the production of commodities outside the home had several influences on the character of women's work. It led to the development of dual roles for women as paid laborers and as unpaid housewives.

With industrialization, the household was no longer the primary center of production, although women's work in the home was still socially and economically necessary. As the focus of work moved beyond the home, the worth of all persons became measured in terms of their earned wage; therefore, the work of women in the home was devalued. In addition, with for-profit goods (not just for exchange or subsistence) being produced largely outside the home, international mercantilism developed, further eroding the position of women (Dobash and Dobash, 1979).

In a wage system, producing, distributing, and purchasing goods requires cash. Although women and children worked for wages in the factory system, they received less pay than men did and, in fact, were chosen as workers because they were a cheap supply of labor. Male control of the wage-labor system, along with the capitalist pursuit of greater profits, weakened women's earning power (Hartmann, 1976). Because cash resources were needed to survive in the new economy, women became more financially dependent on men (Tilly and Scott, 1978).

African American women in the United States during this period worked primarily as domestic workers. Until 1940, as many as 60 percent of African American women labored as private domestic workers (Rollins, 1985). African

American men worked primarily in agriculture and as service workers, where seasonal unemployment and low wages prevented them from assuming the role of family breadwinner—the mark of masculinity and achievement in White, patriarchal societies.

The history of work for other groups in the United States shows similar patterns of the intersection of race, class, and gender oppression during industrialization and the move to a wage-based economy. In the Southwest, Chicanas were employed in the expanding agricultural market, which often forced whole families to migrate to find seasonal labor. The newly industrializing agricultural economy placed men in mining, railroad work, and agricultural field work as pickers; women were employed in canning and packing houses and in the textile industry; and Chicanas also continued to work as domestics—mainly as servants, laundresses, cooks, and dishwashers (Baca Zinn and Eitzen, 1999).

The experience of Asian women in the United States has been one of exclusion. The Chinese Exclusion Act of 1882 prevented male Chinese laborers from bringing their wives to the United States. Other legislation restricted the entry of Asian immigrants and prohibited marriage between Asians and Whites. Those Chinese, Japanese, Filipino, and Korean women who were in the United States were stereotyped as cheap sex objects and worked in restricted occupations primarily as merchants' wives, domestics, laborers, or prostitutes (Chow, 1987; Amott and Matthaei, 1996).

In the Northeast, White immigrant women filled factory jobs in the textile and garment industries, where wages were low and working conditions hazardous. Other immigrant women worked as domestic workers. In fact, in 1870, one-half of all women wage earners in the United States were domestic workers. By 1920, the percentage of women working as paid domestics declined to 18.5 percent, reflecting employment changes for women as they moved into new fields as clerical workers, teachers, and nurses. Still, domestic work remained a major source of employment for Japanese and Chinese women immigrating to the United States in the first half of the twentieth century (Glenn, 1986). Domestic work continues to be a major means of employment for contemporary immigrant women, particularly Latinas (Romero, 1992) and new immigrants.

As production and commerce grew, management also become more complex, leading to vast increases in clerical and administrative occupations. The invention of the typewriter created a new concentration of women in the clerical labor force. The typewriter was introduced to the public in 1873 and, because there was a shortage of labor for the new jobs it created, women were recruited for typing jobs based on the ideological appeal that they were naturally more dextrous than men (Benet, 1972). In other fields, too, women were recruited when labor shortages necessitated a new work force. As public education was expanded in the late nineteenth century, women were said to be naturally suited for a profession that required patience, nurturing, and the education of children. Similarly, when the middle class organized the public health movement of the early twentieth century to ward off the "contagions" of the poor, female nurses were recruited to serve doctors and to bring "feminine compassion" to the sick (Ehrenreich and English, 1973a).

The Family-Consumer Economy

The third period of economic change is called the **family-consumer economy**. This period, also characteristic of the present, is really an extension of the family-wage system, as it developed through the twentieth century. In this period, technological change increased productivity, and the mass production of goods created households that specialized in consumption and reproduction (Tilly and Scott, 1978). Although in the family-consumer economy economic production goes on outside the home, the labor of family members does contribute to their economic standing. As you have already seen, in this period women's work as housewives is often coupled with their participation in paid labor; in the family-consumer economy, women's economic productivity is even higher than it was in the past (Tilly and Scott, 1978). Although women continue to do the same amount of housework they did in earlier periods (Vanek, 1978), public institutions (such as schools, welfare systems, and the fast-food industry) also take over activities that were once located in the household. Women consequently become defined primarily as consumers, even though, in most cases, their wages are still necessary for household support, and most women of color continued to work for wages.

Throughout the twentieth century, women's labor force participation continued to rise. Much has been made about the dramatic influx of women into the paid labor force during World War II. Popular wisdom has it that because of the need for women's labor, women entered the labor force in unprecedented numbers, only to leave it and return to their homes at the end of the war. In fact, women did respond with enthusiasm to the appeals for wartime work, but three-quarters of those who were employed during the war had worked for wages before. Historians estimate that a sizable group of new women workers would have entered the labor force anyhow; thus, the influx of women to paid work during the war is not as dramatic as usually assumed. Women saw the emergency as an opportunity to get ahead; women of color, professional women, and older women took advantage of the reduction in discrimination to enter well-paying jobs (Kessler-Harris, 1982). During the war, women were employed not so much in unprecedented numbers, but in unprecedented jobs—jobs that were well paid, were industrialized, and gave a new legitimacy and value to the work that women did (Sacks, 1984).

At the conclusion of the war, many women did not leave the paid labor force, but took jobs in other areas—jobs that did not pay as well as those they had left. Women were laid off after the war at a rate double that of men and were shunted into jobs in the clerical and service sectors. Older women, married women, and racial-ethnic women had a hard time finding jobs after the war.

Since World War II, White women have dramatically increased their employment rates, resulting in convergence of the measures of labor force participation between White women and women of color (see Table 5.1). Women continue, however, to work in occupations highly segregated by race and gender, generally working in occupations where more than two-thirds of the workers are women.

TABLE 5.1   Earnings in Selected Occupations: 1997

Occupation	Percent Women	Women's Median Weekly Earnings	Men's Median Weekly Earnings
Executives, administrators, managers	44.3%	$605	$868
Engineers	9.6	837	994
Scientists	31.0	668	878
Teachers, college and university	42.7	829	936
Teachers, elementary	83.9	655	719
Teachers, secondary	58.4	689	764
Lawyers	26.6	959	1267
Physicians	26.2	946	1220
Nurses	93.5	705	778
Social workers	69.3	518	551
Editors/reports	51.2	606	769
Retail sales workers	65.7	266	392
Secretaries	98.6	409	n/a
Waitresses/waiters	77.8	268	328
Bartenders	57.2	293	341
Maids and housemen	80.1	259	292
Plumbers	1.4	n/a	608
Electricians	1.9	n/a	625
Child care workers, private household	96.8	204	n/a
Construction workers	2.4	442	522
Machine operators	37.7	313	449
Farm workers	19.0	247	276

Source: Data from U.S. Department of Labor 1998. *Employment and Earnings*. Washington, DC; U.S. Government Printing Office, pp. 174–179, 209, 214.

In sum, the history of women's labor shows that women's work has been essential to economic productivity. Indeed, women's work, and particularly that of women of color, has been the foundation for the development of economic institutions in the United States. Women of color have always worked outside the home, and thus have had to combine work and family in ways new to some White women. White women, at the same time, have been used as a reserve supply of labor, being kept out of the labor force unless there was a labor shortage or particular demand for cheap workers. As you will see, transitions in the role of women in the paid labor force have also been buttressed by belief systems that make women's labor patterns seem natural and to be expected.

Ideology and the History of Women's Work

In Chapter 3, *ideology* was defined as a belief system that seeks to explain and justify the status quo. The economic and technological changes that marked the transitions from the domestic economy to the consumer economy were historically accompanied by changes in the ideological definition of womanhood. The *cult of true womanhood* (Kraditor, 1968), popularized in the nineteenth century, glorified women's ideal place as the home, where women were seen as having a moral calling to serve their families. The aristocratic lady of leisure became a model to be emulated and set the ideal, although not the reality, for women of the bourgeois class. At the same time, the Protestant ethic, which stressed individualism, success, and competition in the workplace, also encouraged White women to submerge their wills to piety, purity, and submissiveness (Kessler-Harris, 1982). At least in White bourgeois families, women's destiny became defined as a separate sphere in which home, duty to the family, and religion would prevail.

Despite these ideals, working-class women and women of color continued to work both in the public labor force and in the home. The reality of their working lives in the early industrial period stands in contradiction to the myth of true womanhood. Only the most affluent families could maintain an idle woman; most women worked long hours in factories and then at home. While the cult of true womanhood was at its peak, African American women were working as slaves, and no ideal of femininity was bestowed on them. In fact, the myth of the ideal woman could be created only at the expense of other women because African American, immigrant, Latina, Asian, and poor women still performed the necessary household and factory tasks.

For example, around the turn of the twentieth century in the United States, the woman who stayed at home to do her own housework became a symbol of middle-class prosperity (Davis, 1981). Consequently, women of color and immigrant women who had found employment as domestics were expelled from White middle-class homes and replaced by new technological devices that promised to make women's work easy. In fact, some of the advertising campaigns for new products in this period (such as irons) presented explicit images of these new products purging middle-class homes of the alleged germs and social diseases of Black and Chinese women (Cowan, 1976). Homes became depicted during this period as bulwarks of defense against the rapid social changes occurring in the industrial workplace. The new ideology of domesticity portrayed women's place in the home as a moral alternative to the effects of the bustling, nervous organization of public labor. Because many of the industrial changes taking place involved the migration of African Americans, Asians, Chicanos, and immigrants to the cities, it can be said that the cult of domesticity was intertwined with the dynamics of racism. White, middle-class women were not only seen as pious and pure but they were also perceived as the moral antithesis of allegedly inferior women of color and poor women.

At the same time, by the early twentieth century, middle-class women were expected to apply the skills of rational professional men to the maintenance of their homes. Inspired by modern models of rational management, housework (under the guise of the domestic science movement) was to be efficient, sanitary, and technologically streamlined. Order, system, and efficiency were the goals of domestic science, and the housewife was to become an engineer who would keep accurate records, color-code her appliances, maintain an efficient schedule, and, in the modern sense of the word, *manage* her home (Andrews and Andrews,

1974). Once again, clean houses and efficient management were seen as the antithesis of immigrant lives. Racism in this period depicted racial-ethnic groups as slovenly, diseased, and ridden with contagious germs (Higham, 1965; Palmer, 1989). Racist fears about the underclass propelled the middle classes to a new sense of themselves as both the moral agents of society and the social engineers of the future.

It is from this period that we have acquired many of our common household practices today. During the 1920s, many of the household designs that are now commonplace were introduced. Kitchens and bathrooms were to be pretty, as indicated in the following editorial:

> *Time was when kitchens were gloomy and dark, for keeping house was a gloomy business. . . . But now! gay colors are the order of the day. Red pots and pans! Blue gas stoves! . . . It is a rainbow, in which the cook sings at her work and never thinks of household tasks as drudgery.* (Ladies' Home Journal, *March 1928, cited in Cowan, 1976:150–151)*

Old wooden furniture was painted pastel colors, new brides were advised to keep the gray out of their husbands' shirts, and protecting the family from germs became evidence of good maternal instincts (Cowan, 1976). The ideology of domesticity added an emotional dimension to what had previously been the work of servants.

Women's roles in the home were further elaborated by the new importance placed on child care and the psychological life of infants and children. In the early twentieth century, the child became the leading figure in the family, and child psychology experts admonished mothers to turn their attention to their babies' emotional development and security (Ehrenreich and English, 1978). In the end, the concepts of both housewife and motherhood emphasized new standards for women's services in the home. Although technological change created the potential for a reduction in household labor, ideological shifts in the concept of women's roles increased the social requirements for women's work. Whereas housework before had been necessary labor, it now carried ideological significance, as well. As contemporary ads imply, keeping a clean house is not just labor; it is also supposed to be an expression of love. These new standards of housework effectively raise the level of consumption by individual households, leading to the conclusion shared by many social scientists that consumption, not production, is one of the major functions of contemporary household units today.

The preceding discussion shows that an analysis of women's roles in economic production cannot be separated from their roles in family life. Although the family and the economy are usually perceived as separate institutions, they are, both in history and in the present, intertwined through the activities of production and reproduction. Women work both for wages and without wages. This discussion of women and work must be understood in this context; furthermore, understanding the history of women's work means knowing the history of race and class oppression.

≈ *What Is Work?*

There are different ways to think about the concept of work, including looking at the personal questions that individuals ask when thinking about work they do. These include questions like: What kind of work can I find? How can I earn a good income to support myself and those who depend on me? Will I be in a job that recognizes my abilities and promotes my accomplishments? Will I be treated fairly? How can I balance work and the other dimensions of my life—school, family commitments, personal life? All of these are important questions that individuals ask at varying points in their lives.

Sociological questions about work, however, have a different focus. Sociologists are concerned with the quality of individual experiences and the opportunities people have to find meaningful work, but they analyze the social structure of work, meaning how the societal patterns of gender, class, and race shape work experiences. From a sociological point of view, even the individual questions people ask about their jobs reflect gender, race, and class relations. To explain, any employed women might be concerned about balancing work and family, but exactly how these strains are felt and the resources women have to address the problem differ across social classes. A professional middle-class woman might solve part of this problem by paying someone else (most likely, a woman) to clean her house, but the woman who cleans it is not likely to have this option. For her, balancing work and family may mean holding down two or more jobs, finding friends or relatives to care for children, and worrying about having enough money to support her family. The point is that a sociological perspective on work has to analyze the gender, race, and class relations that shape the work experiences of different groups in society.

Studies of work have been much enriched by feminist studies that have sought to explain the specific experiences of women in the labor force. Inspired by many of the personal experiences women have had at work, feminist scholars have used sociological perspectives (and have drawn from fields such as economics, political science, history, anthropology, and psychology) to learn: What is women's role in the labor force? What historical changes have taken place for working women? What is the socioeconomic status of women workers, and how do they fare, relative to men? What factors influence the mobility of women workers? Why do women, on average, still earn less than men? These and other questions are the basis for feminist and sociological studies of gender and work.

Two other questions, however, have emerged from feminist studies of work: How do we define work and how has that definition had to change to recognize the work women do? Many people tend to think of work as that which people do for pay, but as the history of women's work shows, women (and sometimes men) often work without pay. Housewives work but do not get paid; Black women worked as slaves but did not get paid; volunteers work but do not get paid, and, in fact, many women have full-time careers as volunteers (Daniels, 1988). Problems in the concept of work are not just a question of whether work is paid or unpaid, but are fundamental to the question of what constitutes work.

One consequence of feminist studies has been to question the traditional concept of work and its ability to include the full range of women's and men's productive activities. Feminists have pointed out that mothering is work, although it does not fit the criteria imposed by the traditional definition of work; moreover, if mothering is work, should fathering be considered work, as well? In considering the case of housework, feminist sociologists observe that there is an invisible dimension to the work, including not only the fact that it goes unnoticed but also the fact that part of doing housework is the work of "keeping in mind" various aspects of the tasks that constitute housework (DeVault, 1991). Housework involves the physical work of doing tasks as well as the mental efforts of noticing and remembering the chores that need doing, mentally arranging the tasks that need doing, and keeping track of the work to be done. None of this mental work can be actually measured or observed; as a result, it is difficult to share, although it is an essential aspect of the work.

In addition, Hochschild (1983) developed the concept **emotional labor** to refer to the work people do in managing the emotions of others. Emotional labor, she argues, is work that is done for wages and that is meant to achieve a desired emotional effect in others. Emotional labor is done in jobs that require personal contact with the public, wherein creating a given state of mind in the client or user is part or all of the product being sold. Hochschild's research is a study of airline flight attendants, for whom emotional labor is a central part of job training, activity, and evaluation. Hochschild shows that as a result of the shift from a production-based to a service-based economy, and given the fact that women predominate in service-oriented jobs, emotional labor is a growing part of the work that women do. It is monitored by supervisors and is the basis for job rewards and reprimands. She concludes that doing emotional labor often requires putting on a false front; as a result, engaging in emotional labor is a source of workers' stress. Emotional labor is required in an increasing number of jobs and is therefore subject to the rules of mass production, resulting in what Hochschild calls "the commercialization of human feeling."

≈ *Gender and Class Stratification*

Gender stratification refers to the hierarchical distribution by gender of economic and social resources in a society. All societies are organized around a system for the production and distribution of goods. In addition, most societies are marked by a system of social stratification. Sociologists define **stratification** as the process whereby groups or individuals in a society are located in a hierarchical arrangement on the basis of their differential access to social and economic resources. Sociologists also point out that there is nothing inherent in human nature or inevitable in social organization that requires unequal access to social and economic resources. Were inequality an inevitable result of human nature, stratification patterns would not vary in societies to the extent that they do; moreover, we would not find egalitarian societies in the record of human history.

Because differences in stratification are found in different societies, sociologists are very interested in the conditions that generate social inequality. Many point out that socioeconomic inequality emerges when there is a surplus of goods available in the society (Marx and Engels, 1970). Simply put, a surplus of goods creates the possibility that one group of people can appropriate the surplus for themselves. This action forms the initial basis for class systems in which one class controls the resources of other groups in the society.

In most societies, gender is a primary category that stratifies social groups. Women's access to societal rewards is greatly influenced by the degree to which they control the means and forms of social and economic production. In virtually all societies, women's work sustains the economy, although in many societies (such as our own), women's work is either invisible or devalued. Cross-cultural research shows that women tend to have the most egalitarian status in societies in which they directly contribute to the production of goods (Leacock, 1978). In hunting-and-gathering societies, for example, women produce most of the food supply. Their status in these societies is relatively equal to that of men, even though a gender division of labor still exists. In agricultural societies, although women continue to be primary producers, their status deteriorates because land, economic surplus, and, subsequently, political power are concentrated in the hands of male rulers (O'Kelly and Carney, 1986).

In preindustrialized societies, women's labor in the home is a vital part of the productive system because it is in the home that goods are produced; moreover, in these societies, women also have visible roles outside the home, as they distribute their goods in markets or even operate small businesses. As industrialization advances, though, economic production is shifted from the home to the factory, and although working-class and immigrant women hold factory jobs, women's domestic labor becomes both invisible and devalued. In U.S. history, the devaluation of household labor has not only resulted in a loss of status for middle-class women who work at home but has also created a class of the most severely underpaid and socially devalued laborers—African American and Chicana domestic workers (Davis, 1981; Romero, 1992).

It is impossible to understand gender stratification in the United States without also understanding **class stratification,** meaning the institutionalized system by which some groups have more economic resources and power than do others. Class is one of the most important dimensions of women's and men's lives (and therefore an important concept in sociology) because it influences the access different groups have to economic, social, and political resources. Class standing determines how well social institutions serve you; thus, poor women have far less access to good health care, education, or other societal resources than do elite and middle-class women. The class system also places groups in different positions of privilege and disadvantage in society.

Sociologists define and analyze class in different ways, but, simply put, **class** refers to the social structural position groups hold relative to the economic, social, political, and cultural resources of society. Members of a given class have relatively similar resources and tend to share a common way of life. Class matters, not just because of the different opportunities class privilege or disadvantage create for different people, but because society is structured in terms of class relationships. Class is not just a matter of individual resources; it involves the relationship between class groups and whole social systems. The class system is not simply the sum of individual opportunities; it is a structured (or institutionalized) system of privilege and inequality.

Class is indicated by who controls money, who controls the labor process, and who controls the production and distribution of goods and services. Those who have such control are dominant in the class system; those who do not are dominated. Class is more than an economic relationship; it involves power relationships as well as differential access to resources and control, domination, and power. Therefore, classes vary not only in terms of their access to economic resources but also in the degree of control they have over how things are produced, who produces them, and how work is organized and managed. The *working class* has little control over these things; the *middle class*, on the other hand, exercises greater control, and the *elites* have the most control of all. In sum, class is not just a matter of individual income and prestige; rather, class is part of a structured system involving control, power, and differential access to resources (Vanneman and Cannon, 1987; Wright, 1979).

Class can also be seen in terms of levels in a hierarchical system, typically using several common indicators to measure class standing: income, education, occupation, and place of residence. Although these indicators do not define class per se, they can be used to indicate a person's or group's class standing; these indicators also tend to be interrelated. Class is the common position groups hold in a social hierarchy (Wright, 1979; Lucal, 1994).

Class does not stand alone in shaping women's or men's experiences. As this book emphasizes throughout, class intersects both with gender and race in determining group standing in society. Systems of privilege and disadvantage cannot be described by either class, gender, or race alone. The next section reviews contemporary data about women's position in the labor market, with an eye toward understanding how the class system shapes women's economic standing.

❧ The Contemporary Status of Women

Women's status in the labor market on many measures has changed dramatically in recent years. More women are working than ever before, and some women now enter occupations that were previously held only by men. Women's earnings as a percentage of men's have improved, although a significant pay gap remains. At a glance, many might conclude that women's struggle for equality is over; yet, on many measures, women still lag behind. Although they are more likely to work, women remain highly segregated in certain jobs, their earnings are low, and they experience what has popularly been labeled *the glass ceiling*, referring to implicit limits on their ability to move up at work. In fact, in 1995, a government commission (the Glass Ceiling Commission) reported that, despite three decades

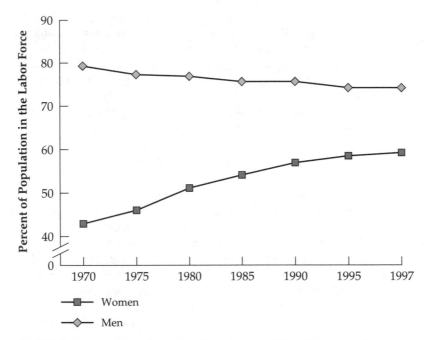

FIGURE 5.1   Labor Force Participation: 1970–1997

Source: Data from U.S. Department of Labor. 1998. *Employment and Earnings.*
Washington, DC: U.S. Government Printing Office, p. 163.

of new policies designed to address gender and race inequality in the labor market, women and racial minorities were still substantially blocked from senior
management positions (Glass Ceiling Commission, 1995). How do women fare in
the labor market?

Labor Force Participation

By 1997, 60 percent of all women were in the labor force, compared with 75 percent of men (see Figure 5.1); moreover, since 1960, married women with children
have nearly tripled their labor force participation. Hispanic women are somewhat
less likely than African American and White women to be employed, but these
data are distorted by the clustering of different groups into one category as
"Hispanic." Mexican American women have the highest employment rates of any
Hispanic women. Puerto Rican women have the lowest labor force participation
rate (U.S. Department of Labor, 1998). Asian American women are even more likely than other women to be in the labor force, but, since their educational levels are
relatively high, most are concentrated in clerical, service, and blue-collar jobs.
Women's work is increasingly necessary because it is only in families where wives
are in the paid labor force that the median income level is reached.

In the future, the labor force is likely to include more women and minority groups. Among women, by the year 2005, Hispanic women are expected to have the highest labor force participation rate, followed by (in order) White women, Asian women, and Black women. While women's labor force participation rate has been increasing, men's has been decreasing. In 1951, 87 percent of men were in the labor force, but by 1997, this had dropped to 75 percent. The decline of men's labor force participation is expected to continue, whereas that of women is expected to continue increasing. Among racial minorities, Hispanics are predicted to have the greatest increase in labor force participation (a projected 75 percent growth rate between 1990 and 2005). Asians and "others" (i.e., Pacific Islanders, Native Americans, and Alaskan natives) are predicted to have a growth rate of 74 percent (Fullerton, 1995).

One of the developments influencing women's position in the labor force is the growth in immigration that the United States has witnessed in recent years. In the late 1990s, approximately three-quarter million immigrants were arriving each year—a rate of immigration not matched since the 1920s, when so many European immigrants arrived. Now, the largest number of immigrants come from Caribbean countries, Mexico, the former Soviet Union, and the Philippines. Other Asian and Latin American countries account for another large share of the total number of immigrants (U.S. Census Bureau, 1997). For women, immigration has a number of consequences for labor force participation. Immigration is typically a family experience, as family units make decisions about who will migrate, who will work, and what impact immigration will have on family well-being. This means that women who may not have been in the labor force before will work for wages, often transforming gender roles within the family that existed prior to immigration (Hondagneu-Sotelo, 1994; Grasmuck and Pessar, 1996; Lim, 1997; Pedraza, 1991, 1996). Immigrant women can also find themselves "niched" in certain sectors of the labor market, such as domestic work or factory production, where wages are low and opportunities for advancement are poor (Repak, 1994; Myers and Crawford, 1998). Still, they may find that employment brings them more independence and more opportunity to exercise influence in family decisions.

Gender Segregation

One of the most significant factors influencing women's class position is gender segregation in the labor market. **Gender segregation** refers to the pattern whereby women and men are situated in different jobs throughout the labor force. Gender segregation is a particular form of *occupational distribution*—a term sociologists use to refer to the placement of workers in different occupations.

Most women work in gender-segregated jobs (see Figure 5.2). That is to say, women work in jobs where most of the other workers are women, and women constitute a numerical minority of workers in many of the jobs that have historically been identified as men's work. This is vividly seen in Figure 5.2, showing the distribution of women, African Americans, and Hispanics in selected occupations. Note that women constitute 98 percent of secretaries, 75 percent of teachers,

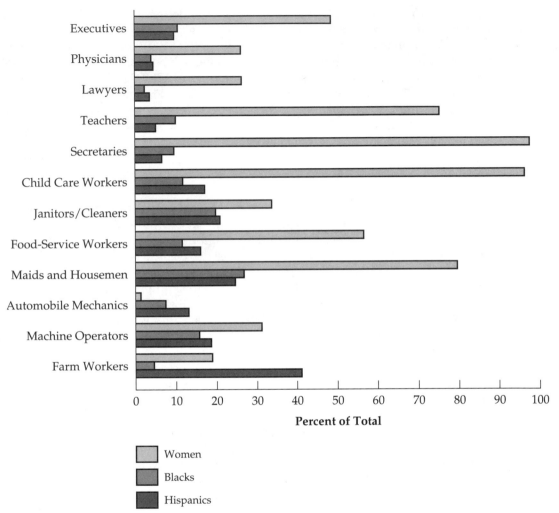

FIGURE 5.2   Occupational Segregation by Gender and Race-Ethnicity: 1997

Source: Data from U.S. Department of Labor. 1998. *Employment and Earnings.* Washington, DC: U.S. Government Printing Office, pp. 174–179.

and 97 percent of child care workers, but only 26 percent of physicians and 27 percent of lawyers (a huge increase since the 1970s, when they were 8 percent of physicians and 12 percent of lawyers; Andersen, 1983). Men are more broadly distributed across the labor market and are more likely located in the higher-paying professions, although this is mitigated by men's racial status.

Women also work in fewer occupational categories across the labor force than do men. As late as 1997, 40 percent of all employed women worked either in clerical or service jobs; almost two-thirds of employed women worked either as health care workers, teachers, sales workers, clerical workers, service workers, or machine operators (U.S. Department of Labor, 1998). These data provide only a glimpse of gender segregation, in part because it is aggregate data—that is, based on large national samples and big groupings of occupations.

Within occupational categories, women are also concentrated in gender-segregated jobs. This is referred to as *internal gender segregation*. Take the example of teachers. Women are 76 percent of teachers (excluding college and university teaching), but they are 98 percent of prekindergarten and kindergarten teachers and 84 percent of elementary school teachers. Likewise, in the category of machine operators, where women are 40 percent of all workers, they are 72 percent of textile machine operators and, within this category, 82 percent of sewing machine operators. Women are internally segregated as professional workers, too. Although they appear from the aggregate data to make up half of professional workers (seeming equality), the majority of women professionals are health care workers or teachers; far fewer are in the more prestigious and better paid professional jobs.

Gender segregation is further complicated by race. Chicanas, for example, are most heavily concentrated in clerical, operative, and nonhousehold service occupations (such as maids and kitchen workers; U.S. Department of Labor, 1998; Segura, 1994). As a result, except for Native American women, the income of Chicanas is less than that of any other group. Like White women, women of color are most likely to work in jobs where more than two-thirds of the other workers are women; African American women and Latinas also work in occupations where nearly one-quarter of the other workers are other people of color; Asian American and Native American women work where most of the other workers are people of color. These numerical facts affect social relations at work, but they also affect women's income, since occupations with high concentrations of women of color are the worse paid of all jobs. This is shown by the fact that, in general, the larger the proportion of women in an occupation, the lower the pay (as shown in Figure 5.3). One frustrating thing about using federal data to examine labor market data is that the government does not include Asian Americans and Native Americans in their summary reports. Occasional reports are sometimes issued specifically about these two groups, but since neither is included in the general reports, it is difficult to compare labor market experience across these categories.

The data on gender and race segregation exposes the myth that women of color are entering the labor market and taking jobs away from White men. Although some individuals see this happen on occasion, the aggregate data reveal that this can be true only in a small number of cases. The general pattern is that women and people of color work in different occupations than do White men. You might ask why it has become such a big public issue when you consider the number of jobs over the years that have gone to White men and not to women and people of color. Criticisms of affirmative action hiring programs make it appear that women and minorities are flooding the labor market, taking jobs away from White men. The data show the contrary. Even with affirmative action policy and equal employment opportunity laws, White women, African American women and men, Hispanics, Asian Americans, and Native Americans are employed in a labor market divided by race and by gender.

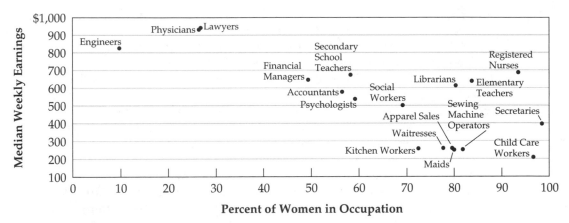

FIGURE 5.3   Income and Gender Segregation: 1997

Source: Data from U.S. Department of Labor. 1998. *Employment and Earnings.* Washington, DC: U.S. Government Printing Office, pp. 174–179, 209–214.

Note: Shown only for selected occupations, 1997.

Aggregate data on gender segregation provide a general view of where women work. To understand fully women's experiences in these different positions of work requires a closer view of women's experiences in various work settings. This gives us a picture drawn not just from government statistics but also drawn from the many studies of women and work that examine in detail the variety of circumstances where women are employed. Next, some of this work will be examined by looking in more detail at some of the broad categories of women's employment. This will also provide more analysis of the combined effects of gender, race, and class in the social and economic organization of work.

Women in the Professions

Women who work in the professions have the advantage of holding the most prestigious and highly paid jobs in the labor market. Women's presence in the professions has increased in recent years, although they are still a numerical minority in many of the most senior positions. Women constitute almost half of those in the census category "Managerial and Professional Specialty," but within this broad category are numerous different occupations with widely varying participation by women. Women represent 10 percent of engineers, 26 percent of physicians, 17 percent of dentists, 31 percent of scientists and mathematicians, 14 percent of clergy, 27 percent of lawyers, and 27 percent of professional athletes. Where women predominate in the professions is in traditionally women's work; thus, they are 94 percent of nurses, 89 percent of dietitians, 98 percent of preschool teachers, 81 percent of librarians, 66 percent of social workers, and 81 percent of educational and vocational counselors (U.S. Department of Labor, 1998).

It is in the professions where women have made some of the most dramatic numerical gains; yet they are still concentrated in the lower ranks and less prestigious specialties. In universities, as you saw in Chapter 3, although women constitute 43 percent of all college and university professors, they are only 18 percent of full professors (the top rank) and they are half of instructors—positions that are temporary, not well paid, and typically without the job benefits and rewards associated with other university appointments (Carter and Wilson, 1998). Likewise, within medicine, women are concentrated in certain specialties that are less prestigious and less financially lucrative than others—pediatrics, family practice, psychiatry, internal medicine, obstetrics/gynecology, anesthesiology, and pathology; women of color who are physicians are even more concentrated in pediatrics and obstetrics/gynecology (American Medical Association, 1994; Titus-Dillon and Johnson, 1989). With the move to managed health care, women physicians are also more likely to work in university or hospital staff positions, not independent practice. Similarly, in law, although women are now more widely distributed across different specialties within law, they are still more likely to be found in certain areas (such as domestic law, real estate, trust, and general practice), and they are twice as likely as men to work in public service law (Epstein, 1993).

These patterns are established early on, as women and people of color often find it difficult to find sponsorship by mentors in the professions. Professions are socially organized like communities and, as such, involve informal roles and practices and tend toward homogeneity and exclusionary relations. Social control in professional life, as well as access to rewards, typically operates through a sponsorship system that feminists have labeled the "old boy network." Within the network, social relations with one's peers and mentors can bring access to jobs, promotions, opportunities, and status.

The woman professional who is excluded from the protégé system is likely to find herself at a disadvantage when it comes to professional opportunities. Additionally, the information and colleagueship shared by those in the network are likely to give professional advantage to those who are "in the know." Whether by exclusion or personal choice, women who are not part of the old boy network are likely to find their careers detrimentally affected (Epstein, 1970).

The climate in graduate and professional schools also influences women's subsequent career patterns. Studies show that the climate in these settings often reflects a male-dominated culture, just as women are likely to find once they enter the profession. Studies of medical school cultures, for example, find that the atmosphere is like a men's club. In medical school, women report discrimination in their clinical experiences, condescending chivalry, sexual harassment, and condescending remarks about feminism (Grant, 1988; Lorber and Ecker, 1983). In law schools, race and gender dynamics in the classroom also discourage participation by women and people of color (Mertz, Njogu, and Gooding, 1998). In addition, the clockwork of professional careers has been developed around male-centered models—that one should uproot one's family and move when opportunities are available, put in long hours independent of family and personal responsibilities, and be available whenever the profession calls for you, regardless of other commitments. Research on lawyers finds, for example, that women have poorer prospects for becoming partners than do men and that different gender expectations for men and women shape their perceived value as partners and thus the likelihood of their achieving partnership. Men are valued for maintaining traditional corporate family images, whereas women are valued for giving priority to work outside the home (Kay and Hagan, 1998).

This professional culture has encouraged women professionals in most fields to establish alternative networks of support, both for professional advancement and for personal encouragement. Groups such as the Association for Women in Science, the Society of Women Engineers, Sociologists for Women in Society, and the Association for Women in Psychology, to name only a few, have flourished. As both professional networks and local support groups for women professionals, these organizations encourage the development of alternative networks to promote the status of professional women.

Women as Clerical Workers

Women make up 80 percent of all administrative support workers, an occupational category of the U.S. census that includes clerical workers. Women are 98 percent of all secretaries, stenographers, and typists. Over the twentieth century, the number of clerical workers has drastically increased, but their prestige has declined—even though the technological skill required to do the job has increased.

Before the mechanization of office work by the invention of the typewriter in the late nineteenth century, skills such as shorthand and accounting were men's trades, and relatively prestigious trades at that. An 1888 book titled *How to Succeed as a Stenographer or Typewriter* was addressed to men, saying, "There are comparatively few verbatim reporters, and the young shorthand writer who has reached that distinction should consider that it gives him the rank of a scholar and a gentleman" (Baker, 1888, cited in Benet, 1972:39). The introduction of mechanized switchboards and typewriters and the corresponding need for new workers brought the rapid introduction of women workers to these jobs. Capitalist owners saved money by tapping the cheap, large, female labor market, and soon women workers experienced a decline in the wages and prestige associated with office work.

To this day, the median weekly earnings for women in administrative support work are low, especially compared with those of men. In 1997, full-time male administrative support workers earned $514 per week, compared to $403 per week for women (U.S. Department of Labor, 1998). A huge supply of women clerical workers is also provided by temporary clerical services, where workers have low wages, little control of their work, minimal social relationships with co-workers, and highly alienated attitudes toward their jobs. Opportunities for advancement are greater for secretaries than for other clerical workers, but mobility for secretaries is often dependent on the promotion of their supervisor, not just their own performance.

Full-time secretaries, except those who work in large typing pools where work is heavily routinized, are tied to individual and patrimonial relationships with their bosses. Their status is then contingent on that of the boss, whose power may determine their own. Although studies find that secretaries most resent doing personal work for their bosses, bosses expect their secretaries to appreciate and provide nonmaterial rewards such as emotional intimacy, praise, and affection. Loyalty and devotion to their employers are often the bases for secretaries' rewards at work (Kanter, 1977).

Clerical work, of course, varies in different settings, but in large companies where there is the most extensive automation and use of a secretarial pool, clerical work is becoming "proletarianized." That is, work is becoming organized more around manual than mental activities, tasks are externally structured and controlled, and relationships among workers more depersonalized. Automation in the form of electronic data processing and word processing means that computers now perform many clerical functions, decreasing the autonomy of workers and increasing fragmentation among clerical workers (Feldberg and Glenn, 1979). The development of word processing increases productivity at the same time that it increases surveillance of clerical work (Machung, 1984). The proletarianization of clerical work leaves workers with less control over the work itself, and makes relationships between workers and supervisors more impersonal. This process also has serious implications for the development of solidarity among clerical workers. As working groups become less interdependent and more physically separated, it is more difficult for workers to know if they share common conditions and occupy comparable positions in the office hierarchy. Although the strains associated with more mechanized work can create cooperation among the workers, the strains also increase workers' vulnerability, sometimes decreasing their desires for personal ties with others (Feldberg and Glenn, 1979).

The increased use of computers has advantages and disadvantages for clerical workers. Computerized technology can eliminate some of the stress from routine, repetitive, and tedious aspects of one's job, but in occupations such as data entry, the work becomes more routinized. Increasingly, large numbers of women, especially women of color, work in "electronic sweatshops" entering keyboard data, with their work electronically monitored. Computer technology also brings new forms of fatigue, physical strain, and stress. Many researchers argue that the negative affects of computers are not the result of the technology per se, but of the way they are used in the workplace (Gutek, 1988). Because clerical workers are seldom given any authority or responsibility for designing their workplace, it is little wonder that they suffer the consequences of poor workplace design and organization.

Women in Blue-Collar Work

Among blue-collar workers, women have been entering the skilled trades at a rapid rate—faster, in fact, than men in recent years—although women still constitute only a small percentage of those in the more highly skilled trades. Women in blue-collar work are more likely to be employed as semiskilled machine operators than as skilled crafts workers; within the occupational categories in which they work, women earn less than men.

Women in blue-collar work also find gender segregation on the job. Even when women are employed in the same occupational category as men, they tend to be located in different industries. Women are more likely to be employed in the nondurable-goods sector, whereas men are more likely employed in manufacturing, where wages and job benefits have traditionally been higher. Although the job crises that men in these industries face cannot be ignored, women (especially minority women) tend to be located in the poorest quality blue-collar jobs available.

In fact, the largest majority of women in blue-collar work are employed in assembly work—jobs with little autonomy and often involving repetitive tasks. Depending on the region of the country, women in assembly work are a disproportionate number of assembly-line workers. In the microelectronics industry in California, 50 to 75 percent of the jobs are estimated to be held by minorities, many of them Latina, Asian, and African American women, even though 90 percent of the managers and owners are White men (Hossfeld, 1990).

Blue-collar workers in the United States, both women and men, are also increasingly affected by global restructuring of the economy. **Global restructuring** refers to the process through which research and management are based in developed countries (e.g., the United States), while assembly-line work is relegated to underprivileged nations (especially in Latin America and Asia). Some have referred to this as the development of the **global assembly line**. In the global assembly line, women workers are relocated from their traditional work in home-based production and are employed in factories as assembly workers. This new work gives women somewhat greater independence from traditional patriarchal arrangements but introduces them to new forms of exploitation in the form of high job turnover, little mobility, low wages, and hazardous working conditions. Their work within these settings is often justified through crude sexist and racist ideologies defining them as "fit" for this demeaning work.

The global assembly line links the experiences of women in poor nations to the consumerism in the United States that "markets gender." Barbie dolls are a good example. Barbie is the "dream girl" of the United States, each version depicting a different fantasy life of beauty, fashion, romance, and play. But most Barbie dolls are manufactured by workers not much older than those who play with her in the United States. For these workers, it would take all of their monthly pay just to buy *one* of the dolls that many U.S. girls collect by the dozens. In China, where more toys are produced than in any other part of the world, workers molding Barbie dolls earn 25 cents an hour, and human rights organizations say violations of basic rights are flagrant. Moreover, this works to the advantage of corporate owners in the United States, such as the chief executive officer of Mattel (the company that produces Barbies), who, in 1995, earned $7 million and an additional $23 million in stock options—far more than the combined salaries of the 11,000 Mattel workers who produce Barbie dolls in China. Indonesian workers making Barbies earn the minimum wage of $2.25 a day; it would take such a worker a full month to earn the money to buy the Calvin Klein Barbie (Press, 1996). Similar analyses can be made of many products—action figures, jeans, and other gendered products—that are manufactured in the global assembly line for sale to an international gendered market.

Within the U.S. economy, women in blue-collar jobs are much less likely than men to be protected by labor unions. Although women's union membership increased during the 1970s, the percentage of all workers represented by unions has declined more recently to only 16 percent of employed persons in 1997; 14

percent of employed women and 16 percent of employed men are represented by unions. As a result of their concentration in blue-collar occupations, African American men and women are more likely to be represented by unions than are White men and women. Hispanic men are less likely than White men to be unionized, although Hispanic women are slightly more likely to be unionized than White women. Women in service occupations and clerical work tend not to be unionized, leaving them subject to the discretionary practices of individual companies and employers.

Despite low rates of union membership, being in a union is significant for employed women and men. Not only does it increase the likelihood of due process and job protection, but median weekly earnings of those represented by unions exceed earnings of nonunion members. For example, women who were members of unions in 1997 had median weekly earnings of $543, compared with $398 for nonunionized employed women (U.S. Department of Labor, 1998).

Within blue-collar labor, male supervisors' gender stereotypes and discomfort at the presence of women shape women's experiences at work. Supervisors may believe, for example, that women should be excluded from some jobs so they do not get hurt; paternalistic attitudes put supervisors in the position of gatekeepers who maintain the status quo by assigning women to gender-typed jobs. Often, the fact that supervisors' reservations about women are paternalistic rather than overt and hostile makes it difficult for women in such jobs to identify or document sexism, for it appears subtle or trivial; nonetheless, such attitudes and behaviors do create barriers to women's mobility. Supervisors' paternalistic attitudes also communicate to male co-workers that sexist behavior is acceptable (Reskin and Padavic, 1988). Studies of desegregation in blue-collar work do show, however, that supervisors often lose their reservations about women's work after supervising more women. One mechanism for eliminating sexism in these occupations is to increase the number of women workers in these jobs (Reskin and Padavic, 1988).

Some people assume that women do not choose to enter traditionally male blue-collar jobs as a result of their gender socialization not to prefer such work. Studies show, however, that although this plays some small part in women's choices about blue-collar work, economic need overrides any learned distaste women may have for such jobs (Padavic, 1991).

Women and Service Work
Service work is the third largest category of women's employment, accounting for 17.4 percent of women in the labor force. Women in service work are among the lowest paid of employed women, yet this is the most rapidly expanding area of work—one where most new jobs are predicted to be found in the future. Included in service work are fast-food workers, waitresses, and health care assistants (e.g., nurses' aides, maids, and various personal service workers). This category of work employs large numbers of women of color, as well as older women workers returning to the labor force after years of working in the home. In 1997, the median weekly earnings for service workers (not including private and protective ser-

vices) were $317 for men and $260 for women (U.S. Department of Labor, 1998); those working in private households earned even less (see Table 5.1).

Service work is highly segregated by gender, even within specific occupational categories. For example, women constitute almost three-quarters of kitchen workers and counter servers but less than one-fifth of protective service workers (e.g., police, firefighters, and guards), where pay is better. High rates of turnover and part-time employment are also common in service work, further limiting women's chances for upward mobility in those occupations (Berheide, 1988).

Service work can also be one of the most degrading forms of work for women. Women service workers are often supervised by men whose attitudes can be patronizing, impatient, and overtly hostile. Sexist expectations also shape women's experiences in these occupations. Waitresses, for example, are often expected to be young and sexy, to dress in provocative clothing, and to treat even the most obnoxious customer with grace and charm. Sometimes, sexist expectations for women service workers are very explicit, as in the old requirements of some airlines that flight attendants not exceed certain weight and height standards. Even when not written into explicit employment practices, these expectations often shape women's opportunities in service occupations. For women of color in these occupations, the combination of sexist and racist attitudes and behaviors can be doubly demeaning.

For many years, employment as a domestic worker was the only choice for women who needed to work, particularly women of color. Now, although other opportunities are available, large numbers of women still work in private households where their labor is unregulated and sometimes unreported. Although it pays poorly, domestic work is often the only work available for incoming groups of immigrant women, women with little education, and women with little choice of occupation. In recent years, refugees from Latin America have entered domestic work, receiving low wages and few, if any, benefits (Repak, 1994). Domestic workers seldom face opportunities for unionization and are rarely given employee benefits such as health care insurance, paid sick leave, retirement, or vacation. Although private-household workers sometimes have the benefit of negotiating their own work schedules and, thus, may have greater flexibility than workers in the public sector, they pay the price in terms of low wages and little job security.

Women who work as domestic workers regard the independence and autonomy of the job as a positive feature of the work, but since domestic workers typically do not have co-workers, loneliness, especially for live-ins, is the most difficult part of the work (Rollins, 1985). Rollins's study of Black domestic workers in the Boston area identifies maternalism as structuring the relationship between domestics and their employers. Rollins, who holds a Ph.D. in sociology, hired herself as a domestic worker as part of her research design. Through her own experiences and her interviews with Black domestic workers, she shows that because the domestic work is based on personal relations, it is both psychologically and economically belittling. Although employers may act caring and protective, the job is still structured as a power relationship. Patterns of deferential behavior, such as referring to the domestic as "girl" and treating the domestic as if she is invisible, reveal the subordination and exploitation in this work.

Farm and Migrant Labor

Farming employs a very small proportion (1 percent) of the total labor force and an even smaller proportion of women workers (0.2 percent), yet it is significant because of the large number of workers in this category who are Hispanic and because of the importance of migrant labor in the contemporary economy. Migrant farm workers are at the very bottom of the occupational ladder, where they face physically demanding jobs, poor working conditions, and extremely low wages. Of farm workers, 21 percent are Hispanic men and women (U.S. Department of Labor, 1998).

Research on migrant workers shows the effect that the structure of this work has on gender roles. Men's and women's roles in families change as the result of the migration experience. Frequently, men move first, living in labor camps of mostly other men, where they have to cook, wash dishes, and manage other household duties. At the same time, separated from their husbands, women act more assertively and autonomously. As a result, when the family is reunited, both find that they have moved in a more egalitarian direction (Hondagneu-Sotelo, 1992, 1994).

A similar pattern has been observed historically among Chinese who migrate to the United States. Although Chinese women traditionally had low rates of labor force participation in China, the necessity of finding employment after migration challenged traditional beliefs that "a woman's place is in the home." Chinese women's work experiences in the United States instead produced a new attitude that married women have an obligation to work to help support their families (Geschwender, 1992).

In sum, research on women and work shows how deeply structured the labor market is along lines of gender, race, and class. Moreover, as the brief portraits shown on these pages have revealed, patterns of segregation in the labor market (by gender and by race) have enormous consequences for all workers. As you will see next, one of the major consequences is in the earnings associated with gender-segregated jobs.

Earnings

Perhaps we would not care if women and men worked in gender- and racial-ethnic-segregated jobs if that fact did not have such enormous consequences for women's earnings (see Figure 5.4). In 1997, women working full time and year round earned 74 percent of what men earned (U.S. Census Bureau, 1998). Women's concentration in gender- and racial-ethnic-segregated occupations is clearly related to this inequality, as shown in Table 5.1 and Figure 5.3. These low earnings have serious consequences for women. Those who head their own families are in an especially precarious position, since they are so likely to be poor (see Figure 5.5).

Why do these earning differentials persist? One explanation is overt discrimination. **Discrimination** refers to practices that systematically disadvantage one or more groups; it can be overt or covert. Overt discrimination occurs when someone treats someone differently simply because of some characteristic of the person

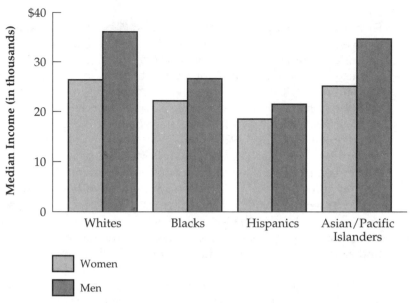

FIGURE 5.4   The Pay Gap: 1997

Sources: Data from U.S. Bureau of the Census. 1998. *Money Income in the United States: 1997.* Washington, DC: U.S. Government Printing Office. Website: <www.census.gov/>; Linda M. Hooper and Claudette E. Bennett. 1998. *The Asian and Pacific Islander Population in the United States: March 1997 (Update),* Table 5. Washington, DC: U.S. Bureau of the Census, Current Population Reports. Website: <www.census.gov/population/socdemo/race/apr97>

Note: Includes only year-round, full-time workers.

(e.g., gender, age, sexual orientation, race, religion, or national origin, to name a few). Paying someone a different wage *because* she is a woman is discrimination, as is not hiring someone presumed to be gay or lesbian. Overt discrimination because of someone's sex, race, or age is illegal. The trick to understanding discrimination is that it is often not overt or conscious, even though, to the receiver, it may seem obvious and apparent. Discrimination is institutionalized, and so it can occur even in the context of individual good will and a seeming absence of overt prejudice or intent to discriminate. For example, there may not be someone in an employment office telling women they cannot apply for certain jobs, but the structural patterns whereby women historically have been denied access to those jobs or whereby women do not receive the education and training needed to qualify for such jobs is a form of institutionalized discrimination. It can be harder to see, because it is not represented by some person making a sexist comment or deliberately blocking access to a job, but it is real, nonetheless.

This situation has caused social scientists to examine pay inequities and gender segregation in the labor market by using social structural, not individualistic, explanations. This does not mean that overt discrimination does not occur. It does. As sociologist Barbara Reskin has pointed out, sometimes men will organize as a group to block women from entering formerly male-dominated organizations. Historically, for example, men in labor unions developed policies excluding

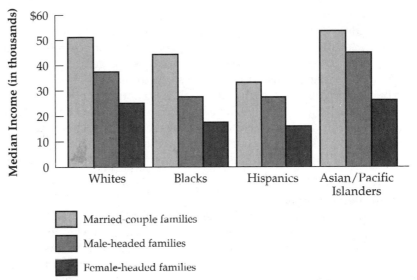

FIGURE 5.5   Gender, Race-Ethnicity, and Household Income

Sources: Data from U.S. Bureau of the Census. 1998. *Money Income in the United States: 1997.* Washington, DC: U.S. Government Printing Office. Website: <www.census.gov/>; Linda M. Hooper and Claudette E. Bennett. 1998. *The Asian and Pacific Islander Population in the United States: March 1997 (Update),* Table 9. Washington, DC: U.S. Bureau of the Census, Current Population Reports. Website: <www.census.gov/population/socdemo/race/apr97/table09.txt>

women and minorities from union membership, thereby excluding them from better-paying union-based jobs (Reskin, 1988). One could interpret the contemporary backlash against affirmative action policies in a similar vein—the mobilization of dominant groups to preserve their historic privilege in the workplace.

Much of what happens to women in the labor market is not, however, caused by overt discrimination. Scholars have looked to other structural causes to explain the underlying reasons for continuing inequities in women's and men's earnings. Two primary explanations have emerged: human capital theory and dual labor market theory.

Human Capital Theory
Human capital theory explains wage differentials as a result of different characteristics of workers. Human capital consists of worker characteristics, such as level of education, marital status, prior experience, training, and so forth—individual level variables. Human capital theory assumes that, in a competitive economic system, wage differences reflect differences in human capital. According to this perspective, the quality of labor supplied by men and women varies because of characteristics of workers themselves. Presumably, high turnover rates, interrupted careers, and shorter participation in the labor force among women lead to their lesser productivity and therefore lower wages.

There is some evidence that human capital theory explains some of the difference in women's and men's wages. Statistical studies of earnings in various occupations typically find that human capital variables explain a portion of the earnings gap, but studies also find a significant portion of the earnings gap unexplained by human capital theory (Firestone, Harris, and Lambert, 1998; Avalos, 1996). As an example, a study of workers in higher education finds that, controlling for the effects of human capital variables, the gender composition of the occupational category also influences salary differential between women and men (Bellas, 1997; Colker, 1997). Although some studies find a strong effect of human capital variables (Tam, 1997), more consistent is the finding that a high percentage of women in a given occupation depresses wages (Kilbourne et al., 1994). Thus, even though human capital theory explains some of the gender gap in earnings, it does not explain the full gap. Dual labor market theory is another rationale.

Dual Labor Market Theory

Dual labor market theory is a second explanation of gender inequality in wages. This perspective sees the labor market as organized around both a primary and a secondary internal market. Jobs in the primary labor market have more stability, higher wages, better working conditions, chances for advancement, and due process in the administration of work roles. The primary labor market restricts entry to a relatively few low-level entry jobs but is organized around long promotion ladders, worker stability, good working conditions, and job security.

Disadvantaged groups, including women and people of color, are employed primarily in the secondary market, which internally is less structured than the primary market and is characterized by numerous points of entry, short or nonexistent promotion ladders, less worker stability, little job security, and arbitrary work rules. The secondary labor market has jobs with low wages, few or no fringe benefits, poor working conditions, high turnover, few chances for advancement, and often arbitrary and capricious supervision.

Within the secondary labor market, the firms where women are employed have lower capital investments, low profit margins, irregular personnel practices, higher turnover, and lower pay, leaving women more at the mercy of economic fluctuations. Even in the less marginal industries where blue-collar women work, the jobs that women hold tend to have the characteristics of the secondary labor market (e.g., poor wages, poor fringe benefits, and unstable employment). The steady supply of women workers, however, discourages employers from paying better wages. The dual labor market perspective causes us to look at occupational distribution by gender as a major factor in the earnings gap between men and women and leads us to conclude that *where* people work, not *what* their individual characteristics are, is a better predictor of income.

Dual labor market theory points to gender segregation as a major cause of wage inequality. Also, studies find that as occupations become more populated by women, wages tend to decline—both for women and men. Such studies suggest that occupations become "feminized" when they are no longer attractive careers (Reskin and Roos, 1990, 1992), as may be currently happening for physicians.

Unlike human capital theory, which looks at characteristics of individuals to explain wage differences among groups, dual labor market theory looks at social structural characteristics to explain the same thing. Thus, such societal level factors as the gender composition of an occupation, economic decline or prosperity, and historical effects are structural explanations of the wage gap. As you will see in a later section, such societal processes have strong effects on the status of women and men—independent (or at least intersecting with) individual level differences.

Structural perspectives caution us against relying too heavily on "differences" as the framework from which to study wage equity, since differences in men's and women's earnings could be substantially reduced through deterioration in the economic status of men and no improvement in the status of women! There is evidence that, indeed, this is happening, as sociologists and economists are reporting that the decreasing wage gap between men and women occurring in recent years is significantly influenced by a decline in male earnings (Bernhardt, Morris, and Handcock, 1995). Measured in constant dollars, White men in the bottom 20 percent of the labor market (as measured by wage level) have seen a 22 percent decline in wages since World War II (Smith, 1998). Structural changes, like the increases in the service industry and the decreases in manufacturing jobs where White men have historically predominated, create changes in the labor market that have a strong impact on gender and race equity.

Promotions

Research on women and work has tended to focus on why women are segregated in the labor market and why they earn less than men. A third important question, though, is whether women advance in work organizations. Studies of employed women, for example, find that when women are asked about their greatest frustrations at work, the problems most likely pointed to are obstacles to being promoted and the sexist perceptions that men at work have of them (Weber and Higginbotham, 1995). The obstacles that women encounter at work have popularly come to be known as the **glass ceiling**. This phrase is meant to convey the fact that, even though most formal barriers to women's advancement have been removed, there are invisible mechanisms that prevent women from advancing. These mechanisms are "invisible" because they are built into the social structure of organizations, and they are not as obvious as formal restrictions and rules that discriminate against women. Still, they are such powerful barriers that, as late as 1995, a federal panel, the Glass Ceiling Commission, appointed by Senate Majority Leader Robert Dole, issued a report concluding that, despite three decades of policies meant to address inequality in the labor market, women and minorities are still substantially blocked from senior management positions (Glass Ceiling Commission, 1995; Naff and Thomas, 1995).

What evidence, or lack thereof, is there of women's advancement in the workplace? Most studies find that women are actually promoted more often than men—that is, if promotion means moving from one job classification to another. However, for women, promotions are most likely to be lateral (i.e., from one location in an occupational system to another of similar rank and status), whereas men's promotions are more likely to be vertical (i.e., upward in the job ranks). Even when men and women have the same qualifications (i.e., education and prior experience), they seldom receive similar promotions. One source of the problem is that men and women may begin in different entry-level positions in an organization, with the positions men enter being those that are more likely to lead to upward mobility in the organization (DiPrete, 1989; H. Smith, 1998). Also, the longer men are in a particular job, the more likely they are to be promoted, but the same is not true for women (White and Althauser, 1984).

Researchers also find that the gender composition of an occupation affects the likelihood of women being hired and promoted in this occupation. Specifically, women are more likely hired and promoted into jobs with a high proportion of women. This is not just a statistical effect, since women are also more likely to be promoted in an occupation when there is a substantial minority of women in the level above. This indicates that women are more likely to be promoted when other women have gone before them (Cohen, Broschak, and Haveman, 1998).

Job ladders in organizations reveal the organization's hierarchy as well as the chances for ongoing promotions in certain positions. This concept of job ladders reflects the fact that some jobs are more likely to be those that lead to mobility than others. Jobs where men predominate are less likely to be dead-end jobs (Baron, Davis-Blake, and Bielby, 1986). Unlike men, women tend to be stuck in jobs with fewer chances for continuing upward mobility. Secretarial work provides a good example. In most organizations, there is a top limit to the "grade" of the highest secretaries in the organization. Beyond that, it is rare for secretaries to move into higher positions where there are additional career ladders. As a result, a secretary might move from being a clerk-typist to an office supervisor, but will seldom move out of this job classification to a job defined as more professional and with more chances for advancement (such as an administrative assistant or manager), even though the skills in these jobs may be the same. This has led observers to say that not only is there is a glass ceiling for women in work organizations but there is also a "sticky floor" (Berheide, 1992).

Whether looking at pay, location, or promotions, research on women and work consistently finds that, despite much change over recent years, structural obstacles to women's advancement in the labor force persist. Although these are not the same formal barriers of the past, they have similar effects. The point is that these barriers are structured into the character of the workplace, not just in the intentions of individual women and men. Although many women choose to work in historically women's work or some choose to put their priorities on personal and family matters rather than career mobility, even more women than in the past perceive that there is discrimination against women in the workplace. Most say that things have improved, but the vast majority also say further changes are needed to make their lives better (Roper Organization, 1995).

Economic Restructuring

The experience of all workers is currently being affected by what has come to be called **economic restructuring**. This is the process by which the economy is becoming less based on manufacturing than on service-based jobs, is being driven by technological change, is becoming more global, and is increasingly driven by what has popularly been referred to as *downsizing* (i.e., having fewer workers do the same amount of work). Economic restructuring is having a major effect on all workers. Many men who assumed they would be in the labor force until they retired are being pushed out of work; young workers are finding it harder to find employment; those without education are facing massive unemployment. However, since economic restructuring is occurring at a time when the work force is becoming more diverse (i.e., more workers are women and members of racial minority groups), there are enormous consequences of this process for women workers.

Economic restructuring means that for many groups, especially women and men in racial-ethnic minority groups and minority teens, there is not enough work; for others, it means there is too much work—long overtime hours, holding more than one job, and piecing together part-time and temporary work. The movement of labor out of the United States leaves many workers at home unemployed, since jobs they formerly held are now being done mostly by women workers in other parts of the world (e.g., Mexico, Asia, the Caribbean) where labor is cheaper, nonunionized, and without the job benefits U.S. workers would likely receive. At home, this has made many workers "disposable" (Sklar, 1994). Although unemployment rates between women and men are not drastically different, women are more likely than men to be unemployed because they are new or reentering the labor market. Black and Hispanic men and women are far more likely to be unemployed than either White women or men and are likely to be unemployed for longer periods of time (U.S. Department of Labor, 1998).

Contingent workers (i.e., temporary employees, contract workers, and part-time workers) have, as a result, become one-third of the U.S. labor force (up from one-quarter in 1988). Contingent workers, who are more likely to be women than men, are less likely to receive job benefits (i.e., vacations, health insurance, unemployment insurance, pensions) and are more vulnerable to harassment and health and safety hazards, since they are less protected than permanent employees.

Corporate downsizing is also part of economic restructuring. Although business leaders have heralded downsizing as a virtuous goal, its purpose is to reduce the costs of labor while maintaining or enhancing business profits. Typically, downsizing means eliminating layers of management within the company—a process that eliminates the career ladders that have recently provided women and racial-ethnic groups (who are often clustered in middle-management positions) some opportunity for advancement. Displaced workers who are reemployed typically earn lower wages than before and, if they are rehired, they tend to be hired into less-skilled work. The longer the joblessness, the greater the loss of wage on reemployment (Moore, 1990).

To date, White men have been the most likely to be laid off by downsizing (either by being fired or given early retirement or some other form of job severance). The primary reason that downsizing has not had as sizable an impact on women and minorities is because there are so few women and minorities in these management positions to begin with (Hamlin, Erkut, and Fields, 1994). An important consequence of downsizing has been that those who are still employed have more performance pressure, often having to work longer hours and do the jobs that used to be performed by more than one person.

In other ways, economic retrenchment is having a severe impact on women and racial-ethic minorities. Women and racial-ethnic minorities are expected to comprise five-sixths of all new workers, meaning that their representation in the labor force will increase even more in the next several years. Many in these groups will not, however, have the education and training necessary to compete in a technologically driven labor force, unless there are massive reforms in the educational system. New job opportunities are most likely to come in technological fields where education (and the scientific training that women often lack) are required. Deindustrialization, meaning the transition from a predominantly goods-producing economy to one based on the provision of services, means that service-based industries—such as banking and finance, retail sales, or personal services—will predominate in the economy. The majority of workers are now employed in what is called the *service sector*. This sector includes two segments: the service-delivery segment (e.g., food preparation and delivery, cleaning, or child care) and the information-processing segment (e.g., banking and finance, computer operation and analysis, or clerical work). The service-delivery segment consists of many low-wage, semi- and unskilled forms of labor and employs high numbers of women and people of color, particularly in some of the least attractive jobs in this segment of the economy.

❧ Poverty and Welfare

One of the consequences of women's status in the labor market is the high rate of poverty among women and their children (see Figure 5.6). The **poverty line** is an index developed by the Social Security Administration. It is based on the lowest cost for a nutritionally adequate food plan (as developed by the Department of Agriculture). The poverty line (based also on family size) is calculated by multiplying the cost of this food plan by three (assuming that a family spends one-third of its budget on food), adjusted by the Consumer Price Index. In 1997, the official poverty line for a family of four was $16,555.

Gender differences in poverty have increased in recent years, partially because of the fact that women now, unlike in the past, are more likely to be financially responsible for their children (McLanahan, Sorenson, and Watson, 1989). This trend toward more of the poor being women and children is called the **feminization of poverty**. In 1997, the median family income for all families was $37,005. In the same year, median family income in family households headed by White women was $25,670; for families headed by Black women, $17,962; and for families headed by Hispanic women, $16,393 (see Figure 5.5). The most prosperous families are White families with both husband and wife present and both working. As you will see in the next chapter, although these families in some ways define the American ideal, they are by no means the statistical norm in contemporary U.S. society.

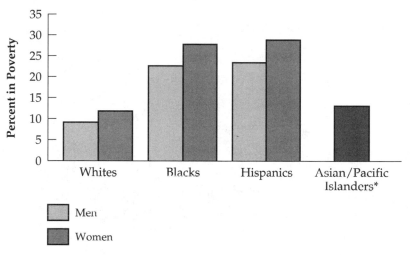

FIGURE 5.6   People in Poverty: 1997

Sources: Data from Joseph Dalaker and Mary Maifeh, U.S. Bureau of the Census, Current Population Reports. Series P-60-201. 1998. *Poverty in the United States: 1997.* Washington, DC: U.S. Government Printing Office. Website: <www.census.gov/>; Linda M. Hooper and Claudette E. Bennett. 1998. *The Asian and Pacific Islander Population in the United States: March 1997 (Update),* Table 5. Washington, DC: U.S. Bureau of the Census, Current Population Reports. Website: <www.census.gov/population/socdemo/race/apr97/table02.txt>

*Note: Data not available by gender for Asian/Pacific Islanders.

In 1997, 31.6 percent of all female-headed households lived below the official poverty line; 39.8 percent of Black female-headed households and 47.6 percent of Hispanic families headed by women lived below the poverty line, compared to 27.7 percent of White female-headed households. One consequence of increasing poverty among women who head families is an ever-growing number of children who are poor. In 1997, 37.2 percent of Black children, 36.8 percent of Hispanic children, and 16 percent of White children lived in poverty (see Figure 5.7; Dalaker and Naifeh, 1998). Among Asian American families, the pattern is somewhat different. Despite images of being the "model minority," poverty rates among Asian Americans are higher than among Whites. Almost 13 percent (12.7) of Asian American families are poor, with poverty being highest among the most recent Asian immigrants (Hooper and Bennett, 1998). Poverty rates among Asians also vary dramatically across different national origins: 61.5 percent of Laotian and Cambodian families in the United States are poor, as are 25 percent of Vietnamese, 24 percent of Chinese, 21 percent of Koreans, 15 percent of Japanese, 11 percent of Asian Indians, and 10 percent of Filipinos (Lee, 1994). Asian American women heading their own households also have a significant economic disadvantage relative to Asian American men.

Limited opportunities for women in the labor market are a major cause of poverty. In addition to their secondary employment status, women's continuing responsibilities for child rearing, in the absence of adequate day care and other social supports, tend to leave them poor. Poverty among women is exacerbated

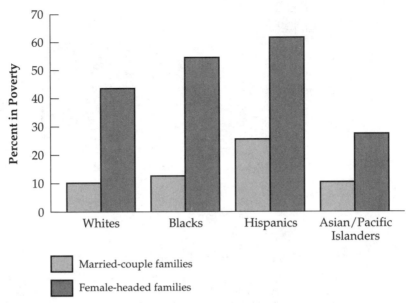

**FIGURE 5.7   Poverty among Households with Children
(under 18 years of age)**

Source: Data from Joseph Dalaker and Mary Maifeh, U.S. Bureau of the Census, Current Population Reports. Series P-60-201. 1998. *Poverty in the United States: 1997.* Washington, DC: U.S. Government Printing Office. Website: <www.census.gov/>; Linda M. Hooper and Claudette E. Bennett. 1998. *The Asian and Pacific Islander Population in the United States: March 1997 (Update)*, Table 5. Washington, DC: U.S. Bureau of the Census, Current Population Reports. Website: <www.census.gov/population/socdemo/race/apr97/table02.txt>

by the high rate of divorce, since women's economic status after a divorce deteriorates significantly (Weitzman, 1985, 1996; Peterson, 1996a, 1996b; Kurz, 1995).

Women in poverty have been the focus of much public debate in recent years—particularly with regard to welfare. Welfare reform has been based on the assumption that welfare recipients need to work, with new welfare laws stipulating work requirements and time limits to welfare receipt. Until 1996, the major national welfare program was Aid to Families with Dependent Children (AFDC). This program was replaced in 1996 with new regulations that place a lifetime limit of five years on receiving welfare and require all welfare recipients to find work within two years—a policy known as *workfare*. Because the vast majority of welfare recipients are women and their children, these policies have had a major impact on poor women and their families.

At the heart of public debate about welfare is the idea that poor people do not want to work and that providing public assistance encourages dependency. Studies show, however, that the low-wage work the poor may find is simply not enough to lift them out of poverty (McCrate and Smith, 1998). Most poor women have to combine low-wage work with public assistance and support from family and friends to make ends meet. Even then, most women on welfare find a wide gap between what they need to support their family and what they have available through welfare support. Contrary to public myths, poor women have aspirations to find better work, move to better neighborhoods, buy their children good clothes, and have a nest egg for emergencies. They just find it impossible to do so on the limited resources available to them (Edin and Lein, 1997).

Moreover, much of the public seems to misunderstand other facts about poor women on welfare. Most women receiving welfare do, in fact, work, and did so even prior to workfare requirements. Studies also find that poor women have left welfare for work, but find themselves in even more difficulty when they do so. The jobs they find tend to be low paying and unattractive and child care is hard to come by (and afford). Given the nature of the jobs most likely available to them, many find that they lose health insurance when they work or may experience violence from boyfriends and husbands who feel threatened by their becoming more independent by working. This results in a pattern for many of "welfare cycling"—going on and off welfare over a period of time (Pavetti, 1993). Sociologists have actually found that the exit from poverty is actually hastened when welfare benefits are higher, since higher payments give welfare recipients the support they need to find job training and child care so that they can make the transition to a decent job (Butler, 1996).

The connection made in the public eye between welfare, work, and poverty also ignores the vast numbers of people (women and men) who are employed and are nonetheless poor—a group known as the *working poor*. The poverty rate among employed women is higher than for men, obviously because of the lower wages women are paid. Among women heading their own families *and* working, 18.6 percent are still officially poor (U.S. Census Bureau, 1998).

Still, the myth abounds that welfare has nothing but negative consequences for women. In one sense, it does, since the stigma associated with welfare makes welfare recipients more secretive about how they put resources together to survive. It tends to affect their own self-esteem, making it more difficult for them to act on their own behalf. Most often, people go on welfare because of life events over which they have little control (unemployment, divorce, poor health, racism, battering, etc.). Constructing a support system that enables people to survive such problems seems a far more humane way to build society than the victim-blaming reforms that have dominated social policy in recent years (Abramovitz, 1996; Dujon and Withorn, 1996).

Many have argued that the poverty rate among female-headed households is high because the male provider role has become "optional," but the preceding analysis suggests something quite different: Only policies specifically designed to improve women's status, not just return men to families or women to the labor force as is, are likely to alleviate the problem of poverty among women and their children.

❧ *Work Environments for Women*

Women's experiences at work are not just a function of earnings, promotions, and placement in the labor force. Within a work organization, one's ability to succeed, to be influential, and to be satisfied with work are also shaped by the organizational climate. Factors such as tokenism, sexual harassment, and workplace culture are important components of the work experience.

Tokenism

The experience of women in organizations is influenced by the proportions in which they find themselves. Rosabeth Moss Kanter (1977) has identified four types of groups in work organizations, based on the numerical proportions in which different kinds of people are represented. The first is the *uniform group*, which has only one kind of person (e.g., all men or all White). *Skewed groups* are those in which there is a great preponderance of one type of person over another (e.g., a group that is 85 percent men and 15 percent women). In skewed groups, those in the numerical minority are identified as tokens. Third are *tilted groups*, in which there are less exaggerated differences, but in which one group still forms a clear majority (e.g., a group in which men constitute 65 percent of the group population and women 35 percent). Kanter argues that in tilted groups, minority members have the opportunity to form alliances with each other and can form coalitions and can begin to affect the culture of the group. Finally is the *balanced group*, one close to a fifty-fifty proportion of social types. Kanter suggests that only in balanced groups will organizational outcomes for individuals depend more on structural and personal factors than on the dynamics established by the group itself.

Most women entering traditionally male-dominated occupations find themselves in skewed groups where they are tokens; the same is true for people of color in predominantly White organizations. In such groups, tokens stand out in contrast to other members of the group; group dynamics will usually reflect these contrasts. The presence of tokens heightens the boundaries between different groups. For instance, members of the dominant group become more self-conscious of what they have in common, and they might "test" tokens to see how they respond to, for example, male culture. This means that in skewed groups, the contrast between tokens and the majority becomes exaggerated in social interaction. In skewed groups, tokens also receive extra attention and are more easily stereotyped than are those found in greater proportions in social groups. Kanter argues that these perceptual tendencies—visibility, contrast, and assimilation—put more performance pressures on tokens, as they live life in the limelight. At the same time, tokens may be more closely supervised, given "silent" treatment, or not be given the training and direction required in a job (Yoder and Aniakudo, 1997).

Tokens respond to these performance pressures in a variety of ways. One response is overachievement, in which tokens try to gain more control over the extra attention given to their actions; this may, however, be difficult to accomplish, especially for those who are new to organizations. It also involves creating a delicate balance between doing well and not causing too much resentment among the majority. Tokens may also try to turn the notoriety of their uniqueness to advantage—for example, by flaunting their "only woman manager in the company" status. Kanter argues, however, that this strategy of response reinforces the dynamics of tokenism and disadvantages other women. Third, she says that tokens may respond to performance pressures by trying to become socially invisible, perhaps through dressing "like a man," keeping a very low social profile, working at home, or avoiding risks.

Kanter's research shows that a mere shift in numbers has the potential to transform the working experience of all members of an organization. Her work also shows, in a unique way, how the structure of groups themselves influences the organizational structure and climate of occupational settings. Some researchers have argued that by focusing on numbers alone, Kanter's work underestimates the backlash that men direct against women upon women's desegregation of traditionally male jobs. Research has shown that the negative consequences of tokenism are far more acute for members of groups who enter occupations defined as inappropriate for them and who have lower social status than the dominant group. Upper-status tokens (such as men who enter traditionally female occupations) actually experience rapid upward mobility and are more likely to be seen as innovators than are women in similar token positions (Yoder, 1991). Such findings do not discount Kanter's analysis but show how the interplay of numbers, dominant group behavior, and social-structural context affect the experience of minorities in the workplace.

Sexual Harassment

Sexual harassment is defined as the unwanted imposition of sexual requirements in the context of a relationship of unequal power. Sexual harassment was first defined as constituting illegal discrimination by Title VII of the Civil Rights Bill of 1964. A landmark Supreme Court decision in 1986, *Meritor Savings Bank* v. *Vinson*, ruled that sexual harassment violates federal laws against discrimination. This decision makes sexual harassment unconstitutional.

There are a number of social myths about sexual harassment, including the myths that it affects only a few, that women ask for it, and that charges of sexual harassment are usually false. As a result of these myths, a woman may find it hard to speak out against sexual harassment because the myths establish the tendency for others to blame her. Often when women have spoken out about harassment, they have been ignored, discredited, or accused of misunderstanding the intentions of the other parties. The unveiling of sexual harassment as a serious issue affecting work environments for women has forced employers to create policies designed to deal with sexual harassment. The Supreme Court has made it clear that sexual harassment is a violation of the law, and public scandals have called attention to the seriousness of the problem.

Although accurate counts of the extent of sexual harassment in the workplace are difficult to establish, surveys of working women indicate that as many as 50 percent say they are currently being harassed at work; 80 to 90 percent say they have been harassed at some point in their careers (Martin, 1989). Between 20 and 25 percent of undergraduate women report experiencing sexual harassment at least once during their college careers (McCormack, 1995). Sexual harassment occurs in every kind of work setting and can deeply influence women's perceptions of themselves as workers (Carothers and Crull, 1984). Especially in an unsupportive context, those who experience sexual harassment may also experience feelings of helplessness, guilt, fear, empathy for the harasser, and ambivalence about the incident (Kaufman and Wylie, 1983). One survey reported that graduate students who were harassed typically did not think of the experience as coercive at the time; however, in retrospect they did see the relationship as coercive, unethical, and costly to their careers (Glaser and Thorpe, 1986).

Researchers also find that the experience of sexual harassment varies, depending on whether it occurs in an area of traditional women's work or in areas where women are entering traditionally male occupations. In traditional women's occupations, sexual harassment is characterized by the threat of losing a job for failing to comply with sexual demands; the harasser in those settings is typically a supervisor. On the other hand, women entering traditionally male occupations encounter more sexual harassment, making it seem that harassment is a form of retaliation directed against women for threatening male economic and social status (Mansfield et al., 1991). In these settings, harassment expresses men's resentment of the presence of women. It can be more difficult for women workers in these jobs to bring charges of harassment, because their harassers are more likely to be co-workers. In female work settings where the harasser is a supervisor, women who are harassed may have less internal conflict about bringing up charges and are more likely to be able to garner support from other women for bringing charges (Carothers and Crull, 1984).

Sexual harassment is fundamentally a matter of the misuse of power and it is deeply linked to gender attitudes. Men are more tolerant of sexual harassment than are women and women are more likely to see things such as sexist comments, verbal sexual advances, invitations for dates, and sexual propositions as sexual harassment than are men (McKinney and Crittenden, 1992).

Workplace Culture

In addition to having interest in the social-structural characteristics of women's work on the employed labor force, feminist scholars are also interested in the cultures in work organizations. Work environments shape the experience of women (and men) at work, just as objective rewards can shape the work experience. Studies of gay and lesbian work experiences show that many fear they will suffer adverse career consequences if co-workers know they are lesbian, bisexual, or gay. This leads many to "pass" as heterosexual at work or keep their private lives secret, but being closeted at work puts workers at a disadvantage, since it isolates them from social networks in the workplace. Studies show, however, that gay employees' relationships with co-workers are less stressful when the employee is "out," since gay workers no longer fear and anticipate rejection. When closeted, gays and lesbians are likely to be distant and avoid interpersonal contact to shield themselves from antagonism, resulting in potentially low performance reviews because they appear to be unfriendly, boring, and withdrawn (Schneider, 1984; Badgett and King, 1997).

Studies of work culture have found that women employ a variety of strategies to resist the male-dominated culture of organizations. Women's work culture is the ideology, rituals, and practices through which women forge a relatively autonomous sphere on the job. By sharing photographs, celebrating birthdays, elaborating informal norms among themselves about office procedures and norms, and developing other forms of women's culture at work, women exercise some control over the meaning and character of their work (Melosh, 1982; Benson, 1978).

Women's culture in the workplace can be the basis for political organization, resistance to oppression, and the creation of solidarity among workers. Recognizing and studying women's culture in the workplace shows how groups that lack power collectively define their positions and use their informal relations to adapt to or resist powerlessness. While these informal relations may soften exploitative work conditions by humanizing the work force (Lamphere, 1984), they can also be the basis for militant job actions (Costello, 1985). As Zavella's (1985) research on Chicana cannery workers shows, in a labor market where workers are divided along race and sex lines, women's culture can create both ethnic and racial solidarity while also generating gender consciousness of exploitative work conditions.

≈ *Intersections of Family and Work*

For many years, studies of work presumed that work was separate from family life—as if work and family were separate spheres of life. This assumption reflected the sexist idea that men's place was in the work world and women's place was in the family. New studies of women and work (and, now, men and work) have shown this not to be the case. Quite the contrary is true: Work and family are strongly intertwined. You will see this further in the following chapter on families, but this relationship is apparent in studying work, especially when considering the amount of work that people do (counting both paid, unpaid, labor force, and household work), and in the process of reconceptualizing housework as work, not just family activity.

The Double Day

Studies of employed women have all concluded that women work a double day. That is, if they are employed for wages in the labor market, when they are home, they work a **second shift** (Hochschild, 1989). This term refers to the work women do at home in addition to time spent in paid employment. As an example, employed mothers now work an average of 76 to 89 hours per week, counting paid labor, housework, and child care (Schorr, 1991). Since this estimate includes only White married couples, the actual hours are probably higher, since the inclusion of African Americans, Latinas, and Asians would raise the hours, given the fact that women in these families are more likely to work outside the home and to hold more than one job. Women who do not work for wages spend about 70 hours per week in housework, about 30 of which are devoted exclusively to child care. The extra work that women do in the second shift means that they both work more and have less leisure than men do; furthermore, it results in a substantial speed-up in the amount of work that women are doing. Economists estimate that the additional hours that people, in general, are working (in the form of extra hours, holding more than one job, the increased length of the work week, and more weeks worked per year) amount to an extra one month of work per year since 1970 for the average employed person. Since women are already estimated, in terms of hours, to have been working an extra month longer than men, one could conclude that women, on average, work an additional two months per year!

Contemporary sociologist Arlie Hochschild has studied the effect of speed-up on families. Based on extensive interviews with women and men in dual-career families, Hochschild found that women develop a variety of strategies for coping with these demands of the second shift. Some feign helplessness over certain tasks as a way to get men to do them. Others avoid conflict by taking on the work themselves. Some cut back on their expectations about what is necessary in the home or reduce their working hours. Often, women turn to women friends and family members for help or, if they have the economic ability, pay other women to work for them. Some try to be "supermoms"; those who do report feeling "numb" and out of touch with their feelings. In any case, women typically pay the greater price of this added household stress (Hochschild, 1989).

Hochschild (1997) has also shown that, as more women have entered the paid labor force, life for most people centers more and more on work. The tensions then created at home mean that many women and men run their families like efficiency experts, having to manage time spent in child care, leisure activity, and household chores as if they were managers of their personal lives. Ironically, Hochschild's research also finds that, even in corporations with "family-friendly" policies (flex-time, child care facilities, etc.), workers underutilize these benefits. Instead, people work more and more, often not using vacation benefits, even when they feel there is a time deficit in their lives. Why? Based on her research, Hochschild concludes that the "time bind" and stress that people feel at home means that they find more satisfaction and pleasure at work than they do at home. In her words, the social worlds of work and home have been reversed, with people feeling more "at home" at work and "at work" when home.

Housework

The second shift shows that not all women's labor is paid labor, but, because the concept of work has been tied to paid employment, housework has long gone unrecognized as work, even though it is socially and economically necessary. The work that housewives do not only takes care of people's basic needs—food, shelter, and clothing—but also socializes new members of the society. Housework benefits employers, too, because housework sustains workers, making it possible for them to return to the labor force (Benston, 1969). Social myths about housework show us the contradictions that pervade our images of the work women do in the home. On the one hand, to be a housewife is idealized as a desirable goal for women; at the same time, however, housework is depicted as drudgery and menial labor. Both images obscure the fact that, for most women, housework is time consuming as well as physically and psychologically demanding, even though it can also be a source of satisfaction.

The glamorous image of the housewife is perpetrated in commercials, where women are surrounded by happy families and a wealth of material goods. The housewife in these ads is usually cheerful, buoyant, and smiling, although pathologically obsessed with cleanliness and food. Although housework is seen as glamorous, housewives are also ridiculed as scatterbrained, lazy, and disorganized. Anyone who has seen comic strip and greeting card depictions of a housewife standing bedraggled with an apron around her waist, a broom in her hand, and a cigarette dangling from her mouth has seen one facet of the contemporary myth about housework.

The artificial picture these myths create about housework is unsupported by social and economic research. To begin with, the role of the housewife is multidimensional and is experienced by women in different ways (Lopata, 1971). Many housewives are overwhelmed by the isolation of their work and by the repetitiveness of their tasks. As a result, many of them experience depression and anxiety. It would be a mistake to see the housewife role as totally oppressive, for many women find this work both creative and satisfying, especially when compared with the jobs most women occupy in the paid labor force. Historians suggest that housework is less alienating than paid labor because it is task-oriented rather than ordered by the timed structures of industrial activity (Thompson, 1967). Because women's work at home is oriented to the needs of others, allows for some personal flexibility, and provides some autonomy, many women prefer it to the alienating labor they would likely encounter in the paid labor force.

Sociological studies of housewives confirm this point. Research finds that housewives dislike the monotony and routinization of their work, but they like the autonomy that housework provides (Lennon, 1994; Gill and Hibbons, 1996). Others find that housewives' work as volunteers also provides them with an independent source of satisfaction and personal expression, although their contentment in these roles is to a large extent dependent on their husbands' affluence (Andersen, 1981). These studies of housewives' roles tell us that the role is both complex and fragile. Many housewives are satisfied with the work they do; others find it stultifying and unsatisfying. Many women see being able to be a full-time housewife as a privilege. Many African American, Asian, Hispanic, and working-class women have never been housewives only, because they have worked at two jobs to support their families—one job in the paid labor force and the other in the home (Davis, 1981). Even for women in privileged classes, the role of affluent housewife is precariously based on the continued economic and emotional support of their husbands. A sudden death, divorce, or economic need can quickly change even the happiest housewife to an anxious and possibly poor woman who must find a way to support herself and her family.

The emotional experience of housework is, however, only one side of the issue. Whatever the woman's response to housework, her work is real, although traditionally it is unrecognized and unpaid. The most detailed pictures of housework have emerged from time-budget studies that record the tasks that make up housework and measure the amount of time used in household labor. These studies show that the contemporary full-time housewife works an average of 57 hours per week on household tasks by preparing and cleaning up after meals, doing laundry, cleaning the house, taking care of children and other family members, shopping, and keeping records, with women doing more housework than men (Schorr, 1991; South and Spitze, 1994; Bird, 1996; Press and Townsley, 1998). Despite changes in gender attitudes over the years, women are still more likely to have the responsibility for planning, remembering, and scheduling the day-to-day activities of children. Half of husbands now participate in this responsibility, but they are nonetheless less likely to be the one arranging child care (Marshall and Barnett, 1995).

Patterns in who does the housework reflect a gender division of labor, one that is related to other patterns in the family regarding employment, presence of children, and gender-role attitudes. Thus, when people form couples (either married or cohabiting), men tend to reduce the time they have previously spent in housework, while women increase their time (Das Gupta, 1998). The amount of housework that women do also increases as they move from being single to being married and to becoming a parent (Sanchez and Thomson, 1997), whereas men's domestic work remains relatively constant over these stages of life (Perkins and Demeis, 1994). The gender gap in housework is also greatest among married couples, particularly when men are defined as the primary breadwinner. Interestingly, having an adult son living at home increases a mother's time spent in housework, but having an adult daughter living at home decreases a mother's housework (South and Spitze, 1994). Within coupled relationships, a woman's relative power (as measured by her employment status) is a strong factor in determining a husband's contributions to housework (Heath and Bourne, 1995). Women who are economically dependent on men are more likely to do a greater share of the work at home (Ferree, Anthony, and Wilkie, 1994).

Tensions over who does the housework are a significant source of conflict within relationships between men and women (Stohs, 1995), and patterns of time spent in housework are related to mental health. There is a clear relationship between time spent in housework and depression, with depression increasing with more time spent in housework (Glass and Fujimoto, 1994). Also, when men increase the time they spend doing housework, their level of stress also increases—a pattern long noted for women (Marshall and Barnett, 1995). In the end, it appears that those with the most egalitarian attitudes are more likely to share in the housework done and therefore the least likely to suffer the consequences of doing otherwise.

Housework is organized in the modern economy as a private service, one that women provide for men and children. It is a gender division of labor in which women not only do more work than men but also do different tasks. The gender division of labor in housework is evident when we look at the tasks that different members of the family do. These tasks can be categorized into two types: work internal and work external to the home. The work that men, including male children, do most frequently is largely external—mowing the lawn, carrying out garbage, raking leaves, and some shopping; the work that women and female children do includes washing and drying dishes, preparing meals, cleaning the house, and doing the laundry.

Contrary to social myth, the advent of modern technology and household appliances has not significantly reduced the time women spend in housework (Hartmann, 1976, 1981a). The earliest information on time spent in housework was gathered in the 1920s under the guise of the new science of home economics and its emphasis on rational management (Vanek, 1978). These studies show that women spent about the same number of hours per week doing housework as they do now. Although the amount of time spent on housework has not changed, the actual character of housework has.

In 1900, most U.S. homes had no electricity and no running water; in 1920, one-third of U.S. families still lived on farms. By the 1920s, a variety of canned and processed foods had become available, reducing the time a housewife spent producing and preparing food. By the 1930s, approximately 60 percent of homes in the United States had electricity, opening the way for mechanical refrigerators and washing machines and gas and electric ranges. By 1940, 70 percent of U.S. homes had indoor plumbing; in the 1950s, automatic washers replaced wringers; and in the 1960s, women's laundry work was changed by the introduction of dryers and wash-and-wear fabrics (Cowan, 1976; Vanek, 1978). In the 1970s, the fast-food industry offered to take the work of the housewife out of the home, although microwave ovens, food processors, and computerized home management systems increased the expectations of women's laboring within the home.

Although these technological and commercial developments created the potential for reducing women's work as housewives, ideological changes as well as actual changes in the requirements of housework have contributed to the demands on the housewife's time. For instance, between 1920 and 1980, the amount of time spent on food preparation, cleaning, and sewing and mending decreased. The introduction of cheaper clothing and linens meant, however, that there was more clothing and linen per household; consequently, the time spent doing laundry increased. The invention of the automobile and the development of suburbs meant that the housewife spent more time transporting family members and shopping. Housewives' managerial tasks in the household have increased as financial and medical records, grocery lists, deliveries, and repairs have become routine work (Vanek, 1978). As child care has become more the work of individuals, not extended families, the amount of time spent on child care has increased.

The evolution of changes in household labor is part of the more general changes that have occurred in the relationship of the household to the economy and is also related to changes in the economic structure of life. The isolation of women's work as housewives is not inevitable; instead, it is a historically specific development that is tied to the modern structure of economic and household relations. Cross-cultural evidence demonstrates that women are not inevitably domestic. In many societies, even when women are engaged in childbearing and child rearing, their role in child care is accommodated to their role in the public economy—not the other way around (Friedl, 1975; Malbin-Glazer, 1976). In such societies, women's contributions to production are recognized and valued. Anthropological evidence indicates that women have more egalitarian roles in those societies where individuals are directly dependent on the well-being of the society as a whole, where there is no structural dichotomy between the public and domestic worlds, and where those who make decisions also carry them out (Leacock, 1978). The modern role of the housewife, isolated and dependent in the private home, is a specific consequence of the historical transition to industrial capitalism. This transition and its consequences for women's roles in families and households are discussed in the following chapter.

❧ *Policies for Gender Equity*

The **Equal Pay Act of 1963** was the first federal legislation enacted requiring equal pay for equal work; it has been extended by various executive orders and civil rights acts to forbid discrimination on the basis of sex. Title VI of the Civil Rights Act of 1964 forbids discrimination against students on the basis of race, color, or national origin in all federally assisted programs. **Title VII of the Civil Rights Bill of 1964**, amended by the Equal Employment Opportunity Act of 1972, forbids discrimination on the basis of race, color, national origin, religion, or sex in any term, condition, or privilege of employment. This law was amended in 1972 to cover all private and public educational institutions, as well as state and local governments. Title VII was a path-breaking law for women, as it established the principle of equal rights in federal law and opened the door for women's participation in education, employment, and athletics, to name some of its major areas of impact. **Title IX of the Educational Amendments of 1972** forbids discrimination on the basis of sex in all federally assisted education programs in all institutions, public and private, that receive federal monies through grants, loans, or contracts.

Although federal laws do forbid discrimination in employment, feminists have argued that because women tend to be located in different occupations than men, equal pay for equal work will by itself be adequate to eliminate wage inequities in the paid labor force. **Comparable worth** is the principle of paying women and men equivalent wages for jobs involving comparable levels of skill. Assessing comparable worth requires measuring the skill levels of comparable jobs and developing correlated pay scales, regardless of the sex of the job occupants. Comparable worth is an important concept for women workers and one that organizes workers for collective action against wage discrimination (Blum, 1986).

Comparable worth goes beyond the concept of equal pay for equal work by creating job evaluation systems that assess the degree of similarity between different kinds of jobs. In places where comparable worth has been used as a method for evaluating women's and men's work, it has improved women's wages (Steinberg, 1992; Jacobs and Steinberg, 1990), but it has also been resisted by businesses, probably because they recognize the economic cost that would come from reassessing and increasing the worth of the work that women do.

Another public policy that has proven of great importance in bringing new opportunities to women and racial minority groups in the labor market is **affirmative action**. Affirmative action has now become one of the most controversial policies for creating better opportunities for members of historically disadvantaged groups. Affirmative action developed as a policy referring to positive efforts taken to open new areas of opportunity to groups who had previously been excluded from such jobs. Typically, an affirmative action program would identify the potential pool of eligible (i.e., qualified) workers in a given occupational category and then require employers to develop recruitment mechanisms to ensure fair opportunities to members of these groups. It includes such actions as advertising for jobs in places where women and minorities are likely to see job postings, instead of relying on word of mouth and "White men's networks" to recruit able applicants. Affirmative action policies have forced organizations to develop fair rules and uniform recruitment procedures so that some groups are not advantaged over others.

Contrary to popular opinion, affirmative action does not set rigid quotas for jobs, although it does set goals or targets for different jobs, depending on the number of qualified women and minorities in the available pool. Affirmative action has also forced employers to think carefully about what the term *qualified* means; perhaps this is what has been most controversial. For example, in some jobs, performance on a written test is an important part of the application procedure, but affirmative action can mean that someone with a somewhat lower score on the test may, for other reasons, be seen as more qualified than someone whose test scores are slightly higher. If the person with the lower score is hired, it does not mean that person is not qualified (since he or she would not be hired with a significantly lower score), only that additional factors constitute the qualifications for the job. Affirmative action has also meant that diversifying the work force is itself a desirable goal.

Affirmative action has been under sharp attack from groups who perceive it as taking away opportunities from Whites and men; it has become one of the most controversial and heated policies for desegregating the workplace. The fact remains, however, that it has been critical to the success of women and people of color. The fact that it is now being so vigorously opposed by previously more privileged groups in the workplace shows that it has had a strong effect in opening opportunities to groups that historically have been disadvantaged because they were not White or male. Whether affirmative action will survive in place remains to be seen. Critics of affirmative action argue that race-blind and gender-blind policies are the only fair way to proceed, but most feminists and civil rights advocates would argue, as the evidence in this chapter would support, that, as long as the society is structured (even in less-visible ways) along gender-, class-, and race-stratified lines, seemingly "neutral" or color-blind policies cannot transform the institutional structures that have developed specifically out of gender and race inequities.

❧ *Summary*

The work women do has been obscured by social myths that devalue women's work, both socially and economically. This history of women's work in industrialized societies is characterized by a shift from the family-based economy to the family-wage economy and, contemporarily, the family-consumer economy. The history of women of color in the United States follows a different, but related, course. Under slavery, Black women's work benefited both their owners and their own families and communities. The work of all women of color was fundamental to the development of social institutions. Ideological changes in the definition of women's work justifies the exploitation of women as wage workers and as houseworkers, although this image varies for women of different racial and class backgrounds.

Feminist perspectives on women's work have transformed sociological concepts such as class, status, and work. *Gender stratification* is the hierarchical distribution of economic and social resources along gender lines. Gender stratification intersects with and overlaps the system of racial stratification.

The contemporary status of women is marked by their increasing labor force participation, gender segregation, occupation, and income inequality. The experience of women workers in the paid labor force is further complicated by the intersection of race, class, and gender. Women are increasingly affected by job displacement and economic restructuring. Poverty is increasing among women, especially among those who head households. The causes of poverty for women are their status in the labor market, their roles in child rearing, and the rising rate of divorce.

The culture of work organizations affects women's chances for success. Sexual harassment is a form of discrimination and is defined as the unwanted imposition of sexual requirements in the context of a power relationship. Women's culture in the workplace generates resistance to exploitation and gives women workers some degree of control over their work conditions.

Current economic trends indicate that women's labor force participation will continue to increase, as will demands for their work both in the paid labor force and in the family, resulting in increased stress and social speed-up for women workers. Women's work as housewives, though unpaid, constitutes a form of work. Women continue to spend far more time doing housework than do men, including men whose wives work for wages. Housework shows the interrelationship of economic and family systems.

🐦 Key Terms

affirmative action
class
class stratification
comparable worth
discrimination
dual labor market theory
economic restructuring
emotional labor
Equal Pay Act of 1963
family-based economy

family-consumer economy
family-wage economy
feminization of poverty
gender segregation
gender stratification
glass ceiling
global assembly line
global restructuring
human capital theory
Meritor Savings Bank v. *Vinson*

poverty line
second shift
sexual harassment
stratification
Title VII of the Civil Rights Bill
    of 1964
Title IX of the Educational
    Amendments of 1972

🐦 Discussion Questions/Projects for Thought

1. Identify an occupation in which you can imagine having a career. Using your college library as a resource, find out what percentage of workers in this field are women and racial-ethnic groups, and, if possible, interview men and women currently working in this occupation. Discuss the evidence (or lack of) of gender and race segregation in this occupation and what that implies about policies needed to achieve equity for workers.

2. Give yourself a monthly budget of $1,379 (the monthly dollar amount that you would have if you lived at the federal poverty line). Imagine that you head your own household, with three children. Using prices from the area where you live, develop a monthly budget to account for everything you have to spend to get by. What would your life be like and what would your children's lives be like? What does this exercise teach you about contemporary images of people on welfare and low-income families?

3. Ask several young men and women how they expect to balance work and family commitments in the future. Then interview several people who are currently employed about how they balance these commitments. What do your interviews about expectations and current realities suggest for future social policies to support families and workers?

🐦 Suggested Readings

Amott, Teresa L., and Julie A. Matthaei. 1996. *Race, Gender, and Work: A Multicultural History of Women in the United States*. 2nd ed. Boston: South End Press.
Based on an analysis of the intersections of race, class, and gender in the labor market, this book presents the histories of the work of women of color and White women workers. It is an excellent introduction to the experiences of different women in the United States.

Dujon, Diane, and Ann Withorn. 1996. *For Crying Out Loud: Women's Poverty in the United States.* Boston: South End Press.
This anthology includes analytical and first-hand accounts of the experience of poverty, including analyses of the impact of welfare reforms on women and their children. The collection also includes articles on social policy and advocacy programs for poor women.

Edin, Kathryn, and Laura Lein. 1997. *Making Ends Meet: How Single Mothers Survive Welfare and Low Wage Work.* New York: Russell Sage Foundation.
Using interviews with almost 400 low-income women, Edin and Lein show how the women struggle to make ends meet, often balancing welfare with low-wage jobs. Their study is an excellent close-hand look at the realities of low-income women's aspirations, economic struggles, and values.

Hochschild, Arlie Russell. 1997. *The Time Bind: When Work Becomes Home and Home Becomes Work.* New York: Metropolitan Books.
Wondering why workers in the corporation she studied seldom took advantage of so-called family-friendly policies, Hochschild argues that people have to structure family life like efficiency experts and act devoted to work—an emotional commitment historically more associated with family life.

Reskin, Barbara, and Irene Padavic. 1994. *Women and Men at Work.* Thousand Oaks, CA: Pine Forge Press.
This is an introduction to gender and work in a book intended for a student readership. The authors explore topics such as the gender division of labor, gender segregation, wage inequality, and trends for the future.

Williams, Christine. 1995. *Still a Man's World: Men Who Do Women's Work.* Berkeley: University of California Press.
Based on interviews with men in the fields of nursing, elementary school teaching, social work, and librarianship, Williams shows how jobs become gendered. She also documents how men experience greater upward mobility in these jobs than women.

Chapter 6
Women and Families

Little more than 100 years ago, a housewife's guide proclaimed:

> Our boys are, in another score of years, to make the laws, heal the soul and bodies, formulate the science, and control the commerce of their generation. Fathers who, recognizing this great truth, do not prepare their sons to do their part toward accomplishing this work, are despised, and justly, by the community in which they live. Our girls are, in another score of years, to make the homes which are to make laws, heal souls and bodies, formulate science, and control the commerce of their generation. (Harland, 1889:202)

The home is woman's place, so the historical legacy tells us. In the period when the above guide was published, the glorification of the home and family was at its historical peak. The home was considered a moral sanctuary, and morality, which flourished in the home, was considered the work of women. It was women who would shape future generations. Although their place was ideally limited to the domestic sphere, within that sphere women were charged with preserving and creating the moral fiber of society.

Today's families may seem quite different from this ideal because the family is one of our most rapidly changing social institutions. Today, for example, only about 10 percent of U.S. families fit the supposed ideal of a two-parent family in which the man works and the woman stays home to care for the children (Baca Zinn and Eitzen, 1999). The vast majority of families in the United States are now either two-earner families, female-headed or single-parent households, postchildbearing couples, or those who have no children. If we consider families to include more alternative forms of household organization, then cohabitors, gay and lesbian couples, singles, and various kinds of communal or cooperative living arrangements have to be included in our picture of contemporary families. In addition, 50 percent of all children can now expect to live in one-parent homes for part of their lives.

Still, the social ideal of the family remains quite different from the realities of contemporary households. The family is still idealized as a private world—one in which family members are nurtured and prepared for their roles in the outside world. The family is also a place where, even if women are employed in the public sphere, they still tend to provide primary care for children and manage the everyday affairs of the household. The realities of contemporary households and the persistence of the family ideal create a series of contradictions, especially for women. On the one hand, the family is idealized as women's world. It is glorified, isolated, and assumed to be detached from public life; it is also seen as an enclave for the development of family members' personalities and for the gratification of their physical and emotional needs. At the same time, families have been undergoing rapid social changes, making clear the fact that families are situated within the larger context of political, economic, and social conditions—all of which are structured in accordance with the gender relations of society.

Although people experience their families in terms of personal, intimate relationships, those relationships are conditioned by events that extend far beyond immediate family life. Families take on great significance in the development of our individual lives, for they are where we first encounter social expectations, where our physical needs are met, where our primary emotional bonds are first established, and where we first encounter systems of authority, power, and social conflict. Although the family seems to be a personal experience, many of the strains associated with family life can be seen as stemming from the conflicts posed by the family's relationship to other social institutions. For example, unemployment, divorce, violence, and the welfare state are all experienced within the family, although they are also a part of broader social conditions.

The relationship of the family to other social institutions is also seen by the importance we give to the family as central to all other social institutions. Pleas for strengthening the family and for "family values" policies signify the threat that contemporary transformations in families pose to traditional ways of life in this society. Although appeals to family values at times stem from genuine concern about troubled families, they also represent a conservative view that regards many new family forms as symbolic of all that has gone wrong with traditional values in the society. Although most people accept the reality that most women will work outside the home, many see this reality as damaging to children, and some advocate the return of man's authority in the home. Contemporary politics surrounding families reveal the extent to which families are not isolated from other social institutions.

❧ *Historical Perspectives on Modern Families*

Families in the Western world today are characterized by an emphasis on child rearing, an assumed separation of home from work, and the idealization of the home as women's world. In addition, the family is also idealized as a private world—one where conflicts are supposed to be self-contained, without the intervention of the state. In reality, of course, the family is heavily entangled not only with economic institutions but also with the political state and its various social agencies.

The history of the Western family reveals the events that have molded contemporary families. Discussion of this history shows how family structures are interwoven with the economy and the state and how the family mediates between individual or personal life and the public collective realm of society (Wermuth, 1981). Without historical analysis, we tend to see the family as an abstract form, void of its real context and social changes (Dobash and Dobash, 1979; Weber, 1947). Knowing the history of a contemporary institution is like knowing the biography of a good friend—it helps you understand the present.

It is impossible to pinpoint the exact time in history when the modern family first emerged. One could trace it to the patriarchal household in the early Roman family, one of the strongest patriarchal systems known. *Patriarchal households*—defined as those where men rule over women—are found throughout Western history. One could also look to the medieval period as an era when courtly love and chivalry marked gender and class relations between men and women.

The modern household in Western society, however, is generally depicted as having its origins (in the Western world) in the transformations of economic and political life found in the postmedieval period, roughly beginning in the fourteenth century. Philip Aries (1962) locates the origins of the modern Western family in a series of gradual transformations that began in the fourteenth century and culminated in the seventeenth and eighteenth centuries. Starting in the fourteenth century, the wife's position in the household deteriorated as she lost the right to replace her husband in the management of household affairs in the event of his death or insanity. By the sixteenth century, the wife was placed totally under the authority of her husband—any acts she performed without the authority of her husband or the law were considered null and void. At the end of the sixteenth century, the Church recognized the possibility of sanctification outside of the religious vocation. In other words, it became possible for institutions outside the Church to be seen as sacred at this point, and the family became an object of common piety. The marriage ceremony itself, in the seventeenth century, took on a religious form by becoming like a christening in which families gathered around the bride and groom.

Also in the sixteenth and seventeenth centuries, new importance was placed on the family, as attitudes toward children changed. Greater intimacy between parents and children established a new moral climate and, although the extension of school education made education increasingly a matter for the school, the family began to center its emotional life on that of the child. By the eighteenth century, the family began to hold society at a distance, thereby initiating the idea of the family as an enclave of private life. Even the physical character of the household changed. Homes became less open; instead of being organized around large communal spaces, they became characterized by several rooms, each specialized by function (Aries, 1962). This change is explained as a result of homes becoming more organized around domestic work as commerce and production became increasingly located in the public workplace.

It is important to note that this evolution of family life was specific to the noble and middle classes and wealthy artisans and laborers. Even as late as the nineteenth century, the vast majority of the European population was still poor and lived like the medieval family, with children separated from their parents and the idea of the home and the family, as just described, nonexistent. Beginning in the nineteenth century, however, and continuing through the present, the concept of the family, as it originated in the well-to-do classes, extended through other strata of society. Still, the concept of the family as we know it today—a privatized, emotional, and patriarchal sphere—has its origins in the aristocratic and bourgeois classes.

By the late eighteenth and early nineteenth centuries, these historical transformations led to what U.S. historians have labeled the **cult of domesticity** (Cott, 1977; Kraditor, 1968). The ideology of domesticity gave women a limited and gender-specific role to play—namely, that of the person responsible for the moral and everyday affairs of the home. This ideal, coupled with economic transformations in family life, limited women's idealized experiences to the private world of the family. In actuality, of course, large numbers of women, especially women of color and working-class women, also performed wage labor. The definition of womanhood as idealized femininity, however, stemmed from the bourgeois origins of the cult of domesticity. The cult of domesticity did provide the conditions for women's involvement in moral reform movements and, ultimately, feminism, because it encouraged women's nurturance to be turned toward social improvement (Cott, 1977). In the context of the family, however, the cult of true womanhood limited women's experiences to affairs of the heart, not the mind. This ideal glorified a woman's role as homemaker at the same time that it fragmented the experience of women and men.

The idealized domestic role of women followed the transformations in women's labor (described in the preceding chapter). To review briefly, before the seventeenth century, the work role of women was not marginal to the economy or the household. In fact, as late as the seventeenth century, the household and the economy were one, the household being the basic unit of production. Domestic life in the earlier period was not splintered from public life, and households, as the basic units of economic production, consisted not only of individuals related through marriage but also of individuals with economic relationships, particularly servants and apprentices. In such a setting, women's labor, as well as that of children, was publicly visible, equally valued, and known to be economically necessary.

The emergence of capitalism, with the related rise of mercantilism, industrialization, and a cash-based economy, eroded the position of women by shifting the center of production from the domestic unit to the public workplace. This separation not only devalued women's labor in the home but it also made women more economically dependent on men (Tilly and Scott, 1978). The emergence of a family-wage economy, as distinct from a family-based economy, transformed not only women's work but, equally important, the family and women's role within it (see Chapter 5).

When the workplace became separated from the home, the family, although still economically productive, became a vehicle largely for the physical and social reproduction of workers and for the consumption of goods. As more goods were produced outside the home, the value of workers became perceived in terms of their earned wages. The social value of women, especially those left unpaid as housewives, was diminished.

In addition, the status of women in the family was radically altered not only by changes in the economic organization of the household but also by political changes in the relationship of the family to the state. The displacement of large feudal households by the modern state enhanced the power of the husband over his wife. For example, in sixteenth-century England, the state assumed the powers of justice, punishment, military protection, and regulation of property originally assumed by feudal estates. At the same time, a massive propaganda campaign was initiated in support of the nuclear family. Family members were required to be loyal, subservient, and obedient to both the king and the husband (Dobash and Dobash, 1979). The patriarchal family became the cornerstone—the basic social unit—for the emergence of the modern patriarchal state (Aries, 1962; Foucault, 1967). As capitalism developed further, there was a shift from private patriarchy within the family to public patriarchy centered in industry and government (Brown, 1981). Although individual men may still hold power in families where they are present, the patriarchal state ensures that all women are subject to a patriarchal order. In contemporary society, social welfare systems, family courts, and reproductive policies are dominated by men and patriarchal values, even though their primary effect is on women and children.

Historically, the patriarchal family (and, ultimately, the state) was hierarchically structured around the power of men and morally sanctioned by the patriarchal church. With the Protestant Reformation, an ever-increasing amount of religious socialization occurred within the home. Whereas Catholicism had reluctantly sanctioned family life (and thus forbade it to the clergy), the Puritans embraced the family as an exalted and natural (God-given) order. The Protestant ethic, as it emerged, blessed the family as a unit of material labor. The ideal that one could do God's work in secular vocations encouraged a view of the family as sacred and as the place for spiritual life (Zaretsky, 1976). In the end, the self-consciousness and individualism encouraged by the Protestant ethic helped ensure the subjective importance of the family. With the rise of capitalism, women's lower status in economic production was counterbalanced by their exalted status in the family as God's moral agents.

The split between work and home established by capitalism is related to a second schism—that between personal and public life. Modern capitalism depends on individual consumerism; thus, it encourages modern families to emphasize individualism, self-consciousness, and the search for personal identity. When personal identity is viewed as detached from objective material conditions, one can come to believe that personal liberation can occur without a change in the objective conditions of economic relations. The "plunge into subjectivity" (Zaretsky, 1976:119) and its emphasis on life-style, consumerism, and personal awareness is a form of consciousness specific to, and consistent with, the ideological and economic needs of capitalist economies.

Modern families are also regulated by the patriarchal authority of the state and its various agencies. Especially in poor and working-class families, state agencies and reformers seeking to eliminate deviance regulate personal and family life through the work of professional experts. Even in the middle class, professional experts claim to know more about personal life, thereby defining individual and family needs and the character of contemporary social problems (Ehrenreich and English, 1978; Illich, 1977).

The development of specific family structures varies, depending on the specific historical experiences of given groups in the society. Working-class, ethnic, African American, Asian American, Latino, and Native American families did not develop in exactly the same fashion as did White, middle-class households, as you will see in a later section on racism and families. Transformations in White, middle-class households do, however, set the ideals by which other groups have been judged; the historical development of racial and ethnic families and working-class families has also been shaped by the same transformations in economic and family systems. This historical account of transformations in family life paints only a broad picture of the emergence of family life over time. Specific family histories, like other social experiences, are nested within the class, race, and gender relations of any given historical period.

The history of families shows that the family is an institution that is interconnected with economic and political institutions of society. Although we tend to think of families and personal life within them as relatively autonomous social forms, we cannot understand the sociological character of families without studying the interrelationships of families; the state; the economy; and gender, race, and class relations.

ও⬥ *Feminist Perspectives on Families*

All societies are organized around some form of kinship system, although the definition of family changes in different cultural and historical contexts. Certain common characteristics of the family have been used to define the family. These include economic cooperation, common residence, socially approved sexual relations, reproduction, and child rearing. Anthropologists also add that, in most kinship systems, "marriage exists as a socially recognized, durable, although not necessarily life-long relationship, between individual men and women" (Gough, 1975). It also appears that, in most societies, men have higher status and authority in the family than women (Gough, 1975). Commonsense definitions of the family also define the family to mean blood ties, although as discussed in the following section, many contemporary families do not meet this criterion. In addition, many contemporary families do not meet the criteria of common residence, socially approved sexual relations, reproduction, child rearing, or marriage, as the standard definition implies.

As in the case of work, feminist thinking about families and modern transformations in family and household life have forced some rethinking of the meaning of family. Feminist scholars have suggested a number of themes in thinking about families, including that (1) the family is a social, not a natural, unit; (2) primary emotional commitments occur outside, as well as inside, the family; (3) men and women experience the family in different ways; (4) families are economic, as well as emotional and reproductive, units of society; and (5) the family ideal is an ideological concept that does not necessarily reflect the variety of family forms found in contemporary society (Rapp, Ross, and Bridenthal, 1979).

The Social Basis of Families

From a sociological point of view, the family is a social, not a natural, phenomenon. Feminist scholars say that the study of family life in the past has been biased by assumptions that define the family as a natural unit. Feminist perspectives on the topic lead in several directions, a major one viewing the family as being in a state of constant transformation as it influences, and is affected by, the larger social world.

The assumption that families are natural or biological units prejudices our conceptions of the family by presuming families to be universal and detached from the influence of other social institutions. The idea that the family is "natural" is strongly held by some groups—especially conservative, religious groups. This ideal is often used to argue that women should remain in the family under the authority of men.

In fact, the meaning and character of family systems vary widely. Both historically and in contemporary families, persons designated as kin may extend beyond blood relations; adoption is a case in point. As in the case of illegitimate children, blood relations may sometimes even be excluded from the social network of the family. The traditional assumption that family relations are natural also stems from the ethnocentric attitude that the ideals of our own culture are universally the most appropriate social form.

Even a cursory look at cross-cultural studies of kinship systems reveals a great variety of family forms. For example, traditionally, in poor rural villages of the Dominican Republic, although single-mate patterns were the dominant ideal, women usually had multiple partners, lived on or near the land of their own families, and had their children tended by maternal kin (Brown, 1975). Among the Chuckchee of Siberia, adult women are allowed to marry boys 2 or 3 years of age. The women care for the boys until they are adults, because the Chuckchee believe that parental care will cement the marriage bond. In contemporary Iran, under the rule of Shiite religious leaders, women are defined as dangerous and destructive if they are not controlled by men. When the Shiites took power over Iranian society, they lowered the age of marriage so young girls would be under the control of husbands; children are considered the sole property of a husband and women who commit adultery are guilty of a capital crime (O'Kelly and Carney, 1986).

Within the U.S. culture, family forms over time and among different groups. Carol Stack's (1974) work on poor African American families has shown, for instance, how extended kin networks in the African American community function as systems for social and economic exchange. Kin are recognized as those who share and meet socioeconomic obligations, regardless of blood ties. Among some Native American groups, traditionally, ancestry would be traced through maternal descent; young couples would reside with the woman's parent; and, wherever they lived, the women would assume control of the household—including the distribution of game that her husband caught (Axtell, 1981). In another example, the system of *compadrazgo* among Latinos exemplifies an extended kinship network that extends beyond blood ties. *Compadrazgo* is a family system whereby those defined as kin have very strong connections to the family; in this system, kin includes not only blood relatives but also godparents (Baca Zinn and Eitzen, 1999). The point is that these different family forms show that what seems natural about the Western **nuclear family**—families in which married couples live together with their children—is only that which dominant groups have defined as the ideal and that many have come to take for granted as the only, or best, family form.

Emotional Experiences and the Family

Another assumption that has characterized traditional views of the family but that has been challenged by feminist scholarship is the idea that people's most significant emotional relationships take place exclusively within the family. Although emotional life within the family is surely important, focusing exclusively on the family as the site for emotional connections underestimates the significance of emotional relationships outside the family. The traditional view, for example, assumes that women's primary emotional tie is to husbands and children. Research on women's friendships, however, shows that women may have equally strong, if not stronger, ties to friends; furthermore, this was true in the past, even at the time when women were assumed to be most constrained by family life. Studies of nineteenth-century women, for example, reveal that women's friendships involved passionate and sensual relations (Cott, 1977; Smith-Rosenberg, 1975).

Studies of the importance of emotion in social life also show how emotion, often thought of as internal and uncontrollable states of feeling, is shaped by a variety of social contexts. Assuming that the family is the primary site for strong emotional feeling overlooks the significance of emotion in all of social life. Such a view also is based on gender stereotypes associating women with the family and men with the public world of work—as if the family is the emotional world of women and work is the dispassionate, rational world of men.

Men's and Women's Experiences of Family Life

Feminist scholars studying the family have also shown that men and women experience the family in different ways, unlike earlier assumptions that the family was experienced in similar ways by all members. Jessie Bernard (1972), one of the foremothers of feminist scholarship in sociology, first wrote about how marriage was experienced differently by women and men within the family. Research on families has since shown that not only do women and men experience the family in different ways but they also hold different expectations for marital roles, with men tending to have more traditional expectations than women do (Hiller and Philliber, 1986; Wilkie, 1993). More husbands than wives want to maintain traditional roles in money matters, whereas more wives than husbands believe that the wife should be responsible for domestic matters. In this survey, 43 percent of couples agreed that money earning is the husband's job, and, although two-thirds of the husbands like (or would like) their wives to have a job, 58 percent of husbands think it is important for them to earn more than their wives do. The researchers take these results to mean that few husbands or wives want to give up the prerogatives of traditional roles, yet some are interested in expanding their activities into nontraditional roles. Men's and women's satisfaction in marriage is highly influenced by their gender expectations. When wives within a marriage adopt less traditional gender attitudes, they tend to perceive the quality of their marriage as declining. On the other hand, men who adopt less traditional gender roles tend to see the quality of their marriage as improving (Amato and Booth, 1995).

The assumption that families are based on a harmony of interests is also challenged by research on the power that men and women have within families. For many years, sociologists have been able to show that the amount of power men and women have within families is highly dependent on their relative material resources (Blood and Wolfe, 1960). Wives who are not employed or who do not bring material resources to a marriage are less likely to be able to influence family decision making, although this also depends on the extent to which men consider women's employment a threat or a contribution to the marriage (Pyke, 1994).

Finally, the notion that families are harmonious units is also shattered by the known extent of domestic violence. The vulnerability of women to violence is also a reflection of their relative powerlessness within marriage; this results in the cycle of violence whereby abused women find it difficult to leave violent relationships. If they are emotionally and materially dependent on men, they may have few resources on which to establish a more independent life. Marital violence will be examined later in this chapter; here, the point is that new studies of families, for all of the reasons just cited, challenge the idea that men's and women's experiences within families are the same. There is little wonder, then, that there is such a gender gap in the sources of resentment between men and women, as shown in Figure 6.1.

Economic and Family Systems

The popular conceptualization of the family as a refuge from the public world hides the fact that families serve economic purposes as well as reproductive and emotional ones. As an example, research on contemporary Asian American families shows the importance of family networks to the economic adaptations that groups have to make. Vietnamese refugees, for example, patch together a wide array of resources, based on the belief in family collectivism (i.e., the belief emphasizing collective sharing and exchange, in contrast to individualism). This collectivist attitude encourages households to share economic and social resources as a way of coping with the economic difficulties that immigrant groups

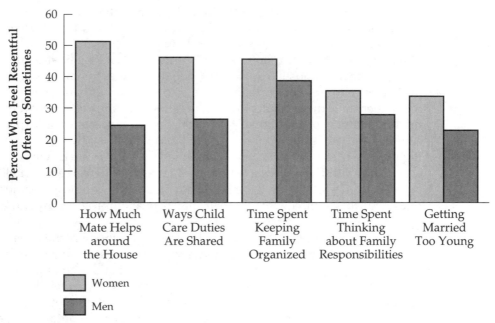

FIGURE 6.1   Sources of Resentment

Source: Data from Roper Organization. 1995. *The 1995 Virginia Slims Opinion Poll.* Storrs, CT: Roper Search Worldwide, p. 82.

face (Kibria, 1994). The family, then, is an important source of economic adaptation, and this example shows how intertwined the family and economy are as social institutions.

Family organization both reflects and reproduces the economic system of society. The availability of work for different family members will affect the family's form, pattern relationships within the family, and shape the family's lifestyle. The economic resources available to family members will also determine much about their experience in the family, in schools, at work, and at play. Just as economic arrangements influence families, so do families influence economic arrangements. In the family, people learn values and personality characteristics that make them suitable as workers; families shape our understanding of economic systems and our aspirations and definitions of ourselves within them.

The role of the state in shaping family life also cannot be underestimated. Particularly for the poor, state intervention in family life is an everyday reality, just as economic policies (e.g., through the tax system) can shape the type of family one creates. In sum, as the preceding history of Western families shows, neither families, economic systems, nor the state can be fully understood without knowing their interrelationships. At the same time that there is an interrelationship between family and work, there are also conflicts and competing demands, many of which fall on women, who bear the brunt of the different demands and needs of the workplace and the home.

Ideology and the Family

Feminist scholars have argued that the label *the family* has a specific and ideological meaning—in particular, "the family" implies a monolithic and unchanging entity. The ideology of the family assumes that all people do or should live in nuclear families, that women have husbands to support them, and that motherhood is women's major role. This ideology of the family mystifies women's work in families and, as a result, reinforces their economic exploitation (Thorne, 1993).

Feminist scholars suggest instead that we think of the idea of the family as distinct from actual households, because each word, *family* and *household*, has a different and distinct connotation. We tend to think of families as involving blood ties; households, on the other hand, imply the existence of a material (or economic) unit. Households are residential units that cannot be analyzed apart from their socioeconomic context. As Rapp, Ross, and Bridenthal describe them, "Households are material units within which people pool resources and perform certain tasks. It is within households that people enter into relations of production, reproduction, and consumption with one another, and on one another's account" (1979:176).

This concept leads to the final point in feminist perspectives on the family. *Family* connotes a particular social ideal, and, because of its singular form, the word implies that there is one dominant form of family life. *Household* underscores the connection between residential units and the economic structure of society, but *family* carries ideological significance, as well (Rapp, Ross, and Bridenthal, 1979). Distinguishing households from families allows us to recognize the diversity in people's lived experiences and frees the discussion of household life from the traditional assumptions that have biased our study of families. Because most households no longer meet the family ideal, it seems appropriate to think of new language and concepts to describe this change. Old traditions die slowly, however, and it seems likely that the word *family* will remain in our consciousness and our analysis. The preceding discussion should point out the importance of recognizing that traditional concepts of the family are no longer adequate to describe the social facts of most people's family experience. At least, the plural form, *families,* is more descriptive of the diverse realities in contemporary U.S. households.

❧ *Portraits of Contemporary Households*

What do U.S. households look like? Statistically, among Western industrial nations, the United States still has the highest rate of marriage. In 1997, 56.4 percent of the population (over age 15) was married. Single persons made up 27.7 percent of the population; 6.6 percent were widowed, and 9.3 percent were divorced (Bryson and Casper, 1998; see Figure 6.2 for a breakdown by gender and Figure 6.3 for a breakdown by race).

The changing character of families is especially visible in divorce statistics and statistics about single female-headed households. The United States has the

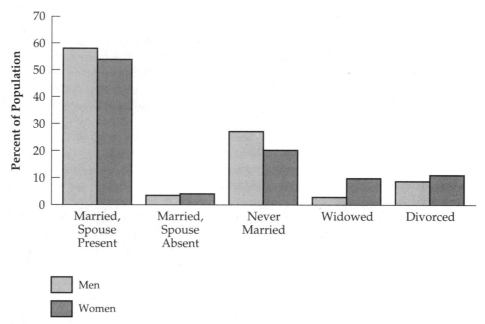

FIGURE 6.2 Marital Status of the Population: 1997

Source: Data from Terry A. Lugalia. 1998. *Marital Status and Living Arrangements: March 1997* (Update). Current Population Reports, Series P20-506 (June). Washington, DC: U.S. Census Bureau, p. 1.

highest divorce rate of any country in the world; for every two marriages in one year, there is one divorce. Annually, there are close to one million divorces. One-quarter of the children under age 18 live with only one parent (Arendell, 1992; Lugalia, 1998).

Measuring Family Status

Changes in family experiences are reflected in the difficulty the U.S. Census Bureau has in counting and categorizing families and households. Before 1980, the national census routinely classified the husband as the head of the family if he and his wife were living together. As the U.S. Census Bureau itself has reported, "Recent social changes have resulted in greater sharing of household responsibilities among the adult members and, therefore, have made the term 'head' increasingly inappropriate in the analysis of household and family data" (U.S. Census Bureau, 1994:B2). Now, the census distinguishes between household, family, family household, householder, and a related subfamily. A **household** is defined as all persons occupying a housing unit; they may or may not be related. A **family** is "a group of two persons or more (one of whom is the householder) related by birth, marriage, or adoption and residing together" (U.S. Census Bureau, 1994:B2). The **householder** is the person in whose name the unit is owned or rented; it may be either a man or a woman. A **family household** is a household maintained by a family and unrelated persons residing together, whereas a related **subfamily** is a

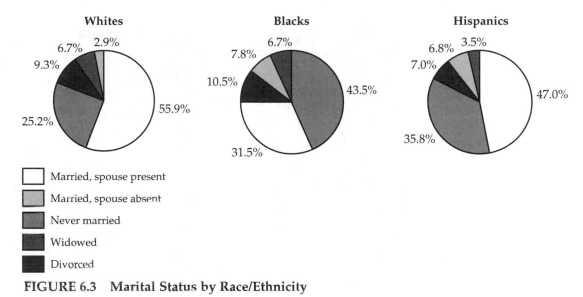

FIGURE 6.3   **Marital Status by Race/Ethnicity**

Source: Data from Terry A. Lugalia. 1998. *Marital Status and Living Arrangements: March 1997* (Update). Current Population Reports, Series P20-506 (June). Washington, DC: U.S. Census Bureau, p. 1–3.

married couple with or without children or one parent with one or more never-married children under age 18 living in a household and related to, but not including, the person who maintains the household (such as a teen mother living with a mother or aunt). Confusing as these definitions may be, they reflect the complex structure of families in the current period and help researchers develop more accurate analyses of family patterns and trends.

In 1997, 18.2 percent of all family households had female heads (see Figure 6.4). Counting all households (i.e., families, singles, and nonrelated individuals), 29.5 percent had female heads. Among Black Americans, 46.6 percent of family households had female heads; 24.3 percent of Hispanics; 14.1 percent of Whites; and, 11.7 percent of Asian/Pacific Islanders (Bryson and Casper, 1998; Hooper and Bennett, 1998). The increase in female-headed households is one of the most significant trends in family structure in recent years and can be accounted for by a number of factors: later age at first marriage, high rates of divorce, less likelihood that pregnant teens will marry, and, in some communities, the high rate of incarceration of young men.

Divorce

It is well known that marriages do not endure, as the ideal implies. The divorce rate in 1998 was 3.9 per 1,000 persons in the population, compared with 2.2 in 1960. Perhaps this divorce figure does not seem so large until you consider that the marriage rate was 8.4 per 1,000 in the same year—thus, an average of about one divorce results for every two marriages. The average marriage lasts only seven years—not exactly the lifelong commitment implied by the ideal. In addi-

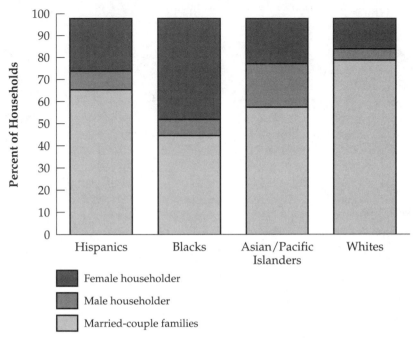

FIGURE 6.4   Household Composition

Sources: Data from Ken Bryson and Lynne M. Casper. 1998. *Household and Family Charac-teristics: March 1997.* Current Population Reports, Series P20-509 (April). Washington, DC: U.S. Census Bureau, pp. 86–91; Linda M. Hooper and Charlotte E. Bennett. 1998. *The Asian and Pacific Islander Population in the United States: March 1997* (Update). Current Population Reports, Series P20-512 (September). Washington, DC: U.S. Census Bureau, Table 5, p. 1. Website: <www.census.gov/population/socdemo/race/apr97>

tion, one-quarter of all marriages formed were remarriages (U.S. Census Bureau, 1997; National Center for Health Statistics, 1998).

Following divorce, women are far more likely than men to obtain custody of children. Because they are also more likely to face reduction in their income and because spousal support is awarded in less than 14 percent of divorces and received in less than 7 percent, women face considerable financial hardship in the aftermath of divorce. In addition, few women (24 percent) receive all of the child support they are owed by fathers (U.S. Census Bureau, 1998). Although this is one of the most fundamental problems for women after divorce, divorce also results in additional work for women—including coping with the legal system, redefin-ing relationships with friends and families, coming to terms with a changed iden-tity, and building a new personal life—while usually carrying the sole burden of child rearing and parenting. Many mothers nonetheless report better relation-ships with their children following a divorce because they have had to redefine their relationships and their new, shared situation. Both women and men report exclusion from their married friends after divorce, but for women the exclusion is exacerbated by the change in their social-class status (Grella, 1990). Women also find it difficult to have a social life outside of their family (Arendell, 1992). Separated and divorced women, however, tend to be better able than men to rebuild and maintain old social bonds. Men are more likely to drop their old ties, whereas divorced women's social ties reproduce their home-centered lives. For a number of men, divorce reproduces the character of young bachelorhood (Gerstel, 1988).

Balancing Family and Work

Changes in family structure are reflected in the beliefs and practices of people about balancing work and family life. Some 55 percent of women want to combine marriage, children, and a career, although that number has declined since the mid-1980s when 63 percent thought so (Roper Organization, 1995). Men are also more likely now to want marriages where they share work, housekeeping, and child care, although nearly one-third of men still think that it is best for men to assume the responsibility for providing for the family while women take care of the house and children. Younger men are more likely to support women's work outside the home, although the greatest change in attitudes toward more egalitarian views is among middle-aged (35–54 years) men (Wilkie, 1993). These changes in attitudes likely reflect the realities faced by couples who combine work and family.

Despite the fact that men and women generally agree about what needs to change to balance work and family demands, the biggest problem lies in the load women carry. As wives' paid work has become an economic necessity in most families, most struggle with the competing demands of work and personal life. Integrating family and work is a balancing act for all employed women, but sociologists have found that the ability to do so varies by class and marital status. Working-class women are more likely to emphasize economic reasons as the rationale for working—not surprising, since they also make higher contributions to family income than professional and managerial women. They nonetheless give their families priority over their work, whereas professional/managerial women see work as more central to their lives. Professional/managerial women either give work a higher priority than their family or rank the two equally. Single mothers or mothers with children who have special problems have the greatest difficulty integrating work and family (Burris, 1991).

Women and men develop a number of strategies for coping with the demands of work and family. At the heart of these demands, however, are deep-seated conflicts about gender ideology—conflicts that are brought on by time pressures felt within relationships, most particularly marriage (Hochschild, 1997). Women respond by trying to redefine their roles—choosing men to marry who plan to share work at home or, following marriage, trying to change the husband's understanding of his role at home. Some women force men's greater involvement in work at home by feigning helplessness over certain kinds of tasks; other women cope by trying not to impose change on their husbands, thereby avoiding conflict. Some women attempt to be "supermoms," but, as Hochschild found in her research on dual-earner families, supermoms pay the price, seeming "out of touch" with their feelings and reporting being "numb" (Hochschild, 1989:196). Others respond by cutting back on work or, very often, redefining what is necessary in the home. Women also respond by seeking outside help, either other female relatives or friends, or, for those with economic privilege, paying other women to do the work at home (Hochschild, 1989).

Balancing work and family is complicated by the power differences between men and women in families. Those power differences, in turn, influence marital satisfaction. Wives are much more likely than husbands to desire change in the areas of domestic labor, children, sexuality, leisure activities, and finance. Power differences within marriage tend to confirm gender roles, with women desiring more change than men. As researchers have reported, "Real changes in marital power can occur only if husbands and wives recognize their stereotyped self-concepts and ways of seeing each other, as well as the discrepancies between their respective perceptions of marital life, and the effect of these stereotypes and discrepancies in maintaining the status quo" (Komter, 1989:214).

The experience of dual-earner couples often puts strains on their relationship because of the adaptations they must make in household responsibilities and decision making. Especially when a traditional marriage evolves into a dual-earner marriage, all members of the family (including the children) may have difficulty adjusting to new roles. While couples face these new issues, there are also positive effects in changing traditional roles. Wives tend to experience greater satisfaction with their jobs, and research indicates that children develop more flexible and less stereotypic gender expectations in dual-career families than in traditional ones (Nadelson and Nadelson, 1980). Such findings are a direct contradiction to the idea, widespread in popular thought, that the children of working mothers experience maternal deprivation. The assumption that working mothers, but not working fathers, deprive their children of emotional bonding is further evidence of the extent to which the family is idealized as the responsibility of women.

Some dual-earner couples, both married and unmarried, find it necessary, because of their job locations, to maintain separate residences. These commuter couples also experience problems posed by their long-distance arrangements, not the least of which are considerable transportation and long-distance telephone expenses, but also lack of daily companionship and emotional support. Researchers find commuter marriages to be less stressful, however, for older couples who have been married longer, where at least one partner has an already established career, and where they are free from child rearing (Gross, 1980). Men and women in commuter marriages report high levels of satisfaction with the relationship and report being equally committed to their partners and careers (Skirboll and Taylor, 1998; Groves and Horm-Wingerd, 1991).

Cohabitation

Recent trends among single persons include a profound increase in the numbers of persons who are cohabiting outside of marriage. Since 1970, the number of unmarried persons living together has tripled, with researchers now estimating that soon a majority of persons will experience this life-style at some point in their lives. Among the more than four million cohabiting couples, only one-third involve two never-married people; most include at least one divorced partner (Lugalia, 1998).

In about three-quarters of cases, cohabitation leads to marriage (Peres, 1998), even though delayed (Spain and Bianchi, 1996). Researchers find that there are similar patterns of interaction among partners in cohabiting relationships and those who marry, and there are similar rates of happiness within these relationships (Brown, 1996). On the other hand, some also find higher rates of violence among cohabitors than among spouses, at least among those who have come from violent households (Jackson, 1996), and those who cohabit prior to marriage have higher divorce rates (Nock, 1995). The likelihood of cohabitation is also related to factors such as educational status, gender-role attitudes, and political orientation, with those most likely to cohabit being more likely to have favorable attitudes toward gender equality and nontraditional gender roles (Lye and Waldron, 1997; Thornton, Axinn, and Teachman, 1995; Barber and Axinn, 1998).

Gay and Lesbian Households

Much of the traditional research on gay men and lesbian women has previously assumed that homosexuality is pathological behavior, but new perspectives are beginning to show a more objective picture of gay and lesbian existence (Allen and Demo, 1995). Research on lesbian experiences finds that lesbian women tend to form extended networks of support that operate at local and national levels. In a sense, these support networks function like a large family, except that, unlike patriarchal families, they tend to be nonauthoritarian and nonhierarchical.

In a study of lesbian co-parents—those who live together raising children—Sullivan (1996) found that lesbian couples tend to have more gender equality within their households than do heterosexual couples, so long as both partners are employed. This confirms earlier research on the same subject (Tanner, 1978; Taylor, 1980). However, when one partner is the primary breadwinner and the other the primary caregiver for children, the partner staying at home becomes economically vulnerable, less able to negotiate with her partner about her needs, and more devalued as a person and a daily contributor—just like the traditional pattern where women stay home and men are the primary breadwinners.

A substantial number of lesbians and gays are raising children, some of whom are from earlier marriages and others of whom are born to lesbian couples or are adopted. Research finds that children of lesbian and gay parents are well adjusted and have no greater likelihood of being gay than children in heterosexual families (Goleman, 1992; Patterson, 1992; Flaks et al., 1995; Gross, 1991). Children of lesbians are usually accepting of their parents' life-style, but they are concerned about external reactions from peers and neighbors (Lewis, 1980). Some research also shows that lesbian mothers are actually more child oriented than heterosexual mothers and that lesbian mothers are more concerned about the long-range development of their children (Miller, 1982). Research on African American lesbian mothers shows that the quality of their relationships with their daughters is contingent on the extent to which mothers have been able to develop intimate relationships, find satisfaction in their work, and acquire a sense of competency and self-worth (Joseph, 1984).

Lesbian mothers may have to protect the custody of their children, although in some recent lawsuits they have won the right to do so by arguing that the quality of parenting, not sexuality, is the most important issue. Feminists argue that when lesbian mothers have left unhappy marriages, the children may be more nurtured in lesbian households, where two women (or more) share the work of child care (Swerdlow et al., 1980).

Fewer children live in gay male households, in part because women are still more likely to get custody of their children, but also because fewer gay men live in long-term unions than do lesbian couples (Vida, 1978). Those gay men who are the most committed to each other are likely to live in the same residence, are more likely to socialize with other gay couples rather than other gay men, place greater emphasis on emotional intimacy than sexual intimacy in the relationship, and are more likely to be sexually faithful to their partners (Joseph, 1979).

The small amount of research that has been done finds that compared to heterosexual fathers, gay fathers tend to be more nurturing, less traditional in their overall parenting practices, and less accepting of the idea that being an economic provider is the main ingredient of good fathering. Research also shows that gay fathers have very positive relationships with their children, that they try to create stable home lives, and that the fathers' sexual orientation is of little importance in the overall parent-child relationship (Bigner and Bozett, 1989). Gay fathers do tend to be more strict than heterosexual fathers and set more limits on their children's behavior; they also place more emphasis on verbal communication with their children (Bigner and Jacobsen, 1989). In sum, there is little evidence that living with a gay or lesbian parent has a negative effect on children.

Motherhood

The child-centeredness of modern families has tended to distract us from thinking about mothers; yet, an examination of motherhood as a social institution reveals both the objective and the subjective dimensions of this experience. Women's roles as mothers are idealized in our culture as all-loving, kind, gentle, and selfless; however, the objective conditions of motherhood in this society fill the role with contradictions, conflicts, and pleasures. Motherhood is, in fact, a social institution—one that is controlled by the systems of patriarchy and the economic relations in which it is embedded (Rich, 1976). Like other institutions, motherhood involves a complex set of social relations organized around specific functions. Once established, institutions also involve a system of power relations, a division of labor, and the distribution of resources (Glenn, Chang, and Forcey, 1993).

Viewing motherhood as an institution distinguishes motherhood as something more than a caring relationship between a woman and her children (Rich, 1976). Mothering involves not just care for children but also situates women in various institutions. Viewing mothering only in the isolated context of the family misses its connections to other social institutions. As an example, research on

Latina and African American mothering finds that low-income women define their mothering as an activist activity when they are engaged in community work that they see as an extension of their mothering role. For these mothers, activism is essential to providing the safety, health care, education, and other services that they know are necessary for their children's welfare (Naples, 1992). Seen in this light, mothering is work that takes place not just within the family, but throughout social institutions. It is a socially constructed practice, one wherein mothers construct an understanding of themselves and their children in relationship to the society around them.

In U.S. society, motherhood is typically characterized by its isolation. Although most young girls are socialized to become mothers, they are seldom prepared for the solitary activity of actually caring for children in the home. Jessie Bernard (1975) suggests, in fact, that when women marry, their early socialization for dependency is reversed, because as wives and mothers they are expected to be responsible for both their husbands and their children. The experience of motherhood then becomes a mixture of satisfaction and pleasure plus anger, frustration, and bitterness (Rich, 1976). The contradictions also appear for children since, as Rich says, "Most of us first know both love and disappointment, power and tenderness, in the person of a woman" (1976:11). Because motherhood is a role exclusively reserved for women, women's identities develop in ways that reproduce mothering qualities.

Nancy Chodorow has explored this issue by asking how the psychological structures of gender emerge from the "asymmetrical organization of parenting" (1978:49; see also Chapter 2). Chodorow notes that the role of women as mothers is one of the few seemingly universal elements of the gender division of labor. Instead of relying on explanations that see motherhood as a natural fact, however, she asks why the psychological characteristics of motherhood are reproduced so that women, and not men, want to be mothers and develop the capacity of nurturing others. According to Chodorow, "Women, as mothers, produce daughters with mothering capacities and the desire to mother. These capacities and needs are built into and grow out of the mother-daughter relationship itself. By contrast, women as mothers (and men as not-mothers) produce sons whose nurturant capacities and needs have been curtailed and repressed" (1978:7).

Chodorow explains this process as the result of both the gender division of labor and the psychological processes it inspires. Both boys and girls, in order to become their own person, must separate—psychologically—from the parent. Because the parent most often present is a woman, the process of individuation is complicated by gender identity. Boys, who identify with the gender of the father, learn that their gender role is one of detachment and distance, because the father is seldom present in the home. Girls, on the other hand, identify with the gender of the mother; thus, their own psychological process of separation and individuation is less complete. Girls, then,

are more continuously embedded in and mediated by their ongoing relationship with their mother. They develop through and stress particularistic and affective relationships to others. A boy's identification processes are not likely to be so embedded in or mediated by a real affective relation to his father. At the same time, he tends to deny identification with and relationship to his mother and reject what he takes to be the feminine world; masculinity is defined as much negatively as possible. . . . Feminine identification processes are relational, whereas masculine identification processes tend to deny relationship. (Chodorow, 1978:176)

As a consequence, gendered personalities both reflect and re-create the gender division of labor in the household. Women become mothers because this role is consistent with their acquired psychological being; the fact that they are mothers, then, re-creates similar personality structures of nurturance in their daughters. In sum, the social organization of parenting creates psychic structures that orient the person to his or her social behavior. To reverse this process, so that men as fathers become more nurturant, will require that men be placed in the household on an equal basis with women. Because the organization of parenthood is tied to the organization of economic production, both the family and the economy must be transformed, however, if we are to eliminate gender inequality.

Chodorow's analysis is psychoanalytic in its orientation; thus, the evidence for her argument is clinical evidence. As her critics point out, clinical evidence is weak because it rests on patients' accounts and psychoanalysts' interpretations of those accounts (Lorber et al., 1981). Beyond these methodological criticisms, some sociologists are concerned that Chodorow overemphasizes psychological processes in lieu of social-structural conditions as the source of women's choice to become mothers. It is ideologically normal in our society for women to become mothers; furthermore, given the inequality in men's and women's incomes, it is reasonable for fathers, not mothers, to be the primary wage earners in families (Lorber et al., 1981:484).

Other questions about the class, race, and culture bias of Chodorow's explanation can also be raised, for she assumes that the mother in the gender division of labor is a devalued woman. Although this is true in many cultures, including the dominant U.S. culture, it is not universally true. An important test of her theory would involve the study of boys and girls who are raised by men or in cultures where women are not devalued and parenthood is more equally shared. Recall that in Chapter 2, Chodorow's work was discussed in the context of Chicano families where researchers have found it provides valuable insights to the women-centered households common among Chicanas (Segura and Pierce, 1993).

The psychoanalytic perspective may not, however, account for variations in the actual practices and relationships of mothers who are raising children. The mother's own personality, as well as the child care arrangements she makes, may alter the degree to which her sons and daughters separate or do not separate themselves from her, and it certainly alters their relationship with her. Still, Chodorow's analysis gives us a provocative account of the formation of gender identity and its relationship to the social structure of the family.

Most importantly, Chodorow points out that the family is "a primary constituent of the male dominant social organization of gender and, as such, is as fundamental a constituent feature of society as a whole—of 'social structure'—as is the economy or the political organization" (Lorber et al., 1981:502). One is not dependent on or contained by the other; people live in families, just as they live in societies. Chodorow's analysis has led us to see the importance of understanding "the gender politics of infancy" (Harding, 1981) and the connection of masculine and feminine personalities not only to the social organization of families but also to self—other distinctions that constitute the basis for domination relations (Chodorow, 1978; Harding, 1981). In sum, although the cross-cultural evidence for Chodorow's work remains to be studied, she provides an insightful explanation of some of the effects of nuclear family relations, in which the woman's work as a mother is isolated from that of other persons and is founded on the norm of exclusivity.

Much of the feminist scholarship on changes in women's roles as mothers has focused on the new definitions that feminist and other social changes have inspired among women. What about mothers who remain in more traditional roles, relying on husbands for financial support? Research finds that they tend to hold social and political beliefs that emphasize the natural basis and moral superiority of gender differences; they definitely see motherhood as more satisfying than paid work. Their perception of the erosion of support for domesticity has left them feeling embattled; they think they must defend choices that were once considered sacred. As a result, some view employed women as selfish and dangerous to children, but they also frown on men who shirk responsibility for their children's support (Gerson, 1990).

Fatherhood

Fathers' roles in the family have traditionally been defined as instrumental. That is to say, fathers were to be the primary breadwinners and the source of authority in the family, while mothers were to fulfill the emotional needs of family members. Just as women have found their traditional roles to be limiting and one sided, many men have tried to redefine their roles as fathers to include more primary care of children. In fact, researchers have learned that role flexibility within the family is necessary to preserve the well-being of all family members (Speigel, 1983).

Research on fathers has traditionally been based on the assumption that fathers have a limited role in families (Robinson and Barret, 1986), although as fathers have assumed more responsibilities in family life, new research has emerged. Still, the research shows that following the birth of a baby, most fathers tend to "help out" rather than share child care and they continue to view caring for the baby as the mother's work (Walzer, 1996; Belsky and Kelly, 1994; La Rossa, 1986). Men express a willingness to help with child care, but do not do so equally (Liss-Levinson, 1981); moreover, mothers say they are unwilling to force the issue because they perceive the price to be too great (Robinson and Barret, 1986). Although the adjustment to parenthood for both men and women is considerable, fathers experience less stress in adapting to parenthood than do mothers (La Rossa and La Rossa, 1981).

Families headed by single fathers have also increased, although they are a small percentage of families. Despite the increase in the number of single and divorced fathers, as well as the greater involvement of many men in their roles as fathers, there are few social support networks for men. Many men continue to feel pressure to put their jobs and careers first, and, although employers give lip service to increased family involvement, workers perceive that choices have to be made between family and career (Greif, 1995). Single fathers also tend to use outside help, typically from women, and to use daughters as mother substitutes—to do child care, housework, and manage household affairs (Grief, 1985). Single fathers feel competent about their skills as parents and demonstrate more mothering behaviors than do married fathers. Compared to men who are still married, single fathers spend more time with their children, report more sharing of feelings between father and child, are more likely to stay home with sick children, and take a more active interest in their children's out-of-home activities (Risman, 1986; Risman, 1987).

Most single fathers are heading their own households as the result of divorce or widowhood, although new research on young unwed fathers adds to our understanding of the difficulties men face as fathers. Despite social stereotypes, many, if not most, young unwed fathers try to take some responsibility for their children, but their economic disadvantage is high. Most young unwed fathers are generally less well educated than other groups, have limited employment prospects, and are more likely to engage in crime (Lerman and Ooms, 1993; Marsiglio, 1995). These conditions, particularly acute among African American men, make it difficult for these fathers to support their children.

Sociological perspectives on fatherhood see fathering, like mothering, as a role, not just a biological connection to one's offspring. In fact, neither kinship nor household membership is always necessary for a man to perform the psychological and instrumental functions associated with a father. Men who have worked to include more expressive and caretaking work in their roles as fathers report considerable rewards in creating fuller relationships with their children, although they also note that society provides little emotional, practical, or financial support for men to spend regular time with their children. Societal support in the form of paternity leaves, new work arrangements for parents, and transformation in our attitudes about gender and parenting are as essential for fathers' roles as for mothers' roles.

🞥 *Race, Gender, and Families*

Families are organized, as you have seen, around gender relations, but they are also shaped by the racial-ethnic organization of society. As in other social institutions, race and gender, along with class, organize the social structure of families and create experiences within families that are connected to the family's location in the system of race, gender, and class relations. This is true for all families—not just so-called minority families, but White families, as well. White families, for example, benefit from some degree of racial privilege in a society that is marked by racial inequality; that privilege, however, is also influenced by the class position of the family. A working-class White family will not have the same access to resources as an African American middle-class family; nonetheless, the African American middle-class family will likely teach family members how to deal with the racism they are likely to experience, even given their class location. Strong sociological analyses of the family thus take race, class, and gender into account in considering how families are organized, how they change, and what different members within families experience.

In the past, studies of racial-ethnic families have been biased by the assumption that families should conform to dominant group norms (Staples and Mirandé, 1980). As scholars and the public have realized that this ideal no longer reflects reality, there has been a greater willingness and ability to understand all families without judging them by some dominant ideal. Scholarship on African American, Latino, Asian American, and Native American families has also transformed many of the assumptions earlier built into family studies. New scholarship on families is also critical to understanding many current social issues—including welfare reform, teen pregnancy, and violence—since public discussions of these problems often miscast minority-group families as "disorganized," "maladjusted," and "breaking down."

Consider, for example, discussions of welfare reform. Many of the policies proposed to solve the problem of welfare target African American women and their family roles as somehow responsible for the flaws in the welfare system. Welfare recipients are portrayed as not wanting to work and as best helped by creating policies that would put men back into the family. These attitudes can be attributed to a deep cultural belief that there is something wrong with women-headed households and to beliefs that women who stay home to care for their children are not working. At the level of social policy, these assumptions can be traced to the Moynihan Report, first published in the mid-1960s, yet still influencing and reflecting many of the assumptions that guide current public opinion and policies affecting the family life of women of color and poor people.

The Moynihan Report, *The Negro Family: The Case for National Action*, was published as a federal study of the Black community in 1965; it cited the breakdown of the Black family as the root cause of social disorganization within Black communities and blamed a presumed **matriarchy** (defined as women holding power) for problems among Black people. Its author, Daniel Patrick Moynihan (an influential senator from New York), stated then, "At the heart of the deterioration of the fabric of Negro society is the deterioration of the Negro family" (p. 5).

Moynihan's report attributed the origins of the family problem to the period of slavery and the social disorganization it created. Other studies of the Black family have also cited slavery as creating female-headed families through the separation of family members by slave sales, the practice of slave breeding, and the disrespect paid to the Black slave community (Frazier, 1948). Others have traced the structure of Black family life to its African origins, where polygamy and birth out of wedlock were more common (Herskovits, 1958). Recent scholarship on the

African American family questions both of these conclusions, noting that locating the causes of contemporary family structure in the past downplays an analysis of family life within contemporary economic and social structures.

Historian Herbert Gutman argues that if Moynihan was right in concluding that the structure of Black families has its origins in the past, then we should expect the family to be less stable as we move backward in time. To test this assumption, Gutman traced five generations of kin as they adapted to the changes of postslavery society in the United States. Part of his research is based on 1925 census data from New York City that show that 85 percent of kin-related Black households at that time were headed by both parents; 32 of the 13,924 families had no father present; and five in six children under age 6 lived with both parents (Gutman, 1976:xix). Based on this information, he concluded that female-headed households are a contemporary phenomenon, not just remnants of the past. His historical research is complemented by that of Genovese (1972), who shows that slave owners used the family as a form of social control. Genovese recognizes that separation of families occurred, but he suggests that it was often to the benefit of slave owners to maintain stable families as a way of preventing slave revolts. The slave family, according to Genovese, was subordinated to the economic interests of the owner. If it benefited him, he would break up families for sale; in fact, most slave owners broke up families when owners were under economic pressure (Genovese, 1972:453).

Both Genovese's and Gutman's analyses indicate that slave families faced oppressive conditions that tested the adaptive capacities of men and women. Within slave communities, a subculture of resistance emerged in which family relations and women's role fostered resistance to dominant White institutions (Davis, 1971, 1981). As a result of the gender division of labor, Black women in slavery provided domestic labor not only in the White households but also in their own. The labor they provided for their own family was the only labor not claimed by the ruling class; it was for the benefit of the slave community. As a result, Black women's labor in the slave community "la[id] the foundation for some degree of autonomy" (Davis, 1971:5), and the Black woman became essential to the survival of the slave community. Because of her indispensable labor in the household of the oppressor, she developed a practical awareness of the oppressor's dependence on her. As Davis says, "The master needs the slave far more than the slave needs the master" (1971:6). Black women's consciousness of their oppression benefited the slave community, as women were responsible for the socialization of future generations. Thus, the women in their roles in the family and community passed on a culture of resistance to oppressed kin (Caulfield, 1974).

The picture of the African American family emerging from these revisions is one of strength and resistance. Ladner (1995) suggests that traditional myths of the Black matriarchy confuse Black women's strength with domination. Because of racism, Black women have not been subjected to the ideals of femininity, as have White women (Davis, 1971). One result is found in the strong self-concept and higher educational and occupational aspirations that Black women have for themselves compared with White women (Jarrett, 1994; Collins, 1998; Dill, 1980).

Instead of explaining patterns in Black families as the result of slavery or individual pathology, it makes sense to analyze the origins of African American family life in terms of the patterns of urbanization, industrialization, and poverty in current society (Billingsley, 1966; Frazier, 1948; Staples, 1971). In the early twentieth century, racial discrimination in the labor force denied African Americans employment using the skills they had acquired in slavery. As a result, men could find only unskilled, often seasonal, and always underpaid, employment; women were more likely to find steady, although also severely underpaid, employment in private domestic labor. In 1920, 41 percent of Black women worked as servants and 20 percent as laundresses (Katzman, 1978:74). Black women's labor thus made them steady providers for their family. As the twentieth century developed, continuing patterns of unemployment, the elimination of Black men through war and imprisonment, and the conditions the social welfare system established for households encouraged the formation of female-centered households.

The contemporary structure of African American households must be understood in terms of both racism and sexism and the economic context in which they are embedded, not in conditions of the past. As we look at African American families without racist and sexist assumptions, we see that even in the poorest of families, systems of cooperation and social exchange characterize the organization of family life (Stack, 1974; Stack and Burton, 1993). The social and community ties that people generate in the face of poverty and oppression, in fact, appear stronger than some of the ties of nuclear families. This fact shows us that African American families are not necessarily disorganized but that they are not always organized according to dominant group ideals. Seen in this way, the role of women in the African American family can be seen for the strength it creates, not the social destruction it allegedly causes. African American women continue to work to support their families and to hold high ideals for their children's future (Dill, 1980). Studies of educated Black women show that those educated women from the lower middle class are less likely to be married than educated Black women from middle-class families because parents in the lower middle class are more likely to encourage their daughters to become educated than to get married (Higginbotham and Weber, 1992). This finding is different from popular images of working-class Black families, in that parents have positive aspirations for their children and hope they will receive more education than the parents themselves have achieved (Wilkinson, 1984). Black working-class families view the education of their children as providing a way to overcome racial discrimination, whereas White working-class families worry that highly educated children will no longer honor family customs and maintain cohesion with their relatives (Willie, 1985).

African American middle-class families promote among their children and through their community activities a strong sense of building a just and equitable society, whereas White middle-class families are likely to encourage family members to become individually better informed and enriched. Willie also points out that a significant difference between African American and White middle-class families is the historically greater likelihood of the middle-class Black mother being in the labor force; in fact, her contribution to family income is essential in maintaining the family's standard of living. This tends to create greater egalitarianism within Black families and promotes the greater participation of Black husbands in child care and household management (Willie, 1985).

These conclusions challenge the stereotype of families as breaking down or deteriorating. They also sensitize us to the different conditions that families face depending on their class location. Although certainly many African American families struggle with problems of poverty, unemployment, and violence, those problems stem from the social structural location of families in a race, class, and gender-stratified society, not from something inherently problematic in women's heading households or in African American values.

Similar transformations of thinking have come from new studies of Latino families. Like past studies of African American families, past studies of Latino families have been founded on the assumption of pathology. *Machismo* in Latino families has been assumed to encourage aggressive, violent, authoritarian behavior in men and saintly, virginal, submissive behavior in women (Staples and Mirandé, 1980). Some researchers see machismo as a more benevolent feature of Latino families, encouraging honor, respect, and dignity among family members (Mirandé, 1979; Murillo, 1971). Research shows that Latino families are more egalitarian than the ideal of machismo suggests (Baca Zinn, 1976; Hondagneu-Sotelo, 1994) and that the Latino family is more woman centered than prevailing stereotypes suggest (Baca Zinn, 1976).

Chicano families have been characterized as close-knit kinship systems, typically explained as a consequence of Chicano culture. Scholars now recognize that these family patterns represent adaptation to a hostile society that excludes Chicanos from full participation and keeps them socioeconomically marginal (Baca Zinn and Eitzen, 1999; Dill, 1994; Baca Zinn, 1990). Especially for women, close kinship networks provide social exchanges and support that are not available elsewhere. Studies of Latino families show considerable differences in family experiences, depending on the different social histories and contemporary status of particular groups categorized as "Latino." Thus, Chicanas (women of Mexican descent born and raised in the United States) are more likely to hold the ideal of stay-at-home motherhood than Mexicanas (Mexican women immigrants residing in the United States). Because Mexicanas are more likely to have mixed family and employment, they are less likely to dichotomize family and work in their understandings of motherhood (Segura, 1998).

For all groups, family experience is bound by the broader systems of race, class, and gender inequality. So, for example, in her study of Chicana cannery workers, Zavella (1987) shows how family life is influenced by the work women do in the canneries. Seasonal work in the canneries necessitates changes in family activities, and the low status and low wages of the job reinforce women's traditional role in Chicano families. Likewise, Puerto Rican families have experienced one of the most rapid rises in female-headed households, largely due to the decline of industrial employment for men in the regions where Puerto Ricans tend to be concentrated (Moore, 1988; Rodriguez, 1989). As a result, although Puerto Rican families are traditionally headed by men, the rate of families headed by females among Puerto Ricans has nearly converged with that of African Americans. This trend is further evidence that societal conditions, not just cultural preferences, shape family structure (Baca Zinn and Eitzen, 1999).

New patterns of family life in the context of widespread immigration illustrate this point well. High rates of immigration in recent years—especially from Central America, the Caribbean, and Southeast Asia—are creating a new classification of family life: **transnational families**. In these families, family members live in different countries, usually at considerable distance from one another, but with a pattern of moving back and forth across national boundaries. Thus, as in Hondagneu-Sotelo's (1997) study of transnational mothers, women may work as domestic workers in Los Angeles, while their children reside in Mexico, El Salvador, or Guatemala. The very structure of the work they do may discourage having children physically present in their new home, thus challenging strong beliefs that mothers should raise their own children. Yet, transnational mothers do not see themselves as abandoning their children; rather, they redefine motherhood to include mothers' obligations to financially support their children and to value the contributions of other caregivers (e.g., grandmothers, aunts, and friends) to the well-being of their children. As Hondagneu-Sotelo concludes, "Transnational mothering radically rearranges mother-child interactions and requires a concomitant radical reshaping of the meanings and definitions of appropriate mothering" (1997:557). Other studies of transnational families show that women negotiate and sustain relationships across national borders because this is how they forge their identity and maintain a sense of security in their homeland in the face of racial oppression and class disadvantage in their new location (Das Gupta, 1997; Alicea, 1997).

Research on Asian American and Native American families is less extensive, but, as with African American and Latino families, family experience in these groups should be seen in the context of the racist policies that discourage strong and cohesive families and in the specific class locations of racial-ethnic groups (Dill, 1988; Baca Zinn and Eitzen, 1999). Asian Americans, for example, are typically stereotyped as the "model minority"—meaning that they have been depicted as highly successful in comparison to other immigrant groups, presumably as a result of their hard work, education, and thrift (and, by implication, the absence of these qualities among other racial-ethnic groups). This simplistic view ignores the barriers to mobility that Asian Americans have encountered and is based on the myth that hard work always reaps commensurate rewards (Woo, 1992). In addition, it overlooks the diversity within Asian American groups.

U.S. policies regarding Asians have encouraged the use of Asians in specific cheap forms of labor, at the same time that they have explicitly discouraged family unity (Lai, 1992). So, for example, in the nineteenth century, young Asian men were seen as desirable workers in agriculture, mining, and railroads; women were not. The Page Law, passed in 1875, intended to exclude Chinese women as prostitutes, was so strictly enforced that it functionally excluded Chinese women from coming to the United States. The Chinese Exclusion Act of 1882 prohibited the entry of Chinese laborers (men or women) and forbade wives of resident laborers from entering the United States (Takaki, 1989). Later, the Immigration Act of 1924 prohibited the entry of any Chinese women to the United States, making it impossible for families of Chinese men to join them.

In addition to explicit laws restricting immigration, many Asian immigrants believed that their work in the United States would be temporary; so, in accordance with tradition, wives remained at home. In the elite classes, the practice of footbinding also limited women's ability to travel. As a result, the large number of men in Chinese communities in the United States made them bachelor societies. Only in Hawaii, where sugar planters thought Chinese women could control Chinese laborers through their taming influence, were women encouraged to immigrate.

Before 1868, as part of its isolationist policy, the Japanese government forbade its citizens to leave; however, with a new emperor in 1868, Japan encouraged select classes to seek education abroad. Economic depression in the 1880s encouraged many small farmers to seek opportunities in the United States, where wages were high compared to those in Japan and hard work held the promise of enabling workers to return to Japan as wealthy people—a promise that rarely came true. Japanese immigrants to the United States tended to come from middle-class backgrounds and, on the whole, were better off economically than other Asian and European immigrants to the United States. Like the Chinese, the earliest immigrants were mostly men who worked in unskilled labor in agriculture, mining, railroads, and lumber. They, too, believed their work in the United States was temporary (Glenn, 1986).

Japanese women were allowed to come to the United States under the terms of the Gentlemen's Agreement of 1908. This law restricted the entry of Japanese laborers but allowed parents, wives, and children of those already in America to settle here. This law also encouraged the practice of "picture brides," particularly among Japanese and Korean immigrants. Consistent with the traditional practice of arranged marriage, Asian men in the United States would marry women who, hopeful of upward mobility, applied and were displayed in offices in many of the port cities (Takaki, 1989). Until ruled unconstitutional in 1967, **antimiscegenation** laws barred marriages between Whites and "Mongolians," or laborers of Asian origins (Chow, 1987). Such policies made it difficult, if not impossible, for stable Asian American families to form. This history reveals that family stability is as much a result of policies and practices that promote family life as it is of the culture and characteristics of different groups.

Among Native Americans, family life-styles vary widely, as diversity among groups is a key element of culture. The attempt to impose Western family forms on these people complicates the picture of Native American family life. Interference in these cultures by social workers, the federal government, and other outsiders might have done more to promote family and cultural disorganization than to assist these groups. Among Native American families, urbanization contributes to high rates of unemployment and dependence on public welfare (Miller, 1975). Left to their own culture, Native American families tend to rely on extended family networks to fulfill family functions (Redhorse et al., 1979; Staples and Mirandé, 1980). The imposition of Western standards on these traditional forms creates stress for the community and the family, because adapting to both traditional and dominant societal values poses difficulties for both individuals and families.

The problems faced by diverse families underscore the point that families do not exist in a cultural and economic vacuum. Economic changes, racial and cultural conflicts, and gender relations interact to produce family systems. In sum, we can see that no single model of family life characterizes *the* American family, in spite of ideological beliefs to the contrary. Even the feminist perspective that family life is debilitating for women seems questionable when we consider the role of the family in the cultural resistance of minority groups. Sociological perspectives on family life should be sensitive to the interaction of the family with other social institutions and should keep in mind that the ideology of the family often, if not always, departs from the actual structure of both dominant- and subordinate-group family systems. Understanding family experiences for all groups requires an understanding of the intersections of race, class, and gender oppression in the structuring of family life.

❧ *Families and Social Problems*

Violence in the Family

The tensions experienced within families are no more clear than in recognizing the extent of violence that occurs within families. These once-hidden problems now seem disturbingly common. Although accurate measures of the extent of family violence are difficult to establish, researchers estimate that the problem is widespread across families in all classes and races. With regard to wife battering and child abuse, indirect evidence of their extent also comes from police records of domestic disturbances, hospital emergency room files, family court records, homicide rates of women killed by husbands and lovers, and the great number of divorces that cite violence as the primary reason for ending the marriage. Information on incest is even harder to obtain because social taboos against it make incest one of the most hidden of social problems. As victims of incest have spoken out, we have begun to see its high incidence across class and race. Although we have tended to think of violence as most prevalent in lower classes and among minority groups, it is important to point out that it occurs in all groups, although the middle and upper classes have more ability to keep violence secret.

Partner Violence
Studies indicate that the overwhelming amount of domestic violence is directed against women (Kurz, 1989). Coupled with the idea that violence is purposeful behavior, this fact leads to the conclusion that violence against wives is a form of social control—one that emerges directly from the patriarchal structure and ideology of the family. Historically, wife beating has been a legitimate way to express male authority. Scholars contend that the transformation from the feudal patriarchal household to the nuclear family had the effect of strengthening the husband's

power over his wife by placing systems of authority directly in the hands of individual men, not in the indirect rule of the state. Throughout the seventeenth, eighteenth, and nineteenth centuries, men could, within the law, beat their wives, and there was little community objection to their doing so as long as the method and extent of violence remained within certain tacit, and sometimes formally documented, limits. For example, eighteenth-century French law restricted violence against wives to "blows, thumps, kicks, or punches on the back if they leave no traces" and did not allow the use of "sharp edged or crushing instruments" (Castan, 1976, cited in Dobash and Dobash, 1979:56–57). One ancient code, from which we get the phrase *rule of thumb*, allowed a man to beat his wife with a stick no thicker than his thumb (Dobash and Dobash, 1977).

The historical context of wife beating provides a perspective with which to view the contemporary problem. Now, although wife beating is socially abhorred, it is also widely legitimated through its humorous portrayal and through attitudes protecting privacy in marriage. Additionally, the attitude that wives bring violence on themselves (by not leaving) seems to discourage social intervention in violent relationships. As a result, the phenomenon of violence is widely misunderstood. Dobash and Dobash's (1979) early study of Scottish wives gives us some understanding of how violence emerges in marriage and how it is tied to the social isolation and powerlessness of women in the family.

Dobash and Dobash traced the course of 109 relationships that resulted in battering, beginning with the initial courtship phase. During the period when couples first met, both maintained separate lives, including an independent social life with friends and individual commitments to their family, jobs, and education. As the couples' commitments to each other increased, the partners modified their social lives, although women did so more than men. One-quarter of the women went out with their own friends once a week or more, compared with nearly half of the men. The more serious the relationship became, the less time women spent with their own friends.

Prior to marriage, the women reported that sexual jealousy was the major conflict in the relationship, although arguments over jealousy seem to have had the purpose of confirming the couple's commitment to each other. The women became increasingly isolated from their friends before the marriage, and they reported believing that love would take care of any problems that existed in the relationship. Both partners entered marriage with ideals about how the marriage would work, although after a time it was clear that the husband's ideals would rule. Marriage, for the wife, involved an extreme constriction of her social world, and the husband began to believe that he could monopolize his wife, although she could not put similar demands on him. He, as the representative to the outside world, was supposed to have authority, independence, and freedom; she could not question his movements.

In this study, 41 percent of the wives experienced their first attack within six months of the wedding; another 18 percent experienced an attack within the first year of marriage. The wives' response was one of surprise, shock, shame, and guilt, although both partners treated the incident as an exception and assumed, without discussion, that the issue had been resolved. As the marriage continued, however, conflicts repeatedly surfaced. Nearly two-thirds of the couples reported sexual jealousy and expectations about domestic work as the source of conflict leading to violent episodes. The women reported that their social world moved more apart from their husbands' as the marriage went on. The wives were mostly involved in the everyday matters of household management and child care, whereas the husbands were involved in their own work. The husbands, though, still expected their wives to meet their immediate needs.

What is striking about these case studies is how common the patterns in these relationships are. Clearly, wife battering emerges from institutional arrangements that isolate women in the home and give men authority over them. Once a pattern of violence is established, wives believe they have no options. Most will, at some point, leave—even if temporarily—but their feeling that they have no place to go is usually a realistic assessment of their economic situation and their powerlessness to effect changes within the relationship. When wives do stay in abusive relationships, they tend to rationalize the violence to themselves. Research on women who do not leave after battering finds that they use several types of rationalizations, including believing that the man can be "saved" and denying the battering by seeing it as the result of external forces.

In the courts, battered wives are faced with the problem of having to prosecute a man who is both their husband and, possibly, the father of their children. Even if the wife brings charges, when the husband is released, he returns to the home perhaps more angry than when the violence began (Martin, 1976; Miller, 1997). The movement to establish refuges for battered women has assisted many victims in responding to battering, and such centers have proliferated in communities throughout the country. Difficulties in funding such centers have caused many to close, and current cutbacks in social services funding seem likely to pose additional setbacks. Finally, the attitude that family problems are a private matter, to be resolved between two equal partners and within the confines of the home, creates resistance to social changes that could assist battered wives.

Scholars estimate that approximately one-third of all couples have at least one episode of violence at some point in their relationship; ongoing violence is less common. Violence is not confined to marriage, nor to heterosexual couples. Studies show that approximately one-quarter of dating couples experience violence in the relationship (Sugarman and Hotaling, 1991), and comparable rates of violence have been found in same-sex relationships as in heterosexual relationships (West, 1998; Renzetti, 1997). A number of risk factors contribute to the likelihood of violence in any relationship, especially power imbalances that occur between partners, with the least powerful and most dependent partner being most at risk. In addition, patterns such as a prior history of violence (including within one's family of origin), substance abuse, and attempts to end a relationship (separation and divorce) are linked to the likelihood of violence (Kantor and Jasinksi, 1998). Studies of same-sex violence are rare, and conclusions about the causes of violence in lesbian and gay relationships have typically been extrapolated from studies of heterosexual couples, but it appears that the causes of violence in these relationships are similar to those in heterosexual relationships, with the addition of the influence of homophobia. Some have pointed out that homophobia may be used as a weapon in gay and lesbian relationships, such as in threatening to expose the relationship to parents or employers. Internalized homophobia can also lead to patterns of violence (West, 1998; Renzetti, 1997).

The consequences of violence are many, ranging from psychological harm to death. Wives' risk of homicide from family violence is three times that of husbands' (Hampton and Coner-Edwards, 1993) and women are far more likely to be injured through violence. Even when men are the victims of family violence—a phenomenon that has been exaggerated in the media, but does occur—men are less likely to be seriously injured than are women in violent relationships (Brush, 1990). Studies also link numerous health problems to domestic violence (Fischbach and Herbert, 1997). For children, witnessing family violence has a strong effect. Researchers estimate that 11 to 20 percent of children report having witnessed parental violence when they were young (Hennig et al., 1996). This can lead to emotional and physical distress, personality and adjustment problems, disciplinary problems, and educational underachievement, to say nothing of putting children in physical danger (Wolak and Finkelhor, 1998).

Feminist scholars argue that violence is a weapon men use to control women and that gender-neutral explanations ignore the specific patriarchal relationships from which violence stems (Kurz, 1989). This perspective puts the cause of domestic violence in the power dynamics existing between men and women in the family. According to this argument, men abuse their wives as an expression of their power. This has been investigated in a number of studies, particularly those that examine whether women's and men's contributions to family economic resources are related to violence against women. Some studies find that men are more likely to be violent when their financial power in the family is eroded (whether because of low income, unemployment, or a shift in the balance of what husbands and wives contribute to total family income). Violence becomes one way that men maintain their power over women, even when their economic power is diminished (McCloskey, 1996).

Marital Rape

Marital rape is defined as "forced sexual activity demanded of a wife by her husband" (Frieze, 1983). Legal definitions of marital rape vary from state to state, and in many states forced sex is still not considered a crime in marriage. Historically, the "right" to sex was fundamental to the legal definition of marriage (Ryan, 1995). Many still view rape as something that cannot happen in marriage, as shown in studies of undergraduates who minimize the seriousness of rape by a husband compared to rape by a stranger (Monson, Byrd, and Langhinrichsen-Rohling, 1996).

Estimates of marital rape are hard to come by, but most studies find it occurring in 10 to 14 percent of married couples—more common than rape by a stranger. Most wives experiencing marital rape have experienced it multiple times in the marriage (Mahoney and Williams, 1998).

Marital rape is associated with other forms of violence in the relationship. Sometimes wives who have experienced sexual assault in marriage report being forced to engage in sex with their children, with other people, or in public. Sexual assault often occurs when the couple is in the process of separation or divorce or when the husband suspects sexual infidelity. Marital rape has also been found to be common when the wife is ill, pregnant, or has just given birth. Studies of offenders find that themes of power, control, dominance, and humiliation are common among these men and that they are likely to believe rape myths, such as that their wives enjoyed being forced to have sex. Male offenders also typically do not understand the harm they have caused as the result of their violence (Mahoney and Williams, 1998).

Wives in these marriages have few resources of their own to draw on, exacerbating their powerlessness in this situation; moreover, the belief that sexual access is a right in marriage allows the idea that they have not been raped. The evidence on marital rape nonetheless shows the extent to which the definition of women as the property of men continues to affect marital relationships.

Incest and Sexual Abuse

Accurate estimates of the extent of incest and sexual abuse are very difficult to establish. Russell's (1986) study, the most widely cited, indicates that 16 percent of women have been sexually abused by a relative by the time they are 18 years old; other forms of incest range between 4 and 12 percent of the population. Girls are far more likely to be abused than boys and, when they are, to experience greater harm (Nelson and Oliver, 1998).

Feminist clinicians who have studied incest have challenged traditional Freudian assumptions about incest, which presume that children lie or fantasize about incestuous sexual encounters. Those subjected to incest do try to stop the incest by seeking help or striking back, although often they are not believed. Research from feminist clinicians has shown that families in which incest occurs tend to share several characteristics, the most significant of which is the estrangement of mother and daughter.

Mothers may be aware of incestuous abuse, but they are typically powerless to stop it. A mother may become a silent bystander because her emotional and/or economic dependence on her husband prevents her from confronting the situation (Armstrong and Begus, 1982). Particularly in families where mothers are unusually powerless as a result of battering, disability, or mental illness there is an especially high risk of sexual abuse, especially among daughters who have taken on the household responsibilities. In such families, the daughter is often led to believe that she must comply with the father's demands if she is to hold the family together (Herman and Hirschman, 1977). Molested daughters in this situation are still dependent on their fathers for care and, since this may be the only affection they receive, they often report warm feelings for their fathers, who make them feel special (Herman, 1981).

This research finds that the father/assailant feels no contrition about his behavior. When mothers are incapacitated, fathers do not take on the nurturing functions, nor do they express nurturing feelings for the child or understand the destructiveness of the incest. Fathers typically blamed their wives or their daughters for the incest and, distressingly, Herman finds that daughters often reinforce this view, blaming the mothers and themselves, while exonerating the fathers (Herman, 1981).

This portrait of incestuous behavior underscores that the intersection of power and gender relations in families is a contributing fact in incestuous behavior. Researchers also are only now beginning to see the multiple consequences of sexual abuse. For example, childhood abuse is linked to a variety of social problems, including delinquency, substance abuse, developmental problems, and later violence in relationships (Milner and Crouch, 1993; Hernandez, 1995; Conte, 1993). These findings also suggest that sexual abuse is important for practitioners to consider when developing treatment programs for other social problems concerning women and young girls.

Feminists have pointed to violence as the logical result of both women's powerlessness in the family and a male culture that emphasizes aggression, domination, and violence. The modern form of the family leads women to be economically and emotionally dependent on men, and, as a result, the traditional family is a source of social conflict and a haven only for men (Hartmann, 1981a). The phenomenon of violence in the family shows clearly the problems that traditional family structures create for women. Feminist criticism of the family rests, in part, on the psychological, physical, and economic threats families pose for women, and it is for those reasons that feminists argue for a change in traditional family structures. These changes, intended to empower women, would not necessarily abolish the family, but they would create new values regarding women's work in the family and new rewards for women in the family, regardless of whether they are also working in the public labor force.

Teen Pregnancy

Since 1990, the teen birth rate has actually been declining, although at a rate of 58.9 births per 1,000 women, the rate is much higher than it was in 1980 (53 per 1,000 women). Contrary to popular stereotypes, the rate of increase in teen births is higher among White teens than any other racial group (U.S. Census Bureau, 1997). The most significant change has been in the rate of births to unmarried women—a phenomenon affecting all age groups, but most pronounced among White women, where the rate of birth to unmarried women increased from 17.6 per 1,000 women in 1980 to 38.2 in 1994. In the same period, the rate for Black women actually went down, although not by much—from 82.9 per 1,000 to 82.1 per 1,000 (U.S. Census Bureau, 1997). Teen mothers face higher medical risks in pregnancy and are more likely to have low-birth-weight babies, which, in turn, is a major cause of infant mortality. The recent increase in infant mortality rates, which had previously been on the decline since 1940, is probably due in large part to the increase in teenage pregnancy.

In addition to the health problems, teenage parents face chronic unemployment or, when they work, low earnings and low-status jobs. In 1997, the unemployment rate for Black teenage males was 36.5 percent; for White teenage males, 14.3 percent; and for Hispanic teenage males, 20.8 percent. For teenage females, unemployment was 28.7 percent for Blacks, 12.8 percent for Whites, and 22.7 percent for Hispanics (U.S. Department of Labor, 1998). It is little wonder that, despite the fact that teen parents initially perceive welfare to be only a temporary means of providing for their children, their situation encourages long-term welfare dependency (Ladner, 1986).

Approximately 85 percent of teenage mothers continue to live with their families, many of whom are themselves single-female heads of household who were also teenage mothers. One-third of teen mothers live in poverty, regardless of race; those who live on their own are more likely to be poor. Regardless of their race and class background, teen mothers do value marriage as an ideal, but they are not sure they will ever marry. Compared to teen mothers of the past, present-day teen mothers from all races and classes feel much less pressure to marry. Although they do regard childbearing as a marital event, they also see sex as separated from marriage. Teens no longer think that marriage is necessary to legitimate a birth. They remain unmarried because they think fathers are unwilling or not ready to marry, because they are not ready for marriage, and because their families counsel them against marrying precipitously (Farber, 1990).

Poor African American teen women also tend to be more cynical about men than are White teen women. Poor African American teen women do not expect that men will be responsible for their families; although they want men to be committed to them, they do not expect their hopes to be fulfilled (Farber, 1990). Considering the high rates of imprisonment and unemployment among young African American men, these doubts are realistic. Ladner's study of two generations of teenage mothers (where grandmothers are only in their thirties and one is only age 29) shows that they feel resigned to their plight. Compared with a similar population whom Ladner studied more than 30 years ago, these women's futures are harsher and bleaker than those of their earlier counterparts who had high hopes for positive and productive futures (Ladner and Gourdine, 1984).

Working-class and middle-class teens (both African American and White) have career expectations that act as an incentive to keep them unmarried; they are likely to see marriage as an impediment to further education and job experience (Farber, 1990). African American teen mothers, however, are more likely than White or Hispanic teen mothers to continue attending school (Trent and Harlan, 1990).

Sociological studies of African American teen mothers show that, contrary to stereotypical views, the Black community does not condone teen pregnancy. Elaine Kaplan (1997) has done detailed ethnographic research in two communities in the San Francisco Bay Area: East Oakland and Richmond, both communities with a large African American population. These neighborhoods are characterized by high rates of unemployment, poverty, inadequate schools, crime and drug-related violence and high numbers of single-parent households. Kaplan spent several months in the community, working as a volunteer in a community teen center, "hanging out" with a group of teen mothers. She interviewed the teen mothers and, when she could, their mothers and, sometimes, the fathers of their children. Kaplan found that, unlike what stereotypes would suggest, the teens were embarrassed by being pregnant and had numerous conflicts with their mothers, who saw their daughters' pregnancies as disrupting the hopes they had for their daughters' success. The teen mothers were also ashamed of having to go on welfare and, if they did, they tried to hide that they needed welfare to make ends meet. These conclusions are directly counter to the public image that such women do not value success and live in a culture that promotes welfare dependency.

The high rate of teenage pregnancy has caused much concern over the issue of birth control and the sexual behavior of young people. Since the early 1970s, birth control has become widely available, and evidence shows that an increasing number of women and men now engage in sexual intercourse before marriage. About four in five people have sexual intercourse while they are teenagers, most initiating sex in their mid to late teens. About two-thirds use a contraceptive during their first experience with intercourse—a number that has increased in recent years because of an increase in condom use among teens.

Among teens using birth control, the most frequent contraceptive is the pill (44 percent), followed by the condom (38 percent), injectable birth control (10 percent), withdrawal (4 percent), and the implant (3 percent). The number of teens using birth control has increased in recent years, perhaps due to widespread publicity about AIDS and safe sex, perhaps contributing to the recent decline in teen pregnancy. Ease of use, such as with "the shot" (injectable birth control), has likely increased effective use of contraceptives by younger women. Women under age 24 are the group most likely to use the injectable and the implant for birth control (Alan Guttmacher Institute, 1998).

Still, a large number of young women have sex without birth control (35 percent). A sexually active teen who does not use contraception has a 90 percent chance of getting pregnant within one year (Alan Guttmacher Institute, 1998). Many have argued that a sociological reason for young women not using birth control is that the regular use of contraceptives requires conscious recognition of oneself as sexually active (Luker, 1975). Teenage sex tends to be episodic; for a young woman to make calculated plans for contraceptive protection requires her to see herself as a sexually active person. Cultural and legal proscriptions that encourage the denial of sexuality to young women seem likely only to exacerbate this situation.

Many also argue that sex education does not filter down to adolescents before they start having sex. Girls often have little or no information about their bodies and are often seriously misinformed about sex (for example, believing they cannot get pregnant if they are standing up during intercourse!). The fact that mothers, not fathers, talk to their children about sex also spreads the message that men have no responsibility in this area, discouraging young men from being responsible for birth control and resting the decision to avoid pregnancy only on young girls. Researchers find that pregnant teens romanticize the demands of motherhood, and many believe they can give their babies a better life than they received. Because adolescent pregnancy disproportionately affects poor and minority youth, having children may be their only way of achieving masculinity or femininity in a society that denies them the expression of these traits in adult roles (Ladner, 1986; Horowitz, 1995).

Adolescents who do get pregnant are more traditional in their gender-role orientation than other sexually active young teens. They perceive themselves as competent in highly gender-typed activities, have lower aspirations and grades, and have less of a sense of personal control. Teenagers who get pregnant are also more likely to rely on God to determine the course of their lives, indicating that both traditional gender roles and religious beliefs influence the problem of teenage pregnancy (Ireson, 1984). This should lead us to conclude that programs and policies designed to alleviate the problems of teenage pregnancy must recognize the importance of gender relations in understanding the character of this growing social problem. It has been demonstrated that more egalitarian gender-role attitudes are associated with the belief in contraceptive use; moreover, young men with egalitarian gender-role attitudes are more likely to use contraceptives in premarital intercourse than are young men with more sexist attitudes (MacCorquodale, 1984).

Child Care

Child care in the United States is, by virtue of the character of the family, largely a system of private care. The parent-child unit is allegedly self-sufficient and, given the gender division of labor, the responsibility for child care falls heavily on individual women. The experience of mothers (or other caregivers) is based on the assumption that children are best cared for by their biological mother. Exceptions to this design do exist, although even then the arrangements for child care are usually managed by the mother, and it is other women who do the work. Although it is more and more impractical to do so, mothers usually have the major responsibility for the everyday care of their children.

The privatized and exclusive character of child care seems especially inappropriate when we consider the labor force participation rate of mothers. As already noted, recent increases in the labor force participation rate are highest among women with children, especially women with children of preschool age.

Women's access to child care can significantly influence their prospects for employment. Since the cost of child care can be a significant deterrent to women seeking employment (see Figure 6.5), many must rely on kin or other volunteers for child care. A study of Puerto Rican and African American single mothers, for example, found that having relatives aged 16 to 64 and other young children at home made it more likely that Puerto Rican and African American single mothers would be employed (Figueroa and Melendez, 1993). Such findings show how important extended kin networks can be in facilitating women's access to jobs of their own and indicate the role families play in providing a kind of volunteer welfare system.

In another vein, it has been found that women who rely on their husbands for child care are more likely to quit paid jobs than are women who have other child care arrangements. This research finds that men resist caring for children for any length of time when their wives are employed. Low-income women are especially likely to leave paid jobs under these circumstances, since they likely have fewer options for child care than do women of greater means (Maume and Mullin,

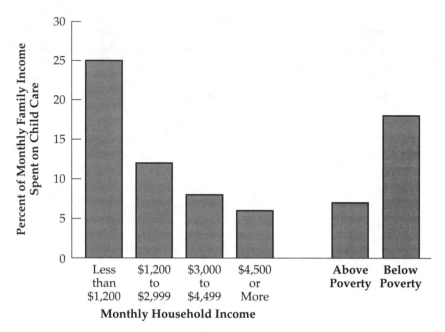

FIGURE 6.5   The Cost of Child Care (as Percent of Monthly Family Income)

Source: Data from Lynne M. Casper. 1995. "What Does It Cost to Mind Our Pre-schoolers?" Washington, DC: U.S. Census Bureau, p. 4; Website

1993). In general, however, the demand for child care is greater than the supply. Employed women then use a variety of arrangements to care for their children, with most being cared for by another relative (see Figure 6.6). Note that for non-school-aged children, two-thirds are cared for either in their homes or in another private home. Fewer than one-third are tended in organized child care facilities (Casper, 1995).

These facts suggest the need to imagine new models and policies for child care in society. Historically, depression and war have provided the major impetus for establishing public child care facilities in the United States. Public child care in the United States first originated in the Works Progress Administration (WPA) of the New Deal. In the 1930s, WPA day care and nursery schools were designed to provide employment for needy teachers, child care workers, cooks, janitors, nutritionists, and clerical workers during the Depression. By the end of the Depression and the beginning of World War II, when jobs were no longer in short supply, the WPA nurseries were eliminated. In 1941, the Lanham Act (also known as the Community Facilities Act) was passed by Congress to meet the day care needs of mothers in wartime employment. The Lanham Act made matching federal funds available to states for the expansion of day care centers and nursery schools. Following World War II, when women were no longer needed in the labor force,

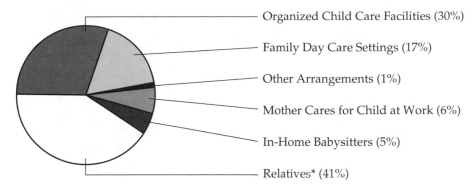

Organized Child Care Facilities (30%)

Family Day Care Settings (17%)

Other Arrangements (1%)

Mother Cares for Child at Work (6%)

In-Home Babysitters (5%)

Relatives* (41%)

*Includes fathers, siblings, grandparents, and other relatives

FIGURE 6.6   Child Care for Preschoolers

Source: Data from Lynne M. Casper. 1995. "What Does It Cost to Mind Our Preschoolers?" Washington, DC: U.S. Census Bureau; Website

Congress withdrew funds for day care, and most of the Lanham Act nurseries closed (Baxandall, 1979).

Since World War II, federally funded day care programs have been established for the poor. For example, Project Head Start, funded through the Office of Economic Opportunity, was designed primarily for children from families below the poverty line. In the past, public attitudes toward funded child care were stigmatized by the association of federally supported child care with welfare services, but support for increased availability of child care services now runs high.

The public has become far more accepting of mothers being employed, and most women and men believe that society is now less critical of women being employed while they raise children. At the same time, women and men also accept that having two employed parents is stressful for the family and that these parents miss out on sharing more time with their children. But men and women also see that there are positive benefits to children of having both parents employed, including that they learn to be more responsible and are more open-minded about the roles of women (Roper Organization, 1995).

That women are still socially defined as primarily responsible for children is well illustrated by the now widely recognized phenomenon of *deadbeat dads*—those who, following a custody and support agreement, abandon financial support of their children. What kind of child support do women receive following divorce? Only 24 percent of women actually receive the full amount they are due. In the rare cases where women owe men child support, men are more likely to receive it. Yet, women are more economically dependent on receiving support for their children; support payments, on average, constitute 17 percent of the women's total income (only 7 percent for men). Fewer than half of all awards made include health benefits for the children (U.S. Census Bureau, 1995). In these situations, women can feel stuck. They are unlikely to have the resources needed to pursue legally what they are owed. In many cases, particularly those involving young, uneducated men, the father may be unable to pay.

With the number of young people increasing in society and the rate of poverty now being highest among young people, there is a compelling argument for more socially supported programs for child care and child support. Without this, a new generation of people will face economic hardship and the social disadvantage that follows. Simply leaving child care needs for individual women and men to handle on their own, although reflecting beliefs about women's responsibility for family life, will not serve the overall needs of children and their society well.

❧ Summary

Historical legacies glorify the home as a refuge and idealize women's roles within the home. Today, the family is a rapidly changing institution, and the traditional family ideal is realized by only a small minority of U.S. families. Modern families are characterized by an emphasis on child rearing, assumed separation of work from home, and idealization of the home as women's world. The emergence of capitalism has affected family structure by shifting economically valued labor outside of the home and into public workplaces. Patriarchal societies regulate women's roles in the family by making men the basis for authority. The historical development of families is situated in race, class, and gender relations in the society.

Feminists distinguish between families and households to emphasize the economic functions of households. The family is an ideological concept. Feminists also see families as social, not natural, units and note that men and women experience families in different ways.

Contemporary U.S. households are characterized by high rates of divorce and an increase in the number of households headed by women. Households consist of many types, including married couples, cohabitors, dual-career couples, gay and lesbian couples, and singles, to name some. Each of these types of households has a unique sociological reality that shapes the experience and consciousness of its members. Balancing work and family commitments is increasingly difficult and calls for redefinition of traditional gender roles, as well as increased societal support systems for personal and family needs.

Race, class, and gender influences shape family experiences. African American, Chicano, Puerto Rican, Asian American, and Native American families have been subjected to policies that have destabilized families. Although minority families have been characterized in terms of cultural pathology, societal conditions of racism and sexism shape family structure.

A number of contemporary social problems are located in families. Violence against women in the family—in the form of battering, marital rape, and incest—reflects the powerlessness of women in society. Adolescent pregnancy is also increasing and results in higher rates of poverty among female-headed households. Finally, changes in family organization have created greater societal needs for child care. Resistance to organized child care stems, in part, from the continuing belief that only biological mothers can best care for children. In sum, new policies are needed that provide supports for the diverse needs of families and recognize the new demands placed by changing systems of work and family life.

❧ *Key Terms*

antimiscegenation	household	nuclear family
cult of domesticity	householder	subfamily
family	marital rape	transnational family
family household	matriarchy	

❧ *Discussion Questions/Projects for Thought*

1. Identify two families that could be described as having different structural characteristics (i.e., married working couple, commuting marriage, divorced head of household, lesbian couple, single-parent household, etc.) and interview each family member (including any children) about who does what work in the family, including finances, child care, housework, managing social relations, and so on. What does your project tell you about gender and the household division of labor?

2. Identify a group of working mothers and/or fathers and interview them about their child care practices, including questions such as: Who cares for the child when the parent(s)

work? What happens when the child is sick? How much does the child care cost and who pays? When do problems arise and how are they solved? What does your research on this reveal about gender and child care? What new policies would you recommend to provide affordable child care to working parents?

3. Find out if there is a shelter for battered women in your community. If so, interview some of the workers there and ask them about the patterns they see among those who come to the shelter. What do they think would stop violence against women? Do you agree?

❧ *Suggested Readings*

Baca Zinn, Maxine, and Stanley D. Eitzen. 1999. *Diversity in American Families*. New York: Addison Wesley Longman.
This comprehensive text reviews all aspects of family life from a sociological perspective and with a focus on the importance of race, class, and gender in shaping different family experiences.

Hansen, Karen V., and Anita Ilta Garey, eds. 1998. *Families in the U.S.: Kinship and Domestic Policies*. Philadelphia: Temple University Press.
This anthology is a comprehensive review of research on diverse family forms and experiences. It is an excellent introduction to social-science research on families and also

utilizes a historical perspective to frame an understanding of families in the United States.

Jasinski, Jana L., and Linda M. Williams, eds. 1998. *Partner Violence: A Comprehensive Review of 20 Years of Research.* Thousand Oaks, CA: Sage.

Reviewing the empirical and theoretical research on violence, the authors in this anthology document and analyze the violence that occurs in different kinds of relationships, including marriage, parent-child violence, and violence within gay and lesbian relationships.

Kaplan, Elaine Bell. 1997. *Not Our Kind of Girl: Unraveling the Myths of Black Teenage Motherhood.* Berkeley: University of California Press.

Kaplan's study of African American teenage mothers challenges social myths and stereotypes about these young women and their families. Her ethnographic study provides an empathetic portrait of the experience of these young women in confronting racism, sexism, and class disadvantage.

Kurz, Demi. 1995. *For Richer, For Poorer: Mothers Confront Divorce.* New York: Routledge.

This study of divorced mothers shows the economic and sociological impact of divorce on women. It provides a feminist framework for family policies that would be more supportive of women and children.

O'Tolle, Laura L., and Jessica R. Schiffman, eds. 1997. *Gender Violence: Interdisciplinary Perspectives.* New York: New University Press.

This anthology includes articles from a wide variety of perspectives, all of which are intended to help understand diverse forms of violence against women, children, and, in some cases, men. Together, the essays provide a comprehensive review of current thinking about gender and violence.

Stacey, Judith. 1996. *In the Name of the Family.* Boston: Beacon Press.

Based on a feminist perspective, Stacey examines the family values debate, pointing to areas where social policy could improve the status of women.

Weston, Kath. 1991. *Families We Choose: Lesbians, Gays, Kinship.* New York: Columbia University Press.

Weston challenges traditional views of kinship by developing an analysis of gay and lesbian families. Her work helps us conceptualize how families are defined and how to think about family social policy to incorporate all family forms.

Chapter 7
Women, Health, and Reproduction

Almost any day on the news, you might hear a report about a new medical research study that gives new insight into some aspect of a disease or health problem. Have you ever stopped to ask who such studies represent and what the implications of this research are for women? If you did, you might very well find out that all of the subjects in the study were men and that the same insights or procedures that medical researchers are heralding as advancing medical science have not been at all considered for their implications for women's health. Such was the case when the Office of Research on Women's Health of the National Institutes of Health (NIH) was founded in 1990. NIH founded this office in response to criticism that women had been routinely excluded from research sponsored by NIH, including such now well-known studies as the one showing that taking one aspirin per day can prevent some heart attacks. The research sample for this study was 22,000 men, all of them doctors; women were excluded on the grounds that there were not enough women doctors to include them in the research sample. As a result, despite this study's revelations, we simply do not know what effect taking aspirin each day might have on women, relative to heart attacks. Perhaps it would not make any difference if we did know, since another study found later that doctors treat women with heart disease less aggressively than they treat men with heart disease. Women with heart disease are far less likely to undergo common diagnostic procedures for heart conditions, and they are less likely to have bypass surgery or angioplasty, even though women in the study tended to have more advanced heart disease than the male subjects (Steingart et al., 1991; Ayanian and Epstein, 1991).

Consider the attention given to Viagra, the drug that treats male impotency and for which the scientists who did the basic research underlying its functioning were given the Nobel Prize. Would fewer women be dying from breast cancer if such resources were poured into its study? Would women be healthier if the resources were directed toward dieting, battering, eating disorders, or the prevention of smoking?

Physical health is one of the most basic of life's privileges. Although we tend to think of our bodies as best cared for through personal hygiene and individual diet and health habits, in fact, physical health is heavily influenced by sociological factors. One of those factors, gender, plays a significant part in determining physical well-being and in influencing our bodily experience, as do race and class.

For instance, the likelihood that one will encounter stress, become overweight, experience hypertension, or die of certain diseases is significantly affected by one's gender. National health statistics show that hypertension is more common among women than men (at all ages). National data also show that, under age 45, men are more likely to be overweight than women, although the reverse is true after this age. In all cases, along with gender and age, racial status is a complicating factor in predicting health. For example, African Americans are far more likely to experience disability, to develop hypertension, and to suffer from poor nutrition (U.S. Census Bureau, 1997; National Center for Health Statistics, 1998).

These data indicate that physical health is mediated by social and cultural organizations. For this reason, gender influences not only what we will become but also how long our lives will be and how we are likely to die. Gender, along with race and class, also affects access to health care. Men are less likely to be covered by medical insurance than are women, for example (U.S. Census Bureau, 1997). Gender relations in the society are also reflected in institutional patterns of health care systems. Health care institutions in this society are dominated by men, even though healing and caring for others have traditionally been defined as the work of women. Because of the structure of health care in this society, women have had little control over their own reproductive lives. Throughout this chapter, you will see that gender relations are important in determining the character of health and reproduction in contemporary U.S. society.

❧ The Social Structure of Health

Gender Roles and Health

Male and female health patterns change according to the social arrangements of the time. For instance, in the late nineteenth century, illness was quite fashionable for women—at least those of the upper-middle and upper classes. Women in these classes were expected to be idle and faint; consequently, retiring to bed because of "nerves" was not only acceptable but actually encouraged by medical practitioners (Ehrenreich and English, 1973a).

Differences in life expectancy for men and women did not emerge in U.S. society until the beginning of the twentieth century. Even now, longer life expectancy for women occurs primarily in highly industrialized Western societies. Gender differences in mortality rates are because of a number of factors, most of which are culturally shaped by gender relations. Changes in women's roles mean that women now approximate men in the rate of death by heart disease, whereas as recently as 1980, men were far more likely to die by this cause (U.S. Census

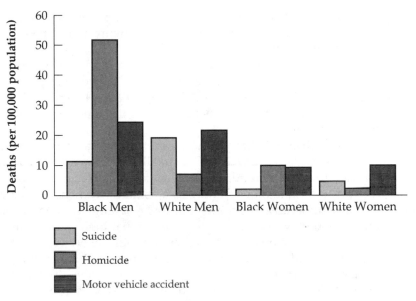

FIGURE 7.1   Death Rates: 1996

Source: Data from National Center for Health Statistics. 1998. *Health, United States, 1998.* Hyattsville, MD: U.S. Government Printing Office, p. 83.

Bureau, 1997). Mortality differences between men and women are determined by men's greater risk of death by accident (see Figure 7.1), itself a function of men's engagement in risky behavior, violent activity, and alcohol consumption (Harrison, Chin, and Ficarrotto, 1988).

Women's health, like men's, varies according to the sociological features of their lives. Studies have indicated, for example, that there are higher rates of reported illness among housewives than among women working outside the home, indicating that employment generally has positive effects on women's health. This effect, however, is mediated by other variables. For example, the characteristics of the work site (i.e., job demands, rewards and deprivations, physical environment, and social support) also influence the well-being of workers, regardless of gender (Loscocco and Spitze, 1990).

There is little evidence that combining employment and motherhood has harmful health effects (Waldron, Weiss, and Hughes, 1998). What is significant in predicting women's health and mental health are such factors as income, life satisfaction, and social contacts. Thus, women who at mid-life feel they have fallen short of their career aspirations experience higher levels of depression than women who feel more fulfilled (Carr, 1997). Financial strain for all groups is not only related to poor physical health but also to increased stress and depression. In one study examining mental health differences among married and unmarried mothers, researchers found that mothers who become employed experience little change in their levels of stress, since increases in the the stress of managing caregiving activities are offset by a decline in financial stress (Ali and Avison, 1997).

Generally speaking, whether a woman is employed or not, depression is associated with having to do routine things repeatedly and being responsible for things beyond one's control (Lennon, 1994). For housewives, depression is also reduced if women have a range of social contacts; thus, women with young children at home or those with limited social support networks experience higher rates of depression (Shehan, Burg, and Rexroat, 1986). Together, these studies demonstrate the significance of gender in shaping life conditions, and therefore women's physical and mental health.

Mental health is strongly associated with gender, race, and class status. Most studies indicate higher rates of mental illness for women than for men, at least as indicated by hospital admissions, clinical treatment, and the duration of treatment. Some explain this finding as a result of women's secondary status in society, which, because it produces stress, results in women becoming mentally ill more frequently than men. Others argue that high rates of mental illness among women reflect the fact that women are more likely to report mental problems, seek help, and think of themselves as emotional and lacking self-control. This explanation interprets women's higher mental-illness rate as the consequence of learned gender-role behavior. Both explanations are probably correct, underscoring the point that mental as well as physical health is connected to the status in society. These data suggest the need for change in women's traditional status—a point that is underscored by a study showing that women living in nontraditional relationships are less depressed than women living in traditional ones. Men living in nontraditional relationships are more depressed than comparable women (Rosenfield, 1980), which may indicate the personal needs and services that women in traditional relationships provide for men but not for themselves.

❧ Race, Class, and Health

Racial-ethnic and class oppression in U.S. society further complicate patterns of health in men and women. Examination of health statistics by race shows significant differences in the patterns of health for different groups, with death rates by cerebrovascular disease, homicide, and diabetes, for example, significantly higher for Black Americans than for White Americans. In all age groups, hypertension among Black women exceeds that of both White and Hispanic women; for all women, the rates of hypertension increase as they age (National Center for Health Statistics, 1998; see Figure 7.2). Although maternal death from the complications of pregnancy has decreased since 1960, women of color are twice as likely to die from causes related to pregnancy as are White women (Horton, 1995); the rate of death from ectopic pregnancy is five times as high among women of color as among White women, in part because Black, American Indian, and Hispanic women are less likely to receive prenatal care than White and Asian American women (Horton, 1995; Centers for Disease Control, 1998). Racial patterns also appear in studying the incidence of cancer among different populations, with a greater incidence of most forms of cancer among White women than women of color (National Cancer Institute, 1998).

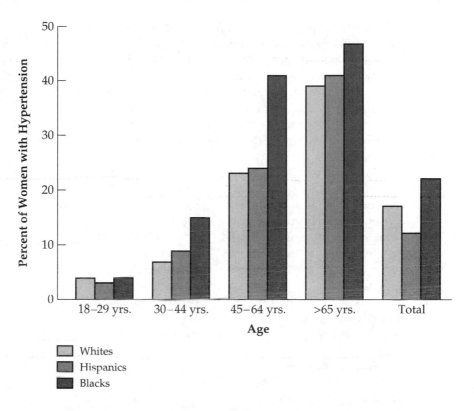

FIGURE 7.2   Women with Hypertension (percent by age)

Source: Data from Jacqueline A. Horton (Ed.). 1995. *The Women's Health Data Book.* Washington, DC: The Jacobs Institute of Women's Health, p. 58.

The effects of racial inequality on health are dramatically shown by data on accidental deaths. As shown in Figure 7.1, death caused by accident is greater among Black men than White men. Note the very high rate of death by homicide among Black men. Suicide rates among Black men are lower than among White men, although suicide among Black men has been increasing in recent years. Suicide rates for Black women are half those for White women. In would appear that, although violent death is more common for Black Americans, cultural values and the economic dependence of families on Black women's work influence the lesser degree of suicide among them.

Native Americans' health is also affected by the degree of oppression they experience. Their mortality rates are especially high among the young, particularly young men; moreover, Native Americans are twice as likely to die by homicide than are others in the general population (Snipp, 1996).

Among women, race and social class significantly affect chances for good health and for exercising some degree of control over their own bodies. Poor women do not have the same expectations as middle-class women of being able to alter their birth experiences. As a result, they are less likely to question some of the obstetrical practices (such as separating the mother and the newborn baby) that middle-class women have challenged (Hurst and Zambrana, 1980).

Infant mortality, one of the major indices of the health of a population, is still almost twice as high for African Americans as for Whites. Although infant mortality rates have been decreasing over recent years, the rate of decline in infant mortality, especially among African Americans, has slowed. Black and Puerto Rican Americans are also more likely to have low-birth-weight babies, a fact that contributes to infant mortality and represents the health problems faced by these mothers.

Both historically and now, women of color and poor women have been denied control over their reproductive lives. Studies indicate that very high percentages of poor and minority women have been sterilized, often without their consent. African American and Hispanic women are more likely than White women to have been sterilized (Horton, 1995). Although this may be voluntary, poor women are often coerced into sterilization. One study, conducted in the 1970s, found that 42.3 percent of the women living in East Harlem had had either a tubal ligation or a hysterectomy. In most cases, the doctor had recommended it to the patient but had given her incorrect information about the consequences (Hurst and Zambrana, 1980). Other studies indicate that among samples of welfare mothers, approximately half have been sterilized; welfare women have had approximately one-third more sterilizations than other women (Gordon, 1977).

Much of the difference in health along lines of race is also attributable to social class. Social class has long been shown to have a strong influence on both physical and mental health, with poverty, in particular, having a strong influence on both access to health care and actual physical and mental well-being. Chronic illness is higher among less prosperous groups, as are disabilities, infectious diseases, and, as we have seen, infant mortality. There is little wonder that the higher one's social class, the better one's chance of a long and healthier life. The fact that racial inequality in this society results in higher rates of poverty for Native Americans, Latinos, and African Americans is a major factor in considering the health care of these diverse populations (Williams, 1998; Council of Economic Advisors, 1998).

✿ Women, Work, and Health

As the discussion of race, class, and health shows, health is influenced by the social context in which people live. Sociological studies of health look to the environment in which people are located to understand the various health risks that different groups experience. Work environments are an important site for understanding the health risks faced by women and men; moreover, because work organizations are shaped by gender, work may have a different impact on health for women than for men.

The mythology of work in U.S. culture is that it provides an avenue for self-expression and the realization of personal goals. We have increasingly come to see, however, that work can be hazardous to physical and mental health. Toxic chemicals in the workplace produce risks for workers, although, typically, public attention to those risks for women has focused primarily on their reproductive health. Stress is also a significant health problem for workers in different environments; for women, this is more acute because of the double day employed women experience at work and at home. Studies of different occupational health hazards also reveal how these health risks are structured by the gender segregation that characterizes the workplace.

Work Environments and Health

Gender-biased definitions have caused us to ignore the work environments of many women. One telling example comes from national surveys of cancer mortality in various occupational groups. These studies typically do not consider housework to be an occupation, and consequently have provided no data comparing cancer rates among housewives and other workers. One early study showed, however, that housewives have a far greater death rate by cancer than any other occupational group of women (Morton and Ungs, 1979). The work that women do in the home exposes them to a wide variety of toxic substances; moreover, none of these substances is subject to the control systems advocated for use in industrial settings, nor are the workers who use them instructed to wear protective equipment or to be periodically screened for toxic contamination. Additionally, although these substances are often used together during household cleaning, little is known about their potentially hazardous combination. Because housework is seldom considered to be real work, little public attention has been given to the carcinogens and toxic substances used, nor has the high death rate by cancer among housewives been widely discussed.

Obviously, the health risks for both male and female workers are great. Both men's and women's work involves stress and physical dangers other than toxic risks. Job-related stress leads to an increased risk of disease even without direct physical hazard on the job, and stress can be caused by a host of factors, including monotony, human relations, time demands, insecurity, and relative powerlessness.

The increasing use of video display monitors in the workplace, for example, poses new questions about workers' health. Millions of workers in the United States use computers, and their numbers are increasing at a very rapid rate. Given the fact of gender segregation in jobs where computers are most extensively used, the majority of workers using computer monitors are women. Workers who work at computers for long periods of time, many of whom are women, are subject to carpal tunnel syndrome, eye strain, and back problems.

Reproduction and Protective Legislation

When considering issues of work and health, it is easy to see that work and gender are closely bound together. As noted previously, concern about women's work and health has almost exclusively focused on women's reproductive health (Novkov, 1996; McCammon, 1995; Crenshaw, 1995). Interestingly, however, few ever consider how reproductive hazards for men are related to their work, leading to the erroneous conclusion, based on sexist premises, that only women reproduce. Clearly, occupational toxic agents and carcinogens can equally affect male sperm; yet **protective legislation** against reproductive hazards is almost always aimed at women workers.

In the 1920s, the Women's League for Equal Opportunity staunchly opposed the protective legislation proposed by groups such as the Women's Trade Union League and the Consumer League of New York. They argued that consumer restrictions on the conditions of labor should be based on the nature of the industry, not on the sex of the worker (Stellman, 1977:36); yet, history shows that protective laws apply specifically to women workers. The Supreme Court decision in *Muller* v. *Oregon*, for example, held in 1908 that it was constitutional to restrict the work day to 10 hours for women only. Protecting workers from long work days and unhealthy environments is a reasonable action, but when applied only to women, these laws exclude women from jobs under the benign guise of protection (Chavkin, 1979).

Contemporary protective legislation has also been used to exclude women from work in trades in which the hazards seem no greater than those in some traditionally gender-segregated female occupations. For instance, Title VII of the 1964 Civil Rights Act prohibited employment discrimination on the basis of sex, race, color, religion, and national origin. It also provided for bona fide occupational qualification (BFOQ), which made it lawful to hire on the basis of sex when sex is a reasonable qualification for performance on the job (Hill, 1979). For instance, the BFOQ clause allowed women to be excluded from jobs exceeding weight-lifting limitations set only for women. That weight restrictions on women's work are based on gender stereotypes is clearly shown by the fact that such restrictions do not appear in occupations that are typically female (such as waitressing) and that involve strenuous physical effort.

Subsequent court cases made it clear that the BFOQ clause could be applied only in a very restricted way. In both *Weeks* v. *Southern Bell Telephone and Telegraph Company* and *Rosenfeld* v. *Southern Pacific Company*, the courts ruled that individual women, like individual men, have to be given the opportunity to show that they are physically qualified for a job (Hill, 1979). Overall, however, Title VII has been the basis for eliminating much protective legislation. In 1991, the Supreme Court ruled (in *Automobile Workers* v. *Johnson Controls*) that it was discriminatory to bar women from high-risk jobs in which there was potential harm to a fetus or reproductive system. Prior arguments for protective legislation assumed that pregnant women and fetuses are especially susceptible to toxic chemicals, radiation, and other risks. Although there is little doubt that these hazards do affect pregnant women and fetuses, they affect the reproductive health of men, as well. Legislation or company practices that apply to women only rest on the faulty assumption that only women reproduce. There is evidence of the damaging effects of lead poisoning on male sperm, the excess of chromosomal aberrations among male vinyl chloride workers, and the causal relationship between the pesticide dibromochloropropane (DBCP) and male sterility (Wright, 1979). Wives of male chloride workers also have excessive rates of stillbirths and miscarriages

(Infante, 1975). Removing only women from jobs in which they may be exposed to these substances clearly does not protect the reproductive health of the population.

Gender-biased assumptions in protective regulations are intricately bound to the gender-segregated character of the labor force. Concern for women's health has not caused companies to remove workers from jobs traditionally considered women's work—in spite of known risks from mutagens, teratogens, and toxic substances that are found in occupations employing mostly women. For example, women who work in hospital operating rooms as nurse-anesthetists, anesthesiologists, and scrub personnel have higher rates of miscarriages and birth malformations than other groups of workers, but no one has argued that women should be excluded from these jobs (Hunt, 1979; Wright, 1979). Protective policies that restrict women from hazardous jobs seem to emerge only in higher-paying and traditionally male occupations in which women are now beginning to be employed (Chavkin, 1979). Other occupations that pose equally serious hazards, yet are poorly paid and are filled by women, are usually excluded from protective legislation. Similarly, risks to the male reproductive system seldom are used to restrict their employment opportunities. In fact, one bizarre suggestion has been made that male workers exposed to sterility-causing DBCP might consider it a novel form of birth control (Wright, 1979)!

Limiting occupational health hazards solely to women or solely to reproductive effects is to overlook the complexities of work and the various health hazards it creates. All workers need protection from health hazards posed by their jobs. Included would be policies that protect the reproductive health of men and women and provide a good system of reproductive leave for both sexes (Wright, 1979). Toxic substances and radiation have a hazardous effect not only on workers in industrial plants but in surrounding communities, as well. As Supreme Court Justice Felix Frankfurter said in 1916:

> *Once we cease to look upon the regulation of women in industry as exceptional, as the law's graciousness to a disabled class, and shift the emphasis from the fact that they are* women *to the fact that it is* industry *and the relation of industry to the community which is regulated, the whole problem is seen from a totally different aspect. (1916:367, cited in Hill, 1979)*

Discussion of women's health and work also cannot ignore the fact that in spite of real risks to health posed by contemporary jobs, employed women, as far as we can tell, are healthier on the average than women who are unemployed. Only the future will reveal the long-range effect of carcinogens, toxic substances, and radiation on human life, but current data indicate that employment has positive effects on women's health. There are higher rates of illness among housewives than among women who work for wages, but even with the additional burden of the double day, women who work for wages have better physical and mental health than women who do not.

In sum, research on women's health and their work environments reveals a host of social problems. Although the specific hazards that workers face will vary depending on the type of work and the specific work conditions they face, there is a serious need for careful study of work-related health hazards. Policies that single out women as a restricted class do not solve this problem, nor does ignoring the complexities of gender relations in the workplace. In the end, safe workplaces, both in industry and in the home, must be constructed for men and women alike.

❧ Gender, Health, and Social Problems

Women, Weight, and Food

The culture that we live in is one that is obsessed with weight and thinness. In the United States, women, and men as well, are taught to dislike their bodies; no matter what their shape, size, or form, women's bodies seem never to meet the cultural ideal, especially as it constantly changes over time.

Beginning in the twentieth century, U.S. culture began to regard fleshiness as not sexy. Sexy bodies are now depicted as thin ones; in fact, cultural images of weight have projected an increasingly thin image, resulting in a very high rate of anorexia among models and actresses who portray these ideals. Being thin is also increasingly associated with wealth and class, because idealized sex objects also portray class images (Millman, 1980). In an odd sense, only rich women can "afford" to be thin, since poor women are much more likely to be overweight. Fat on women and men also violates gender roles, as we tend to think of overweight women as having improperly indulged themselves, and overweight men are derided for seeming passive, vulnerable, and soft (Millman, 1980).

One consequence of this cultural obsession with weight and thinness is the high rate of anorexia nervosa, bulimia, and compulsive eating among women and, increasingly, men. Although anorexia nervosa generally occurs among White, adolescent females, men and minorities are increasingly being affected. Black and Hispanic women, however, are still more likely to be overweight, especially those near poverty, than are White women (National Center for Health Statistics, 1998).

Anorexia nervosa is characterized by severe weight loss; anorexics also have delusions about their body images, thinking of themselves as fat when they are, in actuality, dangerously thin. They typically do not recognize signs of nutritional need and may, literally, starve themselves to death. Feminist psychotherapists who work with anorexic clients have shown that these are women who have fully internalized cultural ideals of womanhood. Seen in the context of a whole array of practices designed to reduce women's body size—such as stomach stapling, diet fads, breast reduction surgery, and other extreme procedures—anorexia is even to be expected in a culture so obsessed with thinness (Bruch, 1978; Chernin, 1981, 1985; Lawrence, 1984).

Other eating problems, such as bulimia and compulsive overeating, also stem from the culture's definition of idealized womanhood. **Bulimia**, the syndrome in which women (typically) binge on huge amounts of food and then purge themselves by vomiting, use of laxatives, or extreme fasting, seems to be rapidly increasing, especially among the young and college students (Boskind-White, 1985). Researchers estimate that 4 to 18 percent of college students are bulimic (Boskind-White, 1985). A national poll of women found that while only 25 percent were actually overweight, 41 percent were unhappy with their bodies, 80 percent felt they had to be slim to be attractive to men, and a majority were ashamed of their stomachs, hips, and thighs. It is no wonder, then, that the survey also revealed women's intense desperation about weight control and found that half of the respondents used diet pills, 27 percent used liquid formula diets, and 18 percent used diuretics for weight loss (Whitney, 1984:198–201).

Women's concern with weight and body image can affect self-esteem and academic performance. Research finds that the less attractive a woman perceives herself to be and the more weight she wants to lose, the greater is her sense of academic, social, and psychological impairment (Hesse-Biber, Clayton-Matthews, and Downey, 1987). Ironically, eating disorders, although contributing to poor academic performance and lowered self-esteem, are most common among women who value physical appearance, strive for success in multiple roles, and come from families where their daughters have insecure attachments to their parents (Hart and Kenny, 1997).

Most studies of eating disorders have been based on the experiences of White women, and their conclusions should be judged accordingly. Latino, Native American, and African American women have never been portrayed as the "ideal woman"; their problems with weight are conditioned by the specific intersections of race, class, and gender in their experience. Thompson's (1994) research on compulsive eating among women of color finds, for example, that African American women overeat to soothe the rage, fear, and disappointment in their lives. She also found that over two-thirds of the women in her study who were overeaters had also been sexually molested during childhood.

Thompson's (1994) work suggests that emphasis on the culture of thinness as the explanation for eating problems among women is too narrow. Aspects of African American culture, for example, do not hold the same thin ideals for African American women that are found in the dominant culture; quite the contrary, there are many positive images within the African American community of large women who enjoy food. As in other cultures of the society (e.g., Jewish), the preparation and enjoyment of food has a positive and valued place within the culture. A more multicultural approach to understanding the origins of women's eating problems, Thompson suggests, is one that directly links eating problems among women to the multiple forms of oppression they experience. Thompson's study of African American, Latina, and White lesbian women found that compulsive eating, bulimia, and anorexia are not so much linked to women's obsession with appearance as they are responses the women have developed to soothe the distress they feel as the result of poverty, sexual abuse, racism, and/or homophobia. Although these women are not isolated from dominant cultural images of thinness, Thompson suggests that the origins of eating problems have to be seen in the broader context of class oppression, racism, homophobia, and the sexual abuse of women (Thompson, 1994).

Gender and Substance Abuse

With the widespread use of drugs in U.S. culture beginning in the 1960s, it was generally believed that "the drug revolution" would eventually eliminate differences in patterns of substance abuse between women and men. People assumed that as women took on more "male" roles, such as working in the paid labor force, women's use of alcohol and drugs would more nearly approximate men's. This has not generally occurred (Robbins, 1989), although there is some convergence in drinking rates among young people, particularly college students.

Alcohol

With regard to alcohol, men drink more frequently than women and drink more on any given occasion. Men are more likely to be classified as problem drinkers. A recent survey on college campuses found that, although men are more likely to drink heavily than women, a large percentage of both women and men college students are binge drinkers (50 percent of men; 39 percent of women)—binge drinking being defined as heavy, episodic drinking. Another 35 percent of men and 45 percent of women students drank, but not as binge drinkers (Wechsler, 1995).

Among women, the frequency of drinking and the volume of consumption decrease with education. National surveys find that the highest rate of drinking problems among women are found among those who are unsuccessfully looking for work, followed by women who, because of their position in the labor force, face the stress of dead-end, low-income jobs (Sandmaier, 1980). Still, women drink less than men do, and drinking is less likely to become a problem for them (National Center for Health Statistics, 1998).

National surveys find that African American and Hispanic women are more likely to abstain from drinking and are less likely to be heavy drinkers than White women; Asian American women have low rates of alcohol use, but Native American women have high rates of use, as reflected in high alcohol-related mortality among American Indian and Alaskan Native women (Horton, 1995). White women are more likely to be drinkers if they are single, have high incomes, and are employed. African American women are more likely to drink if they are young and employed. Some have argued that women's employment makes them more likely to drink because it gives them greater independence and exposes them to cultural norms and expectations like those men experience. Marital status is also a reasonable predictor of drinking patterns, although its effect varies for White and African American women. Researchers have found no single explanation for differences in drinking patterns for White women and women of color except that the drinking behavior of both groups is dependent on the complex interaction of their race, age, income level, and marital and employment status (Herd, 1988).

When women do drink, they are more likely to drink alone, in private, or with a spouse. Women also tend to be introduced to alcohol by men and are encouraged by men to drink. There is some evidence that employed women drink more than unemployed women, although no association has been found between drinking and the role conflicts experienced by women who are married and working for wages (Parker et al., 1980). The greatest amount of problem drinking occurs among women aged 18 to 20; moreover, drinking among young women has dramatically increased in recent years, nearly closing the gender gap between male and female drinkers (Sandmaier, 1980; Wechsler, 1995).

Drugs

Although women are less likely than men to be drug abusers, there are significant health risks for women with substance abuse problems. An estimated 200,000 women die annually from illnesses related to substance abuse (more than those who die from breast cancer). Legal and illegal drugs, alcohol, tobacco, and caffeine are among the most prominent causes of health problems for premature death among both women and men. Nearly one in three women in the United States uses an illegal drug at least once in her life; the rate is higher among women of childbearing age. It is estimated that 15 percent of all women aged 15 to 44 are currently abusing drugs or alcohol. Three-fifths of people admitted to treatment facilities for addiction to tranquilizers and sedatives are women (Blumenthal, 1998).

One explanation of the differential patterns of substance abuse among men and women is that gender roles encourage different social responses to drug and alcohol use by men and by women. There is no evidence that confusion about one's gender identity is a cause of substance abuse; in fact, for both men and women, patterns of substance abuse are consistent with images of masculinity and femininity in the culture. According to traditional gender roles, women are not expected to drink and use drugs to the same extent as men. Indeed, women who become alcoholics tend to be perceived as more masculine and "hard" than other women, indicating that this behavior violates expected roles for women. Women heroin addicts are also seen as more deviant, more reprehensible, and less treatable than male addicts. Although traditional gender roles may protect women from substance abuse, they also pose constraints on the treatment and societal reaction to women with substance abuse problems.

The problem of drug abuse is not just a problem with illegal drugs. Women are more likely than men to be prescribed tranquilizers, sedatives, and amphetamines. In part, high rates of legal drug use among both men and women are attributable to the belief that technological advancements make relief available for every condition and disease (Klass, 1975), but the particularly high rates of prescribed drug use among women also require a gender-specific explanation. Some suggest that women are more often prescribed tranquilizing drugs because they are more likely to seek help for their problems than are men (Nathanson, 1975). According to this explanation, women are freer, as a result of their social roles, to report pain, both physical and emotional, than are men; physicians are also likely to expect women to be emotional, whereas they tend to regard men as more stoic (Cooperstock, 1971). Others say that because of structured inequality, women's roles are more stressful and, as a result, women have more real complaints (Fidell,

1973). While these are plausible explanations, the fact is that powerful economic and political interests capitalize on women as a market for drugs that brings massive profits to their producers.

Smoking

Although tobacco has not been considered an addictive drug, and therefore has not been regulated to the same extent as other substances, it has come under increasing public attention as an addictive health hazard. For women, cigarette smoking has also been manipulated by advertisers as a sign of women's independence, even though tobacco is significantly linked to multiple negative health consequences for all users.

Historically, men have been more likely to smoke than women. Although the rate of smoking for both women and men in the United States has declined in recent years, one in four women and men smoke; among women, the percentage who are heavy smokers has increased. Once women start to smoke, they are also more likely than men to continue, making the initiation of smoking especially significant for women. Among high school seniors, 37 percent of males and 35 percent of females smoke, more than at any time in history, despite the known risks. An alarming 20 percent of eighth-graders (males and females) now smoke (see Figure 7.3; National Center for Health Statistics, 1998; Horton, 1995).

Smoking patterns among women and men seem significantly affected by gender roles. Researchers studying smoking behavior among adolescents have found, for example, that although peer pressure is significant for both boys and girls in the initiation of smoking, it is more significant for girls. Young men, on the other hand, are more influenced by "sensation seeking" (Martin and Robbins, 1995; Chassin, Presson, and Sherman, 1989). At the same time, girls (and, later, women) are more likely to say that they smoke to control their weight (Logio-Rau, 1998). For both groups, appearance before others—whether it to be appear adult-like, to be slim, to be "tough," or to go along with the crowd—are significant risks to health. Clearly, despite knowledge about the effects of smoking, gender and social status override rational decisions about health risks.

Women and AIDS

Originally identified as a disease affecting primarily gay men, AIDS (Acquired Immune Deficiency Syndrome) has taken on new dimensions. Although most of those initially having AIDS were White, middle-class, homosexual or bisexual men, the current incidence of AIDS is 2 to 3 times higher for African American and Hispanic homosexual men than for White homosexuals; among heterosexuals, the rate is 20 times higher among African Americans and Hispanics than Whites (Williams, 1990). AIDS is no longer a disease only among men. In 1997, 22 percent of all new AIDS infections in U.S. adults were in women. Worldwide, the number of women with AIDS is predicted to soon equal the number of men, with 6 to 8 million women infected. AIDS is already the fourth leading cause of death for women worldwide and is the leading cause of death for women of reproductive

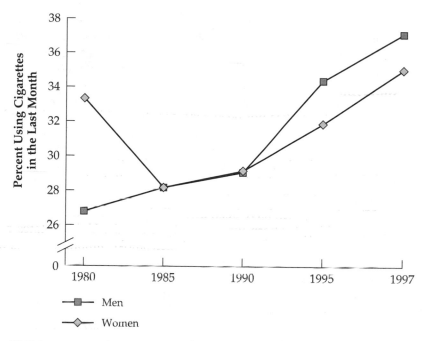

FIGURE 7.3 Cigarette Smoking among Teens

Source: Data from National Center for Health Statistics. 1998. *Health, United States, 1998.* Hyattsville, MD: U.S. Government Printing Office, p. 277.

age in several major U.S. cities (Blumenthal, 1998; Schneider and Stoller, 1995; National Center for Health Statistics, 1998).

In the United States, AIDS is currently spreading faster among women than among men, although men are still a majority of cases. In 1997, 84 percent of AIDS cases were men and 16 percent were women. AIDS falls especially hard on women of color, as three-quarters of all AIDS cases among women are among African American women, American Indians, Asian Americans, and Latinas. AIDS is already the leading cause of death for African American women, ages 15 to 24, in two states: New Jersey and New York. AIDS also falls disproportionately among women in their childbearing years, with nearly two-thirds of all AIDS cases among women in the age group of 25 to 39 years (Horton, 1995; Schneider and Stoller, 1995; National Center for Health Statistics, 1998).

Half of all cases of AIDS among women are the result of drug injection, itself an activity highly related to poverty. More recent cases of infection, however, are most likely to be the result of sexual transmission from male carriers. Women have typically not been included in clinical trials on AIDS; instead, most medical research on AIDS among women has been on pregnant women, with a particular focus on the implications for pediatric AIDS cases. Although this area is surely an important avenue for research, studying women relative only to pediatric AIDS leaves unanswered many questions about the more general implications of AIDS for women.

These facts suggest the urgency of understanding AIDS in the context of a gender and race analysis. To begin with, women's social, sexual, and economic standing clearly influences their susceptibility to AIDS. Especially when seen in a global context, women's lack of access to education, medical care, and economic support makes them unable to protect themselves from this serious disease. Conditions of poverty among women of color in the United States contribute to the vulnerability of women to AIDS, as they turn to drugs for relief or have poor access to health and reproductive services that can provide some protection from AIDS. In addition, women's position as sex workers and as vulnerable sexual partners enhances their risk of AIDS. As a consequence, women who have mobilized against AIDS have linked the prevention of AIDS to the necessity of improving women's status worldwide (Schneider and Stoller, 1995).

Health Insurance

With so many known health risks for women, one would hope that national health care policy and health care systems would be able to meet the challenges of keeping women and men healthy. Especially in a nation known for its advanced health care system and in a nation that is affluent relative to other nations in the world, one would expect a health care system that works for total population. Yet, data on health care coverage reveal that women are at risk of being uncovered by health insurance, especially if they are poor, unmarried, and/or a woman of color. Unmarried women are two to three times less likely to be covered by health insurance than married women, who are often covered by the employment of their spouse (Meyer and Pavalko, 1996). Women who are employed are also less likely to be covered by health insurance than are men, because of the structural patterns of gender segregation that place them in occupations with fewer health care benefits (Seccombe and Beeghley, 1992). At all income brackets, Blacks and Hispanic Americans are less likely to be covered by health care insurance than are Whites (see Figure 7.4; National Center for Health Statistics, 1998).

The Politics of Reproduction: Birth Control, Abortion, and Childbirth

Feminist Perspectives on Reproduction

The issues of abortion, birth control, and pregnancy are at the heart of feminist politics and are core issues around which feminist analysis has been built. Contemporary feminists see women's right to control their own bodies as essential to the realization of other rights and opportunities in society. As the Boston Women's Health Book Collective has written, "Unless we ourselves can decide whether and when to have children, it is difficult for us to control our lives or participate fully in society" (1984:291).

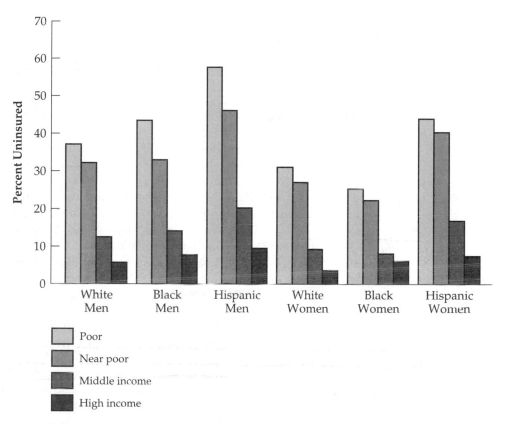

FIGURE 7.4   Health Insurance by Gender, Race-Ethnicity, and Class

Source: Data from National Center for Health Statistics. 1998. *Health, United States, 1998.* Hyattsville, MD: U.S. Government Printing Office, p. 158.

Whether individual women experience pregnancy, abortion, or birth control as stressful or traumatic is at least partially because of how they are socially organized. Reproduction, although it is a physiological event, stands at the junction of nature and culture (Oakley, 1979). Women do not simply get pregnant and give birth in the physical sense alone; they do so within a definite set of social relations (Petchesky, 1980). These social arrangements vary not only historically but also cross-culturally. Feminist arguments about the social control of reproduction clearly take this fact into account. Following her early study of seven Pacific Island cultures, Margaret Mead wrote:

Whether childbirth is seen as a situation in which one risks death, or out of which one acquires a baby, or social status, or a right to Heaven, is not a matter of the actual statistics of maternal mortality, but of the view that a society takes of childbearing. Any argument about women's instinctively maternal behavior which insists that in this respect a biological substratum is stronger than every other learning experience that a female child faces, from birth on, must reckon with this great variety in the handling of childbirth. (Mead, 1962:221)

Female control of reproduction is cross-culturally and historically the dominant social arrangement (Oakley, 1979); yet, in modern Western societies, reproduction is controlled by men. Traditional social theories have also largely ignored the question of reproduction, as if assuming that it is irrelevant in analyses of human experience and social organization.

Feminist perspectives on reproductive issues assert women's right to control their own bodies. Feminists see the medical profession as unresponsive to women's needs and as treating women's bodies as objects for medical manipulation. Not only are feminists distressed by the demeaning treatment women receive in medical institutions but they are also critical of the fact that it is men (either in medicine or in politics) who make decisions about reproductive issues (Ruzek, 1978). Feminists believe that it is women's right to choose their reproductive status. Not only do feminists believe in individual rights on reproductive issues but they also see that reproduction is embedded in systems of social power and social control (Petchesky, 1980). The history of reproductive issues and their contemporary manifestations also show that reproduction is directly entangled with class and race relations, in addition to relations of gender. Changes in federal funding for abortion, a recurring history of sterilization abuse, and the manipulation of powerless women for medical experiments are all evidence of the powerlessness of women to control reproduction. This section reviews the politics of reproduction, focusing on three contemporary issues: birth control, abortion, and racism and reproduction.

Birth Control

Birth control, although a personal matter, is also controlled by decisions of the state, the social organization of scientific and medical institutions, and the normative system of public values and attitudes. Because birth control regulates sexual activity and population size, its significance extends beyond the individual relationships in which it is actually practiced. Moreover, the availability, form, and cultural significance of birth control bear directly on the role of women in society (Gordon, 1977).

Many young women today probably take birth control for granted, although it was not long ago that the right to practice birth control was established in law, especially for the unmarried. A 1965 Supreme Court decision (**Griswold v. Connecticut**) established the first constitutional precedent that the use of birth control was a right, not a crime; however, this decision extended only to married persons. Not until 1972 (in **Eisenstadt v. Baird**) were laws prohibiting the dispensing of contraceptives to any unmarried person, or by anyone other than a physician or pharmacist, held unconstitutional (Goldstein, 1988). This decision was introduced following an incident in which Bill Baird, a long-time birth control activist, handed a package of vaginal foam to an unmarried young woman during a lecture on contraception at Boston University. Baird, in violation of a Massachusetts law that prohibited the distribution of nonprescribed contraceptives, was arrested and convicted of a felony before the case reached the Supreme Court.

Before the establishment of the constitutional right to birth control, laws varied from state to state, and, even in those states where the distribution of birth control devices was legal, actual dispensing depended on the discretion of individual doctors. The effect was to shift the decision regarding birth control from women to men in the medical and judicial professions. Current policies on birth control are shaped by a political context that puts control over these issues into the hands of men and the government. For example, the Adolescent Family Life Law, passed by Congress in 1981, mandated the development of "caring services" to counsel pregnant teenage girls. The bill, however, prohibited the use of funds from its budget for research on contraceptive development, and it barred recipients from providing abortion counseling or services. Research funds allocated by this bill also could not be used for any research on abortion except research that demonstrated its consequences—the strong implication being that research could be supported only when it was to show the negative consequences of abortion.

Adolescent reproductive rights have also been a recent area of judicial rulings. A series of court rulings has upheld the practice of requiring parental notification, as long as there is an adequate bypass when needed (such as allowing authorization by a judge). Although there is flexibility on the issue of a minor's rights to choose abortion, these decisions still place young women in the situation of needing the approval of parents or a court to proceed with an abortion (Goldstein, 1988). Court delays make the timeliness of such decisions critical, but, more fundamentally, such decisions clearly take the control of the woman's body out of her hands.

These directions in law are especially troubling when we consider the research on teenage sexuality, contraception, and parental relationships. Procrastination is the teenager's most frequent reason for delay in initiating contraceptive use; the second most frequent reason is fear that parents will find out. Only 12 percent visit contraceptive clinics prior to becoming sexually active because of this fear (Alan Guttmacher Institute, 1994). Thus, young women are the age group most likely to have abortions (see Figure 7.5). Regulations that limit the options available to young girls (or anyone else) seem unlikely, then, to solve the problems associated with teenage pregnancy.

Abortion

Women's rights to choose abortions were established by the 1973 Supreme Court decision in **Roe v. Wade**. This decision held laws that prohibited abortion unconstitutional, except where such laws are restricted to the last three months of pregnancy or to the stage of fetal viability (Goldstein, 1988). The Court's decision acknowledged that on the issue of abortion, separately legitimate social concerns collided: (1) the constitutional right to privacy, (2) the right of the state to protect maternal health, and (3) the right of the state to protect developing life. The Court thus divided the gestation period into thirds and argued that in the first trimester the woman's right to decide her future privately, without interference from the state, took precedence over the other two rights. In the second trimester, the state

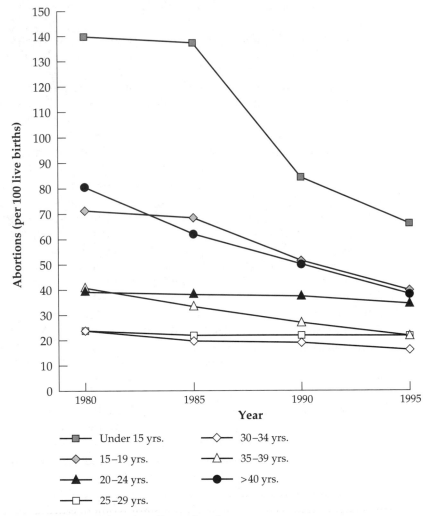

FIGURE 7.5   Abortion Rates by Age

Source: Data from National Center for Health Statistics 1998. *Health, United States, 1998.* Hyattsville, MD: U.S. Government Printing Office, p. 185.

cannot deny an abortion, but it can insist on reasonable standards of medical procedure. In the third trimester, abortion may be performed to preserve the life or health of the mother.

In 1989, the Supreme Court (in *Webster* v. *Reproductive Health Services*) gave states the right to impose substantial restrictions on abortion (such as requiring fetus viability tests, restricting use of public funding for abortion, and refusing to allow public employees to perform abortions in public hospitals). Political pressure from Christian conservatives and the political right threatens to limit abortion rights.

Despite increasing legal restrictions on abortion created by a conservative Supreme Court, public support for abortion has increased, with 56 percent identifying as pro-choice (37 percent as pro-life), although most qualify their position by saying there are some circumstances where they do not support abortion, such as late-term abortion (Gallup Poll, 1996, 1997). Moreover, 58 percent of the public does not want to see *Roe* v. *Wade* overturned—an increase in support since 1985. Support for abortion rights is equal among women and men and among Whites and people of color, although women and White people are more likely to believe abortion should be legal under any circumstances. Support for abortion rights increases with education and is higher among those under 50 years of age. There are also class differences in support for abortion rights, with those earning incomes over $30,000 per year more likely to support abortion rights than those earning less than $20,000 per year. Religious differences are also strong, although perhaps not in the ways one might predict. Half of those identified as born-again Protestants want to see *Roe* v. *Wade* overturned; 41 percent do not; 9 percent have no opinion. Only 24 percent of other Protestants and 38 percent of Catholics want to see *Roe* v. *Wade* overturned. Opinions of those of the Jewish faith were not reported in this survey, although earlier polls (1985) indicated that 91 percent of Jewish people support the *Roe* v. *Wade* decision (Gallup, 1989; Gallup and Jones, 1993).

In the United States, abortion was not viewed as morally wrong (if performed before quickening at four or five months) until the second half of the nineteenth century. Before that time, abortion was a common practice and was often performed using drugs, potions, techniques, and remedies made popular in home medical guides. Abortion was viewed as relatively safe and was commonly assisted by midwives, "irregular" physicians, and physicians of the period. The earliest laws governing abortion were not enacted until 1821 and 1841, but these laws placed guilt only on those who used particular methods feared unsafe for inducing abortion. None of these laws punished women for having abortions; they were intended as regulations to ensure safe methods (Mohr, 1978).

In the mid-nineteenth century, abortion became a widespread phenomenon, especially among White, married, Protestant women. During this period, abortion also became increasingly commercialized. One noted woman entrepreneur, Madame Restell, earned an enormous income from her abortion products and spent as much as $60,000 per year on advertising alone (Mohr, 1978). As both the drug industry and the medical profession grew in the second half of the nineteenth century, more profits could be made by companies seizing control of the abortion market. In addition to eliminating midwives from the practice of abortion, the medical profession created laws and spread propaganda that altered the perception and practice of abortion.

These changes were additionally fueled by shifts in the class, racial, and ethnic structure of U.S. life. The emerging new class of physicians was not only incensed by the flagrant commercialization of abortion but also expressed the fear that the growing rate of abortion among the middle and upper classes would cause immigrants, Black Americans, and the poor to outbreed them. Spurred by the growth of social Darwinism and an increasing nativist movement, the antiabortion crusade appealed to racist fears and portrayed abortion as the work of criminals, backward medical practitioners, and immoral social agents (Mohr, 1978). Beginning in the period between 1860 and 1880 and continuing through the first two-thirds of the twentieth century, antiabortion policies included strict criminal laws about abortion and put absolute control of abortion in the hands of the medical profession. By these laws, women seeking abortions—and their accomplices—were defined as guilty of murder, abortion was defined as a criminal act, and the distribution of abortion and birth control information was deemed illegal. The public moralizing about abortion seen in the late twentieth century emerged historically from new professional groups seeking to control abortion. Only very recently has abortion been seen as a moral issue stemming from religious beliefs.

Racism and Reproduction

The reproductive issues of abortion, birth control, and sterilization have particular significance for women of color. Although the majority of women of color support women's rights to abortion and birth control, history also shows that the birth control movement has been closely linked with racist movements for population control.

In the early twentieth century, when Margaret Sanger was organizing the birth control movement, White birth control reformers were campaigning to prevent so-called racial suicide for themselves through their allowing the overpopulation of Black Americans, immigrants, the poor, and social misfits (Davis, 1981; Gordon, 1977). The campaign for birth control was interwoven with genocidal movements to eliminate racial groups, and appeals for birth control were clearly intended to limit what was perceived as overbreeding among the poor. Sanger herself made this appeal part of her campaign, and thus seemed to support the racist goals of the eugenics movement.

In the contemporary record, information on the sterilization of women of color and poor women confirms that birth control and population control are often linked. As we have already seen, sterilization rates are highest among African American, Native American, and Puerto Rican women and female welfare recipients. These data raise the issue of the blurred distinction between forced and voluntary sterilization. Although forced sterilization is illegal, reports indicate that doctors and clinics do give misleading information to minority and poor clients. Although clients may technically agree to the procedure, they have frequently been misled or misinformed.

Federal investigations have revealed a high incidence of sterilization of minors in other government-sponsored clinics. High rates of sterilization, experimentation on Third World women and U.S. women of color for the development of contraceptives, and the inadequacy of health care for women of color all indicate the extent to which racism, coupled with sexism, is institutionalized in the health care system. White feminists have framed much of their discussion of reproductive health care in the context of individual choice, but for women of color and poor women, choice is restricted by the conditions of oppression they face in health care institutions. In fact, women of color have been sometimes reluc-

tant to become involved in White feminists' movements for rep
dom. People of color have been wary about movements promoting
birth control because historically these movements have been used as racist methods of population control. Women of color are also, however, the most frequent
victims of restrictive reproductive policies because poor women and women of
color are most dependent on public funding of reproductive services; they are
also disproportionately most likely to suffer death and injury if abortion becomes
illegal. This suggests that feminist analyses of reproductive freedom should be
framed by a political perspective wider than individual choice; reproductive freedom should be framed by an understanding of the need for social justice for all
women, not just those with the privilege to make free choices. Rights to privacy
alone probably cannot achieve such freedom, because privacy itself is largely conditioned through the structured inequalities of race, class, and gender oppression
(Petchesky, 1990).

The Politics of Birth: Pregnancy and Childbirth

Historical Perspectives on Childbirth

The emergence of modern medicine is usually seen as a conquest of ignorance
and a triumph over superstition. Modern medical men are imbued with high status in U.S. society and are perceived as learned, rational, and wise. There was a
time when healing was almost solely the province of women. Particularly in matters of birth and childrearing, women were perceived as the experts and birth was
a female-centered, home affair (Dye, 1980). Until the nineteenth century in this
country, women presided over most births, in the presence of female friends and
kin who provided comfort and aid to the childbearing woman (Wertz and Wertz,
1977).

Because childbirth was originally placed in the hands of women as midwives,
developments in the history of childbirth provide a case study in which what was
once a female-oriented process has come to be dominated and controlled by men.
Although this section focuses primarily on childbirth, it also reveals more general patterns in the emergence of modern medicine. In the end, you will see how
particular characteristics of medicine as an institution still take control of reproduction away from women.

Childbirth has a distinctive social history and one that is tied to the emergence of medicine as a profession, as well as to changes in the ideology and structure of women's roles in society. In the colonial United States, childbirth occurred
in the home and in the presence of female family members and friends (Dye, 1980;
Scholten, 1977). During this period, six to eight pregnancies were typical for
women, as was a fear of pain and the possibility of death in childbirth. Female
midwives who attended births generally practiced noninterventionist methods of
delivery and, along with the other females present, provided comfort and emotional support for the laboring mother (Wertz and Wertz, 1977). Records of the
midwives' practices, successes, and failures are hard to find in this period, so it is
difficult to know exactly how skilled or knowledgeable the midwives were.

Information and experiences about childbirth were shared by women, and there is little indication in the historical record that midwives posed dangers for child-bearing women. There are no recorded epidemics of puerperal fever, such as those that killed thousands of women when childbirth was moved to hospitals, and there are few recorded instances of midwives' incompetence in the colonial peri-od (Wertz and Wertz, 1977). Without romanticizing midwives and the process of birth, it appears that, unlike images of midwives that appeared later with the advent of scientific medicine, "the stereotype of the midwife as a curse upon women seems unfitting for colonial midwives" (Wertz and Wertz, 1977:13).

Certainly, the pain associated with childbirth was a significant factor in women's desire for alternative practices. New interventionist techniques promised by the male founders of medical science appealed to women who sought relief from long and difficult labors. Beginning in the mid-eighteenth cen-tury, a slow transition occurred in which birth was shifted from female to male control. Medical men in the United States took their lead from French and English physicians, who described the body as being like a machine and developed instruments or tools to intervene in natural bodily processes. Tools (such as for-ceps) promised to shorten labor and to make difficult labors more manageable, although such techniques were generally resisted by U.S. and English women midwives, who believed that these techniques introduced new dangers and unsafe procedures to the natural process of birth.

In the mid-eighteenth and early nineteenth centuries, there was an open mar-ket for both female midwives and the medical men who were developing new birth techniques. Advances in knowledge about the physiology of labor, as well as various birth techniques, were taught in medical colleges—most of which were located in England and France. Men from the United States learned from these colleges, but, because the government provided no financial support for medical education, women, with fewer financial resources than men, did not attend. Medical education during this period, however, was notoriously poor (Dye, 1980), and many have argued that female midwives continued to have greater skills in birth, based on their practical experience, than did medically trained men (Ehrenreich and English, 1978).

By the mid-nineteenth century, medical men had adopted an increasingly interventionist approach toward birth, whereas female midwives relied more on the normal course of delivery. Mary Wollstonecraft (1759–1797), an outspoken English feminist whom you will study in Chapter 11, deplored the takeover of childbirth by men and insisted that her daughter, Mary Shelley (author of *Frankenstein*), be born with a woman attendant. When the placenta was not deliv-ered, a male midwife was called in, who, upon inserting his hand to withdraw it, caused Wollstonecraft to hemorrhage and later to die of puerperal fever (Flexner, 1972; Wertz and Wertz, 1977). Studies indicate that although physicians gained greater control of childbirth during this period, as late as the early twentieth cen-tury, midwives had high status in their communities (Litoff, 1978), maintained their own apprenticeship systems (Mongeau, Smith, and Maney, 1961), and had better mortality records than medical men (Dye, 1980).

Transformations in childbirth that ultimately resulted in the medical model of contemporary birth were accelerated in the mid-nineteenth century, when obstetrics was first developed as a medical specialty and when Victorian cultural attitudes transformed bourgeois notions of female sexuality. During the Victorian period, pregnancy was treated with shame and concealment in the middle and upper classes. Because the Victorian period severely restricted women's sexuality and because pregnancy directly acknowledged their sexual activity, it became an event to be hidden and concealed. For example, it is reported that Susan B. Anthony's mother was embarrassed by her own pregnancy (Wertz and Wertz, 1977). Like other bourgeois Victorian women, she disappeared from public view when she was pregnant.

At the same time, the emergence of the medical profession provided status to those who could afford new medical treatments. Families who could pay for it, especially in urban areas, began to go to medical specialists. Obstetrics was one of the first of these specialties, although most women continued to employ women midwives because they were more trusting of midwives' noninterventionist techniques and more comfortable in their modesty with other women (Bogdan, 1978). Physicians themselves stated that medical midwifery was the key to a successful practice because, if they could eliminate midwives, physicians would have a dependable market; also, the uncharted knowledge of obstetrics provided a chance for the expansion of physicians' careers (Barker-Benfield, 1976; Scholten, 1977). In keeping with the Victorian sensibilities of the time, the typical obstetrician (so renamed from *male midwives* to symbolize their alleged professionalism) draped his client in cloth and avoided looking at her body; consequently, obstetrics with middle- and upper-class clients was commonly practiced by touch alone. Obstetricians thus gained little knowledge of their female patients and relied on experiments on poor and Black women to advance their field. Following the Civil War, maternity hospitals were established as charitable asylums for poor and unmarried pregnant women. Stating that such places would provide a more moral and sanitary environment than the patients' own homes, doctors provided free medical treatment for poor women (often servants of the upper classes) in return for using these patients as research subjects (Wertz and Wertz, 1977). Because the physicians would have violated the "ladylike" codes of the period by actually examining an affluent woman's body, poor, Black, and immigrant women in the charity hospital became research subjects for medical treatment and observation.

One of the most outrageous cases of experimentation is found in the practice of J. Marion Sims, originator of gynecology and an early president of the American Medical Association. One of his early claims to fame was the discovery of ways to suture tears that occurred between the vagina and bladder and the vagina and anus. He developed these techniques by purchasing Black female slaves, whom he kept in hospital quarters that he built in his own yard (Axelson, 1985). Because he saw Black slaves as enduring, passive, and helpless, he performed countless experimental operations on them without anesthesia. The pain he inflicted on them had to create unimaginable agony, yet this seemed not to faze him in his obsessive search for techniques to build his own career (Barker-Benfield, 1976). Nor did it seem to bother upper-class women, who later erected a statue to him in Central Park because of their gratitude for his surgical method! (They, of course, experienced it only after the development of anesthesia.)

Sims, like other medical men of his day, believed that women's psychology stemmed from their sex organs, and he was anxious to perform clitoridectomies and oophorectomies (removal of the clitoris and ovaries). His drastic use of the knife seemed intended not for the betterment of women but for the enhancement of his own career, for an aspiring specialist, then as now, made his name through the invention and publication of new techniques. Indeed, as one historian has noted, the operating rooms where female surgery was performed in the nineteenth century were essentially "an arena for an exchange between men" (Barker-Benfield, 1976:101). Sims, in fact, developed gynecological procedures as if he were an explorer charting new frontiers; his own writings clearly show this to be his own metaphor about his work. He was the first to develop the speculum and says of it, "Introducing the bent handle of a spoon, I saw everything as no man had ever seen before. . . . I felt like an explorer in medicine who first views a new and important territory" (Barker-Benfield, 1976:95). Other medical men, too, declared his "speculum to be to diseases of the womb . . . what the compass is to the mariner" (Barker-Benfield, 1976:95).

The removal of childbirth from the home and the control of women contradicted the Victorian point of view that birth was a private matter, to be conducted in secrecy and within the domestic world. Initially, delivery by men was seen as a breakdown of moral standards and an offense to female delicacy (Donegan, 1978). Over time, however, as doctors promised safer and less painful births, women began to desire the new techniques they were offered. Most women wanted less painful childbirth, although in the late nineteenth century, the absence of pain in childbirth was associated with supposedly precivilized women—especially Indians and Blacks. Racism in the middle and upper classes defined more "primitive" peoples as closer to nature and therefore unlikely to experience childbirth pain. From the racist perspective of the bourgeois class, to experience pain, and therefore to need relief from it, became a sign of one's civilized nature. Needing relief from childbirth pain was also an indication of the social distance of the upper and middle classes from other strata of the society. Pain, then, became a mark of the "truly feminine"—a fact with its own paradoxical truth because childbirth pain and complications were greatly increased by the "civilized" practices of tight corsets, lack of exercise, fashionable illness, and airless rooms (Wertz and Wertz, 1977).

Rather than change their cultural habits, middle- and upper-class women sought relief from childbirth pain and thus became more interested in the promises of modern medicine. Promises were all many of these techniques gave, however, for although they might have alleviated extreme pain, there is little evidence that childbirth was made any safer by medical men of the early twentieth century. Puerperal fever, later found to be caused by infections generated by unsanitary hospital procedures and interventionist techniques, became a major cause of maternal death (Wertz and Wertz, 1977). Epidemics of puerperal fever killed thousands of women who sought painless deliveries through hospital births.

The number of births occurring in hospitals increased rapidly after the 1930s. Before this time, hospital birth had been primarily an urban phenomenon and, even there, had occurred on a large scale beginning only in the twentieth century. In 1930, only about 25 percent of all births took place in hospitals; by 1990, over 95 percent of all births occurred in hospitals. Today, hospital births represent the ultimate transformation of birth from a female-centered, home activity to one that is male controlled and medically defined. The prevalence of hospital births followed a direct assault on women midwives in the second half of the nineteenth century, when propaganda to make women fear pregnancy and legislation to eliminate midwives combined to generate new definitions of women's place in childbirth and, more generally, in medicine (Barker-Benfield, 1976). Legislation between 1900 and 1930 made licensing for midwives a necessity. To obtain a license, midwives were required to get vouchers of their moral character from a member of the medical profession, to have their homes and outfits inspected by a physician's nurse, and to have attended births under the supervision of a physician. Because few physicians would provide these credentials, the number of practicing midwives radically declined. In New York City, for example, the number of practicing midwives declined from 3,000 in 1908 to 270 in 1939, 2 in 1957, and 1 in 1963 (Barker-Benfield, 1976). In most cases, women were excluded from medical schools and, if they wanted to enter the health care system, were relegated to secondary status as nurses (Ehrenreich and English, 1978). Childbirth and, more generally, women's health had effectively been placed in the hands of male physicians.

The movement of childbirth to hospitals and medical men was further increased by popular racist fears of contagion and germs that were associated with poor, immigrant, and Black people. The fads of genetic science and social Darwinism of the 1920s and 1930s increased middle-class fears of associating with those from the lower strata of society. Coupled with the home economics movement of the 1920s that defined home environments as sources of germs and disease (see Chapter 6), popular opinions laced with racist and class ideologies further generated a social definition of childbirth as a scientific event to be placed under the authority of medical men.

The Medicalization of Childbirth

Physicians now routinely define pregnancy and birth as medical events and, because of this model, they are more likely to prescribe drugs during pregnancy and birth, set strict limits on what is considered a "normal" pregnancy, and define medical intervention as essential during birth. Midwives, on the other hand, define pregnancy as a healthy and normal condition—one that is optimized not by intervention and technological management but by providing the best possible environment for the pregnant woman (Rothman, 1982). Conflict between the medical and midwifery models of childbirth lies at the heart of struggles over the control of childbirth, including political conflicts over the licensing of midwives and the establishment of nonmedical birth settings (Sullivan and Weitz, 1988).

The dominance of the medical model in controlling pregnancy and childbirth can be seen in how pregnancy and childbirth are routinely handled by the medical profession. Birth is most likely located in hospitals, where doctors and the staff, not the mother, have control and authority over the delivery procedures. Even in the birthing rooms, which some hospitals have recently established, ultimate authority lies with the physician, who may (and does) intervene in the birth process at any point. Reinharz (1988) has also shown how the medical model permeates physicians' treatment and women's understanding of miscarriage.

Interventionist practices characterizing the rise of male control over childbirth continue to dominate women's childbirth experiences. This fact is especially evident in the dramatic increase in the number of cesarean sections being performed in hospitals throughout the country. Since 1970, cesarean sections have increased from 5 percent of all births to 23 percent. Some hospitals report that as many as one-quarter of all births are performed by cesarean section (Horton, 1995). In an age when childbirth is supposed to be safer and less threatening than it was in previous years, how do we explain the high proportion of births using a process that clearly increases the risks to both mother and child?

Researchers cite the routine practices of technological monitoring of birth as contributing significantly to the increase in cesarean births. Although some also mention physicians' greed for higher compensation and their desire for predictable schedules as contributing to the incentives to perform cesareans, it seems most likely that the social organization of childbirth around technological intervention is responsible for the increase. Typically, the process of labor is now observed by an electronic fetal-monitoring device that not only replaces the monitoring originally performed by nurses but also keeps the laboring woman passively strapped to the device and immobile throughout the course of labor. Even though changes in the baby's breathing and heartbeat are routine features of the birth process, the close detection of these changes by the electronic fetal monitor results in a high number of false indications of fetal distress (Corea, 1980). As a result of this situation, which is complicated by doctors' fears of malpractice if an actually distressed fetus is missed, doctors seem to react quickly to the slightest indication of change in the fetal condition by performing a vast number of unnecessary cesarean sections.

Other practices in the obstetric management of birth have also been criticized, including the separation of the mother and infant immediately following birth (Rossi, 1977), the overuse of anesthetics that affect the infant's nervous system, and the widespread use of birth positions that immobilize the mother and increase the incidence of episiotomies (Wertz and Wertz, 1977). All of these practices contribute to better hospital management, but they pose clear risks for mothers and their children. It appears that in modern medical practice, the social organization of hospital routines takes precedence over maternal and infant well-being; moreover, the expectation is that maternity patients should maintain a passive attitude while trusting in the doctor's authority and knowledge.

Women have become increasingly critical of the conditions surrounding childbirth, and many groups have organized to create out-of-hospital birthing centers, more licensing and increased use of midwives, and greater consumer education to enhance women's control over childbirth (Sullivan and Weitz, 1988). Although some reforms are being introduced, feminists argue that the process of childbirth still remains one of the fundamental ways in which women's reproductive abilities are subordinated to the definitions, practices, and controls of men. In the concluding section, the character of the modern medical profession and women's place within it will be examined.

Reproductive Technology

New reproductive technologies—including artificial insemination, in vitro fertilization, embryo transfer, cloning, and genetic engineering—raise new concerns and questions about women's control of their bodies. Feminists point out that while some of these technologies seem to offer liberating possibilities, at the same time they make women new targets for the manipulation of reproductive engineers (Arditti, Duelli-Klein, and Minden, 1984).

Donor insemination, for example, means that lesbian women or women who merely want children without men can become pregnant. In vitro fertilization makes it possible for those who are infertile to have children. Amniocentesis and an array of other tests now allow for prenatal evaluation of the embryo, meaning that characteristics such as sex, disability, and disease can be determined before birth. Although these may appear to be laudable developments, they also raise disturbing questions. Why, for example, is biological parenthood so important that we would go to such lengths and costs to bear children? What are the implications of determining sex before birth, especially in cultures where female infants are less valued than males? What does it say about the oppression of people with disabilities and our prejudices against them if we screen for disabilities before birth?

The eugenics movement in the United States in the earlier part of the twentieth century, like that of Nazi Germany, sought to apply the principles of genetic selection to improve the offspring of the human race. In both Nazi Germany and the United States, the process was explicitly racist, including, for example, compulsory sterilization of those defined as "unfit" or "defective." Many feminists equate the contemporary development of reproductive technology with the possibility of a new eugenics movement—one that, although it may not appear blatantly racist, is still embedded in a racist, sexist, and homophobic culture. Would reproductive technology be used, for example, to control the fertility of those deemed unworthy? To whom are reproductive technology and choice over reproduction most likely made available?

Although new reproductive technologies appear to give women choices over how and when they will have children, these technologies do not affect all women equally (Corea, 1985). Some women may have "rights to choose," but the choices women have are structured by race, class, and gender inequality (Petchesky, 1980; Rothman, 1982). Reproductive control can, in fact, become a façade for population control and, in the context of racism, population control is often a mechanism for more social and political control (Corea, 1985; Rothman, 1982).

Such views make the question of power central to any discussion of reproductive technology. Feminists do not necessarily believe that reproductive technology should be eliminated altogether, but they argue that as long as it is controlled by men, women are still denied the rights to control their bodies. Only
organized resistance to the control of women's bodies by men will ensure that
these technologies do not become a new means for the oppression of women.

❧ Women and the Health Care System

Even with an increase in the number of women physicians, when a woman seeks
medical care from a physician, there are 74 chances out of 100 that the person she
sees will be a man. This fact is especially significant because women utilize the
health care system more than do men, as measured by physician visits, hospital
admissions, and the prescription of drugs (U.S. Department of Health and
Human Services, 1998). Women's health care is intricately interwoven with the
power of men in medicine and with the profit structure of modern medicine.
These factors influence the client-physician relationship, the quality of care
received, and the status of women workers within the health care system.
Feminist criticism of medical institutions is a response to this political and economic structure.

Doctor-Patient Relationships

The most immediate context in which power relations can be seen in medicine is
the doctor-patient relationship. Because women are more likely to make physician
visits and the overwhelming majority of doctors are men, this doctor-patient relationship is likely to reflect the gender roles in society as well as the roles of professionals and their clients. Both the doctor and the patient are likely to have
expectations of the other that are conditioned by the status each occupies. Many
doctors are likely to see illness among their women patients as psychologically
based (Wallen, 1979). These definitions reflect gender-role expectations because
they indicate that male doctors are not taking women patients seriously, even
though women tend to view their doctors as all knowing.

In medical schools, physicians are trained to view their patients as individual
cases, not as representatives of their social-structural milieu. Particularly because
physicians' backgrounds are likely to entail gendered assumptions about male
and female patients, the advice they give is influenced by gender-stereotypic roles
and norms. Studies indicate that male doctors encourage male patients to see their
problems as stemming from job stress, while locating women's problems in their
family roles. Doctors are also prone to view women's complaints as psychosomatic, leading them to prescribe psychotherapy and drugs (Waller, 1988) instead
of suggesting situational or structural changes that might alleviate patients' difficulties. Because of the physicians' tendencies to view cases as individual patholo-
gies, neither male nor female patients are encouraged to consider the social structural origins of their difficulties (Barrett and Roberts, 1978). Even with more

women entering the medical profession as physicians, differential care for women and men as patients persists (Verbrugge, 1984).

Other research reveals similar problems in doctor-patient consultations. Observations of consulting patterns reveal that women are given less complete and shorter explanations of their medical problems than are men, in spite of the fact that women ask more questions of their doctors. Because they are more inquisitive but receive less information, women experience frustration in their encounters with doctors. Because doctors see female illness as psychologically caused, they are also more pessimistic about the patients' recovery and may give less information about their condition (Wallen, 1979).

Women as Health Care Workers

Women constitute 90 percent of health care service workers, yet they are systematically found in the least prestigious and most poorly paid positions in this field. Among doctors, women constitute a 26 percent minority; however, 94 percent of registered nurses are women. African American and Hispanic women in health care are concentrated in the lowest paying of these occupations.

Women who are nurses do not face the problem of existing in a male-dominated occupation, but their position relative to that of male professionals creates its own set of problems. Women of color in these fields also face the problems of racism and discrimination, which hamper their career development. Nurses and other health care workers are put in the position in which male professionals hold authority over them, in addition to receiving greater material benefits. Moreover, men who enter nursing tend to progress to higher echelons than do women within the profession (compounding the problem of sexism that women in this field face).

Despite recent increases in their salaries, nurses face sexist attitudes that define their work as less valuable than that of men. On the job, nurses are subordinate to the doctors in authority; innumerable accounts have described the sexist put-downs, innuendoes, and insults that some doctors have directed toward the nursing staff. More generally, physicians maintain a monopoly over medical knowledge and medical practice, even though nurses have more actual contact with hospitalized patients (Ehrenreich and English, 1973b). Such working conditions lead to a high sense of dissatisfaction among nurses and, as a result, high job turnover.

The subordination of the nursing profession to the authority of doctors has resulted in a split between the activities of curing and caring. Stereotypically, nurses are alleged to provide nurturing, whereas doctors maintain the expertise in healing. Such a myth not only belittles the professional knowledge of nurses but also creates an atmosphere that may not work in the best interest of patients. As alternative medical practices have shown, a patient's health involves a complex configuration of physiological, emotional, and social systems. It appears that a more useful system of medicine is one that integrates the process of healing with the complexities emerging from the interaction of these systems.

Among women who enter higher-status jobs (such as that of physician), most end up in the least prestigious specialties, such as pediatrics, obstetrics/gynecology, and general practice. There is, however, evidence of some change. By the late 1990s, women made up 37 percent of medical students. Because of the long period of training, internship, and residence, the impact of these changes on the composition of practicing physicians is only beginning to be felt.

Some see these changes as signs of major breakthroughs for women in medicine, but this generation is not the first to witness such changes. At the turn of the twentieth century, women were a significant proportion of all physicians, with some cities reporting almost 20 percent of all physicians to be women (Walsh, 1977). The entry of women into medicine is historically closely aligned with feminism and the new opportunities it encouraged for women. Although the feminist movement at the turn of the century was quite different from contemporary feminism, it did encourage women, at least of the upper and middle classes, to use their skills, especially in areas perceived as helping professions. Since the turn of the century, women have been excluded from medicine through overt discrimination (denied entrance to medical schools) and through informal practices whereby they received little encouragement or support, were channeled into nursing schools, encountered hostility from peers, and were excluded from the old boy network that placed persons in their careers.

More pertinent to the status of women as physicians is a consideration of the structure of medical education and medical work as creating obstacles to women's advancement. Research cites the incidence of lack of sponsorship, sexual tracking systems, nonsupportive peer environments, and overt ridicule as contributing to the demise of women's medical careers (Lorber, 1991; Grant, 1988). There has been a reduction in women's attrition rates in medicine as government policies prohibiting gender discrimination have disrupted the autonomy of male-dominated professional enterprises. The current women's movement has helped create a climate of mutual support among women students and professionals, leading to the creation of an environment more conducive to women's success. Only the future will show us if these recent changes will continue to be effective in enhancing women's status. The historical record of women's decline in medical careers indicates that none of these gains can be taken for granted. Continual lobbying, network building among women, and federal support for women's medical education are all necessary for stabilizing the role of women in this profession.

The Women's Health Movement

The women's health movement has suggested various alternatives to traditional medical care, ranging from more consumer information to feminist self-help clinics (Ruzek, 1978; Lewin and Olesen, 1985). As a social movement, the women's health movement has resulted from a reaction to the sexism of the medical profession and the criticism of traditional medical practices that deny women control of their own reproductive lives and physical health.

Numerous groups in the women's health movement are also organized to provide health care to women without the high-handed authority of traditional medical practitioners. Many of these organizations disseminate health care information, some offer direct services, and others work primarily as lobbying organizations, attempting to create changes in the health care system and its policies.

Altogether, the women's health movement has the goals of reducing differences in knowledge between patient and practitioner, challenging the mandate of physicians as the sole providers of health care, reducing the professional monopoly over goods and services, increasing the number of women practitioners, and organizing clients around health issues (Ruzek, 1978). The emergence of the women's health movement is indicative of the dissatisfaction women have shown in health care institutions and over issues involving reproduction and health. As this chapter has shown, feminist perspectives on health and reproduction insist on women's right to control their own bodies. As long as the power to control women's bodies remains predominantly in the hands of men, feminists are likely to continue organizing on these issues.

ᐧᐤ *Summary*

Physical health is influenced by gender roles. Patterns of male and female health change according to historical conditions. Health studies indicate that mortality and illness rates are associated with gender roles in society. Racial and class oppression also influence the likelihood of physical health and illness, as well as the likelihood of death by accident, hypertension, and other diseases.

Occupational health and safety must also be seen in the context of gender relations. Women and men workers are exposed to a wide variety of occupational health hazards; health hazards vary according to occupation. Protective legislation against reproductive hazards has typically been aimed at female workers, although reproductive hazards are incurred by male workers, as well. Protective legislation has also often been used to exclude women workers from high-paying, high-status, traditionally male occupations.

Social problems associated with health are also conditioned by the culture's gender expectations. Cultural obsession with thinness creates a high rate of anorexia, bulimia, and other eating problems, although for women of color and lesbian women, eating disorders are a response to stress. Women's gender roles also influence their use of alcohol and drugs. Women are less likely to engage in alcohol and substance abuse than are men.

Feminists believe in women's right to control their own bodies. Female control of reproduction has been historically and cross-culturally the most prevalent social arrangement. Modern Western cultures have put reproductive control in the hands of male medical authorities. Birth control is a right that women have achieved through judicial reform. Abortion was made legal by the 1973 Supreme Court ruling in *Roe* v. *Wade*. Public support for abortion has increased in recent years. Population control and sterilization abuse have been used to exploit women of color.

Childbirth occurs in this culture within institutions that are controlled and organized by men. The medical model defines childbirth as a medical event requiring intervention and technological supervision. Interventionist practices have resulted in an increase in the number of cesarean section births. New reproductive technologies raise liberating possibilities for women and men but, to date, have not been controlled by women. Reproductive technologies also can be linked to eugenics movements for population control.

Gender relationships influence the doctor-patient relationship, because the majority of doctors are men and the majority of patients are women. Women's treatment by the medical profession stems from stereotypes physicians may hold about women clients. Gender stratification in the health care system keeps women, for the most part, in lesser-status jobs and gives them less control than men have over medical decisions and medical knowledge. The women's health care movement is a social movement that is critical of male control of health care systems and that is organized to help women resist medical exploitation.

❧ Key Terms

anorexia nervosa
Automobile Workers v. *Johnson
    Controls*
bulimia

Eisenstadt v. *Baird*
Griswold v. *Connecticut*
infant mortality
Muller v. *Oregon*

protective legislation
Roe v. *Wade*

❧ Discussion Questions/Projects for Thought

1. Identify a group of women workers in the health care field (nurses, women physicians, medical technologists, radiologists, physicians' assistants, etc.) and interview them about their work. What opportunities are available to them? Are their jobs segregated by gender and race/ethnicity? How do they see themselves relative to men they work with? What happens to those who try to move up? Are they satisfied with their jobs? If not, why not; if so, why? What do your interviews tell you about the social structure of gender in the health care field?

2. Using a recent sampling of the magazines read most frequently by your peers, describe what the magazine conveys as the ideal image for women's bodies. How does this influence the eating behavior of those who read it? How extensive are eating disorders among women and men on your campus? What do you think are the origins of these problems?

3. Identify a group of women and men on your campus who smoke. Interview them about when they started smoking, why they do so, and what they perceive it as doing for them. Are they aware of the risks of smoking to their health? When you analyze the answers to your questions, ask yourself how gender influences the smoking patterns of people on your campus.

❧ *Suggested Readings*

Boston Women's Health Collective Staff. 1998. *Our Bodies, Ourselves for the New Century.* New York: Simon and Schuster.
Written by a feminist group of health care providers, this book includes sound medical information, as well as psychological and sociological insights about women's health and well-being. It is the single-most useful handbook about many health issues, including birth control, pregnancy, sexuality, menopause, and other topics.

Butler, Sandra, and Barbara Rosenblum. 1991. *Cancer in Two Voices.* San Francisco: Spinsters Book Company.
This book is a moving, firsthand account of the experience of two women lovers—a professional therapist and a sociologist—as one of them dies of cancer. The authors provide an intimate view of the relationship of the lovers, exploring how illness and death affect personal relationships and doing so with both a sociological eye and a strong feeling of love.

Clarke, Adele E., and Virginia L. Olesen. 1998. *Revisioning Women, Health, and Healing: Feminist, Cultural and Technoscience Perspectives.* New York: Routledge.
The authors provide a comprehensive review of feminist issues about women's health, with an eye to providing alternative perspectives to the dominant medical model.

Diamond, Timothy. 1992. *Making Gray Gold: Narratives of Nursing Home Care.* Chicago: University of Chicago Press.
Based on qualitative research in nursing homes, the book explores the dynamics between nursing assistants and nursing home residents. Situated in the context of the commercialization of nursing homes as profit centers, Diamond also explores the caregiving roles of women of color as attendants to White, elderly women. This unique exploration of power relationships and the influence of capitalism on aging is a moving sociological portrayal of both populations of women.

Rothman, Barbara Katz. 1989. *Recreating Motherhood: Ideology and Technology in a Patriarchal Society.* New York: Norton.
This book examines the ideology of motherhood in a society characterized by sexism. It particularly looks at how technology has transformed the experience of motherhood in ways that disempower women.

Ruzek, Sheryl B., Virginia Olesen, and Adele E. Clarke, eds. 1997. *Women's Health: Complexities and Differences.* Columbus, OH: Ohio State University Press.
This anthology provides an overview on topics about women's health, showing how gender, race, and class shape health care experiences and institutions.

Schneider, Beth E., and Nancy E. Stoller. 1995. *Women Resisting AIDS: Feminist Strategies of Empowerment.* Philadelphia: Temple University Press.
This anthology studies various ways that women have organized on behalf of AIDS prevention and research. It not only provides valuable information about AIDs, with an emphasis on its effect on women, but it also explains how women are making a difference in AIDS education, prevention, and care.

Sullivan, Deborah A., and Rose Weitz. 1988. *Labor Pains: Modern Midwives and Home Birth.* New Haven, CT: Yale University Press.
Based on interviews with lay midwives and obstetricians, this book is a comprehensive analysis of the growth of home birth in the contemporary United States and the revolt against medicalized birth that this movement represents. The book reviews the legal status of midwifery, as well as public controversies surrounding this transformation of the birthing process.

Thompson, Becky W. 1994. *A Hunger So Wide and So Deep: American Women Speak Out on Eating Problems*. Minneapolis: University of Minnesota Press.

Based on intensive interviewing with African American, Latina, and White lesbian women, Thompson's study challenges medical and psychological understandings of eating problems among women and revises feminist accounts that emphasize a "culture of thinness" as the primary origin for eating problems.

White, Evelyn C. 1990. *The Black Women's Health Book: Speaking for Ourselves*. Seattle: The Seal Press.

This collection of essays examines numerous facets of African American women's health, placing the origins of health problems in the racial and gender inequality of U.S. society. The book has important implications for developing comprehensive national health care policies that will serve all women.

❧ *Chapter* **8**
Women and Religion

In 1895, Elizabeth Cady Stanton, a passionate feminist, close friend of Susan B. Anthony, and founder of equal rights and suffrage associations during the first wave of feminism in the nineteenth century, wrote:

> *From the inauguration of the movement for women's emancipation the Bible has been used to hold her in the "divinely ordained sphere," prescribed in the Old and New testaments. The canon and civil law; church and state; priests and legislators; all political parties and religious denominations have alike taught that woman was made after man, of man, and for man, an inferior being, subject to man. Creeds, codes, Scriptures and statutes, are all based on this idea. The fashions, forms, ceremonies and customs of society, church ordinances and discipline all grow out of this idea. (Stanton, 1895/1974:7)*

More than 100 years later, Stanton's words still ring true. Certain religious beliefs have aroused conservative political movements that threaten many of the rights that women have won as the result of feminism, and in many religions, women continue to be excluded from positions of leadership. In those where they are now permitted to hold positions of leadership, they are still a small minority. Both in the United States and worldwide, some religious beliefs are the core of sexist ideologies that promote women's exclusion from the public world and that maintain women's subordination in the home. In the United States, the Judeo-Christian tradition is the foundation for laws governing marriage, divorce, contraception, abortion, and sexuality that feminists argue have oppressed women. Feminists also contend that the church provides the basis for the double standard of male and female sexuality. Women's role models in the Christian church are defined through women's sexual behavior and dichotomize women into two polar types: Eve, the temptress, and Mary, the virginal mother (Burlage, 1974).

Religion is a powerful source for the subordination of women in society; yet, across the years religion has also been an important source for the feminist movement and other social and political movements for human liberation. This is evident in the African American community, where religion has been a powerful instrument for social change and where women's roles in the church have provided African American women with opportunities for leadership, education, and the development of organizational skills. In addition, religious belief in the Black community rests on a strong faith in justice, fairness, and equality. The liberating effects of religion are also evident in Judaism—one of the most conservative religions in its doctrine about women—yet, its religious faith has spawned feminism and liberalism.

Although religion has been a repressive force in women's lives, it has also been a source of liberation. Bernice Johnson Reagon, Black feminist and performer, reflects on her religious experience in childhood, writing in her autobiography:

> *Everybody in church talked about/Miss Nana's relationship with God/People thought she had a sort of audacity/Everybody else would say/"Now, Lord, here comes me your meek and undone servant and you know me and you know my condition"/This was a way of saying/"Now Lord, I don't even need to go over my situation/Let us start now with where I am and what I need today"/ . . . /Miss Nana was grateful for what she got but she didn't let up on God for what she wanted/God had already given her a soul, right?/But then she'd say,/"That ain't all I need, Lord/You are not off the hook/I expect you to be here on time tomorrow night." (1982:90–91)*

Our understanding of these dual tendencies of repression and liberation will be best developed through exploring sociological and feminist perspectives on religion. The sections that follow explore several themes in the feminist critique of religion, including the historical relationship of women, religion, and feminism; women's religious beliefs and status within churches; the role of the church in minority communities; and new perspectives inspired by feminist spirituality and theology.

❧ Sociological Perspectives on Religion

For most people, religion is something they hold dear, sometimes so much so that they see it as the only possible view of the world. Paul Tillich (1957), a liberal theologian, defines religion as the expression of humanity's ultimate concerns, the articulation of longing for a center of meaning and value and for connection with the power of being. Sociologists who study religion take another approach. They are not so much interested in the truth or falsity of a religious belief system but in how belief systems and religious institutions shape social behavior and reflect the collective experience of society's members.

From a sociological perspective, religion provides a culture with powerful symbols and conceptions that are deeply felt and shape a group's view of the world around them. Religious belief is often the basis for cultural and societal conflict and is frequently so strongly felt that people will fight and die for it. Religion is also the basis for in-group membership, sometimes strongly protected by sanctions against interfaith marriages, although more than three-quarters of

Americans approve of marriages between Catholics and Protestants or between Jews and non-Jews (McMurray, 1985).

Sociological perspectives on religion also take the institutional structure of religion as significant in a variety of ways. Like other institutions in society, religious institutions socialize their members through enforcing group norms that dictate many aspects of everyday life, including what men and women wear; how life events (such as birth, puberty, marriage, and death) are defined and ritualized; and how men and women are defined in terms of home, work, child care, politics, and the law. Religious institutions also include power structures and, like other social institutions, are characterized by a system of stratification, which is clearly demarcated by gender, race, and class. Feminists have also described patriarchal religions as legitimating widespread violence against women, as in the case of Indian suttee, African clitoral circumcisions, and the burning of women as witches (Daly, 1978).

Religious belief is a particularly important part of our sexual experience. Researchers find that religion, more than any other sociological factor, plays the strongest influence on women's sexual behavior. The frequency and number of a woman's sexual encounters is highly related to her religious faith. In a classic study of human sexual behavior, Kinsey and colleagues (1953) showed that the most devout women are those who are the least sexually active, whereas the least religious are much more sexually active. This finding has held up over time, as sociological studies have reported an inverse relationship between religious behavior and premarital sexual behavior (Woodruff, 1985), meaning that those who are most religious are those who are least likely to engage in premarital sex. Others have also argued that the practice of confession in the Catholic church is a form of social control and regulation of sexual life (Zaretsky, 1980).

These studies indicate that sex and gender are not just a matter of secular social relations. Despite an overall decline in religious faith in U.S. society, religion continues to be a powerful influence on gender relations in contemporary society. For feminist scholars, one of the beginning points of their analysis of religion is the fact that, as measured by a variety of indicators, women are more religious than men in U.S. society. Women are more likely to attend church than men are and to attend on a regular basis; women express higher degrees of religiosity, but, as feminists have pointed out, despite the fact that women outnumber men in religious faith and in attendance at worship services, it is men, regardless of religious denomination, who maintain religious authority. In Christian churches it is men, for the most part, who are the priests and clergy, and they are typically backed up in the institution by men as deacons, elders, and vestry of the church. Orthodox Jews and Roman Catholics still deny ordination to women, and, although their numbers are growing, women are a numerical minority in seminaries of all faiths.

These patterns of gender inequality in religious institutions have raised the question of the extent to which religious traditions contribute to the subjugation of women. Feminist scholars have also examined the alliance between religion and other oppressive social systems (Hargrove, Schmidt, and Davaney, 1993). Religion is clearly one of the foremost forces in society to preserve traditions, conserve established social order, stabilize world views, and transmit values through generations, but religion is equally important in social transformation. Religious beliefs can and do frame new sources of human potential and possibility, and organized religious groups can release enormous bursts of political energy (Falk, 1985). This is well demonstrated in the history of the civil rights movement, with its organizational center in African American churches. The civil rights movement demonstrates that religious institutions can provide liberation movements with the leadership, organizational structure, and values that provide both the support network for social movements and the visions for new futures that such movements need.

❧ Religion and Social Control

From a sociological perspective, religion is one of the forces that holds society together. Although it is also a source of conflict, both within and between different groups and societies, religion is an integrative force in that it shapes collective belief and therefore collective identity. Religious rituals—such as weddings, christenings, and bar and bat mitzvahs—promote group solidarity and symbolize group cohesion. Promoting identification with a religious group gives members a feeling of belonging; at the same time, it also promotes feelings of exclusionary or outsider status to those outside of the group. Jewish or Muslim people living in a predominantly Christian society therefore feel estranged from the dominant culture, yet, their religious faith creates their own awareness of group identity.

Because religion is such a powerful source of collective identity, it also is a form of social control. Religious sanctions, whether formal or informal, chastise those who violate religious norms. Religious beliefs, if internalized (i.e., learned and developed as part of one's self-concept and moral development), direct individual and group beliefs and behaviors. In this way, religion controls the development of self and group identity. At the societal level, religion also can be a form of social control. In the extreme, groups who deviate from religious proscriptions may be tortured, executed, or excommunicated; in more subtle ways, religious deviants may be ridiculed, shunned, or ostracized. In the history of Western religion, the persecution of witches is a good illustration of the connections between religion, social control, and gender.

During the Middle Ages in western Europe, it is estimated that between 30,000 and 9,000,000 women were killed or tortured as witches (Daly, 1978). The breadth of this estimate indicates how difficult it is to pinpoint the number of witch persecutions. Toward the end of the seventeenth century in the United States, another 20 persons (7 of whom were men) were tried and executed as witches. Although the scope of this experience hardly matches that of the witch craze that swept Europe during the period of the Inquisition, the sociological impetus was the same. In both places, witches were believed to be women influenced by the devil, and they were perceived to be threats to social purity.

In western Europe, the *Malleus Maleficarum*, issued by the Catholic church in 1484, defined the church's position on witches. This document defined witchcraft, described the alleged practices of witches, and standardized trial procedures and sentencing for those persecuted as witches throughout Europe. The *Malleus Maleficarum* defined witchcraft as stemming from women's carnal lust; women were seen as instruments of Satan because of their insatiable desire. According to the *Malleus Maleficarum*, "All witchcraft comes from carnal lust, which is in women insatiable. Quoting Proverbs XXX: "There are three things that are never satisfied, yea, a fourth thing which says not, it is enough; that is, the mouth of the womb" (*Malleus Maleficarum*, cited in Dworkin, 1974:133). People believed that witches collected male organs for use in satanic rituals and stole semen from sleeping men. They were also believed to cast spells over male organs so that the organs disappeared entirely!

Who were these women, and what was happening in history that there was such organized madness to eradicate them? Historians explain the witch hunts as stemming from the historical movement of the Catholic and Protestant churches to establish themselves as supreme authorities over sacred and secular matters. The period of the witch hunts in western Europe was a period of the solidification of church authority. Women who were singled out as witches were women who deviated from the religious norms of the time; they were healers, wise women, and midwives. Those who formed witch cults were women who had a strong sense of people as a part of nature and who, because of this belief, gave animals a prime place in some of their rituals. Such a belief system, with its integrated view of human life and nature, was anathema to the patriarchal and hierarchical structure of the church. As feminists have argued, because the church was the ultimate representation of male power, witchcraft also symbolized men's fears of female sexuality, its assumed relationship to nature, and its unbounded expression. Feminists describe the witch hunts as a means of men's desire to control women's sexuality (Daly, 1978; Dworkin, 1974). Women defined as witches also were often widows and spinsters—in other words, single women who were living independently of men (Anderson and Gordon, 1978; Szasz, 1970). In sum, the witch hunts were a mechanism for ensuring the social control of women by men, as represented in the emerging hegemony of organized patriarchal religion.

The persecution of women as witches is a historical case of the imposition of serious sanctions against women who lived outside the developing control of patriarchal religious bodies and outside the control of men. Modern sociologists see the persecution of witches as the persecution of sexual and religious deviants (Szasz, 1970). Although in retrospect this may seem like an extreme case, there are contemporary equivalents. The so-called ethnic cleansing in Bosnia-Herzogovinia that has resulted in the mass murder and rape of Bosnian Muslims by the Serbs can be interpreted as an example of ethnic conflicts that originate, in part, in religious differences. Analyses of Muslim fundamentalism have shown a link between Muslim concepts of female sexuality and the political, social, and economic subordination of Muslim women (Mernissi, 1987). Fundamentalist Christians are more likely than other religious groups to believe in sexual abstinence before marriage. Numerous such examples show the link between religious belief and the social control of women.

❧ Religion and the Emergence of Feminism in the United States

Discussion of religion as a form of social control may create an assumption that religion is only a negative force in women's lives. Religion, however, is also a source of resistance to oppression. This duality is well illustrated by the history of feminism in the United States.

In the United States, the power of the Protestant and Catholic faiths was well established during the colonial period, and, although women outnumbered men in the churches, the church hierarchy was exclusively male (Cott, 1977). Not until the nineteenth century in the United States do historians typically see the beginnings of significant social change in women's religious roles and the seeds of developing feminism. Two particular developments in the nineteenth century in the United States have major significance for the role of women in religion and the development of the feminist movement: the evangelical spirit of the Second Great Awakening and the widespread belief in the cult of womanhood that defined and restricted women's world to the world of domesticity (Hargrove, Schmidt, and Davaney, 1993).

The **Second Great Awakening** was a social movement in the early nineteenth century that emphasized a revivalist and egalitarian spirit in religion. During this period, ministers and laypersons began to see religion as a route to salvation on earth and they used this belief to teach the restraints they believed were necessary for an orderly society (Cott, 1977). Occurring in the aftermath of the French Revolution and in the midst of worries about the destructive influence of growing urban populations and Catholic immigration, the Second Great Awakening had a democratic impulse—reaching out to the urban poor and western frontier residents. The Second Great Awakening created a lay missionary spirit in which conversion and religious benevolence were seen as the solution to the social ills generated by widespread social transformations affecting the fabric of American society (Cott, 1977).

During this period, Christianity was softened (or "feminized"); rather than stressing dogma, it instead exalted meekness. Christians also began to reinterpret Christ as embodying these more gender-typed images of love, forgiveness, and humility. The "feminization" of American culture and religion meant that, among other things, by the middle of the nineteenth century, women were the majority in American religion (Douglas, 1977; Welter, 1976). During this time, women were defined as the keepers of the private refuge of the home—the place where piety and religious spirit were to prosper. In this domestic refuge, women's purity and piety were seen as vehicles for redemption; women were seen in opposition to the aggressiveness and competition of the public sphere that was identified with men. Although these images exalted the traditional status of women, many have suggested that they also provided women with positive roles and images—at least ones that did not degrade and denigrate women's culture. The exaltation of women's culture encouraged women to speak in prayer meetings and congregations and encouraged them to participate in voluntary religious associations.

Women's religious societies were especially successful at fund-raising, and these societies became the basis for a developing sense of sisterhood among women. Local missionary activities trained women for what was defined as a life of social usefulness, teaching them hygiene, citizenship, family values, and social relationships and engaging them in fieldwork in the cities. As a consequence, women's religious activities engaged them in other social reform movements.

During the nineteenth century, women were considered to be more spiritual and more naturally prone to religious observance and piety than were men. The belief that women were naturally good also influenced the development of the feminist movement in this period. Women's alleged moral superiority was perceived to have a potentially benevolent impact on the more callous and harsh realities of the public world. Some feminists argued that extending the values of the domestic or private sphere to the public would create a more compassionate public world—a theme now resounded among some contemporary feminists, as well (Miller, 1977). Throughout the nineteenth century women's movement, religious faith played an important part in articulating feminist concerns. Women in the Women's Christian Temperance Union, one of the first feminist organizations, extolled the virtues of women and blamed the impersonal and competitive culture of the male public world for a variety of social ills.

Belief in the virtues of women's culture led early feminists to use the values of the home as the basis for crusading in the public world and for demanding women's rights. At the same time, as the suffrage movement developed, men (and some women) also used arguments from the Bible against women's suffrage and other changes in women's status. They maintained that the Scripture ordered a different and higher sphere of life apart from public life and that this "higher" sphere was the responsibility and, in fact, nature of women. As a result, many feminists eventually gave up on the traditional churches and turned to experimental religious societies, such as the Quakers, for more inner-directed spiritual experiences.

For most early feminists in the United States, religious faith was a significant part of their feminist ideology. Elizabeth Cady Stanton was herself relatively alone in seeing the domination of women as having religious roots. By the late nineteenth century, when Stanton first published *The Woman's Bible*, the influence of Darwin's thought was also paramount in U.S. culture. Stanton had likely been influenced by the more relativistic view of culture that Darwin's work inspired. Darwin's work had encouraged the development of anthropological relativism—a system of thought that saw ideas in society as emerging from culture. Such a belief made it possible to doubt that the Bible had been divinely inspired. While Stanton herself seemed to be influenced by this developing social consciousness, other feminists of the period did not share her perspective.

The first publication of *The Woman's Bible* in 1895 (reprinted in 1898) reflected Stanton's belief that domination of women had deep ideological and religious roots. Other feminists, however, did not share her sense of its importance. Members of the National American Women Suffrage Association, with the exception of Susan B. Anthony and a few others, repudiated any connection with this view (Hole and Levine, 1971). Afterwards, *The Woman's Bible* went into obscurity, not to be rediscovered until the 1970s during the second wave of feminism in the United States.

Historians of religion have since asked why Christianity was a basis for women's progressive movements in the nineteenth century when in the twentieth century, Christianity is more often perceived as an enemy to feminists than a friend (Reuther and Keller, 1986). The answer lies in observing the social transformations occurring in the nineteenth century. Throughout the nineteenth century, the process of industrialization meant that men had entered a new secular world. Even when women worked in the industrial sector, the cultural ideology of the time defined women's world as being in the home. Religion was defined as a part of women's culture, although, for women, religion was one of the few dimensions of public culture in which they were allowed to participate.

By the early twentieth century, White women's winning of the vote coincided with shifts in the boundaries between religious and secular domains. White women in the twentieth century entered the public world with men. Feminist social reformers of the 1920s and 1930s were more likely to use the language and philosophy of social science than they were to use theology to articulate their concerns. In the twentieth century, religion for women, if they believed it at all, had become more a private culture. At the same time, secularization resulted in the increasing conservatism of churches on women's issues. Churches, particularly Evangelical and Catholic churches, perceived secularism as having a pernicious influence on society. As a result, the churches politicized religious culture by using religious doctrine as a platform against women's equality—including their social, legal, and reproductive rights.

By the time of the emergence of the second wave of feminism in the 1970s, women's religious roles had changed dramatically. Although many feminists were still active in religious life, their critical distance from religious institutions and their understanding of religion's sexist roots created a new basis for feminist criticism of religion and a new basis for feminist transformation of religious thought.

❧ Women and Religiosity

Images of Women in Religion

Feminists have contended that the traditional view of women in most religious faiths idealizes and humiliates women (Daly, 1978). Images of women in religious texts reflect and create stereotypical gender roles and legitimate social inequality between men and women. The New Testament of the Bible, for example, urges women to be subordinate to husbands, thereby fulfilling the assumed proper hierarchy of women as subordinate to men as men are subordinate to God. Jewish feminists have also repudiated the traditional Jewish morning prayer in which a man blesses God for not creating him as a woman, while a woman blesses God for creating her in accordance with His will.

The humiliation of women through religious texts is especially clear in religious depictions of female sexuality, defined by both Christianity and Judaism as a dangerous force to be feared, purified, and controlled by men. In Orthodox Judaism the myth that women are unclean during menstruation and seven days thereafter also reflects a negative view of female sexuality. Feminists see **misogyny**, meaning the hatred of women, depicted in the creation stories in male-dominated cultures that assign women responsibility for evil. In most of these legends women are seen as sexually alluring, curious, gullible, and insatiable. The biblical story of Adam and Eve is, of course, the classic example. Eve is depicted as cajoling Adam into eating the apple, thereby dooming them to live in a world of trouble and evil. Hebrew myth depicts Lilith, the first woman, as equal to Adam in all ways, but she refused to do what he wanted her to do. As this myth goes, in response to Adam's demands, the Lord created Eve from Adam's rib and made her inferior and dependent. One version of this legend in Hebrew tradition is that it was Lilith who persuaded Eve to eat the apple from the Tree of Knowledge. Feminists suggest that this creates dual stereotypes of woman—one as evil, the other as gullible. Either way, women are defined through these myths as bad (McGuire, 1997).

Religious Texts as Interpretive Documents

Whether a group of religious believers accepts their religious tradition as literally true and divinely ordained by God or whether the group sees their religious text as subject to interpretation influences the group's acceptance of transformed religious roles for women. Sociologists see all religious texts, including the Bible and the Torah, as cultural and historical documents. That is to say, sociologists see these texts as not containing truth per se, but as cultural artifacts—records of particular cultural beliefs, historical practices, and societal legends. The legends and beliefs that the texts communicate are the basis for what Durkheim called the **collective consciousness** of a society—the system of beliefs in a society that create a sense of belonging to the community and the moral obligation to live up to the society's demands. Sociologists see these histories and texts as neither true nor false, but as symbols, powerful as they may be, of group belief and collective consciousness; consequently, they are subject to interpretation and symbolic use by religious groups.

Seeing the Bible as a document to be interpreted, not just the literal word of God, is probably the most contentious point between sociologists of religion and those with strong and traditional commitments to religious world views. The use of Christianity to justify slavery shows, however, how Christianity and the Bible have been interpreted to support human oppression. European explorers who traveled to African cultures in the sixteenth century encountered societies having religious practices and beliefs quite unlike the Christian traditions of western Europe. Their response to such practices was to define African people as heathens and savages who worshipped pagan gods (Jordan, 1968). Europeans' identification of Africans as heathens led them to believe that Black women and men were lustful, passionate, and sexually aggressive; this became the basis for racial and sexual stereotypes of Black men and women. White beliefs in Black men's sexual prowess created fears among White men that were the basis for extreme measures of social control—including lynching—throughout U.S. history. The identification of Black women as lustful also established White men's belief in their rights to sexual relations with Black women.

Christian beliefs played a central role in legitimating the exploitative treatment of African people. Slave traders and owners believed that Africans needed Christian salvation. Slaveowners saw their exploitation of slaves as the justifiable and necessary conversion of heathens, even going so far as to think that the slaves could not take care of themselves. Slaveowners reasoned it was their Christian duty, although a burden, to care for the slaves (Genovese, 1972).

Although Christianity was a tool of the oppressing class, used to justify and legitimate the economic and cultural exploitation of millions of African American slaves, it also reinforced slaves' own belief in their rights as human beings. As a result, Christianity provided the basis for slaves' political resistance to exploitation. The slaves came to believe in the Christian values that slaveowners taught them, and therefore continued to believe in their own humanity and their rights to social justice. So, while Christianity was interpreted by slaveowners to justify slavery, for the slaves Christianity was also a source of salvation.

Understanding the relationship between Christianity, slavery, and emancipation also helps us understand why feminists who reject the misogynist traditions of religious beliefs and institutions sometimes see Christianity as providing the theological and philosophical basis for advocating women's liberation. In the sections that follow, we examine more carefully the role of women in religion and the new ways that feminist theologians have transformed traditional theology to generate new meaning systems intended for the liberation of human beings.

Gender and Religious Beliefs

As we have already seen, studies show that women are more religious than men, both in expressed religious faith and in women's participation in worship services (see Figures 8.1 and 8.2). This difference has persisted over time, despite the fact that church attendance has declined in U.S. society. In 1997, 58 percent of all Americans identified themselves as Protestant, 27 percent as Catholic, and 3 percent as Jewish; 9 percent claimed other religious preferences, and 5 percent said they had no religious preference (Gallup Poll, 1997).

In the United States, 70 percent of the population say they are members of a church or synagogue, although considerably fewer say they attend church weekly—33 percent of women and 26 percent of men (Gallup Poll, 1997; Moore, 1995). Because in polls more people report church membership than the churches themselves report to data-gathering agencies, poll data are not totally reliable. Nonetheless, the poll data indicate the public importance people attribute to religious affiliation and polls are a sound measure of where people place their religious identification.

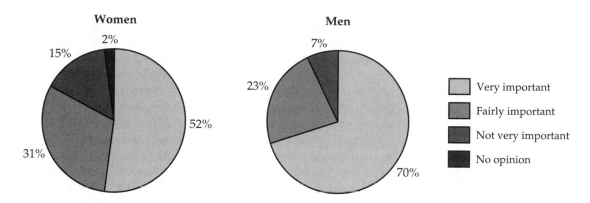

Women

Men

Very important

Fairly important

Not very important

No opinion

Question: How important would you say religion is in your life?

FIGURE 8.1   The Significance of Religion

Source: Data from Roper Organization. 1997. *The Gallup Poll.* Storrs, CT: Roper Organization.

Despite the historical decline in religious faith and attendance at worship services, religion still plays a significant role in U.S. society. Religious belief influences a wide array of other social attitudes and behaviors. As previously discussed, this is especially evident on matters involving sexual attitudes and behaviors. For example, a majority of men and women who say that religion is very important in their lives believe that premarital sex is wrong, while 80 percent of

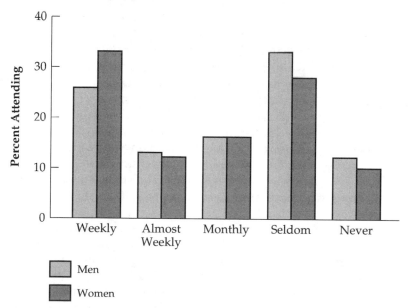

FIGURE 8.2   Frequency of Religious Attendance: 1994

Source: Data from *The Gallup Poll Monthly,* "Who Are the Religious Americans?" Storrs, CT: Roper Organization, p. 20.

those who say religion is not very important to them also believe there is nothing wrong with premarital sex (Gallup, 1985). In addition to influencing sexual attitudes, religious belief and affiliation also affect a broad range of opinions on social and political questions, with those of the Jewish faith typically being more socially and politically liberal. Church attendance and fundamentalist Protestant religious identification also tend to preserve more traditional gender role attitudes, whereas youth, labor force participation, and educational attainment contribute to more egalitarian views (Thornton, Alwin, and Camburn, 1983). Religion also influences the perpetuation of gender differences in occupational choices, with the most gender-segregated preferences appearing among men and women in religious denominations with the greatest degree of gender inequality in the church (Rhodes, 1983).

Attention to women's religious beliefs shows, however, that women may have a slightly different understanding of religion than do men. The General Social Survey, a national opinion poll taken among U.S. men and women, asked people to identify their images of God. The population as a whole ranked their images of God in the following order: creator, healer, friend, redeemer, father, master, king, judge, lover, liberator, mother, and spouse. On closer look, men were more likely than women to emphasize the paternal images of God (e.g., father, master, king), whereas women were more likely to identify with the more feminine images of God (e.g., healer, friend, lover, mother, and spouse). In recent years, the more feminine images of God have become increasingly popular among the entire population, although for both men and women they are still secondary to paternal images (Roof and McKinney, 1987).

These data suggest that women's understandings of religion may differ from those of men and that women may adopt those aspects of religious belief that speak best to their situations (McGuire, 1997). The data also raise the question as to whether women see themselves as their religion sees them. Although the traditional image of women in religious texts is one that sees women as more passive, docile, and pious, women may be more active agents in the construction of their religious identity and beliefs than has typically been assumed. Although sexist images in religious thought remain, it may well be that women adapt them to their own circumstances, indicating that women's religious faith is not as passive or meek as the images in religious texts suggest.

This has been demonstrated in a study of contemporary, well-educated women who have returned to Orthodox Judaism. In her study of these women, Lynn Davidman, a feminist sociologist, asked how women who have the modern options of a career would turn to a traditional religious faith, one that professes very traditional roles for women. Such a conversion seems contrary to societal movement toward women's greater independence and new gender roles—transformations one would especially expect to see among well-educated women. Davidman found, however, that joining an orthodox religious community where they retreated from the public world was one way her respondents avoided the difficulties faced by other women who have to balance the competing definitions of womanhood generated by dual and competing roles for women in the family and at work. For the women she studied, religious orthodoxy provided meaning and a sense of self that was less fragmented than more modern and evolving definitions for career women. Davidman (1991) is careful to point out that the construction of women's identities, including their religious identities, is an active and conscious decision the women make. This perspective sees women not as mere victims of religious and gender roles but as active agents in the construction of their own identities and religious world views.

In recent years, there has been a dramatic resurgence of traditional evangelical Christianity. Evangelicals, popularly known as "born-again Christians," are those who claim to have been born again through conversion, who accept Jesus as a personal savior, who believe the Scriptures are the authority for all doctrine, who feel urgency in spreading their faith, and who claim to have had a dramatic witnessing of the presence of a divine spirit (Flowers, 1984; Pohli, 1983). They also hold highly traditional views of womanhood. By 1996, 43 percent of the U.S. population identified themselves as "born again," an increase from 17 percent in 1981. The resurgence of this movement has created a consequent rise in the political power of this group. More women than men identify themselves as evangelical Christians; women are 54 percent of all evangelical Christians. Although the vast majority of evangelical Christians are White (74 percent), 36 percent of all nonWhites are evangelical Christians, compared with 16 percent of Whites. Compared with the rest of the national population, evangelical Christians are less educated, older, and more likely to live in small communities. Fifty-three percent of evangelical Christians have no college education; 46 percent began, but did not graduate from, college (Gallup Poll, 1993; 1996). Studies also find that young women have a more positive attitude toward Christianity than young men and that among both young men and women a positive attitude toward Christianity is associated with belief in more traditional gender roles (Francis and Wilcox, 1998).

Careful examination of the world views and social attitudes and experiences of women in the evangelical churches finds that women's opinions in these faiths are "received ones," meaning that women are more likely to internalize religious views imposed by others. Studies of evangelical women find that becoming an evangelical Christian involves the narrow constriction of women's world views and opinions about the world and social issues (Pohli, 1983). As you will see in a subsequent section, belief in evangelical Christianity among women is also a source for their antifeminist political activities.

❧ Women's Status in Religious Institutions

Women's Roles

Measures of church attendance and identification alone do not fully reveal the extent of women's religious participation. Although observers can easily document that women have been excluded from positions of religious leadership, nonetheless it is women who constitute the vast bulk of church activity. Many of these activities are difficult to measure numerically, but observations of women's activities in religious organizations show that women run the church bake sales, dinners, and bazaars. Women also teach Sunday schools, babysit during religious services, visit the sick, join prayer circles, and arrange and staff church social events. In fact, women have historically been those who raise funds for churches and temples. Although Orthodox Judaism defines women's religious role as centered in the home, women in Reform temples participate fully in the life of the temple and they engage in a wide array of volunteer religious, educational, and philanthropic activities (Hargrove, Schmidt, and Davaney, 1993).

These activities in different religious organizations make important social ties for women, but they also reflect a gender division of labor within religious institutions. In Protestant churches, women rarely preach, serve as trustees, control funds, or make decisions about the pastor, church, or church programs. In Roman Catholic churches, men have held all the positions of religious authority. This patriarchal structure is so pervasive that Roman Catholicism has even been described as a sexual caste system. This means that despite the greater participation and faith of Roman Catholic women, the organizational structure, beliefs, ritual expressions, and prescribed norms of the Catholic Church are patriarchal (McGuire, 1997).

Gender segregation in religious institutions is also evident in the nontraditional religious cults. In the Hare Krishna, Sikh, and Divine Light Mission religious cults, women's roles have been described as those of a housemother. These cults are male authority systems in which women serve the men in exchange for the rewards of emotional gratification. The very intense nature of commitment in these nontraditional groups can lead to extremely repressive aspects. Women in these cults typically have domestic obligations required as demonstration of their religious commitment, and they are often expected to engage in sexual relations with the men of the cult. Whereas male devotees have access to positions of power as a means of bonding and sustaining their group affiliation, love and devotion are seen as leading to spiritual fulfillment for women in these movements. Women in these cults are often subjected to psychological, physical, and sexual abuse, as they are expected to be devoted to the religious leaders. Those who have studied women who leave such movements have noted, in fact, that the destruction of romantic idealism is a significant part of the women's decision to leave these movements (Jacobs, 1984).

Despite the patriarchal structure of religious institutions, women develop organizational and leadership skills through their work in these institutions. Although their contribution is often trivialized, there is a heavy dependence on women's labor in religious organizations; however, in most churches and temples, it seems that women are in the background. They play the support roles, but not the leadership roles. The Catholic church, for example, relies heavily on the work of nuns in the church, the schools, and the community, but, until the mid-1960s when Vatican II modernized the role of nuns by allowing them to discard their habits and take on a more public role, nuns were cloistered and were kept silent. Now they are among the active women within the church and are urging that women be ordained and given access to real power in the Catholic church.

Women as Clergy

The restriction of women to support positions in the church and their exclusion from making policies has led women to organize for the ordination of women in all the major denominations. Women now constitute 14 percent of all clergy, an increase from the past, but still a small proportion, especially considering that women are 62 percent of all religious workers. Even in the Catholic church, where women cannot be ordained, women serve as parish leaders in many places where there is no priest present (Wallace, 1992).

The entry of women into the clergy is not entirely new, although its magnitude is certainly unprecedented. Throughout the nineteenth century, women were licensed as evangelists, and, beginning in the 1880s, African American women began to press for ordination in the mainline Protestant denominations. The African Methodist Episcopal Zion Church ordained women as early as 1884, and the African Methodist Episcopal Church began ordaining women in 1948, but Harvard Divinity School did not even open its doors to women until 1955.

Holiness and Pentecostal denominations account for the largest share of all clergywomen. Those who have examined women's role as clergy in Holiness and Pentecostal churches claim that the higher status of women as clergy in these churches stems from the faiths' rejection of the practices of the mainline churches, including their role definitions for women. Their emphasis on charismatic or prophetic ministry, rather than the more "priestly" ministry of male-dominated religious institutions, means that the ministry is more open to women's participation (Barfoot and Sheppard, 1980; Carroll, Hargrove, and Lummis, 1981). As these churches evolve into more traditional and bureaucratic organizations and away from more spiritual symbolic roles, the proportion of women in positions of clerical leadership does decrease (Barfoot and Sheppard, 1980).

Evidence of the increasing role of women in the clergy is also seen by the substantial increases in their enrollments in divinity schools (see Figure 8.3). In 1972, women were only 10.2 percent of divinity students, compared with 33 percent by the 1990s. These increases reflect more than an increasing proportion of women as divinity students; they reflect large increases in the absolute numbers of women in divinity school (Baumgaertner, 1986). By 1994, women received 25 percent of all Ph.D.s in theology, compared with 2.3 percent in 1970 (U.S. Bureau of Commerce, 1997).

More people now support having women in positions of religious leadership, with 75 percent of Lutherans, Methodists, Episcopalians, and Presbyterians supporting equality in church leadership. Half of Catholics now endorse this idea, but members of more conservative Christian denominations (e.g., Southern Baptists and Assemblies of God) are unlikely to support women's roles as leaders. Religious faiths that give a more priestly role to leadership and define women as supporters, rather than as leaders, are at least likely to support women as clergy (Hoffman, 1997; Nason-Clark, 1987; Jelen, 1989). People are also more likely to endorse the idea of women's leadership in the church once they have experienced having a woman in this role. Women, young people, and those with more formal education are also most likely to support women's ordination (Dudley, 1996).

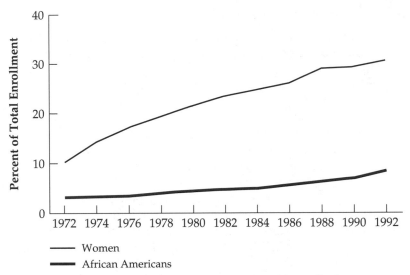

FIGURE 8.3 Women and African Americans Enrolled in U.S. Seminaries

Source: Data from Robert Famighetti, ed. 1995. *The World Almanac and Books of Facts, 1995.* Mahwah, NJ: Funk & Wagnalls Corporation, p. 736.

Generally, as the women's movement has changed the public perception of women's roles, resistance to women as clergy has declined over time (Chaves and Cavendish, 1997). Because women are more liberal on critical issues facing religious organizations, such as abortion and the acceptance of gays and lesbians, an increase in women's leadership may well influence church positions on abortion and other issues in the future (Finlay, 1997).

Those who advocate women's greater leadership in religious institutions often do so by asserting that women will bring a more woman-centered approach to these leadership roles. Studies of women ministers and rabbis find that women in these roles do tend to have a more collaborative style than men and that there are gender-specific approaches to women's leadership roles. Women ministers also tend to be more open to a wide variety of service-oriented roles, whereas male clergy are more likely to want a high-status clientele (Finlay, 1996). How women specifically define their roles depends somewhat on their faith. Women rabbis, for example, are more likely to emphasize the secular aspects of their leadership (as teacher, counselor, and community leader), whereas women ministers emphasize the more spiritual components of their role (saying they are a "moral voice" and emphasizing that they have been "called" to the ministry). In either case, women believe they carry out their role differently from male colleagues, saying they are more engaging, less formal, more people-oriented, and less concerned about power struggles (Lehman, 1994; Wallace, 1992; Simon, Scanlan, and Nadell, 1994).

🕊 *Religion, Racism, and Social Change*

The Role of the Church in African American Communities

Within African American communities, the church has historically provided a buffer against segregation, discrimination, and bigotry. Some sociologists have also suggested that African American churches provide for the release of emotion that cannot be expressed in the dominant White racist society (Blackwell, 1991). Most recognize that the church is, along with the family, the most important institution in African American society. It is the one institution over which African Americans have their own control (Frazier, 1964), and it is an important source of social cohesion. African American churches are often described as the organizational and expressive core of African American culture and community (Dodson and Gilkes, 1986), where the church performs a variety of social and community functions (Blackwell, 1991).

African American churches are instruments for the development of Black leadership, and they provide a cohesive institutional structure within African American communities. They are also the basis for community action and act as charitable institutions on behalf of African American people. As a result of the churches' many functions, Black ministers (and, when the ministers are men, their wives) play roles as both social workers and political, personal, and religious advisors. The Black church has a function of supporting education and being an institution for the transmission of community values, historically stressing the value of the family, mutuality, and responsibility. The educational function of the African American church is illustrated by the fact that more than one-half of all historically Black colleges are funded by religious bodies. The church in African American communities can also be an agency for the development of business ventures, a situation especially well illustrated by the economic entrepreneurship of Black Muslims.

The Role of Women in African American Churches

Within the African American community, as in other communities, it is the work of African American women that holds the church together. It is estimated that Black churches are 75 percent female. In the **sanctified church**—the term used to refer to Holiness and Pentecostal churches—women are 90 percent of the congregation. Women's activities are crucial to African American churches, and Gilkes (1985) contends that all African American churches have been influenced by the militancy of women in the sanctified church. Gilkes also points out that historically men have rarely matched the financial contributions of women in the sanctified church.

African American women, like White women, seem to have greater participation in decision making in churches with smaller, not larger, congregations (Grant, 1982). Interviews with African American male ministers, however, reveal continuing prejudices against African American women in the ministry, resulting in unfair expectations and unjust treatment of women ministers whom they encounter (Grant, 1982). Thus, although African American women have played a central role in the church, they too have been excluded from many positions of authority and leadership.

Gilkes's (1985) studies on the role of women in the sanctified church give us a detailed picture of African American women's participation in religious activity and institutions. The sanctified church elevates women to roles as heroines, both as spiritual and professional role models. Gilkes identifies a feminist infrastructure in the sanctified church that has its origins in women's racial uplift movements of the late nineteenth and early twentieth centuries. She also shows that the collectivist orientation of these churches has emerged from the relationship of African American culture and its churches to the dominant culture. They have rejected the patriarchal organization of major denominational churches, which has, in turn, encouraged a cooperative model of gender relations and pluralistic political practices within the church. In this sense, these churches provide a feminist model of institutional organization and practice for the larger society.

Religion and Social Justice

The role of African American churches is multidimensional and includes religious, as well as social and political, work. Because the central theme of Black theology is liberation (Flowers, 1984), African American churches are meeting places for protest strategy and have been highly significant in the historical development of Black protest. The liberatory function of the African American church is evidenced by the fact that African Americans define the education of both oppressed people and oppressors as central tasks of Christian missions. Black spirituals and sermons are full of protest symbolism. The musical ministries of African American women have advanced and institutionalized their forms of creative expression (Dodson and Gilkes, 1986). There is, in fact, enormous cultural significance to African American church music; almost every popularly recognized indigenous musical style in the United States has antecedents in the oral tradition of African American worship services.

Despite the liberatory functions of the African American church, sociologists have also shown that religion can serve as an "opiate" for social protest. In other words, sociologists use **religion as opiate** to describe Black churches as also discouraging social protest. Some sociological research has shown that despite the connection of Black theology to movements for social justice, there is an inverse relationship between religious piety and political militancy (Marx, 1967).

Still, for racial and ethnic groups, religion is often the basis for group identity. For Jewish women and men, religious and ethnic identities are fused as a public and political culture. For Native Americans, Latinos, and African Americans, religion is one way to affirm one's ethnic subculture, while creating a basis for political and social organizing.

Latino experience is typically seen as heavily influenced by the religious traditions of the Catholic Church, although sociologists note that patterns of urbanization have restricted the influence of religion in people's lives. Among Latinas, religion helps sustain ties to family and friends in the face of more industrialized and bureaucratic public life. Although the Catholic Church has been seen as oppressive to Latinas, religion also plays a positive role in their relationships with friends, family, and community. Among both Catholic and Protestant Latinas, the influence of religion varies by social class, with the working class more committed to religious beliefs than is the professional class (Williams, 1990). For all groups, religion can be the basis for racial, ethnic, and gender identity, although it does not typically have a monolithic influence. The influence of religion should be seen in relationship to other social systems, in order to better understand the simultaneous ways that religion can have a conservative influence and be the basis for positive forms of social identity and movements for social justice.

≉ Religion as a Basis for Antifeminism

The Religious Right and Antifeminism

The rise of the religious right in recent years has generated a new period of religious activism. Conservative politics have stemmed, in part, from the organizational support and political mobilization of conservative Christian groups whose religious beliefs have fostered strong opposition to abortion rights and feminist principles of multicultural education and who foster a wide array of conservative social positions, ranging from opposition to sex education in the schools to the banning of books in the schools. Many aspects of this new nexus of religion and politics are deeply antithetical to feminist values.

The religious right sees the church as the defender of public morality, perceiving feminism, liberalism, and humanism as threatening to Christian values of family life and as violating the hierarchy of God to man to woman. Women, they believe, should be subordinate to their husbands. So, for example, the Eagle Forum, a national organization of women and men headed by Phyllis Schlafly, defines itself as a group "who believe in God, Home, and Country, and are determined to defend the values that have made America the greatest nation in the world" (Eagle Forum, cited in Conover and Gray, 1983:74). The National Right to Life Committee takes as its motto, "For God, for Life, for the Family, for the Nation."

The antifeminist activities of the religious right have been particularly well organized in the antiabortion movement, and they are also opposed to reproductive freedom, sex education, equal rights for women, and pornography. They support prayer in the public schools, preferred tax status for Christian schools, and other policies that would ensure women's subordination to male authority.

The religious right views the battle over family values as "the most significant battle of the age-old conflict between good and evil, between the forces of God and forces against God, that we have seen in our country" (*Conservative Digest*, 1980:15, cited in Conover and Gray, 1983). One of the reasons the right has been so politically effective is that it has established an organizational infrastructure through the support of Protestant and Catholic churches. The support of evangelical churches makes available a massive communication network which, through television preachers, aids in the mobilization of voters, a powerful source for conservative social changes. Allied with the most conservative segments of the Republican Party, the religious right has effectively given power to right-wing politicians such as Pat Buchanan, Pat Robertson, Newt Gingrich, and others.

Sociological and political scientists have examined the extent to which religious faith predicts people's support for conservative political positions. One study of right-wing activists found, for example, that those who oppose abortion and the **Equal Rights Amendment (ERA)** have more traditional moral codes, support traditional gender roles in the family, and place responsibility for women's status on individual women (Conover and Gray, 1983). Membership in Catholic or fundamentalist Protestant churches per se does not predict support for right-wing attitudes, but there is a strong relationship between church attendance in these groups and conservative political attitudes.

One of the puzzling features of the religious and political right is that many of its activists are women. How can women be so numerous in a movement that to many seems so antagonistic to women's interests? Studies of these women right-wing activists find that the antifeminist women tend to be White, middle-aged housewives (married or widowed) who are new to politics and focus on a single issue, but they are not monolithic in their beliefs. Some define their political activism in terms of gender roles, defending traditional roles in the family, which they see under siege by feminist transformations of recent years. Others take a more laissez-faire approach, arguing that government in all forms should not be involved in the lives of individuals—whether men or women. Their politics are not a defense of traditional gender arrangements per se, although many find themselves in coalition with socially conservative women (Klatch, 1988).

The Abortion Debate: The Conflict of Religious World Views

One of the most active programs of the religious right has been its organized opposition to abortion rights for women. Spurred by the 1973 Supreme Court case *Roe* v. *Wade* (see Chapter 7), many women who previously had not been politically active were prompted into antiabortion activism. These were predominantly women with high school educations (and occasionally some college), who were married, had children, were not employed outside the home, and tended not to have been politically active in other groups or unions. Most had not been active in the PTA, church groups, scouting, or other activities typically associated with their traditional homemaker roles. These women believe that men and women are intrinsically different and that women are best suited to raise children, manage homes, and love and care for their husbands. They also believe that men are best suited for the public world of work.

The sociological literature identifies several explanations for antifeminist activities. Kristin Luker's work, based on a study of California prochoice and antiabortion activists, depicts the debate over abortion as a debate over conflicting world views. Antiabortion activists tend to believe that giving women control over their fertility (through abortion or birth control) breaks up the set of relationships in traditional families where women care for the home and children and men go into public work. Antiabortion activists also define sex as sacred and are disturbed by social changes in values that secularize and profane sex. Unlike prochoice women, they believe that one becomes a parent by being a parent and that the purpose of sexuality is to have children. Their world view also includes the idea that the availability of contraception only encourages teens to have sex; therefore, to halt teenage pregnancy and what they believe is immoral behavior, they argue that sex education and birth control should be eliminated.

The world view of prochoice women, on the other hand, is one that sees women's control over reproduction as essential for women to have control over their lives. Prochoice women do not see reproduction as the primary purpose of sex; instead, they think of sex as a means of communication between partners and, if they think of it as sacred at all, it is because they see sex as a mystical experience that breaks down the boundaries between self and other. Prochoice activists see nothing natural about masculinity and femininity; rather, they see persons and their gender roles as learned and emergent, just as they see parenthood as a learned role. To prochoice activists, parenting means giving a child emotional, psychological, social, and financial resources—not just biologically bearing a child.

Prochoice and antiabortion activists differ not only in their world views, but also in their sociological characteristics. Prochoice activists are generally better educated and less likely to be married than those against abortion. Antiabortion activists generally have less income than prochoice activists (whose income also tends to be their own). Prochoice women are much more likely to be working in the paid labor force and, if married, their husbands also usually have above-average incomes. In fact, the incomes of prochoice women place them in the top 10 percent of women earners, whereas antiabortion women are generally situated in the lowest income groups and are more often employed in traditionally female occupations.

Luker (1984) found that the single-most dramatic difference between these two groups is in the role religion plays in their lives—a fact supported by other research (Himmelstein, 1986). Three-quarters of the prochoice people in Luker's study say that formal religion is either unimportant or completely irrelevant to them. Only 25 percent ever attend church, and they do so only on occasion. In contrast, 69 percent of those opposed to abortion say that religion is important in their lives; 22 percent of them say it is very important. Half attend church once a week; 13 percent attend more often. Only 2 percent of those opposed to abortion never attend church.

Luker argues that those who are actively against abortion see a societal decline in religious commitment and, more broadly, a decline in the sense of a common community. They believe that the absence of belief in a supreme being leads to a "do your own thing" attitude, whereas the prochoice world view is one centered around the belief in the highest abilities of human beings. The struggle over abortion, in Luker's thinking, is a struggle over the meaning of motherhood itself. She writes that abortion "strips the veil of sanctity from motherhood" (1984:205).

Luker and others depict antiabortion activism and antifeminism as stemming from the status anxiety some groups experience when social and economic changes in the society threaten their social and cultural status (Ehrenreich, 1983; Luker, 1984). Antifeminism is not seen as just a direct function of socioeconomic variables like age, education, and class, but is explained by the fact that some groups are especially vulnerable to the social, cultural, and economic changes that feminism and the transformation of men's and women's roles in society have generated. Their anxiety about these threats to their status is the basis for their support of right-wing movements (Himmelstein, 1986).

This helps explain a fact that has puzzled many—that so many of the activists in antifeminist causes are women. While some suggest that women in these movements are the "foot soldiers," not the leaders, it is clear that women are a large portion of antifeminist activists. Seeing their antifeminist activities as a result of status anxiety explains why antifeminism is more prevalent among women who are the most vulnerable to and dependent on men. Their profamily position is one that sees the traditional family, in fact, as a fortress that protects women from men's declining commitment and ability to meet their traditional breadwinner role (Ehrenreich, 1983).

Religious activism has not, however, been restricted to the religious right. Although most feminists do not express or act on strong religious beliefs, some have developed their feminist politics through religious faith. For them, although they have been critical of patriarchal religion and its subordination of women, their reexamination of religious faith has created the framework through which their feminist world view has been constructed. The concluding section of this chapter reviews the work of feminist theologians who are actively working to construct new forms of faith and spirituality intended to provide the grounds for women's liberation.

Faith, Feminism, and Spirituality

Feminism and Religious Reform

The feminist critique of religion has at its heart a deep-felt sense of injustice (Christ and Plaskow, 1992). This is particularly evident in the personal accounts some feminist scholars have written of their experiences in divinity school. Judith Plaskow, a noted feminist theologian, describes the reaction of her thesis advisor at Yale Divinity School when she said she wanted to do her thesis on theology and women's experience. " 'Fine,' he told her; it was a good subject as long as she dropped all the references to women" (Christ and Plaskow, 1992:i–ii). Both she and Carol Christ, another feminist theologian and scholar, were told by divinity faculty that the history of Christian attitudes toward women was not an important area for study (Christ and Plaskow, 1992).

Theologians such as Christ and Plaskow nonetheless persisted in their studies of women and religion. The first feminist analyses of religion during feminism's second wave in the 1970s criticized the explicit statements of female inferiority found in religious texts, the subordination of women in the church, and the exclusion of women from ministry. Christian women, for example, rejected the biblical teaching that women must be subordinate to their husbands as indicated in, among other things, the passage in wedding ceremonies that women must obey their husbands. They also criticized the image of God as male and have developed new images for feminist worship. Feminists came to believe that the church and theology will transcend sexist ideologies only when women are granted full spiritual, theological, and ecclesiastical equality. They are not hesitant to acknowledge the interest-laden character of feminist theology, since they have openly declared the commitments out of which it emerges.

Beyond this reform position, however, lies a deepening analysis of the ***androcentrism,*** or male-centered view, of traditional theological views. This developing analysis is one that is critical of the theological world view of biblical faith and that sees sexism in religion as integrally tied to the dualistic and hierarchical mentality of traditional Christian theology (Reuther, 1979). From this analytical perspective, feminist transformation of patriarchal religion will take more than eliminating or changing sexist images in religious thought and admitting women to positions of religious leadership. The more radical feminist critique suggests that the patriarchal models of patriarchal religions cannot be simply rehabilitated to include women. Instead, the radical perspective understands the exclusion and domination of women to be fundamental to the very nature of patriarchal systems of religious thinking. The radical view sees sexism as so deeply embedded in the theology of patriarchal religion that reforms alone could never create the postpatriarchal future that feminist theologians seek (Christ and Plaskow, 1992).

This position in radical feminist theology sees the need for revolutionary changes in religious thought, practices, and organizations and refuses even to accept the possibility of the male messiahs of Christian tradition. Whereas many feminists believe that traditional religions can be reformed by identifying sexist language and symbols and giving women full status in places of worship, more radical feminist theologians say that women should simply discard patriarchal religious traditions and forge new visions of women's spirituality—ones that are distinctively based on women's experiences.

Radical Feminist Theology

Several themes emerge from this radical theological stance: that patriarchal religions rest on and re-create the domination of women by men; that women, like nature, are degraded and seen as needing control; that patriarchal religion forms the basis for other patriarchal institutions; that patriarchal religion has emerged historically through the suppression of female power; and, finally, that spirituality based on women's experience is the only way of reclaiming a fully human faith and liberatory vision of the future.

Two of the most noted radical feminist theologians are Rosemary Reuther and Mary Daly. Reuther (1979) has articulated the feminist view that Christian theology is centered on a domination model. She argues that traditional Christian theologies depict the soul and spirit as opposed to the human body—flesh, matter, and nature. This world view sees human beings as standing between God and nature and teaches human beings that they must subdue the irrational desires of the flesh to spiritual life. This creates a model for domination—one that sees human life as dominated by God, just as some human lives are dominated by others; furthermore, because Christianity depicts the desires of the flesh as needing suppression, the domination model of Christianity has justified the historical domination of those seen by Christians as more carnal (including Jews, African Americans, and Native Americans). Reuther contends that Christianity encourages a world view characterized by dualisms—such as the ethnocentric "we/they" view of the world that sees one group as superior and all others as inferior and in need of salvation and civilization. As a result, the missionary spirit of Christianity feeds the historical development of racism and the development of imperialistic power by seeking to create a monolithic empire.

Similarly, Daly argues that the "widespread conception of the 'Supreme Being' as an entity distinct from this world but controlling it according to plan and keeping human beings in a state of infantile subjection has been a not too subtle mask of the divine patriarch" (1979:56–57). Unmasking the patriarchal character of religious traditions causes us to see the powerful alliance between religion and oppressive social structures. Patriarchal theologies have in this way directly contributed to the oppression of women.

This more radical feminist critique of patriarchal religion leads to more fundamental changes in feminist visions of faith and spirituality—ones that are stimulated by asking what it would mean if women's experience were the basis for theological and religious world views. Experience is the key term in this developing feminist analysis. Feminist religious scholars take experience to mean the fabric of life as it is lived. In keeping with the feminist practice of consciousness-raising and defining the personal as political, they believe there is something unique about women's experience and that women's faith and spirituality should be centered on those experiences (Saiving, 1979).

This has also led such thinkers to distinguish between religion and spirituality. They claim that religion is that which is historically associated with established and institutionalized structures and ideologies, whereas spirituality suggests a vital, active, and energizing interior perception of the power of being (Yates, 1983). This vision of spirituality is exemplified in Ntozake Shange's play, *for colored girls who have considered suicide/when the rainbow is enuf*: "i found god in myself/& i loved her/i loved her fiercely" (1975:63).

Because religion has such a deep hold on the human psyche, radical feminist theologians believe one cannot afford to leave it in the hands of men. They see that men's control of religion emerged only with the suppression of female power and symbolism through the historical demise of goddess worship. They argue that there is nothing natural about patriarchal religion, pointing out that the introduction of male gods and messiahs occurs at specific historical points in the development of human experience and that before the introduction of male messiahs, goddess worship was a nearly universal phenomenon. The earliest artifacts of human culture, they suggest, are female statues and symbols, indicating the awe our ancestors felt for women and their bodily mysteries (Spretnak, 1994).

The creation of new symbols, legends, myths, and rituals centered on women's experiences is central to new forms of feminist worship. Often, these woman-centered rituals are explicitly linked to attempts by women to release anger and fear and to increase a sense of power and community. One study found that participation in such rituals helped women recover from sexual victimization and improved their mental health (Jacobs, 1994). For contemporary women spiritualists, reclaiming the goddess has become symbolic of the affirmation of female power and the female body, the celebration of female will, and the recognition of women's bonds and heritage (Christ, 1979). Positive attitudes about women's bodies are an essential dimension to this new feminist spirituality, and affirmation of the female body and the life cycle expressed in it have become the basis for new feminist rituals. The positive value of female will is also expressed by newly celebrated practices such as women's spellcasting and witchcraft.

According to feminist theology, reclaiming goddess imagery is a way of acknowledging female power as beneficent and independent. This is, of course, in radical contrast to the patriarchal perception of women's power as inferior and dangerous. The significance of the goddess for reevaluating women's bonds and heritage is that "as women struggle to create a new culture in which women's power, bodies, will, and bonds are celebrated, it seems natural that the Goddess would reemerge as symbol of the newfound beauty, strength, and power of women" (Christ, 1979:285).

In sum, the emphasis in radical **feminist theology** is not just to point out the androcentric bias of traditional religious world views, but to fundamentally change theology and religion to represent women's experiences in all its forms. Some have criticized radical feminist theology as reflecting a White, middle-class, and Christian or post-Christian perspective. Jewish women have also criticized some feminist theology for its anti-Semitic framework (Hargrove, Schmidt, and Davaney, 1985). The many attempts to re-create systems of faith to acknowledge the presence and power of women are indicative of the far-reaching attempts of feminist thinkers to create new visions and world views that will provide the foundations for building a feminist society.

๛ *Summary*

Religion is a powerful source for the subordination of women. At the same time, religion has historically been a powerful instrument for social change. For women, religion has a dual tendency to be both oppressing and potentially liberating.

Sociologists see religion as a system of beliefs and an organized institution that provides groups with symbols and concepts that define their world view and shape other social institutions. Religion provides group norms that influence the everyday behavior of members of a society. As such, religion is strongly associated with sexual attitudes and behaviors and can operate as a system of the social control of sexuality.

The burning of witches during the European Middle Ages represents the growth in the authority of the church and its takeover of women's traditional power. Women who were persecuted as witches were those who were sexual and religious deviants. In the United States, religious belief has played a strong role in the development of feminism. During the nineteenth century, women were believed to be more pious and spiritual than men, and religion was used to justify their exclusion in the domestic sphere. Religion also was important to some of the early feminists, although others saw religion as a source of women's oppression.

Images of women in religious texts produce stereotypical gender roles and have defined women as subordinate to men. Whether a religious group defines its religious tradition as literal or interpretive is related to the group's acceptance of nontraditional religious roles for women. Christianity has historically been used to justify slavery and the sexual exploitation of African American men and women. At the same time, Christian theology has been used by minority groups as the basis for strong beliefs in social justice.

Gender inequality in religious institutions has segregated women into the least powerful and influential religious roles. Even though women are the majority of church participants and tend to be more religious than men, they play a support role in most church activities. Gender segregation in houses of worship for different faiths has given women secondary status in religion, although the number of women clergy in most denominations has increased in recent years. African American churches provide cohesion and fulfill important sociological functions in the African American community. African American women's work in the church holds the church together.

In recent years, the religious right has become especially politically active on antifeminist issues. Antifeminists in the religious right hold different world views about sexuality and women's role than do activists who are prochoice on the issue of abortion. Religious identification is one of the major distinctions between those who are prochoice and those who are against abortion.

Some feminist theologians have a reform perspective on religion. They believe that eliminating sexism in religious images of women in religious texts and admitting women to positions of religious leadership can transform religious institutions and belief systems. Radical feminist theologians have constructed new theologies that begin with women's experience and construct new rituals, legends, myths, and spiritual practices based on women's experiences. Both reform and radical feminists see faith as an important dimension to the construction of a new feminist society.

❧ Key Terms

androcentrism
collective consciousness
Equal Rights Amendment
   (ERA)

feminist theology
misogyny
religion as opiate

sanctified church
Second Great Awakening

❧ Discussion Questions/Projects for Thought

1. Talk with a group of people from different religious backgrounds (this could be a discussion group in class) and ask the men and women in the group what their religion taught them about women's roles. How did these ideas influence each person's self-concept?

2. Select a group of students who are opposed to abortion and another group who are pro-choice. Interview people within each group, asking them about their religious beliefs and their attitudes toward women's roles. Do you find support for Luker's idea that those who are prochoice have less religious commitment and that those who are opposed to abortion are more traditional in their attitudes about women's roles?

3. Attend the religious services of a group with which you are unfamiliar. While there, observe who is in attendance and what they are doing and also observe the teachings of this religious group. What do your observations tell you about the role of women and men in this particular faith?

❧ Suggested Readings

Allen, Paula Gunn. 1986. *The Sacred Hoop: Recovering the Feminine in American Indian Traditions*. Boston: Beacon Press.
   Allen's book examines the woman-centered perspectives of American Indian faith. Her work provides alternative visions of more feminist religious practices, not just within religion but in new forms of social organization.

Beck, Evelyn Torton, ed. 1989. *Nice Jewish Girls: A Lesbian Anthology*, 2nd ed. Boston: Beacon Press.
   These essays examine the influence of Judaism on growing up as a woman and as a lesbian. The focus is on the tensions and continuities some Jewish women find between their Jewish identity and feminist values.

Davidman, Lynn. 1991. *Tradition in a Rootless World: Women Turn to Orthodox Judaism*. Berkeley: University of California Press.
   Based on a detailed ethnographic study, Davidman examines the lives of contemporary young women who have returned to Orthodox Judaism. She questions how women in an otherwise liberated era would be attracted to a traditional faith and she explores the meaning that Judaism gives to these women's lives.

Kaufman, Debra Renee. 1991. *Rachel's Daughters: Newly Orthodox Jewish Women*. New Brunswick, NJ: Rutgers University Press.
   Based on interviews with 150 Orthodox Jewish women, Kaufman explores the meaning that religion has in the lives of highly traditional women.

Lincoln, C. Eric, and Lawrence H. Mamiya. 1990. *The Black Church in the African-American Experience*. Durham, NC: Duke University Press.
This is a comprehensive analysis of the influence of diverse religious groups and experiences in the history of African American people. It also examines the connections between religion in the African American community and movements for social justice.

Mernissi, Fatima. 1987. *Beyond the Veil: Male-Female Dynamics in Modern Muslim Society*. Bloomington, IN: Indiana University Press.
Mernissi explores the implications of Muslim religion for men's and women's roles in the Muslim world. She focuses especially on how the Muslim faith shapes conceptions of women's sexuality and the relations between men and women that result.

Spretnak, Charlene, ed. 1994. *The Politics of Women's Spirituality: Essays on the Rise of Spiritual Power within the Feminist Movement*, 2nd ed. Garden City, NY: Anchor Books.
This anthology of writings by feminist theologians provides a good overview of the new analyses and questions feminism brings to the study of religion.

Swatos, William H., Jr. 1994. *Gender and Religion*. New Brunswick, NJ: Transaction Publishers.
This anthology examines women's status, primarily in the Protestant, Catholic, and Jewish religious institutions, and also examines, in various contexts, women's experiences with religions.

Wallace, Ruth A. 1992. *They Call Her Pastor: A New Role for Catholic Women*. Albany, NY: State University of New York Press.
This analysis of the role of women in the Catholic church is based on studies of 20 Catholic parishes. It examines women's leadership in the Catholic church and the appointment of women as lay administrators of parishes that have no priests.

C h a p t e r 9

Women, Crime, and Deviance

In 1995, Susan Smith was convicted of murdering her two young sons, aged 3 years and 14 months. Prior to her arrest, Smith had claimed, before the national media, that her car had been carjacked by an African American man and her two children kidnapped by him. As the truth unfolded, Smith was tried and convicted for this ghastly murder and the public learned that Smith had driven the boys to a remote lake, pushed the car into the water, and watched them drown—strapped into their safety belts in the backseat of the car.

This crime made Susan Smith one of the most notorious women criminals in recent years, and the public wondered how any mother could so coldheartedly murder her children. As the details of Susan Smith's life became known, people learned that she herself was a victim of her stepfather's sexual abuse and was in the midst of a divorce. Raised working class and marginally poor most of her life, Susan Smith had worked in a mill, eventually working her way up to an office job. One week before the murder of her sons, she had received a "Dear John" letter from the man she had been dating, the son of the wealthy mill owner, in which he said he was breaking up because he was not yet ready for children (Bragg, 1994).

Smith's case has all the elements of an extraordinary sociological event: A woman is abused by her father, is involved in a failed marriage, and has a love affair that crosses class differences; she appropriates racial stereotypes in her initial accusation that her sons were kidnapped by a Black man. This event begs an analysis of women's criminal behavior as it is influenced by gender, race, and class relations.

Consider another less notorious and less violent crime. Sandra is a hustler. As described in Eleanor Miller's *Street Women* (1986), she is a White woman, 23 years old, who grew up in a strict family household. When she was 9 years old, her father, a heavy drinker, accused her of being a whore. His fury and her mother's passivity led her to run away from home. By the time she was age 12, a juvenile court had labeled her "uncontrollable" and she was sent to a delinquent home for girls.

She repeatedly ran away from institutions in which she was placed and, as a young teenager, started working the streets as a prostitute. When one of her girl-friends was found dead, she started paying a pimp for protection. She used drugs with him, but when he was high, he beat her and the other women who worked for him. After beating one woman to death, he was given a life sentence. Sandra paid the maitre d' of a hotel so she could safely work the hotel as a prostitute. She also worked in a topless bar for a while, but her big success, in her eyes, came through an escort service she established with a female partner.

They accumulated a lot of money through their entrepreneurship, and Sandra began hanging out with a gambler. When he was arrested, she and the woman working with her were also arrested and their attorney's fees wiped them out financially. Sandra went to work for a house of prostitution, where she earned money that she sent to her boyfriend's lawyer. She then became involved with another man who was a heavy drug user and became a serious drug user herself. She was sent to prison, having been busted for marijuana and carrying a concealed weapon (a knife).

She plans to enter the state university on her release from prison; however, she says she doubts she will stop hustling. In her words, "If the opportunity comes up and someone offers me enough money, I'll do it. . . . I don't think I'll ever walk the stroll again, but I'll do anything else. If I have to feed my baby, I will, you know? I know I can. I know I can survive anywhere" (Miller, 1986:54).

Is Sandra a serious criminal? Unlike Susan Smith's crimes, Sandra's crimes are victimless; yet, like Susan Smith's, her life story has common elements of sexual abuse, attempts to get ahead financially, and troubled relationships with men. These cases illustrate how patterns in women's crime are connected to gender relations in society and to women's position in the class system. Race affects women's participation in crime, too; African American women and Latinas are more likely to commit crimes than are White women because, sociologists argue, of their disadvantaged position in the class system. Understanding women's crime reveals much about the effects of gender, race, ethnicity, and class stratification in society.

This chapter begins with a review of sociological perspectives on crime and deviance, particularly as they have been developed to explain criminal and deviant behavior among women. Two sections follow that discuss women and social deviance, and women and crime. As each of these sections shows, many of the assumptions made about women's crime and deviance are based on gender expectations about women's roles in society. Furthermore, patterns of gender relations are also reflected in the actual crimes that women commit. The feminist movement has called attention to the fact that gender relations in this society generate a high degree of violence against women. The chapter also examines women as victims of crime and discusses the theoretical perspectives used to explain violence against women. Finally, women's position within the criminal justice system is discussed, particularly as the system treats women offenders.

❧ *Origins of Deviance Theory*

Women's crime and deviance have only recently come to the attention of academic scholars. A few early studies (Lombroso, 1920; Pollak, 1950; Thomas, 1923) appear in the sociological literature, but most of them depict women's deviance as rooted in their biological and psychological predispositions. Contemporary feminist research has taken critical examination of these assumptions as a starting point for analysis. Examining these early assumptions introduces the contemporary issues surrounding crime and deviance among women.

Lombroso's work in the 1920s, although by now discredited, was one of the earliest studies of female crime. His highly racist and sexist ideas depicted crime as based on biological differences between women and men, White and Black Americans, the fit and the unfit. Lombroso believed that crime represented the survival of primitive traits; his theory was explicitly linked to popular racist and sexist notions of the time (Higham, 1965). He explained female crime by arguing that women are less highly evolved than White men, and thus are more susceptible to primitive urges. He also depicted women as less varied in their mental capacities and, in general, more passive and sedentary than men (Klein, 1980). As he said, "Even the female criminal is monotonous and uniform compared with her male companion, just as in general woman is inferior to man" (Lombroso, 1920:122, cited in Klein, 1980:78).

In Lombroso's work, the cause of crime is located within individuals and their biology, not within their social circumstances. W. I. Thomas, an early sociologist, paid more attention to the role of social circumstances in producing crime. Thomas's work is of great importance to sociological thinking, although his work on female deviance is seriously flawed. Like Lombroso, he traced women's crime to biological differences between the sexes and to deep-seated psychological "wishes" that he defined as unique to young girls. In his early work, Thomas claimed that females are biologically "anabolic"—motionless and conservative—whereas males are "katabolic"—destructive of energy, yet creative because of the outward flow of this drive. (As an aside, Thomas also saw monogamy as an accommodation to these basic urges because he believed that through monogamy women become domesticated and men become leaders!)

Thomas's later work (*The Unadjusted Girl*, 1923) contained an important sociological insight—that female delinquency is a normal response to certain social conditions. He still emphasized, however, that social behavior is a result of "primary wishes" that are derived from biological instincts. He identified these wishes as the desire for new experience, security, response, and recognition; for women, there is the added wish for maternalism. In Thomas's view, middle-class people are less likely to commit crimes because they are more likely to control their natural desires; delinquents are driven to crime because they long for new experiences. Girls, in particular, he says, engage in deviance in order to manipulate others, and their maternal instincts lead them to crimes such as prostitution, in which he claims they are seeking love and tenderness (Klein, 1980).

In sum, Thomas attributed motivational differences between men and women to internal, even biological, differences between the sexes. Although this biological explanation for sex differences is inadequate (see Chapter 2), Thomas did recognize differences in the attitudes of men and women and attempted to use these differences to explain patterns of delinquency and crime. His work, although seemingly crude now, has left an important message for more recent sociological work. He attempted to find a behavioral basis for sex differences in delinquency, and he tried, even if unsuccessfully, to relate those differences to attitudes that we now see as reflecting gender socialization. Whether patterns of women's crime can be properly attributed to gender socialization is an important question that is explored further in this chapter.

The major problem in Thomas's work—other than the crude gender stereotypes he used by seeing women as more manipulative, emotional, and desirous of love and tenderness than men are—was that he portrayed gender differences as internal to individuals, not as a product of their social environment. He had an important insight even on this point, however, because he thought that internal wishes and motivations could be directed by socialization and manipulation of the social environment. Thus, Thomas's work provides a foundation for the liberal tradition in criminology that sees individual rehabilitation as the best solution to problems associated with deviant behavior. The liberal solution "requires that individual offenders be treated as undersocialized, as not fully adapted to the social values of society which represent their interests, and ultimately as being 'sick' rather than inherently evil or rationally opposed to the dominant values of society" (Smart, 1977:37). The efficacy of such a view can, in fact, be questioned, but no doubt it is fundamental to many of the rehabilitative programs and treatment modes of contemporary practitioners.

Later, Otto Pollak (1950) tried to explain women's crime, based on sexist assumptions. Like Lombroso and Thomas, Pollak traced women's deviance to their biological and psychological being; however, he reduced women's criminal behavior to sexuality and to what he assumed to be the natural character of sexual intercourse (Klein, 1980). Pollak claimed that the basis for female crime is women's passive role in sexual intercourse. According to Pollak, women are able to conceal their sexual arousal from men and, because of this physiological manipulation, women become socially deceitful. His major concern with women's crime was the "masked" character of female criminality; he argued that the real extent of female crime is hidden from the public's view. Women, he argued, are deceitful and duplicitous; he saw them as the masterminds behind crime, manipulating men into committing offenses while they themselves remain immune from prosecution. Pollak saw women as liars and interpreted the hidden nature of their criminality as a reflection of their cunning behavior (Smart, 1977). In Pollak's view, men have been so duped by women that they protect women through chivalry and thus fear to charge and convict them for their crimes.

Although the views of Lombroso, Thomas, and Pollak appear quite outlandish now, the issues they raised continue to be addressed in current research and theory. Many still assume that delinquency can be traced to different emotional states in men and women, and these theorists have looked to sexual character as the root of women's criminality. Some who interpret female crime as a rebellion against gender roles want to decrease women's crime by restoring women to their "proper" place in the social system (Klein, 1980; Smart, 1977). There is even a revival of biological explanations of crime which, although resting on highly questionable suppositions, have received much attention in the public media.

Wilson and Herrnstein argue that social scientists overly rely on social and environmental causes of crime and ignore genetic predispositions toward criminal behavior. They insist that sex differences in crime among men and women must be understood as a function of aggression, which they see as rooted in the hormonal constitution of the sexes: "Knowledge has not yet advanced to the point where it can be said positively that human sex differences in aggression have been directly traced to differences in hormones. Yet, the evidence for some sort of connection is stronger than the . . . objections may suggest" (1985:119).

Why do women commit fewer crimes than men? In the words of Wilson and Herrnstein, "Our best guess centers on the difference in aggression and perhaps other primary drives that flow into the definition of sex roles" (1985:124). While they do admit that social and cultural arrangements may have some influence on the gender gap in crime, they see biological differences as establishing differences that go deeper than social structure: "The underpinnings of the sexual division of labor in human society, from the family to commerce and industry to government, may not be rigidly fixed in the genes, but their roots go deep into the biological substratum that beyond certain limits they are hard to change" (1985:125).

Wilson and Herrnstein's work has been soundly criticized by other scholars for its simplistic view of biology and culture as opposing systems, its misuse of scientific research, its confusion of correlates (such as gender, race, and crime) with genetic cause, and its omission of white-collar and corporate crime in their definition of crime (Kamin, 1986). The popularity of recurring arguments about the genetic basis for criminal behavior cannot be ignored, however. As we have already seen, biologically reductionist arguments tend to flourish in periods marked by radical changes in traditional social relations. Biologically based explanations of women's crime need to be understood in this political context.

❧ Sociological Perspectives on Crime and Deviance

New research and theory on crime and deviance provide new directions for understanding the significance of gender in exploring criminal and deviant behavior. Several questions are the basis for this work, including some of the same questions asked by early theorists. Answers to these questions now typically take quite a different direction in relating women's and men's crime and deviance to gender relations.

Beginning questions include: Do women commit less crime than men and, if so, why? Are there distinctive characteristics of women deviants? How has criminological research been influenced by sexist assumptions? Why is female deviance typically seen as sexual deviance and women's crime seen as caused by physiological differences or internal motivations?

From a feminist perspective, female crime and deviance must be seen within the context of gender, race, and class relations; otherwise, any account of crime that is produced is liable to be misleading. Although feminists recognize that individual women may commit crimes or engage in deviant behavior, they see these acts as related to the status of women in society. Any explanation of crime that views individual behavior as causally significant overlooks the more complex origins of deviant and criminal behavior; moreover, feminist perspectives on crime and deviance are also beginning to discover the influence of gender relations on men's criminal and deviant behavior.

From a feminist perspective, the traditional questions that sociologists ask about women's crime and deviance are incomplete. For example, before the feminist movement, few criminologists asked about the experience of women as victims of crime, and they did not inquire about how societal gender relations generated crimes usually committed against women (e.g., rape, wife battering, and incest). In fact, traditional studies of women as criminals and deviants have largely been limited to topics that feminists do not see as crime and deviance, such as prostitution, teenage promiscuity, and lesbianism. As we have seen in discussing the meaning of work and families, feminist analyses and questions have also led us to reexamine the meaning of crime and deviance. The following sections discuss theory and research about gender, crime, and deviance.

Although deviance is a concept with many popular connotations, sociological definitions of deviance are based on three primary points: (1) deviance is social behavior that departs from conventional social norms; (2) deviance involves a process of social labeling; and (3) deviance becomes recognized within the context of social institutions that reflect the power structure and gender, racial-ethnic, and class relations of society.

Defining Deviance

From a commonsense point of view, deviance is behavior that is bizarre, unconventional, and perhaps hard to understand; from a sociological perspective, however, this definition is inadequate and misleading. First of all, what is unusual in one situation may be quite ordinary in another; second, even the most extraordinary behavior can often be understood if we know the context in which it occurs. Sociologists define **deviance** as behavior that departs from conventional norms, noting that norms vary from one situation to another; consequently, sociologists see deviance as located in a social context. Knowing and understanding this context is essential to understanding deviant behavior.

Although deviance is defined as behavior that departs from conventional norms, deviant behavior, like conventional behavior, is often guided by norms and rules, both formal and informal. In fact, deviance may be practiced in subcultures in which the social norms of the group encourage members to engage in deviant acts. One example comes from the research on gang rape, which shows that violence escalates when there is peer pressure to show off one's "masculini-ty" through increased aggression and abuse of the victim (Brownmiller, 1975).

Another commonsense definition of deviance is that it is behavior of which people disapprove. This idea, too, is inaccurate because deviance is subject to social definition, and whether it is approved or disapproved depends on who is doing the defining. Because deviance is situationally specific, it is sometimes dif-ficult to distinguish deviant behavior from conventional behavior (Matza, 1969). In fact, there is probably more overlap between deviant and conventional behav-ior than one might think. Most people engage in deviant behavior, sometimes on a regular basis. Whether they become identified as deviant may be a function of their social standing (including their gender, race, and class), the context of their deviant acts, and their ability to maintain a conventional identity.

For example, many would consider that the enjoyment of pornography is deviant behavior. It offends many people's moral sensibilities (including that of some feminists, who see it as portraying women in a degrading and dehumaniz-ing way). The easy availability of pornography, its widespread consumption, and its appearance in even the most respectable settings, however, make it seem that pornography is a normal feature of everyday life. Whether one is perceived as deviant for reading or watching pornography depends on one's social standing and the social context in which pornography is viewed. This fact is evident when we consider the deviant label attached to a frequenter of peep shows or pornog-raphy houses, in contrast to the socially legitimate label afforded to the young bachelor who keeps a copy of *Playboy* on his coffee table or bathroom reading rack. When we analyze pornography as an economic industry, we see that its social organization is very similar to (although perhaps more coercive than) that of other industries in which workers are exploited for profit and products are marketed by the use of women as sex objects.

Labeling and Social Deviance

This discussion brings us to the second major point that sociologists make about deviant behavior: Deviance involves a social labeling process (Becker, 1963). One cannot be called deviant without being recognized as deviant, and sometimes persons become labeled as deviant regardless of whether they have actually engaged in deviant behavior. Becoming deviant involves societal reactions to one's behavior—or alleged behavior. **Labeling theory** emphasizes that some groups with the power to label deviance exercise control over what and who is considered deviant. Police, courts, school authorities, and other agents of the state thus wield a great amount of power through their control of institutions. For example, social workers, psychiatrists, or other agents of the state who define a woman as mentally ill can have a drastic effect on her behavior, identity, and life options.

Sociologists who work from the labeling perspective point out that in the absence of a deviant label, actual deviant behavior may have no consequences at all, but the process of being labeled as deviant may involve real changes in a per-son's self-image as well as his or her public identity. Sociologists note that once people are labeled deviant, they are likely to become deviant. This new identity, however, usually does not emerge suddenly or as the result of a single act. Instead, it involves a process of transformation wherein people adapt their self-images and behavior to the new identity being acquired (Lemert, 1972). For example, in becoming a prostitute, a woman may slowly change her identity from a nondeviant status as a sexually active woman to a deviant status as a prostitute by exaggerating to herself that the exchange of sexuality for economic favors is typical of nondeviant women (Rosenblum, 1975).

Deviance, Power, and Social Conflict

Labeling theory helps us see that deviance occurs in the context of social institutions. People in these institutions have the power to label some as deviant and others as not. This fact is especially true to the degree that the official agents of these institutions carry gender, race, and class stereotypes or biases that make them more likely to discover deviance in some groups than in others. These agents include the police, judges, lawyers, prison guards, and others who may enter the official process of labeling deviant behavior (e.g., psychologists, psychiatrists, counselors, social workers, and teachers). Because these official agents of social institutions have the power to label some groups and persons as deviant and others as not, and because these institutions reflect the power structure and the systems of race, class, and gender relations in the society, deviance tends to be a label that falls most frequently on powerless people in the society. The labeling of deviant behavior can thus be seen as a form of social control.

Sociologists who focus on deviance have suggested that it be studied from the point of view of the deviant actor (Becker, 1963; Matza, 1969). This method would allegedly prevent sociologists from seeing deviance only through official eyes and would create a more accurate portrayal of the deviant's social world. Many feminists studying deviance share this point of view, adding that, traditionally, women's deviance has been viewed through men's eyes.

Prostitution, for example, has traditionally been described in terms of men's demands for sexuality and women's supply of this "service" (McIntosh, 1978). Although this is an apt description of the economic nature of prostitution, it also makes ideological assumptions about both men's and women's sexuality. Women are depicted as merely providing an outlet for male sexual needs and remaining sexually passive, while men are defined as having greater sexual urges than women. Prostitution is a gender-specific crime that punishes women, not men, for not subordinating their sexuality to monogamous marital relationships (McIntosh, 1978). Were sociologists to study prostitution from the point of view of the prostitute, other questions would likely emerge (Chancer, 1993; Jolin, 1994).

For example, we might ask about the typical relationship between pimps and prostitutes and how prostitutes view their pimps. One such study found that prostitutes laughed at the notion of having a pimp and said that they used men only to give them backup protection. The men, on the other hand, thought they were pimps, even though the women did not think so (Pottieger, 1981). Another issue that might be studied from the point of view of prostitutes is how they

define their sexuality. Young delinquent girls, for example, have a more differentiated set of sexual mores than the simple virgin/whore dichotomy that is usually imposed on them (Tolman, 1994). This fact suggests that prostitutes, as well as
delinquent and other girls, define their own sexual codes of conduct and negotiate them in social interaction.

A feminist perspective on prostitution also encourages interest in the woman-
centered subculture among prostitutes. Typically, this subculture is assumed to be
competitive and distrustful; yet, in reality, prostitutes work together and are
dependent on each other for safety and support. Instead of assuming that they
exploit each other, we might ask how their group culture is established and maintained (Millman, 1975). One study finds, for example, that clusters of four to five
call girls maintain emotionally and financially reciprocal relations with each
other. An exchange of clients is necessary to cover appointments if they are busy,
to provide more than one woman if needed for their clients, or to aid financially
troubled friends (Rosenblum, 1975). Prostitutes are also frequent victims of sexual assault, but they develop a number of resistance strategies to assault, including
fighting back, "street justice" (i.e., revenge), and sometimes calling the police.
Contrary to the idea that prostitutes have weak and exploitative relationships
with each other, this research discovers an essential network existing among them
and shows that they are victims of others, but agents of their own lives.

Feminist Perspectives on Deviance

Feminist perspectives on deviant behavior are critical of traditional studies for
their content, their omissions, their interpretations of women's deviance, and
even their assumptions about what counts as deviance. To a large extent, the
study of women's deviance has been ignored, thus allowing more easily for sexist interpretations of deviance to persist. When women's deviance is studied, it is
often relegated to a few categories of deviant behavior that evoke sexist stereotypes. Studies of female deviance have typically been limited to behaviors that are
linked with women's sexuality (e.g., prostitution and promiscuity) or to behaviors
seen as stemming from women's alleged inability to control their emotions (e.g.,
mental illness, alcoholism, and drug abuse). Interpretations of women's deviance
have been clearly tied to the sexual status attributed to women in this society. This
tendency seems especially true when comparing the alleged deviance of women
with that of men. A double standard of morality marks some behaviors as deviant
in women that are not considered deviant when performed by men. A good example is the issue of teenage promiscuity—a value-laden concept, yet one that policymakers and official institutions take quite seriously. The double standard of
morality marks promiscuity as a social problem only among young girls. Teenage
boys are expected, if not encouraged, to be aggressive in their sexual encounters;
girls who do the same thing are labeled as "loose" and are likely to be seen by officials as constituting a social problem.

The sexual status attributed to women deviants is also evident in the frequently made assumption (particularly among official agents of correctional and
counseling institutions) that all women deviants are also sexually deviant. For

example, women junkies and alcoholics are frequently presumed to be sexually promiscuous as well, and, in many jurisdictions, female delinquents charged with nonsexual deviant offenses may be routinely checked for virginity and/or venereal disease (Chesney-Lind, 1981; Strouse, 1972).

Another assumption that feminists criticize is the idea that women engage in less deviance and delinquency than do men. If fewer women are detected, then it may simply be because we assume that they are less deviant; thus, this assumption can become a self-fulfilling prophecy. In addition, if women are seen to be usually less deviant than men, then those women whose deviance is detected may be seen as more abnormal than their male counterparts (Smith, 1978). This helps explain the fact that when a woman is defined as deviant, more strict sanctions may be brought against her because she has greatly violated her gender role (Haft, 1980).

In studying deviance, sociologists have also tended to ignore issues that may appear mundane but are important in establishing complete accounts of the social world of the deviant. For instance, few have considered the effect that deviance might have on the lives of those in the deviant's social circle (Millman, 1975). It is often these people—the family and friends of deviant actors—who must accommodate the consequences of social deviance (including social stigma, embarrassment, ostracism, or imprisonment). Because sociologists focus on the public aspects of deviance, they ignore its emotional dimension and the accommodations that friends and families make for it.

Sociological interpretations of deviance have often rested on sexist assumptions about men's and women's behavior. Many studies of women's deviance assume either that these women have lost control of their emotions or sexuality, or that they are exploitive, impulsive, or "doing it all for love" (Millman, 1975). In addition, women's deviance is often equated with sexual pathology; thus, the causes of female deviance are often attributed to individual maladjustment or a poor family background. It is true that some deviance (including sexual deviance) does involve the individual's psychosexual adjustment. Often, in fact, child abuse, particularly sexual abuse by the father or other male kin, results in damage to female self-concepts and sexual identities (Jaget, 1980). Such experiences may provoke a woman to engage in deviant behavior, but these events in her biography (which are by no means true for all female deviants) are not always the sole or the primary cause of deviant behavior.

Feminist scholars have also suggested that much of women's deviance, including that of girls and young women, is the result of the social context in which they live. Studies of girls' gangs, for example, have shown that young women find in gangs the solidarity that they may not experience in their home environments (Joe and Chesney-Lind, 1995). A good illustration comes from a study of Puerto Rican girls' gangs. Many young Puerto Rican girls live in a relatively confined social environment. They have little opportunity for educational or occupational advancement, and their community expects them to be "good girls" and to remain close to their families. Joining a gang is one way to reject the racial-ethnic, class, and gender role into which the girls have been cast (Campbell, 1989). From a feminist perspective, these young women are doing the best they can to adapt to their situation. Others have also argued that gangs provide a haven for young girls to cope with the many problems they have because of the sexism, racism, and class inequality that they face (Joe and Chesney-Lind, 1995). These kinds of analyses place women's deviance squarely in the gender, racial-ethnic, and class relations of society.

In sum, explanations of women's deviance have tended to be gender specific, particularly because deviance in women, but seldom in men, is seen to emerge from problems in the woman's sexual identity or sexual behavior. This fact underscores the point that women's deviance has traditionally been linked to women's sexuality.

The deviant label typically attached to lesbianism makes it appear that there is something perverted about loving persons of one's own sex. Much of the research on lesbianism and homosexuality assumes that this sexual preference is pathological. As a consequence, the prevailing mode of explanation has been one of individual maladjustment, but lesbianism can just as well be seen as conscious resistance to conventional heterosexuality whereby women are defined as the adjuncts of men and female sexuality is seen as passive acquiescence to male demands. The volumes of research asserting that homosexuality needs correction are strong evidence of the compulsory nature of heterosexual institutions in the society (Rich, 1980). Lesbianism and homosexuality are seen by some as deviant, not because gay men and lesbian women are sick, but because they exist outside of the dominant expectations of a patriarchal and heterosexist society. It is the heterosexist structure of institutions that defines lesbians as deviant, invisible, and abhorrent. Inside lesbian-feminist communities, lesbian existence is viewed as a healthy response and a conscious resistance to patriarchal domination.

In conclusion, sociological work on female deviance challenges the gender-stereotypic assumptions that have guided earlier work on the topic. Feminist research has produced new perspectives for investigating the social problems that female deviants face.

ꙮ *Women as Criminals*

In general, women commit much less crime than do men and women's crimes tend to be less serious than men's; however, women's participation in some crimes has increased in recent years, although not at the rapid rate implied by popular accounts. Central questions asked in the research on women and crime are: Has women's crime increased and, if so, for what types of crime? Is the amount of crime by women beginning to approximate the amount of male crime? How are women's crimes linked to gender relations, and have changes in gender roles created more opportunities for women to commit crimes?

The Extent of Criminality among Women

Available information on female crime comes primarily from official statistics (the FBI's *Uniform Crime Reports*), from self-report surveys, and from national victim-

TABLE 9.1   Total U.S. Arrests by Sex: 1997

	Percent Male	Percent Female
Murder	89.7%	10.3%
Forcible Rape	98.7	1.3
Robbery	90.2	9.8
Aggravated Assault	81.2	18.8
Burglary	88.1	11.9
Larceny	65.4	34.6
Motor Vehicle Theft	85.0	15.0
Arson	85.0	15.0
TOTAL: Violent Crime	83.8%	16.2%
Other Assaults	78.7%	21.3%
Forgery/Counterfeiting	61.4	38.6
Fraud	53.9	46.1
Embezzlement	52.9	47.1
Vandalism	85.1	14.9
Prostitution and Commercialized Vice	39.8	60.2
Sex Offenses	90.9	9.1
Drug Violations	82.7	17.3
Gambling	90.2	9.8
Offenses against Family and Children	76.1	23.9
Driving under the Influence	84.7	15.3
Disorderly Conduct	77.9	22.1
Vagrancy	79.8	23.2
Curfew Violations	69.2	30.8
Runaways	41.8	58.2
TOTAL: All Arrests	78.4%	21.6%

Source: Data from Federal Bureau of Investigation. 1997. *Crime in the United States, 1997.* Washington, DC: U.S. Government Printing Office, p. 239.

ization and crime surveys (see Table 9.1). Although each data source reveals different kinds of information, together they give a consistent picture of women's crime.

Data on arrests show that the proportion of women arrested (as a percentage of all arrests) has increased slightly over the last decade. Arrest data must be interpreted with caution, however, because arrest rates measure police activity and may not reflect the actual commission of crime. Apparent increases and decreases in crime among different social groups are as much an indication of the law-and-order mentality of the time as they are accurate measures of actual crime.

Violent crime by women has increased notably since the late 1980s, with the percentage increase of violent crime by women exceeding that of men. This should be interpreted cautiously, however, because the low absolute rates of crime by women in this category create small absolute increases into large percentage increases. Still, the proportion of violent crimes committed by women has also increased in recent years.

The gap in male-female property crime rates has also narrowed substantially, with arrest rates for property crimes by women increasing and those by men decreasing. Women approximate men now in committing fraud and embezzlement. Some suggest that these crimes have increased for women because there are more opportunities for women to commit these crimes as their status in the labor market improves (Simon, 1975). The evidence shows, however, that although women are approximating men in terms of total arrests for both fraud and embezzlement, women are far more likely to engage in fraud than they are embezzlement. In addition, most women arrested for fraud are involved in small-profit offenses such as minor confidence games, welfare fraud, or being an accessory to fraudulent business practices.

Embezzlement for women is also largely a petty crime. Most of the thefts in this category for women are for small sums of money (under $150). Although changes in women's position in the labor force may explain some of the increase in female embezzlement, large embezzlement schemes are still mostly the work of men, who are in higher-level occupational positions and therefore have more opportunity to engage in white-collar crime.

Causes of Women's Crime

What, then, can we make of the relationship between women's roles and their participation in crime? Many criminologists suggest that patterns of crime among women represent extensions of their gender roles. Activities such as shoplifting, credit card fraud, and the passing of bad checks result from the opportunities women have as consumers. Likewise, the crimes that are less frequent for women (e.g., armed robbery, aggravated assault, and major embezzlement) involve either physical strength or economic opportunities associated with men's gender roles.

These associations have led some to conclude that women's involvement in criminal behavior changes when there are changes in their social roles (Adler, 1975). Many have, in fact, attributed increases in women's crime in recent years to the development of the women's movement. Adler argues that shifts in gender roles make women more willing to participate in crime and that this explains recent increases in crime among women. Others say that objective changes in women's situation, particularly their greater labor force participation, make more criminal opportunities available to women. Is either of these a valid explanation of increases in women's crime?

Even with increased economic opportunity for women in the labor force, the vast majority of women remain in low-paid, low-status jobs; thus, it is an exaggeration to say that women's opportunities for crime are related to women's rapid advancement in the labor force. Second, increases in women's crime that show up in the arrest statistics do not necessarily reflect an increase in the actual extent of crime; rather, these statistics may reflect an increase in the detection of women's crimes. This increased detection can occur in several ways.

It is possible that the feminist movement has created changes in public attitudes about women's crime. Although the amount of crime may remain the same, the police may be more likely to arrest women for offenses they commit. A second possibility is that changes in the rate of women's crime do not result from changes in gender roles per se, but instead from broad structural changes in the economy, technology, legal systems, and law enforcement procedures. (Steffensmeier, 1981). Greater reliance on electronic transactions, credit cards, and self-service markets have increased the opportunities for crime for all consumers. At the same time, detection systems (including national information systems, technological surveillance, and an expansion of private security forces) have increased the amount of social control and law enforcement. "The greater willingness of business officials to prosecute, the trend toward computerized records, and improvements in the detection of offenses such as shoplifting, bad checks, credit card fraud, and forged prescriptions would also tend to increase female, more than male, arrests for larceny, fraud, and forgery" (Steffensmeier, 1981:63).

Miller (1986) makes the most compelling and reliable argument about the causes of women's crime. She reminds us that increases in crime among women in recent years have been almost entirely in property crimes. Rather than attributing the causes of women's crime to the women's movement and the changes it engenders, she argues that the women's movement coincides with (and, in fact, stems from) other structural changes that best explain women's criminal behavior, as well. Those who have associated increases in women's crime with the rise of the women's movement do so because the women's movement and increases in women's crime can be marked in the same period of time; however, according to Miller, those who argue the association overlook important facts about women's employment status and high rates of poverty.

Miller notes that the increased labor force participation of women beginning in the mid-1960s was especially marked among better-educated women with children and who had never worked. Occupational segregation also depresses the wages of all women workers and raises their unemployment rate; consequently, the entry of older, White, middle-class women into the labor force may disadvantage minority, poor, and younger women at the same time that the unskilled, domestic, and laborers' jobs these women might have held are becoming more scarce. The effect is to create an underclass of women, for whom criminal activity is the only means of supporting themselves and their children. This argument is also supported by historical evidence that there are significant increases in property crimes by women in periods of economic depression.

Women's crime, Miller argues, cannot be understood separately from the crime of the men for whom they often work. Her research on women hustlers shows (as seen in the opening case of Sandra) that women's crime often benefits men—directly and indirectly. The street hustlers in Miller's study worked in the context of street networks, controlled by men having lengthy criminal records. Further encounters with the criminal justice system will likely lead to long prison sentences for these men, so their major source of income may be derived from the work of the women. The men create street networks in which women do the crime and they take the money, maintaining their criminal activity, without as great a risk of prosecution.

Miller's explanation of women's crime places the causes of women's crime much more in the context of rising rates of poverty among women, thereby also supporting the long-standing association sociologists have seen between poverty, unemployment, and crime. This explanation of crime is particularly compelling because it explains women's and men's crime in the context of structural characteristics that involve class, race, and gender relations (Simpson, 1989).

Feminist scholars studying women's crime have also pointed to the strong connections between women's involvement in crime and women's victimization. What Daly (1994) calls *the reproduction of harm* means that women who have been emotionally and sexually abused, raised in families that are marginalized by poverty, and subjected to violence in relationships with men are more likely to become deviant or engage in criminal behavior. Engagement in deviant and criminal activity for some women and young girls may also be a strategy for coping with oppression—an argument that has been used to understand the deviance of young Black women. Arnold's (1994) research on African American women in prison, for example, found that African American women who are habitual criminals were abused as children, had few social networks to assist them in overcoming abuse, and grew up with a profound sense of powerlessness and isolation, feeling alienated both at home and school. Without what Arnold calls "structural supports" and with few skills, little education, and no occupational training, they turn to alcohol abuse, drug addiction, and criminal involvement as a form of rebellion against their marginal status.

Likewise, new research by Richie (1996) suggests that many women are coerced into crime by their male partners. Her study of African American women in jail focuses on women who were battered by their male partners. Richie argues that women who are marginalized in the culture because of their race, ethnicity, class, and gender are vulnerable to abusive relationships. Although the women she studied aspired to "normal" family relationships, they were unable to establish these relationships, and instead became subjected to escalating violence—ultimately coerced into the patterns of crime resulting in their incarceration. Richie's analysis, like that of Arnold and Miller, locates the causes of women's crime in the societal factors that shape women's conduct, not simply in flawed character types or individual maladjustment.

Defining Crime

Feminist perspectives on crime define crime and the criminal justice system as systems of social control. What is considered crime is established by powerful persons in the society, who define some acts as criminal in order to protect their own interests (Messerschmidt, 1986). Criminal acts, particularly crimes against property, are thus defined primarily as the crimes of the powerless. Laws defining crime are made by the rich and politically powerful; at the same time, laws are created that allow for the legal acquisition of money by the wealthy.

From this perspective, we might ask why some behaviors are considered crimes and others are not. For feminists, this question is also important. For instance, historical changes in the law sometimes defined abortion as criminal behavior and other times did not (see Chapter 7). These changes in abortion policy benefited medical doctors who sought to gain control of the abortion market

(Mohr, 1978). Those who define crime do so for their own interests, and these interests have often worked against the interests of women. Consider, for instance, who would be considered criminal if our definition of crime included the control of another person's body. From this perspective, some of the normal practices of the medical profession might be considered criminal (see Chapter 7), as would the acts of corporations whose products proved unsafe to women's health. The act of rape provides another case in point because, even now, in many states, rape within marriage is not legally defined as rape.

Feminist perspectives on crime and gender take a broadly based view of criminal behavior. Much criminological research generally asks who committed the crime and why; feminists see crime within a holistic context of social power, gender relations, and economic stratification. From a feminist perspective, it is inadequate to ask simply why women commit fewer crimes than men. Feminists have directed attention not only to the crimes committed by women, but even more to the crimes committed against women. A discussion of gender and crime is incomplete without an inquiry about women as victims of crime.

❧ Women as Victims of Crime

Statistics indicate that, overall, women are less likely to be victimized by crime than are men. National data on victimization rates are taken from **victimization surveys** based on a national sample of households and businesses in which persons are asked to report crimes by which they were victimized in the preceding months. The fact that the surveys include crimes against businesses may distort the gap between male and female victimization because men are more likely to own businesses. Faulty recall among some research subjects and the fact that many crimes might not be reported to the survey interviewers also potentially distort these data. Particularly in the case of rape, it is quite possible that, if a woman never reported it to the police, she is also unlikely to report it to a researcher.

Given these qualifications in the data, how can we characterize the victimization of women by crime? Women are less likely to be victimized by crime than men; however, there are some groups of women and some crimes in which victimization rates are higher for women than they are for men. Some women are also more likely to be victimized than others, and these categories reveal how victimization by crime is related to the political and economic powerlessness of women in society.

Victimization surveys show that a large amount of the violence directed against women (and for men, as well) is committed by those with whom they have an intimate relationship. Using a strict definition of *intimate* to include husbands, ex-husbands, boyfriends, girlfriends, ex-boyfriends, and ex-girlfriends, 29 percent of violent crimes against women (rape, sexual assault, robbery, and assault) were committed by intimates (see Figure 9.1). If one extends this defini-

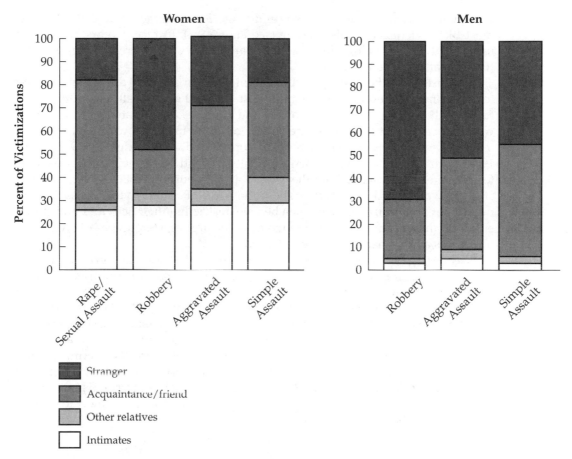

FIGURE 9.1   Violent Crime and Victim-Offender Relationship

Source: Data from Ronet Bachman and Linda E. Saltzman. 1995. *Violence against Women: Estimates from the Redesigned Survey.* Washington, DC: Bureau of Justice Statistics, p. 3.

tion to include other relatives and acquaintances and friends, another 49 percent of violent crimes against women are committed by those they know (i.e., 23 percent of violent crimes against women are committed by strangers). Thus, women murder victims are more likely to have been killed by an intimate partner than is true for men. The highest rate of intimate violence is directed against women aged 16 to 24. Robbery is the crime most likely to be committed by a stranger; rape is the least likely (Bachman and Saltzman, 1995; Greenfield, 1998).

Victimization by crime is strongly influenced by gender and race. For example, data show young African American men (ages 16 to 19, and increasingly ages 12 to 15) to be the most likely victims of violent crime. Among women, African American and Hispanic women are far more likely to be victims of violent crime than White women. Young women (under age 20) of all races/ethnicities are the most likely victims of violent crime (see Figure 9.2). In recent years, the rate of unmarried women being killed by their partners has also increased significantly (Browne and Williams, 1993).

Regardless of their actual victimization, women at every age have a greater fear of crime than do men. Race, marital status, and age are all related to fear of rape, with African American women and widowed, separated, and divorced women being most fearful. Women's fear of crime increases with age, the most fearful being elderly women who live alone (Gordon and Riger, 1989; Madriz, 1997). Fear of rape affects women especially by restricting their freedom, as the fear dictates when and where they travel and go out in public. Madriz's (1997) study of women and fear of crime shows how fear of crime is a form of social control in that it organizes how women behave, restricting their activities and differentiating their behavior relative to men. As she argues, stereotypes of women as powerless and vulnerable are perpetuated.

Crimes against women reflect women's powerlessness. Divorced and separated women are more likely to be crime victims than are married women. Women who have never been married are also victimized more than married women (U.S. Department of Justice, 1997). One should not take these data to mean, however, that married women are safe from victimization. Research on violence against wives indicates a high degree of violence within the privacy of the household. That these events do not show up in public records of crime should not lead us to the complacent conclusion that marriage protects women from crime and violence. Instead, empirical data on women and crime suggest that women's isolation (both inside and outside the home) is a common feature of crimes of violence against women.

Rape

The case of rape illustrates how isolation and powerlessness make women vulnerable to crime. Women report 500,000 rapes and sexual assaults per year, but this figure is the subject of debate. Because rape is underreported, the FBI has estimated that only one in four rapes actually shows up in the official statistics that are published in the *Uniform Crime Reports*; moreover, the *Uniform Crime Reports* do not includes rapes that end in death, since those are reported as homicides. (U.S. Department of Justice, 1997). Perhaps the important thing is not to know exactly how many rapes there are, but to understand how the official data on rape can be distorted by the different factors that result in underreporting.

Specific data on which women are more likely to be raped show the connection of rape to women's status in society; women of the lowest status are the most vulnerable to rape. Victimization surveys show that African American and Hispanic women are more likely to be raped than White women and that divorced, separated, and never married women are much more likely to be raped than women who are married or widowed. For all women, the rape rate is higher for those with incomes under $7,500 per year. The likelihood of rape has been

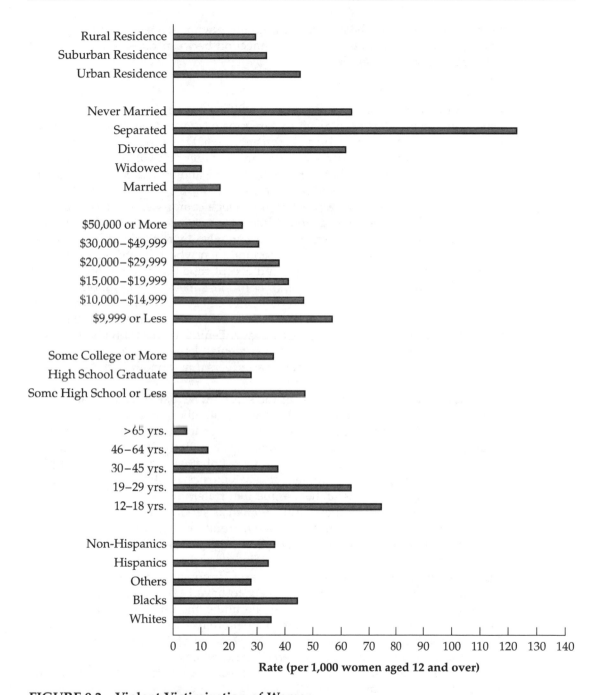

FIGURE 9.2   Violent Victimization of Women

Source: Data from Ronet Bachman and Linda E. Saltzman. 1995. *Violence against Women: Estimates from the Redesigned Survey.* Washington, DC: Bureau of Justice Statistics, p. 4.

shown to be related to the amount of time these women spend in public places (Bowker, 1981). These data show the connection between rates of victimization and women's status in society.

Date Rape

Stereotypical images of rape associate it with strangers in public places. Yet, increasing attention has been given to **date rape** or *acquaintance rape*—defined as forced, unwanted intercourse by a known aggressor. Date rape is the most under-reported form of rape and thus is much more widely prevalent than statistics alone show. Young women between the ages of 15 and 25 are the most frequent targets of date rape (Hughes and Sandler, 1987).

Date rape is particularly a problem on college campuses. Surveys of college students find that college men are more likely than college women to believe that heterosexual relations are adversarial. Men are also more likely to blame those who are raped than are women; furthermore, men who tolerate sexual harass-ment, hold adversarial sexual beliefs, and accept rape myths are more likely to victimize women (Reilly et al., 1992). In addition, rape tolerance among college men is related to the extent to which they have images of men as dominant and women as passive (Hall, Howard, and Boezio, 1986), revealing an attitudinal cli-mate prone to sexual violence against women. Feminist education about rape is effective in reducing the extent to which students blame the victim, accept rape myths, and define heterosexual relations as adversarial (Fonow, Richardson, and Wemmerus, 1992).

Changing attitudes is only part of the solution. Sexual violence is also more likely to occur in some organizational contexts than others. Fraternities, for exam-ple, often have an organizational culture that is ripe for sexual violence. As social groups, fraternities are based on an ethic of masculinity. When masculinity is associated with competition, violence, and alcohol abuse and is further coupled with gender stereotyping of women, sexual violence is likely to occur—some-times on a group basis. Researchers argue that fraternities are conducive to vio-lence against women when they define women as serving men or as sexual prey. Whenever rape occurs in a fraternity context, group loyalty, protection, and secre-cy also make it difficult to prosecute the perpetrators because brothers' protection of each other can interfere with their willingness to cooperate with university, legal, and criminal justice officials (Martin and Hummer, 1989). Researchers have found that sorority women are more likely to have been forced to have sexual intercourse through physical force or while under the influence of alcohol and drugs. At the same time, sorority women are more likely to believe certain myths about rape and are more accepting of interpersonal violence as to be expected than is the case of other college women (Kalof, 1993).

Whereas all forms of rape are traumatic, some argue that rape by someone you know is particularly traumatic because it erodes a trusting relationship. Victims may also be part of a friendship circle that includes the assailant, making it even more difficult to talk about it with friends. As with other forms of rape, vic-tims of date rape may fear being alone, become depressed, have sexual problems, or feel guilt and anxiety.

This information gives a compelling picture of women's experience and its relationship to violence as a system of social control. Explanations of violence against women have usually suggested that its cause lies within the personalities and social backgrounds of individuals who commit violence, but the empirical data on women as victims indicate that the causes of violence lie not in the characteristics of offenders but in the social status of their victims. This is not to say that women are responsible for the violence committed against them. Quite the opposite; it locates the causes of violence within the political and economic status of women in society. How one understands the causes of rape is significant—not just for understanding rape, but because different causal explanations have different implications for change. Rape crisis centers, for example, may see the causes of rape in individualist or social structural terms; this is significant in what they advocate and how they assist victims (Fried, 1994; Martin, 1997). Theoretical explanations of rape can be broadly categorized into four groups: psychological theories, the subculture of violence theory, gender socialization theory, and political-economic theory (Andersen and Renzetti, 1980).

Psychological Explanations of Rape

Psychological theories of rape look to individual characteristics of personality maladjustment and psychosexual development as the origins of men's motivation to rape. Explaining rape as a matter of individual psychopathology conforms to stereotypic notions of rapists as psychopathic and deviant, but it does not fit the evidence. That is, empirical studies have been unable to find consistent personality differences between men who rape and those who do not (Albin, 1977). Because the vast majority of rapists go unidentified by official agencies, there is a tremendous bias in such studies. The men included in the studies are those who are most likely to be detained or incarcerated for rape, and because these men are more likely to be African American, Hispanic, or poor, studies of rapists tend to be biased by both class and race. The suggestion in the psychological studies that only abnormal men rape thus carries an implicit class and race bias that defines these men as deviant and psychologically deranged. At the same time, such studies underemphasize the causal contribution of the social environment to the occurrence of rape.

Subculture of Violence

A second theory of the causes of rape comes from the **subculture of violence** perspective in criminology. This theory sees the social environment as the origin of violent behavior, but it is extremely biased by its differential emphasis on the behavior of African American, Hispanic, and working-class men. The subculture of violence theory claims that violence is a cultural way of life in working-class and minority communities; thus, its members come to take violence for granted, and it becomes a routine feature of everyday life. In this perspective men's violence and aggression are explained as adaptations to poverty, but the emphasis is placed on the collective psychological maladjustment of minority and working-class populations (Wolfgang and Feracuti, 1967; Amir, 1971). The problem with the subculture of violence thesis is not that violence in these communities is not a problem, but that this theory blames the presumed pathological culture of these people for violent behavior.

Such a perspective begs the question of whether violence is more widespread in poor and working-class communities or whether it is just less hidden. Criminologists have frequently pointed out that the higher rape and violence rates found among minority and poor men largely reflect race and class discrimination in the criminal justice system. It is important to note that the most violent crimes (rape and homicide) show smaller race differences than the less violent crime of robbery (U.S. Department of Justice, 1997). This fact seemingly discredits the subculture of violence theory. Critics of this perspective also point out that violence is equally extensive in the dominant culture; it is just more easily hidden or legitimized as appropriately masculine behavior. In the end, the subculture of violence theory gives us an inadequate explanation of violence against women because, in its focus on society's underclasses, it does not explain why violence is also symptomatic of the dominant culture.

Gender Socialization as a Cause of Rape

The third perspective used to explain rape comes from gender socialization theory. Feminists have suggested that the causes of rape can be traced to the dominant culture and its emphasis on masculinity as a learned pattern of aggression and domination. Unlike psychological and subcultural theories that emphasize deviations from the mainstream culture, feminist explanations show rape as an exaggeration of traditional gender roles. Gender socialization theory provides a perspective on rape that is sensitive to the variety of contexts in which it occurs. For example, a large proportion of rapes are committed by persons who are known to the victim. Many of these violent events occur in the context of a date or some other relationship between the person being raped and the rapist. Researchers have noted that heterosexual relations typically involve some degree of seductive coercion on the part of the man, whereas women are expected to resist sexual relations (Clark and Lewis, 1977).

There is support in the research literature for this explanation. Men who rape are more likely to have attitudes that see sexual aggressiveness as legitimate (Scully, 1990), and the presence of sexually aggressive friends is also the best predictor of whether a man will act sexually aggressive, indicating that men's image among other men is an important context for understanding their willingness to rape. This perspective also helps us understand the commonly reported finding that men who rape typically do not think they have done anything wrong. Convicted rapists typically justify rape in a variety of ways. They see the women as seductresses, think that women say no to sex when they really mean yes, think that those raped eventually relax and enjoy the rape, believe that nice girls do not get raped, or see what they did as only a minor wrongdoing (Scully, 1990). Scully's research on rapists also shows that men who rape see it as a means of revenge and punishment; those raped are thought to represent all women. Other rapists see rape as an afterthought, like a bonus after a burglary or robbery. Others define rape as recreational and say that it boosts their self-images (Scully, 1990).

From the perspective of gender socialization theory, rape occurs because men have learned that forcing women to have sex is legitimate and normal behavior. Understanding rape from this perspective helps us see how traditional gender reactions encourage the high incidence of rape in this culture, but we cannot limit our understanding of rape only to socialization and interpersonal relations. Although it is correct to see rape as connected to learned patterns in the culture, this perspective is inadequate without an understanding of how the cultural concepts of masculinity and femininity emerge from the status of women and men in the society.

Rape and the Political-Economic Status of Women

Feminists suggest a fourth perspective on rape that explains violence against women as founded on the political and economic status of women in patriarchal and capitalist societies. This political-economic theory states that women historically have been defined as the property of men in these societies. For example, the rape of African American women by White slaveowners is evidence of the relationship between rape and the property status of women. Although women in contemporary society are no longer explicitly defined as the property of men, their use as sexual objects in advertising reduces their sexuality to a commodity. Images of violence against women in advertising and the popular media legitimate violent behavior against women and reiterate their status as sexual objects. To become an object is to become a piece of property, and this status, according to feminists, dehumanizes women and makes them an object for male violence.

The fact that most rapists do not believe they have done anything wrong shows that violence against women carries some degree of legitimacy within the society. Those women who are perceived as the least valuable in the society are apparently most likely to be raped. This fact explains why African American, Hispanic, poor, unemployed, and unmarried women are those most frequently raped. The evidence is that high rates of poverty and divorce have the strongest relationship to the likelihood of rape (Smith and Bennett, 1985). This is a suggestive finding, since we have already seen the increasing linkage between divorce and poverty.

Cross-cultural evidence discloses that the level of violence against women is lowest in those societies where women have the most social, political, and economic autonomy (Friedl, 1975; Sanday, 1994). In patriarchal societies, where men rule women, women lose their autonomy and are encouraged to be dependent on men. Research on women who are raped shows that women who are not identified as belonging to a man (i.e., women who are alone in public, single, divorced, separated, or living with nonfamily members) are raped most often. At the same time, increasing social isolation seems to be a pattern in the phenomenon of wife beating (Dobash and Dobash, 1979), and, in the case of incest, the isolation of women in the privacy of family life keeps that act a closely guarded secret.

Feminist research on rape has shattered the myths surrounding the crime. Still, women are told by male experts and authorities that they should not resist, that giving in is safer than fighting to avoid rape. Bart and O'Brien's (1985) research refutes this. Their study of women who had been attacked shows that women who confront rapists both physically and verbally and who resist in a variety of strategies are most likely to avoid rape. Subsequent research has confirmed that those who resist are much less likely to have rape completed; furthermore, most forms of resistance are not associated with higher rates of injury, as women may fear. The only forms of resistance associated with increased injury are unarmed forceful resistance and arguing with the rapist (Kleck and Sayles, 1990).

Violence against women is based on the economic and political powerlessness of women living in patriarchal societies. Understanding violence against women requires an analysis that shows the relationship of violence to the structure of major social institutions. In this sense, stopping violence against women is intricately connected to the liberation of women from oppressive social and economic relations. In sum, violence against women is supported through the institutions of society (Bart and Moran, 1993). Cultural institutions ideologically promote violence against women; patriarchal social institutions encourage violence against women; criminal justice institutions minimize or cover up violence against women; and legal institutions resist radical change in policies to protect women from violence.

❧ Women in the Criminal Justice System

What happens to women when they enter the criminal justice system—either as victims or as defendants? Women in the criminal justice system are treated differently from men both as offenders and as victims. Although justice is symbolized by a blindfolded woman, equality of treatment by the law seems not to exist for women (Moulds, 1980).

Gender and the Courts

Research, particularly in the area of rape, shows that women victims are not equally credible before the law. For example, in many rape trials, the victim's past sexual history is often introduced to discredit her testimony against her assailant. Many states have reformed their legal statutes to make a woman's past sexual history inadmissible as evidence in a rape trial, but, despite legal reforms, trial evidence indicates that lawyers' allegations about a woman's character are still used to discredit her testimony or to make her appear to have an illegitimate claim. Even before trial, police and prosecutors make judgments about the victim's credibility and the prosecutive merit of her case. If she had a prior relationship with her assailant; if she delayed reporting the crime; if she was under the influence of drugs or alcohol; or if she is a prostitute, a woman of color, a welfare recipient, or a hitchhiker—her case may be seen as unsubstantiated (Clark and Lewis, 1977; Wood, 1981). How well a particular case fits prosecutors' preexisting ideas of what constitutes rape determines whether a case even goes to trial (Frohmann, 1991). Studies have repeatedly shown that gender stereotypes about rape victims affect the likelihood that a case will be brought to trial and, following that, the likelihood of sentencing (LaFree, Reskin, and Visher, 1985). Moreover, rape experiences that do not conform to stereotypes of rape are thus less likely to be prosecuted (Martin and Powell, 1994). Thus, rape survivors who prosecute their assailants often have to challenge the prevailing assumptions that judges, juries, and attorneys hold about rape, and they have to prepare extensively to confront a legal system that doubts their credibility (Konradi, 1996).

The racial composition of victim-assailant dyads is significant in understanding official reactions to rape. African American men charged with assaulting White women are not more likely to be arrested or found guilty than White men who rape White women, but, once arrested, they receive more serious charges than other defendants. If found guilty, they also receive more serious sanctions. This research suggests that the race of the defendant, studied alone, is insufficient in understanding its influence in the processing of rape cases (LaFree, 1980).

Women's perceptions of the criminal justice system clearly influence their willingness to report rape. They are much more likely to report rape when they see a high probability of conviction (Lizotte, 1985) and when the rape fits prevailing definitions of a "classic" rape—that is, rape involving use of a weapon, rape by a stranger, rape in a public place, or rape with a break in to the victim's home (Williams, 1984).

Further research finds gender bias for women in the courts, in roles as both adjudicators and as defendants. The eighteenth-century legal scholar Blackstone, whose work provides the cornerstone for English and American law, thought women were rightfully prohibited from jury service because of the defect of sex. Although women are now being fairly represented on juries, until very recently they were severely underrepresented on juries and were often permitted exemptions from jury service simply because of their sex. Women are still selected as forepersons of juries much less often than would be expected, given their numbers on juries. White men with college degrees, high-status occupations, and previous jury service are much more likely to be selected as jury forepersons (Hans and Vidmar, 1986).

Gender bias in the courtroom also affects the disposition of jury cases, although not directly because of the gender of jurors. In cases of rape, jurors' beliefs about rape influence their willingness to convict or acquit. Men are more likely than women to believe in rape myths (Reilly et al., 1992), and women tend to have greater empathy for those raped while men are more likely to see the defendant's point of view (Deitz et al., 1982). As a result, the greater representation of women on juries has resulted in a higher rape conviction rate in recent years. Women and men do however recommend similar punishments for defendants found guilty of rape (Hans and Vidmar, 1986).

For women offenders brought before the criminal justice system, a number of factors influence the disposition of cases. Some have argued that judges are more lenient toward women defendants as a result of chivalrous and paternalistic attitudes toward women. The bias of judges may also come into play when women engage in behaviors judged inappropriate for their gender, since there is some indication that when convicted for the same crime, women receive more serious sanctions than do men (Haft, 1980). Most recently, sociologists have explained gender differences in sentencing in terms of two factors: (1) the influence of defendants' work and family obligations on judges' determinations of sentencing and (2) the interaction of race and gender.

Specifically, Daly (1989) found that a defendant's work and family situations influenced sentencing of both men and women. Judges perceive men on a continuum, ranging from "good" men, who work and support dependents, to "irresponsible" men, who may or may not have a job and dependents but who do not contribute support. These irresponsible men, along with those who do not have jobs or dependents, are more likely to be sentenced. Similarly, women are judged along a similar continuum—the "good" woman being one who has dependents for whom she cares regularly (regardless of whether she holds a job) and the "irresponsible" woman being one who has dependents but does not care for them regularly. As with men, women judged to be irresponsible are more likely to be sentenced. This research concludes that judges seek to protect children and families, not women per se, as prior arguments about judicial paternalism and chivalry have implied.

This conclusion is further elaborated by subsequent research finding that the influence of work and family relations in sentencing varies by race. The results here are complicated but, generally speaking, African American women are given leniency only when they are perceived as providing support to dependents and doing it well (Bickle and Peterson, 1991). White women seem to be more quickly presumed to be good mothers by virtue of marital status. By examining race and gender simultaneously in analyses of sentencing patterns, researchers have shown the significance of not generalizing from either race or gender alone, because patterns of sentencing emerge from the interactive effects of race and gender.

Gender and Juvenile Justice

There is a wide gap between the amount of juvenile crime committed by young men and that committed by young women. Male juvenile delinquents are much more likely to engage in serious crime (including property and violent crime) and in petty property crime, with the exception of larceny. Arrests for young women are highest for larceny and running away.

Typically, juvenile female offenders are high school dropouts, come from single-parent households, have experienced foster care placement, are substance abusers, and are victims of sexual and/or physical abuse and exploitation. Over half are African American or Hispanic (Bergsmann, 1991). Experts predict that almost 90 percent of juvenile female offenders will become single heads of household who will have to spend 80 percent of their income on housing and child care (Sarri, 1988). Given their class and race background, they will suffer from racism and sexism and are unlikely to have opportunities that will improve their situation and that of their children.

Research on the juvenile justice system finds that there is differential treatment between young women and young men. Female delinquents are more likely than males to be incarcerated for noncriminal offenses. They are more likely to be arrested for what are called **status offenses** (e.g., running away, incorrigibility, waywardness, and curfew violations) than are boys (see Table 9.1). Because girls are expected to conform to traditional roles, they are more likely than boys to be locked up for sexual promiscuity. The courts also see girls as more in need of the protection of the courts, and thus courts tend to give more severe sanctions to females than males for noncriminal offenses (Chesney-Lind, 1981).

These particular children are those who are most "at risk" in the society. The educational system has failed them, they have few marketable skills, and, in many cases, they are ignored by the juvenile justice system. Training programs and educational opportunities are needed to improve the life chances of both young men and young women, but, in addition, attention must be given to the underlying causes of the trouble they find themselves in. Most typically, this trouble results from the gender, race, and class oppression that falls especially hard on young people. Unless these fundamental problems are addressed, the situation for juvenile offenders is unlikely to improve.

Women and Prison

The number of women in prison is a small percentage (6.4 percent) of all state prisoners (Gilliard and Beck, 1998); however, the female prison population has increased at a faster rate than the male prison population. A disproportionate number of women in prison are members of racial minority groups; almost half of women prisoners are African American and 14 percent are Latinas (McQuiade and Ehrenreich, 1998). The highest rates of imprisonment of women are for those between 25 and 39 years of age—years when they are also likely to be mothers. Two-thirds of women in prison have at least one child under age 18; about half of these children live with grandparents, and about one-fourth live with their fathers. Consistent with patterns of crime, a greater percentage of women are imprisoned for property and drug offenses than is the case for men, who are more likely imprisoned for violent offenses. Two-thirds of women serving sentences for violent offenses victimized someone they knew—a relative, an intimate, or someone else they knew; men, on the other hand, are more likely imprisoned for violent offenses against strangers (Snell, 1994).

Once women are in prison, little attention is paid to their special needs. Some have argued that this is because, until recently, there have been so few women in prison that it is costly to develop special programs for them. Instead, they are "confined in a system primarily designed, built, and run by men for men" (Church, 1990:20). Prisons are "gendered institutions," where organizational policies and practices are modeled on men's needs and interests, even while such practices (such as job training) are assumed to be gender neutral (Britton, 1997). Gender stereotypes also shape the vocational training women get in prison; the prison experience typically leaves women marginalized upon their exit (Morash, Harr, & Rucker, 1994). Although men in prison may be trained in relatively well-paying trades (e.g., mechanics, carpentry, etc.), job training for women, to the extent that it exists, is for poorly paid, gender-segregated jobs that offer little hope for advancement (e.g., laundress, homemaker, or beautician). Women's prisons are smaller than men's prisons but have also become increasingly overcrowded. Increasingly, however, women in prison are being treated no differently than men—a mixed message, since this means that women are now subject to much of the same degradation as male prisoners (Chesney-Lind, 1997).

Health care in women's prison is also notoriously poor, particularly in meeting needs specific to women's medical and reproductive care. Many women enter prison with existing medical problems, including drug addiction, psychiatric illness, hypertension, and respiratory disease. One in four is pregnant or has recently given birth. Although some women remain sexually active while in prison, they may lose the right to use contraceptives. Many prisons do not permit women to use particular birth control devices (such as diaphragms and IUDs); if women become pregnant while in prison, they may have a long wait for medical care, making abortion a potentially high risk. Some facilities do not allow abortions at all. Should a woman prisoner carry through her pregnancy, she may not receive adequate prenatal care and, when she gives birth, is likely to be separated from her child (Resnik and Shaw, 1981; Ingram-Fogel, 1991, 1993; McQuiade and Ehrenreich, 1998).

Women in prison say that separation from their children is the most difficult part of their sentence and they see few alternatives for their children's care. They typically give them up for adoption, release them to foster care, or leave them with relatives (the choice most often selected). There are also differences in the support women prisoners receive from family and friends on the "outside," compared to men. Men in prison receive frequent visits from wives and girlfriends, but men seldom visit women in prison. Allyn Sielaff, the Corrections Commissioner of New York City, reports that "boyfriends and brothers usually drop a woman convict 'like a hot potato' " (Church, 1990:21). As a result, women turn to other women prisoners for comfort and company.

In sum, the conditions in women's prisons often lead them to fend for themselves. In the face of these conditions, research indicates that women's own social networks in prison are more supportive and affectionate than those formed in male prisons. Giallombardo's early study (1966) found that women in prison form pseudofamilies, with prisoners taking different roles in relation to each other (e.g., mother, daughter, and sister). Her observation has since been replicated by others (Culbertson and Fortune, 1991). Many have interpreted this phenomenon as a reflection of the external values and cultural expectations that society has for all women. According to this argument, women in prison have external norms, values, and beliefs that define women in stereotypic family roles, these norms and roles are then reflected in prison subcultures.

An alternative explanation emphasizes women's active construction of a supportive subculture rather than their passive acquiescence to external gender roles. Women prisoners form a conscious culture of resistance like those of other oppressed groups who, in the context of domination, create and maintain networks of mutual support (Caulfield, 1974). Cultures of resistance often take the form of conscious affirmation of cultural differences in the face of external domination. Although women in prison do not all come from similar cultural backgrounds, the subcultures they form in prison exhibit resourcefulness, flexibility, and creativity in the social relations they develop. The perspective of a culture of resistance emphasizes that they are not merely passive victims of their situation; instead, they develop adaptive strategies to cope with the conditions they face.

Women are more likely than men to form interracial friendships in prison. Men more commonly segregate themselves by race and interact on a competitive, sometimes violent, basis (Church, 1990). Part of women's prison subculture is reflected in the lesbian relationships that emerge between some women prisoners. Compared with homosexuality among male prisoners, which tends to be founded on coercion or prostitution, women prisoners put more emphasis on love than physical sex in lesbian relations. Because lesbian relations in women's prisons occur in the context of love, sexual coercion is a rare event (Bowker, 1981); moreover, many loving relationships which are not overtly emerge between women in prison subcultures. Such relationships are less evident in men's prisons (Bowker, 1981).

❧ *Summary*

Women's crime and deviance historically have been explained as the result of women's biological and psychological characteristics. Early sociologists looked to social circumstances as instrumental in producing crime. Sexist assumptions about women's character still permeate some explanations of crime. Biological explanations of crime, although unsupported by scientific evidence, have recently been revived, but receive little support from sociological research.

Women's deviance should be interpreted in the context of gender relations in society. Sociologists define deviance as behavior that departs from conventional norms and that is labeled deviant; becoming deviant involves societal reactions to behavior. Deviance occurs in the context of social institutions that have the power to label some as deviant, others as not. Feminist perspectives on social deviance look to the point of view of the deviant actor for understanding deviance. Feminists are critical of the sexual labeling of deviant girls, and also point to a double standard that sees behavior as deviant in women that is not seen as deviant in men.

Data on crime show some increase in female crime, especially in the category of property crimes. Some attribute the causes of women's increased crime to the women's movement. A more reliable explanation sees the causes of women's crime as located in high poverty rates among women and the development of an underclass of women. Feminists see crime as involving a system of social control.

Women are less likely to be victimized by crime than are men, except for rape. Women's victimization by crime varies by race, class, age, and marital status. Women's fear of crime restricts their freedom. Rape reflects the powerlessness of women in society. Four perspectives are used to explain rape: psychological explanations, a subculture of violence theory, gender socialization, and the political and economic status of women.

Women in the criminal justice system are treated differently from men as offenders and as victims. Gender bias affects the courtroom process. Male delinquents are more likely to be involved in serious crime; female delinquency is primarily for status offenses. Women in prison are a small proportion of all prisoners. Conditions faced by women in prison include poor health care, separation from families, insufficient job training, and lack of educational opportunity. Women's subcultures in prisons reflect adaptive strategies designed to cope with oppressive conditions.

❧ Key Terms

date rape	labeling theory	subculture of violence
deviance	status offenses	victimization surveys

❧ Discussion Questions/Projects for Thought

1. Think of a time when you engaged in some activity that was considered deviant for someone of your gender. Alternatively, without putting yourself at risk, do something that violates the routine expectations associated with your gender. How do people react to you? How does this make you feel? What does your experiment tell you about the concepts of deviance, gender, and social control?

2. What services does your campus or community offer to assist women who are victims of violence? Contact some of those who work (or volunteer) in one such organization and ask them what they have learned about violence against women. Based on these discussions, what links do you see between violence and women's status?

3. Follow the daily newspaper for one week, noting the stories involving criminal activity. What evidence of men's and women's crime do you see and how do your anecdotal observations support (or not) the data on gender and crime reported in this chapter?

❧ Suggested Readings

Bart, Pauline B., and Eileen Geil Moran, eds. 1993. *Violence Against Women: The Bloody Footprints.* Thousand Oaks, CA: Sage.
This collection of articles explores different dimensions of violence against women, showing how violence is linked to the status of women in a patriarchal society.

Madriz, Esther. 1997. *Nothing Bad Happens to Good Girls: Fear of Crime in Women's Lives.* Berkeley: University of California Press. Madriz's research is based on focus groups and interviews with African American,

Latina, and White women of different ages. She shows how fear of crime is a source of the social control of women, particularly for African American women and Latinas.

Miller, Eleanor. 1986. *Street Women.* Philadelphia: Temple University Press.
This important book examines women's participation in criminal activities, arguing that women's economic status is the most important source of women's deviance. The study is based on interviews with women in a halfway house.

Miller, Susan L. 1999. *Crime Control and Women: Feminist Implications of Criminal Justice Policy.* Thousand Oaks, CA: Sage.

Miller's analysis of current criminal justice policies shows the consequences for women of such concepts as "three strikes, you're out" and mandatory sentencing for battering. Her analysis carefully links the consequences of social policy to patterns or racial, class, and gender inequality.

Price, Barbara Raffel, and Natalie J. Sokoloff, eds. 1995. *The Criminal Justice System and Women: Offenders, Victims and Workers,* 2nd ed. New York: McGraw-Hill.

This anthology provides a good overview of women's participation in crime, women as victims of crime, and women as workers in the criminal justice system.

Rafter, Nicole Hahn. 1990. *Partial Justice: Women, Prison and Social Control,* 2nd ed. New Brunswick, NJ: Transaction Publishers.

Rafter's study of women's prisons provides a historical overview of their development, showing how the development of women's prisons is intricately linked to gender ideologies in different historical periods.

Richie, Beth E. 1996. *Compelled to Crime: The Gender Entrapment of Battered Black Women.* New York: Routledge.

Based on extensive interviews with African American battered women in prison, Richie analyzes whey women participate in crime. She argues that they become dependent on men who encourage their criminal activity, because the women are both traditional in their gender ideology and trapped by the oppression of their race, class, and gender status. The life stories of the women she studies provide vivid evidence of the connection between women's criminality and social inequality.

Chapter 10

Women, Power, and Politics

During the 1990s, record numbers of women were elected to national office. More women serve in the U.S. Congress today than during any prior period. Indeed, prior to 1992, there was no women's bathroom near the Senate floor and one had to be installed for the women serving in the Senate.

Social scientists project that women will increasingly be elected to public office (Darcy, Welch, and Clark, 1994). At the same time that more women are running for and being elected to political office, they continue to encounter numerous barriers to their full political participation. Even with their increased representation, women remain vastly outnumbered by men in government and in other institutions that comprise the political system. Although women may be reaching new heights of political power, old attitudes and stereotypes remain, and women who become powerful are frequently ridiculed, as if there is only one proper role for political women—to be the support system behind political men.

This is vividly communicated in the presumed proper role for the nation's First Lady (a term laden with sexist connotations). Public images of the First Lady show her in traditional women's roles—volunteering at social service organizations, promoting volunteer work, being an advocate for human issues, and supporting her husband, even if at the expense of her own interests. The persistence of this helpmate image is all the more obvious when some first ladies try to act otherwise; thus, when Hillary Rodham Clinton was appointed by the president to lead the nation in health care reform, she was publicly ridiculed and hailed as out of line for trying to share power with her husband. Soon thereafter, her advisors tried to soften her image, and a new Hillary Clinton appeared in the press—a woman whose primary interests were children and whose identity was most often described in terms of her hairstyle! Following President Clinton's affair with Monica Lewinsky, public sympathy for Hillary Clinton increased, but mostly because the public saw her as a victim of her husband's infidelity, not because of her own achievements. At a time when many think women might be reaching new heights of political power, the message is clear: Some women can move into politics, but it is still a man's world—where women are not expected to exercise equal power.

How do we describe women's political behavior? As you will see, feminists have challenged traditional concepts of political behavior, arguing that the usual focus on formal political institutions ignores the variety of ways that women act politically; thus, one of the major contributions of feminist thought has been to redefine *political* and to expand this concept to include otherwise invisible activities in women's lives. In addition, feminist scholars have shown how deeply gender influences political behavior, political attitudes, and the structure of political institutions. In studying women's roles in political institutions—including local government, federal government, and political action groups—feminists have discovered numerous ways that gender shapes power and politics. The examination of women, power, and politics must also include analysis of the women's movement—one of the most important and far-reaching political movements of our time.

ᨒ *Defining Power*

Power has traditionally been believed to be the province of men. Indeed, judging from some indicators, this is little changed—just notice how few women are heads of state, particularly in the major world powers. Women, instead, have been seen as exercising power primarily at home (a myth exposed by considering men's power in the family; see Chapter 6). Women have also been stereotyped as holding the "power behind the throne," as if women's power comes primarily from their presumed manipulation of men and as if women's primary political role is to remain invisible and out of public view.

Sociologists define **power** as the ability to influence others. Power comes in many forms. It can be exercised by individuals or groups and within and outside of formal social institutions. Power can come through persuasion, charisma, law, political activism, and coercion. It is not just an individual attribute, even though some individuals may be more powerful than others. Power in society comes as the result of a social process and social relationships; the use of power cannot be understood without reference to this social context (Bookman and Morgan, 1988). To explain further, although an individual may have characteristics that make him or her more powerful (i.e., the person's race, gender, age, religion, social class, education, etc.), it is the value that society has placed on these characteristics that gives the person power. Moreover, exercising power means people have to be situated such that they can mobilize the resources needed to influence others.

Consider the subject of men's power. Feminists describe men's power as a system of patriarchy, meaning an organized social structure whereby men as a group hold more power than women. Patriarchal societies give men power and authority over women; this can be institutional and/or individual. Societies will differ in exactly how patriarchal power is structured. For example, in a monarchy, an individual man (e.g., as a king or an emperor) may have ultimate power and authority; in a democratic society, power is determined through law and the various regulatory institutions that uphold and enforce the law. If men control the law-making process and the institutions that implement the law, however, they hold institutional power. In this sense, patriarchy becomes part of the structure of the society, even if power is not held by a single or particular man. In such a system, patriarchy structures the many social institutions that regulate and determine the nature of women's lives. In this sense, the United States is a patriarchal society.

Men's power does not stem from the mere fact of their being biologically male, nor does having institutions that are patriarchal mean that every individual man is a patriarch. Patriarchy in an institutional sense means that social institutions have been organized over time to give men more advantage than women (recognizing that this advantage is also influenced by other factors, such as one's social class, religion, race, etc.). It is the structural supports given to men's power that constitute the institutional basis of patriarchy.

To understand this, think about the subject of marital violence. Feminists explain men's violence against women as an expression of men's power, a power manifested in the actual marital relationship where violence occurs. Beyond the relationship between these two people, feminists have pointed out, other institutions are organized to support men's power. Women who turn to these institutions for help often find that the system does not work on their behalf. Understanding violence against women, then, is a matter of understanding both individual power relationships and institutional power relationships.

Power is not all one-sided, however. People can mobilize to challenge existing power arrangements in society, and individuals can work to create more egalitarian relationships. Power does not come only from within existing institutions. People can mobilize to alter the structural supports that give power to some groups and not others; thus, social movements and other forms of political action are means of challenging and transforming the status quo. While the existing system may give certain power resources to certain groups, people can develop the resources to alter social institutions. Power can come through mobilization of vast numbers of people (such as in mass movements); through effective use of strategies such as boycotts, civil disobedience, or media campaigns; and through the exercise of law, including, if needed, legal reforms. Although groups can be described as more or less powerful than others, these forms of political action can change the circumstances even of those considered to be the most powerless. The women's movement, as an example, has mobilized women and men to make a number of changes that have altered the power that women hold both as a group and as individuals. Likewise, the civil rights movement involved the mass mobilization of African American people who were otherwise quite powerless—unable to vote, unable to use public accommodations, and without access to the best educational institutions. Although as a group Whites still hold more power than do people of color and men as a group hold more power than do women, these political movements have altered the power base of race and gender in the United States.

Sociologists also distinguish the concepts of power and authority. **Authority** is power that is perceived by others as legitimate and that is structured into specific social institutions. Authority comes not just because a person or group exercises power, but because their constituents believe their power is legitimate and because there are institutional supports in place that make this authority legitimate. The recognition of authority varies across societies, depending on the structure of that society. In a monarchy, for example, the king or queen has authority over all matters; in a totalitarian society, the dictator or emperor has total authority over all affairs. In a democratic society based on the rule of law, the law serves as the system of authority, with those who interpret and execute it as the primary agents of authority. In the United States, some forms of authority are also perceived as more legitimate than others. Science, for example, is increasingly taken to be a source of authority—hence the reason feminists have been so critical of science when its biases against women have been revealed. One of the further consequences of patriarchy is the tendency to see men and men's activities as more authoritative in the areas deemed to be most important.

ᨠ *Women and the State*

The institution that embodies the official power system is the *state*. Sociologists use the term **state** to refer to the organized system of power and authority in society. This is different from the ordinary meaning of the term as a geographic area (e.g., California, Missouri, or Georgia). As a concept, the state refers to all of the institutions that represent official power and authority in society. The state regulates many societal relations, ranging from individual behavior and interpersonal conflicts to international affairs. Different institutions make up the state, including formal systems of government, the military, and the courts and the law.

Feminist thinking about the state begins from the premise that an analysis of gender is critical to understanding the state. Feminists see the state as a *gendered institution*—that is, an institution that embeds within it the characteristics associated with a particular gender. Feminists conceive of the state as embodying the masculine characteristics of presumed rationality, detachment, power, forcefulness, and impersonality. As one of the most bureaucratic of all institutions, the state operates as if it were neutral, when, in fact, according to feminists, it is organized on quite gender-specific grounds. Not surprisingly, then, some of the specific institutions comprising the state (e.g., the military and the police) are the most masculine (in the cultural sense) and male dominated of all social institutions.

Because the state represents the imposition of power and authority in society, it is characterized by feminists as a source of oppression. That is, it represents men's interests more than women's and it is an imposing force in many women's lives. Women living on welfare, for example, have the state intruding in their affairs more than happens for women with more class privilege. The state may regulate how one lives, whether one is forced to work, how one cares for children, and what kind of health care is available. For all women, the state is also a source for laws that govern many features of everyday life, ranging from reproductive rights to rights to work and rights for equal protection.

Two primary theoretical models have been used by social scientists to explain how the state operates. The first, the **pluralism** model, sees the state as representing the plural interests of different groups in society. According to this model, the state tries to balance the different interest groups in society. Interests groups are those that are organized around a specific cause or purpose, such as the National Gay and Lesbian Task Force, the National Women's Political Caucus, the National Abortion Rights Action League (NARAL), Planned Parenthood, and the National Organization for Women (NOW). This model interprets the state as representing the diverse interest groups in society. These groups mobilize to achieve political results and use their influence to achieve their political ends.

The other model of the state is known as the **power elite**. According to this perspective, a powerful ruling class controls the actions of the state. The power elite consists of those who hold power in the economy, the executive branch of the government, and the military. Elites in these institutions share common interests and shape the political agendas in the society. Since this powerful group is primarily men, the power elite model represents men's interests as shaping the major decisions in society. This model also sees a strong alliance between government and corporate business, since the power elite, through their role in government, shape decisions that protect the interests of big business. The power elite model sees the state as part of the structure of domination in society, including gender domination, racial domination, and class domination.

Feminists have supplemented these models of state theory with the argument that the state essentially reflects men's interests, not only because men are those most likely to be in the power elite but also because men control most of the major interest groups that influence the workings of the state. Feminist theory sees the state as fundamentally patriarchal—that is, representing the power of men over women. Some have concluded that despite the presence of some women in positions of authority in the state, on the whole, the state promotes men's interests. As Catharine MacKinnon, a noted feminist legal scholar, puts it, "the state is male" (1983:644).

The argument that "the state is male" was perhaps most clear to the public during the 1991 hearings to confirm Judge Clarence Thomas to the Supreme Court. The Senate Judiciary Committee that heard Anita Hill testify that she had been sexually harassed by Thomas was a committee of all men. Feminists argue that, as an all-male group, the Senate Judiciary Committee could not understand Hill's testimony and would act to protect men's interests.

Ironically, although some feminists analyze the state as essentially oppressive to women because the state represents men's interests, feminists also see the state as the only institution to which disadvantaged groups can turn for redress. Both the women's movement and the civil rights movement have used state power to enforce existing laws or to work to change the law. While the state can (and does) support gender inequality—for example, by denying women the right to vote or, as was the case in the early history of this country, denying women the right to speak in public—the state is also the institution that guarantees women equal protection under the law. Legislation that has brought women civil rights, defined sexual harassment as illegal, and provided some degree of reproductive freedom has been developed through the state. It is important to point out, however, that this state action has come only as the result of political mobilization by feminist groups.

≈ *Women and the Law*

Law is the written system through which state authority is defined; thus, the study of law is extremely significant in feminist analysis. Like the state, the law is both a source for the denial of women's rights and one of the avenues to which feminists have turned to address the problems of women's inequality. Significant scholarship in women's studies has developed both to describe the changes in law that have stemmed from the women's movement and to understand the process by which the law has encoded men's interests. Recently, feminist legal scholars have also developed the analysis of feminist jurisprudence—that is, they have developed studies of law that interpret the law as reflecting men's power but that try to revise legal doctrine to be consistent with feminist theory and practice. These studies have shown that although the law is a significant source of change for women, it is also limited in its ability to transform women's lives (Smart, 1989).

Since the 1960s, women's position relative to the law has changed dramatically. Whereas historically the law officially excluded women from full citizenship, now the law has taken a neutral position on gender. Early on, there was no protection for those women who departed from traditional roles in family. Laws overtly prohibited women from entering certain professions and treated men and women differently at every level. The Equal Pay Act of 1963, which required equal pay for equal work, was the first law to begin breaking this discriminatory framework. Strengthened by the Civil Rights Bill of 1964 and subsequent pieces of legislation, the law now, at least in theory, gives women equal civil rights to men.

As they are written, laws provide some basis for the equal treatment of men and women before the law. How the law is interpreted and implemented, however, may be another matter. Even with an equal rights framework in place, executing the law is a function of many sociological factors, including how police, lawyers, and judges interpret and execute the law and how the legal system is structured to give legal advantage to some groups and not others.

On the first point, feminists have pointed out that women are underrepresented among those who are responsible for interpreting and exercising the law. For example, women make up 30 percent of judges; women of color are a smaller proportion still (3.4 percent), although women of color more equally approximate the number of men of their own race who serve as judges. Although there is more gender equity between men and women of color than between White women and White men as judges, this fact probably affects only minimally the execution of justice before the law. As lawyers, women have dramatically increased their representation in recent years, now comprising 27 percent of lawyers. As you saw in Chapter 5, however, women lawyers are more likely to practice some areas of law than others, and although they are more widely distributed across legal specialties than in the past, they are more likely to work in the least prestigious area of public service law, where salaries are also lower (Epstein, 1993).

Judges, like lawyers, have considerable power in the interpretation of the law. The fact that women are underrepresented as judges means that in practice the law likely embodies men's perspectives and values—even though the law and its execution are allegedly neutral. This has been a major point in feminist analyses of the law, since it gets to the crux of how some feminists see the law as encoding men's power. First, it means that the execution of the law is significantly influenced by gender prejudice. There is ample empirical evidence of this in the research literature. Like racial prejudice, gender prejudice means that women may be treated differently before the law, depending on the bias of the lawyers, the judges, and perhaps the jury. A number of states have documented this bias against women in the courts, as have research studies on the disparaging way that women lawyers are treated in court (Rosenberg, Perlstadt, and Phillips, 1993). Several states, for example, have appointed task forces to examine gender discrimination in the courts and have found discrimination against women in the courts at several levels, including differential treatment of women in the court environments (including how women lawyers are treated) and prejudicial standards in the interpretation of the law (Associated Press, 1992).

Feminist critique of the law has generated the question: Are equal rights enough? As you will see in Chapter 11 on liberal feminism, although many feminists take the position that creating equal rights for women is the best strategy for social change, others argue that this strategy neither recognizes the different conditions of women's lives that make unique solutions for women necessary nor addresses the fundamental ways that gender, race, and class structure the basic institutions of society, including courts and the law. Some feminists have also raised the question of whether treating everyone theoretically the same under the law is appropriate, given women's unique life experiences. For example, should women be given special treatment before the law for pregnancy and maternity? This is a source of debate within the feminist literature. Some feminists, for instance, have been opposed to protective legislation that has excluded pregnant women from certain occupations (see Chapter 7). Under current law, maternity has no special place; it is defined as a disability. Is this an adequate framework for the legal protection of pregnant women?

Beyond these questions of whether women should be treated the same or differently by the law are more radical questions. Some feminists have argued that the presumed neutrality of the law is problematic for women, because under the guise of legal neutrality, the law protects men's power. They claim that the law takes men's experience as its reference point (Smart, 1989).

As an example, consider rape law. First, most state laws define rape as occurring only when penetration has taken place—a definition that feminists would argue takes a phallocentric position, as if sexual intercourse has only taken place when a man inserts himself (or an object) into a woman. In addition, despite changes in actual law, women are still sexualized during rape trials; men are not. In rape cases, the law also makes consent the crux of whether the assailant is guilty, thereby making most rape trials as much a trial for the victim as for the rapist. In a society where women are defined as sexual objects, any number of factors can influence whether consent is perceived by the police, the defense attorney, the judge, or the jury. A woman is easily discredited on the issue of consent, particularly if she had been drinking or was under the influence of drugs at the time of the assault or if she had any prior relationship (including marriage) with the assailant. What the woman was wearing, where she was walking, how she earns her income, and any number of other factors influence people's judgments about consent.

What if a different standard existed in the law and it was not assumed, going into trial, that the woman's consent was the most significant issue? For example, how would rape laws and trials be different if men's dominance was the major point to prove? This is the kind of thinking that feminist scholars consider when they argue that the law, presumably neutral, is masculine in its very framework.

Finally, feminists also argue that the legal method reflects masculine culture. Legal interrogation is adversarial, based on rational argument, outdoing one's opponent, and arguing minute details. Think again of a rape trial; the method of interrogation is so masculine that rape victims report that the trial feels like a repetition of the rape. Some feminists have concluded that the legal method—debate and argument—is a masculine mode of thinking and acting. The reliance on former precedent and case law also replicates gender inequities, since this reliance gives weight to tradition without looking at the gendered context in which that tradition was constructed.

In sum, feminist studies of the law have both analyzed the legal reforms that have produced more equity for women and, as well, have criticized the gendered basis of the law. As you will see in the chapters to come, different theoretical and political positions underlie feminist arguments and form a substantive debate around the use of the law as a framework for liberating social change for women.

❧ Women in Government

One way to change women's standing before the law is to increase the number of women who are lawmakers; thus, one of the major feminist political strategies in recent years has been to expand the number of women serving in public political office. In the past, women were explicitly barred from political office. In the early history of the nation, political rights were based on birth, property, age, and religion. Basic political rights that have defined this nation as democratic were not originally extended to women; women were denied rights to free speech and property, and the right to assemble. They were effectively excluded from participating—not just as political officials, but in sharing the same political rights as White men. For women, the American Revolution was actually a loss of political status, since it eliminated the customs that allowed some women to participate in political life and brought universal suffrage to men (White men), thereby officially excluding women from the right to vote (Darcy, Welch, and Clark, 1994:8).

With this history behind us, feminists now ask why there continue to be so few women elected to formal political office in the United States. Compared to most other democratic, industrialized nations, women in the United States are an amazingly small number of elected officials (see Figure 10.1), although since the 1990s, women's representation in government has been increasing (see Figure 10.2). The number of women in the U.S. House of Representatives reached an all-time high in 1998 (56 women of 434 members); 9 women (the historic high) serve

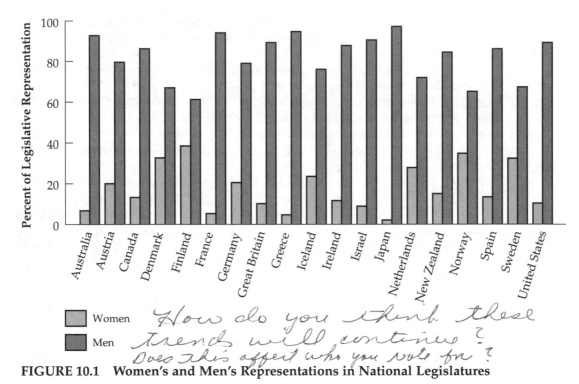

Women

Men

How do you think these trends will continue? Does this affect who you vote for?

FIGURE 10.1   Women's and Men's Representations in National Legislatures

Source: Data from R. Darcy, Susan Welch, and Janet Clark. 1994. *Women, Elections, and Representation.* Lincoln: University of Nebraska Press, p. 78.

with 91 men in the Senate. Although these numbers have increased and reached record highs, they are still a small portion of the national Congress.

Women fare somewhat better in statewide offices; in 1998, 8 percent of state legislators were women. There has been an actual decrease, however, in the number of women governors since the 1980s, with only three serving as of 1998 (Center for the American Woman and Politics, 1998). In general, the more powerful the political office, the fewer women there are in it. This means that matters of greatest national importance are determined by men. Since holding a state office is also typically a route to mobility in the political system, being underrepresented there has consequences for women's likelihood of being elected to higher office.

Mobility

Why are there so few women elected officials? Research offers a number of possible explanations. One explanation is that sheer prejudice has taught people to think that women are not well suited to politics. This is reflected in the attitude that women are best suited for taking care of their families and in beliefs that women do not have the personality characteristics that suit them for politics. Although only a small minority of people in the United States explicitly believe this, the attitude does persist in some people's minds. Men more than women are likely to think that women do not have the characteristics that suit them for politics, although the gap between men and women on this point is small. For example, as late as the 1990s, 22 percent of women and 26 percent of men thought that

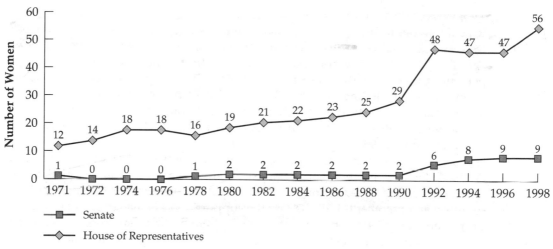

FIGURE 10.2   Women in the U.S. Congress

Source: Data from Center for the American Woman and American Politics. 1995. *Fact Sheet on Women's Political Progress.* New Brunswick, NJ: Rutgers University; Center for the American Woman and American Politics. 1998. *Women's Electoral Success: A Familiar Formula.* New Brunswick, NJ: Rutgers University. Website: <www.rci.rutgers.edu/~cawp/98electpress.html>

most men are emotionally better suited for politics than are women; 15 percent of women and 20 percent of men thought that women were not tough enough for politics (Roper Organization, 1990).

These attitudes, however, are changing. In the early 1970s, 40 percent of women and 50 percent of men said they would be less likely to vote for a woman candidate if a man and a woman with equal qualifications were running for office. Now, however, most men and women say whether the candidate were a man or a woman would make no difference at all. Four times as many women as before say they would now be more likely to vote for the woman. Men have not changed in saying they would be more likely to vote for the woman; they are more likely to have moved from saying they would be less likely to vote for the woman to saying now that it would not make any difference (Roper Organization, 1990).

More than half of men think women would do a worse job than men in directing the military, although 75 percent thought so 25 years ago. Attitudes are changing. Most people think women would do a better job in handling a variety of issues important to social and public policy, including education, poverty, health, homelessness, support for senior citizens, and encouraging the arts. Men think, however, that women cannot be as capable in dealing with the "harder" issues, such as prison reform, dealing with big business, and overseas trade. Women do not agree with men on these points, since they think women would be equally capable of handling difficult issues.

A second explanation of the small number of women in politics is that gender-stereotyped socialization does not encourage women to see themselves as potential political candidates. A large number of people think that women do not enter politics because as girls growing up, they are not encouraged to do so.

Almost 40 percent of women and men believe that young girls are not encouraged to aspire to political careers; 20 percent of women and men still think men are better suited for politics. At the same time, the public perceives that there is a shortage of role models for women considering politics; 46 percent of women and 41 percent of men think there are too few women in high political office to inspire other women, including young girls, to run. Most people (90 percent of women and 88 percent of men) now say that they would vote for a woman for president if she were qualified for the job (Roper Organization, 1990; National Opinion Research Center, 1994).

Explaining women's underrepresentation in politics as a matter of prejudice and socialization, however, does not expose the social structural factors that discourage women's greater political participation. Being successful in politics requires, among other things, having the support of party leaders; if those leaders do not encourage women to run for office, there is little likelihood of women's success as politicians. A study of judges found, for example, that women judges are more likely to have an interest in seeing more women run for public office than is true for male judges; 90 percent of women judges wanted to see more women run for office, compared to 53 percent of male judges (Martin, 1990).

Other social structural factors also influence the likelihood of women winning political office. Being an incumbent, regardless of one's gender, carries a huge advantage in political elections. As new entrants to politics, women are at a disadvantage in challenging those who already hold office; as one example of the power of incumbency, political scientists have found that 90 percent of political action committee contributions go to incumbents (Malcolm, 1993).

One of the ways that people succeed in politics, as in other high-level careers, is through the use of social and political networks. These networks are important resources for people in positions of influence, since they provide systems of support for information, communication, and acquaintances where associates can be counted on for help. In any high-level job, networks are critical. Women, however, tend to have less extensive networks than do men and to be isolated from the male-centered networks where the most power lies. Having fewer women in political office also gives women fewer ties than men have, since people often form their networks based on gender similarities. On the other hand, having fewer women in these offices at least encourages more gender integration, since the low proportion of senior women ensures that women have to form networks with male co-workers (Moore, 1990, 1992). If these men hold sexist attitudes, however, it cuts women off from the circles of power that are critical to political success.

Campaign financing is another area where women are at a structural disadvantage, relative to men. Political campaigns are notoriously expensive; women, who as a group have lower incomes than men and fewer economic resources, are not likely to have the financial resources necessary to mount expensive political campaigns. One way that women have organized to counter this disadvantage is through groups like Emily's List. Emily is an acronym for "Early Money Is Like Yeast." Begun in 1985, Emily's List is a national organization whose purpose is to raise funds that are used to support women's election campaigns. In 1996, Emily's

List raised $6.5 million to support prochoice, Democratic women running for office. Other groups are now engaging in similar fund-raising efforts on women's behalf, including Sisters United, a New Jersey organization that supports Black Democratic women.

Finally, women's dual roles in work and the family may put them at a disadvantage in running for political office. As long as women hold the primary responsibility for family care, it is difficult for them to meet the time and energy requirements of political office. Numerous studies have shown that women's family obligations, including the availability of child care, interfere with their ability to take on political jobs. One study of women judges, however, found that 80 percent of women judges report their spouses are very favorable toward their careers; male judges are far less likely to say this. This may reflect the fact that strong spousal support is prerequisite for women to seek public office. In the past, women were more likely than men to feel conflict between their marriage and career aspirations; now, parental roles are more likely to be a source of conflict than marital roles (Martin, 1990).

Despite the structural barriers to women's increased role in politics, women are making numerous inroads to political power. Their increased representation in formal government is partially the result of a concerted effort by many groups to increase women's political power in formal political systems. Without such political activism on behalf of more women in politics, one wonders if there would have been much change at all.

The Gender Gap

Studying women and politics is not just a matter of studying women as elected officials. Gender is also a major social factor influencing political attitudes and behavior. The term **gender gap** refers to the differences in women's and men's political behavior and political attitudes. One indication of the gender gap is that women are more likely than men to hold and support liberal views—and to identify and vote themselves as Democrats. The development of the gender gap is a recent phenomenon, however. For many decades, men were more likely to vote than women, and, when asked, women reported voting like their husbands or fathers. Now, this trend is reversing. In the 1998 national elections, men were more likely to vote Republican than women. Black men and women voters overwhelmingly vote for Democratic candidates.

Women are now equally likely to vote as men do, but there are significant differences between their political outlooks. The gender gap is widest on issues involving violence and the use of force. Women, for example, are more likely than men to be peace-seeking and to support gun control. The gender gap is also evident on so-called compassion issues; women are more likely to support government spending for social service programs and they are more liberal on issues such as abortion, gay and lesbian rights, and women's rights.

Although the gender gap has been most noted and studied within the United States, there is some evidence that it is present in other nations, as well. Interestingly, there is no gender gap between African American women and African

American men, most likely because African American men are more liberal on political and social issues than are White men (Welch and Sigelman, 1989).

Do Women Make a Difference?

The other important question that feminists ask about women's representation as elected officials is whether women's political participation makes a difference. Some argue that women's increased representation in government will bring a more compassionate view to politics. Gender differences between women and men suggest that women might bring different interests and different values to their work as elected officials. Do women have a different view? Does their participation in politics differ from that of men?

Some certainly hope so. For example, during the confirmation hearings of now Supreme Court Justice Clarence Thomas, held before the U.S. Senate Judiciary Committee in 1991, Anita Hill accused Judge Thomas of sexual harassment during the time she worked for him at the U.S. Equal Opportunity Commission. Hill had to testify before an all-male committee whom many argued could not understand sexual harassment as a woman's issue. In the following year, this opinion seemed to hold sway, since in the national election that followed more women than ever were elected to public office.

Research on women politicians indicates that they tend to be most active in areas traditionally associated with women, including education, health, and welfare. Women state legislators are now equally active to men in public speaking and floor activity, and they are actually more likely to succeed in getting their priority legislation passed (Darcy, Welch, and Clark, 1994). Women legislators are more likely than men legislators to support feminist issues such as the Equal Rights Amendment, government-subsidized child care, and abortion rights (Mandel and Dodson, 1992). Women are also more liberal and more feminist than their male counterparts, even controlling for political party and age. On a variety of issues, women differ from men—for example, in being less likely to support the death penalty, not trusting the private sector to solve economic problems, and opposing laws requiring parental consent for minors to have an abortion. Women are also more likely than before to make women's issues a priority. In public opinion polls, women also are more pacifist than men and they hold less militaristic values. Some feminists argue that women's traditional roles as mothers and caregivers produce these different value systems (Ruddick, 1989). Carol Gilligan's work on women's moral values, for example, suggests that women have different moral values than men and make value judgments by different sets of criteria—using an ethic of caring rather than absolute judgments about moral right and wrong, which is more characteristic of men (Gilligan, 1982).

These contrasts suggest that women will make a difference as they move further into the political area. Some feminists caution us about such an expectation, however, claiming that arguments about women's different ways of being are based in an *essentialist position,* meaning one that too easily assumes fixed differences between women and men. Although those who argue that women are different recognize the socially constructed nature of these differences, their critics argue that some too easily base women's differences from men in their reproductive roles and their psychosexual makeup. This ignores how women's distinctive consciousness is shaped by history and the specific politics of race, class, and gender that create diverse experiences for different groups of women.

Those who claim that there are basic differences between women and men do tend to ignore or understate differences among women. Critics of the essentialist position suggest that the gender gap in women's attitudes and behaviors may be explained by other factors. For example, some of the largest differences in political opinion are those between middle-class and working-class women; since middle-class women are more likely to get elected to political office, this may confound some of the research results purporting to find a gender gap.

The fact is that having such a small number of women in elected office makes it difficult to tell if their presence makes a difference in political outcomes, since they are typically a numerical minority and can be treated like tokens. If the numbers of women in office truly represented women's proportion in the population, perhaps there would be a big difference in political agendas, but we also have to be cautious about using gender stereotypes to assume that women will inevitably be different from men once they enter dominant social institutions.

🐚 Women and the Military

When Shannon Faulkner, a young 18-year-old woman, entered The Citadel in the fall of 1995, she was the first woman allowed to enroll in this previously all-male military college. She was able to do so only after a 2½–year legal battle, through which she sought to meet her lifelong dream of being a military cadet. Although she was finally admitted, she left after the first week, known as "hell week," when cadets are subjected to extremely rigorous physical exercise, this particular year during an extreme heat wave. Faulkner succumbed to exhaustion and, along with three of the male cadets, was in the infirmary for a few days before she resigned.

For some, this may have confirmed their suspicions that women cannot endure the physical strain of military training. Others, however, noted that none of the men who entered had to undergo the stress and public notoriety of a 2½–year legal struggle to gain admission, nor had they been forced to endure the jeers and harassment of the other cadets and some of the military leadership at The Citadel. During her brief stay at The Citadel and throughout the year prior, when she was allowed to attend classes as a day student, she was harangued by male cadets. Upon her leaving, cadets chanted and whooped in glee, banging pipes against their window sills in celebration (Manegold, 1995). Since Shannon Faulkner's efforts, other women have entered these formerly all-male institutions. They are breaking down barriers that have made the military one of the most male-dominated institutions in the nation.

The Status of Women in the Military

It was only in 1976 that women were first allowed into any of the military academies. Since then, there have been profound changes in the presence of women in the military. The percentage of women has increased from a mere 1.6 percent in 1973 to 14 percent in 1997. There are an additional 151,000 women in the reserves, not including the Coast Guard and its reserves.

Women are very much underrepresented as military officers; 14 percent of officers are women. Minority women are 19 percent of women officers—a much larger percentage than minority men represent relative to all men in the military (see Table 10.1), although, overall, White women are more likely than women of color to be officers. While 80 percent of women officers are White, 87.8 percent of male officers are White (U.S. Department of Defense, 1992, 1997).

Women in the military are generally better educated than their male counterparts. Nearly all women (99.8 percent) in the military are high school graduates (not much different from men, 98 percent of whom are high school graduates), but women are more likely than men to have attended college—27 percent of women versus 21 percent of men (Becraft, 1990).

Although women's roles in the military are rapidly changing, gender segregation marks the distribution of women and men in military occupations. Only 9 percent of women in the military work in the occupational group of power- and mechanical-equipment workers, compared to 23 percent of enlisted men. Men are also twice as likely as women to work in electrical-equipment repair jobs; the largest concentration of women workers is in the category of support and administration (more than two-thirds of all enlisted women personnel work in this category, compared to only 14 percent of men). Women are also three times more likely than men to work in health care within the military. Among officers the patterns of gender segregation are even more stark—45 percent of women officers work in health care, compared to 13 percent of men; 47 percent of male officers work in tactical operations, compared to only 7.6 percent of women (U.S. Department of Defense, 1992).

The end of the Cold War and the resultant downsizing of the U.S. military means than there is more emphasis in the military on noncombat roles. This should increase the opportunities for women within the military. At the same time, the creation of higher technical job requirements means that military service is an opportunity for women to get the technical training and experience that can lead to more lucrative employment in the civilian world, as well (Knouse, 1991). The patterns of gender segregation that persist in military work, however, mitigate against these possibilities.

Laws continue to prohibit women's assignment to ships and aircraft engaged in combat, although all Coast Guard jobs are open to women. The exclusion of women from full participation in the military has been justified by the belief that women need protection by men and that they can best carry out their womanly duties as mothers and wives. The fear among conservatives that women might have to serve in combat was also one of the major ideological reasons for defeat of the Equal Rights Amendment. Women, however, are actively serving in com-

TABLE 10.1   Women and Men in the U.S. Military

	Women	Men
U.S. Army		
Black	48.7%	29.1%
Hispanic	3.5%	4.9%
White	42.6%	60.8%
Other minority	5.2%	5.2%
U.S. Navy		
Black	26.8%	16.7%
Hispanic	8.3%	6.8%
White	61.2%	70.4%
Other minority	3.7%	6.1%
U.S. Marine Corps		
Black	28.5%	18.5%
Hispanic	8.4%	7.9%
White	58.6%	70.3%
Other minority	4.5%	3.3%
U.S. Air Force		
Black	23.7%	15.9%
Hispanic	3.5%	3.8%
White	69.3%	77.0%
Other minority	3.5%	3.3%

Source: Data from Department of Defense. 1995. "Women in the U.S. Military: Selected Data." Washington, DC: Defense Manpower Data Center. Website: <www.inform.umd.edu:8080/EdRes/topic/WomensStudies/Government Politics/MilitarySelected-data> (April 1996), p. 1.

bat-related roles in the military, despite these public reservations. Some 41,000 women served in combat during the Persian Gulf War, when 7.2 percent of active combat forces were women (Holm, 1992). The Defense Authorization Act of 1992 also allows women to fly combat aircraft, traditionally a male-only option. The increased visibility of women soldiers during the Persian Gulf War also shifted public opinion about women's service in combat positions. Following the Gulf War, polls found that the majority of Americans thought women should be able to serve in combat if they want to (Wilcox 1992; Enloe, 1993; Cooke and Woollacott, 1993).

There are, nonetheless, significant racial and gender differences in support for women's roles in combat and other nontraditional military employment. African Americans are less supportive of women's roles in combat than are Whites, and women are more supportive than men (see Figure 10.3). White men who have been in combat are the group least likely to support women's roles in combat. Attitudes toward other egalitarian gender roles are the best predictors of people's positions on roles for women in military service; those who support women's expanded roles in the military see the matter as one of equal opportunity (Wilcox, 1992).

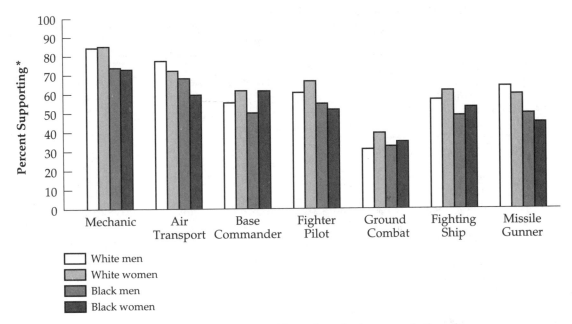

* Indicates percent of people supporting specific combat roles for women in the military

FIGURE 10.3   Support for Women in Combat (by Race-Ethnicity and Gender)

Source: Data from Clyde Wilcox. 1992. "Race, Gender, and Support for Women in the Military." *Social Science Quarterly* 73 (June): 315.

Currently, women are still barred by law from direct combat in the air force, navy, and the army; however, women are increasingly allowed in "combat-related" tasks. The United States is not the only country that bars women from combat, although numerous countries allow women in combat and many nations have rescinded their laws restricting women from combat. In Canada and Denmark, women are trained as fighter pilots; in fact, the U.S. Air Force has actually trained Danish women as fighter pilots even though, ironically, the Air Force will not train U.S. women in the same capacity (Becraft, 1990). Israeli women, like Israeli men, are subject to military conscription and are assigned to combat units; however, if the unit is deployed on a combat mission, the women are evacuated. The only NATO countries to exclude women from the military are Italy and Spain.

Gender relations in the military extend beyond looking at women who serve in the military. The experience of military wives, for example, is greatly affected by their husbands' employment as soldiers. Frequent moving means that military wives are less competitive in the labor market. They have both lower labor force participation than their women peers and, for their own educational level, lower economic returns (Enloe, 1993; Moskos, 1992; Payne, Warner, and Little, 1992). Comparable research has yet to be done regarding the experience of husbands of military women.

Gays and Lesbians in the Military

Prejudices against women in the military pale beside the related prejudices that characterize gay and lesbian experiences in the military. There has been a long-standing policy to exclude gays and lesbians from the military, although gays and lesbians have made significant contributions to the nation's armed forces. Until recently, they have had to remain deeply closeted, however. Gays and lesbians have served in all branches of the U.S. armed forces for years. Now, military policy is a "Don't ask, don't tell" policy, adopted by the Clinton administration. According to this policy, recruiting officers cannot ask about sexual preference and individuals should not reveal their sexual preference; those who reveal that they are gay or lesbian can be excluded from military service, based on their sexual orientation.

A different wall of silence

Critics of this policy have argued that it effectively keeps gays in the closet by forcing them to keep their sexual identities secret. Although the policy does not allow the explicit discharge of individuals because of homosexuality, nor does it allow the military to screen recruits based on being gay, neither does it fully acknowledge the civil rights of gays and lesbians. Gay soldiers and potential recruits have filed several lawsuits against the U.S. government to overturn these exclusionary rules; whether they will win the right to full military inclusion remains to be seen.

Those who oppose gays in the military argue, among other things, that the presence of gays affects the morale of the troops and thereby makes them less effective. Supporters of a ban against gays and lesbians in the military argue that the morale of other soldiers will drop if they are forced to serve alongside gay men and lesbian women. They also claim it will "threaten national security" and that having *known* homosexuals serving in the military would upset the status quo. Citing the "tight quarters" where recruits live and work, opponents of gay rights seem to assume that gays and lesbians cannot control their sexuality when living so close to members of the same sex. Their assumption is that gays and lesbians are out to convert all others to their life-style. Fear and misunderstanding about AIDS has fueled these homophobic ideas.

Irony — who doesn't have control over sexual behavior

Ironically, there seems to be more cause for worry about sexual harassment, in general, in the military—particularly the harassment of heterosexual men toward military women. The Tailhook scandal and the exposure of sexual harassment at the Army's Aberdeen Proving Ground site have exposed this issue before the public. Unlike the homophobic arguments that gays should be excluded from the military because they cannot control their sexuality and might affect military morale, no one has argued that some heterosexual men have this problem.

Ideas like those being used to exclude gays and lesbians from the military were also used earlier in history to exclude African Americans from military service. Opponents of desegregating the armed services argued that it would lower military morale and that it would be difficult for Whites and Blacks to live together in close quarters. In fact, when President Truman ordered the racial desegregation of the military by executive order in 1948, he showed that these arguments were not true. Although racial integration in the military has not been fully achieved, the military is one of the most desegregated institutions in the nation.

Feminism and Militarism

Feminists have criticized the military not just for its discriminatory treatment against women and gays and lesbians, but also for the masculine character of the institution as a whole. Earlier, the concept of a *gendered institution* was discussed—a gendered institution being one that embodies the characteristics of a specific gender. The military is a perfect example of a gendered institution in that it is characterized as a most masculine institution, one emphasizing hierarchy, force, violence, and aggression (Connell, 1992). This can be seen in a variety of ways.

First, national involvement in war and military aggression is often justified in terms of a nation being "tough," "supreme," and "heroic"—all characteristics associated with men's gender role. Numerous examples throughout history also show how military propaganda utilizes images of threatened manhood to rationalize a nation's engagement in war. Aggression and the capacity for violence are seen as indicating national strength, just as they are seen as indicating the strength of individual men. As two feminist men have written, "Violence is the accepted masculine form of conflict resolution" (Kokopeli and Lakey, 1995:453). While men's violence occurs in day-to-day interactions, in its most escalated form it results in war and organized terrorism.

Militaristic values also legitimate much violence and sexual aggression against women, especially that which accompanies war and military occupation. The large-scale rape of women by invading armies in war-torn Bosnia is an example of how military conquerors tend to see sexual violation of women as their right following a military victory. Rape is common in war, as is the widespread use of women sex workers in brothels and as prostitutes in occupied territories and war zones (Enloe, 1989).

The strong association between militarism and masculinity is also evident in military training practices where homophobic socialization forces military recruits to be tough, aggressive, and strong as a way of proving their masculine heterosexuality. Labeling as "faggots" those perceived as weak is one way that military recruits are initiated into military roles.

❧ Rethinking the Political

Reviewing the workings of state institutions—including courts and the law, government, and the military—raises many new questions for feminist analysis. One of the primary questions to have emerged from feminist studies in this area is a rethinking of what *political* means. When most people think of something political, they likely think in terms of formal election politics and the workings of official government. In this sense, political behavior is only that which occurs within public political institutions. Feminist scholars, on the other hand, have defined the term *political* more broadly and have argued that traditional concepts of the political have been marked by an incorrect conceptual dichotomy between the public and private spheres of life. Assuming that the political is only that which occurs in the formal, public sphere overlooks significant political activity by women in other arenas, and limits our understanding of the political only to those institutions where men have predominated. In addition, feminist scholars argue that the conceptual separation of the public and private spheres leads to oversight of how the public and private spheres intersect, as, for example, in understanding how women's work in the private sphere supports public institutions, even when that work is devalued and ignored.

Redefining the political to include a broader spectrum of behavior encourages thinking of political behavior in new ways. Women's community activism is one such area that has long been overlooked by those studying politics, but which, on closer look, reveals the many ways that women engage in political behavior. As examples, Gilkes (1980) has shown how African American women who have careers as community workers use their work both to help their communities in everyday survival and to transform social institutions. Although these women are seldom recognized as "political women," their work in social service organizations, on the boards of local organizations, and as directors of agencies has important political ramifications for the African American community. Their political work stems not from their activity in dominant institutions but from their commitments to change and their mobilization of resources in service of the Black community. In a similar vein, Naples (1992) has studied low-income Latina and African American mothers, finding that they see their community work as stemming from their desire to improve the lives of their families and neighbors; the specific problems around which they organize include health care, housing, crime and safety, and sanitation. As activist mothers, their political action is part of the continuum of their caregiving activities.

These are but two examples of how women engage in political action, but from the grass roots. This gives political activism a different meaning than that which is associated with mainstream politics. In both cases, the distinction between women's private work in their families and communities is blurred with their public work as political actors.

Although women's grass-roots activism is rarely the substance of evening news headlines, as is the formal political work of men, it is nonetheless significant in women's contributions to political life. Feminists argue that the media have obscured much of women's political activism, thereby lending the impression that women are not interested in politics or are ineffective in mobilizing on behalf of their interests. Furthermore, redefining the political to include the work that women do sheds more light on the political activism of working-class women and women of color—groups whose political contributions are largely ignored in the dominant culture, despite the fact that working-class women and women of color have a rich history of political organizing. Women work politically in the contexts in which they are found—local communities, workplaces, churches, and social service organizations, to name a few.

Because women's political action has been understudied and misunderstood, theories of political behavior typically fail to deal with gender as a central concept (Bookman and Morgen, 1988); moreover, political theory has only in rare cases made women major subjects for analysis (Laslett, Brenner, and Arat, 1995). As a consequence, much political analysis has made women invisible as political actors and made politics appear to be gender neutral. As two feminist scholars note, "Politics is conventionally understood as the activities of elected officials and the workings of government, both out of the reach of ordinary people" (Bookman and Morgen, 1988:4). Such portrayals also create, among many women, a sense of disenfranchisement and alienation from mainstream politics, especially the working-class and poor women who are most disaffected by dominant institutions. This means that working-class and poor women have to make gains outside of traditional electoral politics—in factory organizing, in churches, on the streets, and through other grass-roots activities—areas of political life that have been largely ignored by academic scholars.

Within grass-roots politics, women are much more likely to contend with the intersecting politics of race, class, and gender (Bookman and Morgen, 1988). Grass-roots politics rest on individual resistance to the dominant culture and, sometimes, to mass political mobilization. Through such political behavior, women challenge the dominant power relations of society and recognize the systematic forces that oppress women. Often through grass-roots politics, women also change their ideas about the sources of their powerlessness and act to change conditions of their lives (Bookman and Morgan, 1988).

In sum, women are not as peripheral to politics as they might appear in an analysis of women and politics in the electoral world alone. Understanding the full range of women's political behavior means also seeing how working-class women and women of color have a long history of political activism, despite their invisibility in recorded history. These groups have also had a very feminist analysis, supporting women's independence and activism, even when this kind of feminism differs from—and is sometimes in conflict with—the feminism of White, middle-class women (Hine, 1995). For all women engaged in the feminist work, however, phrases like *the personal is political* and *sexual politics* show how women have linked their everyday lives to their political action and beliefs.

The Women's Movement

Women's political activism can be found on any number of issues, particularly beyond the formal political system. Women have been important in the work of many political groups that are organized on social and political issues, including environmental-action groups, groups uniting to fight racism, gay and lesbian movements and organizations, abortion rights groups, and many others too numerous to mention. The women's movement, or the feminist movement, was one of the most significant and influential movements in the twentieth century. There are probably few women or men in this country who have not been touched by some aspect of the women's movement, and, although many are reluctant to call themselves feminists, opinion polls show that the majority of people in the United States support the values and programs that the women's movement has encouraged and supported.

Sociologists define **social movements** as groups that act to promote or resist changes in society. Movements often emerge because of their members' perceived sense of injustice and their wish to effect changes that will redress such injustices (Turner and Killian, 1972). Social movements involve the sustained activity of organized groups, and they often include a network of organizations that, although they may have different goals and members, have a shared sense of belonging to the movement. Sociologists who study social movements also try to identify the societal conditions that foster the development of the movements. In the case of the contemporary women's movement, the development of feminism can be traced to the development of the nineteenth-century women's movement.

American Feminism in the Nineteenth Century

In the United States, many of the early feminists were women who advocated the equal rights of women to acquire an education. One of the earliest advocates of education for women was Emma Willard, who campaigned actively for the establishment of colleges for women in the 1920s. Frances Wright also was an active spokeswoman for the establishment of equal educational training for women. Education for women, these women argued, would extend the "rights of man" to all persons and therefore make for general and human improvement. As the result of their efforts, Oberlin College was the first college to admit women in 1833. Mount Holyoke College opened in 1837, Vassar in 1865; both Smith and Wellesley in 1875; Radcliffe in 1879; and Bryn Mawr in 1885 (Flexner, 1975). Although extending education primarily to women of the upper class, these institutions nonetheless created an educated class of women, many of whom worked on behalf of women's rights.

Feminism did not, however, have its origins only in the activism of educated White women. Its political origins also lie in the abolitionist movement of the 1830s and the efforts of African American and White women and men to struggle for the abolition of slavery and women's rights. Charlotte Forten (1784–1884), an African American woman reformer and abolitionist, was a founder of the Philadelphia Female Anti-Slavery Society. She tutored her three daughters, Margaretta, Harriet, and Sarah Louise, each of whom was also active in the abolitionist and feminist movements. The Grimke sisters, Sarah (1792–1873) and Angelina (1805–1879), were daughters of a slaveholding family who traveled and spoke out vigorously against slavery in the 1830s. Both the Grimke sisters and Sarah Forten were delegates to the first Anti-Slavery Convention of American Women held in 1837. The correspondence between Sarah Forten and Angelina Grimke records their friendship and their strong sentiments about both **abolitionism** and feminism (Sterling, 1984).

Frederick Douglass, a former slave and ardent abolitionist, supported women's rights for many years and was a strong supporter of women's suffrage. He and other male abolitionists believed that women's suffrage was necessary for

[handwritten marginalia: "What would a social movement be about today. race? class? gender?"]

the full enfranchisement of all citizens, although racism among White women and men in the women's rights movement forced Douglass and other abolitionists to subordinate the issue of women's suffrage to that of Black suffrage (DuBois, 1978). The abolitionists saw clear links between freedom for slaves and freedom for women, although as the women's rights movement developed, White women discriminated against Black women in the movement and used racist appeals to argue for the extension of voting rights to White women.

From their work in the abolitionist movement, women learned how to organize a political movement. They challenged the assumption of the natural superiority of men and understood that suffrage was an important source for self-respect and social power. Historian Ellen Carol DuBois has concluded that

> *abolitionism provided [American women] with a way to escape clerical authority, an egalitarian ideology, and a theory of social change, all of which permitted the leaders to transform the insights into the oppression of women which they shared with many of their contemporaries into the beginnings of the women's rights movement. (1978:32)*

In 1840, a World Anti-Slavery Convention was held in London. The mere presence of women delegates at this convention generated excitement about the potential power of women, although women were relegated to the galleries and were prohibited from participating in the proceedings. Their exclusion from the proceedings generated an increased awareness among women of the need for a women's movement. When they returned to the United States, two of the women attending the convention, Lucretia Mott and Elizabeth Cady Stanton, continued to meet and discuss strategies for establishing women's rights. On July 14, 1848, they called for a Woman's Rights Convention to be held in Seneca Falls, New York, five days later. Despite such short notice, 300 men and women came to Seneca Falls and there approved a Declaration of Sentiments, modeled on the Declaration of Independence. The Declaration of Sentiments declared that "all men and women are created equal; that they are endowed by their Creator with certain inalienable rights; that among these are life, liberty, and the pursuit of happiness" (Hole and Levine, 1971:6). Those attending the Seneca Falls Convention also passed 12 resolutions, one of which resolved to grant women the right to vote.

The Seneca Falls Convention has since been heralded as the official beginning of the women's suffrage movement in the United States. Other women's rights conventions were held throughout the United States, including one in 1851 in Akron, Ohio, where Sojourner Truth, a former slave, challenged the popular doctrine of women's delicacy and physical inferiority. She exhorted:

> *Nobody ever helps me into carriages or over puddles, or gives me the best place—and ain't I a woman? . . . Look at my arm! I have ploughed and planted and gathered into barns, and no man could head me—and ain't I a woman? I could work as much and eat as much as a man—when I could get it—and bear the lash as well! And ain't I a woman? I have born thirteen children, and seen most of 'em sold into slavery, and*

when I cried out with my mother's grief, none but Jesus heard me—and ain't I a
woman? (Hole and Levine, 1971:191)

In the beginning, the women's movement was not just a single-issue movement. Feminists saw the issue of suffrage as one aspect of women's rights and advocated full equality for women. The momentum of the women's movement was stalled somewhat by the Civil War, but after the war, feminists worked hard to get the word *sex* added to the Fifteenth Amendment. The Fifteenth Amendment declares that the right to vote cannot be denied or abridged by race, color, or previous condition of servitude, but it did not extend to women—either White or African American. Although feminists' efforts to get the term *sex* added did not succeed, this setback furthered their resolve for suffrage; in 1869, Susan B. Anthony and Elizabeth Cady Stanton organized the National Woman Suffrage Association (NWSA), which embraced the broad cause of women's rights. A few months later, Lucy Stone and others organized the American Woman Suffrage Association. This organization restricted itself more narrowly to the suffrage issue, trying to avoid more controversial issues like marriage and the church.

Suffrage, however, was not the only issue for which early feminists fought. The **temperance movement** in the late nineteenth century was organized by women with a strong feminist consciousness. The motto of the Women's Christian Temperance Union (WCTU), under one of its early presidents, Frances Willard, was "Do everything!" Willard organized departments in the WCTU, each with its own programs of activity, including work in prisons, in kindergarten, and with the shut-in sick; other departments were concerned with physical culture and hygiene, prostitution, and motherhood. One department, the most effective, worked for suffrage. The temperance movement pressed for laws restricting the sale and consumption of alcohol; women were encouraged to join because their status as married women gave them no legal protection against abuse or abandonment by a drunken husband (Flexner, 1975).

In 1890, the American and National Woman's Suffrage associations merged to become the National American Woman Suffrage Association (NAWSA). By this time, the women's movement had become a single-issue movement. Feminist efforts were devoted to gaining women's right to vote—a right they believed would open other opportunities and give women full rights as citizens. Shortly after the turn of the century, a second generation of U.S. feminists appeared, including women like Carrie Chapman Catt, president of NAWSA. Also, Alice Paul, a young militant woman, became active in the suffrage movement. She formed a small radical group, the Congressional Union, to work solely on federal suffrage for women. The Congressional Union used tactics such as parades, mass demonstrations, and hunger strikes to further their cause. The combined efforts of the Congressional Union, NAWSA, and local suffrage groups and activists were eventually successful. On August 26, 1920, the Nineteenth Amendment, guaranteeing women the right to vote, was adopted.

With the success of the suffrage movement, the women's movement lost much of its public momentum and, many say, lay dormant for the years between passage of the Nineteenth Amendment and the rebirth of feminism in the United

States in the 1960s. Others have shown, though, that feminist activities through this period did not totally disappear. Many women continued to pursue feminist goals in a variety of organizations and contexts; their work provided continuity between the early women's movement and contemporary feminism. Although only a few organizations from the 1920s to the 1960s embraced explicitly feminist goals, the birth control and family planning movement, the settlement house movement, the establishment of organizations working to improve working conditions for employed women, and the founding of professional women's groups (including the National Federation of Business and Professional Women's Clubs, the League of Women Voters, and the American Association of University Women) set the stage for feminist developments in later years (Ferree and Hess, 1985). Even in the post–World War II period, when cultural ideology strongly defended the idea that a woman's proper place was in the home, the National Women's Party, organized by Alice Paul, continued to fight for improving the status of women. The National Women's Party had one major plank in its platform—passage of the Equal Rights Amendment (ERA). Since 1923, when the ERA was first introduced in Congress, Paul and other members of this organization worked to garner support from other women's organizations, lobbied Congress, and sought publicity for the amendment. Most other women's organizations opposed passage of the ERA, believing it would legitimate protective legislation for women. Despite their differing goals and philosophies, all of these organizations provided strong support networks for women in the particularly hostile environment of post–World War II sexist ideology (Rupp and Taylor, 1987).

The Emergence of the Contemporary Women's Movement

Several transformations in women's roles occurring during the 1950s and 1960s influenced the development of contemporary feminism. These included changes in women's labor force participation, a change in women's fertility patterns, increases in women's educational level, and ideological patterns that glamorized women's domestic life. In the 1950s, White women were idealized as happy housewives whose primary purpose was to care for their husbands and children. In that decade, women were marrying younger, but they were also having fewer children because widespread use of contraception gave women control over their fertility. At the same time, White, middle-class women were better educated and, although their education was intended to make them better wives and mothers, they were acquiring many of the same skills as men. For women in the home, technological changes in housework simplified physical tasks, but the increased consumption and new patterns of family life in automobile-based suburbs complicated the role of housewives. Although there was less physical labor associated with housework, housewives were supposed to be constantly available to their children. Whatever time was saved by labor-saving appliances was more than replaced by increased shopping, transporting of children, and nurturing of family members. The dominant ideology of housework and motherhood told middle-class women that their work in the home would bring them fulfillment and gratification, but, in fact, many found the experience to be depressing, isolating, and boring.

This situation created a crisis for White, middle-class family women that was brought to the widespread attention of the public by the appearance of Betty Friedan's best-seller, *The Feminine Mystique*, in 1963. Friedan identified "the problem that has no name"—the isolation in the family—as the source of women's discontent. Friedan's book critically assailed the establishment (including mass advertising, women's magazines, and Freudian psychology) as contributing to women's problems. The chord she struck was soon repeated by a number of critical assessments of women's roles that appeared in academic and popular literature (Evans, 1979).

In addition to experiencing a crisis in domestic life, women were, at the same time, appearing in the labor force in greater numbers. Throughout the 1950s, women from middle-income families entered the labor force at a faster rate than any other group. They were working not just in the years before marriage but later, in addition to their marriage and family roles. Although married women's work experience was defined in terms of helping their families, it broadened their horizons at the same time that it made them conscious of discrimination in the workplace. The decade of the 1950s and the early 1960s created a self-conscious cohort of women who lived in the contradictions of a society that idealized their role and promised them opportunity and gratification while it devalued their labor and denied them self-expression.

Professional women working within established institutions began pressuring politicians to recognize the problems facing women in the United States. In 1961, although it was likely done for political reasons, President John F. Kennedy appointed a Presidential Commission on the Status of Women, chaired by Eleanor Roosevelt. The commission was charged with documenting "prejudices and outmoded customs that act as barriers to the full realization of women's basic rights" (Hole and Levine, 1971:18) and with making recommendations designed to alleviate the problem. The commission report, *American Women*, was released in 1963, the same year that Friedan's *The Feminine Mystique* appeared.

The commission's report made a number of recommendations involving employment and labor discrimination. It was the basis for the Equal Pay Act of 1963, requiring that men and women receive equal pay for equal work performed under equal conditions (Hole and Levine, 1971:28ff). Problems in enforcing this law and exemptions that were later attached to it prohibited the act from making the radical changes it implied; thus, the commission's work had only a moderate effect. The commission also held steadfastly to the idea that the nuclear family was the foundation of U.S. history and that women's role in the family was an invaluable and necessary resource. Although recognizing the contribution that women made to the home, the commission ignored the effects of home life on women that Friedan's book so strikingly portrayed.

These developments within both the government and the society provided the context for women to begin to question their traditional roles, but it remained for major social movements of the period to crystallize the vague discontent that women felt. The birth of contemporary feminism must be seen as also stemming from the civil rights movement and, later, the anti–Vietnam War and student movements.

Feminism and the Civil Rights Movement

The civil rights movement was initiated within African American communities of the South during the 1950s as a challenge to public racial segregation and White racial prejudice. Like the nineteenth-century U.S. feminists who had developed their feminist politics through participation in the abolitionist movement, White women working in the civil rights movement soon saw their own oppression as similar to the racial injustices against which they were organizing. White women worked in the civil rights movement out of their felt need to remedy the inequities of racial injustice, which they saw as a moral issue calling for their humanitarian participation. For White women and men, joining the civil rights movement required a radical departure from the dominant beliefs and practices of White society. Their challenge to the status quo on racial issues was soon to influence the way they also interpreted other social issues (Evans, 1979).

Between 1963 and 1965, White liberals from the North (especially male and female college students) went to the South in great numbers to assist in the civil rights struggle. The nonviolent direct-action projects in which they engaged (voter registration drives, protest marches, and sit-ins) forced them to encounter institutional racism and generated a new consciousness not only of racial issues but of the institutional structure of society in the United States (Rothschild, 1979). Most important, the civil rights movement's emphasis on examining the roots of oppression caused many White people to look into their own experience so as to comprehend their relationship to dominant institutions. In so doing, White women in the movement began to see the origins of their own oppression—both as they had learned sexism in their own lives and as it was reflected in the public institutions of society.

In spite of a growing feminist consciousness, sexual politics within the civil rights movement divided Black and White women for two reasons. First, White women in the movement sometimes tried to prove their social liberalism by having sexual relations with Black men. Although this action was encouraged by the permissive atmosphere in the movement, it discouraged solidarity between Black and White women (Rothschild, 1979). Second, both White and Black women believed that the movement had failed to address the issue of sexual inequality. Black women in the Student Non-Violent Coordinating Committee (SNCC) wrote position papers protesting the fact that women in the movement were relegated to clerical work, were not given leadership and decision-making positions, and were belittlingly referred to as "girls." White women, supporting the idea that the movement should be led by Blacks, were reluctant to present their own analysis of sexism, and distrust between Black and White women prevented their alliance against male sexism (Evans, 1979).

Throughout the summers of 1964 and 1965, the position of Whites in the civil rights movement became increasingly precarious. Black disillusionment with

White liberals and the ideology of Black power eventually resulted in the exclusion of Whites from SNCC in 1965. As a result, at the very time that women were becoming more conscious of their ties to each other, both White and Black women ended up working in movements that were even more male dominated and less open to an examination of gender inequality. For Black women, the Black power movement explicitly appealed to the power of Black men and the role of Black women as supporters of men. White women, after their exclusion from the Black power movement, organized around antiwar and student issues, but in groups that were typically male dominated. These movements once again relegated them to traditionally women's work and treated them as sexual objects for the pleasure of radical men. By applying the analysis of racial injustice they had learned in the civil rights movement to their own oppression as women, White feminists emerged from the ranks of other activist groups (Evans, 1979).

The feminism of Black women emerged under similar conditions, although as in the nineteenth century, Black women's feminist politics are much more situated in their antiracist activities. Increasing educational levels and transformation of the employment status of Black women throughout the 1960s and 1970s, however, created the sociological conditions through which their evolving feminist consciousness can be seen.

Surveys of Black women show that they are more likely than White women to hold feminist values, although they do not necessarily identify with the feminist movement. Black women's political consciousness is often situated in the context of their community work, where they identify themselves as working to empower the African American community—through both professional and political work (Gilkes, 1980). For African American women, the concept of sisterhood has not been the basis for a political identity, as it has been for White women. African American women's political identity has more likely been formed around the issue of race, and as a result, they see feminist issues in a different context than do White women (Dill, 1983). Whereas White women tend to see themselves oppressed as a sexual group, African American women are more likely to see race, class, and gender exploitation as intersecting in their lives (Collins, 1990).

The Second Wave of Feminism

By the late 1960s, feminism in the United States had developed as a full-fledged movement, with a variety of organizations, local consciousness-raising groups, and political strategies intended to advocate transformations in women's status in society. Referred to as "the second wave of feminism" (in contrast to the nineteenth century "first wave"), the women's movement in the 1960s and 1970s had diverse origins, philosophies, and strategies for change.

Two major branches of the feminist movement evolved: the *women's rights* branch and the *women's liberation* branch. The women's rights branch took an "equal rights" strategy—working to extend equal rights to women, particularly through legal reform and antidiscrimination policies. From this perspective, the inequality of women is seen as the result of past discriminatory practices, and is thus best remedied by creating gender-blind institutions in which all persons, regardless of sex (or race, religious preference, sexual preference, or physical disability), are given equal privileges. The women's liberation branch of the feminist movement, on the other hand, took a more far-reaching analysis, seeing that transformation in women's status requires not just legal and political reform but radical transformation of basic social institutions, including, to name a few, the family, sexuality, religion, and education. Women's rights and women's liberation are not separate movements, but the analytical distinction between the two shows the different political and social theories on which feminism is built. As you will see, the women's rights approach is more centered in the context of liberal political theory, while women's liberation has its roots in more radical philosophical theory.

Each wing of the feminist movement attracted different constituencies and developed different strategies for change. The women's rights wing (identified as *liberal feminism*) tended to attract older, professional women. The organizational structure of equal rights groups also reflected the more traditional style of their politics. These feminist organizations, especially as they have evolved over time, are typically more formal, with hierarchical leadership and authority structures, and with more formal procedures and rules for membership (Freeman, 1973).

The style and organization of women's liberation groups, on the other hand, reflected their more radical ideological base. Participants tended to be younger than their liberal counterparts, and the organization of these groups was deliberately nonhierarchical, mass based, and with informal procedures and networks (Freeman, 1973). The looser, more flexible style of discussion in women's liberation groups encouraged analyses that were not only more critical of establishment systems but also more person oriented and more likely to engage individuals in examining their own experience and its relationship to institutionalized sexism. This more radical branch of feminism recognized that personal life was tied to the structure of public institutions and would be altered only as these institutions changed.

The more radical feminist groups often emerged from the New Left and drew their participants from women who were critical of the often sexist and patronizing behavior of radical men (Evans, 1979). Their early political analysis was forged from the appeals to justice that the civil rights and leftist movements had articulated and that women felt were being denied to them. Women in the antiwar and student movements of the 1960s were radicalized not only by the philosophies of these movements but also by the sexist behavior of men within the movements. African American women whose leadership had been central in the civil rights movement were often relegated to secondary status in the Black power movement, as the movement became more influenced by Black nationalism. Women's participation in all of these movements had the effect of further radicalizing White and African American women's feminist perspectives.

Still, African American women did not fully embrace the feminist position of White women; White women were more likely to see all men as the problem and were less sensitive to the class and race differences among men that gave them differential access to power. The feminist alliance between White women feminists and women of color is still imperfect, in part because of this issue and also because of racism among White women.

Feminism for the Twenty-First Century

With the evolution of the feminist movement over time, early distinctions between the equal rights and women's liberation branches of feminism have blurred, although diverse political beliefs and strategies among feminists remain. Some of those who were radical feminists in the 1960s and 1970s—then younger women, students, and movement activists—now work in positions of some power and influence. At the same time, liberal feminist organizations, although they work within the existing political system, are influenced by more radical feminist thought. Race, class, *and* gender have also become more central to feminist politics and feminist analyses. Although tensions continue to exist between White women and women of color, the feminism of women of color has become more elaborated, and more White women have worked to challenge their own racism and to build analyses that are inclusive of race, class, and gender.

In the 1990s, feminists faced two new challenges: the identification of a so-called postfeminist generation and a backlash against feminism, both from the mainstream media and from the rise of the new religious and political right. The dominant media generated a strong image of feminism as no longer necessary and a thing of the past (Faludi, 1991). In addition, the media created a stereotype of feminism that stigmatized it in the eyes of many, especially younger women. This image of feminists as antimale, lesbian, humorless, and politically correct ideologues made feminism seem unapproachable to many, including those who otherwise supported its values and goals (Whittier, 1995).

The rise of the religious right also promoted values specifically opposed to the feminist agenda. The right's advocacy of "traditional family values" endorsed an antifeminist stance, one promoting a strong connection of women to the home, little tolerance of diverse family forms, and many extremely homophobic platforms directed against gays and lesbians (such as some of the ballot initiatives in different states to deny civil rights to gays and lesbians). The influence of this significant conservative movement means that feminism has lost ground on important issues like abortion rights, gay and lesbian rights, and state or federal support for any number of social programs that support women and their children. This conservative movement also generated a climate far less tolerant of diverse life-styles and feminist modes of thinking; the right-wing attack on being "PC" (i.e., "politically correct") has thus been strongly directed at women's studies programs and scholars, as well as those who promote more democratic, antielitist, and multicultural education.

In this context, there is little wonder that younger women may find themselves confused by feminism. Although the media has portrayed this generation as a "postfeminist" one, a more careful look finds that young women and men are those most likely to support feminist values, even though they may be reluctant to call themselves feminists. Ironically, the image of young women and men as uninterested in feminism has been most prevalent at the same time that enrollments in women's studies courses have soared on most college campuses over the past twenty years. It is probably more accurate to say that young women are not so much antifeminist as they are cautious about being identified with a movement so reviled in the media and that they see as stemming from the concerns of a different generation.

Young women who grew up in the 1980s and 1990s have had very different experiences from those of their mothers' generation, who established the second wave of feminism. Younger women have grown up in a period dominated by conservative, not progressive, values. They have also benefited from the gains made by the second wave of feminism, so they do not have to worry so much about access to birth control, rights to education and employment, or exclusion from formerly men-only occupations and organizations—some of the issues that activated the second wave of feminism. Still, issues about women's safety from violence, men's and women's sexual identities, work and family roles, and other opportunities still haunt us and are by no means resolved. Young people have also grown up in a context where the politics of personal identity—gender identity, racial-ethnic identity, and sexual identity—have been a vocal topic in the political world. The generational differences between young women and their feminist foremothers thus shape the reactions of young women to feminist politics (Whittier, 1995). At the same time, however, the shape of the third wave of feminism will be determined by the political action taken by younger women and men who define feminism in the context of their own life experiences and needs (Walker, 1995).

There has been no demise of the women's movement. Quite the contrary, the women's movement remains one of the most influential sources of social change, even though there is not a single national organization that is identified as representing feminism. Some of the most radical feminist activities occur at the grass-roots level, where women struggle against poverty, violence, harassment, and exploitation. At the same time, more mainstream feminist organizations continue to work on behalf of women's health and welfare, safety and security, and educational and employment rights (Whittier, 1995). Just as the feminist movement has ebbed and flowed with different emphases and different agendas over the past 100 years or more, so will its future be influenced by the needs of diverse women in their own times.

❧ Summary

Several themes emerge from the study of women, power, and politics. First is to recognize that women are underrepresented in every institution of the state. Whether it is the government, the courts, or the military, women are a significant minority of those who occupy positions of power and authority; moreover, within these institutions, women tend to work in gender-segregated occupations. As politicians, women are more likely to be found in local office, not national office; in the courts, one of the areas where women have been most successful, women are still a minority of judges; and, in the military, one of the most masculine institutions, women are still formally excluded from some positions.

Throughout the study of women in state institutions runs the question of whether women's increased presence in diverse roles will transform these institutions. There is evidence, for example, that women vote differently from men, that they hold different and more liberal positions on a number of social and political issues, and that they tend to be politically active around issues affecting family, work policies, and other social issues, including feminism. Assuming, however, that having more women in positions of influence will change these institutions can be a sexist judgment, since such an argument often relies on stereotypes about women's connection to reproductive and family roles. We should not underestimate the extent to which institutions shape the people within them, although it is probably also true that the increased presence of women in positions of power and authority will alter social and political life.

Studies of state institutions also reveal how deeply these institutions are structured by masculine culture; that is, they are gendered institutions—each in their own way being based on principles of rational argument, hierarchy, and power. Feminists have questioned whether such institutions can protect women from the patriarchal systems that are also the source of women's oppression. This reveals a fundamental contradiction in thinking about state power: that the same institutions to which women and other oppressed groups turn for redress against historical patterns of exclusion themselves embody these same patterns.

In the end, transformation of social institutions tends to come not from within these institutions but from organized political action and social movements. The women's movement is one of the most significant social movements in recent years. Through feminist action, women, and the men who support feminism, have altered all social institutions, although much remains to be done if we want a world structured on principles of fairness, equity, and justice.

✿ *Key Terms*

abolitionist	pluralism	social movement
authority	power	state
gender gap	power elite	temperance movement

✿ *Discussion Questions/Projects for Thought*

1. Watch the national evening news for one week, keeping notes on which stories are reported and when women are mentioned. How frequently do women appear in the news? When they do, what is being reported? Are women depicted as active political news makers or are they "on the sidelines" of the news? What does this tell you about gender and politics?

2. Contact the military base nearest to you and inquire about services for military wives. What services are provided? What does this teach you about the experiences of women associated with the military? In what ways is the military a gendered institution?

3. Take a current piece of legislation being debated by your state legislature or the federal government, and ask yourself: What are the implications of this law for women? Are the implications being considered as part of this political debate? If so, in what terms? If not, why not?

ᘒ *Suggested Readings*

Bookman, Ann, and Sandra Morgan, eds. 1988. *Women and the Politics of Empowerment.* Philadelphia: Temple University Press.
This anthology examines women's political activism and redefines political behavior to include work that women do outside of formal political institutions.

Enloe, Cynthia. 1989. *Bananas, Beaches, and Bases.* Berkeley: University of California Press.
Enloe's book presents a feminist perspective on international relations. Her compelling analysis studies the role of gender in peace, war, international development, and the social structure of the military.

MacKinnon, Catharine. 1989. *Toward a Feminist Theory of the State.* Cambridge, MA: Harvard University Press.
MacKinnon defines the state as "male," meaning that it is based on, and represents, men's power. Her radical feminist analysis is a powerful critique of dominant political institutions.

Mansbridge, Jane. 1986. *Why We Lost the ERA.* Chicago: University of Chicago Press.
This case study of the politics of the Equal Rights Amendment explains how women and men organized the ERA campaign. It also explains the sources of resistance to this constitutional amendment.

Martin, Patricia Yancey, and Myra Marx Ferree. 1995. *Feminist Organizations: Harvest of the New Women's Movement.* Philadelphia: Temple University Press.
This anthology explores the diverse organizations that are engaged in feminist activism. Written from a sociological perspective, the articles examine how feminist organizations are structured and how the feminist perspective of the members influences their action and work.

Shilts, Randy. 1993. *Conduct Unbecoming: Gays and Lesbians in the U.S. Military.* New York: St. Martin's Press.
This book provides a historical overview of gays and lesbians in the military and analyzes public and government response to this issue.

Stiehm, Judith Hicks. 1996. *"It's Our Military, Too!": Women and the U.S. Military.* Philadelphia: Temple University Press.
This anthology covers a wide range of issues about women and the military, centering on the premise that one should understand the structure of the military to engage in current issues about violence, sexual harassment, and women's roles in the military.

Whittier, Nancy. 1995. *Feminist Generations: The Persistence of the Radical Women's Movement.* Philadelphia: Temple University Press.
This book examines the different generations in the women's movement, including the so-called postfeminist period of the 1980s. Whittier's analysis focuses on the persistence of feminism across the years.

Williams, Patricia. 1991. *The Alchemy of Race and Rights.* Cambridge, MA: Harvard University Press.
Using literature, legal scholarship, and an imaginative form of presentation, Williams's analysis of race and gender shows both the limitations and the possibilities of law as a vehicle for social change.

Chapter 11
Women and Social Reform
Liberal Feminism

As a social movement, feminism has brought many changes to society—not the least of which is change in intellectual life. Although perhaps to many in the public, intellectual life seems like a rarified thing—distant, aloof, disconnected from reality—intellectual thought guides many of the changes that we see in the world around us. As policymakers debate reforms in labor relations, family policy, social welfare, education, or any other arena of life, they often draw on the knowledge of experts to guide their work as agents of change. These experts come from a variety of intellectual and political perspectives—thus, the great debates that characterize some of the more difficult and pressing issues of our times. In the absence of feminist theory, few of these changes are likely to be informed by an analysis that understands the implications of such change for women.

In addition, sometimes people advocate changes with an implicit, and perhaps even unconscious, set of assumptions built into their ideals for change. For example, you will see in this discussion of liberalism that despite negative stereotypes about this label, liberalism is the dominant political philosophy in the United States—including in some conservative thought. A basic premise of liberalism is that all people should be treated alike, with no formal barriers to opportunity and equal rights before the law. Consciously or not, liberalism guides many of the changes people advocate in contemporary times.

Feminist theory has also guided some of the basic transformations in women's and men's lives in recent years. Feminism is both a way of acting and being in the world, as well as a way of thinking. Feminist theory is the social and political thought that lies behind much of feminist politics. It forms the basis for social policies and social actions that have driven change in recent years. The development of feminist theory is not separated from the women's movement; indeed, the two are inextricably linked. Behind feminist politics lie modes of analysis (i.e., feminist theory) that guide and inform social and political action. These modes of thought are as diverse as the feminist movement itself, but they can be roughly categorized into broad categories, including liberal feminism, socialist feminism, and radical feminism—the major theoretical orientations that are examined in these chapters. Recently, new directions in feminist thinking are building on the foundation established by these theoretical perspectives, as feminists grapple with new questions about the intersections of race, class, and gender in society, gay and lesbian studies, and the implications for feminist scholarship of what is known as *postmodernist theory*.

As you will see in this chapter, throughout history feminist theory has been tied to broad intellectual and social changes in society. The social thought of influential European thinkers in the eighteenth and nineteenth centuries (Mary Wollstonecraft, John Stuart Mill, and Harriet Taylor Mill) laid the groundwork for contemporary liberal feminism. During the nineteenth century, Karl Marx, whose writings changed the course of world history, also influenced the development of feminist thought. Within the United States, social movements—including abolition, temperance, and the women's suffrage movement—have also influenced the development of feminist theory. At the same time, social changes taking place in society—including industrialization, geographic expansion, expanding educational opportunities for women, and the growth of social reform movements—have all influenced the development of feminist thought over time. In the chapters that follow, you will examine this thought, with the goal of understanding the underlying assumptions in diverse theoretical perspectives, since these same assumptions shape the imaginations people have for envisioning social change.

❧ Frameworks of Feminist Theory

To many people, the idea of theory implies a way of thinking that is highly abstract and perhaps void of any connection to the "real" world. Many tend to think of theories as ideas that hold a certain degree of fascination for intellectuals but that are not particularly relevant for the ordinary person's understanding of life or the world. Most of us, however, do have ideas about the way society is organized. Although we may not think of ourselves as theorists, we hold many assumptions, unexamined as they may be, about the organization of society and the possibilities for social change.

Sociological theory attempts to explain the relationship between social facts, like many of those you have observed in preceding chapters, and the social structure of society and culture. Feminist theory similarly attempts to situate the everyday events of women's and men's lives in an analysis that links our personal and collective experience to an understanding of the structure of gender relationships in society and culture. Feminists also claim that what we know, both intellectually and practically, is thoroughly infused with gendered assumptions about the character of the social world, its problems, its inhabitants, and its meaning.

The purpose of **feminist theory** is to help us understand the conditions in society and to envision the possibilities for liberating social changes. Feminist theory is not written about and discussed just for its own sake but rather for what it suggests about political change, as well. While theoretical analyses may seem complex and sometimes abstract, their purpose is to help understand the character of social structure and therefore the possibilities for social change. As we can see by examining the various frameworks of feminist theory and their relationship to feminist politics, different political frameworks in the feminist movement rest on different theoretical assumptions. Although these assumptions are not always evident in political discourse, understanding them can sharpen political analyses and inform strategies for social change.

For example, since feminism has moved into the mainstream of life in the United States, many people identify themselves as feminists with little understanding of the liberal framework they assume (Eisenstein, 1981). Whether one assumes a liberal or a radical feminist stance, examining the intellectual roots of different feminist perspectives provides a more complete understanding of the assumptions of a given perspective, as well as the different programs for social change that given perspectives imply. Careful study of particular feminist frameworks enables us to more accurately answer questions about women's status in society, and therefore allows for a better assessment of possible directions for social change.

The theoretical and political frameworks of feminist thought emerge from some of the classical traditions of social and political theory. As you will see, in considering issues about women's lives, feminists have revised some of these classical perspectives to better explain the position of women in society. Like the intellectual traditions from which feminist thought stems, feminist theory is organized around varying assumptions about social organization and social change. These assumptions also guide the way in which we interpret the empirical observations of social research, such as that reviewed in earlier chapters of this book. Depending on the theoretical position used to understand data, the data may take on a different meaning. Facts do not usually speak for themselves; they are interpreted within the context of assumptions made about their meaning and their relationship to other facts. Theories guide this interpretation and are therefore an integral part of the process of knowledge construction.

This chapter focuses on the framework of liberal feminism, a long-standing and far-reaching framework for feminist social change. Liberal feminism is rooted in the history of liberalism as a mode of political theory and it is centered on the premise of equality and the capacity for existing democratic social institutions to create equal rights and equal opportunity for all. As the foundation for democracy, liberalism promotes the removal of particularistic barriers—that is, practices that discriminate based on particular characteristics such as gender, race, and religion. Although to many this seems like an ideal solution for promoting gender equality, you will see that there are some fundamental limitations to this approach.

Liberal feminism emphasizes social and legal reform through policies designed to create equal opportunities for women. In addition, it emphasizes gender socialization as the origin of gender differences, thereby assuming that changes in socialization practices will result in more liberated and egalitarian gender relations.

Liberal feminism differs from other feminist theoretical perspectives in accepting the basic structure of democratic social institutions as conducive to social change. As you will see in the subsequent chapter, socialist feminism is a more radical perspective—one that interprets the origins of women's oppression in the systems of capitalism and patriarchy. Radical feminism analyzes patriarchy as the primary cause of women's oppression. Socialist feminism and radical feminism are examined in Chapter 12. As you will see, no single perspective provides the singularly most correct analysis of women's place in society. As the text will show, each perspective has its own conceptual strengths and weaknesses, and thus is able to answer some questions better than others. Together, these feminist theoretical perspectives provide a rich and engaging analysis of women in society.

The adequacy of each perspective should be assessed, in part, in terms of its ability to address several fundamental issues in feminist thought. Most important, because feminism purports to liberate *all* women, a sound feminist analysis must be able to address the interrelationship of race, class, and gender. The adequacy of a given theoretical and political framework must be judged according to the perspective it provides on these relationships.

In addition to explaining how race, class, and gender intersect in women's experiences, feminist perspectives must address some of the central issues that are encountered in thinking about women. These issues follow from the topics that have organized the preceding chapters of this book. They include understanding the issue of nature versus nurture (including the process of gender socialization); interpreting women's status in work and the family; explaining the social control of female reproduction, health, and sexuality; comprehending female crime and deviance and their connection to gender relations; and relating the ideology of sexism to the social institutions in which it is produced.

❧ *The Liberal Basis of Modern Feminism*

This review of feminist theory begins with liberal feminism—the most mainstream feminist perspective. In political and sociological theory, *liberal* has a particular meaning quite different from its common usage to mean open-minded, tolerant, or socially nontraditional. The specific philosophical meaning of **liberalism** lies behind the political liberalism of certain kinds of activist groups. Liberalism in this sense is characterized by an emphasis on individual rights and equal opportunity. Liberal groups are those that attempt to reform social systems for the purpose of giving all groups equal opportunities.

As was stated earlier, liberalism is the dominant political philosophy in the United States. Those who might never consider themselves liberal—in the sense the label has come to imply—nonetheless are likely to believe that the best society is one in which no group receives special treatment based on its race, color, religion, national origin, or gender. Indeed, this philosophy is the very foundation for modern civil rights legislation. It is a position that advocates a color-blind and gender-neutral society. Many take this position to the extreme, thinking that to even acknowledge another's gender or race is to be sexist or racist. This attitude stems from the underpinnings of liberal social thought.

As a political and social theory, liberalism has generated quite specific programs for social change—notably, eliminating any practices or laws that either discriminate against particular groups and, as is the movement among current conservatives, trying to eliminate any programs that have race- or gender-specific components (e.g., affirmative action, minority scholarships, and incentive programs for women and minorities starting their own businesses). As you will see, the philosophy behind such actions, although they have very different proponents, is based in the ideals of liberalism as a social and political theory.

The liberal politics of the women's movement include a range of organizations and issues, perhaps best exemplified by the National Organization for Women (NOW), founded in 1966. As a national organization, NOW works within the established economic and political systems to advocate for social changes on behalf of women. Other liberal feminist organizations such as the National Women's Political Caucus and the National Abortion Rights Action League also work within the existing political system through extensive lobbying and agendas for legislative reform. The gains inspired by liberal feminism in recent years have made significant changes in women's lives. On issues ranging from equity in employment to reproductive rights, liberal reforms have resulted in increased opportunities for women and increased public consciousness of women's rights. The fact that liberal feminism works largely within existing institutions has, most likely, contributed to its broad-based support.

Because liberalism is such a popular strand of feminist thought and is fundamental to the assumptions of some feminist politics, it is important that we carefully examine its intellectual roots. The origins of liberal philosophy lie in western Europe and the societal transitions of the eighteenth and nineteenth centuries. By examining this context and the social thought produced within it, you will see the theoretical tenets of the liberal perspective, as well as its connection to the evolution of feminist thought. Although you have already reviewed the growth of feminism in the United States in the nineteenth and twentieth centuries, this historical analysis of liberal thought will give a more detailed and analytical vision of the liberal basis of some feminist beliefs and politics.

❧ *Liberalism as a Mode of Social Thought*

The origins of contemporary liberal feminism reach back to the seventeenth- and eighteenth-century **Age of Enlightenment** in western Europe (also known as the *Age of Reason*). This period fostered an array of political, social, and intellectual movements, most of them characterized by an explicit faith in the capacity of human reason to generate social reform. As the setting for the early philosophies of feminism, the Age of Enlightenment is noted for its libertarian ideals, its pleas for humanitarian reform, and its conviction that "reason shall set us free" (Rossi, 1973).

The philosophy of the period provided the theme for major changes in Western social organization (including the French and American revolutions), and it set the stage for the eventual development of social-scientific thought and the emergence of sociology as an academic field. The historical context of early feminist thought is found in conditions that inspired more general appeals to social reform through the application of human reason. It is worthwhile to examine some of the transformations that mark the period and that provide the historical arena for the emergence of contemporary liberal feminism.

Sociologists cite two notable developments that influenced broad-scale change in the West: the consolidation and expansion of a world system of capital (Wallerstein, 1976) and a decline in the traditional sacred authority of religion (Nisbet, 1970). The development of Western capitalism created new systems of inequality marked by the displacement of the poor from rural land and the concentration of wealth in the hands of the new capitalist class. The related developments of urbanization and industrialization also planted the seeds of the social problems that continue to confront us today: urban crowding and the development of slums, pollution and waste, poverty, crime, and new tensions in family life. In the Age of Enlightenment, political thinkers who observed these changes also delighted in the decline of the influence of the sacred authority of the church and the secular feudal state. Enlightenment thinkers fostered the hope that the human ability to reason would provide societies with reasonable solutions to the new problems they encountered.

One of the central tenets of Enlightenment philosophy and the political-social thought it inspired was that free, critical inquiry was to be the cornerstone for the future. At heart, the Enlightenment thinkers were optimists, and they seemed undaunted by the vast problems surrounding them. Although, in retrospect, they can be criticized for their naive faith in human rationality, their work is also praised for its emphasis on nondogmatic discussion and open inquiry (Hughes, 1958).

The Enlightenment libertarian ideals challenged the power of feudal elites and assumed that the future was in the hands of the masses. As they considered the development of history, they envisioned a decline in the brutal and "uncivilized" physical abuses of the past (de Tocqueville, 1945). They believed that the church, identified by most Enlightenment thinkers as the villain of past repression, would continue to decline in its authoritarian influence; modern society would instead be regulated by the rational construction of democratic government.

The influence of the Enlightenment extends beyond the eighteenth century, laying the foundation for the development of social science in the nineteenth and twentieth centuries and influencing later thinkers such as John Stuart Mill in the nineteenth century. Sociology, in particular, is indebted to the Enlightenment for its emphasis on the application of reason and the scientific method to the solution of social problems. Early sociological thinkers such as Auguste Comte (1798–1857) and Henry Saint-Simon (1760–1825) believed that social knowledge would take the form of social laws, telling us how the social world operated and how we could therefore engineer positive changes. The simplicity of their faith in sociology as the ultimate science is now apparent, but their influence on the positivist methods of sociology is immeasurable. The positivism they inspired and that others have developed since assumes that the techniques of scientific observation in the physical sciences can be used in the discovery of social behavior. Their insistence on the application of sociological knowledge for engineering social change continues to influence the activities of modern social planners.

The philosophy of liberalism emerging in this period rests on two central principles: the concept of individual liberty and the emphasis on human reason as the basis for humanitarian social change. In liberal feminism, these philosophical ideals are the basis for the principle of equal opportunity and social reform. Much of the focus of social change among liberal feminist groups lies in the construction of legislation and in the regulation of employment practices. According to the liberal perspective, the obstacles to equal rights for women (as well as other groups) lie in traditional laws and practices that deny the same individual rights to women that men already have.

The liberal perspective assumes that persons can create humanitarian change through the use of human rationality. Injustice is viewed as the result of irrationality and ignorance. Reason and the pursuit of knowledge are believed to be the source of social change; consequently, liberal policies for change rely on a faith in the process of social reform. Liberal feminists' practical solutions to inequality include programs that prohibit discrimination (e.g., equal opportunity policies). Liberal feminism also seeks the reform of individuals through, for example, the resocialization of children and the relearning of appropriate social roles for adults. A central emphasis of the liberal perspective is that all persons' abilities are culturally learned; therefore, egalitarian gender relations will follow from relearning traditional gender-role attitudes and behaviors.

The popularity of the liberal perspective makes it difficult to identify as a specific social and political philosophy. It is the philosophical backdrop to many contemporary programs for change, and it has been widely adopted by diverse groups working for legal and economic reform. Liberalism also encourages the acceptance of diverse life-styles, because it sees life-style as a matter of individual choice. Within the liberal perspective, persons and the societies they create should be tolerant and respectful of the choices persons make. Because persons have civil rights to exercise their freedom, societies should not erect barriers to individual liberties. The liberal perspective, like other feminist perspectives, rejects the conservative view that persons assume their status in life because of ascribed (biological) characteristics and attributes the different statuses that people acquire to social learning and the denial of opportunity. Liberal feminists (along with other feminists) thus reject the conservative belief that women are bound to particular roles and statuses because of their biological capacity to bear children.

In sum, liberal feminism assumes that the inequality of women stems both from the denial of equal rights and from women's learned reluctance to exercise their rights. The goal of liberal feminism is equality—the construction of a social world where all persons can exercise individual freedom. At its heart, the liberal perspective is a philosophy based on the principle of individual liberty. In the liberal framework, every person should be allowed to exercise freedom of choice, unfettered by either public opinion or law. In effect, all persons should be given equal opportunities, and civil rights should be extended to all. Liberal feminist philosophy lies behind the call for reforms such as the ERA, which, if it had been enacted, would amend the Constitution to state: "Equality of rights under the law shall not be denied or abridged by the United States or by any state on the basis of sex." One indication of the nation's unwillingness to fully embrace liberal feminist ideals is the fact that such an amendment has never been ratified, so as to make it the law of the land.

❧ An Enlightenment for Women?

The legacy of the Enlightenment, as it is recorded in the historical record, was a period characterized by the ascendency of reason over tradition, the outreach of humanitarianism to dispossessed groups, and general improvement in the condition of humanity. The Enlightenment period is often interpreted as the origin of contemporary social thought.

We are not sure what the Enlightenment was like for women, because its recorded history has been largely that of men's accomplishments. We do know that women's historical experience differs significantly from men's (Kelly-Gadol, 1976), and feminist historians have suggested that the Enlightenment is no exception. They would argue that the Age of Reason is a reference only to the reason of certain men. During this same era, women's work was idealized as belonging in the emotional world of the home; nevertheless, women's labor (both in the home and outside of it) constituted a major part of the society's economic productivity. Most women still produced marketable goods in the home and, as factories became the sites for production, women and children were employed for long hours at low wages.

Seen in the context of women's lives, the period of Enlightenment takes on a different meaning. Both women and the working class seem to have been left out of the Age of Reason, because the intellectual movement of the Enlightenment was largely based on the thought of bourgeois White men. During this same period in the United States, most African American women and men were still enslaved and, although slavery was one of the concerns of the men of the Enlightenment, histories of feminist thought rarely look to the thoughts of African American women, slave or free, as an origin for early feminist work. The development of feminist thought cannot be placed exclusively though in the Enlightenment. African American women such as Charlotte Forten, Maria Stewart, Sojourner Truth, and Ida Bell Wells articulated some of the early principles of feminist thought (Lerner, 1973; Sterling, 1984; Collins, 1990). Maria Stewart, a former servant to a clergy family in New England, was the first woman in the United States to deliver a public lecture (in Boston on September 21, 1832). Although rarely recognized in the histories of feminism, her exhortations to women domestic workers and day laborers to improve their minds and talents, which she saw as thwarted by women's servitude, are clear and passionate feminist ideals. When she left Boston because of hostile public response to her work, she delivered a parting speech ardently defending the right of women to speak in public (Sterling, 1984). To exclude women such as Stewart and the many other African American thinkers and activists of this early period from the history of feminist thought is to take White European and American philosophers as creating *the* history of feminism and to see African American women's feminist ideas only as secondary or as a reaction to White thought (Gilkes, 1985).

This interpretation does not mean we should disregard the influence of Enlightenment thought on the history of feminism, but it does cast this history in a different light. The legacy of the Enlightenment as the triumph of man's reason is a celebration of the growing preeminence at this time of men's rational power. Women during this period were identified with the irrational and emotional side of life. The ascent of rationality, which the Enlightenment celebrates, can then be seen as the ascent of male rational power over the presumed emotionality and inferiority of women.

This revision puts the thinkers of the Enlightenment period into a different context and also reveals different aspects of their work. Feminist historians who have studied the major Enlightenment philosophers (Rousseau, Diderot, and Condorcet, for example) conclude that although the Enlightenment philosophers had the potential to decry the sexist ideas of sacred traditions, most of the Enlightenment thinkers ignored the revolutionary potential of their ideas for change in women's lives (Kleinbaum, 1977). Still, the thinkers of the Enlightenment did have a strong influence on the development of modern feminism, although a more complete history of feminist thought, as it also evolves through the work of women of color, has yet to be written. Women in this period, in both Europe and the United States, produced some of the earliest feminist work, although many of the White women never escaped the class-biased boundaries of their own experience.

Later (in the nineteenth century), John Stuart Mill was to become an exception among male philosophers, as he adopted a strikingly feminist position on the emancipation of women. Together with his collaborator, Harriet Taylor Mill, John Stuart Mill produced a series of essays that have now become the cornerstone of modern liberal feminism. (The Mills' work is studied later in this chapter.) The roots of liberal feminism in western Europe are first traced to the work of Mary Wollstonecraft.

❧ Mary Wollstonecraft

Mary Wollstonecraft (1759–1797) provides part of the philosophical foundation for modern feminism. Her essay *A Vindication of the Rights of Women*, first published in London in 1792, was so provocative that editions of it quickly appeared in Dublin, Paris, and New York (Poston, 1975). So astutely did she outline the position of women that her essay was equally provocative to White, middle-class women who discussed it in consciousness-raising groups in the 1960s and 1970s. Her words continue to inspire women almost 200 years after the original edition was published—a testimony to the influence Wollstonecraft has had.

Wollstonecraft left her home as a teenager in 1778. Distressed by her father's excessive demands for obedience and her family's continued poverty, she wandered from town to town in the countryside of Wales and England (Rossi, 1973). Her independence and self-sufficiency established a lifetime pattern of refusing to submit to authority—both in her life and in her writings. She later wrote:

> *I will venture to affirm, that a girl, whose spirits have not been damped by inactivi-ty, or innocence tainted by false name, will always be a romp, and the doll will never excite attention unless confinement allows her no alternative. Girls and boys, in short, would play harmlessly together, if the distinction of sex was not inculcated long before nature makes any difference. I will go further and affirm, as an indisputable fact, that most of the women, in the circle of my observation, who have acted like ratio-nal creatures, or shown any vigour of intellect, have accidentally been allowed to run wild. (Wollstonecraft, 1792/1975:43)*

Her concern with subservience to authority recurs as a central theme in her work, and it is tied to her argument that learning and socialization are responsi-ble for the formation of mind. Foretelling generations of feminists to come, Wollstonecraft argued that gender role characteristics were the result of education (used broadly in her work to mean all social learning). What appeared to be the natural weakness of women was the result of their lack of liberty and their depen-dence on men. She wrote, "All the differences that I can discern, arise from the superior advantage of liberty, which enables the former to see more of life" (Wollstonecraft, 1792/1975:23). She went on to say:

> *It is vain to expect virtue from women till they are in some degree independent of men; nay, it is vain to expect that strength of natural affection which would make them good wives and mothers. Whilst they are absolutely dependent on their hus-bands they will be cunning, mean and selfish, and the men who can be gratified by the fawning fondness of spaniel-like affection have not much delicacy, for love is not to be bought; its silken wings are instantly shriveled up when anything besides a return in kind is sought. (1792/1975:144)*

Throughout her essay, Wollstonecraft emphasized that blind submission to authority not only limits social and political freedom but also inhibits the devel-opment of mental reasoning. Like others in the Enlightenment, she imagined that the downfall of tyranny would occur as society became organized around the principle of rational thought. She wrote, "Tyrants would have cause to tremble if reason were to become the rule of duty in any of the relations of life, for the light might spread till perfect day appeared" (1792/1975:150).

Wollstonecraft equated the life of a dutiful soldier to that of a well-socialized woman:

> *They both acquire manners before morals, and a knowledge of life before they have, from reflection, any acquaintance with the grand ideal outline of human nature. The consequence is natural; satisfied with common nature, they become a prey to preju-dices, and taking all their opinions on credit, they submit blindly to authority. So that,*

if they have any sense, it is a kind of instinctive glance, that catches propositions, and decides with respect to manners but fails when arguments are to be pursued below the surface, or opinions analyzed. (1792/1975:24)

More than other early White feminists, Wollstonecraft was sensitive to the issue of social class and the artificial distinctions among persons that she believed social class created. She directed her arguments especially to leisure-class women, for, she said, it is in that class that women are most dependent on men. She held in contempt the idleness of mind and attention to gentility that she believed wealth produced: "The education of the rich tends to render them vain and helpless, and the unfolding mind is not strengthened by the practice of those duties which dignify the human character" (1792/1975:9). "The preposterous distinctions of rank, which render civilization a curse by dividing the world between voluptuous tyrants and cunning envious dependents, corrupt, almost equally, every class of people, because respectability is not attached to the discharge of the relative duties of life, but to the station" (1792/1975:144). Although she recognized that her observations were of a particular social class, she gave little, if any, attention to women of other classes and cultures.

Wollstonecraft's outspoken portrayals of femininity, authority, and property relations earned her a lifetime of insults and insinuations about her bad character. Her contemporaries indexed articles written about her under the topic "prostitution" (Rossi, 1973; Wardle, 1951); more recently, her feminist beliefs have raised charges that she was "pitifully weak," "consumed with penis envy," and an "extreme neurotic" (Lundberg and Farnham, 1947). These same critics wrote, "Out of her illness arose the ideology of feminism, which was to express the feelings of so many women in years to come" (Lundberg and Farnham, 1947:145–159).

Wollstonecraft's work is a powerful criticism of women's role and its connection to power and social control. Her writing typifies the passion with which the Enlightenment thinkers pursued their condemnations of traditional authority, and it stands as one of the most persuasive accounts of the effects of women's subservience on their powers of thought, behavior, and self-concept. Her statement that more egalitarian education was needed to liberate women sounds as if it could have been written yesterday. It is a tribute to Wollstonecraft's own capacities for reason and her unchecked passion for justice that her words continue to inspire two centuries after they were written.

❧ Harriet Martineau

Not long after Wollstonecraft's death in 1797, another woman was born who could appropriately be called the mother of sociology. Little recognized in contemporary histories of sociological thought, English woman Harriet Martineau (1802–1876) was one of the first to use field observation as a method for the development of social knowledge. She was the translator of Auguste Comte's (the father of sociology) *Positive Philosophy*; and, like her counterpart, Alexis de

Tocqueville, she traveled widely in the United States, producing a descriptive and analytic account of her observations in her book *Society in America* (1837). Her other book, *How to Observe Manners and Morals* (1838), was the first methodology book in sociology, for in it she detailed the method of participant observation as she developed it in her own work (Lipset, 1962; Rossi, 1973).

Like many of the early feminists, Martineau matched her concern for women's emancipation with her support for the U.S. abolition movement. Her outspokenness on the slavery issue, coupled with her daring to travel as a single woman in the nineteenth century, generated threats against her life. She was eventually forced to restrict her travels to the northern section of the country, but in her analysis she insisted on the right of women to speak their conscience. She wrote:

> *The whole apparatus of opinion is brought to bear offensively upon individuals among women who exercise freedom of mind in deciding upon what duty is, and the methods by which it is to be pursued. . . . The reproach in all the many similar cases I know is, not that the ladies hold anti-slavery opinions, but that they act upon them. The incessant outcry about the retiring modesty of the sex proves the opinion of the censors to be that fidelity to conscience is inconsistent with retiring modesty. If it be so, let the modesty succumb. (1837:158–159)*

As Marx and Engels were also later to proclaim, she also wrote, "If a test of civilization be sought, none can be so sure as the condition of that half of society over which the other half has power" (1837:156).

The connection Martineau made between the abolition and feminist movements is indicative of the association that early feminists had with their antislavery movement in the United States. White women's dissatisfaction with their position likely led to their involvement in and appreciation for the abolitionist cause (DuBois, 1978). Their involvement in the antislavery movement taught White feminists how to understand and change their situation.

African American women in the antislavery movement were more likely to put racial prejudice at the center of their feminist analyses. Sarah Forten, for example, writing in 1837, discussed the influence of prejudice on her life. She said:

> *It has often embittered my feelings, particularly when I recollect that we are innocent victims of it . . . and [I] consequently seek to avoid as much as possible mingling with those who exist under its influence. I must also own that it has often engendered feelings of discontent and mortification in my breast when I see that many were preferred before me, who by education—birth—or worldly circumstance were not better than myself—their sole claim to notice depending on the superior advantage of being white. (Sterling, 1984:124)*

White women who worked in the abolition movement gained an understanding from African American women of the concept of institutional power and adopted the political conviction of natural rights for all individuals, regardless of race or sex. Their analysis of racial and sexual oppression, however, remained at the level of analogy. Early White feminists did not develop an understanding that took account of the historical specificity of the African American experience in the United States, nor did they ever make the kind of analysis that could adequately account for class and other cultural differences among women (DuBois, 1978). As a result, the liberal tradition of feminism that was established by leaders such as Elizabeth Cady Stanton (1815–1902) and Susan B. Anthony (1820–1906) began and continued with an inadequate comprehension of race and class issues in women's experience.

Martineau's own analysis of race and class is filled with contradictions. She appealed to justice and freedom, yet maintained the ethnic stereotypes typical of her period. She wrote:

> *The English, soon find it impossible to get American domestic help at all, and they are consigned to the tender mercies of the low Irish; and everyone knows what kind of servants they commonly are. Some few of them are the best domestics in America; those who know how to value a respectable home, a steady sufficient income, the honour of being trusted, and the security of valuable friends for life; but too many of them are unsettled, reckless, slovenly; some dishonest, and some intemperate. (1837:171–172)*

Martineau's work stands as an example of early White feminist thought, complete with its class and race contradictions. More generally, in spite of appeals to reason, free will, humanitarianism, and liberty, liberal feminism has never adequately addressed the issues of race and class inequality. In stating that racism and sexism are analogous forms of oppression, liberal feminism suggests an analysis that would take race, class, and gender into account, but, as the concluding section of this chapter shows, this analysis is not provided by liberal White feminists, leaving the theoretical and political task of comprehending race, class, and gender oppression to other thinkers.

❧ *John Stuart Mill and Harriet Taylor Mill*

No thinkers have been more influential in the development of liberal feminism than John Stuart Mill (1806–1873) and Harriet Taylor Mill (1807–1858). *The Subjection of Women*, first published in 1851, was the philosophical inspiration for the British suffrage movement and, like Wollstonecraft's *A Vindication of the Rights of Women*, continues to be studied. The analysis that the Mills developed is the philosophical backbone of liberal feminist politics. Their essays go further than Wollstonecraft's or Martineau's in that they relate women's oppression to a systematic critique of liberty and the relations between the sexes. A review of the Mills' work provides an analysis of the particular assumptions and modes of thinking that are characteristic of liberal feminism.

From an early age, John Stuart Mill was steeped in the rigors of intellectual thought and disciplined study. Under his father's stern supervision, he began a course of study at age 3 that created his intellectual genius at the same time that it apparently robbed him of emotional gratification (Rossi, 1970). His life was one of continuous intellectual production mixed with political activism and long struggles with emotional depression. His father's intense emphasis on rational thought left Mill with a long struggle to "cultivate the feelings," an accomplishment perhaps best made through his strong relationship with Harriet Taylor (later to become Harriet Taylor Mill).

The relationship between John Stuart Mill and Harriet Taylor is one that matches romantic commitment and intellectual collaboration with a fervor for individual liberty; so passionate and unusual was their life together that it is still the subject of discussion (Rossi, 1970). Through their correspondence and conversation with each other, their published ideas were formed. Mill himself wrote that the ideas in *The Subjection of Women* (published after Harriet's death) belonged to his wife and had emerged from their vast discussions on a topic dear to them both (Rossi, 1970). Over the years, scholars have seldom given Harriet Mill the recognition she deserves for her contribution to these works or, for that matter, to her own writing. The fact that Harriet Taylor Mill has so seldom been cited in the many detailed reviews of the Mills' work underscores the sexist character of philosophical criticism and points out how little credit has been given to women thinkers of the past. Alice Rossi has made a convincing case that the Mills' work was a joint effort, even though it was published under his name. She also argues that *Enfranchisement of Women* (published in 1851) was actually written by Harriet Mill (Rossi, 1970).

Taken together, the Mills' essays provide the most comprehensive statement of the liberal perspective of feminist thought. The issues they raise can be grouped into several key areas—the logic of inquiry, gender differences, work and the family, and the process of modernization and social change.

The Logic of Inquiry

The logic of the Mills' arguments is typical of that inspired by the rational perspective of the Enlightenment thinkers. Convictions, the Mills claimed, fare poorly in argumentative debate, for the resistance of conviction to reason makes rational argument impossible. Strong feelings, they maintained, are impenetrable by rational debate; consequently, those who argue against almost universally held opinions will, most certainly, have a hard time being heard. In discussing the subordination of women, the Mills clearly argued that open inquiry—especially listening to women's voices—is a prerequisite to establishing knowledge of women's lives. They wrote:

> We may safely assert that the knowledge which men can acquire of women, even as they have been and are, without reference to what they might be, is wretchedly imperfect and superficial and always will be so, until women themselves have told all they have to tell. . . . Let us remember in what manner, up to a recent time, the expression, even by a male author, of uncustomary opinions, or what are deemed eccentric feelings, usually was, and in some degree still is, received; and we may form some faint conception under what impediments a woman, who is brought up to think custom and opinion her sovereign rule, attempts to express in books anything drawn from the depths of her own nature. (cited in Rossi, 1970:152–153)

Knowing that their ideas in *The Subjection of Women* would be controversial, the Mills placed the burden of proof to the contrary on those who would oppose human liberty:

> *The burden of proof is supposed to be with those who are against liberty, who contend for any restriction or prohibition, either any limitation of the general freedom of human action, or any disqualification or disparity of privilege affecting one person or kind of persons, as compared with others. The* a priori *presumption is in favor of freedom and impartiality. (Mill, 1970:3)*

The starting point of their argument, as well as the central concept in the liberal perspective, is that all persons have equal liberty, and therefore human institutions should treat all alike. Their words provide the philosophy behind the modern practice of equal employment opportunity and equality before the law. They wrote, "The law should be no respector of persons, but should treat all alike, save where dissimilarity of treatment is required by positive reasons, either justice or of policy" (1970:4). They defined human liberty as a natural right and one that should not be denied on the basis of any individual or group characteristics. As their writing shows, the rational style of their argument is coupled with a passionate emphasis on the necessity for liberating social changes.

Gender Differences and Social Learning

The Mills showed how social conditions create gender-specific attitudes and arrangements that conservatives use to discredit the claim of women's equality. By imagining new alternatives, the Mills showed how a change in the relationship between men and women would likely alter the characteristics usually thought to be natural differences. They argued that there is no reasonable defense for the current state of affairs and that the creation of liberty for women would benefit not just women but society as a whole. The social benefits of liberation would include "doubling the mass of mental faculties available for the higher service of humanity" (1970:153), overcoming the selfish attitudes and self-worshipping characteristics of humanity (1970:148), and enhancing the "softening influence" (1970:156) of women's moral tendencies.

What is considered to be natural is only what is taken for granted, they argued. Foretelling the thoughts of contemporary feminists, they wrote:

> *Was there ever any domination which did not appear natural to those who possessed it? There was a time when the division of mankind into two classes, a small one of masters and a numerous one of slaves, appeared, even to the most cultivated minds, to be a natural, and the only natural, condition of the human race. . . . Did not the slave owners of the Southern United States maintain the same doctrine, with all the fanaticism with which men cling to the theories that justify their passions and legitimate their personal interests? (Mill, 1970: 20–21)*

They continued:

> *The smallest acquaintance with human life in the Middle Ages shows how supreme-*
> *ly natural the dominion of feudal nobility over men of low condition appeared to the*
> *nobility themselves, and how unnatural the conception seemed, of a person of the infe-*
> *rior class claiming equality with them, or exercising authority over them. It hardly*
> *seemed less so to the class held in subjection. The emancipated serfs and burgesses,*
> *even in their most vigorous struggles, never made any pretension to a share of author-*
> *ity; they only demanded more or less of a limitation to the power of tyrannizing over*
> *them. So is it that unnatural generally means only uncustomary, and that everything*
> *which is usual appears natural? The subjection of women to men being a universal*
> *custom, any departure from it quite naturally appears unnatural. (Mill, 1970: 22–23)*

Like contemporary social scientists, the Mills saw that what appears natural is primarily the result of social learning. They continued by saying that one can know what persons actually are only by comprehending their social experience. In their words, "We cannot isolate a human being from the circumstances of his condition, so as to ascertain experimentally what he would have been by nature; but we can consider what he is, and what his circumstances have been, and whether the one would have been capable of producing the other" (1970:126).

Because women had been held in such an unnatural state of submission and domination, the Mills believed it was impossible to make claims about natural gender differences. All that we see as masculinity or femininity, they contended, is the result of learned, not actual, differences. They wrote, "Women have always hitherto been kept, as far as regards spontaneous development, in so unnatural a state, that their nature cannot but have been greatly distorted and disguised" (1970:104–105). They went on, "I deny that any one knows, or can know, the nature of the sexes, as long as they have only been seen in their present relation to one another" (1970:38), and said, "One thing we may be certain of—that what is contrary to women's nature to do, they will never be made to do by simply giv-ing their nature free play" (1970:48).

The Mills made the case for liberty by identifying the detrimental effects of social learning or, in their words, education and custom, under a state of subjec-tion. They assumed that persons construct their social arrangements and social identities, although some may have more power than others to do so. Human beings, they argued, are rational and creative. Only by removing constraints and obstacles to liberty can the free expression of rational choice and humane social development be encouraged. According to the Mills, human beings have a natur-al right to self-expression that unnatural systems of authority and rule take away.

The Mills' concept of liberty rests on the idea of voluntary contracts among human actors. Accordingly, they argued that marriage ties should be based on free and voluntary choice and that law, in marriage and other areas, should treat all alike—giving no unnatural advantage to one group or another. The purpose of *The Subjection of Women* is, in fact, to show the following:

The principle which regulates the existing social relations between the two sexes—and legal subordination of one sex to the other—is wrong in itself, and now one of the chief hindrances to human improvements; and that it ought to be replaced by a principle of perfect equality, admitting no power or privilege on the one side, nor disability on the other. (Mill, 1970:1)

Harriet Taylor Mill, in her own essay, *Enfranchisement of Women*, argued, in addition, that "we deny the right of any portion of the species to decide for another portion, or any individual for another individual, what is and what is not their proper sphere" (Rossi, 1970:100). Although the Mills differed on their opinions about women's place in marriage, their attitude toward self-determination was clearly one that denies the right of any one group to restrain another. As they wrote, "The law which is to be observed by both should surely be made by both; yet, as hitherto, by the stronger only" (Rossi, 1970:68). This premise in their work is also the foundation for their ideas on women's position in the workplace and the family.

Work and the Family

The Mills' belief in individual liberty is also seen in their arguments on women's occupations. They believed in the laissez-faire operation of the economic market, meaning that they favored a nonintervention approach to economic processes. Their assumption was that if persons are free to choose their occupations, then the best qualified will fill the positions most appropriate to their talents. Then the occupational system will work in the best interests of all.

These assumptions are grounded in the earlier work of the British economist Adam Smith. Smith maintained that the economic market should be based on open competition and a lack of regulation or interference. According to Smith, this laissez-faire policy best suits the laws of the market. He identified the laws of the market as stemming from the self-interest of individuals and reasoned that open competition between individuals will establish a harmony of interests as individuals mutually compete to establish reasonable prices for the sale of goods. Because Smith believed this process to be the natural law of the market, he concluded that the most effective policy is a hands-off, or laissez-faire, approach.

Although the Mills did not speak so directly about the laws of the economy, they similarly assumed that free competition is the key to economic equity—at least in terms of occupational choice. In *The Subjection of Women*, they wrote:

It is not that all processes are supposed to be equally good, or all persons to be equally qualified for everything; but that freedom of individual choice is now known to be the only thing which procures the adoption of the best processes, and draws each operation into the hands of those who are best qualified for it. . . . In consonance with this doctrine, it is felt to be an overstepping of the proper bounds of authority to fix beforehand on some general presumption, that certain persons are not fit to do certain things. (Mill, 1970:32)

The Mills' arguments about an open choice of occupation have one important qualifier, however. In spite of their general position on the emancipation of women, John Stuart Mill and Harriet Taylor Mill disagreed about women's preferred occupation. John Stuart Mill believed that the occupation women should (and would) choose is marriage. He argued that in marriage, women's work is to be the moral educators of children and to make life beautiful; thus, regardless of his advocacy of an open marketplace, in his correspondence with Harriet Taylor, he wrote:

It does not follow that a woman should actually support herself because she should be capable *of doing so: in the natural course of events she will* not. *It is not desirable to burden the labour market with a double number of competitors. In a healthy state of things, the husband would be able by his single exertions to earn all that is necessary for both: and there would be no need that the wife should take part in the mere providing of what is required to* support *life: it will be for the happiness of both that her occupation should rather be to adorn and beautify it. (John Stuart Mill and Harriet Taylor Mill,* Early Essays on Marriage and Divorce, *in Rossi, 1970:74–75)*

Later, in *The Subjection of Women*, Mill wrote:

In an otherwise just state of things, it is not, therefore, I think, a desirable custom that the wife should contribute by her labour to the income of the family. . . . Like a man when he chooses a profession, so, when a woman marries, it may in general be understood that she makes choice of the management of a household, and the bringing up of a family, as the first call upon her exertions, during as many years of her life as may be required for the purpose; and that she renounces, not all other objects and occupations, but all which are not consistent with the requirement of this. (Mill, 1970:88–89)

In other words, in spite of his general arguments to the contrary, John Stuart Mill thought that women were more self-sacrificing than men and that they would *by nature* want marriage. Only a free market, however, will sort out which individuals have this nature and which do not. Still, he would prefer not to change the traditional activities of women in the family. He wrote, "The education which *does* belong to mothers to give . . . is the training of the affections. . . . The great occupation of women should be to beautify life" (Rossi, 1970:76).

Harriet Taylor Mill seriously disagreed with Mill on this subject, and her arguments show her to be the more radical of the two. In *The Enfranchisement of Women*, she argued, "To say that women must be excluded from active life because maternity disqualifies them for it, is in fact to say, that every other career should be forbidden them in order that maternity may be their only resource" (Rossi, 1970:105). In the same essay, she said, "Let every occupation be open to all, without favour or discouragement to any, and employments will fall into the hands of those men or women who are found by experience to be most capable of worthily exercising them" (Rossi, 1970:100–101)

The disagreement between John Stuart Mill and Harriet Taylor Mill indicates one of the shortcomings in this philosophy of emancipation. He stops short of advocating full equality for women, because he does not support major changes in family relations. Harriet Taylor Mill's analysis is more far-reaching because she argues for the unqualified equality of women with men. Both of them, however, fail to make a radical analysis of women's status because their assumptions ignore the limits to individual free choice that are created by the system of stratification.

The Mills' analysis of occupation is characterized by meritocratic assumptions. A **meritocracy** is a system in which persons hold their positions allegedly on the basis of their individual talents and achievement. Although meritocracies supposedly resist ascriptive hierarchies (i.e., those based on characteristics such as gender or race), they still maintain hierarchical organization (Harding, 1979). Because the Mills' analysis ignores questions such as how talent is distributed, how talent is created or recognized, and how merit is defined, they do not analyze how social systems are marked by unequal powers, privileges, and rewards. In short, their analysis does not overcome inequality; it simply replaces educational, occupational, and legal inequality by gender with other forms of distinction.

Because the Mills do not develop a theory of social class or a perspective on racism, their view of the emancipation of women is based primarily on the optimistic belief that social progress is marked by the increased liberty of the individual. As a central tenet in liberal philosophy, this concept of individual liberty leaves unanswered the question of how institutions are structured around collective inequality. At the same time, the liberal perspective implies that individual liberty will result in the social transformation of the whole society.

Modernization and Social Change

The picture of the future that liberalism portrays tends to be an optimistic one; likewise, its view of history assumes that modern Western civilization is more progressive than Western civilization in the past because, in the Mills' language, the modern, advanced state leaves behind the tyrannies and repressions of the past. The Mills conceptualized history in terms of progressive improvement, and they imagined the future as lacking the subjugation and repression of the past.

In keeping with the Enlightenment perspective, the Mills assumed that the historical rule of force is ending with the development of modern rationalized institutions. History, they argued, replaces the use of force with the use of reason. Accordingly, social organization is no longer based on ascriptive roles, but rather on the achieved merit of individuals. The Mills wrote:

> *For what is the peculiar character of the modern world—the difference which chiefly distinguishes modern institutions, modern social ideas, modern life itself, from those of times long past? It is, that human beings are no longer born to their place in life, and chained down by an inexorable bond to the place they are born to, but are free to employ their faculties, and such favourable chances as offer, to achieve the lot which may appear to them most desirable. (Mill, 1970:29–30)*

The Mills' attitude toward this alleged change is consistent with their desire for equality of choice. Their plea for the enfranchisement of women was based on the argument that women are the only exception to an otherwise emancipated world. They wrote:

> *At present, in the more* improved *countries, the disabilities of women are the only case, save one, in which laws and institutions take persons at their birth, and ordain that they shall never in their lives be allowed to compete for certain things. The one exception is that of royalty. . . . The disabilities, therefore, to which women are subject from the mere fact of their birth, are the solitary examples of the kind in modern legislation. (Mill, 1970:35; emphasis added)*

Although this essay was published following the emancipation of the slaves in the United States, the Mills' arguments reveal naive optimism about the actual disenfranchisement of many social groups. Although broad-scale legislation had struck down many ascriptive barriers in the law, in practice a large majority of society remained oppressed. The Mills' naiveté in considering that inequality of rights was a "relic of the past" (1970:30) rests solely on their belief that rationality provides a new moral base for society. The Mills envisioned the Western world as the most advanced of all forms of civilization; yet this view is both **ethnocentric** (meaning that it regards one's own group as superior to all others) and is founded on class- and race-based assumptions about the desirability of present social arrangements. The Mills' commitment to rationality as a moral basis for society blinded them to the facts of continuing inequality and oppression of underprivileged peoples in the contemporary Western world.

The Mills' optimism about social change also led them to assume that women's status had necessarily improved over time. They wrote:

> *Experience does say, that every step in improvement has been so invariably accompanied by a step in raising the social position of women, that historians and philosophers have been led to adopt their elevation or disbasement as on the whole the surest test and most correct measure of the civilization of a people or an age. Through all the progressive period of human history, the condition of women has been approaching nearer to equality with men. (Mill, 1970:37)*

Feminist studies have shown that women's status has not necessarily improved with time (Kelly-Gadol, 1976). In Western culture, women's status has fluctuated, depending on developments in industrialization, capitalism, the advent of technology, and transformations in patriarchal relations. The Mills' assumption that the position of women was necessarily improving is a reflection of their sincere commitment to bringing about that change. Because they did not study specific historical developments in women's roles created by capitalism and patriarchy, however, their analysis of social change has a hollow ring.

These criticisms aside, the Mills' arguments for the emancipation of women still stand as provocative, replete with insightful ideas on the relationship of gender inequality to other systems of unjust authority and to the repression of individual freedom. Their failures result from what they did not explain, not from the errors of their inquiry. It is uncanny how truthful the Mills' ideas seem today.

Apart from the particular eloquence of their style, their words could be those of a contemporary feminist. This discovery is, in fact, rather disheartening, for it indicates how unchanged are many of the structures resulting in women's inequality, despite the many changes that have occurred.

≈ *The Critique of Liberalism*

The problems in the Mills' philosophy typify the limitations of the liberal perspective. Liberalism seeks changes in the way individuals are treated in social systems. In fact, the strengths of the liberal feminist position are its insistence on individual freedom, its toleration for diverse life-styles, and its support of economic, social, and political reform. These strengths reflect the bourgeois origins of liberal thought, which emphasize the importance and autonomy of the individual. One reason liberalism is accepted as the norm for feminists is that its philosophy reflects Western cultural values of individualism and personal achievement (Eisenstein, 1981). Liberalism's strengths are also its weaknesses, for each of these positions has serious limitations that the liberal framework does not address. Consider, for example, the issues of individual liberty and tolerance liberals accord to diverse life-styles. Many probably agree that it is important to tolerate the individual's right to choose his or her life-style. The liberal perspective encourages us to say, for example, that gays and lesbians are entitled to live as they please. What liberalism does not do is to recognize that heterosexuality is institutionalized in this society and, thus, is made compulsory for all except those who are deviant. From a liberal perspective, lesbianism is tolerated as a choice, but it is not seen as a positive alternative to the patriarchal control of female sexuality.

Similarly, the liberal perspective fails to explain the institutionalized basis for race and class oppression. By claiming that all persons—regardless of race, class, or gender—should have equal opportunities, liberals accept the existing system as valid, often without analyzing the structured inequality on which it is based. From a liberal feminist perspective, experiences of women of color are some among many. Explaining how White women's and White men's experience is also conditioned by racism is not part of the liberal program. Liberal feminism sees race as a barrier to individual freedom, but it does not see that the position of White women is structurally tied to that of women of color. This connection remains for other theoretical perspectives to make.

Liberal feminism's perspective on individual rights does remind us that social change must provide the basis for individual well-being; therefore, liberal feminism is premised on humanistic ethics for social change. Some feminists also argue that liberal feminism recognizes that women form a sexual class (Eisenstein, 1981). Because liberal feminism is based on the premise that individuals are autonomous beings, it does recognize that women are independent of men. Early feminists (such as Wollstonecraft and the Mills) viewed women as having an independent and collective existence apart from men; they are not merely different as individuals. Liberal feminist programs for change leave this point underdeveloped. They offer solutions that would simply grant individual rights; therefore, liberal feminism to some extent denies the connections between individuals and leaves its political goal as one of equality. In saying that women should be equal to men, liberal feminism does not specify which men women want to be equal to; thus, it glosses over the class and race structure of societal relations (Eisenstein, 1981).

As a result, liberal feminism leaves much unanswered. It does not explain the emergence of gender inequality, nor can it account, other than by analogy, for effects of race and class stratification in women's lives. Its analysis for change tends to be limited to issues of equal opportunity and individual choice. As a political ethic, it insists on individual liberty and also challenges any social, political, and economic practice that discriminates against persons on the basis of group or individual characteristics. The major change advocated by liberal feminists is that more women should be admitted to the existing political and economic systems; consequently, **discrimination** (i.e., differential treatment) is a key concept within the liberal framework, as is the conceptualization of women's oppression as the result of learned gender roles. The liberal perspective emphasizes gradual reform and assumes that progress can be accomplished within the structure of existing political, social, and economic institutions.

The limits of liberal feminism are also clear in contemporary political arguments about affirmative action. Whereas affirmative action was developed to root out the effects of historic discrimination, its opponents argue that it promotes race-specific and gender-specific policies and that these are counter to the premises of civil rights—that no one should be treated differently *because of* their race, gender, or religion. Ironically, opposition to affirmative action stems from conservatives, but the framework of the argument against affirmative action is founded on the liberal premise of race-blind and gender-blind remedies. As a result, liberals who have supported affirmative action to promote social change are left with little argument to counter the conservative movement against race-specific and gender-specific policies. It remains for more radical perspectives to analyze how remedies can be found that directly confront the fundamental problems in social institutions that create and perpetuate gender and other forms of injustice.

❧ Summary

Sociological theory explains the relationship between observed social fact and the social structure of society and culture. Feminist theory purports to understand the conditions women and men face in society and to seek ways to liberate women and men from oppressive societal conditions. Feminist theory emerges from both liberal and radical traditions. Three theoretical perspectives have emerged in feminist theory: liberal feminism, socialist feminism, and radical feminism. Liberal feminists emphasize social and legal reform through policies designed to create equal opportunities for all.

The origins of contemporary liberal feminism are in the Age of Enlightenment, which valued critical inquiry and the ability of men's rationality to achieve social justice. Feminists have criticized the Enlightenment thinkers for excluding women from their philosophies and have depicted the Enlightenment as a period celebrating man's rational power. Mary Wollstonecraft was one of the earliest European feminists. She argued that gender roles were the basis for women's experience and thinking and she rejected arguments asserting natural differences between the sexes. Harriet Martineau is a founding mother of sociology whose work established some of the early principles of sociological thought. John Stuart Mill and Harriet Taylor Mill's liberal philosophy is a basis for modern liberal feminism. Their work provides the basis for arguments promoting equal opportunity for women and the removal of barriers standing in the way of women's achievements.

The strength of liberal feminism is its emphasis on individual liberty, but it is weak in its analysis of the intersections of race, gender, and class in social structure. The emphasis on individual rights in liberal theory encourages changes that would admit more women to the existing political and economic system, but liberalism does not challenge the fundamental structure of existing institutions.

ᘔ♠ *Key Terms*

Age of Enlightenment	feminist theory	meritocracy
discrimination	liberal feminism	
ethnocentric	liberalism	

ᘔ♠ *Discussion Questions/Projects for Thought*

1. Identify a nineteenth-century African American woman whose works have been published. (See the collections by Anne Sterling, *We Are Your Sisters*, New York: Norton, 1984, or Gerda Lerner, *Black Women in White America*, New York: Vintage, 1973.) How would you describe the political theory of this thinker? How does her thinking compare to the feminism of White women during this period?

2. Identify one of the feminist organizations in your local community or state. Ask the organization for any material it has describing its goals and orientation. How would you describe the political orientation of this group? Is it based in liberal, socialist, or radical feminism? Identify the specific political ideals and actions that explain your answer.

3. Suppose that Mary Wollstonecraft were to return today and observe gender relations. How might she revise her feminist theory? What would she retain in her thinking?

❧ *Suggested Readings*

Berry, Mary Frances. 1986. *Why ERA Failed: Politics, Women's Rights, and the Amending Process of the Constitution*. Bloomington: Indiana University Press.
This case study of the Equal Rights Amendment (ERA), written by the former director of the U.S. Civil Rights Commission, is an illustration of liberal politics, how they work, and why the passage of the ERA failed, despite its widespread support.

Eisenstein, Zillah. 1981. *The Radical Future of Liberal Feminism*. New York: Longman.
Although liberalism is typically criticized for its inability to make radical social change, Eisenstein shows the underlying radical philosophy of liberal feminism and its connection to fundamental social change.

England, Paula, ed. 1993. *Theory on Gender/Feminism on Theory*. New York: Aldine de Gruyter.
This collection of articles examines contemporary sociological theory from a feminist perspective and engages the reader in seeing what feminists contribute to contemporary theory and what these theories contribute to the sociology of gender.

Frye, Marilyn. 1983. *The Politics of Women's Reality*. Trumansburg, NY: The Crossing Press.
As a major feminist philosopher, Marilyn Frye illustrates the significance of feminist theory for analyzing society and women within society.

Jaggar, Alison M., and Paula S. Rothenberg, eds. 1993. *Feminist Frameworks: Alternative Theoretical Accounts of the Relations between Women and Men*, 3rd ed. New York: McGraw-Hill.
This collection of articles is organized around seven theoretical perspectives: conservatism, liberalism, classical Marxism, socialist feminism, radical feminism, multicultural feminism, and global feminism. It is one of the best anthologies to present the different theoretical positions of feminism and to do so by exploring how different theories explain certain issues in women's lives, including sexuality, work, and family.

Rossi, Alice, ed. 1970. *Essays on Sex Equality*. Chicago: University of Chicago Press.
This book includes reprints of the major essays on women by John Stuart Mill and Harriet Taylor Mill. Rossi's introduction provides the biographical and historical context for interpreting their work and their collaboration.

Sterling, Anne, ed. 1984. *We Are Your Sisters: Black Women in the Nineteenth Century*. New York: Norton.
This collection of writings is an outstanding sampler of the social and political thought of African American women in the nineteenth century. Although few of them have ever been formally recognized as major intellectuals, the anthology makes clear their major contributions to American thought.

Radical Alternatives
Socialist and Radical Feminism

Radical perspectives in feminist theory arise from the critique of liberalism and also from a dialogue with Marxist perspectives on women's position in society. Two radical alternatives to liberal feminism are socialist feminism and radical feminism. **Socialist feminism** interprets women's oppression as primarily based in capitalism and its interrelationship with patriarchal gender relations. **Radical feminism** analyzes patriarchal social relations as the primary cause of women's oppression.

Whereas the liberal framework emphasizes learned gender roles and discrimination as the primary causes of women's oppression, both of these more radical perspectives attempt to explain how gender develops and persists as a social, economic, and political category. The radical analysis goes beyond the goal of including women in existing societal institutions by arguing that dominant institutions are organized through gender, race, and class oppression. Interpreting the specific process by which this oppression occurs is the divergence between socialist and radical feminist perspectives.

Radical feminists criticize liberal feminists for assuming that sexism is largely a remnant of traditional beliefs and practices. Because of their indignation over the continuation of past practices, liberal feminists have widely documented the effects of discrimination and have tried to locate the institutional practices and policies that foster continuing discrimination. As shown in the previous chapter, the liberal feminist perspective takes women's equality with men as its major political goal. In distinct contrast to this perspective, socialist and radical feminism challenge the social, political, and economic analysis of the liberal perspective. Equality, these alternatives suggest, would only put some women on a par with men without transforming the conditions of oppression that produce gender as well as class and race relations. This chapter reviews socialist and radical feminism and shows how each emerges from an ongoing debate with Marxist theory and its analysis of gender, class, and race relations.

At first glimpse, socialist and radical feminism may seem extreme to those considering them for the first time. The popular association of socialism with communism makes it seem an anathema to U.S. students who have been raised in a strong anticommunist culture. Nonetheless, socialist feminist theory reveals much about the social organization of capitalism and its particular impact on women. Likewise, radical feminism conjures up images of man-hating and extremism when, in fact, radical feminism has produced some of the best explanations of and solutions to high rates of violence against women. It is important to discard negative stereotypes of socialist and radical feminists in trying to understand these important theoretical viewpoints. As you will see, socialist and radical feminist analyses have contributed much to our understanding of women's (and men's) experiences in society.

The focus of this chapter is on the contemporary issues posed by these perspectives, although their intellectual origins are rooted in the nineteenth century and in an ongoing dialogue with Marx since that time. As feminist analysis has shifted from liberal concerns with equality and gender roles, new questions have arisen regarding gender as a social, political, and economic category. In relation to Marxist theory, feminist theory asks how gender is socially produced and reproduced and how it is related to class analysis. It asks, further, whether women's oppression is a consequence of class oppression and how patriarchy—simply defined as rule by men—is linked to class relations. Each of these analytical questions is developed in this chapter, but first, some additional background to the emergence of radical feminism and a review of classical Marxist analysis are presented.

❧ *The Political Context of Radical Feminism*

Just as liberal feminism has its roots in the historical frameworks of liberal thought, so do radical feminist perspectives have earlier intellectual and political roots. In the nineteenth century, the same political and economic changes that fostered the development of liberal political philosophy also stimulated the emergence of more radical perspectives, most notably the work of Karl Marx (1818–1883) and his collaborator, Friedrich Engels (1820–1895). Marx and Engels's major essay, *The Communist Manifesto*, was published in Paris in 1848, the same year and city as John Stuart Mill's primary work, *On Liberty*. The differences between the radical perspective of Marx and Engels and the liberal perspective of Mill point to the profound controversies over the analysis of social structure and social change that historical changes in the structure of Western society were generating at this time.

The middle and second half of the nineteenth century in western Europe and the United States were marked by the vast growth of capitalism and the rapid expansion of industrialization, along with widespread social and political changes inspired by the French Revolution and, in the United States, by the elimination of slavery, the expansion of western territories, and urbanization. The climate of social reform that began in this period set the stage for the British suffrage movement and the American feminist movement of the late nineteenth and early twentieth centuries. The political discourse that this period fostered created a diversity of political and social thought that fostered the growth of sociological theory (Bramson, 1961; Zeitlin, 1968).

Nineteenth-century feminism is typically characterized as a reform movement whose ideas are rooted in the liberal thought of persons such as John Stuart Mill and Harriet Taylor Mill, but the politics of this movement also emerged through debate and action between radical and reform leaders. Some groups in the nineteenth- and early twentieth-century feminist movement were as much influenced by class and union politics as they were by the spirit of moral reform characterizing the women's rights approach of nineteenth-century feminism. Case studies of both the suffrage movement (DuBois, 1978) and the women's trade union movement (Dye, 1975) in the United States reveal the complexities of the movements' attempts to grapple with the complexities of class, race, and gender politics. In the end, however, most nineteenth-century feminists were unable to transcend the class biases of their middle-class majority leadership. Some feminist leaders, such as Susan B. Anthony, also used prevailing racist and anti-immigrant sentiments to attract members and to articulate movement ideologies (DuBois, 1978; Dye, 1975). These failures to unite women across class and race limited the effectiveness of nineteenth century feminism, but some feminists in this period established a radical tradition for alliances with working-class women and articulated the beginnings of an analysis linking gender, race, and class oppression.

Many of the feminists of this period and the early twentieth century were also socialists who worked for radical causes, in addition to their feminist politics. Charlotte Perkins Gilman (1860–1935) developed a socialist feminist analysis in *Women and Economics* (published in 1898). She proposed that housework should be communally organized, particularly for working mothers, who were entering the paid labor force at this time. She suggested that apartment houses have one common kitchen where all families could be served and that cleaning, child care, nursing, and teaching should be paid professional work. The responsibility for this work should not fall on individual families, she thought, but instead on apartment house managers (Rossi, 1973). Other radical thinkers of the time, such as Emma Goldman (1869–1940) and Agnes Smedley (1892–1950), did not define feminism as their primary cause, but they clearly linked the oppression of women to other forms of economic and political oppression.

Although not all contemporary radical feminists have a Marxist analysis of women's oppression, the framework of Marxist thinking is extremely important in the evolution of feminist thinking, particularly for socialist feminism. Reviewing Marxist thought thus provides a starting point for understanding later analytical frameworks in feminist thought.

❧ *The Marxist Perspective*

Karl Marx

Marxist thought is one of the most influential and insightful analyses in modern intellectual history. Some argue that most sociological theory even developed as a dialogue with the ideas that Karl Marx (1818–1883) inspired (Zeitlin, 1968). Certainly, for modern feminism, Marx's ideas are pivotal.

Marx himself began writing as a student, first at the University of Bonn (1835–1836) and then at the University of Berlin (1836–1841), where he was involved in some of the most politically and intellectually controversial movements of his time. He was active in a group known as the Young Hegelians, who based their studies and activities on the work of the German philosopher Georg Wilhelm Friedrich Hegel (1770–1832). Hegel's philosophy is based on the idea that persons create their world through reason; thus, rational ideas form the objective reality through which human beings construct their world. Hegel's philosophy, furthermore, sees the "real" as emanating from the "divine" (Giddens, 1971:3), and Christian theology is an important foundation for his work. The Young Hegelians followed Hegel's concern with theology and adopted his philosophical perspective, until their outlook was radically transformed by the appearance of Ludwig Feuerbach's work *The Essence of Christianity* in 1841. Feuerbach (1804–1872) reversed the philosophy of ideas in Hegel's work by arguing that ideas follow the existence of human action. Feuerbach wrote, "Thought proceeds from being, not being from thought" (Giddens, 1971:3). From Feuerbach's thesis, the divine is a construction of human thought; human activity, not ideas, provides the basis for social reality.

This philosophy led Marx's teacher and sponsor, Bruno Bauer (1809–1882), to assert that the Bible was a historical document and that Christian theology was a social and historical myth. Bauer was consequently dismissed from the university, as he was declared to be dangerous to the state. In a university system where one's future was dependent on academic sponsorship, Bauer's dismissal meant the end of Marx's academic career. Although Marx received his doctorate of philosophy from the University of Jena in 1841, he, who had once been predicted to be the most outstanding professor of his time, was never to hold a university post. The remainder of his life was spent in political exile and in poverty. He continued to write, working occasionally as a journalist, but he was forced to move from Germany to Paris and later to London as he was expelled by various governments.

In 1849, Marx moved to London, where he was to spend the last 34 years of his life. His family was extremely poor; several of his children died of malnutrition and disease. When his sixth child was born, he saw the birth as a catastrophe, because two of his children had already died and a third was gravely ill. He was scarcely consoled when the child was born a girl, Jenny Julia Eleanor, as he announced to his friend and collaborator Friedrich Engels that the child was "unfortunately of the sex par excellence" and "had it been a male the matter would be more acceptable" (Kapp, 1972:21). Loans from Engels supported the family, along with Marx's occasional journalism jobs. Throughout this difficult time, Marx continued writing and studying, and he produced several works that would change the course of world history and the history of social thought.

Historical Materialism

The ideas Marx developed always reflected the early influences of Hegel and Feuerbach and resulted in a theoretical perspective often called **historical materialism** (also referred to as **dialectical materialism**). The central thesis of historical materialism is that the material conditions of people's lives shape their behavior and their beliefs; human consciousness and behavior are formed by the interplay between persons as subjects and as objects in the world in which they live. Because human beings have the capacity to reflect on their actions, their ideas (and ideals) are reflections of their material world. People's relationship to their environment and what they think of it are mediated by the particular historical and social milieux of which they are a part. The possibilities for human existence are shaped by the choices and constraints imposed by material organization. Specifically, for Marx, the materialist thesis saw human production—what men and women actually do—as the basis for social structure. The cause of social change, for Marx, lay not in ideas and values that are abstracted from human experience. Instead, he saw societal change as emerging from the social relations and activities that themselves emerge through human labor and **systems of production** (Giddens, 1971).

The method of dialectical materialism, unlike that of many other sociological theories, is not deterministic. In other words, Marx did not see human history and experience as determined by particular features of social structure but rather thought that social structure and social change are always emerging and reemerging according to the choices human beings make. In addition, Marx said that this means there will always be contradictions within society and in the experience of human beings in society. That is to say, because social life is not simply determined, it will always involve inconsistencies and the tendency for conflict. Social change, according to Marx, arises from these contradictions and the action of human groups in trying to solve them. The dialectical method is "an approach to problems that visualizes the world as an interconnected totality undergoing a variety of changes due to internal conflicts of opposing forces with opposing interests" (Sokoloff, 1980:71).

Marx also assumed that human beings are distinguished from animals because they produce their means of survival. Through their productive work, humans also create new needs. He concluded that if human work is oppressive, then all social life is distorted. Human beings do more than merely exist; they reach their full human potential for creative living through social consciousness and their struggle against oppression. According to Marx, systems of production that distort human potential and, consequently, deny the realization of the species must be transformed by changing social relations and, consequently, through revolution.

Marx explicitly rejected a biologically determinist view of human nature, because he saw human production and reproduction as interacting with social and physical environments. Different forms of social organization produce different social relations, because, in Marxist theory, the systems of human production and reproduction create the conditions for everyday life. Marx and Engels defined **production** as the labor humans perform to satisfy their immediate needs and **reproduction** as the physical re-creation of both the species and the social systems in which human beings reproduce. In Engels's words, production and reproduction are the central features of human society:

According to the materialistic conception, the determining factor in history is, in the final instance, the production and reproduction of immediate life. This, again, is of a two-fold character: on the one side, the production of the means of existence, of food, clothing and shelter and the tools necessary for that production; on the other side, the production of human beings themselves, the propagation of the species. The social organization under which the people of a particular historical epoch and a particular country live is determined by both kinds of production: by the stage of development of labor on the one hand and of the family on the other. (Engels, 1884/1972:71–72)

Feminists have argued that Marx and Engels never fulfilled their promise of developing a materialist perspective to account for productive *and* reproductive activity (Eisenstein, 1979; Flax, 1976). Marx and Engels also clearly place reproduction solely within the family. They devote most of their analysis to class relations and systems of production, the alienation of human labor, and the struggle of the working classes against capitalism. In spite of their recognition of the dual importance of production and reproduction, their analysis subordinates reproduction and the family to economic systems of production. They consider production to be primary because it is necessary for maintaining the material basis for satisfying the most immediate requirements for survival. As you will see, classical Marxism sees women's oppression as a reflection of the more fundamental form of oppression by class; thus, sexism is a secondary phenomenon and, assumedly, will disappear with a revolution in class relations. It is on this point that socialist and radical feminists depart from classical Marxist feminists, because they would argue that the oppression of women itself is fundamental (Jaggar and Rothenberg, 1993).

Class and Capitalism

The materialist perspective of Marx and Engels sees human activity (as it is engaged in productive relations) as the mainspring of social change and as the determining feature of social organization. In Marx's analysis, the economic mode of production forms the **infrastructure** of social organization; other institutions form the **superstructure**, meaning that they reflect the essential character of the economic system.

In the Western capitalist societies that Marx observed, the economic infrastructure was marked primarily by class struggle—the division of society into groups characterized by their relationship to the means of production. Under capitalism, two new major classes emerge: *capitalists*, who own the means of production, and the *proletariat* (or working class), who sell their labor to capitalist owners in exchange for wages. Two minor classes also exist: the bourgeoisie (merchants, managers, and artisans, for example), who become functionally dependent on capitalism, although they do not own the means of production; and the lumpenproletariat, who have no stable social location because they are individuals from a variety of classes and social locations. In Marx and Engels's words, they form "the 'dangerous class,' the social scum, that passive rotting mass thrown off by the lowest layers of old society" (Tucker, 1972:25).

The Marxist concept of class differs significantly from that of non-Marxist social scientists, who use it to refer to stratified status or income hierarchies (see Chapter 5). **Class**, in the Marxist sense, refers specifically to the relationship of a group to the societal means of production; thus, it indicates a system of relationships, not a unit of like persons. Similarly, the concept of "ownership" refers not primarily to the accumulation of goods (which in Marxist theory may occur in any class), but to the actual ownership of a society's productive enterprises.

Society emerges, according to Marxist thought, through class struggle; according to Marx and Engels, "The history of all hitherto society is the history of class struggles" (1970:16). Classes emerge as a society produces a surplus; as a division of labor emerges, thereby allowing for surplus production, the accumulation of a surplus can be appropriated by one group. As a result, this group stands in an exploitative relationship to the mass of producers, and class conflict is established (Giddens, 1971). Marx and Engels point out that the first division of labor is the division of labor by sex for the purpose of propagating children and controlling women's labor in the household; gender thus provides the first class antagonism. They (and most subsequent Marxist thinkers), however, leave this point without further development.

As capitalism develops, the capitalist class appropriates the wealth produced by the subordinate classes because the capitalists have the power to control the conditions under which other classes work. The working class owns only its labor, which it must sell for wages; the capitalists, in turn, exercise the power to determine what wages they will pay and the conditions under which people work. As capitalists try to increase their profits, they do so at the increasing expense of laborers. Profit comes from the fact that workers produce more value than the wages they receive. The craft of distinctive workers becomes less important than the value of mass-produced commodities. Material objects, then, take on greater value than the workers who produce them. In effect, in Marxist analysis, the value of individual human activity decreases as the material value of the created products increases.

Human beings, then, become alienated from the process, in the sense that they do not control or own the products of their labor; they choose neither the form nor the use of the products they make. Additionally, workers are alienated from each other, and they become alienated from themselves because they do not exercise the human ability to transform nature to their own design.

Politically, according to Marx, workers must end the tyranny of private ownership of the means of production by reorganizing the means of production (and, feminists would add, reproduction); the accumulation of profit in the hands of a few must be eliminated. Marxists see that social changes that do not strike at the material basis of social life—capital accumulation by the owning class—will be insufficient because they will not change the underlying causes of social organization.

Ideology and Consciousness

The materialist thesis of Marx is also central to the perspective on consciousness and ideas that is developed throughout Marxist theory. Systems of knowledge take their historical form in response to the mode of production. Marx argued that the ideas of a period are a reflection of the interests of the ruling class (see Chapter 3). Marx wrote:

> *The production of ideas, of conceptions, of consciousness, is at first directly interwoven with the material activity and the material intercourse of men, the language of real life. . . . We do not set out from what men say, imagine, conceive nor from men as narrated, thought of, imagined, conceived, in order to arrive at men in the flesh. We set out from real, active men, and on the basis of their real life-process we demonstrate the development of the ideological reflexes and echoes of this life process.* (Marx, The German Ideology, *in Tucker, 1972:118–119)*

Basic to this perspective on the sociology of knowledge is the proposition that "it is not the consciousness of men that determines their being, but, on the contrary, their social being that determines their consciousness" (Marx, *A Contribution to the Critique of Political Economy*, in Tucker, 1972:4). Those who own the means of production also determine the ruling ideas of the period.

Consciousness is determined by class relations, for even though persons will normally try to identify what is in their best interest, under capitalism the ruling class controls the production of ideas. Also, even though humans create practical ideas from experience, most of their experience is determined by capitalist relations of production. The ideas that are disseminated through communication systems, including language, serve to authorize a reality that the ruling class creates. In this sense, ideas become **ideology**—understood to mean a system of beliefs that legitimate and maintain the status quo (see also Chapter 3).

For feminists, Marx's work on ideology is fundamental to their understanding of sexism. Sexism, as an ideology that justifies the power of men over women, emerges not in the best interest of women but as a defense of male domination. Like other ideologies, sexist ideology is a means by which one class rules a society and sanctions the society's social relations. The extent to which women believe in the precepts of sexist ideology is only a reflection of sexist social relations that include the powers of coercion (whether subtle or overt) and social control.

False consciousness emerges as the subordinate group accepts the world view of the dominant class. Because consciousness changes with historical change, at the time that workers see the nature of their exploitation, false consciousness is transformed into **class consciousness** and workers take the revolutionary struggle into their own hands.

Marx's theory is more than an academic analysis, because the idea that theory must be connected to social and political practice (*praxis*, in his words) is central to his work. Revolutionary theory is to be created by intellectuals who emerge from and are associated with the working class. Social criticism has no value unless coupled with material change. In *The German Ideology*, he wrote:

> *All forms and products of consciousness cannot be dissolved by mental criticism, by resolution into "self-consciousness" or transformation into "apparitions," "spectres," "fancies," etc., but only by the practical overthrow of the actual social relations which gave rise to this idealistic humbug; that not criticism, but revolution is the driving force of history. (cited in Tucker, 1972:128)*

Marx saw human beings as potentially revolutionary because their capabilities for creative work and social consciousness far exceed those allowed them under capitalist organization (Eisenstein, 1979). This fact provides the basis for optimism in Marx's work, because it lays the foundation for radical change and the transformation from human oppression to human liberation.

The Question of Women

Marx and Engels's analysis of women's oppression is drawn mostly from their writing on the family, especially Engels's essay *The Origin of the Family, Private Property, and the State*, published in 1884 after Marx's death. Feminists who, in the beginning of the contemporary women's movement, were looking for alternative analyses to the liberal perspective began with this classical Marxist perspective. Their later criticisms of Marx and Engels are based primarily on the discussion of the family proposed by Engels.

Although Engels stated in the preface to *The Origin of the Family, Private Property, and the State* that production and reproduction together are the determining factors of history, he saw family relations as derived from the economic mode of production. From a Marxist perspective, in capitalist societies, forms of the family change as class relations change, thus making family relations secondary to economic and class relations. In keeping with their perspective on the social origins of ideas, Marx and Engels would say, however, that the social image of the family is an idealized one that disguises the real economic structure of family relations.

They described the family under capitalism as a microcosm of the society's larger class relations; so, particularly in bourgeois families, the wife is the proletariat. Engels wrote:

> *In the great majority of cases today, at least in the possessing classes, the husband is obliged to earn a living and support his family and that in itself gives him a position of supremacy, without any need for special legal ties and privileges. Within the family he is the bourgeois and the wife represents the proletariat. (1884/1972:137)*

Monogamous marriage, Marx and Engels argued, develops as part of the formation of private property. Particularly in the bourgeois family, the development of private property creates the need to determine lineage for the purpose of inheritance. Engels wrote:

> *Monogamy arose from the concentration of considerable wealth in the hands of a single individual—a man—and from the need to bequeath this wealth to the children of that man and of no other. For this purpose, the monogamy of the woman did not in any way interfere with open or concealed polygamy on the part of the man. (1884/1972:138)*

Engels did not explain how men and not women came to control property; therefore, feminists have criticized the Marxist perspective for not explaining the origins of patriarchy.

Marx and Engels discussed marriage as being, for women, a form of prostitution. Engels wrote:

> *Marriage is conditioned by the class position of the parties and is to that extent always a marriage of convenience.... This marriage of convenience turns often enough into crassest prostitution—sometimes of both partners, but far more commonly of the woman, who only differs from the ordinary courtesan in that she does not let out her body on piece-work as a wage-worker, but sells it once and for all into slavery. (1884/1972:134)*

Marx and Engels defined marriage as based on economic relations, although they made it clear that they would have preferred to see it based on individual sex-love. In marriage and the family, Marx and Engels recognized the woman's role is to be responsible for household management and child care. They argued that household work becomes a private service under advanced capitalism, because it loses the public character it has in earlier forms of economic life. In advanced capitalism, the work of the housewife is both a private service to the male head of the household and an unpaid economic service to the society as a whole. Marx and Engels concluded that "the modern individual family is founded on the open or concealed domestic slavery of the wife, and modern society is a mass composed of these individual families as its molecules" (Engels, 1884/1972:137).

Based on their analysis of the family, Marx and Engels saw emancipatory social change in family relations as occurring only with the abolition of private property. Although they maintained a wish for monogamous relationships, they wanted monogamy to be the expression of a sexual commitment based on love, not property; furthermore, although they did not use the modern language of double standards, what they hoped for was monogamy for *both* men and women, not masked polygamy for men and monogamy for women.

Because Marx and Engels saw male supremacy in the family as originating with the accumulation of property and the development of class relations, they suggested that the liberation of women will occur as the result of class struggle. Women's status is derived from the economic organization of society; therefore, the liberation of women will follow with the revolution of the workers and the abolition of private property. Although Marx and Engels noted that the gender division of labor is the first class oppression, their analysis assumes that women's oppression is secondary to oppression by class and that women will be liberated when class oppression is ended.

It is on this point that socialist and radical feminists begin their critique of Marx. These feminists agree with much of Marx and Engel's analysis, but they disagree that the oppression of women is secondary to class oppression. Socialist feminists essentially agree with Marx's theory of class relations, although they believe that gender relations are equally important in the determination of historical social relations.

Radical feminists, on the other hand, identify patriarchy as an autonomous historical fact and consider gender relations to be the fundamental form of oppression. Class and racial-ethnic oppression, radical feminists argue, are extensions of patriarchal inequality. Accordingly, radical feminists see the abolition of male supremacy as their primary political goal. Although radical feminists differ in the extent to which they use Marxist theory, both socialist and radical feminists would agree that Marx and Engels ignored their own observations on gender oppression. The Marxist assumption that gender oppression would disappear with the abolition of private property too easily assumes that gender is of secondary importance in the determination of social, political, and economic relations.

❧ Socialist Feminism

The Critique of Marx

The emergence of *socialist feminism* in the 1970s stemmed largely from feminists' dissatisfaction with classical Marxist perspectives on women and the family. Marx and Engels, socialist feminists argued, did not seriously consider their own point that sexual division of labor is the first form of class antagonism. As a result, they too easily assumed that economic class relations are the most critical relations defining women's place in society. Too many questions—cross-cultural, historical, and contemporary—stand in the way of such a theoretical assumption. Are women subordinated to men in preclass societies? Why does women's oppression continue even in socialist societies? Where, in advanced capitalist societies, do women fit into the Marxist definition of class?

Questions such as these lead socialist feminists to conclude that women's oppression cannot be reduced to capitalism alone, although capitalism remains as a highly significant source of women's oppression. The socialist feminist perspective begins with the point that although economic class relations are important in determining women's status, gender relations may be equally important. Socialist feminists see that class and gender relations intersect in advanced capitalist societies (Hartmann, 1976) and that class relations alone do not account for the location of women and men in social life (Jaggar and Rothenberg, 1993). According to this perspective, eradicating social class inequality alone will not necessarily eliminate sexism as well.

As feminists have asked these new questions, they have had a dialogue with Marxist theory and an independent theoretical tradition in feminist studies. Feminist theory questions how biological and social reproduction are tied to the mode of production; how patriarchal relations are tied to the development and maintenance of class relations; whether women's oppression is primarily a question of gender or class; and how systems of race, class, and gender oppression interact with each other.

On the first point, feminists argue that Marx and Engels ignored their statement that forms of production and reproduction constitute the basis for social organization. Marxist theory defines reproduction as the social (as well as physical) production of workers. The family is the place, in advanced capitalism, where workers are restored (through food and shelter) so as to be able to reenter the labor force on a daily basis. Reproduction in the family includes the socialization of workers to capitalist values and personalities. Implicit in the classical Marxist argument is the idea that the family is a separate force in history, although one subordinate to the forces of production. Although Marx and Engels noted historical changes in the family as a productive unit, they did not develop an analysis of women's place in the family, nor did they explain the gender politics of male-female relations in the family in any terms other than property relations.

✎ Family and Economy in Capitalist Society

One of the first extended analyses of Marxist theory to women's place in society was that of Juliet Mitchell. Because her work has been so influential in the development of socialist feminism, it is elaborated in detail here. Mitchell's work, like that of other Marxist feminists, analyzes the interrelationship between the economy and the family, placing the origins of the family in the dynamics established by the economics of capitalism.

Mitchell begins with the classical Marxist premise that the economic mode of production is the defining factor of social organization, but she argues that, in Marx and Engels's theory, the liberation of women remains an abstract ideal, not a problem to be explained. Marx and Engels assumed that the liberation of women would occur with the transition from capitalism to socialism, but Mitchell contends that a specific theory of women's oppression is needed if the liberation of women is to occur with the transition from capitalism to socialism. Although women's role in production is central to their oppression, Mitchell argues that the subordination of women involves the interplay of women's role in reproduction, sexuality, and the socialization of children with the economic mode of production.

The structure of production embraces the structure of the family, which, in turn, includes the structures of sexuality, reproduction, and socialization. Mitchell writes:

> *The contemporary family can be seen as a triptych of sexual, reproductive, and social-*
> *izatory functions (the women's world) embraced by production (the man's world)—*
> *precisely a structure which in the final instance is determined by the economy. The*
> *exclusion of women from production—social human activity—and their confinement*
> *to a monolithic condensation of functions within a unity—the family . . . is the root*
> *cause of the contemporary social definition of women as natural beings. (1971:148)*

Mitchell argues that women were excluded from production in the past because of their presumed physical weakness and the involuntary character of childbearing. Technological developments and automation have now lessened the necessity for physical strength in labor, and the development of contraception makes childbearing a voluntary act. Because contraception makes it possible to separate sexual and reproductive activity, Mitchell maintains that the ideological basis of family life as the unit of sexual and reproductive activity is destroyed, and because biological and social parentage need not be performed by the same person, she concludes that the development of technology and industrialization now makes the liberation of women a possibility. She concludes that "probably it is only in the highly developed societies of the West that an authentic liberation of women can be envisaged today" (1971:121).

Based on her theory, Mitchell assumes that "the entry of women fully into public industry and the right to earn a living wage" (1971:148–149) must be a fundamental goal of women's emancipation movements. The exclusion of women from public industry, their restriction to the private world of the family (where socialization, reproduction, and sexuality are located), and their lack of control over women's work form the basis for their subordination. The ideological assumption of women's dominance in the family obscures their inferior role in production, she argues. Women's full entry into the system of production, coupled with policies to transform the character of family relations, forms the practical implication of the argument she develops.

Mitchell raises a number of issues that remain central to feminist theory. For one, she opens the feminist discussion of the relationship of the family to the economy. The family has both an economic and an ideological role in capitalist systems. As industrial capitalism of the nineteenth and twentieth centuries developed, the family changed from a unit of production to a unit of consumption. As a result of how the family controls women's work in reproduction, sexuality, and socialization, several specific consequences of the family's economic-ideological functions occur for women. The process of consumption obviously supports economic life, but in more subtle ways, it affects the status of women. Sexuality, for example, becomes intermixed with a consumption ethic; under modern capitalism, sexuality becomes marketable. Although this fact supposedly means more sexual freedom for women, it clearly increases their use as sexual objects (1971:142). The economic function of the modern family is also reflected in socialization and reproductive practices because it is in the family that workers are created and sustained for their labor force participation. A capitalist work force supports capitalist enterprises by leaving women with the responsibility for creating the personalities that are appropriate to a capitalist labor force.

In addition, Mitchell argues that the family's ideological role supports the rationale and the inherent contradictions of advanced capitalist societies. The ideology of the family supports values of individualism and personal freedom at the same time that it favors individual accumulation of property. The family becomes typified as a "haven in a heartless world" (Lasch, 1977), where persons are free to be themselves and to consume goods at their pleasure. An essential contradiction of capitalism lies in the fact that as capitalism develops, private property, as well as the real choices necessary for personal freedom, are taken away from the masses. The individualism and freedom that the ideology of the family promises stand in opposition to the fact that capitalism makes these social and economic ideals impossible to realize.

The result is a self-contradictory system in which, ideologically, women are asked to hold together a system that cannot operate as it is supposed to. Mitchell writes, "The family is a stronghold of what capitalism needs to preserve but actually destroys: private property and individualism. The housewife-mother is the guardian and representative of these. She is a backward, conservative force—and this is what her oppression means" (1971:161). According to Mitchell, the one area of women's power—the socialization of children—becomes a mystique for their own oppression.

Marxist feminists attribute the cause of women's oppression directly to the development of capitalism. Their solution to women's oppression is to eliminate the division of labor by gender and, ultimately, to support the transition from capitalism to socialism.

The Question of Separate Spheres

Women have traditionally been associated with the private sphere (the domestic world of home, children, reproduction, and sexuality) and men have been associated with the public sphere (paid work, institutionalized religion, and political authority). Women's work and activity in the private world have also been invisible. One of the accomplishments of feminist theory has been to make the activities of both men and women in the private sphere more visible. Feminist theory has criticized traditional sociological and political theory for focusing primarily on the public world and assuming the public world to be the only place where history, social life, and culture are made. Because the private sphere has been identified with women, it has been perceived as inferior; the public sphere, superior. This conceptualization of the public and private spheres reaches deep into our consciousness, as reflected, for example, in the attitude that women's relationships with each other in the private sphere are insignificant or trivial in the making of history, society, and culture.

The relationship of the public and private spheres is an important theme in the development of feminist theory. Women's relegation to the private, domestic sphere excludes them from public life, and thus from equal access to social and economic resources, although the increasing entry of middle-aged, married women and mothers into the labor force makes it less true that women are confined to the home. Still, women's work in public labor is often said to mirror and extend the private services they provide in the home. Others have also argued that women's confinement to the private sphere is largely a White, middle-class phenomenon; the assumption of a public/private split is therefore a race- and class-bound argument. Without arguing that women's exclusion from the public sphere is the primary basis for their subordination, feminists continue to point out that a theory of women's position must account for the relationship of the private, domestic realm to the public realm of social and economic life (Sacks, 1975).

Zaretsky (1976), for example, argues that the supposed split in the public and private spheres obscures the economic role of the family. The production of food, shelter, and emotional nurturance is a basic material necessity, along with sexuality and reproduction, consequently, even if it is unpaid, housework constitutes socially necessary labor. The idea that the private labor of women is separate from publicly productive labor is, in Zaretsky's analysis, specific to the historical development of capitalism. He argues that the idea of the family as separate from the productive world—*and* as the sphere of women—originated in the nineteenth century with the rise of industrial capitalism. At that time, women's work was ideologically defined as taking place in the home (Cott, 1977), even though most working-class, poor, and minority women continued to work in factories, domestic service, agriculture, and other forms of public labor. Whereas others trace the division of the public and private spheres to earlier historical periods, Zaretsky's work points to the specific dynamics of this split under advanced capitalism.

What is innovative in his work is his equation of the public-private split with a second division—that between the newly emerging concept of personal life and the collective life as found in the social division of labor. Zaretsky writes, "This 'split' between the socialized labour of the capitalist enterprise and the private labour of women in the home is closely related to a second 'split'—between our 'personal' lives and our place within the social division of labour" (1976:29). Personal life, emerging under capitalism, appears to be an autonomous process—as if persons' private lives were governed by their own internal laws. Accordingly, Zaretsky argues that human relations become seen as an end in themselves, detached from the material world of economic fact. Individuals appear unique, and the subjective sphere of self and life-style takes preeminence over the economic relations that, for Zaretsky, define social organization.

Zaretsky's analysis shows how, in the advanced capitalist family, women's primary responsibility is for an emotional world that is ideological in character. Like Mitchell, he sees that advanced capitalism eliminates the production of goods as the basis of the family, but he adds to her analysis that the seeming independence of personal life is a falsehood. Socialist feminist theory and practice must therefore include the elimination of capitalism *and* the transformation of the family and personal life.

The socialist feminist position makes the important point that change in women's status will come only through the transformation of capitalist relations, along with independent efforts to transform family relations as well. Socialist feminism shares with classical Marxism the idea that the oppression of women is primarily an economic fact, although it is buttressed by ideological delusions about the family. Socialist feminism makes the additional point that women's oppression must be related to their position in the private world of reproduction and the family. In sum, socialist feminism suggests that women's oppression extends beyond the area of economic production. As you will see, socialist feminists have recently incorporated an analysis of patriarchy into their theoretical analysis, but the inclusion of patriarchy follows from the analysis developed by radical feminists. It is to their ideas that we now turn.

ɣ Radical Feminism

Patriarchy and the Domination of Women

Socialist feminists argue that class and capitalism are the basis of women's oppression, whereas radical feminists argue that male domination per se is the basis for women's oppression. Radical feminists define **patriarchy** as a "sexual system of power in which the male possesses superior power and economic privilege" (Eisenstein, 1979:17), and they view patriarchy as an autonomous social, historical, and political force. Whereas socialist feminism emphasizes the economic basis of gender relations, radical feminism emphasizes male power and privilege as the bases of social relations. Radical feminism sees patriarchal relations as more fundamental than class relations in determining women's experiences.

Since its inception, the radical feminist position has taken several different directions, some of them more explicitly tied to Marxism than others. Some current radical feminist thought is totally apart from the materialist thesis in Marxist work, locating the causes of oppression solely within patriarchal culture and its control of women (Daly, 1978). Much of radical feminism, however, has developed specifically because of the failure of Marxist perspectives to explain adequately the emergence and persistence of patriarchy. Some early radical feminists attempted to explain the origins of patriarchy by claiming that women controlled many of the early hunting and gathering societies, but men organized themselves to conquer women by force, thereby also gaining control of originally woman-centered forms of social organization. This position is spelled out by Charlotte Bunch:

> *The first division of labor, in pre-history, was based on sex: men hunted, women built the villages, took care of children, and farmed. Women collectively controlled the land, language, culture, and the communities. Men were able to conquer women with the weapons that they developed for hunting when it became clear that women were leading a more stable, peaceful, and desirable existence. We do not know exactly how this conquest took place, but it is clear that the original imperialism was male over female: the male claiming the female body and her service as his territory (or property). (1975:37)*

The claim that matriarchal society predates the emergence of patriarchy is a debatable point. Popular feminist accounts often claim a universal matriarchal history in human social organization (Davis, 1971), but anthropological evidence gives a more cautious interpretation. Research on the transition from primate to human society indicates a high level of cooperation between men and women in early human societies (Zihlman, 1978); studies of early hunting and gathering societies show that, although many groups were matrilineal, they tended to be egalitarian, not matriarchal (Leacock, 1978). Anthropologists conclude that more careful conceptual definitions of power, authority, influence, and status are needed before we can accurately describe women's role in the evolution of human society (Webster, 1975) and before we can make claims about the existence of matriarchal societies. Women's social position has not always been, in every society or in every way, subordinate to that of men (Sacks, 1975). The arrangements between women and men vary widely from society to society and across history. It has taken a great amount of new anthropological research to untangle the early history of male-female relations (Reiter, 1975); moreover, in traditional anthropological accounts, scholars have often projected contemporary assumptions of male supremacy and female social roles into the pasts they have studied. Only now are scholars beginning to find answers to the questions that arise from considering the origins of women's oppression.

The question posed is: How did men gain control of the systems of production and reproduction, and how is women's oppression tied to the development of class systems? Radical feminists concentrate on the first half of the question. They argue that men's control of women cannot be simply explained as based on class oppression and, as the feminist anthropologist Gayle Rubin has written, "No analysis of the reproduction of labor can explain foot-binding, chastity belts, or any of the incredible array of Byzantine, fetishized indignities, let alone the more ordinary ones, which have been inflicted upon women in various times and places" (1975:163). In part, the strength of the radical feminist position is that it is better able to explain men's violence against women and the many cultural practices designed to control female sexuality and reproduction. Radical feminists see patriarchy as having emerged from men's control of female sexuality.

The Sex/Gender System

Rubin's own work on the genesis of women's oppression centers on the concept of the **sex/gender system** as the "set of arrangements by which a society transforms biological sexuality into products of human activity, and in which these transformed sexual needs are satisfied" (1975:159). For Rubin, the oppression of women lies in social systems that create male solidarity, not simply in systems of economic production. Kinship systems, as the observable form of sex/gender systems, relate persons through social categories that may or may not have their basis in biological relations. Beginning with Levi-Strauss's theory in which the essence of kinship systems is the exchange of women (usually through marriage), Rubin goes on to say that "the subordination of women can be seen as a product of the relationships by which sex and gender are organized and produced"

(1975:177). The solidarity expressed through the exchange of women represents solidarity between men. According to Rubin, "the 'exchange' of women is a . . . powerful concept. It . . . places the oppression of women within social systems, rather than in biology. Moreover, it suggests that we look for the ultimate locus of women's oppression within the traffic in women, rather than within the traffic in merchandise" (1975:175).

Rubin also develops the idea that gender is a socially imposed division of the sexes that is reproduced through the production of gender identities. As socialization theory has argued, persons are not created in a gender-neutral process. Their personalities represent the gendered categories around which kinship systems are organized. In the radical feminist analysis, the production of gender sets the preconditions for other forms of domination (Harding, 1981). Men first learn to dominate women, setting a pattern for the domination of others. Economic systems may determine who these others are, but sex and gender systems establish the preconditions for domination to emerge. In the end, radical feminism sees systems of domination based on class, race, or nationality as extensions of the underlying politics of male supremacy (Bunch, 1975).

Radical feminists also see patriarchal institutions as creating myths and forms of social organization that constrain women to exist in male-centered worlds (Daly, 1978). One radical feminist solution to women's subordination is the establishment of women-centered beliefs and systems. For some, this movement has produced the separatist philosophy of radical lesbian feminism, whereby a woman-identified world is created through the attachments women have to each other, not to men.

Sexuality, the State, and Radical Feminism

MacKinnon proposes a radical feminist analysis that takes men's control of women's sexuality as the central fact of the domination of women. As she puts it, "Sexuality is to feminism what work is to Marxism" (1982:515). MacKinnon describes sexuality as a social process that creates, organizes, and directs desire; the process of directing the expression of desire creates the social beings we know as women and men, and their relations create society. She reminds us that through gender socialization, women and men come to identify themselves not just as social beings but also as sexual beings.

Sexuality is the primary sphere of men's power in MacKinnon's radical feminist analysis. Through rape, sexual harassment, incest, and violence against lesbians, men exercise their sexual power over women. Heterosexuality is the institution through which men's power is expressed; gender relations and the family are the specific forms of compulsory heterosexuality. Because this analysis sees heterosexuality as institutionalizing male dominance, men's control of women's sexuality is the linchpin of gender inequality.

As seen in Chapter 10, MacKinnon (1983) departs from both liberal and Marxist thinking about the **state** in analyzing state authority as masculine authority. She argues that liberals see the state as disembodied reason, while Marxists see the state primarily as a reflection of material interests. As a result, liberal analyses of the state see women as simply another interest group and treat women as abstract persons with rights, but they do not see women as a specifically gendered group. In Marxist analyses, the state is a tool of dominance and a force that legitimates ideology; women in this analysis are relegated to just another subordinated group.

MacKinnon argues that the law sees and treats women the way men see and treat women—that is, the state is coercive and ensures men's control over women's sexuality; thus, although the state assumes objectivity as its norm, in practice, women are raped by the state just as they are raped by men. The implication of MacKinnon's analysis is that as long as the "state is male"—meaning that its meaning systems, its mode of operations, and its underlying assumptions are based in men's power—women will be unable to overcome their subordination through actions of the state.

MacKinnon's analysis helps us understand some of the complexities of feminist positions on state intervention. Although many feminists have demanded state intervention in areas such as sexual abuse, discrimination, and family policy, radical feminist analysis suggests that women cannot entrust their liberation to the state. This analysis also demonstrates how thoroughgoing feminist criticism of social structure and social theory is. By challenging the limited and male-centered frameworks of previous theoretical analyses, feminists—including liberals, socialists, and radicals—have forged new questions and new directions for sociological theory and political action.

In sum, whereas socialist feminism sees women's oppression as stemming from their work in the family and the economy, radical feminism sees the oppression of women as the result of men's control of female sexuality and the patriarchal institutions that structure the sex/gender system. The radical feminist therefore takes male domination as the primary fact of women's oppression, whereas socialist feminists see capitalist social structure as the starting point for feminist analysis. Although there are important differences between these two frameworks of feminist thinking, contemporary feminist theory often involves a synthesis of the two perspectives, which is discussed next.

🜲 *Intersections of Capitalism and Patriarchy*

The assumption in radical feminist analyses that gender relations are more fundamental than class relations has posed important questions for feminist theory. The dialogue between radical feminists and socialist feminists has formulated new insights that reject the ahistorical and universalist claims in some radical feminist accounts, but that reckon with the empirical observation that patriarchal relations do precede and exist independently of class relations. Although women in general are not equal to men in class societies, anthropological research shows that property ownership is not the sole basis for men's supremacy (Sacks, 1975). Within this new synthesis, socialist feminists who might earlier have rejected the radical feminist perspective as a causal theory do take seriously radical feminist perspectives on patriarchy. Although socialist feminists still reject the universalist and ahistorical assumptions sometimes found in radical feminist accounts (Rosaldo, 1980), they are grappling with the fact that the oppression of women predates the development of class society, and are therefore trying to relate gender domination more carefully to patriarchal relations and other forms of oppression.

Hartmann's (1981b) analysis of the interaction of patriarchal structures and the development of capitalism is one such work to make this synthesis. Hartmann, a socialist feminist theorist, argues that feminists must identify patriarchy as a social and historical structure if we are to understand Western capitalist societies. She says that Marxist analyses take the relationship of women to the economic system as their central question, but that feminist analyses must take their central question as the relationship of women to men. Understanding capitalism alone will not illuminate women's situation unless we recognize that capitalism is also a patriarchal system of social organization. Hartmann sees the partnership of patriarchy and capitalism as the critical starting point for feminist theory.

In precapitalist societies, Harman argues, men controlled the labor of women and children in the family and "that in so doing men learned the techniques of hierarchical organization and control" (Hartmann, 1976:138). As larger systems of exchange formed beyond local communities, men were faced with the problem of maintaining their control over women. Through the long-standing institution of patriarchy, men learned techniques of social control that, when capitalism emerged in Western societies, were transformed from direct and personal systems of control to indirect and impersonal systems of social control. Hartmann's analysis sees capitalism as emerging in interaction with—and reinforcing—patriarchy but with patriarchy not as the sole cause of gender inequality. Many have pointed out, in fact, that the categories of capitalist systems are potentially gender-blind. Gender stratification developed as a particular hierarchy under capitalism because the precondition of the gender division of labor was extended to newly emerging systems of wage labor.

Hartmann's analysis continues by arguing that "job segregation by sex . . . is the primary mechanism in capitalist society that maintains the superiority of men over women" (1976:139). She documents her argument through historical review of the change from cottage and farm production to industrial factory systems and the transformation of household industry, pointing out that the development of capitalism had a more severe impact on women that it did on men. Not only was women's productive role in the family altered, but they became more economically dependent on men. The gender division of labor was thus transformed from one of interdependence to one of the dependence of women on men. The crux of Hartmann's research lies in her analysis of men's control of the wage-labor market, where she says the reason men excluded, rather than organized, women workers "is explained, not by capitalism, but by patriarchal relations between men and women: Men wanted to assure that women would continue to perform the appropriate tasks at home" (1976:155). Men both benefit from the higher wages they receive *and* from the household division of labor in which they receive women's services.

Although Hartmann's analysis explains much about job segregation by gender and about the interplay of capitalism and patriarchy, it still does not explain the origins of gender stratification. In fact, her work concludes, as earlier suggested by radical feminists, that we will not be able to eliminate the gender division of labor until we have understood and transformed the process of the social production of gender.

The synthesis of radical and socialist feminism shows how the gender division of labor is related to women's position in society as a whole. Where a gender division of labor exists, women's roles are often seen as "complementary and equal" to those of men (Lamphere, 1977; Matthiasson, 1974), leading many to conclude that women's power in society is directly related to their contribution to production and the extent to which they control the resources they produce (Friedl, 1975; Leacock, 1978; Sanday, 1973).

The Status of Women in Socialist Societies

Questions about the relationship of women's oppression to capitalism and patriarchy beg the question of whether women's status improves under socialism. Socialist feminists have had a vision of societies in which women would have full equality before the law, in which they would enter economic production on a par with men, in which private household work would be transformed to a public enterprise through the collectivization of housework and child care, and in which the subjection of women to men would end. Many socialist societies—including Cuba, the People's Republic of China, and African socialist societies such as Zimbabwe—have declared these to be their goals. Most, however, have fallen short of reaching them (Nazzari, 1983). Why? First, it is difficult to sustain economic socialism in the penetrating context of global capitalism, as the move to privatization and capitalism in the People's Republic of China shows. Moreover, the patriarchal totalitarianism of the state in socialist societies has produced political resistance, not necessarily to socialism per se, but to the absence of political freedom. This development is not necessarily reflective of the failure of socialism so much as it is a failure of the antidemocratic political organization.

Can socialism liberate women? Many feminists have asked this question and have concluded that women's status does improve under socialism, but that other factors may limit the progress of women in socialist countries. Cuba is a good example. Before the Cuban revolution, most Cuban women were housewives, not laborers. Castro early spoke of the need to free women from domestic slavery so that they could participate equally in the revolution and share its benefits. Cuba provided increased educational opportunities for women, encouraged their labor force participation, and provided more public services to reduce women's domestic chores in the household. In 1975, Cuba passed the Cuban Family Code, making husband and wife equally responsible for housework and child care. Individual men resented this change, however, and studies of housework in Cuba indicate that men continue to spend far less time on housework than either employed women or housewives.

Men's recalcitrance does not by itself fully explain the difficulties encountered in creating equality between men and women in Cuba. Cuban law requires that men and women must be paid equal wages for equal work, but there are differences in wages for employees in different job classifications. The fact that women tend to be concentrated in the service sector means that, at least for minimum-wage workers, women earn less than men; thus, many women still rely on men's financial support to be able to support their children. Cuban law also requires that men work; women are more likely to be part of a labor reserve. This exacerbates women's economic dependence on men for the support of their families. The government no longer provides free day care, so working mothers have to bear the cost of providing child care. In addition, rules that require businesses to provide paid maternity leave to women may discourage businesses from hiring women when it would be cheaper to hire men. Finally, absenteeism among women workers indicates that many Cuban women still find it difficult to work for wages while they carry out household duties (Nazzari, 1983).

Probably the biggest change for Cuban women as the result of the Cuban Revolution was access to education. One of the early reforms of the revolution was universal access to education, which led increasing numbers of women both into school and into the labor force. Women now consistently surpass boys in scores on exams for entrance to higher education and have become 65 percent of Cuba's professional people and technicians. These gains have led scholars to conclude that Cuba has made significant progress in establishing equality for women. But equality is undercut both by the persistence of patriarchal authority in Cuba and, recently, the economic crisis that has eroded earlier gains. Rural women report having to obtain their husbands' permission to participate in any activity outside the home, including shopping. A distinct gender division of labor also remains—in agricultural labor as well as industrial labor. The economic crisis of the 1990s has also meant that earlier state services have been reduced, university admissions cut in half, and food difficult to get. As a result, women's activism in Cuba, as in other nations where basic needs are critical, is more likely to focus on work and personal safety than on the sexual politics that has characterized U.S. feminism (Smith and Padula, 1996; Padula, 1996; Ramirez, Rojas, and Fraga, 1989; Leiner, 1993; *The Economist*, 1998).

The situation in the People's Republic of China is somewhat different. When the Chinese Communist Party came to power in 1949, China was primarily a patriarchal peasant society. Land reform was the cornerstone of the Communist Party's political platform, and peasants were encouraged to be disobedient to traditional landlords. To win peasants over to the revolutionary cause, the Communist Party embraced the ideals of the traditional patriarchal structure. The communist revolution had the effect of making the patriarchal family available to almost all men, instead of a privileged few, but it did little to liberate women from the domination of this familial form (Stacey, 1983).

In the People's Republic of China, women have been given higher legal status and much has been said about the need to liberate women in this new society. During the period of land reform, land was distributed to heads of families, based on the number of dependents in the family. Individual members of a family unit were given work points that were credited to the family unit, but women were given fewer work points than men for a day's work. Fathers retained control over the family economy and family members.

The People's Republic of China has made efforts to socialize domestic work by providing social services such as public dining rooms, child care centers, and food-processing facilities, but services to relieve the pressures of women's work were the first services cut back when other tensions appeared. As a result, women continue to bear the main burden of domestic chores (O'Kelly and Carney, 1986). Now, the antidemocratic posture of the state makes it difficult to imagine the liberation of women or men. This apprehension was reflected in the concerns about human rights violations that were apparent during the 1995 International Women's Conference in Beijing, sponsored by the United Nations.

In Russia, formerly the Soviet Union, observers have often been struck by the number of women in wage labor and their central position in industrial, professional, and agricultural work. When the government was established in 1917, programs were introduced to give women control over their fertility; to provide economic support for wives, widows, and divorcees; and to provide many public services that would enable women to work outside the home. The state established nurseries and boarding schools, as well as canteens and laundries, intended to reduce the domestic work of women. Despite the effort to reduce household labor, however, these services are inadequate to meet the current needs of working women. Families in Russia continue to produce most of their own food and must provide their own child care, which creates a serious conflict in women's productive and reproductive roles.

A final example of women's status in socialist societies is found in Zimbabwe. During the colonial period, British rulers in Zimbabwe (then Rhodesia) used a system of passes and permits (similar to that used under apartheid in South Africa) to keep women and children on tribal trust lands, while men were used as laborers on White-owned mines and farms. Women on the tribal trust lands were responsible for feeding their own families. During the movement for independence during the 1970s, women worked in the guerrilla forces as support staff, food producers, cooks, and supply carriers. By the end of the war, however, women and men in the guerrilla movement shared all tasks in common, including military fighting. Women's participation in the movement for independence challenged traditional attitudes toward women. Many women, influenced by the Western feminist movement, also began to articulate explicit feminist ideals. When the Zimbabwe African National Union came to power in 1980, many party leaders believed that only socialism would provide the material basis for equality between women and men.

It is not clear to what extent feminist ideas are actually represented now in the government. Most women (82 percent) continue to live in rural areas, where they are responsible for meeting most of their families' needs. The government has seemed unwilling to change the existing family structure and its control over women's sexuality and reproduction. Although the government has established a Ministry of Community Development and Women's Affairs, it is a weak unit. As a result, women in Zimbabwe are caught in a contradictory position in which feminist ideals were a part of the revolutionary struggle, but in which the government has done little to make actual structural changes in traditional gender arrangements; moreover, little has been done to give women greater control over reproduction (Seidman, 1984).

Analysis of women's roles in socialist societies underscores the point made by feminists that women's roles in reproduction and their work in the "second shift" have consequences for their involvement in all other spheres of life (Benéria and Sen, 1982; Massey, Hahn, and Sekulić, 1995). Neglect of women's roles in reproduction and domestic life makes any socialist revolution incomplete. Transitions to socialism without the elimination of patriarchal forms of organization and rule mean that women are still subjected to oppressive social forces. Only with transformations in women's roles in production and reproduction—and with the elimination of patriarchal social control—can women be fully liberated and will we find the possibility for true equality between women and men.

Women's Status in Egalitarian Societies

Anthropological work on women's roles in egalitarian societies begins to shed light on the necessary conditions for egalitarianism between women and men. Can groups maintain a gender division of labor and still have economic, political, and social freedom for women and men? Can women remain different but equal, or must differences between the sexes be eliminated altogether? Can changes in the gender division of labor eliminate women's subordination, or must we also consider transformations in the social production of gender? How, in effect, is the social production of gender tied to the modes of economic life that have emerged in modern societies?

In studying the social organization of hunting-and-gathering societies having relatively egalitarian gender relations, Leacock identifies three social structural conditions that seem necessary to produce egalitarianism: (1) the ties of collective economic dependency link *all* individuals directly to the well-being of the group as a whole; (2) the public and private spheres are not dichotomized; and (3) decisions are made by those who will also carry them out (1978:247).

On the first point, Leacock emphasizes that all members of an egalitarian society would be necessary to the system of production. They need not, it would seem, all contribute in the same way, but they would all be seen as equally valuable—quite a contrast to the socially and economically devalued labor of women under capitalism. Second, Leacock shows how the separation of the public and the private invites the restriction of women to the family. Other anthropologists, too, argue that the restriction of women to domestic work is an important precondition for the subordination of women. Domestic labor is production for the use of society's members, whereas public production creates goods for exchange. Because production for exchange takes on greater value than production for use, any group that is restricted to production for use is likely to be devalued (Sacks, 1975). In modern societies, the separation of the public and the private also invites the ideological oppression of women. Claims that women are more fit for domestic life mean they are more likely to be restricted to the domestic sphere.

Finally, Leacock's analysis suggests that no group should have authority over the experience of others. Were women to be involved in the decision-making processes that affect them, they would exercise control over their own lives. Again, this arrangement would be the reverse of the contemporary situation, in which men rule even on matters that greatly influence the course of women's experience, such as female reproduction. The development of modern patriarchy puts men in positions of authority in public and private institutions. The historical shift placing more authority in industry and government has meant that men control (through public patriarchy) areas that deeply affect women's lives—family law, welfare practices, reproductive policy, work policies, and the prosecution of men's violence (Brown, 1981). Leacock's analysis raises the question of how different gender relations might be in a society where women and men controlled decisions pertinent to their lives, where persons engaged in equally valuable labor, and where all members of the society were equally responsible for household work. Chodorow's (1978) work on the production of gender (see Chapter 6) suggests that such a society would produce men and women with less stereotypical personalities and, consequently, more flexibility in creating new social arrangements.

⮞ *Comparing Liberal and Radical Feminism*

Theoretical issues in feminist analysis are not simply academic exercises. Feminists from each of the perspectives you have reviewed—liberal, socialist, and radical feminism—agree that theoretical analyses are intended to sharpen political analyses and inform strategies for social change. Liberal, socialist, and radical feminism each make unique contributions to our understanding of the situation of women. Although for purposes of analysis the three are distinct from one another, in practice, feminist politics are often informed by all three; moreover, these theoretical viewpoints are not always as easily distinguished from each other, as the preceding analytical discussion may indicate. Each of the feminist frameworks illuminates different dimensions of political and analytical issues, and no single perspective provides a complete understanding of the many issues feminists have raised.

This review of feminist theory suggests that we ground discussion of women's position in the dynamics of the gender division of labor, the emergence of class systems, the formation of patriarchal relations, and the social organization of the family. In all, a complete theory of women's oppression must explain not only women's role in production but also the patriarchal control of reproduction and sexuality. Feminist theory, from a radical perspective, directs us to look at the material conditions of women's lives and, in so doing, to explain the basis for women's oppression not only by gender but also by race and by class.

The theoretical perspectives reviewed here make the point that social change is informed by different premises about the social organization of society. Different feminist perspectives suggest different kinds of social change; therefore, for feminists to realize their goals for an egalitarian society requires careful examination of the underlying assumptions of given theoretical and political perspectives. As Karl Mannheim suggests, "A theory is wrong if in a given practical situation, it uses concepts and categories which, if taken seriously, would prevent man from adjusting himself at that historical stage" (1936:95).

Liberal feminism emphasizes that social change should establish individual civil rights so that no one is denied access to the existing socioeconomic system based on sex, race, or class. Liberal feminism also tells us that sexism is the result of past traditions and learned psychology, and consequently suggests reform in gender socialization practices, putting much of its faith in the raised consciousness of future generations. The political tactics of liberal feminism are primarily those of interest-group politics in which liberal feminists attempt to increase the political influence and power of women. Their political strategy involves building coalitions that align the issues of feminism with other political causes, thereby increasing the strength of the women's movement. This strategy also has its costs, however, because political compromises mean that only the most moderate feminist demands can gain the support necessary for a solid coalition.

Socialist and radical feminism, on the other hand, locate the cause of sexism in the fundamental character of political and economic institutions. These perspectives pose a challenge to the very basis of our social existence by suggesting that revolutionary changes need to be made in the systems of capitalism and patriarchy.

Socialist feminists make the issue of social class central to their theoretical analysis and argue that classical Marxist theory has obscured the economic and social roles of women. In their dialogue with the theories of Marx and Engels, socialist feminists go beyond seeing women as just another victim of capitalism by making women's liberation central to all struggles for revolutionary change. They suggest that the issue of class alone cannot account for the complex relationship between the family, reproduction, and productive relations in the society; nonetheless, the class analysis that socialist feminists include does necessitate understanding the experience of women of all classes and racial-ethnic backgrounds. Both socialists and radical feminists take a material perspective on social life—that is, they see things (including those with subjective value, such as ideas, personalities, and social values) as taking on objective value through the relations of human production and reproduction. In the materialist perspective, the actual work and activity of men and women constitute the social world; therefore, to change that world requires a change in the actual labor and reproductive relations among human beings.

As a result of their Marxist perspective, socialist feminists often align themselves with other oppressed groups in their programs for social change. Their politics remain Marxist in tone, but with the added issue of ending women's oppression in ways that traditional Marxists overlook. Their strategies, then, are analytical and practical—seeking to find the common grounds of oppression and trying to establish collective ways to solve the problems that communities and individuals experience.

Distinct from socialist feminism, radical feminism locates the development of sexism in the independent existence of patriarchy and the social relations that patriarchy generates. The radical feminist perspective, then, asks us to look at the structure of consciousness—not just as it is reproduced through gender roles but specifically as it reflects the patriarchal organization of society. Radical feminism suggests that only the elimination of patriarchy will result in the liberation of women in society. Much of the strategy of radical feminist programs for change has been to redefine social relations by creating a women-centered culture. Radical feminists emphasize the positive capacities of women by focusing on the creative dimensions of women's experience. Radical feminists celebrate the creative dimension of women's lives, specifically because they see women's culture and experience as resisting patriarchal social relations.

The distinctions drawn here between these three feminist perspectives are in no way a perfect description of any. In theory and in practice, there are as many shared ideas and politics among feminists as there are differences. Discussion of the different feminist perspectives demonstrates that the questions that feminists raise have different answers and that they are as complex as the systems they seek to change. As you will see in the concluding chapter, the analyses of liberal, socialist, and radical feminism are themselves incomplete and partial. New questions for feminist thought stem from the experiences of women of color and more inclusive forms of feminist thinking. In addition, contemporary feminist theories are supplementing liberal and radical feminism with new modes of thought, as you will see.

❧ *Summary*

Radical perspectives in feminist theory stem from a critique of liberal thought as too much bound by the status quo. Socialist and radical feminism explain the oppression of women as stemming from the character of basic social institutions.

Socialist feminism has its intellectual origins in the work of Karl Marx and Friedrich Engels, although feminists are critical of Marx and Engels for having too limited an analysis of women's oppression. Marxist theory is known as historical materialism—a thesis that social organization and social change stem from the particular lived experience of human beings organized in a system of production. One major focus of Marxist theory is the analysis of class relations under capitalism. A second major point drawn from Marxism is that the ruling ideas of a period, such as sexism, are those that support the status quo.

Socialist feminists have challenged Marxism for ignoring women and have developed Marxist feminist theories that analyze the relationships of women's oppression to capitalism. Radical feminism interprets patriarchal relations as more fundamental to women's oppression than are the economic relations of capitalism. Radical feminists see men's social control of women's sexuality as the root cause of women's oppression. The debate between radical and socialist feminists has produced a third perspective emphasizing the intersecting nature of patriarchy and capitalism.

Theoretical discussion about the effects of patriarchy and capitalism on women's status is best examined within the context of socialist and egalitarian societies. Women's status is improved in socialist societies, but neglect of the specific experience of women in these societies has limited the degree of change brought in women's roles. Anthropological work has helped identify the structural conditions that are necessary for groups to live in more egalitarian forms.

Feminist theories suggest different possibilities for social change. Although no one of these theories—liberal, socialist, or radical feminism—is complete, each guides the possible direction for liberating social changes for women.

❧ Key Terms

class	infrastructure	sex/gender system
class consciousness	patriarchy	socialist feminism
dialectical materialism	production	state
historical materialism	radical feminism	superstructure
ideology	reproduction	systems of production

❧ Discussion Questions/Projects for Thought

1. Find a group of women in a working-class occupation (domestic workers, fast-food workers, blue-collar women, etc.) and ask them about their work conditions. What does a socialist feminist analysis explain about the status of these women, their opportunities for success, and their relationship to other workers?

2. Imagine that Karl Marx has returned to the world as a woman. How might he revise his theory if he was analyzing capitalism and gender relations today?

3. Radical feminism has been vital to the growing awareness of violence against women and the role that men's power plays in generating such violence. Do you think that patriarchy is a continuing feature of contemporary society? If so, what influence does it have on violence against women? If you think it is not so relevant as radical feminists do, what other framework might you use to explain the high rates of violence against women?

❧ Suggested Readings

Bunch, Charlotte. 1987. *Passionate Politics: Essays, 1968–1986: Feminist Theory in Action.* New York: St. Martin's Press.
As one of the major leaders of the radical feminist movement, Bunch's essays provide a framework for understanding the perspective of radical feminism and for seeing the emergence of her thinking and politics over time.

Engels, Friedrich. 1942/1972. *The Origin of the Family, Private Property, and the State.* New York: International Publishers.
This statement of the relationship of the family, capitalism, and private property is the standard reference for interpreting classical Marxist perspectives on women's status under capitalism.

hooks, bell. 1984. *Feminist Theory: From Margin to Center*. Boston: South End Press.
This book is one of the first written to analyze the relationship of African American women to feminist thought. As a major Black feminist writer, hooks (her pseudonym) is also one of the most influential contemporary feminist thinkers.

MacKinnon, Catharine. 1987. *Feminism Unmodified: Discourses on Life and Law*. Cambridge, MA: Harvard University Press.
This collection of essays outlines the radical feminist perspective of another of the major feminist thinkers in the contemporary period. MacKinnon is often cited as one of the primary theorists within radical feminism.

Meyering, Sheryl L., ed. 1989. *Charlotte Perkins Gilman: The Woman and Her Work*. Ann Arbor: University of Michigan Press.
This collection of Charlotte Perkins Gilman's work shows the influence she has had on the development of feminism and provides still a new vision for a society based on equality for women.

Mies, Maria. 1986. *Patriarchy and Accumulation on a World Scale: Women in the International Division of Labour*. Atlantic Highlands, NJ: Zed Books.
This socialist feminist analysis examines the position of women in international development. It provides a strong understanding of socialist feminism, within the context of specific national experiences.

Mitchell, Juliet. 1974. *Woman's Estate*. New York: Pantheon.
Juliet Mitchell's book was one of the first to use a classical Marxist perspective to interpret women's place in Western societies. Although it is old, it still stands as one of the strongest and clearest statements of Marxist feminism.

Sargent, Lydia, ed. 1981. *Women and Revolution: A Discussion of the Unhappy Marriage of Marxism and Feminism*. Boston: South End Press.
This collection of essays is a classic, providing the positions from which feminists argued for an understanding of women's experience in the context of both capitalism and patriarchy.

Chapter *13*

Conclusion

New Directions in Feminist Theory

At the heart of all feminist theory lies the idea that prior knowledge about women, society, and culture has been distorted by the exclusion of women from academic thought. The beginning chapters of this book discussed the male-centered perspectives of knowledge that have been challenged by feminist concepts and research. The review of feminist theory further showed that research and theory in the academic disciplines need fundamental reconstruction if they are to work on behalf of women.

Current developments in feminist theory stem from the fundamental recognition that knowledge is socially constructed, and must therefore be seen in the context of the social relations in which knowledge production occurs. In this regard, feminist epistemology is one of the new modes of feminist thought. Recognition of the socially constructed nature of human society and relationships is also reflected in and forms the basis of new work in feminism and postmodernism—a particular form of social theory examined in this chapter. Postmodernism has especially influenced new questions about sexuality and the social construction of gender. Some feminist questions about sexuality have been examined in earlier chapters, but the postmodernist approach to sexuality is raising new ways of thinking about sexuality and the body. As you have also seen throughout this book, knowledge is also incomplete without considering the multiple experiences of diverse groups in society and how their experiences are interrelated. This recognition has brought increased attention within feminist thought to race, class, and gender and the interrelationships between these different axes of social experience. Although each of these developments in feminist thought is only briefly reviewed here, they suggest some of the future directions for feminist theorizing.

❧ *Feminist Epistemology*

Social experience and consciousness are conditioned by the location of our existence. Because men and women have quite different life situations, their consciousness, culture, and ideas are also different. As Dorothy Smith (1987, 1990) argues, the activity of women (and, by implication, men) forms the basis for their ideas. Because sex/gender systems organize social relations and because intellectual thought is shaped by social relations, the sex/gender system shapes our perspectives as social thinkers and researchers.

Epistemology refers to the ways of knowing that form systems of social thought. This idea emphasizes that knowledge is socially constructed and that ways of thinking are embedded in a variety of assumptions—implicit and explicit—that guide their shape and form. Feminist epistemology, a relatively recent development in feminist theory, is the examination of how gender relations shape the production of thought, including feminist theory itself. Feminist epistemology raises new questions, both about the systems of thinking that have been derived from androcentric (i.e., male-centered) ways of knowing and about new ways of constructing knowledge to be more inclusive of and centered in women's experiences.

One major area of discussion in feminist epistemology is the social construction of science, a particularly important subject because of the deep and central ways that scientific knowledge shapes Western ways of knowing. In the seventeenth century, as modern science began, scientific inquiry was justified for its specific social value; moreover, the legitimacy of scientific inquiry rested on the same principles of reform that today sound like feminist social practices—antiauthoritarianism, progressiveness, antielitism, educational reform, humanitarianism, and the unity of experience and knowing (Van Den Daele, 1977). Contemporary debates about the social and political application of scientific knowledge (such as the examples of nuclear energy and the atomic bomb) also indicate that even in scientific circles the question of scientific purpose is not separate from the practice of scientific inquiry.

Historically, the scientific movement also emerged in specific opposition to the canons of traditional belief, especially as a challenge to the state and the political authority of the church. As historians of science write, "The breakdown of older patterns of authority and traditionally-held dogmas or consensus positions allows much broader boundaries for exploration and the staking out of positions previously proscribed—either tacitly or implicitly" (Mendelsohn, Weingart, and Whitely, 1977:10). By removing the blinders of earlier commitments, scientists have argued that more objective inquiry would provide the new facts and new perspectives needed to meet the needs of emerging social institutions.

Feminists argue that the neutral claims of traditional scholarship mask nonobjective interpretations of women's lives that have been produced. According to feminist inquiry, new perspectives on women's lives—and specifically ones that challenge sexist assumptions—will result in more accurate explanations of women's experiences. Feminists still use scientific methods in their studies, but they claim that their work is more objective because it is more inclusive of all persons' experiences.

A central question in feminist scholarship is the issue of objectivity and its relationship to the process of knowing (Harding, 1986, 1991). According to standard arguments about sociological research, rigorous observation and the use of the **scientific method** eliminate observer bias, but feminists argue that the observer is not a neutral party. Because knowledge is socially produced, the particular experiences and attitudes that observers bring to their work influence what they study, how they study it, and what they conclude about it. Untangling the relationship between the knower and the known is essential, according to feminist scientists.

Smith (1990) and Hartsock (1983) note that all research is done from a particular standpoint or location in the social system. The world is known from the perspective of the researcher. In any given research project, we must know both the subjects' and the researcher's points of entry to the project. Most often, sociologists enter research projects through official institutions (e.g., schools, police, social welfare agencies, etc.); consequently, the work they do may support the status quo and be distorted by the view of official agencies. Smith suggests, then, that most objective inquiries can be produced only by those with the least interest in preserving the status quo.

She explains this idea by using an example from the German philosopher Hegel. Suppose we want to comprehend the world of a master and a slave. Both of them live in the same world, but their experience within that world is quite different. The master takes the slave's labor (in fact, the slave's very existence) for granted; thus, the master's needs are immediately satisfied through slave labor. The slave, on the other hand, conforms to the master's will; his or her labor is an object of the master's consciousness. The organization of this relationship is invisible to the master. If the master were describing the world they both inhabit, his account would be less objective because the structures of that world are invisible to him. The slave's description of the world, on the other hand, would include the master, plus the fact of his or her own labor and its transformation to the status of an object. As a result, the slave is more objective because his or her account is both more complete and more directly related to the empirical events within the relationship and the world in which it is located.

When we begin describing the world by examining women's experiences, the knowledge we create does not merely add to the already established constructs of sociological thought. The experience of women, like that of the slave, has been invisible. Women inhabit the same world as men; in fact, women's labor shapes men's experience in the world (through housework and the maintenance of social and bodily relations). Women's labor makes men's mode of operation—detached and rational—possible; yet, it remains invisible to men as the dominant class. An objective sociological account of reality must make sense of both women's and men's experiences and must therefore be constructed from the vantage point of both.

Smith (1987) also argues that sociological research and theory must situate social actors within their everyday worlds. In other words, unless research begins with the ordinary facts of lives, then the knowledge that sociologists construct will be both alienating and apart from the actual experiences of human actors. Sociological analysis begins with the immediate experience of social actors but goes beyond that experience by discovering the social-institutional context of their lives. Although the institutional context of everyday experience is not immediately visible to those who live it, the sociological perspective makes this context available, and thus is a powerful agent of social change. Like the perspective of C. Wright Mills, Smith's objective is to establish the relationship between social structure and everyday life. This relationship is especially important in comprehending women's experiences, because the affairs of everyday life are the specific area of women's expertise. Given the gender division of labor, women are charged with maintaining everyday life. To overlook that fact or to treat it as insignificant is to deny women's reality (Reinharz, 1983; Smith, 1987).

Feminist **standpoint theory** suggests that the specific social location of the knower shapes what is known and that not all perspectives are equally valid or complete. Again, think of the master and the slave. Because the master takes the slave's existence for granted, he cannot see the world as the slave sees it—including the world that constructs the relationship of the master and the slave. The slave's view is not as partial, or as incomplete, as that of the master, and it is likely to produce a less distorted account of the world in which both the slave and the master live.

Likewise, feminist standpoint theory argues that women's specific location in patriarchal societies is actually a resource in the construction of new knowledge (Harding, 1991; Collins, 1998). This does not result from the biological fact of being a woman but from the unique experience of women as an oppressed group confronting a patriarchal society. Standpoint theory assumes that systems of privilege are least visible to those who benefit the most from them and who, at the same time, control the resources that define dominant belief systems. Whites, for example, are more likely to deny that racism exists; people of color both see the assaults racism produces and understand the nuances of racism in everyday life. Similarly, men can more easily deny the presence of patriarchy than can women, even when women do not fully grasp the workings of sexist oppression. It takes the standpoint of oppressed groups to see and recognize systems of race, class, and gender privilege. Dominant groups can, of course, learn to see how race, gender, and class privilege structure social relations, but they do so through analysis and observation, not simply from the conditions of their own experience.

Standpoint theory does not mean that we have to take the word of oppressed groups at face value to know how society is structured. Systems of oppression also shape the consciousness of the oppressed. Theory constructed from the observed experiences of dominant and subordinate groups yields the insight that produces liberating knowledge.

❧ *Feminism and Postmodernism*

Feminist standpoint theory, and the epistemological assumptions on which it rests, has grown from a theoretical framework known as postmodernism. **Postmodernism** is a form of contemporary social theory that explains all knowledge as stemming from the specific historical period and the conditions in which it is produced and that interprets society not as an objective thing but as a fluid and illusive construction of alternative meaning systems. To postmodernists, society is only a series of stories that emerge from a variety of points of view and experiences. Unlike social scientists, who see social structure as a thing that one can observe and know, postmodernists oppose the idea of structure, thinking it is a reified category that is real only because people believe it is and construct ideas to support that belief. To postmodernists, reality is all simulated, and thus this perspective is particularly attractive in a world marked by highly technological forms of communication that increasingly penetrate everyday life.

Postmodernism recognizes that socially constructed assumptions are built into the knowledge frames that are characteristic of any given historical period or cultural context (Nicholson, 1990). Postmodernist theory goes beyond simply understanding the influence of culture (a view common to all social sciences) by arguing that there is not a singular, monolithic social order (i.e., society); rather, society is a series of images and meaning systems over which people struggle (Fraser, 1989). Postmodernists see reality as constituted through a broad range of **discourses**—that is, all that is written, spoken, or otherwise represented through language and communication systems. Whether it is science, the media, or other cultural artifacts, postmodernists see these discourses as framing knowledge and reality; in addition, these discourses can be systems of social control. Gender ideology, as an example, is a form of social control represented in the discourses (science, language, cultural images) that have embedded within them specific constructions of what it means to be male and female.

Postmodernism has arisen primarily from the field of literary criticism and also from the critiques of science symbolized by feminist standpoint theory. Within literary criticism, the basic idea of postmodernism is that texts do not stand alone as objective entities apart from either the author's construction of the text or the reader's response to it. Because the focuses of postmodernism are on alternative discourses and meaning systems, not goals, choices, behavior, and attitudes, emphasis is placed on what are called *texts*—whether those be actual literary texts like books *or* conversations, media images, and other cultural forms. The concept of a text in postmodernist theory is thus more than the literal text; it refers to the contested meaning systems that appear in all of social reality. A conversation between two people or the nightly news is considered a text; indeed, from the postmodernist perspective, society itself is only a text in that it is constructed out of the interpretive processes that constitute it. The major method used in postmodernism is to examine texts as socially constructed objects. This has resulted in a new field of study, known as *cultural studies*.

In the social sciences, postmodernism emerges from criticisms of positivist science—that is, the idea that society can be known through systematic observation and generalization. Postmodernist theorists debunk this idea, because they assume it is impossible to reflect on something and see the world without presuppositions (Agger, 1991). Postmodernists reject the scientific point of view that through detached measurement one can observe a world that is "out there." They would argue, to the contrary, that science is a specific world view, with its own assumptions about the world built into its framework; moreover, postmodernists would argue that science has a widening sphere of influence within the modern period. Postmodernists see science, like everything else, as constructed; they do not see it as providing knowledge that is any more real or objective than literature. Instead, postmodernists see science, like literature, as a series of texts; the work of intellectuals is to "deconstruct" the meanings embedded in these texts. Unlike other social scientists, postmodernists are wary about generalization, thinking instead that the world consists of diverse, multiple, and unique experiences.

There are serious challenges posed by postmodernist thought for feminists and sociologists or other social scientists who work within the scientific method—that is, thinking that one can use controlled observation and rigorous study to reveal the workings of something known as social structure. Postmodernism is founded on a distrust of some of the ways of thinking that are basic to the social scientific approach to understanding society and social life.

For feminists, postmodernism has had much appeal because of some commonly shared assumptions in both feminist and postmodernist theory. One of the basic premises of feminist thought is that gender is socially constructed; furthermore, one of the fundamental goals of feminist theory is to examine gender relations, see how they are constituted, and study how they are thought of or not thought of (Flax, 1990). This critical attitude makes postmodernism appealing to feminists because feminism and postmodernism are fundamentally skeptical about existing knowledge. Each also recognizes the embedment of social assumptions in such things as language, cultural images, and the ideas of a given period. Because feminists see how ideas and images have been used to oppress women, they want to criticize these discourses, not take them for granted, and, like postmodernist theorists, they see gender and society as socially constituted.

Another basic insight of postmodernism and a reason for its attractiveness to feminists is that postmodernists think there is nothing essentially male or female; rather, there are socially constructed categories that emerge from specific cultural and historical contexts, not from anything fundamental about male or female biology. Postmodernists even challenge the idea that there are real biological categories to begin with, since they understand "male" and "female" only as constructed through human definition. In other words, postmodernists take the social construction of gender to its ultimate extreme—denying that biological differences are anything more than social constructions. The body itself, from a postmodernist perspective, is something that is understood only through social interpretation (Nicholson, 1994). Some feminist postmodernists argue that the distinction other feminists make between sex and gender (see Chapter 2) is a false one because it still accepts biological differences as real. Instead, postmodernist feminists argue that biological sex differences are only a function of our knowledge, not necessarily objectively significant.

A good way to explain this point is to use the metaphor of a coat rack, suggested by Linda Nicholson, a postmodernist feminist thinker. The coat rack metaphor assumes that the body is a rack upon which differing cultural artifacts are hung. In other words, the idea is that there is some constancy to nature but that culture elaborates this basic difference into different societal forms (Nicholson, 1994). Postmodernists question whether the coat rack itself is anything other than a cultural construction. In other words, they deny that there is any essential difference in men and women other than those we construct as significant. As a result, postmodernist feminists challenge the very categories of "man" and "woman," seeing these instead as fluid, artificial, and malleable. Like other postmodernists, feminist postmodernists are skeptical about any categories, since they see all categories and definitions as humanly imposed (Bordo, 1992).

A third premise for the connection between feminism and postmodernism is the insight of both on the social construction of language. Postmodernist theorists understand language as not just a technical device for describing something "out there." Rather, they see language itself as actually constituting the thing it allegedly describes (Agger, 1991). Postmodernist analyses of language rest on the idea that language, like other forms of knowledge, is not pure; instead, language reflects the social categories and practices that characterize a given time and cultural period. For example, calling someone a *man* or a *woman*, just like calling someone *White* or *Black*, has a specific socially constituted meaning that makes no sense outside of its cultural time and place. Because this insight has been central to feminist thought (in that feminists have long deconstructed and exposed the sexist basis of language), many feminists find postmodernist arguments attractive.

In sum, postmodernist feminists see indeterminacy—not determinism—as characteristic of society. They emphasize diversity—not unity—in experience, and the unique—not the general. This perspective makes social science more subjective and tentative, since postmodernism is a more relativistic way of viewing the world. Some have argued that one of the reasons postmodernism is so appealing to contemporary intellectuals is that it reflects the disillusionment of the current generation (Rosenau, 1992). Postmodernism causes people, including scholars, to examine their assumptions in constructing knowledge and formulating a worldview. Its theorists also deny that a singular voice defines all experience, as has been the case in androcentric and ethnocentric scholarship. Through their recognition that various disciplines encode value positions, like standpoint theory, postmodernists helps us deconstruct the gendered basis of knowledge.

The Critique of Postmodernism

One of the criticisms of postmodernist theory is its very high level of abstraction—what one sociologist has called work that is "incredibly, extravagantly convoluted" (Agger, 1991). Almost as a way of emphasizing the contextual nature of all that is known, postmodernists have often purposefully produced work that is obtuse and difficult to understand. As a consequence, the essence of postmodernism is typically inaccessible to those without a high degree of schooling in its interpretation. This fact has led many feminists to charge that postmodernist theory is elitist, since it disallows one of the objectives of feminist theory—accessibility to wide audiences, particularly women who may not have access to the elite educational institutions in which postmodernism is produced.

Postmodernism makes it difficult ever to generalize about any characteristic or experience—as if all the world were merely individual discourses or voices. This is strikingly at odds with the basic principles of social sciences—that one can generalize through careful observation and analysis. Postmodernist thinkers are opposed to the concept of social structure as something that is "there." By criticizing an overly determinist view of gender, race, and class, they actually can "deconstruct gender right out of operation" (Bordo, 1992:160), as if it hardly existed at all. Postmodernist theory has the advantage of emphasizing diversity and thus has added to new work on race, class, and gender, but it does so in a way that denies the reality of structurally based oppression. This makes it limited in its ability to explain structured inequality—whether by gender, race, class, or by all three (Collins, 1998). It is as if studying race, class, and gender is just a matter of different voices, since it reduces the experience of oppression to cultural analysis texts and discourses alone. By denying the concept of social structure, postmodernism limits the framework through which one can understand oppression by gender, race, and class; furthermore, it makes social science only a matter of accounting for diverse social experiences (Agger, 1991), instead of being committed to studying general principles of social structure and organization.

Feminist Theory and Sexuality

The influence of postmodernist theory has been especially strong in new feminist scholarship on sexuality. In part because feminists have wanted to break down taken-for-granted categories of sexual differentiation, postmodernist thought is consistent with the value placed on the fluidity of sexual categories. Postmodernist feminist theorists have thus found subjects like cross-dressing, transvestitism, and the crossing of sexual categories represented in some new forms of gay and lesbian studies to be fascinating and to provide new theoretical constructs for all feminist thought.

Postmodernist theorists understand sex and the body as purely social concepts. That is, the discourses and practices of popular and scientific thought construct sex and the body in particular ways; therefore, interpreting sex and the body is a matter of challenging how sexual categories and understandings of the body are socially developed. From a postmodernist standpoint, as one sociologist writes, "sex is viewed as fundamentally social: the categories of sex—especially heterosexuality and homosexuality, but also the whole regime of modern sexual types, classifications, and norms—are understood as social and historical facts" (Seidman, 1994:171).

One of the arguments, from a postmodernist perspective, is that categories such as *homosexual* and *heterosexual* have emerged as particular social types only in modern Western societies. We have seen this in the studies of earlier work on sexual categories in other cultures (see Chapter 2). Beyond the recognition of cross-cultural differences in the social construction of sexuality, however, postmodernists make a more fundamental point: The categories of *homosexual* and *heterosexual* themselves have been constructed through particular scientific discourses—namely, the work of sexologists and others who have labeled sexual behaviors in dichotomous categories. Furthermore, these "discourses" have assumed an authoritative stance, with systems of power enforcing these labels. To postmodernists, sexual power is embodied in various aspects of social life (popular culture, scientific writings, literary texts, and daily conversations, to name a few); these "texts" establish sexual boundaries that regulate sexual behavior and identities.

One of the major contributions of postmodernist theories of sexuality is to deconstruct sexual categories—that is, to question their presumed natural basis, arguing instead that all sexual identities are composites of multiple components (Stein and Plummer, 1994). The construction of a category such as *homosexual* imposes a particular construction of sex on its subjects and presumes the existence of some other normal and taken-for-granted category—that is, *heterosexual.*

Postmodernist theorists also criticize traditional empirical studies of sexuality for being unreflective about the categories upon which such research is based. Studies of sexuality that compare men and women—or gays, bisexuals, and straights—presume these different types have some fixed meaning; instead, postmodernist theory interprets these as highly fluid categories (Seidman, 1994). This mode of thinking shifts the analysis of sexuality away from dualistic categories to a more fluid understanding of difference. At the same time, it challenges the assumption (one even made within the gay and lesbian community) that there is some natural basis to homosexuality. From this point of view, no one sexual identity is privileged over another; rather, sexual identity is all performance and meaning (Butler, 1990).

There are important implications of postmodernist theory for political action by groups who want to challenge the oppression of gays and lesbians. Postmodernists are less inclined to support the civil rights strategy that has characterized the gay and lesbian political movement. The *civil rights strategy* is one that recognizes gays and lesbians as a minority group and contests that this group has rights, just as do other minority groups in society. Instead, the politics of a more postmodernist approach are to transgress and challenge sexual categories (Stein and Plummer, 1994). Groups such as Act Up and Queer Nation use gender parodies as ways to subvert the dominant sexual order to resist and rebel against taken-for-granted sexual categories (Butler, 1990). Their political strategy is to act in ways that challenge sexual categories, even when their behavior appears outrageous to others (e.g., by cross-dressing and having "kiss-ins"). The shock and outrage that such acts produce are deliberate ways of making people face the socially constructed assumptions about sex that they would normally take for granted. Often, such political behavior takes a playful and risqué attitude, again reflecting the postmodernist appeal to seeing sexual identities as scripts or per-formances.

Not all new feminist studies of sexuality use a postmodernist framework, nor do all gay and lesbian political action groups use the approaches inspired by this theoretical framework. Indeed, as you have seen throughout this book, much of the new scholarship on sexuality has used existing frameworks of sociological and feminist research and theory to explore various questions about sexuality and its relationship to gender. Many feminists are, indeed, critical of the postmod-ernist approach to sexuality, arguing that it does not provide a political perspec-tive that challenges the real structural basis of sexual oppression (Kitzinger and Wilkinson, 1994). In their criticisms, feminists are arguing that structural systems of heterosexual privilege and power are real and cannot be reduced to texts, dis-courses, and performance. As in other areas of feminist thought, there are multi-ple frameworks for understanding sexuality; postmodernist theory is only one such approach.

➤ Feminism and the Analysis of Race, Class, and Gender

Feminist theory is itself incomplete without an analysis of the intersections of race, class, and gender in society. To date, this has been one of the greatest limita-tions of feminist theory, and it stems from the fact that much of feminist theory has been constructed from the particular experiences of White, middle-class women. Some feminist analyses have simply excluded the experiences of women of color—with much the same result as androcentric analyses. At other times, feminist theory has made an implied analysis of race and class, but not one that was explicitly developed or evaluated. For example, each of the theoretical per-spectives reviewed here—liberal feminism, socialist feminism, and radical femi-nism—has a different set of assumptions regarding race and class and their rela-tionship to gender.

Liberal feminism shares many of the assumptions of an assimilationist or civil rights perspective, assuming that the basic cause of inequality (be it race, class, or gender) is discrimination; thus, the remedies proposed are those sought through courts and administrative agencies, as provided under law. This perspective assumes that as barriers of race and gender discrimination are removed, minori-ties will move into the system and become assimilated into the dominant culture and institutions. The goal of liberalism is to establish a system blind to gender and race. This vision of change is a popular and appealing one, although it has a num-ber of limitations, as we have seen.

Socialist feminism provides a somewhat better starting point for an analysis of race, and it has a strong analysis of class; however, it, too, has its limitations. Socialist feminism explains the experience of all women as inextricably linked to the development of class relations; moreover, the development of class relations under capitalism produces much of the basis for the exploitation of racial-ethnic groups. The economic perspective of socialist feminism also reminds us that the liberation of White women from domestic labor has rested on the exploited labor of women of color (Dill, 1980). With its emphasis on class, socialist feminism, however, tends to see both gender and race as secondary to class. As a result, socialist feminism understates the independent, although intersecting and interlocking, operation of race and gender relations.

Radical feminism assumes that gender is the primary form of oppression and that class and race are extensions of patriarchal domination (Daly, 1978). This perspective is perhaps the most problematic in providing a theory of race oppression. In assuming that patriarchy is the cause of women's oppression, it divides minority women and men and takes the experience of White American women as the universal social experience. In placing the causes of oppression in the domination of men over women, radical feminism provides little explanation of the powerlessness that people of color experience together. Its insistence that eliminating sexism is the key to eliminating racism has a hollow ring to women of color, who face oppression on both counts and who have experienced racism as a more fundamental (or at least equally fundamental) fact of their lives. Radical women of color clearly recognize that sexism exists in their communities, but attributing the primary cause of their experience to patriarchy ignores the racism they encounter not only from men but also from White feminists (Moraga and Anzaldúa, 1981).

Given the inadequacies in existing categories of feminist theory, it has taken the independent development of feminist theory by women of color to produce new analyses, grounded in the experiences of women of color, that provide a new starting point for feminist thought and action. The experience of women of color, most usually Black women, has been typically described as *double jeopardy*—a term meant to suggest the cumulative effect of experiencing both race and gender exploitation. Although this phrase is descriptively valuable, it is analytically limited, suggesting that the racism that women of color experience is simply added to sexism, when, in fact, race, class, and gender are systems of oppression experienced simultaneously, not additively, by women of color (Combahee River Collective, 1982; Andersen and Collins, 1998).

Conceptualizing feminist theory from the experience of women of color requires analyses that interpret race, class, and gender as intersecting and interlocking systems of oppression; moreover, it requires shifting the starting point for the development of feminist thinking. Centering knowledge in the experiences of those who have traditionally been excluded causes us to question all of the assumptions made in studying people of color as well as people in dominant groups. This approach is more likely to give us a rich account of the experience of oppressed groups, not simplistic unidimensional analyses that treat all groups as if they were alike.

For example, Collins writes that if we want to know the thoughts and lives of African American women as intellectuals, we have to revise our way of thinking about who is an intellectual. African American women have historically been denied access to formal education; they have not had the privilege of finding publishers and public platforms for their ideas. To recover the work of African American women intellectuals, we must look to new sources and find intellectual thought in the everyday activities of Black women. Collins writes, "Reclaiming the Black female intellectual tradition also involves searching for its expression in alternative institutional locations and among women who are not commonly perceived as intellectuals" (1990:14).

As we begin to think more inclusively about race, class, and gender as intersecting systems, we begin to see the experiences of all groups, not just those of women of color, differently. Race, class, and gender affect the experience of all groups, not just those who are their victims. Thus, in studying race, we should be studying Whites as well as people of color, just as studying gender brings new insights about men as well as women (Andersen and Collins, 1998). The exclusion of people of color from systems of social thought and from the institutions in which thought is produced will continue to distort what we know and how we are able to effect social change on behalf of all groups.

Integrating race, class, and gender into feminist thinking requires a process of transformation in which we move from simply adding women of color into existing analyses to seeing race, class, and gender in relational ways. There are rich empirical studies, as well as historical and political analyses, that provide the basis for doing so. The challenge for feminist theorists in the coming years is to continue developing such work; without it, feminists cannot hope to generate programs for social change designed for the liberation of all women and men.

∂ *Key Terms*

discourse
epistemology

postmodernism
scientific method

standpoint theory

∂ *Discussion Questions/Projects for Thought*

1. Interview students on your campus, asking men and women about their experiences studying science. What evidence do you find in their reports about the patriarchal structure of science as an institution?

2. Postmodernist studies in feminism have analyzed the social construction of gender, particularly as reflected in cultural images of gender. Using one example from any cultural form (film, television, print, art), describe the gendered images that this cultural artifact produces. What evidence of change do you see in the construction of gender over time in the culture at large?

3. Using any one of the subjects discussed in this book, discuss how an analysis of race, class, *and* gender provides a more complete account of this topic.

∂ *Suggested Readings*

Andersen, Margaret L., and Patricia Hill Collins. 1998. *Race, Class, and Gender: An Anthology.* Belmont, CA: Wadsworth.
This anthology explores the diverse ways that race, class, and gender shape group experiences in the United States. Some of the articles also include personal narratives that help students empathize with those from backgrounds other than their own.

Collins, Patricia Hill. 1998. *Fighting Words: Black Women and the Search for Social Justice.* Minneapolis, MN: University of Minneapolis Press.
Using Black women's standpoint as the point of orientation, Collins explores such topics as Afrocentrism, critical social theory, and postmodernist thought to ask how Black women's knowledge can inform analyses of social justice.

Harding, Sandra. 1991. *Whose Science?/Whose Knowledge? Thinking from Women's Lives.* Ithaca, NY: Cornell University Press.
Harding's work is known for elaborating feminist standpoint theory and for challenging the patriarchal biases in Western science. This book asks how knowledge would be different if it were centered in women's lives.

Nicholson, Linda, ed. 1990. *Feminism and Postmodernism.* New York: Routledge.
Nicholson's anthology provides a grounding in the perspective of feminist postmodernist thought, including some of the articles that have best articulated this complex area of social theory.

Rothenberg, Paula S. 1998. *Race, Class, and Gender in the United States*, 4th ed. New York: St. Martin's Press.
This anthology provides not only a contemporary perspective on the workings of race, class, and gender in the United States but it also provides excerpts from important historical documents that have framed racial, gender, and class oppression.

Smith, Dorothy E. 1990. *The Conceptual Practices of Power.* Boston: Northeastern University Press.
Smith's work as a sociologist has defined feminist standpoint theory from a sociological point of view. She also analyzes how traditional sociological scholarship has developed from an androcentric perspective.

❧ *Glossary*

abolitionism nineteenth-century movement organized to oppose slavery

affirmative action policy referring to positive efforts taken to open new areas of opportunity to groups who have historically been disadvantaged in the labor market

Age of Enlightenment period in seventeenth- and eighteenth-century Europe marked by a belief in the ability of human reason to be used for humanitarian social change

androcentrism thought that is centered in men's experiences only

anorexia nervosa condition characterized by severe weight loss and delusions about one's body size

antimiscegenation the prohibition of marriage between different racial groups

authority power that is perceived by others to be legitimate and that is structured into specific social instituions

Automobile Workers v. Johnson Controls Supreme Court decision in 1991 holding that it is discriminatory to bar women from high-risk jobs in which there is potential harm to a fetus or reproductive system

biological determinism faulty reasoning assuming that a single condition inevitably determines a given outcome

biological reductionism faulty argument that reduces a complex phenomenon to a singular cause

bulimia eating disorder in which people, typically women, binge on huge amounts of food, followed by their purging through vomiting, laxatives, or extreme fasting

class social structural position that groups hold, relative to the economic, social, political and cultural resources of a society

class consciousness in Marxist theory, understanding that develops as class groups comprehend their relationship to the system of production

cognitive-developmental theory theory, based on the work of Jean Piaget, that explains children's development of the mental categories formed through interaction with others

collective consciousness system of beliefs, within a society, that create a sense of belonging to the community and convey the moral obligation to live up to the society's demands

comparable worth principle of paying women and men equivalent wages for performing jobs involving comparable levels of skill

compulsory heterosexuality institutionalized practices that presume women are innately sexually oriented toward men and that support privileges associated with heterosexuality

content analysis research method by which researchers analyze the content of documents or other artifacts

cult of domesticity Victorian ideal that made women responsible for the moral and everyday affairs of the home

culture patterns of expectations, beliefs, values, ideas, and material objects that define the taken-for-granted way of life for a society or group

date rape sexual assault where the assailant is an acquaintance of the victim

deviance behavior that departs from conventional norms and is labeled and so recognized by groups with the power to do so

dialectical materialism *see historical materialism*

discourse term used by postmodernist theorists to refer to all that is written or spoken and that requires analysis by social theorists

discrimination act or practice of systematically disadvantaging one or more groups

"doing gender" sociological perspective that sees gender as an activity accomplished through routine social interaction

dual labor market theory gender inequality is explained as the result of a labor market organized into two segments: the primary and secondary market—where jobs in the primary labor market are more valued and more valuable than those in the secondary labor market

economic restructuring process by which the economy is becoming less based on manufacturing than on service jobs, is driven by technological change, is increasingly global, and where workers are being reduced through downsizing

Eisenstadt v. Baird Supreme Court decision (1972) extending unmarried persons the right to use birth control

emotional labor work people do to manage the emotions of others and which is part of one's work evaluation

epistemology term derived from the philosophy of science, referring to a theoretical way of knowing

Equal Pay Act of 1963   first federal legislation requiring equal pay for equal work

Equal Rights Amendment   proposed amendment to the U.S. constitution that would prohibit the denial of rights based on sex (i.e., gender)

essentialism   argument that men and women are basically different and that this shows up in contrasting patterns of social behaviors

ethnocentric   seeing one's group as superior to all others; taking one's own group experience as the starting point for understanding all other experiences

false consciousness   Marxist concept that subordinated groups accept the world view of dominant groups

family   a social ideal, generally referring to a unit of economic cooperation, typically thought to be related by blood, but revised by feminists to include those forming an economically cooperative, residential unit bound by feelings of common ties and strong emotion

family household   U.S. Census Bureau term for a household maintained with a family or unrelated persons residing together

family-based economy   form of economic production wherein the household is the basic unit of the economy and the site for most economic production and distribution

family-consumer economy   form of economic production in which mass production of goods leads to increased consumerism in families and households

family-wage economy   form of economic production in which production moves out of the household into a factory system, where a wage-based system of labor is created

faulty generalization   mode of thinking that takes knowledge from one group's or person's experiences and incorrectly extends it to another

feminism   belief and action based in diverse political theories and principles, but advocating social changes intended to free women from oppressive social structures; also based on the idea that women's position in society is the result of social, not biological, factors

feminist theology   new models of religious belief founded in feminist ethics

feminist theory   analyses explaining the position of women in society, intended also to provoke the possibilities for liberating social changes

feminization of poverty   trend by which a growing proportion of the poor are women and their children

fetal sex differentiation   the developmental phase of an embryo whereby sex identity and male/female genitalia are formed in utero

gender   the socially learned behaviors and expectations associated with men and women

gender identity   definition of self, based on an understanding of what it means to be a woman or a man

gender gap   differing political opinions and voting patterns between women and men

gender roles   patterns of behavior in which women and men behave, based on the cultural expectations associated with their gender

gender segregation   pattern whereby women and men are located in different categories of jobs throughout the labor force

gender socialization   process by which gender roles are learned

gender stratification   hierarchical distribution, by gender, of economic and social resources in a society

gendered institution   total pattern of gender relations embedded in societal institutions

glass ceiling   popular phrase referring to the invisible mechanism that discourages women's advancement in organizations

global assembly line   popular phrase referring to the employment of Third World women in the Third World economy

global restructuring   process by which research and management are based in developed nations, while assembly-line (or production) work is relegated to underprivileged nations

Griswold v. *Connecticut*   first Supreme Court decision (1965) allowing married couples to use birth control

hermaphroditism   condition resulting when the fetus develops as neither totally male nor female; person is born with mixed sex characteristics

heterosexism   institutionalized set of behaviors and beliefs that presume heterosexuality to be the only acceptable form of sexual expression

historical materialism   theoretical position postulating that the material organization of the world (i.e., economic systems) shapes people's behavior and beliefs; the basis for Marxist social theory

homophobia   fear and hatred of homosexuals

household   economic unit of those residing together, with a common economic base

householder   term used by U.S. Census Bureau to refer to the person in whose name a household unit is owned or rented

human capital theory   explanation of wage differentials as the result of different characteristics of workers

identification theory   theory of socialization that explains children's learning of gender-appropriate behaviors through identifying with the same-sex parent

ideology   system of beliefs that distorts reality at the same time that it provides justification for the status quo

infant mortality   the rate of infant death within a population

infrastructure   derived from Marxist theory, refers to the system of economic production as the determining feature of social organization

institutions   established patterns of behavior with a particular and recognized purpose (i.e., work, the family, religion, and so on)

labeling theory   theoretical perspective in sociology, emphasizing that some groups with the power to label deviant behavior exercise control over who and what is considered deviant

liberal feminism feminist theoretical position that interprets the origins of women's oppression as in blocked opportunities and legal obstacles to equal participation in society

liberalism political philosophy characterized by an emphasis on individual rights and equal opportunity; the basis for liberal feminism

marital rape forced sexual activity demanded of a wife by her husband

matriarchy system in which women hold power

matrix of domination particular race, class, and gender configuration in society, which establishes a system of oppression

men's studies a field of study focusing on men and challenging patriarchal biases in traditional scholarship

meritocracy social systems in which persons hold their particular positions on the basis of individual talents and achievements

Meritor Savings Bank **v.** *Vinson* Supreme Court decision in 1986 ruling that sexual harassment is a form of discrimination and, therefore, is unconstitutional

misogyny hatred of women

Muller **v.** *Oregon* Supreme Court decision in 1908 holding it constitutional to restrict the working day to ten hours only for women

nuclear family family structure in which husband and wife reside together with their children

object relations theory theory of psychological development that sees children as identifying with their same-sex parent but forming their own identities through detaching from the parents

patriarchy institutionalized power relationships that give men power over women

personal troubles problematic events in the immediate experience of an individual

phallocentric thinking thinking that assumes women need men for sexual arousal and satisfaction

pluralism model of the state that interprets political action as the result of balancing the needs and actions of diverse interest groups

popular culture beliefs, practices, and objects that are part of everyday traditions

postmodernism form of contemporary social theory positing that society is not an objective entity and that all knowledge is situated in specific assumptions stemming from the historical period in which they develop; a theoretical perspective that sees society as not unitary, but instead composed of socially constituted and highly unstable images and selves

poverty line index developed by the U.S. Social Security Administration that defines the official rate of poverty

power individual or group ability to influence others

power elite model of the state that sees power as stemming from the influence of a powerful ruling class

production in Marxist feminist theory, labor in which human beings engage to satisfy their needs

protective legislation laws and policies prohibiting women from participating in certain jobs because of perceived risks to their reproductive health—generally thought to be discriminatory, since such protections have not been directed toward men as workers

public issues events that originate beyond general immediate experience and that have their origin in the social structure of society

queer theory the belief that sexual identity is socially constructed and that categories of sexuality can be changed

radical feminism feminist theoretical position positing that male power is the source of women's oppression

reflection hypothesis explanation of the depiction of women in the mass media that assumes the mass media reflect the values of the population

religion as opiate idea that religion is a form of social control that discourages social protest by oppressed groups

reproduction in Marxist feminist theory, both the physical and social re-creation of human life

Roe **v.** *Wade* 1973 Supreme Court decision upholding women's right to abortion

role-learning theory explanation of media images of women and men that assumes that these images encourage role modeling by men and women observing the images

sanctified church term used to refer to Holiness and Pentecostal churches within the African American community

scientific method method of reasoning common to the practice of science, including systematic observation, analysis of data, and generalization

Second Great Awakening social movement in the early nineteenth century, emphasizing a revivalist and egalitarian spirit in religion

second shift work women do at home, in addition to paid labor

sex biological identity of a person

sex chromosomes the chromosomal pairs determining the biological sex of an offspring

sex/gender system social-structural arrangements in society that transform biological sex differences into socially meaningful sex and gender relationships

sexism beliefs that see women as inferior and defend their traditionally subordinated place in the world

sexual harassment unwanted imposition of sexual requirements in the context of a relationship of unequal power

sexual politics link between sexuality and power

sexuality sexual behaviors, identities, meaning systems, and institutional practices

sexually dimorphic traits differences appearing between males and females

social construction of gender processes by which the expectations associated with being male and female are passed on through society

social constructionist approach perspective viewing people as constructing gender through their ongoing interaction with others

social learning theory theory of socialization emphasizing the significance of environment in explaining the socialization process

social movement work of groups organized to promote or resist change in society

social structure concept referring to the organization of society that shapes social behavior

socialist feminism feminist theoretical position that interprets the origins of women's oppression in the system of capitalism; some socialist feminists also analyze the intersections of capitalism and patriarchy

socialization process by which social roles are learned

sociological imagination ability to conceptualize the relationship between individuals and the society in which they live

sociology of knowledge field of study within sociology that examines how ideas and knowledge are produced

standpoint theory feminist theoretical argument postulating that the specific social location of the knower shapes what is known and that not all perspectives on social life are valid or complete

because of the different positions of knowers within systems of power and privilege

state organized and institutionalized system of power and authority in society, including the government, the police, law, and the military

status offenses behavior assumed to be deviant because the offender violates the presumed status associated with his or her group

stratification process by which groups or individuals in a society are located in a hierarchical arrangement on the basis of their differential access to social and economic resources

subculture of violence idea that violence stems from the cultural attributes of particular groups

subfamily U.S. Census Bureau term given to a married couple with or without children—or one parent with one or more never-married children under age 18—who live in a household and are related to, but are not included with, the person who maintains the household

superstructure in Marxist theory, institutions of society as they reflect the economic system (law, family, and the like)

symbolic interaction theoretical perspective in sociology that interprets social behavior as stemming from the meanings people attribute to things, including how they act

systems of production means and methods of organized economic production in society

temperance movement a nineteenth-century social movement with feminist values, organized to oppose alcohol abuse

Title VII of the Civil Rights Bill of 1964 federal law prohibiting discrimination on the basis of race, color, national origin, religion, or sex, in any terms, conditions, or privileges of employment

Title IX of the Educational Amendments of 1972 law forbidding discrimination on the basis of sex in all federally assisted education programs

transnational families families whose members live in different countries, usually at a considerable distance from one another, but with a pattern of moving back and forth across national boundaries

victimization surveys studies based on large, national samples that estimate the extent of crime victimization among particular groups

The Woman's Bible published in 1895 by Susan B. Anthony, the first attempt to rewrite the Bible, from a feminist perspective

women's studies field of study grounded in research and theory about women's lives which sees this knowledge as part of the process of changing women's lives for the better

ಎ Bibliography

Abramovitz, Mimi. 1996. "Dependent on the Kindness of Strangers: Issues Behind Welfare Reform." Pp. 287–294 in *For Crying Out Loud: Women's Poverty in the United States,* edited by Diane Dujon and Ann Withorn. Boston: South End Books.

Acker, Joan. 1992. "Gendered Institutions: From Sex Roles to Gendered Institutions." *Contemporary Sociology* 21 (September): 565–569.

Acuña, Rodolfo. 1988. *Occupied America: A History of Chicanos,* 3rd ed. New York: HarperCollins.

Adler, Freda. 1975. *Sisters in Crime.* New York: McGraw-Hill.

Agger, Ben. 1991. "Critical Theory, Poststructuralism, Postmodernism: Their Sociological Relevance." Pp. 105–131 in *Annual Review of Sociology,* Vol. 17, edited by W. Richard Scott and Judith Blake. Palo Alto, CA: Annual Reviews, Inc.

Alan Guttmacher Institute. 1994. *Sex and America's Teenagers.* New York: Alan Guttmacher Institute.

Alan Guttmacher Institute. 1998. "Facts in Brief." New York: Alan Guttmacher Institute.

Albin, R. 1977. "Review Essay: Psychological Studies of Rape." *Signs* 3 (Winter): 423–435.

Ali, J., and W. R. Avison. 1997. "Employment Transitions and Psychological Distress: The Contrasting Experiences of Single and Married Mothers." *Journal of Health and Social Behavior* 38 (December): 345–362.

Alicea, Marixsa. 1997. "'A Chambered Nautilus': The Contradictory Nature of Puerto Rican Women's Role in the Social Construction of a Transnational Community." *Gender & Society* 11 (October): 597–626.

Allen, Katherine R., and David M. Demo. 1995. "The Families of Lesbians and Gay Men: A New Frontier in Family Research." *Journal of Marriage and the Family* 57 (February): 111–127.

Allen, Paula Gunn. 1986. *The Sacred Hoop.* Boston: Beacon Press.

Amadiume, Ifi. 1987. *Male Daughters, Female Husbands: Gender and Sex in an African Society.* London: Zed Books.

Amato, Paul R., and Alan Booth. 1995. "Changes in Gender Role Attitudes and Perceived Marital Quality." *American Sociological Review* 60 (February): 58–66.

American Association of University Women Educational Foundation. 1992. *How Schools Shortchange Girls.* Washington, DC: American Association of University Women.

American Medical Association. 1994. *Physician Characteristics and Distribution in the U.S.* Chicago: Survey and Data Resources, American Medical Association.

Amir, M. 1971. *Patterns of Forcible Rape.* Chicago: University of Chicago Press.

Amott, Teresa L., and Julie A. Matthaei. 1996. *Race, Gender, and Work: A Multicultural History of Women in the United States,* rev. ed. Boston: South End Press.

Andersen, Margaret L. 1981. "Corporate Wives: Longing for Liberation or Satisfied with the Status Quo?" *Urban Life* 10: 311–327.

———. 1983. *Thinking About Women: Sociological and Feminist Perspectives.* New York: Macmillan.

———. 1987. "Moving Our Minds: Studying Women of Color and Reconstructing Sociology." *Teaching Sociology* 16 (April): 123–132.

Andersen, Margaret L., and Patricia Hill Collins. 1998. *Race, Class, and Gender: An Anthology,* 3rd ed. Belmont, CA: Wadsworth.

Andersen, Margaret, and Claire Renzetti. 1980. "Rape Crisis Counseling and the Culture of Individualism." *Contemporary Crises* 4: 323–339.

Anderson, A., and R. Gordon. 1978. "Witchcraft and the Status of Women—The Case of England." *British Journal of Sociology* 29: 171–184.

Andrews, W., and D. C. Andrews. 1974. "Technology and the Housewife in Nineteenth Century America." *Women's Studies* 2: 309–328.

Arditti, R., R. Duelli-Klein, and S. Minden. 1984. *Test-Tube Women: What Future for Motherhood?* Boston: Pandora Press.

Arendell, Terry. 1984. "Divorce: A Woman's Issue." *Feminist Issues* (Spring): 41–61.

———. 1992. "After Divorce: Investigations into Father Absence." *Gender & Society* 6 (December): 562–586.

———. 1995. *Fathers & Divorce.* Thousand Oaks, CA: Sage.

Aries, Philip. 1962. *Centuries of Childhood.* New York: Vintage.

Armstrong, Pamela, and Sarah Begus. 1982. "Daddy's Right: Incestuous Assault." Pp. 236–249 in *The Family, Politics and the State,* edited by I. Diamond. New York: Longman's Press.

Arnold, Regina. 1994. "Black Women in Prison: The Price of

Resistance." Pp. 171–184 in *Women of Color in U.S. Society*, edited by Maxine Baca Zinn and Bonnie Thornton Dill. Philadelphia: Temple University Press.

Associated Press. 1992. "Court That Attacks Sex Bias Is Reported Often Guilty of It." *The New York Times*, August 7, p. A17.

Atchley, Robert C. 1997. *Social Forces and Aging: An Introduction to Social Gerontology*, 8th ed. Belmont, CA: Wadsworth.

Avalos, Manual. 1996. "Gender Inequality: Sorting out the Effects of Race/Ethnicity and Gender in the Anglo Male-Latino Female Earnings Gap." *Sociological Perspectives* 39 (Winter): 497–515.

Axelson, D. E. 1985. "Women as Victims of Medical Experimentation: J. Marion Sims' Surgery on Slave Women, 1845–1850." *Sage* 2 (Fall): 10–13.

Axtell, J. 1981. *The Indian Peoples of Eastern America: A Documentary History of the Sexes*. New York: Oxford University Press.

Ayanian, J. Z., and A. M. Epstein. 1991. "Differences in the Use of Procedures Between Women and Men Hospitalized for Coronary Heart Disease." *New England Journal of Medicine* 325 (July 25): 221–225.

Baca Zinn, Maxine. 1976. "Chicanas: Power and Control in the Domestic Sphere." *DeColores* 2 (Fall): 19–31.

———. 1982a. "Chicano Men and Masculinity." *Journal of Ethnic Studies* 10 (Summer): 29–44.

———. 1982b. "Mexican-American Women in the Social Sciences." *Signs* 8 (Winter): 259–272.

———. 1990. "Family, Feminism, and Race in America." *Gender & Society* 4 (March): 68–82.

Baca Zinn, Maxine, and D. Stanley Eitzen. 1999. *Diversity in Families*, 5th ed. New York: Harper-Collins.

Bachman, Ronet. 1995. *Violence Against Women: Estimates from the Redesigned Survey*. Washington, DC: U.S. Department of Justice.

Bachman, Ronet, and Linda E. Saltzman. 1995. *Violence against Women: Estimates from the Redesigned Survey*. Washington, DC: Bureau of Justice Statistics.

Badgett, M. V. Lee. 1995. "The Wage Effects of Sexual Orientation Discrimination." *Industrial and Labor Relations Review* 48 (July): 726–739.

Badgett, M. V. Lee, and Mary C. King. 1997. Pp. 73–86 in *Homo Economics: Capitalism, Community, and Lesbian and Gay Life*, edited by Amy Gluckman and Betsy Reed. New York: Routledge.

Barber, Jennifer S., and William G. Axinn. 1998. "Gender Roles Attitudes and Marriage among Young Women." *Sociological Quarterly* 39 (Winter): 11–31.

Barfoot, C. H., and G. T. Sheppard. 1980. "Prophetic vs. Priestly Religion: The Changing Role of Women Clergy in Classical Pentecostal Churches." *Review of Religious Research* 22 (September): 2–17.

Barker-Benfield, G. J. 1976. *Horrors of the Half-Known Life*. New York: Harper & Row.

Baron, James, Allison Davis-Blake, and William Bielby. 1986. "The Structure of Opportunity: How Promotion Ladders Vary Within and Among Organizations." *Administrative Science Quarterly* 31: 248–273.

Barrett, M., and H. Roberts. 1978. "Doctors and Their Patients." Pp. 41–52 in *Women, Sexuality, and Social Control*, edited by C. Smart and B. Smart. London: Routledge & Kegan Paul.

Bart, Pauline. 1979. "The Loneliness of the Long-Distance Mother." Pp. 245–261 in *Women: A Feminist Perspective*, edited by Jo Freeman. Palo Alto, CA: Mayfield.

Bart, Pauline, and Patricia O'Brien. 1985. *Stopping Rape: Successful Survival Strategies*. New York: Pergamon Press.

Bart, Pauline B., and Eileen Geil Moran, eds. 1993. *Violence Against Women: The Bloody Footprints*. Newbury Park, CA: Sage.

Basow, Susan. 1992. *Gender: Stereotypes and Roles*, 3rd ed. Belmont, CA: Brooks/Cole.

Baumgaertner, W., ed. 1986. *Fact Book on Theological Education for the Academic Year 1985–86*. Vandalia, OH: Association of Theological Schools.

Baxandall, R. F. 1979. "Who Shall Care for Our Children? The History and Development of Day Care in the United States." Pp. 134–149 in *Women: A Feminist Perspective*, edited by Jo Freeman. Palo Alto, CA: Mayfield.

Becker, Howard. 1963. *The Outsiders*. New York: Free Press.

Becraft, Carolyn. 1990. "Women in the Military." Washington, DC: Women's Research and Education Institute.

Bellas, Marcia L. 1997. "Disciplinary Differences in Faculty Salaries: Does Gender Bias Play a Role?" *Journal of Higher Education* 68 (May–June): 299–321.

Belsky, Jay, and John Kelly. 1994. *The Transition to Parenthood*. New York: Delacorte Press.

Bénéria, L., and G. Sen. 1982. "Class and Gender Inequalities and Women's Role in Economic Development—Theoretical and Practical Implications." *Feminist Studies* 8 (Spring): 157–176.

Benet, M. K. 1972. *The Secretarial Ghetto*. New York: McGraw-Hill.

Benokraitis, N., and J. Feagin. 1995. *Modern Sexism*, 2d ed. Upper Saddle River, NJ: Prentice-Hall.

Benson, S. P. 1978. "'The Clerking Sisterhood': Rationalization and the Work Culture of Saleswomen in American Department Stores, 1890–1960." *Radical America* 12 (March–April): 41–55.

Benston, M. 1969. "The Political Economy of Women's Liberation." *Monthly Review* 21: 13–27.

Berger, Peter. 1963. *Invitation to Sociology*. Garden City, NY: Doubleday-Anchor.

Berger, Peter, and Thomas Luckmann. 1966. *The Social Construction of Reality*. Garden City, NY: Doubleday-Anchor.

Bergsmann, Ilene R. 1991. "The Forgotten Few: Juvenile Female Offenders." Pp. 496–507 in *The Dilemmas of Corrections: Contemporary Readings*, edited by Kenneth C. Haas and Geoffrey P. Alpert. Prospect Heights, IL: Waveland Press.

Berheide, Catherine White. 1988. "Women in Sales and Service

Occupations." Pp. 241–257 in *Women Working*, 2d ed., edited by Ann Helton Stromberg and Shirley Harkess. Mountain View, CA: Mayfield.

———. 1992. "Women Still 'Stuck' in Low-Level Jobs." *Women in Public Services: A Bulletin for the Center for Women in Government* 3 (Fall). Albany, NY: Center for Women in Government, State University of New York.

Berke, Richard L. 1994. "Defections Among Men to G.O.P. Helped Ensure Rout of Democrats." *The New York Times*, November 11, pp. A1, A27.

Bernard, Jessie. 1972. "Marriage: His and Hers." *Ms.* 1: 46ff.

———. 1975. *Women, Wives, Mothers: Values and Options*. Chicago: Aldine.

Bernhardt, Annette, Martina Morris, and Mark S. Handcock. 1995. "Women's Gains or Men's Losses? A Closer Look at the Shrinking Gender Gap in Earnings." *American Journal of Sociology* 101 (September): 302–328.

Best, R. 1983. *We've All Got Scars*. Bloomington, IN: Indiana University Press.

Bethel-Powers, Ann. 1996. "Relationships among Older Women Living in a Nursing Home." *Journal of Women and Aging* 8: 179–184.

Bickle, Gayle S., and Ruth D. Peterson. 1991. "The Impact of Gender-Based Family Roles on Criminal Sentencing." *Social Problems* 38 (August): 372–394.

Bienen, L. 1977. "Rape II." *Women's Rights Law Reporter* 13 (Spring/Summer): 90–137.

Bigner, Jerry J., and Frederick W. Bozett. 1989. "Parenting by Gay Fathers." *Marriage and Family Review* 14: 155–175.

Bigner, Jerry J., and R. B. Jacobsen. 1989. "Parenting Behaviors of Homosexual and Heterosexual Fathers." *Journal of Homosexuality* 18: 173–186.

Billingsley, Andrew. 1966. *Black Families in White America*. Upper Saddle River, NJ: Prentice-Hall.

Bird, Chloe E., 1996a. "Gender, Paid and Unpaid Work, and Depression." Paper given at the Annual Meetings of the Society for the Study of Social Problems.

Bird, Sharon. 1996b. "Welcome to the Men's Club: Homosociality and the Maintenance of Hegemonic Masculinity." *Gender & Society* 10 (April): 120–132.

Blackwell, James. 1991. *The Black Community: Diversity and Unity*. New York: HarperCollins.

Blackwood, Evelyn. 1984. "Sexuality and Gender in Certain Native American Tribes: The Case of Cross-Gender Females." *Signs* 10 (Autumn): 27–42.

Blake, C. Fred. 1994. "Footbinding in Neo-Confucian China and the Appropriation of Female Labor." *Signs* 19 (Spring): 676–712.

Blakemore, J. E. O. 1998. "The Influence of Gender and Parental Attitudes on Preschool Children's Interest in Babies: Observations in Natural Settings." *Sex Roles* 38 (January): 73–94.

Bleier, Ruth. 1984. *Science and Gender*. New York: Pergamon Press.

Blood, Robert, and Donald Wolfe. 1960. *Husbands and Wives: The Dynamics of Married Living*. New York: Free Press.

Blum, Linda. 1986. "Women and Advancement: Possibilities and Limits of the Comparable Worth Movement." Paper presented at the Annual Meetings of the American Sociological Association, New York City, September.

Blumenthal, Susan J. 1998. "Women and Substance Abuse: A New National Focus." Pp. 13–32 in *Drug Addiction Research and the Health of Women*, edited by Cora Lee Wetherington and Adele B. Roman. Washington, DC: National Institute on Drug Abuse.

Blumstein, Philip, and Pepper Schwartz. 1983. *American Couples*. New York: William Morrow.

Bogdan, J. 1978. "Care or Cure? Childbirth Practices in Nineteenth-Century America." *Feminist Studies* 4: 92–99.

Bookman, Ann, and Sandra Morgan. 1988. *Women and the Politics of Empowerment*.

Philadelphia: Temple University Press.

Bordo, Susan. 1992. "Feminist Skepticism and the 'Maleness' of Philosophy." Pp. 143–162 in *Women and Reason*, edited by Elizabeth D. Harvey and Kathleen Okruhlik. Ann Arbor: University of Michigan Press.

Boskind-White, M. 1985. "Bulimarexia: A Sociocultural Perspective." Pp. 113–126 in *Theory and Treatment of Anorexia Nervosa and Bulimia*, edited by S. Emmet. New York: Brunner/Mazel Publishers.

Boskind-White, M., and W. C. White, Jr. 1983. *Bulimarexia: The Binge-Purge Cycle*. New York: Norton.

Boston Women's Health Book Collective. 1984. *The New Our Bodies, Ourselves*. New York: Simon and Schuster.

Bowen, Lawrence, and Jill Schmid. 1997. "Minority Presence and Portrayal in Mainstream Magazine Advertising: An Update." *Journalism and Mass Communication Quarterly* 74 (Spring): 134–146.

Bowker, L. H. 1981. "Gender Differences in Prison Subcultures." Pp. 409–419 in *Women and Crime in America*, edited by Lee Bowker. New York: Macmillan.

Brabant, S., and L. A. Mooney. 1997. "Sex Role Stereotyping in the Sunday Comics: A Twenty Year Update." *Sex Roles* 37 (August): 269–281.

Bradford, J., Ryan, C., and E. D. Rothblum. 1994. "National Lesbian Health Care Survey: Implications for Mental Health Care." *Journal of Counseling and Clinical Psychology* 62: 228–242.

Bragg, Rick. 1994. "Life of a Mother Accused of Killing Offers No Clues." *The New York Times*, November 6, p. A1.

Bramson, Leon. 1961. *The Political Context of Sociology*. Princeton, NJ: Princeton University Press.

Britton, Dana M. 1997. "Gendered Organizational Logic: Policy and Practice in Men's and Women's Prisons." *Gender & Society* 11 (December): 796–818.

Brod, Harry, and Michael Kaufman, eds. 1994. *Theorizing Masculinities*. Thousand Oaks, CA: Sage.

Brown, C. 1981. "Mothers, Fathers, and Children: From Private to Public Patriarchy." Pp. 239–267 in *Women and Revolution*, edited by Lydia Sargent. New York: South End Press.

Brown, J. D., and K. Campbell. 1986. "Race and Gender in Music Videos: The Same Beat But A Different Drummer." *Journal of Communication* 36 (Winter): 94–106.

Brown, S. E. 1975. "Love Unites Them and Hunger Separates Them." Pp. 322–332 in *Toward an Anthropology of Women*, edited by Rayna Reiter. New York: Monthly Review Press.

Brown, Susan L. 1996. "Relationship Quality and the Transition to Marriage among Cohabitors." Paper presented at the Annual Meetings of the American Sociological Association.

Browne, Angela, and Kirk R. Williams. 1993. "Gender, Intimacy and Lethal Violence Trends from 1976 through 1987." *Gender & Society* 78 (March): 78–98.

Browne, Malcolm W. 1998. "Can't Decide if That Centerfold Is Really a Perfect 10? Just Do the Math." *The New York Times*, October 20, p. D5.

Brownmiller, S. 1975. *Against Our Will*. New York: Simon and Schuster.

Bruch, H. 1978. *The Golden Cage: The Enigma of Anorexia Nervosa*. London: Open Books.

Brush, Lisa D. 1990. "Violent Acts and Injurious Outcomes in Married Couples: Methodological Issues in the National Survey of Families and Households." *Gender & Society* 4 (March): 56–67.

Bryson, Ken, and Lynne M. Casper. 1998. *Household and Family Characteristics: March 1997*, Current Population Reports, Series P20-509 (April). Washington, DC: U.S. Census Bureau.

Bunch, Charlotte. 1975. "Lesbians in Revolt." Pp. 29–38 in *Lesbian-*

ism and the Women's Movement, edited by N. Myron and C. Bunch. Oakland, CA: Diana Press.

———. 1987. *Passionate Politics: Essays 1968–1986—Feminist Theory in Action*. New York: St. Martin's Press.

Burgess, A. W., and L. L. Holmstrom. 1978. *The Victim of Rape: Institutional Reactions*. New York: Wiley.

Burlage, D. 1974. "Judaeo-Christian Influences on Female Sexuality." Pp. 93–116 in *Sexist Religion and Women in the Church*, edited by A. L. Hageman. New York: Association Press.

Burris, Beverly H. 1991. "Employed Mothers: The Impact of Class and Marital Status on the Prioritizing of Family and Work." *Social Science Quarterly* 72 (March): 50–66.

Butler, Amy C. 1996. "The Effect of Welfare Benefit Levels on Poverty among Single-Parent Families." *Social Problems* 43 (February): 94–115.

Butler, Judith. 1990. *Gender Trouble: Feminism and the Subversion of Identity*. New York: Routledge.

Calasanti, Toni M. 1992. "Working 'Over-Time': Economic Restructuring and Retirement of a Class." *Sociological Quarterly* 33 (Spring): 135–152.

Califia, Pat. 1997. *Sex Changes: The Politics of Transgenderism*. San Francisco: Cleis Books.

Cameron, Deborah. 1998. "Gender, Language, and Discourse: A Review Essay." *Signs* 23 (Summer): 945–974.

Campbell, Anne. 1989. *Girls in the Gang*. Cambridge: Basil Blackwell.

Cancian, Francesca. 1987. *Love in America: Gender and Self-Development*. New York: Cambridge University Press.

Carothers, S. C., and P. Crull. 1984. "Contrasting Sexual Harassment in Female- and Male-Dominated Occupations." Pp. 209–228 in *My Troubles Are Going to Have Trouble With Me*, edited by Karen B. Sacks and Dorothy Remy. New Brunswick, NJ: Rutgers University Press.

Carr, D. 1997. "The Fulfillment of Career Dreams at Midlife: Does It Matter for Women's Mental Health?" *Journal of Health and Social Behavior* 38 (December): 331–344.

Carrington, C. H. 1980. "Depression in Black Women: A Theoretical Appraisal." Pp. 265–272 in *The Black Woman*, edited by L. F. Rodgers-Rose. Beverly Hills, CA: Sage.

Carroll, J. W., B. Hargrove, and A. T. Lummis. 1981. *Women of the Cloth*. San Francisco: Harper and Row.

Carter, Deborah, and Reginald Wilson. 1998. *Minorities in Higher Education*. Washington, DC: American Council on Education.

Casper, Lynn M. 1995. "What Does It Cost to Mind Our Preschoolers?" Washington, DC: U.S. Census Bureau. <www.census.gov>

Caulfield, Mina Davis. 1974. "Imperialism, the Family, and Cultures of Resistance." *Socialist Revolution* 20: 67–85.

———. 1985. "Sexuality in Human Evolution: What is 'Natural' in Sex?" *Feminist Studies* 11 (Summer): 343–364.

Center for the American Woman and American Politics. 1995. *Fact Sheet on Women's Political Progress*. New Brunswick, NJ: Rutgers University.

———. 1998. *Women's Electoral Success: A Familiar Formula*. New Brunswick, NJ: Rutgers University.

Centers for Disease Control. 1998. "Fastats A to Z: Prenatal Care." <www.cdc.gov/nchswww/fastates/prenatal.htm>

Chancer, Lynn S. 1987. "New Bedford, Massachusetts, March 6, 1983–March 22, 1984: The 'Before and After' of a Group Rape." *Gender & Society* 1 (September): 239–260.

Chancer, Lynn. 1993. "Prostitution, Feminist Theory, and Ambivalence: Notes from the Sociological Underground." *Social Text* 37 (Winter): 143–171.

Chassin, Laurie, Clark C. Presson, and Steven J. Sherman. 1989. "'Constructive' vs. 'Destructive' Deviance in Adolescent Health-Related Behaviors." *Journal of*

Youth and Adolescence 18: 245–262.

Chaves, Mark, and James Cavendish. 1997. "Recent Changes in Women's Ordination Conflicts: The Effect of a Social Movement on Intraorganizational Controversy." *Journal for the Scientific Study of Religion* 36 (December): 574–584.

Chavkin, W. 1979. "Occupational Hazards to Reproduction: A Review Essay and Annotated Bibliography." *Feminist Studies* 5 (Summer): 310–325.

Chernin, Kim. 1981. *The Obsession.* New York: Harper Colophon.

———. 1985. *The Hungry Self: Women, Eating, and Identity.* New York: Times Books.

Chesler, P. 1972. *Women and Madness.* Garden City, NY: Doubleday.

Chesney-Lind, Meda. 1981. "Judicial Paternalism and the Female Status Offender." Pp. 354–366 in *Women and Crime in America,* edited by Lee Bowker. New York: Macmillan.

———. 1986. "Women and Crime: The Female Offender." *Signs* 12 (Autumn): 78–96.

———. 1997. "Equity with a Vengeance." *The Women's Review of Books* 14 (July): 5.

Chodorow, Nancy. 1978. *The Reproduction of Mothering.* Berkeley: University of California Press.

Chow, Esther. 1987. "The Development of Feminist Consciousness Among Asian American Women." *Gender & Society* 1 (September): 284–299.

Christ, Carol. 1979. "Why Women Need the Goddess: Phenomenological, Psychological and Political Reflections." Pp. 273–287 in *Womanspirit Rising,* edited by C. P. Christ and J. Plaskow. New York: Harper and Row.

Christ, Carol P., and Judith Plaskow, eds. 1992. *Womanspirit Rising,* 2nd ed. New York: Harper and Row.

Chronicle of Higher Education Almanac, The. 1998. Volume 45 (August 28).

Church, George J. 1990. "The View From Behind Bars." *Time* 136 (Fall): 20–22.

Churchill, Ward. 1993. "Crimes Against Humanity." *Z Magazine* 6 (March): 43–47.

Clark, L., and D. Lewis. 1977. *Rape: The Price of Coercive Sexuality.* Toronto: Women's Press.

Clark, Roger, Rachel Lennon, and Leanna Morris. 1993. "Of Caldecotts and Kings: Gendered Images in Recent American Children's Books by Black and Non-Black Illustrators." *Gender & Society* 7 (June): 227–245.

Clarkberg, Marin, Ross M. Stolzenberg, and Linda J. Waite. 1995. "Attitudes, Values, and Entrance into Cohabitational versus Marital Unions." *Social Forces* 74 (December): 609–632.

Clarke, E. 1873. *Sex in Education; Or, A Fair Chance for the Girls.* Boston: Osgood and Company.

Clay, V. S. 1977. *Women: Menopause and Middle Age.* Pittsburgh: Know, Inc.

Cohen, Lisa E., Joseph P. Broschak, and Heather A. Haveman. 1998. "Sex Composition and the Hiring/Promotion of Women Managers." *American Sociological Review* 63 (October): 711–727.

Colker, Brian D. 1997. "Wage Inequality in the Staff Workforce at UCLA." Paper presented at the Annual Meetings of the American Sociological Association, Toronto.

Collins, Patricia Hill. 1986. "Learning From the Outsider Within: The Sociological Significance of Black Feminist Thought." *Social Problems* 33 (December): 514–532.

———. 1987. "The Meaning of Motherhood in Black Culture and Black Mother-Daughter Relationships." *Sage* 4 (Fall): 3–10.

———. 1990. *Black Feminist Theory: Knowledge, Consciousness and the Politics of Empowerment.* Boston: Unwin Hyman.

———. 1998. *Fighting Words: Black Women and the Search for Social Justice.* Minneapolis: University of Minnesota Press.

Collins, Patricia Hill, Lionel Maldonado, Dana Tagaki, Barrie Thorne, Lynn Weber, and Howard Winant. 1995. "Symposium: Doing Difference." *Gender & Society* 9 (August): 491–505.

Colman, A., and L. Colman. 1981. *Earth Father/Sky Father: The Changing Concepts of Fathering.* Upper Saddle River, NJ: Prentice-Hall.

Coltrane, Scott, and Michele Adams. 1997. "Work-Family Imagery and Gender Stereotypes: Television and the Reproduction of Difference." *Journal of Vocational Behavior* 50 (April): 323–347.

Combahee River Collective. 1982. "A Black Feminist Statement." Pp. 13–22 in *But Some of Us Are Brave,* edited by Gloria T. Hull, Patricia Bell Scott, and Barbara Smith. Old Westbury, NY: The Feminist Press.

Connell, Bob. 1992. "Masculinity, Violence, and War." Pp. 176–183 in *Men's Lives,* 2nd ed., edited by Michael S. Kimmel and Michael A. Messner. New York: Macmillan.

Conover, P. J., and V. Gray. 1983. *Feminism and the New Right.* New York: Praeger.

Conte, Jon R. 1993. "Sexual Abuse of Children." Pp. 56–85 in *Family Violence: Prevention and Treatment,* edited by Robert L. Hampton, Thomas P. Gullotta, Gerald R. Adams, Earl H. Potter III., and Roger P. Weissberg. Newbury Park, CA: Sage.

Cooke, Miriam, and Angela Woollacott, eds. 1993. *Gendering War Talk.* Princeton, NJ: Princeton University Press.

Cooper, V. W. 1985. "Women in Popular Music: A Quantitative Analysis of Feminine Images Over Time." *Sex Roles* 13 (November): 499–506.

Cooperstock, R. 1971. "Sex Differences in the Use of Mood-Modifying Drugs: An Explanatory Model." *Journal of Health and Social Behavior* 12: 238–244.

Corea, Gena. 1980. "The Caesarian Epidemic." *Mother Jones* 5: 28ff.

———. 1977. *The Hidden Malpractice.* New York: William Morrow.

———. 1985. *The Mother Machine: Reproductive Technologies from Artificial Insemination to Artificial*

Wombs. New York: Harper and Row.

Costello, C. B. 1985. "'WEA're Worth It!' Work Culture and Conflict at the Wisconsin Education Association Insurance Trust." *Feminist Studies* 11 (Fall): 497–518.

Cott, Nancy. 1977. *The Bonds of Womanhood.* New Haven, CT: Yale University Press.

Council of Economic Advisors. 1998. *Changing America: Indicators of Social and Economic Well-Being by Race and Hispanic Origin.* Washington, DC: U.S. Government Printing Office.

Cowan, R. S. 1976. "Two Washes in the Morning and a Bridge Party at Night: The American Housewife Between Wars." *Women's Studies* 3: 147–171.

Crabb, Peter B., and Dawn Bielawski. 1994. "The Social Representation of Material Culture and Gender in Children's Books." *Sex Roles* 30 (January): 69–80.

Cramer, K. M., and K. A. Neyedley. 1998. "Sex Differences in Loneliness: The Role of Masculinity and Femininity." *Sex Roles* 38 (April): 645–653.

Craven, Diane. 1994. "Sex Differences in Violent Victimization, 1994." Washington, DC: Bureau of Justice Statistics.

———. 1996. "Female Victims of Violent Crime." Washington, DC: Bureau of Justice Statistics.

———. 1997. *Sex Differences in Violent Victimization, 1994.* Washington, DC: Bureau of Justice Statistics.

Crawford, Mary. 1995. *Talking Difference: On Gender and Language.* Thousand Oaks: Sage.

Crawford, Mary, and M. MacLeod. 1990. "Gender in the College Classroom: An Assessment of the 'Chilly Climate' for Women." *Sex Roles* 23: 101–122.

Crenshaw, Carrie. 1995. "The 'Protection' of 'Woman': A History of Legal Attitudes toward Women's Workplace Freedom." *Quarterly Journal of Speech* 81 (February): 63–82.

Croteau, James M. 1996. "Research on the Work Experiences of

Lesbian, Gay, and Bisexual People: An Integrative Review of Methodology and Findings." *Journal of Vocational Behavior* 48 (April): 195–209.

Crowley, John E. 1983. "Longitudinal Effects of Retirement on Men's Psychological and Physical Well-Being." Pp. 147–173 in *Retirement Among American Men,* edited by Herbert S. Purnes. Lexington, MA: D. C. Heath.

Culbertson, Robert G., and Eddyth P. Fortune. 1991. "Women in Crime and Prison." Pp. 105–120 in *The Dilemmas of Corrections: Contemporary Readings,* edited by Kenneth C. Haas and Geoffrey P. Alpert. Prospect Heights, IL: Waveland Press.

Currie, Dawn. 1997. "Decoding Femininity: Advertisements and Their Teenage Readers." *Gender & Society* 11 (August): 453–477.

Dalaker, Joseph, and Mary Naifeh, U.S. Bureau of the Census, Current Population Reports, Series P60-201. 1998. *Poverty in the United States: 1997.* Washington, DC: U.S. Department of Commerce. <www.census.gov>

Daly, Kathleen. 1989. "Rethinking Judicial Paternalism: Gender, Work-Family Relations, and Sentencing," *Gender & Society* 3 (March): 9–36.

———. 1994. *Gender, Crime and Punishment.* New Haven, CT: Yale University Press.

Daly, Mary. 1975. *The Church and the Second Sex.* New York: Harper and Row.

———. 1979. "After the Death of God the Father: Women's Liberation and the Transformation of Christian Consciousness." Pp. 53–62 in *Womanspirit Rising,* edited by C. P. Christ and J. Plaskow. New York: Harper and Row.

———. 1978. *Gyn/Ecology: The Meta-Ethics of Radical Feminism.* Boston: Beacon Press.

Daniels, Arlene Kaplan. 1988. *Invisible Careers.* Chicago: University of Chicago Press.

Darcy, R., Susan Welch, and Janet Clark. 1994. *Women, Elections, and Representation.* Lincoln: University of Nebraska Press.

Das Gupta, Monisha. 1997. "'What Is Indian about You?': A Gendered, Transnational Approach to Ethnicity." *Gender & Society* 11 (October): 572–596.

Davidman, Lynn. 1991. *Tradition in a Rootless World: Women Turn to Orthodox Judaism.* Berkeley: University of California Press.

Davis, A. J. 1984. "Sex-Differentiated Behaviors in Nonsexist Picture Books." *Sex Roles* 11 (July): 1–16.

Davis, Angela. 1971. "Reflections on Black Women's Role in the Community of Slaves." *The Black Scholar* 3: 2–15.

———. 1981. *Women, Race and Class.* New York: Random House.

Davis, Donald M. 1990. "Portrayals of Women in Prime-Time Network Television: Some Demographic Characteristics." *Sex Roles* 23: 325–332.

Deaux, K., L. White, and E. Farris. 1975. "Skill Versus Luck: Field and Laboratory Studies of Male and Female Preferences." *Journal of Personality and Social Psychology* 32: 629–636.

DeFrancisco, Victoria Leto. 1991. "The Sounds of Silence: How Men Silence Women in Marital Relations." *Discourse and Society* 2: 413–423.

Deitz, S. R., K. T. Blackwell, P. C. Daley, and B. J. Bentley. 1982. "Measurement of Empathy Toward Rape Victims and Rapists." *Journal of Personality and Social Psychology* 43 (August): 372–384.

Delaney, J., M. J. Lupton, and E. Toth. 1988. *The Curse: A Cultural History of Menstruation.* Urbana: University of Illinois Press.

Dellinger, Kirsten, and Christine L. Williams. 1997. "Makeup at Work: Negotiating Appearance Rules in the Workplace." *Gender & Society* 11 (April): 151–177.

de la Torre, Adela, and Beatriz Pesquera, eds. 1993. *Building With Our Hands: New Directions in Chicana Studies.* Berkeley: University of California Press.

D'Emilio, John, and Estelle B. Freedman. 1988. *Intimate Matters: A History of Sexuality in America.* New York: Harper and Row.

Denzin, Norman K. 1993. "Sexuality and Gender: An Interactionist/Poststructural Reading." Pp. 199–221 in *Theory on Gender/Feminism on Theory*, edited by Paula England. New York: Aldine de Gruyter.

de Tocqueville, A. 1945. *Democracy in America*. New York: Knopf.

Deutscher, I. 1973. *What We Say/What We Do*. Glenview, IL: Scott, Foresman.

DeVault, Marjorie L. 1991. *Feeding the Family: The Social Organization of Caring as Gender Work*. Chicago: University of Chicago Press.

Diamond, Milton, and H. K. Sigmundson. 1997. "Sex Reassignment at Birth: Long-Term Review and Clinical Implications." *Archives of Pediatric and Adolescent Medicine* 151 (March): 298–304.

Dickens, W. J., and D. Perlman. 1981. "Friendship over the Life Cycle." Pp. 91–122 in *Personal Relationships, Vol. 2, Developing Personal Relationships*, edited by S. Duck and R. Gilmour. New York: Academic Press.

Dietz, T. L. 1998. "An Examination of Violence and Gender Role Portrayals in Video Games: Implications for Gender Socialization and Aggressive Behavior." *Sex Roles* 38 (March): 425–442.

Dill, Bonnie Thornton. 1979. "The Dialectics of Black Womanhood." *Signs* 4 (Spring): 543–555.

———. 1980. "'The Means to Put My Children Through': Childrearing Goals and Strategies Among Black Female Domestic Servants." Pp. 107–123 in *The Black Woman*, edited by L. F. Rodgers-Rose. Beverly Hills, CA: Sage.

———. 1983. "Race, Class, and Gender: Prospects for an All Inclusive Sisterhood." *Feminist Studies* 9 (Spring): 131–150.

———. 1988. "Our Mothers' Grief: Racial Ethnic Women and the Maintenance of Families." *Journal of Family History* 13: 415–431.

———. 1994. "Fictive Kin, Paper Sons, and *Compadrazgo*." Pp. 149–170 in *Women of Color in U.S.*

Society, edited by Maxine Baca Zinn and Bonnie Thornton Dill. Philadelphia: Temple University Press.

Dines, Gail, and Jean M. Humez, eds. 1995. *Gender, Race, and Class in Media*. Thousand Oaks, CA: Sage.

DiPrete, Thomas. 1989. *The Bureaucratic Labor Market: The Case of the Federal Civil Service*. New York: Plenum Press.

Dobash, R. E., and R. Dobash. 1977. "Love, Honor, and Obey: Institutional Ideologies and the Struggle for Battered Women." *Contemporary Crises* 1: 403–415.

———. 1979. *Violence Against Wives*. New York: Free Press.

Dobash, Russell, R. Emerson Dobash, Margo Wilson, and Martin Daly. 1992. "The Myth of Sexual Symmetry in Marital Violence." *Social Problems* 39 (February): 71–91.

Dodson, J. E., and C. T. Gilkes. 1986. "Something Within: Social Change and Collective Endurance in the Sacred World of Black Christian Women." Pp. 80–130 in *Women and Religion in America, Volume 3: 1900–1968*, edited by R. Reuther and R. Keller. New York: Harper and Row.

Donegan, J. 1978. *Women and Men Midwives: Medicine, Morality and Misogyny in Early America*. Westport, CT: Greenwood Press.

Donzelot, J. 1979. *The Policing of Families*. New York: Pantheon.

Douglas, A. 1977. *The Feminization of American Culture*. New York: Knopf.

Douglas, P. 1984. "Minority Groups Push Olympic ABC-TV Hirings." *The National Leader* (December 29): 5.

Draper, R. 1986. "The History of Advertising in America." *New York Review of Books* 33 (June 26): 14–18.

DuBois, Ellen Carol. 1978. *Feminism and Suffrage*. Ithaca, NY: Cornell University Press.

Dudley, Roger L. 1996. "How Seventh-Day Adventists Lay Members View Women Pastors." *Review of Religious Research* 38 (December): 133–141.

Dugger, Karen. 1988. "The Social Location of Black and White Women's Attitudes." *Gender & Society* 2 (December): 425–448.

Dujon, Diane, and Ann Withorn, eds. 1996. *For Crying Out Loud: Women's Poverty in the United States*. Boston: South End Books.

Dworkin, Andrea. 1974. *Woman Hating*. New York: E. P. Dutton.

Dye, Nancy Schrom. 1975. "Creating a Feminist Alliance: Sisterhood and Class Conflict in the New York Women's Trade Union League, 1903–1914." *Feminist Studies* 2: 24–38.

———. 1980. "History of Childbirth in America." *Signs* 6: 97–108.

Eagly, A., and L. Carli. 1981. "Sex of Researchers and Sex-Typed Communications as Determinants of Sex Differences in Influenceability: A Meta-analysis of Social Influence Studies." *Psychological Bulletin* 90: 1–20.

Economist, The. 1998. "Brother Fidel and the Women of Cuba." 346: 42.

Edin, Kathryn, and Laura Lein. 1997. *Making Ends Meet: How Single Mothers Survive Welfare and Low-Wage Work*. New York: Russell Sage Foundation.

Ehrenreich, Barbara. 1983. *Hearts of Men*. Garden City, NY: Anchor.

Ehrenreich, Barbara, and Deidre English. 1973a. *Complaints and Disorders*. Old Westbury, NY: Feminist Press.

———. 1973b. *Witches, Midwives, and Nurses: A History of Women Healers*. Old Westbury, NY: Feminist Press.

———. 1978. *For Her Own Good*. Garden City, NY: Anchor-Doubleday.

Eisenstein, Zillah, ed. 1979. *Socialist Feminism and the Case for Capitalist Patriarchy*. New York: Monthly Review Press.

———. 1981. *The Radical Future of Liberal Feminism*. New York: Longmans.

———. 1988. *The Female Body and the Law*. Berkeley: University of California Press.

Elkins, Leigh E., and Christopher Peterson. 1993. "Gender Differences in Best Friendships." *Sex Roles* 29 (October): 497–500.

Emmet, T. 1879. *Principles and Practices of Gynaecology.* Philadelphia: Lea.

Engels, Friedrich. 1884 [1972]. *The Origins of the Family, Private Property and the State,* edited by Eleanor Leacock. New York: International.

English, D. 1980. "The Politics of Porn." *Mother Jones* 5: 20ff.

Enloe, Cynthia. 1988. *Does Khaki Become You? The Militarization of Women's Lives.* London: Pandora.

———. 1989. *Bananas, Beaches, and Bases: Making Feminist Sense of International Politics.* Berkeley: University of California Press.

———. 1993. *The Morning After: Sexual Politics at the End of the Cold War.* Berkeley: University of California Press.

Epstein, C. 1970. *Woman's Place: Options and Limits in Professional Careers.* Berkeley: University of California Press.

———. 1993. *Women in Law.* Chicago: University of Chicago Press.

Espin, Oliva M. 1984. "Cultural and Historical Influences on Sexuality in Hispanic/Latin Women: Implications for Psychotherapy." Pp. 149–164 in *Pleasure and Danger,* edited by Carole Vance. Boston: Routledge & Kegan Paul.

Evans, S. 1979. *Personal Politics: The Roots of Women's Liberation in the Civil Rights Movement and the New Left.* New York: Knopf.

Ex, Carine T. G. M., and Jan M. A. M. Janssens. 1998. "Maternal Influences on Daughters' Gender Roles Attitudes." *Sex Roles* 38 (February): 171–186.

Falk, N. 1985. "Introduction." Pp. xv–xxi in *Women, Religion and Social Change,* edited by Y. Y. Haddad and E. B. Findly. Albany: State University of New York Press.

Faludi, Susan. 1991. *Backlash: The Undeclared War on American Women.* New York: Crown.

Famighetti, Robert, ed. 1995. *The World Almanac and Book of Facts, 1995.* Mahwah, NJ: Funk & Wagnalls.

Farber, Naomi. 1990. "The Significance of Race and Class in Marital Decisions among Unmarried Adolescent Mothers." *Social Problems* 37 (February): 51–63.

Fausto-Sterling, Anne. 1992. *Myths of Gender,* 2nd ed. New York: Basic Books.

Federal Bureau of Investigation. 1997. *Crime in the United States, 1997.* Washington, DC: U.S. Government Printing Office.

Fee, Elizabeth. 1983. "Woman's Nature and Scientific Objectivity." Pp. 9–28 in *Woman's Nature,* edited by Marion Lowe and Ruth Hubbard. New York: Pergamon Press.

Feldberg, Roslyn L., and Evelyn Nakano Glenn. 1979. "Job vs. Gender Models in the Sociology of Work." *Social Problems* 26 (June): 524–538.

Ferree, Myra Marx. 1984. "Sacrifice, Satisfaction, and Social Change: Employment and the Family." Pp. 61–79 in *My Troubles Are Going to Have Trouble with Me,* edited by Karen B. Sacks and Dorothy Remy. New Brunswick, NJ: Rutgers University Press.

Ferree, Myra Marx, Denise Anthony, and Jane Riblett Wilkie. 1994. "Economic Dependency, the Breadwinner Role and the Division of Household Labor." Paper presented at the International Sociological Association.

Ferree, Myra Marx, and Beth Hess. 1985. *Controversy and Coalition: The New Feminist Movement.* Boston: Twayne Publishers.

Fidell, L. S. 1973. "Put Her Down on Drugs: Prescribes Drug Usage in Women." Paper presented at the Western Psychological Association Meeting, Anaheim, CA.

Figueroa, Janis Barry, and Edwin Melendez. 1993. "The Importance of Family Members in Determining the Labor Supply of Puerto Rican, Black, and White Single Mothers." *Social Science Quarterly* 74 (December): 867–883.

Finlay, Barbara. 1996. "Do Men and Women Have Different Goals for Ministry? Evidence from Seminarians." *Sociology of Religion* 57 (Fall): 311–318.

———. 1997. "Future Ministers and Legal Abortion: Gender Comparisons among Protestant Seminary Students." *Women and Politics* 17: 1–15.

Firestein, Beth, ed. 1996. *Bisexuality: The Psychology and Politics of an Invisible Minority.* Thousand Oaks, CA: Sage.

Firestone, Juanita M., Richard J. Harris, and Linda C. Lambert. 1998. "Gender Role Ideology and the Gender Based Differences in Earnings" Paper presented at the Annual Meetings of the American Sociological Association, San Francisco.

Fischbach, Ruth L., and Barbara Herbert. 1997. "Domestic Violence and Mental Health: Correlated and Conundrums within and across Cultures." *Social Science and Medicine* 45 (October): 1161–1176.

Flaks, D. K., I. Fischer, F. Masterpasqua, and G. Joseph. 1995. "Lesbians Choosing Motherhood: A Comparative Study of Lesbians and Heterosexual Parents and Their Children." *Developmental Psychology* 21: 105–114.

Flax, Jane. 1976. "Do Feminists Need Marxism?" *Quest* 3 (Summer): 46–58.

———. 1990. "Postmodernism and Gender Relations in Feminist Theory." Pp. 39–62 in *Feminism and Postmodernism,* edited by Linda J. Nicholson. New York: Routledge.

Flexner, Eleanor. 1972. *Mary Wollstonecraft: A Biography.* New York: Coward, McCann, and Geoghegan.

———. 1975. *Century of Struggle: The Woman's Rights Movement in the United States.* Cambridge, MA: Harvard University Press.

Flowers, R. B. 1984. *Religion in Strange Times: The 1960s and 1970s.* Macon, GA: Mercer University Press.

Floyd, Kory, and Malcolm R. Parks. 1995. "Manifesting Closeness in the Interactions of Peers: A Look at Siblings and Friends." *Communication Reports* 8 (Summer): 69–76.

Fonow, Mary Margaret, Laurel Richardson, and Virginia A. Wemmerus. 1992. "Feminist

Rape Education: Does it Work?" *Gender & Society* 6 (March): 108–121.

Foucault, M. 1965. *Madness and Civilization: A History of Insanity in the Age of Reason.* New York: Vintage.

Fox, L. H., E. Fennema, and J. Sherman, eds. 1977. *Women and Mathematics: Research Perspectives for Change.* Washington, DC: National Institute of Education.

Fox, M., M. Gibbs, and D. Auerbach. 1985. "Age and Gender Dimensions of Friendship." *Psychology of Women Quarterly* 9: 489–502.

Francis, L. J., and Clyde Wilcox. 1998. "Religiosity and Femininity: Do Women Really Hold a More Positive Attitude toward Christianity?" *Journal for the Scientific Study of Religion* 37 (September): 462–469.

Fraser, Nancy. 1989. *Unruly Practices: Power, Discourse, and Gender in Contemporary Social Theory.* Minneapolis: University of Minnesota Press.

Frazier, E. Franklin. 1948. *The Negro Family in the United States.* New York: Citadel Press.

———. 1964. *The Negro Church in America.* New York: Schocken.

Freedman, Estelle, and Barrie Thorne. 1984. "Introduction to 'The Feminist Sexuality Debates.'" *Signs* 10 (Autumn): 102–105.

Freeman, Jo. 1973. "The Origins of the Women's Liberation Movement." *American Journal of Sociology* 78: 792–811.

Frey, K. 1981. "Middle-Aged Women's Experience and Perceptions of Menopause." *Women and Health* 6: 31–36.

Fried, Amy. 1994. "'It's Hard to Change What We Want to Change': Rape Crisis Centers as Organizations." *Gender & Society* 8 (December): 562–584.

Friedl, E. 1975. *Women and Men.* New York: Holt, Rinehart and Winston.

Friedman, M., and R. H. Rosenman. 1974. *Type A Behavior and Your Heart.* New York: Knopf.

Frieze, I. H. 1983. "Investigating the Causes and Consequences of

Marital Rape." *Signs* 8 (Spring): 532–553.

Frieze, I., J. Parsons, P. Johnson, D. N. Ruble, and G. Zellman, eds. 1978. *Women and Sex Roles.* New York: Norton.

Frieze, I., and S. J. Ramsey. 1976. "Nonverbal Maintenance of Traditional Sex Roles." *Journal of Social Issues,* 32: 133–141.

Frohmann, Lisa. 1991. "Discrediting Victims' Allegations of Sexual Assault: Prosecutorial Accounts of Case Rejections." *Social Problems* 38 (May): 213–226.

Frye, Marilyn. 1983. *The Politics of Reality.* Trumansburg, NY: Crossing Press.

———. 1992. *Willful Virgin: Essays in Feminism.* Freedom, CA: Crossing Press.

Fullerton, Howard N., Jr. 1985. "The 1995 Labor Force: BLS' Latest Projections." *Monthly Labor Review* 108 (November): 17–25.

———. 1995. "The 2005 Labor Force: Growing, but Slowly." *Monthly Labor Review* 118 (November): 29–45.

Furnham, A., and L. Gasson. 1998. "Sex Differences in Parental Estimates of Their Children's Intelligence." *Sex Roles* 38 (January): 151–162.

Gagnon, John. 1995. *Conceiving Sexuality: Approaches to Sex Research in a Postmodern World.* New York: Routledge.

Gallup, George, Jr. 1993. *The Gallup Poll: Public Opinion 1993.* Wilmington, DE: Scholarly Resources.

Gallup, George, Jr., and Sarah Jones. 1989. *100 Questions and Answers: Religion in America.* Princeton, NJ: Princeton Religion Research Center.

Gallup Poll. 1996. Storrs, CT: Roper Organization.

Gallup Poll. 1997. Storrs, CT: Roper Organization.

Gallup Poll. 1998, September 21. Storrs, CT: Roper Organization

Gallup Poll Monthly. 1995. "Who Are the Religious Americans?" Storrs, CT: Roper Organization.

Gallup Report. 1985. *Religion in America 50 Years: 1935–1985.* Princeton, NJ: Gallup Poll.

Gamson, Joshua. 1995. "Must Identity Movements Self-

Destruct? A Queer Dilemma." *Social Problems* 42 (August): 390–407.

Gardner, Jennifer M., and Diane E. Herz. 1992. "Working and Poor in 1990." *Monthly Labor Review* (December): 20–28.

Garrett, G. R., and H. M. Bahr. 1976. "The Family Backgrounds of Skid Row Women." *Signs* 2 (Winter): 369–381.

Genovese, Eugene. 1972. *Roll, Jordan, Roll.* New York: Pantheon.

Gerbner, G. 1978. "The Dynamics of Cultural Resistance." Pp. 46–50 in *Hearth and Home: Images of Women in the Media,* edited by Gaye Tuchman, Arlene Kaplan Daniels, and James Benét. New York: Oxford University Press.

Gerson, Judith. 1985. "Women Returning to School: The Consequences of Multiple Roles." *Sex Roles* 13 (July): 77–91.

Gerson, Kathleen. 1990. "Coping with the Conflicts Between Family and Work." Paper presented at the Annual Meeting of the American Sociological Association, Washington, DC, August.

Gerstel, Naomi. 1988. "Divorce, Gender and Social Integration." *Gender & Society* 2 (September): 343–367.

Gerstel, Naomi, and Harriet Gross. 1984. *Commuter Marriage.* New York: Guilford.

Geschwender, James. 1992. "Ethnicity and the Social Construction of Gender in the Chinese Diaspora." *Gender & Society* 6 (September): 480–507.

Giallombardo, R. 1966. *Society of Women: A Study of a Women's Prison.* New York: Wiley.

Gibbons, Sheila, ed. 1992. *Media Report to Women* 20 (Fall): 5.

Gibbons, Sheila J. 1998. *Media Report to Women* 26 (Winter): 4–5, 10.

Gibson, Diane. 1996. "Broken Down by Age and Gender: 'The Problem of Old Women' Revisited." *Gender & Society* 10 (August): 443–448.

Giddens, Anthony. 1971. *Capitalism and Modern Social Theory: An Analysis of the Writings of Marx, Durkheim, and Max Weber.*

Cambridge: Cambridge University Press.

Gilkes, Cheryl Townsend. 1980. "'Holding Back the Ocean with a Broom:' Black Women and Community Work." Pp. 217–232 in *The Black Woman*, edited by L. F. Rodgers-Rose. Beverly Hills: Sage.

———. 1985. "Together and in Harness: Women's Traditions in the Sanctified Church." *Signs* 10 (Summer): 678–699.

Gill, Gurjeet K., and Ray Hibbons. 1996. "Wives Encounters: Family Work Stress and Leisure in Two-Job Families." *International Journal of Sociology of the Family* 26 (Autumn): 43–54.

Gilliard, Darrell K., and Allen J. Beck. 1998. "Prisoners in 1997." *Bulletin*, August. Washington, DC: Bureau of Justice Statistics.

Gilligan, Carol. 1982. *In a Different Voice*. Cambridge, MA: Harvard University Press.

Glaser, R. D., and J. S. Thorpe. 1986. "Unethical Intimacy." *American Psychologist* 41 (January): 43–51.

Glass Ceiling Commission. 1995. *Good for Business: Making Full Use of the Nation's Human Capital.* Washington, DC: U.S. Government Printing Office.

Glass, Jennifer, and Tetushi Fujimoto. 1994. "Housework, Paid Work, and Depression among Husbands and Wives." *Journal of Health and Social Behavior* 35 (June): 179–191.

Glenn, Evelyn Nakano. 1983. "Split Household, Small Producer, and Dual Wage Earner: An Analysis of Chinese-American Family Strategies." *Journal of Marriage and the Family* 45 (February): 35–46.

———. 1986. *Issei, Nisei, War Bride: Three Generations of Japanese-American Women in Domestic Service*. Philadelphia: Temple University Press.

Glenn, Evelyn Nakano, Grace Chang, and Linda Rennie Forcey, eds. 1993. *Mothering: Ideology, Experience, and Agency.* New York: Routledge.

Gluckman, Amy, and Betsy Reed. 1997. *Homo Economics: Capitalism,*

Community, and Lesbian and Gay Life. New York: Routledge.

Goldstein, Leslie. 1988. *The Constitutional Rights of Women.* Madison: University of Wisconsin Press.

Goleman, Daniel. 1992. "Gay Parents Called No Disadvantage." *The New York Times*, December 21.

Golub, S., ed. 1983. *Menarche: The Transition from Girl to Woman.* Newbury Park, CA: Sage.

Goodman, M. 1980. "Toward a Biology of Menopause." *Signs* 5 (Summer): 739–753.

Gordon, L. 1977. *Woman's Body/Woman's Right.* New York: Penguin Books.

Gordon, Margaret T., and Stephanie Riger. 1989. *The Female Fear.* New York: Free Press.

Gordon, Margaret T., S. Riger, R. K. LeBailly, and L. Health. 1980. "Crime, Women, and the Quality of Urban Life." *Signs* 5: 3 Supplement (Spring): S144–S160.

Gornick, V. 1971. "Woman as Outsider." Pp. 126–144 in *Woman in Sexist Society*, edited by V. Gornick and B. Moran. New York: Basic Books.

Gough, Kathleen. 1975. "The Origin of the Family." Pp. 51–76 in *Toward an Anthropology of Women*, edited by Rayna Reiter. New York: Monthly Review Press.

Gouldner, Helen, and Mary Symons Strong. 1987. *Speaking of Friendship: Middle-Class Women and Their Friends.* Westport, CT: Greenwood Press.

Gow, Joe. 1996. "Reconsidering Gender Roles on MTV: Depictions in the Most Popular Music Videos of the Early 1990s." *Communication Reports* 9 (Summer): 151–161.

Grant, J. 1982. "Black Women and the Church." Pp. 141–152 in *All the Women are White, All the Blacks Are Men, But Some of Us Are Brave*, edited by Gloria Patricia Bell Scott and Barbara Smith. Old Westbury, NY: Feminist Press.

Grant, Linda. 1988. "The Gender Climate in Medical School: Perspectives of Women and Men Students." *Journal of the American*

Medical Women's Association 43: 109–119.

Grasmuck, Sherri, and Patricia Pessar. 1996. "Dominicans in the United States: First- and Second-Generation Settlement." Pp. 280–292 in *Origins and Destinies: Immigration, Race, and Ethnicity in America*, edited by Sylvia Pedraza and Rubén G. Rumbaut. Belmont, CA: Wadsworth.

Graves, Sherryl Browne. 1996. "Diversity on Television." Pp. 61–86 in *Tuning into Young Viewers: Social Science Perspectives on Television*, edited by Tannis M. MacBeth. Thousand Oaks, CA: Sage.

Gray, John. 1994. *Men Are from Mars, Women Are from Venus.* New York: HarperCollins.

Greene, B. 1994. "Ethnic-Minority Lesbians and Gay Men: Mental Health and Treatment Issues." *Journal of Counseling and Clinical Psychology* 62: 243–251.

Greenfield, Lawrence A. 1998. *Violence by Intimates.* Washington, DC: Bureau of Justice Statistics.

Greif, Geoffrey L. 1985. "Children and Housework in the Single Father Family." *Family Relations* 34 (July): 353–357.

———. 1995. "Single Fathers with Custody following Separation and Divorce." *Marriage and Family Review* 20: 213–231.

Grella, Christine E. 1990. "Irreconcilable Differences: Women Defining Class After Divorce and Downward Mobility." *Gender & Society* 4 (March): 41–55.

Gross, Harriet. 1980. "Couples Who Live Apart: Two Types." *Journal of Marriage and the Family* 42: 567–576.

Gross, Jane. 1991. "New Challenge of Youth: Growing Up in a Gay Home." *The New York Times*, February 11.

Groves, Melissa M., and Diane M. Horm-Wingerd. 1991. "Commuter Marriages: Personal, Family, and Career Issues." *Sociology and Social Research* 75 (July): 212–217.

Gutek, Barbara A. 1988. "Women in Clerical Work," Pp. 225–240 in *Women Working*, 2nd ed., edited by Ann Helton Stromberg and Shirley Harkess. Mountain View CA: Mayfield.

Gutman, Herbert. 1976. *The Black Family in Slavery and Freedom.* New York: Vintage.

Haas, Kenneth C., and Geoffrey P. Alpert, eds. 1991. *The Dilemmas of Corrections: Contemporary Readings.* Prospect Heights, IL: Waveland Press.

Hacker, Sally L. 1980. "Farming Out the Home: Women and Agribusiness." Pp. 223–233 in *A Woman's Conflict: The Special Relationship Between Women and Food,* edited by J. R. Kaplan. Upper Saddle River, NJ: Prentice-Hall.

Haft, M. 1980. "Women in Prison: Discriminatory Practices and Some Legal Solutions." Pp. 320–338 in *Women, Crime and Society,* edited by Susan Datesman and Frank Scarpitti. New York: Oxford University Press.

Hall, Eleanor R., Judith A. Howard, and Sherrie L. Boezio. 1986. "Tolerance of Rape: A Sexist or Antisocial Attitude." *Psychology of Women Quarterly* 10: 101–118.

Hall, R. M. 1982. "The Classroom Climate: A Chilly One for Women?" Washington, DC: Project on the Education and Status of Women, Association of American Colleges.

Hamer, Dean H., Stella Hu, Victoria L. Magnuson, Nan Hu, and Angela M. L. Pattatucci. 1993. "A Linkage Between DNA Markers on the X Chromosome and Male Sexual Identification." *Science* 261 (July): 321–327.

Hamlin, Nancy R., Sumru Erkut, and Jacqueline P. Fields. 1994. "The Impact of Corporate Restructuring and Downsizing on the Managerial Careers of Minorities and Women: Lessons Learned From Nine Corporations." Marblehead, MA: Hamlin and Associates.

Hampton, Robert L., and Alice F. Washington Coner-Edwards. 1993. "Physical and Sexual Violence in Marriage." Pp. 113–141 in *Family Violence: Prevention and Treatment,* edited by Robert L. Hampton, Thomas

P. Gullotta, Gerald R. Adams, Earl H. Potter III., and Roger P. Weissberg. Newbury Park, CA: Sage.

Hans, Valerie P., and Neil Vidmar. 1986. *Judging the Jury.* New York: Plenum Press.

Harding, Sandra. 1979. "Is the Equality of Opportunity Principle Democratic?" *Philosophical Forum* 10: 206–223.

———. 1981. "What Is the Real Material Base of Patriarchy and Capital?" Pp. 135–163 in *Women and Revolution,* edited by Lydia Sargent. Boston: South End Press.

———. 1986. *The Science Question in Feminism.* Ithaca, NY: Cornell University Press.

———. 1991. *Whose Science? Whose Knowledge?: Thinking from Women's Lives.* Ithaca, NY: Cornell University Press.

———. 1993. *The Racial Economy of Science.* Bloomington: Indiana University Press.

Hargrove, B., J. M. Schmidt, and S. G. Davaney. 1985. "Religion and the Changing Role of Women." *Annals of the American Academy of Political and Social Science* 480 (July): 117–131.

Hargrove, Barbara, Jean Miller Schmidt, and Sheila Greeve Davaney. 1993. "Religion and the Changing Role of Women." Pp. 3–17 in *Modern American Protestantism and Its World: Women and Women's Issues,* edited by Martin E. Marty. Munich: K. G. Saur.

Harland, M. 1889. *House and Home: The Complete Housewives' Guide.* Philadelphia: Clawson.

Harris, Ian, Jose B. Torres, and Dale Allender. 1994. "The Responses of African American Men to Dominant Norms of Masculinity Within the United States." *Sex Roles* 31 (December): 703–720.

Harris, R. J., and J. M. Firestone. 1998. "Changes in Predictors of Gender Role Ideologies among Women: A Multivariate Analysis." *Sex Roles* 38 (February): 239–252.

Harrison, J. 1978. "Men's Roles and Men's Lives." *Signs* 4 (Winter): 324–336.

Harrison, James, James Chin, and Thomas Ficarrotto. 1988. "Warning: Masculinity May Be Dangerous to Your Health." Pp. 271–285 in *Men's Lives,* 2nd ed., edited by Michael S. Kimmel and Michael A. Messner. New York: Macmillan.

Harry, Joseph. 1995. "Sports Ideology, Attitudes Toward Women, and Anti-Homosexual Attitudes." *Sex Roles* 32 (January): 109–116.

Hart, K., and M. E. Kenny. 1997. "Adherence to the Super Woman Ideal and Eating Disorder Symptoms among College Women." *Sex Roles* 36 (April): 461–478.

Hartmann, Heidi. 1976. "Capitalism, Patriarchy, and Job Segregation by Sex." *Signs* 1: (Spring): 137–169.

———. 1981a. "The Family as the Locus of Gender, Class, and Political Struggle: The Example of Housework." *Signs* 6 (Spring): 366–394.

———. 1981b. "The Unhappy Marriage of Marxism and Feminism: Towards a More Progressive Union." Pp. 1–41 in *Women and Revolution,* edited by Lydia Sargent. New York: South End Press.

Hartsock, Nancy. 1983. "The Feminist Standpoint: Developing the Ground for a Specifically Feminist Historical Materialism." Pp. 231–251 in *Money, Sex and Power,* edited by Nancy Hartsock. New York: Longman.

Hawkes, G., and M. Taylor. 1975. "Power Structure in Mexican and Mexican-American Farm Labor Families." *Journal of Marriage and the Family* 37: 807–811.

Hawkins, R. A., and R. E. Oakey. 1974. "Estimation of Oestrone Sulphate, Oestradiol-17B and Oestrone in Peripheral Plasma: Concentrations During the Menstrual Cycle and in Men." *Journal of Endocrinology* 60: 3–17.

Heath, Julia A., and David W. Bourne. 1995. "Husbands and Housework: Parity or Parody?" *Social Science Quarterly* 76 (March): 195–202.

Helwig, A. A. 1998. "Gender-Role Stereotyping: Testing Theory with a Longitudinal Sample." *Sex Roles* 38 (March): 403–423.

Henley, Nancy. 1989. "Molehill or Mountain? What We Know and Don't Know about Sex Bias in Language." Pp. 59–78 in *Gender and Thought: Psychological Perspectives*, edited by M. Crawford and M. Gentry. New York: Springer-Verlag.

Hennig, K., H. Leitenberg, P. Coffey, T. Turner, and R. T. Bennett. 1996. "Long-term Psychological and Social Impact of Witnessing Physical Conflict between Parents." *Journal of Interpersonal Violence* 11: 35–51.

Herd, Denise. 1988. "Drinking by Black and White Women: Results from a National Survey." *Social Problems* 35 (December): 493–505.

Herman, Judith. 1981. *Father-Daughter Incest*. Cambridge, MA: Harvard University Press.

Herman, Judith, and Hirschman, L. 1977. "Father-Daughter Incest." *Signs* 2 (Summer): 735–756.

Hernandez, Jeanne. 1995. "The Concurrence of Eating Disorders with Histories of Child Abuse among Adolescents." *Journal of Child Sexual Abuse* 4: 73–85.

Herskovits, M. 1958. *The Myth of the Negro Past*. Boston: Beacon Press.

Hess, Beth, and Elizabeth Markson. 1991. *Growing Old In America*, 4th ed. New Brunswick, NJ: Transaction Publishers.

Hesse-Biber, Sharlene, Alan Clayton-Matthews, and John A. Downey. 1987. "The Differential Importance of Weight and Body Image among College Men and Women." *Genetic, Social, and General Psychology Monographs* 113 (November): 509–528.

Heywood, Leslie. 1998. "Hitting a Cultural Nerve: Another Season of 'Ally McBeal.'" *The Chronicle of Higher Education* 45 (September 4): B9.

Higginbotham, Elizabeth. 1981. "Is Marriage A Priority? Class Differences in Marital Options of Educated Black Women." Pp. 259–267 in *Single Life: Unmarried Adults in Social Context*, edited by Peter Stein. New York: St. Martin's Press.

Higginbotham, Elizabeth, and Lynn Weber. 1992. "Moving Up With Kin and Community: Upward Social Mobility for Black and White Women." *Gender & Society* 6 (September): 416–440.

Higham, J. 1965. *Strangers in the Land*. New York: Atheneum.

Hill, A. C. 1979. "Protection of Women Workers and the Courts: A Legal Case History." *Feminist Studies* 5 (Summer): 247–273.

Hiller, D., and W. H. Philliber. 1986. "The Division of Labor in Contemporary Marriage: Expectations, Perceptions, and Performance." *Social Problems* 33 (February): 191–201.

Hilts, Philip J. 1990. "N.I.H. Starts Women's Health Office." *The New York Times*, September 11, p. C9.

Himmelstein, J. L. 1986. "The Social Basis of Antifeminism: Religious Networks and Culture." *Journal for the Scientific Study of Religion* 25: 1–15.

Hine, Darlene Clark. 1995. "Black Women and Men and the U.S. Suffrage Movement." Keynote Address, 19th Amendment Conference. Delaware State University, Dover, November 3.

Hochschild, Arlie Russell. 1983. *The Managed Heart: Commercialization of Human Feeling*. Berkeley: University of California Press.

———. 1989. *The Second Shift: Working Parents and the Revolution at Home*. New York: Viking.

———. 1997. *The Time Bind: When Home Becomes Work and Work Becomes Home*. New York: Metropolitan Books.

Hoffman, Thomas. 1997. "Women in Church Leadership: An Analysis of Religious Beliefs." *Free Inquiry in Creative Sociology* 25 (November): 137–143.

Hole, J., and Levine, E., eds. 1971. *Rebirth of Feminism*. New York: Quadrangle Books.

Holm, Maj. Gen. Jeanne. 1992. *Women in the Military*. Novato, CA: Presidio Press.

Hondagneu-Sotelo, Pierrette. 1992. "Overcoming Patriarchal Constraints: The Reconstruction of Gender Relations Among Mexican Immigrant Women and

Men." *Gender & Society* 6 (September): 393–415.

———. 1994. *Gendered Transitions: the Mexican Experience of Immigration*. Berkeley: University of California Press.

———. 1997. "'I'm Here, but I'm There': The Meanings of Latina Transnational Motherhood." *Gender & Society* 11 (October): 548–571.

Hooper, Linda M., and Bennett, Claudette E. 1998. *The Asian and Pacific Islander Population in the United States: March 1997 (Update)*, Table 5. Washington, DC: U.S. Bureau of the Census, Current Population Reports. <www.census.gov/population/socdemo/race/api97>

Horowitz, Ruth. 1995. *Teen Mothers: Citizens or Dependents?* Chicago: University of Chicago Press.

Horton, Jacqueline A., ed. 1995. *The Women's Health Data Book: A Profile of Women's Health in the United States*, 2nd ed. New York: Elsevier.

Hosken, F. P. 1979. *The Hosken Report: Genital and Sexual Mutilation of Females*. Lexington, MA: Women's International Network News.

Hossfeld, Karen J. 1990. "'Their Logic Against Them': Contradictions in Sex, Race, and Class in Silicon Valley." Pp. 149–178 in *Women Workers and Global Restructuring*, edited by Kathryn Ward. Ithaca, NY: Cornell University Press.

Hoyenga, K. B., and K. Hoyenga. 1979. *The Question of Sex Differences; Psychological, Cultural, and Biological Issues*. Boston: Little, Brown.

Hubbard, Ruth. 1984. "Feminist Science: A Meaningful Concept?" Paper presented at the Annual Meetings of the National Women's Studies Association, New Brunswick, NJ.

Hughes, H. S. 1958. *Consciousness and Society*. New York: Knopf.

Hughes, Jean O'Gorman, and Bernice R. Sandler. 1987. "*Friends Raping Friends": Could It Happen to You?* Washington, DC: Project on the Education and Status of Women, Association of American Colleges.

Hugick, Larry, and Jennifer Leonard. 1991. "Sex in America." *The Gallup Poll Monthly*: 60–73.

Hunt, V. R. 1979. "A Brief History of Women Workers and Hazards in the Workplace." *Feminist Studies* 5 (Summer): 274–285.

Hunter, Andrea, and James Davis. 1992. "Constructing Gender: An Exploration of Afro-American Men's Conceptualization of Manhood." *Gender & Society* 6 (September): 464–479.

Hurst, M., and R. E. Zambrana. 1980. "The Health Careers of Urban Women: A Study in East Harlem." *Signs* 5:3 Supplement (Spring): S112–S126.

Idle, Tracey, Eileen Wood, and Serge Desmarais. 1993. "Gender Role Socialization in Toy Play Situations: Mothers and Fathers with Their Sons and Daughters." *Sex Roles* 28 (June): 679–692.

Illich, I. 1977. *Disabling Professions*. Salem, NH: Boyars.

Infante, P. 1975. "Genetic Risks of Vinyl Chloride." *Lancet* 3: 734–735.

Ingram-Fogel, Catherine. 1991. "Health Problems and Needs of Incarcerated Women." *Journal of Prison and Jail Health* 10 (Summer): 43–57.

———. 1993. "Hard Time: The Stressful Nature of Incarceration for Women." *Issues in Mental Health Nursing* 14 (October–December): 367–377.

Ireson, C. 1984. "Adolescent Pregnancy and Sex Roles." *Sex Roles* 11 (August): 189–201.

Jackson, Nicky-Ali. 1996. "Observational Experiences of Intrapersonal Conflict and Teenage Victimization: A Comparative Study among Spouses and Cohabitors." *Journal of Family Violence* 11 (September): 191–203.

Jacobs, J. 1984. "The Economy of Love in Religious Commitment: The Deconversion of Women from Nontraditional Religious Movements." *Journal for the Scientific Study of Religion* 23 (June): 155–171.

Jacobs, Janet L. 1994. "The Effects of Ritual Healing on Female Victims of Abuse: A Study of Empowerment and

Transformation." Pp. 127–142 in Swatos, William H. Jr. 1994. *Gender and Religion*. New Brunswick, NJ: Transaction Publishers.

Jacobs, Jerry A., and Ronnie J. Steinberg. 1990. "Compensating Differentials and the Male-Female Wage Gap: Evidence from the New York State Comparable Worth Study." *Social Forces* 69 (December): 430–469.

Jacobson, D. 1974. "The Women of North and Central India: Goddesses and Wives." Pp. 99–175 in *Many Sisters*, edited by C. Matthiasson. New York: Free Press.

Jaget, C., ed. 1980. *Prostitutes: Our Life*. Bristol, England: Falling Wall Press.

Jaggar, Alison M., and Paula S. Rothenberg, eds. 1993. *Feminist Frameworks: Alternative Theoretical Accounts of the Relations Between Women and Men*, 3rd ed. New York: McGraw-Hill.

Janus, Samuel S., and Cynthia L. Janus. 1993. *The Janus Report on Sexual Behavior*. New York: Wiley and Sons.

Jarrett, Robin L. 1994. "Living Poor: Family Life Among Single Parent African-American Women." *Social Problems* 41 (February): 30–49.

Jelen, Ted G. 1989. "Gender Role Stereotypes and Attitudes Toward Female Ordination." *Social Science Quarterly* 7 (September): 579–585.

Joe, Karen A., and Meda Chesney-Lind. 1995. "'Just Every Mother's Angel': An Analysis of Gender and Ethnic Variations in Youth Gang Membership." *Gender & Society* 9 (August): 408–431.

Johnston, L. C., G. C. Bachman, and P. M. O'Malley. 1982. *Student Drug Use in America: 1975–1981*. Rockville, MD: National Institute on Drug Abuse.

Jolin, Annette. 1994. "On the Backs of Working Prostitutes: Feminist Theory and Prostitution Policy." *Crime and Delinquency* 40 (January): 69–83.

Jones, J. 1985. *Labor of Love, Labor of Sorrow: Black Women, Work, and the Family From Slavery to the Present*. New York: Basic Books.

Jordan, Winthrop. 1968. *White Over Black*. Baltimore: Penguin Books.

Joseph, Gloria. 1984. "Mothers and Daughters: Traditional and New Perspectives." *Sage* 1 (Fall): 17–21.

Joseph, Harry. 1979. "The 'Marital' Liaison of Gay Men." *The Family Coordinator* 28 (October): 622–628.

Jourard, S. M. 1974. "Some Lethal Aspects of the Male Role." Pp. 21–29 in *Men and Masculinity*, edited by J. Pleck and J. Sawyer. Englewood Cliffs, NJ: Spectrum Books.

Julty, Sam. 1974. "A Case of 'Sexual Dysfunction.'" Pp. 35–40 in *Men and Masculinity*, edited by J. Pleck and J. Sawyer. Englewood Cliffs, NJ: Spectrum Books.

Kalof, Linda. 1993. "Rape-Supportive Attitudes and Sexual Victimization Experiences of Sorority and Non-Sorority Women." *Sex Roles* 29: 767–780.

Kamin, L. J. 1986. "Is Crime in the Genes?" *Scientific American* 254 (February): 22–27.

Kanter, Rosabeth Moss. 1977. *Men and Women of the Corporation*. New York: Basic Books.

Kantor, Glenda Kaufman, and Jana L. Jasinksi. 1998. "Dynamics and Risk Factors in Partner Violence." Pp. 1–43 in *Partner Violence: A Comprehensive Review of 20 Years of Research*, edited by Jana L. Jasinkski and Linda M. Williams. Thousand Oaks, CA: Sage.

Kaplan, Elaine Bell. 1997. *Not Our Kind of Girl: Unraveling the Myths of Black Teenage Motherhood*. Berkeley: University of California Press.

Kapp, Yvonne. 1972. *Eleanor Marx, Volume One*. New York: Pantheon.

Katzman, David. 1978. *Seven Days A Week: Women and Domestic Service in Industrializing America*. New York: Oxford University Press.

Kaufman, S., and M. L. Wylie. 1983. "One Session Workshop on Sexual Harassment." *Journal of the National Association for Women Deans, Administrators, and Counselors* 46 (Winter): 39–42.

Kay, Fiona M., and John Hagan. 1998. "Gender Stratification in Law Firms." *American Sociological Review* 63 (October): 728–743.

Keller, Evelyn Fox. 1985. *Reflections on Gender and Science*. New Haven, CT: Yale University Press.

Kelly-Gadol, J. 1976. "The Social Relations of the Sexes: Methodological Implications of Women's History." *Signs* 1 (Summer): 809–824.

Kessler-Harris, Alice. 1982. *Out to Work: A History of Wage-Earning Women in the U.S.* New York: Oxford University Press.

Kibria, Nazli. 1994. "Household Structure and Family Ideologies: The Dynamics of Immigrant Economic Adaptation Among Vietnamese Refugees." *Social Problems* 41 (February): 81–96.

Kilbourne, Barbara Stanek, George Farkas, Kurt Beron, Dorothea Weir, and Paula England. 1994. "Returns to Skill, Compensating Differentials, and Gender Bias: Effects of Occupational Characteristics on the Wages of White Women and White Men." *American Journal of Sociology* 100 (November): 689–719.

Kimmel, Michael S., and Michael A. Messner, eds. 1998. *Men's Lives*, 4th ed. Boston: Allyn and Bacon.

———. 1989. *Men's Lives*. New York: Macmillan.

Kinsey, A. C., et al. 1953. *Sexual Behavior in the Human Female*. New York: Pocket Books.

Kitzinger, Celia A., and Sue Wilkinson. 1994. "Virgins and Queers: Rehabilitating Heterosexuality?" *Gender & Society* 8 (September): 444–462.

Klass, A. 1975. *There's Gold in Them Thar Pills*. London: Penguin Books.

Klatch, Rebecca. 1988. "Coalition and Conflict Among Women of the New Right." *Signs* 13 (Summer): 671–694.

Kleck, Gary, and Susan Sayles. 1990. "Rape and Resistance." *Social Problems* 37 (May): 149–162.

Klein, D. 1980. "The Etiology of Female Crime: A Review of the Literature." Pp. 70–105 in *Women, Crime, and Justice*, edited

by Susan K. Datesman and Frank R. Scarpitti. New York: Oxford University Press.

Kleinbaum, A. R. 1977. "Women in the Age of Light." Pp. 217–235 in *Becoming Visible: Women in European History*, edited by R. Bridenthal and C. Koonz. Boston: Houghton-Mifflin.

Kluckhohn, C. 1962. *Culture and Behavior*. New York: Free Press.

Knouse, Stephen B. 1991. "Introduction to Racial, Ethnic, and Gender Issues in the Military: The Decade of the 1990s and Beyond." *International Journal of Intercultural Relations* 15: 385–388.

Kohlberg, Lawrence. 1966. "A Cognitive Developmental Analysis of Children's Sex Role Concepts and Attitudes." Pp. 82–166 in *The Development of Sex Differences*, edited by Eleanor Maccoby. Stanford, CA: Stanford University Press.

Kokopeli, Bruce, and George Lakey. 1995. "More Power Than We Want: Masculine Sexuality and Violence." Pp. 450–456 in *Race, Class, and Gender: An Anthology*, 2nd ed., edited by Margaret L. Andersen and Patricia Hill Collins. Belmont, CA: Wadsworth.

Kolata, Gina. 1991. "Studies Say Women Fail to Receive Equal Treatment for Heart Disease." *The New York Times*, July 25, p. A1.

Komter, Aafke. 1989. "Hidden Power in Marriage." *Gender & Society* 3 (June): 187–216.

Konradi, Amanda. 1996. "Preparing to Testify: Rape Survivors Negotiating the Criminal Justice Process." *Gender & Society* 10 (August): 404–432.

Kraditor, E. 1968. *Up from the Pedestal: Selected Writings in the History of American Feminism*. Chicago: Quadrangle Books.

Kramer, Cheris, Barrie Thorne, and Nancy Henley. 1978. "Perspectives on Language and Communication." *Signs* 3: 638–651.

Kurz, Demie. 1989. "Social Science Perspectives on Wife Abuse: Current Debates and Future Directions." *Gender & Society* 3 (December): 489–505.

Kurz, Demie. 1995. *For Richer for Poorer: Mothers Confront Divorce*. New York: Routledge.

Ladner, Joyce A. 1986. "Teenage Pregnancy: The Implications for Black Americans." Pp. 65–85 in *The State of Black America 1986*, edited by James D. Williams. New York: National Urban League.

———. 1995. *Tomorrow's Tomorrow*. Lincoln: University of Nebraska Press.

Ladner, Joyce A., and R. M. Gourdine. 1984. "Intergenerational Teenage Motherhood: Some Preliminary Findings." *Sage* 1 (Fall): 22–24.

LaFree, G. 1980. "The Effect of Sexual Stratification by Race on Official Reactions to Rape." *American Sociological Review* 45 (October): 842–854.

Lafree, Gary D., Barbara F. Reskin, and Christy A. Visher. 1985. "Jurors' Responses to Victims' Behavior and Legal Issues in Sexual Assault Trials." *Social Problems* 32 (April): 389–407.

Lai, Tracy. 1992. "Asian American Women: Not for Sale." Pp. 163–171 in *Race, Class and Gender: An Anthology*, edited by Margaret L. Andersen and Patricia Hill Collins. Belmont, CA: Wadsworth.

Lambert, H. H. 1978. "Biology and Equality: A Perspective on Sex Differences." *Signs* 4 (Autumn): 97–117.

Lamphere, Louise. 1977. "Anthropology" *Signs* 2 (Spring): 612–627.

———. 1984. "On the Shop Floor: Multi-Ethnic Unity Against the Conglomerate." Pp. 247–262 in *My Troubles Are Going to Have Trouble With Me*, edited by Karen B. Sacks and Dorothy Remy. New Brunswick, NJ: Rutgers University Press.

La Rossa, Ralph. 1986. *Becoming a Parent*. Beverly Hills: Sage.

La Rossa, R., and L. Rossa. 1981. *Transition to Parenthood*. Beverly Hills: Sage.

Lasch, C. 1977. *Haven in a Heartless World: The Family Besieged*. New York: Basic Books.

Laslett, Barbara, Johanna Brenner, and Yesim Arat. 1995. *Rethinking* the Political: Gender, Resistance, and the State.* Chicago: University of Chicago Press.

Laumann, Edward O., John H. Gagnon, Robert T. Michael, and Stuart Michaels. 1994. *The Social Organization of Sexuality: Sexual Practices in the United States.* Chicago: University of Chicago Press.

Lawrence, M. 1984. *The Anorexic Experience.* London: The Women's Press.

Leacock, E. 1978. "Women's Status in Egalitarian Society." *Contemporary Anthropology* 19: 247–275.

Lee, Janet. 1994. "Menarche and the (Hetero)sexualization of the Female Body." *Gender & Society* 8 (September): 343–362.

Lee, Sharon M. 1994. "Poverty and the U.S. Asian Population." *Social Science Quarterly* 75 (September): 541–559.

Lehman, E. C., Jr. 1980. "Patterns of Lay Resistance to Women in Ministry." *Sociological Analysis* 41 (Winter): 317–338.

———. 1982. "Organizational Resistance to Women in Ministry." *Sociological Analysis* 42 (Summer): 101–118.

———. 1994. "Gender and Ministry Style: Things Not What They Seem." Pp. 3–14 in *Gender and Religion*, edited by William H. Swatos, Jr. New Brunswick, NJ: Transaction Publishers.

Leiner, Marvin. 1993. *Sexual Politics in Cuba: Machismo, Homosexuality, and AIDS.* Boulder, CO: Westview Press.

Lemert, E. 1972. *Human Deviance, Social Problems, and Social Control.* Upper Saddle River, NJ: Prentice-Hall.

Lemon, J. 1978. "Dominant or Dominated? Women on Prime-Time Television." Pp. 51–68 in *Hearth and Home: Images of Women in the Mass Media*, edited by Gaye Tuchman, Arlene Kaplan Daniels, and James Benét. New York: Oxford University Press.

Lennon, Mary Clare. 1994. "Women, Work, and Well-Being: The Importance of Work Conditions." *Journal of Health and Social Behavior* 35 (September): 235–247.

Leong, Russell, ed. 1996. *Asian American Sexualities: Dimensions of the Gay and Lesbian Experience.* New York: Routledge.

Lerman, Robert I., and Theodora J. Ooms. 1993. *Young Unwed Fathers: Changing Roles and Emerging Policies.* Philadelphia: Temple University Press.

Lerner, Gerda. 1973. *Black Women in White America: A Documentary History.* New York: Vintage.

———. 1976. "Placing Women in History: A 1975 Perspective." Pp. 357–367 in *Liberating Women's History*, edited by Berenice Carroll. Urbana: University of Illinois Press.

Lewin, Ellen, and Virginia Olesen, eds. 1985. *Women, Health, and Healing: Toward a New Perspective.* New York: Tavistock Publications.

Lewin, M., ed. 1984. *In the Shadow of the Past: Psychology Portrays the Sexes.* New York: Columbia University Press.

Lewis, K. G. 1980. "Children of Lesbians: Their Point of View." *Social Work* 25 (May): 198–203.

Lewis, S. G. 1979. *Sunday's Women: A Report on Lesbian Life Today.* Boston: Beacon Press.

Lim, In-Sook. 1997. "Korean Immigrant Women's Challenge to Gender Inequality at Home: The Interplay of Economic Resources, Gender, and Family." *Gender & Society* 11 (February): 31–51.

Limbaugh, H. Rush, III. 1992. *The Way Things Ought to Be.* New York: Pocket.

Lindsey, E. W., J. Mize, and G. S. Pettit. 1997. "Differential Play Patterns of Mothers and Fathers of Sons and Daughters: Implications for Children's Gender Role Development." *Sex Roles* 37 (November): 643–661.

Lips, Hilary M. 1988. *Sex & Gender: An Introduction.* Mountain View, CA: Mayfield.

Lipset, S. M. (ed.) 1962. *Harriet Martineau: Society in America.* New York: Doubleday.

Liss-Levinson, W. 1981. "Men Without Playfulness." Pp. 19–28 in *Men in Difficult Times: Masculinity Today and Tomorrow*, edited by R. A. Lewis. Upper Saddle River, NJ: Prentice-Hall.

Litoff, J. B. 1978. *American Midwives: 1860 to the Present.* Westport, CT: Greenwood Press.

Livson, F. B. 1977. "Cultural Faces of Eve." Paper presented at the Annual Meeting of the American Psychological Association, San Francisco.

Lizotte, A. 1985. "The Uniqueness of Rape: Reporting Assaultive Violence to the Police." *Crime and Delinquency* 31 (April): 169–190.

Locksley, A. 1980. "On the Effects of Wives' Employment on Marital Adjustment and Companionship." *Journal of Marriage and the Family* 42: 337–346.

Logio-Rau, Kim. 1998. *Here's Looking at You, Kid: Gender, Race, Body Image and Adolescent Health.* Ph.D. Dissertation, University of Delaware.

Logue, Barbara, J. 1991. "Women at Risk: Predictors of Financial Stress for Retired Women Workers." *The Gerontologist* 31: 657–665.

Lombroso, N. 1920. *The Female Offender.* New York: Appleton.

Longino, Helene, and R. Doell. 1983. "Body, Bias, and Behavior: Comparative Analysis of Reasoning in Two Areas of Biological Science." *Signs* 9 (Winter): 206–227.

Lopata, Helene Z. 1971. *Occupation: Housewife.* New York: Oxford University Press.

Lopata, Helene Z., and Barrie Thorne. 1978. "On the Term 'Sex Roles.'" *Signs* 3 (Spring): 718–721.

Lorber, Judith. 1991. "Can Women Physicians Ever Be True Equals in the American Medical Profession?" *Current Research on Occupations and Professions* 6: 25–37.

———. 1994. *Paradoxes of Gender.* New Haven, CT: Yale University Press.

Lorber, Judith, and Martha Ecker. 1983. "Career Development of Female and Male Physicians." *Journal of Medical Education* 58: 447–556.

Lorber, Judith, Rose L. Coser, Alice S. Rossi, and Nancy Chodorow. 1981. "On 'The Reproduction of

Mothering': A Methodological Debate." *Signs* 6: 482–514.

Loscocco, Karyn A., and Glenna Spitze. 1990. "Working Conditions, Social Support and the Well-Being of Female and Male Factory Workers." *Journal of Health and Social Behavior* 31 (December): 313–327.

Lowe, M. 1983. "The Dialectic of Biology and Culture." Pp. 39–62 in *Woman's Nature*, edited by Marion Lowe and Ruth Hubbard. New York: Pergamon Press.

Lucal, Betsy. 1994. "Class Stratification in Introductory Textbooks: Relational or Distributional Models?" *Teaching Sociology* 22 (April): 139–150.

Lugalia, Terry A. 1998. *Marital Status and Living Arrangements: March 1997* (Update), Current Population Reports, Series P20-506 (June). Washington, DC: U.S. Census Bureau.

Luker, Kristen. 1975. *Taking Chances*. Berkeley: University of California Press.

———. 1984. *Abortion and the Politics of Motherhood*. Berkeley: University of California Press.

Lundberg, F., and M. Farnham. 1947. *Modern Woman: The Lost Sex*. New York: Harper.

Lye, Diane N., and Ingrid Waldron. 1997. "Attitudes toward Cohabitation, Family, and Gender Roles: Relationships to Values and Political Ideology." *Sociological Perspectives* 40 (Summer): 199–225.

MacCorquodale, P. L. 1984. "Gender Roles and Premarital Contraception." *Journal of Marriage and the Family* 46 (February): 57–62.

MacFarlane, Kee. 1978. "Sexual Abuse of Children." Pp. 81–109 in *The Victimization of Women*, edited by Jane Roberts Chapman and Margaret Gates. Beverly Hills, CA: Sage.

Machung, A. 1984. "Word Processing: Forward for Business, Backward for Women." Pp. 124–139 in *My Troubles Are Going to Have Trouble With Me*, edited by K. B. Sacks and D. Remy. New Brunswick, NJ: Rutgers University Press.

MacKinnon, Catharine. 1982. "Feminism, Marxism, Method, and the State: An Agenda for Theory." *Signs* 7 (Spring): 515–544.

———. 1983. "Feminism, Marxism, Method, and the State: Toward Feminist Jurisprudence." *Signs* 8 (Summer): 635–658.

Macklin, E. D. 1978. "Nonmarital Heterosexual Cohabitation." *Marriage and Family Review* 1: 1–12.

Madriz, Esther. 1997. *Nothing Bad Happens to Good Girls: Fear of Crime in Women's Lives*. Berkeley: University of California Press.

Mahoney, Patricia, and Linda M. Williams. 1998. "Sexual Assault in Marriage: Prevalence, Consequences, and Treatment of Wife Rape." Pp. 113–162 in *Partner Violence: A Comprehensive Review of 20 Years of Research*, edited by Jana L. Jasinkski and Linda M. Williams. Thousand Oaks, CA: Sage.

Malbin-Glazer, N. 1976. "Housework." *Signs* 1 (Summer): 905–922.

Malcolm, Ellen R. 1993. "Reining Big Givers." *The New York Times*, March 30, p. A23.

Mandel, Ruth, and Debra Dodson. 1992. "Do Women Officeholders Make a Difference?" Pp. 144–177 in *American Women, 1992–93: A Status Report*, edited by Paula Ries and Anne Stone. New York: Norton.

Manegold, Catherine S. 1995. "Female Cadet Quits the Citadel, Citing Stress of Her Legal Battle." *The New York Times*. August 19, p. A1.

Mannheim, K. 1936. *Ideology and Utopia*. New York: Harcourt, Brace, and World.

Mansfield, Phyllis Kernoff, Patricia Barlalow Koch, Julie Henderson, Judith R. Vicary, Margaret Cohn, and Elaine W. Young. 1991. "The Job Climate for Women in Traditionally Male Blue-Collar Occupations." *Sex Roles* 25 (July): 63–79.

Markens, Susan. 1996. "The Problematic of 'Experience': A Political and Cultural Critique of PMS." *Gender & Society*, 10 (February): 42–58.

Marshall, Nancy L., and Rosalind C. Barnett. 1995. "Child Care, Division of Labor, and Parental Emotional Well-Being among Two-Earner Couples." Paper presented at the Annual Meetings of the American Sociological Asssociation.

Marsiglio, William. 1995. "Young Nonresident Biological Fathers." *Marriage and Family Review* 20: 325–348.

Martin, D. 1976. *Battered Wives*. San Francisco: Glide.

Martin, Elaine. 1990. "Men and Women on the Bench: Vive la Difference?" *Judicature* 73 (December–January): 204–208.

Martin, Emily. 1991. "The Egg and the Sperm: How Science Has Constructed a Romance Based on Stereotypical Male-Female Roles." *Signs* 16 (Spring): 485–501.

Martin, Patricia Yancey. 1997. "Gender, Accounts, and Rape Processing Work." *Social Problems* 44 (November): 464–483.

Martin, Patricia Yancey, and Robert A. Hummer. 1989. "Fraternities and Rape on Campus." *Gender & Society* 3 (December 1989): 457–473.

Martin, Patricia Yancey, and R. Marlene Powell. 1994. "Accounting for the 'Second Assault': Legal Organizations' Framing of Rape Victims." *Law and Social Inquiry* 19 (Fall): 853–890.

Martin, Steven S., and Cynthia Robbins. 1995. "Personality, Social Control and Drug Use in Early Adolescence." Pp. 145–161 in *Drugs, Crime and Other Deviant Adaptations*, edited by Howard B. Kaplan. New York: Plenum.

Martin, Susan Erhlich. 1989. "Sexual Harassment: The Link Joining Gender Stratification, Sexuality, and Women's Economic Status." Pp. 57–86 in *Women: A Feminist Perspective*, 3rd ed., edited by Jo Freeman. Palo Alto, CA: Mayfield.

Martineau, Harriet. 1837. *Society in America*. Paris: Baudry's European Library.

———. 1838. *How to Observe Manners and Morals*. London: C. Knight.

Marx, G. 1967. "Religion: Opiate or Inspiration of Civil Rights Militancy Among Negroes." *American Sociological Review* 32 (February): 64–72.

Marx, K., and F. Engels. 1970. *The Communist Manifesto*. New York: Pathfinder Press.

Marzolf, Marion Tuttle. 1993. "Deciding What's Women's News." *Media Studies Journal* 7 (Winter/Spring): 33–48.

Massey, Garth, Karen Hahn, and Dusko Sekulic. 1995. "Women, Men, and the 'Second Shift' in Socialist Yugoslavia." *Gender & Society* 9 (June): 359–379.

Masters, W. H., and V. E. Johnson. 1966. *Human Sexual Response*. Boston: Little, Brown.

Matthiasson, C. 1974. *Many Sisters*. New York: Free Press.

Matza, D. 1969. *Becoming Deviant*. Upper Saddle River, NJ: Prentice-Hall.

Maume, David J., and Karen R. Mullin. 1993. "Men's Participation in Child Care and Women's Work Attachment." *Social Problems* 40 (November): 533–546.

McCammon, Holly J. 1995. "The Politics of Protection: State Minimum Wage and Maximum Hours Laws for Women in the United States, 1870–1930." *Sociological Quarterly* 36 (Spring): 217–249.

McCloskey, Laura A., and Lerita M. Coleman. 1992. "Difference Without Dominance: Children's Talk in Mixed- and Same-Sex Dyads." *Sex Roles* 27 (September): 241–258.

McCloskey, Laura Ann. 1996. "Socioeconomic and Coercive Power within the Family." *Gender & Society* 10 (August): 449–463.

McCormack, Arlene Smith. 1995. "Revisiting Sexual Harassment of Undergraduate Women: 1989 and 1993." *Violence against Women* 1 (September): 254–265.

McCormack, A., M. D. Janus, and A. W. Burgess. 1986. "Runaway Youths and Sexual Victimization: Gender Differences in an Adolescent Runaway Population." *Child Abuse and Neglect* 10: 387–395.

McCrate, Elaine, and Joan Smith. 1998. "When Work Doesn't Work: The Failure of Current Welfare Reform." *Gender & Society* 12 (February): 61–80.

McCreary, Donald R. 1994. "The Male Role and Avoiding Femininity." *Sex Roles* 31 (November): 517–531.

McGuire, M. B. 1997. *Religion: The Social Context*, 4th ed. Belmont, CA: Wadsworth.

McIntosh, M. 1978. "Who Needs Prostitutes?" Pp. 63–64 in *Women, Sexuality, and Social Control*, edited by C. Smart and B. Smart. London: Routledge & Kegan Paul.

McIntosh, Peggy. 1983. "Interactive Phases of Curricular Re-Vision: A Feminist Perspective." Working Papers Series. Wellesley, MA: Wellesley Center for Research on Women.

McKinney, Kathleen, and Kelly Crittenden. 1992. "Contrapower Sexual Harassment: The Offender's Viewpoint." *Free Inquiry in Creative Sociology* 20 (May): 3–10.

McLanahan, Sara S., Annemette Sorenson, and Dorothy Watson. 1989. "Sex Differences in Poverty, 1950–1980." *Signs* 15 (Autumn): 102–122.

McMurray, Colleen, ed. 1985. *Gallup Report, Religion in America 50 Years: 1935–1985*. Princeton, NJ: Gallup Poll.

McQuiade, Sharon, and John H. Ehrenreich. 1998. "Women in Prison: Approaches to Understanding the Lives of a Forgotten Population." *Affilia: Journal of Women and Social Work* 13 (Summer): 233–247.

Mead, Margaret. 1949. *Sex and Temperament in Three Primitive Societies*. New York: Dell.

———. 1962. *Male and Female*. London: Penguin.

Mehrabian, A. 1971. "Verbal and Nonverbal Interaction of Strangers in a Waiting Situation." *Journal of Experimental Research in Personality* 5: 127–138.

Meier, A., and Rudwick, E. 1966. *From Plantation to Ghetto*. New York: Hill & Wang.

Meigs, C. D. 1847. *Lecture on Some of the Distinctive Characteristics of the Female: Delivered before the Class of the Jefferson Medical College*. Philadelphia: Collins.

Melosh, Barbara. 1982. *"The Physician's Hand": Work Culture and Conflict in American Nursing*. Philadelphia: Temple University Press.

Mendelsohn, E., P. Weingart, and R. Whitely, eds. 1977. *The Social Production of Scientific Knowledge*. Dordrecht, The Netherlands: Riedel.

Mernissi, Fatima. 1987. *Beyond the Veil: Male-Female Dynamics in Modern Muslim Society*. Bloomington: Indiana University Press.

Mertz, Elizabeth, W. Njogu, and S. Gooding. 1998. "What Difference Does Difference Make? The Challenge for Legal Education." *Journal of Legal Education* 48 (March): 1–87.

Messner, Michael A. 1998. "The Limits of 'The Male Sex Role': An Analysis of the Men's Liberation and Men's Rights Movements' Discourse." *Gender & Society* 12 (June): 255–276.

Messerschmidt, James. 1986. *Capitalism, Patriarchy, and Criminology: Toward a Feminist Criminology*. Totowa, NJ: Rowman and Littlefield.

Messing, K. 1983. "The Scientific Mystique: Can a White Lab Coat Guarantee Purity in the Search for Knowledge About the Nature of Women?" Pp. 75–88 in *Woman's Nature*, edited by M. Lowe and R. Hubbard. New York: Pergamon Press.

Meyer, Jan. 1990. "Guess Who's Coming to Dinner This Time? A Study of Gay Intimate Relationships and the Support for Those Relationships." *Marriage and Family Review* 14: 59–82.

Meyer, M. H., and E. K. Pavalko. 1996. "Family, Work, and Access to Health Insurance among Mature Women." *Journal of Health and Social Behavior* 37 (December): 311–325.

Michael, Robert T., John H. Gagno, Edward O. Laumann, and Gina Kolata. 1994. *Sex in America: A Definitive Survey*. Boston: Little, Brown.

Middlebrook, Diane. 1998. *Suits Me: The Double Life of Billy*

Tipton. Boston: Houghton Mifflin.

Milkman, R. 1986. "Women's History and the Sears Case." *Feminist Studies* 12 (Summer): 375–400.

Mill, J. S. 1970. *The Subjection of Women*. New York: Source Book Press.

Miller, D. 1975. *American Indian Socialization to Urban Life*. San Francisco: Institute for Scientific Analysis.

Miller, D., D. Danaber, and D. Forbes. 1986. "Sex-related Strategies for Coping with Interpersonal Conflict in Children Five and Seven." *Development Psychology* 22: 543–548.

Miller, Eleanor. 1986. *Street Women*. Philadelphia: Temple University Press.

Miller, J. B. 1977. *Toward a New Psychology of Women*. Boston: Beacon Press.

———. 1982. "Psychological Recovery in Low-Income Single Parents." *American Journal of Orthopsychiatry* 52 (April): 346–352.

Miller, Susan. 1997. "The Unintended Consequences of Criminal Justice Policy." Talk presented at Research on Women Series, University of Delaware, Women's Studies Program.

Millman, Marcia. 1975. "She Did It All for Love." Pp. 251–279 in *Another Voice*, edited by Marcia Millman and Rosabeth Moss Kanter. Garden City, NY: Doubleday-Anchor.

———. 1980. *Such A Pretty Face: Being Fat in America*. New York: Norton.

Millman, M., and R. M. Kanter, eds. 1975. *Another Voice*. Garden City, NY: Doubleday-Anchor.

Mills, C. Wright. 1959. *The Sociological Imagination*. New York: Oxford University Press.

Milner, Joel S., and Julie L. Crouch. 1993. "Physical Child Abuse." Pp. 25–55 in *Family Violence: Prevention and Treatment*, edited by Robert L. Hampton, Thomas P. Gullotta, Gerald R. Adams, Earl H. Potter, III, and Roger P. Weissberg. Newbury Park, CA: Sage.

Minnich, Elizabeth Kamarck. 1990. *Transforming Knowledge*. Phila-

delphia: Temple University Press.

Mirandé, A. 1979. "Machismo: A Reinterpretation of Male Dominance in the Chicano Family." *The Family Coordinator* 28: 447–479.

Mirandé, Alfredo. 1982. "Machismo, Rucas, Chingasos, y Chingaderas." *De Colores* 6 (1 & 2): 17–31.

Mitchell, Juliet. 1971. *Woman's Estate*. New York: Pantheon.

Mitchell, G., Stephanie Obradovich, Fred Herring, Chris Tromborg, and Alyson L. Burns. 1992. "Reproducing Gender in Public Places: Adults' Attention to Toddlers in Three Public Locales." *Sex Roles* 26 (September): 323–330.

Modleski, T. 1980. "The Disappearing Act: A Study of Harlequin Romances." *Signs* 5 (Spring): 435–448.

Mohr, J. 1978. *Abortion in America*. New York: Oxford University Press.

Money, John. 1988. *Gay, Straight, and In-Between: The Sexology of Erotic Orientation*. New York: Oxford University Press.

———. 1995. *Gendermaps: Social Constructionism, Feminism and Sexosophical History*. New York: Continuum.

Money, J., and A. A. Ehrhardt. 1972. *Man, Woman, Boy and Girl: The Differentiation and Dimorphism of Gender Identity from Conception to Maturity*. Baltimore: Johns Hopkins University Press.

Mongeau, B., H. L. Smith, and A. C. Maney. 1961. "The 'Granny' Midwife: Changing Roles and Functions of a Folk Practitioner." *American Journal of Sociology* 66: 497–505.

Monson, Candice M., Gary R. Byrd and Jennifer Langhinrichsen-Rohling. 1996. "To Have and to Hold: Perceptions of Marital Rape." *Journal of Interpersonal Violence* 11 (September): 410–424.

Moore, David W. 1995. "Most Americans Say Religion Is Important to Them." *The Gallup Poll Monthly* (February): 16–21.

Moore, Gwen. 1990. "Structural Determinants of Men's and Women's Personal Networks."

American Sociological Review 55 (October): 726–735.

———. 1992. "Gender and Informal Networks in State Government." *Social Science Quarterly* 73 (March): 46–61.

Moore, Joan. 1988. "An Assessment of Hispanic Poverty: Does a Hispanic Underclass Exist?" *Tomas Rivera Center Report* 2: 8–9.

Moraga, Cherríe, and Gloria Anzaldúa. 1981. *This Bridge Called My Back: Radical Writings by Women of Color*. Watertown, MA: Persephone Press.

Morash, Merry, Robin N. Harr, and Lila Rucker. 1994. "Comparison of Programming for Women and Men in U.S. Prisons in the 1980s." *Crime and Delinquency* 40 (April): 197–221.

Morgan, M. 1987. "Television, Sex-Role Attitudes, and Sex-Role Behavior." *The Journal of Early Adolescence* 7: 269–282.

Morin, S. F., and E. M. Garfinkle. 1978. "Male Homophobia." *The Journal of Social Issues* 34 (Winter): 29–47.

Morton, W., and T. Ungs. 1979. "Cancer Mortality in the Major Cottage Industry." *Women and Health* 4 (Winter): 305–354.

Moskos, Charles. 1992. Pp. 40–54 in *Women in the Military*, edited by E. A. Blacksmith. New York: H. W. Wilson.

Moulds, E. F. 1980. "Chivalry and Paternalism: Disparities of Treatment in the Criminal Justice System." Pp. 277–299 in *Women, Crime, and Justice*, edited by S. Datesman and F. Scarpitti. New York: Oxford University Press.

Moynihan, D. P. 1965. *The Negro Family: The Case for National Action*. Washington, DC: U.S. Government Printing Office.

Murillo, N. 1971. "The Mexican American Family." Pp. 97–108 in *Chicanos: Social and Psychological Perspectives*, edited by N. Wagner and M. Hang. St. Louis: Mosby.

Myers, Dowell, and Cynthia J. Crawford. 1998. "Occupational Mobility of Immigrant and Native-Born Latinas." *American Sociological Review* 63 (February): 68–93.

Nadelson, C., and T. Nadelson. 1980. "Dual-Career Marriages: Benefits and Costs." Pp. 91–109 in *Dual-Career Couples*, edited by F. Pepitone-Rockwell. Beverly Hills: Sage.

Naff, Katherine C., and Sue Thomas. 1995. "The Glass Ceiling Revisited: Determinants of Federal Job Advancement." *Policy Studies Review* 3–4 (Autumn–Winter): 249–272.

Nanda, Serena. 1998. *Neither Man Nor Woman: The Hijras of India*. Belmont, CA: Wadsworth.

Naples, Nancy A. 1992. "Activist Mothering: Cross-Generational Continuity in the Community Work of Women from Low-Income Urban Neighborhoods." *Gender & Society* 6 (September): 441–464.

Nason-Clark, Nancy. 1987. "Are Women Changing the Image of Ministry? A Comparison of British and American Realities." *Review of Religious Research* 28 (June): 330–340.

Nathanson, C. 1975. "Illness and the Feminine Role: A Theoretical Review." *Social Science and Medicine* 9: 57–62.

National Cancer Institute. 1998. "Cancer Incidence in the United States." <www.rex.nci.nih.gov/NCI_Pub_Interface/rasterisk/rates12.html>

National Center for Educational Statistics. 1994. *Digest of Educational Statistics 1994*. Washington, DC: U.S. Department of Education.

National Center for Health Statistics. 1998. *Health, United States, 1998 with Socioeconomic Status and Health Chartbook*. Hyattsville, MD: U.S. Government Printing Office.

National Opinion Research Center. 1994. *General Social Survey*. Chicago: National Opinion Research Center.

Nazzari, M. 1983. "The 'Woman Question' in Cuba: An Analysis of Material Constraints on the Solution." *Signs* 9 (Winter): 246–263.

Nelson, Andrea, and Pamela Oliver. 1998. "Gender and the Construction of Consent in Child-Adult Sexual Contact:

Beyond Gender Neutrality and Male Monopoly." *Gender & Society* 12 (October): 554–577.

Nicholson, Linda E., ed. 1990. *Feminism and Postmodernism*. New York: Routledge.

———. 1994. "Interpreting Gender." *Signs* 20 (Autumn): 79–105.

Nisbet, Robert. 1970. *The Social Bond*. New York: Knopf.

Nock, Steven L. 1995. "A Comparison of Marriages and Cohabiting Relationships." *Journal of Family Issues* 16 (January): 53–76.

Novkov, Julie. 1996. "Liberty, Protection, and Women's Work: Investigating the Boundaries between Public and Private." *Law and Social Inquiry* 21 (Fall): 857–899.

Oakley, A. 1974. *The Sociology of Housework*. London: Mertin Robertson.

———. 1979. "A Case of Maternity: Paradigms of Women as Maternity Cases." *Signs* 4 (Summer): 607–631.

O'Kelly, C. G., and L. S. Carney. 1986. *Women and Men in Society*, 2nd ed. Belmont, CA: Wadsworth.

Padavic, I., and B. Reskin. 1988. "Supervisors as Gatekeepers: Male Supervisors' Responses to Women's Integration in Plant Jobs." *Social Problems* 35 (December): 536–550.

Padavic, Irene. 1991. "Attractions in Male Blue-Collar Jobs for Black and White Women: Economic Need, Exposure, and Attitudes." *Social Science Quarterly* 72 (March): 33–49.

Padula, Alfred. 1996. "Gender, Sexuality, and Revolution in Cuba." *Latin American Research Review* 31 (Spring): 226–236.

Palmer, Phyllis. 1989. *Domesticity and Dirt: Housewives and Domestic Servants in the United States, 1920–1945*. Philadelphia: Temple University Press.

Parker, D., E. Parker, M. Wolz, and T. Harford. 1980. "Sex Differences and Alcohol Consumption: A Research Note." *Journal of Health and Social Behavior* 21: 43–48.

Patterson, Charlotte. 1992. "Children of Lesbian and Gay

Parents." *Child Development* 63: 1025–1042.

Pavetti, LaDonna Ann. 1993. "The Dynamics of Welfare and Work: Exploring the Process by Which Women Work Their Way Off Welfare." Malcolm Weiner Center for Social Policy Working Papers: Dissertation Series. Cambridge, MA: Malcolm Weiner Center for Social Policy, Harvard University.

Payer, M. 1977. "Is Traditional Scholarship Value Free? Toward a Critical Theory." Paper presented at the Scholar and the Feminist IV, Barnard College, New York.

Payne, Deborah M., John T. Warner, and Roger D. Little. 1992. "Tied Migration and Returns to Human Capital: The Case of Military Wives." *Social Science Quarterly* 73 (June): 324–339.

Pedraza, Sylvia. 1991. "Women and Migration: The Social Consequences of Gender." *Annual Review of Sociology* 17. 303–325.

———. 1996. "Origins and Destinies: Immigration, Race, and Ethnicity in American History." Pp. 1–20 in *Origins and Destinies: Immigration, Race, and Ethnicity in America*, edited by Sylvia Pedraza and Rubén G. Rumbaut. Belmont, CA: Wadsworth.

Peres, Yochanan. 1998. "Cohabitation: A Contemporary Alternative to Marriage?" Paper presented at the International Sociological Association.

Perkins, Wesley H., and Debra K. Demeis. 1994. "Gender and Family Effects on the 'Second Shift' Domestic Activity of College-Educated Young Adults." Paper presented at the Annual Meetings of the American Sociological Association.

Petchesky, Rosalind. 1980. "Reproductive Freedom: Beyond a Woman's Right to Choose." *Signs* 5 (Summer): 661–685.

———. 1981. "Antiabortion, Antifeminism and the Rise of the New Right." *Feminist Studies* 7 (Summer): 206–246.

————. 1990. "Giving Women a Real Choice." *The Nation* (May 28): 732–735.

Peters, Debra K., and Peggy J. Cantrell. 1993. "Gender Roles and Role Conflict in Feminist Lesbian and Heterosexual Women." *Sex Roles* 28 (April): 379–392.

Peterson, Richard R. 1996a. "A Re-Evaluation of the Economic Consequences of Divorce." *American Sociological Review* 61 (June): 528–536.

————. 1996b. "A Re-Evaluation of the Economic Consequences of Divorce: Reply to Weitzman." *American Sociological Review* 61 (June): 539–540.

Pharr, Suzanne. 1988. *Homophobia: A Weapon of Sexism*. Little Rock, AR: Chardon Press.

Phillips, Lynn. 1998. *The Girls Report: What We Know and Need to Know About Growing Up Female*. New York: National Council for Research on Women.

Piotrkowski, Chaya S., and Rena L. Repetti. 1984. "Dual-Earner Families," *Journal of Marriage and Family Review* 7 (Fall-Winter): 99–124.

Pohli, C. V. 1983. "Church Closets and Back Doors: A Feminist View of Moral Majority Women." *Feminist Studies* 9 (Fall): 529–558.

Pollak, Otto. 1950. *The Criminology of Women*. Philadelphia: University of Pennsylvania Press.

Poston, C., ed. 1975. *A Vindication on the Rights of Woman*. New York: Norton.

Pottieger, A. 1981. Personal correspondence, March 1981.

Powers, Bethel-Ann. 1996. "Relationships among Older Women Living in a Nursing Home." *Journal of Women and Aging* 8: 179–198.

Power, Marilyn. Spring 1984. "'Falling through the Safety Net': Women, Economic Crisis and Reaganomics." *Feminist Studies* 10: 31–58.

Powers, M. 1980. "Menstruation and Reproduction: An Oglala Case." *Signs* 6 (Autumn): 54–65.

Press, Eyal. 1996. "Barbie's Betrayal." *The Nation* (December 30): 11–16.

Press, Julie E., and Eleanor Townsley. 1998. "Wives' and Husbands' Housework Reporting: Gender, Class, and Social Desirability." *Gender & Society* 12 (April): 188–218.

Project on the Education and Status of Women. 1978. *Sexual Harassment: A Hidden Issue*. American Association of Colleges, Washington, DC, June.

Purcell, P., and L. Stewart. 1990. "Dick and Jane in 1989." *Sex Roles* 22: 177–185.

Purifoy, F., and L. Koopmans. 1980. "Androstenedione, Testosterone, and Free Testosterone Concentration in Women of Various Occupations." *Social Biology* 26: 179–188.

Pyke, Karen D. 1994. "Women's Employment as a Gift or Burden? Marital Power across Marriage, Divorce, and Remarriage." *Gender & Society* 8 (March): 73–91.

Raag, T., and C. L. Rackliff. 1998. "Preschoolers' Awareness of Social Expectations of Gender: Relationships to Toy Choices." *Sex Roles* 38 (May): 675–700.

Radway, Janice. 1984. *Reading the Romance: Women, Patriarchy, and Popular Literature*. Chapel Hill: University of North Carolina Press.

Raeburn, Nicole. 1997. "The Rise of Lesbian, Gay, and Bisexual Rights in the Workplace: Employee Activist Groups and Institutional Opportunity Structures." Paper delivered at the Annual Meetings of the American Sociological Association, Toronto, August.

Ramirez, Ravenet, Niurka Perez Rojas, and Marta Toldeo Fraga. 1989. *La Mujer Rural y Urbana: Estudios de Casos*. Havana: Editorial de Ciencias Sociales.

Rapp, R., E. Rosse, and R. Bridenthal. 1979. "Examining Family History." *Feminist Studies* 5 (Spring): 174–200.

Reagon, B. J. 1982. "My Black Mothers and Sisters or On Beginning a Cultural Autobiography." *Feminist Studies* 8 (Spring): 81–96.

Redhorse, J. G., R. Lewis, M. Feit, and J. Decker. 1979. "American Indian Elders: Needs and Aspirations in Institutional and Home Health Care." Manuscript, Arizona State University.

Reeves, B., and M. M. Miller. 1978. "A Multidimensional Measure of Children's Identification with Television Characters." *Journal of Broadcasting* 22 (Winter): 71–86.

Reilly, Mary Ellen, Bernice Lott, Donna Caldwell, and Luisa DeLuca. 1992. "Tolerance for Sexual Harassment Related to Self-Reported Sexual Victimization." *Gender & Society* 6 (March): 122–138.

Reinharz, Shulamit. 1983. "Experiential Analysis: A Contribution to Feminist Research." Pp. 162–191 in *Theories of Women's Studies*, edited by G. Duelli-Klein and R. Duelli-Klein. Boston: Routledge & Kegan Paul.

————. 1988. "What's Missing in Miscarriage?" *Journal of Community Psychology* 16 (January): 84–103.

Reiter, R. R., ed. 1975. *Toward an Anthropology of Women*. New York: Monthly Review Press.

Reitz, R. 1977. *Menopause: A Positive Approach*. Radnor, PA: Chilton.

Relman, Arnold S., 1989. "The Changing Demography of the Medical Profession." *New England Journal of Medicine* 321 (November 30): 1540–1541.

Renzetti, Claire M. 1997. "Violence in Lesbian and Gay Relationships." Pp. 285–293 in *Gender Violence: Interdisciplinary Perspectives*, edited by Laura L. O'Toole and Jessica R. Schiffman. New York: New York University Press.

Repak, Terry A. 1994. "Labor Recruitment and the Lure of the Capital: Central American Migrants in Washington, DC." *Gender & Society* 8 (December): 507–524.

Reskin, Barbara. 1988. "Bringing the Men Back In: Sex Differentiation and the Devaluation of Women's Work." *Gender & Society* 2 (March): 58–81.

Reskin, Barbara F., and Irene Padavic. 1988. "Supervisors as Gatekeepers: Male Supervisors'

Response to Women's Integration in Plant Jobs." *Social Problems* 35 (December): 536–550.

———. 1994. *Women and Men at Work*. Thousand Oaks, CA: Pine Forge Press.

Reskin, Barbara, and Patricia Roos. 1990. *Job Queues, Gender Queues: Explaining Women's Inroads into Male Occupations*. Philadelphia: Temple University Press.

———. 1992. "Occupational Desegregation in the 1970s: Integration and Economic Equity?" *Sociological Perspectives* 35 (Spring): 69–91.

Resnik, J., and N. Shaw. 1981. "Prisoners of Their Sex: Health Problems of Incarcerated Women." *Prison Law Monitor* 3 (Winter): 55ff.

Reuther, R. 1979. "Mothercarth and the Megamachine: A Theology of Liberation in a Feminine, Somatic, and Ecological Perspective." Pp. 43–51 in C. P. Christ and J. Plaskow. *Womanspirit Rising*, edited by C. P. Christ. New York: Harper and Row.

Reuther, R. R., and R. S. Keller, eds. 1986. *Women and Religion in America, Volume 3: 1900–1968*. New York: Harper and Row.

Rhode, Deborah L. 1995. "Media Images, Feminist Issues." *Signs* 20 (Spring): 685–710.

Rhodes, A. L. 1983. "Effects of Religious Denomination of Sex Differences in Occupational Expectations." *Sex Roles* 9 (January): 93–108.

Rich, Adrienne. 1976. *Of Woman Born: Motherhood as Experience and Institution*. New York: Norton.

———. 1980. "Compulsory Heterosexuality and Lesbian Existence." *Signs* 5 (Summer): 631–660.

Rich, Melissa K., and Thomas F. Cash. 1993. "The American Image of Beauty: Media Representations of Hair Color for Four Decades." *Sex Roles* 29 (July): 113–124.

Richie, Beth E. 1996. *Compelled to Crime: The Gender Entrapment of Battered Black Women*. New York: Routledge.

Risman, Barbara. 1986. "Can Men 'Mother'? Life as a Single Father." *Family Relations* 35 (January): 95–102.

———. 1987. "Intimate Relationships from a Microstructural Perspective: Men Who Mother." *Gender & Society* 1 (March): 6–32.

Risman, Barbara J., and Pepper Schwartz, 1989. *Gender in Intimate Relationships: A Microstructural Approach*. Belmont, CA: Wadsworth.

Rist, Darrell Yates. 1992. "Are Homosexuals Born That Way?" *The Nation* 255 (October 14): 424–429.

Robbins, Cynthia. 1989. "Sex Differences in Psychosocial Consequences of Alcohol and Drug Abuse," *Journal of Health and Social Behavior* 30 (March): 117–130.

Robbins, Cynthia, and Richard R. Clayton. 1989. "Gender-Related Differences in Psychoactive Drug Use Among Older Adults." *Journal of Drug Issues* 19 (Spring): 207–219.

Robinson, B. E., and R. L. Barret. 1986. *The Developing Father*. New York: The Guilford Press.

Rodriguez, Clara E. 1989. *Puerto Ricans*. Winchester, MA: Unwin Hyman.

———. 1997. *Latin Looks: Images of Latinas and Latinos in the Media*. Boulder, CO: Westview Press.

Rollins, Judith. 1985. *Between Women: Domestics and Their Employers*. Philadelphia: Temple University Press.

Romero, Mary. 1992. *Maid in the U.S.A.* Philadelphia: Temple University Press.

Roof, Wade Clark, and William McKinney. 1987. *American Mainline Religion: Its Changing Shape and Future*. New Brunswick, NJ: Rutgers University Press.

Roper Organization. 1985. *The 1980 Virginia Slims American Women's Opinion Poll*. Storrs, CT: The Roper Center.

———. 1990. *The Virginia Slims American Women's Opinion Poll*. Storrs, CT: Roper Organization.

———. 1995. *The 1995 Virginia Slims Opinion Poll*. Storrs, CT: Roper Search Worldwide.

———. 1997. *The Gallup Poll*. Storrs, CT: The Roper Organization.

Rosaldo, M. Z. 1980. "Use and Abuse of Anthropology: Reflections on Feminism and Cross-cultural Understanding." *Signs* 5 (Spring): 389–417.

Rosenau, Pauline Marie. 1992. *Postmodernism and the Social Sciences: Insights, Inroads, and Intrusions*. Princeton, NJ: Princeton University Press.

Rosenberg, J., H. Perlstadt, and W. R. F. Phillips. 1993. "Now That We Are Here: Discrimination, Disparagement, and Harassment at Work and the Experience of Women Lawyers." *Gender & Society* 7: 415–433.

Rosenberg, R. 1982. *Beyond Separate Spheres: Intellectual Roots of Modern Feminism*. New Haven, CT: Yale University Press.

Rosenblum, K. E. 1975. "Female Deviance and the Female Sex Role: A Preliminary Investigation." *British Journal of Sociology* 26: 169–185.

Rosenfield, Sarah. 1980. "Sex Differences in Depression: Do Women Always Have Higher Rates?" *Journal of Health and Social Behavior* 21: 33–42.

Rossi, Alice. 1970. *Essays on Sex Equality*. Chicago: University of Chicago Press.

———. 1973. *The Feminist Papers*. New York: Columbia University Press.

———. 1977. "Toward a Biosocial Perspective on Parenting." *Daedalus* 106 (Spring): 1–31.

Rossi, Alice S., and Rossi, P. E. 1977. "Body Time and Social Time: Mood Patterns by Menstrual Cycle Phase and Days of the Week." *Social Science Research* 6: 273–308.

Rossiter, M. 1982. *Women Scientists in America*. Baltimore: Johns Hopkins University Press.

Rothman, Barbara Katz. 1982. *In Labor: Women and Power in the Birthplace*. New York: Norton.

———. 1989. *Recreating Motherhood: Ideology and Technology in a Patriarchal Society*. New York: Norton.

Rothschild, M. A. 1979. "White Women Volunteers in the Freedom Summers." *Feminist Studies* 5 (Fall): 466–495.

Rubin, G. 1975. "The Traffic in Women." Pp. 157–211 in *Toward an Anthropology of Women*, edited by R. Reiter. New York: Monthly Review Press.

Rubin, Z., F. J. Provenzano, and C. T. Hull. 1974. "The Eye of the Beholder: Parents' Views on Sex of Newborns." *American Journal of Orthopsychiatry* 44: 512–519.

Ruddick, Sara. 1989. *Maternal Thinking: Toward a Politics of Peace*. Boston: Beacon Press.

Rupp, Leila, and Verta Taylor. 1987. *Survival in the Doldrums: The American Women's Rights Movement, 1945 to the 1960's*. New York: Oxford University Press.

Russell, Diane E. H. 1982. *Rape in Marriage*. New York: Macmillan.

———. 1986. *The Secret Trauma: Incest in the Lives of Girls and Women*. New York: Basic Books.

Rust, Paula. 1993. "'Coming Out' in the Age of Social Constructionism: Social Identity Formation among Lesbian and Bisexual Women." *Gender & Society* 1 (March): 50–77.

———. 1995. *Bisexuality and the Challenge to Lesbian Politics*. New York: New York University Press.

Ruzek, S. 1978. *The Women's Health Movement: Feminist Alternatives to Medical Control*. New York: Praeger.

Ryan, Rebecca. 1995. "The Sex Right: A Legal History of the Marital Rape Exemption." *Law and Social Inquiry* 4 (Fall): 941–1001.

Sacks, Karen. 1975. "Engels Revisited: Women, the Organization of Production, and Private Property." Pp. 211–234 in *Toward an Anthropology of Women*, edited by R. Reiter. New York: Monthly Review Press.

———. 1984. "Generations of Working Class Families." Pp. 15–38 in *My Troubles Are Going to Have Trouble With Me*, edited by K. B. Sacks and D. Remy. New Brunswick, NJ: Rutgers University Press.

Sadker, M., and D. Sadker. 1994. *Failing at Fairness: How America's Schools Cheat Girls*. New York: Charles Scribner's Sons.

Saiving, V. 1979. "The Human Situation: A Feminine View." Pp. 25–42 in *Womanspirit Rising*, edited by C. P. Christ and J. Plaskow. New York: Harper and Row.

Sanchez, Laura, and Elizabeth Thomson. 1997. "Becoming Mothers and Fathers: Parenthood, Gender, and the Division of Labor." *Gender & Society* 11 (December): 747–772.

Sanchez-Ayendez, Melba, 1986. "Puerto Rican Elderly Women: Shared Meanings and Informal Supportive Networks." Pp. 172–186 in *All-American Women: Lines That Divide, Ties That Bind*, edited by Johnetta Cole. New York: Free Press.

Sanday, Peggy. 1973. "Toward a Theory of the Status of Women." *American Anthropology* 75: 1682–1700.

Sanday, Peggy R. 1994. *Many Mirrors: Body Image and Social Relations*. New Brunswick, NJ: Rutgers University Press.

Sandmaier, M. 1980. *The Invisible Alcoholic: Women and Alcohol Abuse in America*. New York: McGraw-Hill.

Sarri, Rosemary C. 1988. Keynote Address, Conference on Increasing Educational Equity for Juvenile Female Offenders. Washington, DC: Council of Chief State School Officers.

Sattel, Jack. 1983. "Men, Inexpressiveness and Power." Pp. 119–124 in *Language, Gender, and Society*, edited by Barrie Thorne, C. Kramarae, and Nancy Henley. Rowley, MA: Newbury House.

Sayers, S. L., Baucom, D. H., and A. M. Tierney. 1993. "Sex Roles, Interpersonal Control, and Depression: Who Can Get Their Way." *Journal of Research in Personality* 27: 377–395.

Sayre, Anne. 1975. *Rosalind Franklin and DNA*. New York: Norton.

Schneider, Beth. 1982. "Consciousness about Sexual Harassment among Heterosexual and Lesbian Women Workers." *Journal of Social Issues* 38: 75–98.

———. 1984. "Perils and Promise: Lesbians' Workplace Participation." Pp. 211–230 in *Women-Identified Women*, edited by Trudy Darty and Sandee Potter. Palo Alto, CA: Mayfield.

Schneider, Beth E., and Nancy E. Stoller. 1995. *Women Resisting AIDS: Feminist Strategies of Empowerment*. Philadelphia: Temple University Press.

Scholten, C. M. 1977. "On the Importance of the Obstetric Art: Changing Customs of Childbirth in America." *The William and Mary Quarterly* 34: 426–445.

Schorr, Juliet B. 1991. *The Overworked American: The Unexpected Decline of Leisure*. New York: Basic Books.

Schwartz, Pepper, and Virginia Rutter. 1998. *The Gender of Sexuality*. Thousand Oaks, CA: Pine Forge Press.

Scully, Diana. 1990. *Understanding Sexual Violence: A Story of Convicted Rapists*. Cambridge, MA: Unwin Hyman.

Seccombe, Karen, and Leonard Beeghley. 1992. "Gender and Medical Insurance: A Test of Human Capital Theory." *Gender & Society* 6 (June): 283–300.

Segura, Denise. 1994. "Inside the Work Worlds of Chicana and Mexican Immigrant Women." Pp. 95–112 in *Women of Color in U.S. Society*, edited by Maxine Baca Zinn and Bonnie Thornton Dill. Philadelphia: Temple University Press.

———. 1998. "Working at Motherhood: Chicana and Mexican Immigrant Mothers and Employment." Pp. 727–744 in *Families in the U.S.: Kinship and Domestic Politics*, edited by Karen V. Hansen and Anita Ilta Garey. Philadelphia: Temple University Press.

Segura, Denise A., and Jennifer L. Pierce. 1993. "Chicana/o Family Structure and Gender Personality: Chodorow, Familism, and Psychoanalytic Sociology Revisited." *Signs* 19 (Autumn): 62–91.

Seidman, G. 1984. "Women in Zimbabwe: Postindependence Struggles." *Feminist Studies* 10 (Fall): 419–440.

Seidman, Steven. 1994. "Symposium: Queer Theory/Sociology:

A Dialogue." *Sociological Theory* 12 (July): 166–177.

Seltzer, Richard. 1992. "The Social Location of Those Holding Antihomosexual Attitudes." *Sex Roles* 26: 391–398.

Shange, Ntozake. 1975. *For colored girls who have considered suicide/when the rainbow is enuf.* New York: Bantam Books.

Shehan, Constance L., Mary Ann Burg, and Cynthis A. Rexroat. 1986. "Depression and the Social Dimensions of the Full-Time Housewife Role." *Sociological Quarterly* 27 (September): 403–421.

Shelton, Beth Anne. 1992. *Women, Men, and Time: Gender Differences in Paid Work, Housework, and Leisure.* New York: Greenwood Press.

Signorielli, Nancy. 1989. "Television and Conceptions About Sex Roles: Maintaining Conventionality and the Status Quo." *Sex Roles* 21: 341–360.

———. 1991. *A Sourcebook on Children and Television.* New York: Greenwood Press.

Silverstein, B., and A. D. Lynch. 1998. "Gender Differences in Depression: The Role Played by Paternal Attitudes of Male Superiority and Maternal Modeling of Gender-Related Limitations." *Sex Roles* 38 (April): 539–555.

Simmel, G. 1950. "The Stranger." Pp. 402–408 in *The Sociology of Georg Simmel,* edited by Kurt Wolff. New York: Free Press.

Simon, R. 1975. *Women and Crime.* Lexington, MA: Lexington Books.

———. 1981. "American Women and Crime." Pp. 18–39 in *Women and Crime in America,* edited by Lee Bowker. New York: Macmillan.

Simon, Rita J., Angela R. Scanlan, and Pamela S. Nadell. 1994. "Rabbis and Ministers: Women of the Book and the Cloth." Pp. 45–52 in *Gender and Religion,* edited by William H. Swatos. New Brunswick, NJ: Transaction Publishers.

Simpson, Sally. 1989. "Feminist Theory, Crime, and Justice." *Criminology* 27: 605–631.

Skirboll, Esther, and Rhoda Taylor. 1998. "Two Homes, Two Jobs, One Marriage: Commuter Spousal Relationships." Paper presented at the International Sociological Association meetings.

Sklar, Holly. 1994. "Disposable Workers." *Z Magazine* (January): 36–41.

Slevin, Kathryn F., and C. Ray Wingrove. 1998. *From Stumbling Blocks to Stepping Stones: The Life Experiences of Fifty Professional African American Women.* New York: New York University Press.

Slater, A. S., and S. Feinman. 1985. "Gender and the Phonology of North American First Names." *Sex Roles* 13 (October): 429–440.

Smart, C. 1977. *Women, Crime and Criminology: A Feminist Critique.* London: Routledge & Kegan Paul.

———. 1989. *Feminism and the Power of Law.* New York: Routledge.

Smedley, A. 1974. "Women of Uder: Survival in a Harsh Land." Pp. 205–228 in *Many Sisters,* edited by C. Matthiasson. New York: Free Press.

Smith, Barbara. 1997. "Where Has Gay Liberation Gone? An Interview with Barbara Smith." Pp. 195–208 in *Homo Economics: Capitalism, Community, and Lesbian and Gay Life,* edited by Amy Gluckman and Betsy Reed. New York: Routledge.

Smith, Dinitia. 1998. "One False Note in a Musician's Life." *The New York Times,* June 2, pp. B1, 4.

Smith, Dorothy E. 1974. "Women's Perspective as a Radical Critique of Sociology." *Sociological Inquiry* 44: 7–13.

———. 1987. *The Everyday World as Problematic: A Feminist Sociology.* Boston: Northeastern University Press.

———. 1990. *The Conceptual Practices of Power: A Feminist Sociology of Knowledge.* Boston: Northeastern University Press.

Smith, Heather. 1998. "Ladders, Ceilings, and Trap Doors: The Promotion of Women and Men." Ph.D. Dissertation, University of Delaware.

Smith, James P. 1998. "Race and Ethnicity in the Labor Market: Trends over the Short and Long Run." Paper presented at the Research Conference on Racial Trends in the United States, National Academy of Sciences, Washington, DC, October.

Smith, L. S. 1978. "Sexist Assumptions and Female Delinquency." Pp. 74–86 in *Women, Sexuality, and Social Control,* edited by C. Smart and B. Smart. London: Routledge & Kegan Paul.

Smith, Lois M., and Alfred Padula. 1996. *Sex and Revolution: Women in Socialist Cuba.* New York: Oxford University Press.

Smith, M. D., and N. Bennett. 1985. "Poverty, Inequality and Theories of Forcible Rape." *Crime and Delinquency* 31 (April): 295–305.

Smith-Rosenberg, C. 1975. "The Female World of Love and Ritual: Relations Between Women in Nineteenth Century America." *Signs* 1 (Fall): 1–29.

Snell, Tracy L. 1994. "Women in Prison." Special Report, March. Washington, DC: Bureau of Justice Statistics.

Snipp, C. Matthew. 1996. "The Size and Distribution of the American Indian Population: Fertility, Mortality, Residence, and Migration." Pp. 17–52 in *Changing Numbers, Changing Needs: American Indian Demography and Public Health,* edited by Gary D. Sandefur, Ronald R. Rindfuss, and Barney Cohen. Washington, DC: National Academy Press.

Sokoloff, N. 1980. *Between Money and Love: The Dialectics of Women's Home and Market Work.* New York: Praeger.

South, Scott J., and Glenna Spitze. 1994. "Housework in Marital and Nonmarital Households." *American Sociological Review* 59 (June): 327–347.

Spain, Daphne, and Suzanne M. Bianchi. 1996. *Balancing Act: Motherhood, Marriage, and Employment among American Women.* New York: Russell Sage Foundation.

Spanier, G. 1983. "Married and Unmarried Cohabitation in the U.S.: 1980." *Journal of Marriage and the Family* 45 (May): 277–288.

Speigel, D. 1983. "Mothering, Fathering, and Mental Illness." Pp. 95–110 in *Rethinking the Family: Some Feminist Questions,* edited by Barrie Thorne. New York: Longmans.

Spender, Dale. 1989. *The Writing or the Sex.* New York: Pergamon.

Spitze, Glenna. 1988. "Women's Employment and Family Relations: A Review," *Journal of Marriage and the Family* 50 (August): 595–618.

Spretnak, C., ed. 1994. *The Politics of Women's Spirituality: Essays on the Rise of Spiritual Power Within the Feminist Movement,* 2nd ed. Garden City, NY: Anchor Books.

Sprock, June, and Carol Y. Yoder. 1997. "Women and Depression: An Update on the Report of the APA Task Force." *Sex Roles* 36 (March): 269–303.

Stack, C. 1974. *All Our Kin: Strategies for Survival in a Black Community.* New York: Harper Colophon.

Stack, Carol B., and Linda Burton. 1993. "Kinscripts." Pp. 405–417 in *Families in the U.S.: Kinship and Domestic Politics,* edited by Karen V. Hansen and Anita Ilta Garey. Philadelphia: Temple University Press.

Stafford, R., E. Backman, and P. Dibona. 1977. "The Division of Labor Among Cohabiting and Married Couples." *Journal of Marriage and the Family* 39: 43–57.

Stacey, Judith. 1983. *Patriarchy and Socialist Revolution in China.* Berkeley: University of California Press.

Stanley, Autumn. 1993. *Mothers and Daughters of Invention: Notes for a Revised History of Technology.* Metuchen, NJ: Scarecrow Press.

Stanley, Harold W., and Richard G. Niemi. 1994. *Vital Statistics on American Politics,* 4th ed. Washington, DC: Congressional Quarterly, Inc.

Stanton, Elizabeth Cady. 1974. *The Woman's Bible.* New York: Arno Press.

Staples, R. 1971. *The Black Family.* Belmont, CA: Wadsworth.

Staples, R., and A. Mirandé. 1980. "Racial and Cultural Variations Among American Families." *Journal of Marriage and the Family* 42: 887–903.

Staples, R., and T. Jones. 1985. "Culture, Ideology, and Black Television Images." *Black Scholar* 16 (May–June): 10–20.

Steenland, Sally. 1989. *Unequal Picture: Black, Hispanic, Asian, and Native American Characters on Television.* Washington, DC: National Commission of Working Women on Wider Opportunities for Women.

Steffensmeier, D. 1981. "Patterns of Female Property Crime, 1960–1978: A Postscript." Pp. 59–65 in *Women and Crime in America,* edited by Lee Bowker. New York: Macmillan.

Stein, Arlene, and Ken Plummer. 1994. "'I Can't Even Think Straight': Queer Theory and the Missing Sexual Revolution in Sociology." *Sociological Theory* 12 (July): 178–187.

Stein, D. K. 1978. "Women to Burn: Suttee as a Normative Institution." *Signs* 4 (Winter): 253–268.

Steinberg, Ronnie. 1992. "Gendered Instructions: Cultural Lag and Gender Bias in the Hay System of Job Evaluation." *Work and Occupations* 19 (November): 387–424.

Steingart, R. M., et al. 1991. "Sex Differences in the Management of Coronary Artery Disease: Survival and Ventricular Enlargement Investigators." *New England Journal of Medicine* 325 (July 25): 226–230.

Steinke, Jocelyn, and Marilee Long. 1996. "A Lab of Her Own? Portrayals of Female Characters on Children's Educational Science Programs." *Science Communication* 18 (December): 91–115.

Stellman, J. M. 1977. *Women's Work, Women's Health: Myths and Realities.* New York: Pantheon.

Sterling, Anne. 1984. *We Are Your Sisters: Black Women in the Nineteenth Century.* New York: Norton.

Stern, M., and K. H. Karraker. 1989. "Sex Stereotyping of Infants: A Review of Gender Labeling Studies." *Sex Roles* 20 (May): 501–522.

Stohs, Joanne Hoven. 1995. "Predictors of Conflict over the Household Division of Labor among Women Employed Full-Time." *Sex Roles* 33 (August): 257–275.

Stoller, Eleanor Palo, and Rose Campbell Gibson, eds. 1997. *Worlds of Difference: Inequality in the Aging Experience.* Thousand Oaks, CA: Pine Forge Press.

Stone, Vernon. 1998. "Minorities and Women in Television News." <www.missouri.edu/~jourvs/gvtminw.html>

Strouse, J. 1972. "To Be Minor and Female: The Legal Rights of Women Under 21." *Ms.* 1: 70ff.

Sugarman, David, and Gerald Hotaling. 1991. "Dating Violence: A Review of Contextual and Risk Factors." Pp. 100–118 in *Dating Violence: Young Women in Danger,* edited by Barrie Levy. Seattle: Seal Press.

Sullivan, Deborah A., and Rose Weitz. 1988. *Labor Pains: Modern Midwives and Home Birth.* New Haven, CT: Yale University Press.

Sullivan, Maureen. 1996. "Rozzie and Harriet? Gender and Family Patterns of Lesbian Coparents." *Gender & Society* 12 (December): 747–767.

Swerdlow, A., R. Bridenthal, J. Kelly, and P. Vine. 1980. *Household and Kin.* Old Westbury, NY: Feminist Press.

Szasz, T. 1970. *Manufacture of Madness.* New York: Dell.

Taffel, S., P. Placek, and M. Moien. 1983. "One Fifth of 1983 Births by Cesarean Section." *American Journal of Public Health* 75 (February): 90.

Takagi, Dana Y. 1996. "Maiden Voyage: Excursion into Sexuality and Identity Politics." Pp. 21–36 in *Asian American Sexualities: Dimensions of the Gay & Lesbian Experience,* edited by Russell Leong. New York: Routledge.

Takaki, Ronald. 1989. *Strangers From a Different Shore: A History of Asian Americans.* New York: Penguin.

———. 1993. *A Different Mirror: A History of Multicultural America.* Boston: Little, Brown.

Tam, Tony. 1997. "Sex Segregation and Occupational Gender Inequality in the United States: Devaluation of Specialized Training." *American Journal of Sociology* 102 (May): 1652–1692.

Tannen, Deborah. 1990. *You Just Don't Understand: Men and Women in Conversation.* New York: William Morrow.

———. 1992. *That's Not What I Meant.* New York: Ballantine.

———. 1998. *The Argument Culture.* New York: Random House.

Tanner, D. M. 1978. *The Lesbian Couple.* Lexington, MA: Lexington Books.

Taylor, Verta. 1980. "Review Essays of Four Books on Lesbianism." *Journal of Marriage and the Family* 42: 224–228.

Taylor, Verta, and Nicole C. Raeburn. 1995. "Identity Politics as High-Risk Activism: Career Consequences for Lesbian, Gay, and Bisexual Sociologists." *Social Problems* 42 (May): 252–273.

Tea, N. T., M. Castanier, M. Roger, and R. Scholler. 1975. "Simultaneous Radioimmunoassay of Plasma Progesterone and 17-Hydroxyprogesterone in Men and Women Throughout the Menstrual Cycle and in Early Pregnancy." *Journal of Steroid Biochemistry* 6: 1509–1516.

Thomas, W. I. 1923. *The Unadjusted Girl.* Boston: Little, Brown.

Thompson, Becky W. 1994. *A Hunger So Wide and So Deep: American Women Speak Out on Eating Problems.* Minneapolis: University of Minnesota Press.

Thompson, E. H., C. Grisanti, and J. Pleck. 1985. "Attitudes Toward the Male Role and Their Correlates." *Sex Roles* 13 (October): 413–427.

Thompson, E. P. 1967. "Time, Work-Discipline and Industrial Capitalism." *Past and Present* 38: 56–90.

Thompson, T. L., and Zerbinos, E. 1997. "Television Cartoons: Do Children Notice It's a Boy's

World?" *Sex Roles* 37 (September): 415–432.

Thorne, Barrie. 1993. *Gender Play.* New Brunswick, NJ: Rutgers University Press.

Thorne, Barrie, and Zella Luria. 1986. "Sexuality and Gender in Children's Daily Worlds." *Social Problems* 33 (February): 176–190.

Thorne, Barrie, ed., with Marilyn Yalom. 1992. *Re-thinking the Family: Some Feminist Questions,* 2nd ed. Boston: Northeastern University Press.

Thornton, A., D. E. Alwin, and D. Camburn. 1983. "Causes and Consequences of Sex-Role Attitudes and Attitude Change." *American Sociological Review* 48 (April): 211–227.

Thornton, Arland, William G. Axinn, and Jay D. Teachman. 1995. "The Influence of School Enrollment and Accumulation on Cohabitation and Marriage in Early Adulthood." *American Sociological Review* 60 (October): 762–774.

Thornton, Bill, and Rachel Leo. 1992. "Gender Typing, Importance of Multiple Roles, and Mental Health Consequences for Women." *Sex Roles* 27 (September): 307–318.

Tillich, P. 1957. *The Dynamics of Faith.* New York: Harper and Row.

Tilly, L. A., and J. W. Scott. 1978. *Women, Work, and Family.* New York: Holt, Rinehart and Winston.

Titus-Dillon, Pauline Y., and Davis G. Johnson. 1989. "Female Graduates of a Predominantly Black College of Medicine: Their Characteristics and Challenges." *Journal of the American Medical Women's Association* 44: 175–182.

Tolman, Deborah L. 1994. "Doing Desire: Adolescent Girls' Struggles for/with Sexuality." *Gender & Society* 8 (September): 324–342.

Tovée, M., J. S. Reinhardt, and J. L. Emery. 1998. "Optimum Body-Mass Index and Maximum Sexual Attractiveness." *Lancet* 352 (August 15): 548.

Tovée, M. J., S. M. Mason, J. L. Emery, S. E. McCluskey, and E.

M. Tovée. 1997. "Supermodels: Stick Insects or Hourglasses?" *Lancet* 350 (November 15): 1474–1475.

Trent, Katherine, and Sharon L. Harlan. 1990. "Household Structure Among Teenage Mothers in the United States." *Social Science Quarterly* 71 (September): 439–457.

Tuan, Yi-Fu. 1984. *Dominance and Affection: The Making of Pets.* New Haven, CT: Yale University Press.

Tuchman, G., A. K. Daniels, and J. Benét. 1978. *Hearth and Home: Images of Women in the Mass Media.* New York: Oxford University Press.

Tuchman, Gaye. 1979. "Women's Depiction by the Mass Media." *Signs* 4 (Spring): 528–542.

Tucker, R., ed. 1972. *The Marx-Engels Reader.* New York: Norton.

Turner, Ralph, and Lewis M. Killian. 1972. *Collective Behavior.* Upper Saddle River, NJ: Prentice-Hall.

Turner-Bowker, D. M. 1996. "Gender-Stereotyped Descriptors in Children's Picture Books: Does 'Curious Jane' Exist in the Literature?" *Sex Roles* 35 (October): 461–488.

U.S. Census Bureau. 1994. *Household and Family Characteristics: March 1993.* U.S. Government Printing Office.

———. 1995. "Who Receives Child Support?" Washington, DC: U.S. Government Printing Office.

———. 1996. *Income and Poverty 1995.* <www.census.gov/ftp/pub/hhes/income/historic/p2.prr>

———. 1997. *Statistical Abstracts of the United States—1997.* Washington, DC: U.S. Government Printing Office.

———. 1998. *Money Income in the United States: 1997.* Washington, DC: U.S. Government Printing Office.

U.S. Department of Defense. 1992. "Women in the U.S. Military: Selected Data." Washington, DC: Defense Manpower Data Center.

———. 1997. *Active Duty Military Personnel by Rank/Grade.* March 31. Washington, DC: U.S. Department of Defense.

U.S. Department of Health and Human Services. 1998. *Health United States 1998*. Hyattsville, MD: National Center for Health Statistics.

U.S. Department of Justice. 1993a. *Sourcebook of Criminal Justice Statistics-1993*. Washington, DC: Bureau of Justice Statistics.

———. 1993b. *Uniform Crime Reports for the United States, 1993*. Washington, DC: Bureau of Justice Statistics.

———. 1997. *Sourcebook of Criminal Justice Statistics*. Washington, DC: U.S. Department of Justice.

U.S. Department of Labor. 1998. *Employment and Earnings*. Washington, DC: U.S. Government Printing Office.

Vance, Carole. 1984. "Pleasure and Danger: Toward a Politics of Sexuality." Pp. 1–28 in *Pleasure and Danger*, edited by Carole Vance. Boston: Routledge & Kegan Paul.

Van Den Daele, W. 1977. "The Social Construction of Science: Institutionalization and Definition of Positive Science in the Latter Half of the Seventeenth Century." Pp. 27–54 in *The Social Production of Scientific Knowledge*, edited by E. Mendelsohn, P. Weingart, and R. Whitley. Dordrecht, The Netherlands: Riedel.

Vanek, J. A. 1978. "Housewives as Workers." Pp. 392–414 in *Women Working*, edited by Anne H. Stromberg and Shirley Harkess. Palo Alto, CA: Mayfield.

Vanneman, Reeve, and Lynn Weber Cannon. 1987. *The American Perception of Class*. Philadelphia: Temple University Press.

Veiel, H. O. F. 1993. "Detrimental Effects of Kin Support Networks on the Course of Depression." *Journal of Abnormal Psychology* 102: 419–429.

Verbrugge, Lois M. 1984. "How Physicians Treat Mentally Distressed Men and Women." *Social Science and Medicine* 18: 1–9.

Vida, G. 1978. *Our Right to Love: A Lesbian Resource Book*. Upper Saddle River, NJ: Prentice-Hall.

Vogel, Dena Ann, Margaret A. Lake, Suzanne Evans, and Katherine Hildebrandt Karraker. 1991. "Children's and Adults' Sex-Stereotyped Perceptions of Infants." *Sex Roles* 21 (May): 605–616.

Waldron, I., C. C. Weiss, and M. E. Hughes. 1998. "Interacting Effects of Multiple Roles on Women's Health." *Journal of Health and Social Behavior* 39 (September): 216–230.

Walker, Rebecca, ed. 1995. *To Be Real: Telling the Truth and Changing the Face of Feminism*. New York: Anchor.

Walker, Sharon. 1995. "'Always There for Me': Friendship Patterns and Expectations among Middle- and Working-Class Men and Women." *Sociological Forum* 10: 273–296.

Wallace, Ruth A. 1992. *They Call Her Pastor: A New Role for Catholic Women*. Albany, NY: State University of New York Press.

Wallen, J. 1979. "Physician Stereotypes About Female Health and Illinois." *Women and Health* 4 (Summer): 135–146.

Waller, Kathy. 1988. "Women Doctors for Women Patients?" *British Journal of Medical Psychology* 61 (June): 125–135.

Wallerstein, I. 1976. *The Modern World System*. New York: Academic Press.

Walsh, M. R. 1977. *Doctors Wanted: No Women Need Apply*. New Haven, CT: Yale University Press.

Walters, Suzanna. 1995. *Material Girls: Making Sense of Feminist Cultural Theory*. Berkeley: University of California Press.

Walzer, Susan. 1996. "Thinking About the Baby: Gender and Divisions of Infant Care." *Social Problems* 43 (May): 219–234.

Wardle, R. M. 1951. *Mary Wollstonecraft: A Critical Biography*. Lawrence: University of Kansas Press.

Ware, M. C., and M. F. Stuck. 1985. "Sex Role Messages vis-a-vis Microcomputer Use: A Look at the Pictures." *Sex Roles* 13 (August): 205–214.

Warr, M. 1985. "Fear of Rape Among Urban Women." *Social Problems* 32 (February): 238–250.

Wasserman, G. A., and M. Lewis. 1985. "Infant Sex Differences: Ecological Effects." *Sex Roles* 12 (March): 665–675.

Watson, James D. 1968. *The Double Helix*. New York: Atheneum.

Weber, Lynn, and Elizabeth Higginbotham. 1995. "Perceptions of Workplace Discrimination Among Black and White Professional-Managerial Women." *Working Papers Series*. Memphis: Center for Research on Women, University of Memphis.

Weber, Max. 1947. *The Theory of Social and Economic Organization*. New York: Free Press.

Webster, P. 1975. "Matriarchy: A Vision of Power." Pp. 141–157 in *Toward an Anthropology of Women*, edited by Rayna Reiter. New York: Monthly Review Press.

Wechsler, Henry. 1995. *Binge Drinking on College Campuses. A New Look at an Old Problem*. Boston: Harvard School of Public Health.

Weisner, Thomas S., Helen Garnier, and James Loucky. 1994. "Domestic Tasks, Gender Egalitarian Values and Children's Gender Typing in Conventional and Nonconventional Families." *Sex Roles* 30 (January): 23–54.

Weitz, Rose. 1996. *The Sociology of Health, Illness, and Health Care: A Critical Approach*. Belmont, CA: Wadsworth.

Weitzman, Lenore. 1985. *The Divorce Revolution: The Unexpected Consequences for Women and Children in America*. New York: Free Press.

———. 1996. "A Re-Evaluation of the Economic Consequences of Divorce: Reply to Peterson." *American Sociological Review* 61 (June): 537–538.

Weitzman, Lenore, D. Eifler, E. Hokada, and C. Ross. 1972. "Sex Role Socialization in Picture Books for Preschool Children." *American Journal of Sociology* 77: 1125–1150.

Welch, Susan, and Lee Sigelman. 1989. "A Black Gender Gap?" *Social Science Quarterly* 70 (March): 120–133.

Welter, B., ed. 1976. *Dimity Convictions*. Athens: Ohio University Press.

Wermuth, L. 1981. "Book Review: The Policing of Families by Jacques Donzelot." *Contemporary Sociology* 10: 414–415.

Wertz, R. W., and D. C. Wertz. 1977. *Lying In: A History of Childbirth in America*. New York: Free Press.

West, Candace, and Sarah Fenstermaker. 1995. "Doing Difference." *Gender & Society* 9 (February): 8–37.

West, Candace, and Don Zimmerman. 1987. "Doing Gender." *Gender & Society* 1 (June): 125–151.

West, Carolyn M. 1998. "Leaving a Second Closet: Outing Partner Violence in Same-Sex Couples." Pp. 163–183 in *Partner Violence: A Comprehensive Review of 20 Years of Research*, edited by Jana L. Jasinkski and Linda M. Williams. Thousand Oaks, CA: Sage.

Westkott, Marcia. 1979. "Feminist Criticism of the Social Sciences." *Harvard Educational Review* 49: 422–430.

White, Robert, and Robert Althauser. 1984. "Internal Labor Markets, Promotions, and Worker Skill: An Indirect Test of Skill ILMs." *Social Science Research* 13: 373–392.

Whitney, Ruth, ed. 1984. "Feeling Fat in a Thin Society." *Glamour* (February): 198–201.

Whittier, Nancy. 1995. *Feminist Generations: The Persistence of the Radical Women's Movement*. Philadelphia: Temple University Press.

Wilcox, Clyde. 1992. "Race, Gender, and Support for Women in the Military." *Social Science Quarterly* 73 (June): 310–323.

Wilds, Deborah J., and Reginald Wilson. 1998. *Minorities in Higher Education*. Washington, DC: American Council on Education.

Wilkie, Jane Riblett. 1993. "Changes in U.S. Men's Attitudes toward the Family Provider Role, 1972–1989." *Gender & Society* 7 (June): 261–280.

Wilkinson, Doris. 1984. "Afro-American Women and Their Families." *Marriage and Family Review* 7 (Fall): 125–142.

Williams, David R. 1990. "Socioeconomic Differentials in Health: A Review and Redirection."

Social Psychology Quarterly 53: 81–99.

Williams, David. 1998. "Racial Variations in Adult Health Status: Patterns, Paradoxes, and Prospects." Paper presented at the National Research Council Research Conference on Racial Trends, 1998: National Academy of Science, Washington, DC, October.

Williams, L. 1984. "The Classic Rape: When Do Victims Report?" *Social Problems* 31 (April): 459–467.

Williams, Norma. 1990. *The Mexican American Family: Tradition and Change*. Dix Hills, NY: General Hall.

Williams, Patricia J. 1991. *The Alchemy of Race and Rights*. Cambridge, MA: Harvard University Press.

Willie, Charles Vert. 1985. *Black and White Families: A Study in Complementarity*. Bayside, NY: General Hall.

Wilson, J. Q., and R. J. Herrnstein. 1985. *Crime and Human Nature*. New York: Simon and Schuster.

Winokur, G., and R. Cadoret. 1975. "The Irrelevance of the Menopause to Depressive Disease." Pp. 59–66 in *Topics in Psychoendocrinology*, edited by E. J. Sachar. New York: Grune and Stratton.

Wolak, Janis, and David Finkelhor. 1998. "Children Exposed to Partner Violence." Pp. 73–112 in *Partner Violence: A Comprehensive Review of 20 Years of Research*, edited by Jana L. Jasinkski and Linda M. Williams. Thousand Oaks, CA: Sage.

Wolff, Kurt H. 1950. *The Sociology of Georg Simmel*. New York: Free Press.

Wolfgang, M., and F. Feracuti. 1967. *The Subculture of Violence: Toward an Integrated Theory in Criminology*. London: Tavistock.

Wollstonecraft, Mary. 1792 [1975]. *A Vindication of the Rights of Woman*, edited by C. Poston. New York: Norton.

Wong, A. K. 1974. "Women in China: Past and Present." Pp. 220–260 in *Many Sisters*, edited by C. Matthiasson. New York: Free Press.

Woo, Deborah. 1992. "The Gap Between Striving and Achieving: The Case of Asian American Women." Pp. 191–200 in *Race, Class and Gender: An Anthology*, edited by Margaret L. Andersen and Patricia Hill Collins. Belmont, CA: Wadsworth.

Wood, P. L. 1981. "The Victim in a Forcible Rape Case: A Feminist View." Pp. 190–211 in *Women and Crime in America*, edited by Lee Bowker. New York: Macmillan.

Woodruff, J. T. 1985. "Premarital Sexual Behavior and Religious Adolescents." *Journal for the Scientific Study of Religion* 25 (December): 343–386.

Wright, M. J. 1979. "Reproductive Hazards and 'Protective' Discrimination." *Feminist Studies* 5 (Summer): 302–309.

Wrong, D. 1961. "The Oversocialized Conception of Man in Modern Sociology." *American Sociological Review* 26: 183–193.

Yates, G. G. 1983. "Spirituality and the American Feminist Experience." *Signs* 9 (Autumn): 59–72.

Yoder, Janice. 1991. "Rethinking Tokenism: Looking Beyond Numbers." *Gender & Society* 5 (June): 178–192.

Yoder, Janice D., and Patricia Aniakudo. 1997. "'Outsider Within' the Firehouse: Subordination and Difference in the Social Interactions of African American Women Firefighters." *Gender & Society* 11 (June): 324–341.

Zaretsky, E. 1976. *Capitalism, the Family, and Personal Life*. New York: Harper and Row.

———. 1980. "Female Sexuality and the Catholic Confessional." *Signs* 6 (Autumn): 176–184.

Zavella, Patricia. 1985. "'Abnormal Intimacy': The Varying Work Networks of Chicana Cannery Workers." *Feminist Studies* 11 (Fall): 541–558.

———. 1987. *Women's Work and Chicano Families*. Ithaca, NY: Cornell University Press.

Zeitlin, I. 1968. *Ideology and the Development of Sociological Theory*.

Upper Saddle River, NJ: Prentice-Hall.

Zihlman, A. L. 1978. "Women and Evolution, Part II: Subsistence and Social Organization Among Early Hominids." *Signs* 4 (Autumn): 4–20.

Zsembik, Barbara A., and Audrey Singer. 1990. "The Problems of Defining Retirement Among Minorities: Mexican Americans." *The Gerontologist* 30: 749–757.

❧ Name Index

Abbott, F., 49
Abramovitz, M., 139
Acker, J., 23
Acuña, R., 106
Adams, L., 57
Adler, F., 271
Agger, B., 381, 382, 383
Albin, R., 279
Ali, J., 197
Alicea, M., 179
Allen, K. R., 169
Allen, P. G., 108, 257
Althauser, R., 134
Alwin, D. E., 242
Amadiume, I., 21
Amato, P. R., 161
Amir, M., 279
Amott, T. L., 106, 108, 109, 151
Andersen, M., 11, 14, 145, 279, 386, 387
Anderson, A., 235
Andrews, D. C., 112–113
Andrews, W., 112–113
Aniakudo, P., 140
Anthony, D., 146
Anthony, S. B., 237, 313, 319, 335
Anzaldúa, G., 386
Arat, Y., 310
Ardetti, R., 223
Arendell, T., 164, 166
Aries, P., 155, 157
Armstrong, P., 185
Arnold, R., 273
Atchley, R. C., 39, 40
Auerbach, D., 96
Avalos, M., 132
Avison, W. R., 197
Axelson, D. E., 219
Axinn, W. G., 169
Axtell, J., 160
Ayanian, J. Z., 195

Baca Zinn, M., 18, 34, 42, 108, 109, 153, 160, 178, 179, 193
Bachman, R., 275, 277
Bacon, F., 76
Badgett, M. V. L., 101, 142
Baird, B., 212

Baker, M. K., 124
Barber, J. S., 169
Barfoot, C. H., 245
Barker-Benfield, G. J., 219–220, 221
Barnett, R. C., 146
Baron, J., 134
Barret, R. L., 173
Barrett, M., 224
Bart, P., 91, 281
Bart, P. B., 282, 288
Bartalow-Koch, P., 142
Barthel, D., 79
Basow, S., 3, 22
Baucom, D. H., 32
Bauer, B., 350
Baumgaertner, W., 245
Baxandall, R. F., 191
Beck, A. J., 285
Beck, E. T., 257
Becker, H., 265, 266
Becraft, C., 304, 306
Beeghley, L., 210
Begus, S., 185
Bellas, M. L., 132
Belsky, J., 173
Benéria, L., 370
Benet, M. K., 109, 124
Bennett, C. E., 130, 131, 137, 138, 165, 166
Bennett, N., 281
Bennett, R. T., 184
Benokraitis, N., 57
Benson, S. P., 143
Benston, M., 144
Bentley, B. J., 283
Berger, P., 23, 31
Berheide, C. W., 128, 134
Bernard, J., 160, 171
Bernhardt, A., 133
Beron, K., 132
Berry, M. F., 346
Bersmann, I. R., 283
Bianchi, S. M., 169
Bickle, G. S., 283
Bielawski, D., 37
Bielby, W., 134
Bigner, J. J., 170

Billingsley, A., 177
Bird, C. E., 94, 146
Blackstone, 283
Blackwell, J., 247
Blackwell, K. T., 283
Blackwood, E., 21
Blake, C. F., 22
Blakemore, J. E. C., 36
Bleier, R., 81
Blood, R., 161
Blum, L., 148
Blumenthal, S. J., 207, 209
Blumstein, P., 97
Boezio, S. L., 278
Bogdan, J., 219
Bookman, A., 291, 310, 322
Booth, A., 161
Bordo, S., 382, 383
Boskind-White, M., 205
Bourne, D. W., 146
Bowen, L., 53
Bowker, L. H., 278, 287
Bozett, F. W., 170
Brabant, S., 38
Bradford, J., 33
Bragg, R., 259
Bramson, L., 349
Brenner, J., 310
Bridenthal, R., 159, 163, 170
Britton, D. M., 285
Brod, H., 15, 18
Broschak, J. P., 134
Brown, C., 157, 371
Brown, J. D., 52
Brown, S. E., 159
Brown, S. L., 169
Browne, A., 276
Browne, M. W., 51
Brownmiller, S., 265
Bruch, H., 204
Brush, L. D., 184
Bryson, K., 163, 165, 166
Buchanan, P., 250
Bunch, C., 11, 362, 364, 374
Burg, M. A., 198
Burlage, D., 231
Burns, A. L., 36
Burris, B. H., 167

Burton, L., 177
Butler, A. C., 139, 384
Butler, S., 229
Byrd, G. R., 184

Cadoret, R., 91
Calasanti, T. M., 40
Caldwell, D., 278, 283
Califia, P., 99
Camburn, D., 242
Cameron, D., 54
Campbell, A., 268
Campbell, K., 52
Cancian, F., 95
Cannon, L. W., 117
Carney, L. S., 116, 159, 369
Carothers, S. C., 142
Carr, D., 197
Carrington, C. H., 33
Carroll, J. W., 245
Carter, D., 123
Cash, T. F., 53
Casper, L. M., 163, 165, 166, 190, 191
Castan, R. E., 182
Castanier, M., 29
Castro, F., 367
Catt, C. C., 313
Caulfield, M. D., 80, 176, 286
Cavendish, J., 246
Chancer, L., 266
Chang, G., 170
Chassin, L., 208
Chaves, M., 246
Chavkin, W., 202, 203
Chernin, K., 204
Chesney-Lind, M., 268, 269, 285, 286
Chin, J., 197
Chodorow, N., 41, 49, 171, 172, 173, 371
Chow, E., 34, 109, 180
Christ, C. P., 252, 253, 255
Church, G. J., 285, 286, 287
Churchill, W., 52
Clark, J., 290, 297, 298, 302
Clark, L., 280, 282
Clark, R., 38
Clarke, A. E., 229
Clarke, E., 70
Clay, V. S., 91, 92
Clayton-Matthews, A., 205
Clinton, H. R., 59, 290
Clinton, W. J., 83, 290
Coffey, P., 184
Cohen, L. E., 134
Cohn, M., 142
Coleman, L. M., 19
Colker, B. D., 132
Collins, P. H., 14, 33, 42, 74, 79, 87, 88, 176, 317, 330, 379, 382, 386, 387, 388

Coltrane, A., 57
Comte, A., 328, 333
Concorcet, 331
Coner-Edwards, A. F. W., 184
Connell, B., 308
Connell, R. W., 104
Conover, P. J., 249, 250
Conte, J. R., 186
Cooke, M., 305
Cooper, V. W., 52
Cooperstock, R., 207
Corea, G., 222, 223
Coser, R. L., 172, 173
Costello, C. B., 143
Cott, N., 156, 160, 236, 361
Couric, K., 59
Cowan, R. S., 112, 113, 147
Crabb, P. B., 37
Craven, D., 2
Crawford, C. J., 119
Crawford, M., 54, 55, 79
Crenshaw, C., 201
Crick, F., 75
Crittenden, K., 142
Croteau, J. M., 101
Crouch, J. L., 186
Crowley, J. E., 40
Crull, P., 142
Culbertson, R. G., 286
Currie, D., 65

D'Emilio, J., 81, 82, 104
Dalaker, J., 137
Daley, P. C., 283
Daly, K., 273, 284, 362, 364, 386
Daly, M., 233, 234, 235, 238, 254
Danaber, D., 19
Daniels, A. K., 56, 57, 60, 114
Darcy, R., 290, 297, 298, 302
Darwin, C., 237
Das Gupta, M., 146, 179
Davaney, S. G., 233, 236, 244, 255
Davidman, L., 242–243, 257
Davis, A., 87, 112, 116, 145, 176, 216
Davis, A. J., 38, 363
Davis, D. M., 57
Davis-Blake, A., 134
de la Torre, A., 106
Decker, J., 180
DeFrancisco, V. L., 54
Deitz, S. R., 283
Delaney, J., 89
Dellinger, K., 45
DeLuca, L., 278, 283
Demeis, D. K., 146
Demo, D. M., 169
Desmarais, S., 37
Deutscher, I., 53
DeVault, M. L., 115
Diamond, M., 27
Diamond, T., 229

Dickens, W. J., 97
Diderot, 331
Dietz, T. L., 38
Dill, B. T., 176, 177, 179, 317, 386
Dines, G., 57, 79
DiPrete, T., 134
Dobash, R., 108, 155, 157, 182, 281
Dobash, R. E., 108, 155, 157, 182, 281
Dodson, D., 302
Dodson, J. E., 247, 248
Doell, R., 77
Dole, R., 133
Donegan, J., 219
Douglas, A., 236
Douglas, P., 57
Douglass, F., 311, 312
Downey, J. A., 205
Dowsett, G. W., 104
Draper, R., 52
DuBois, E. C., 312, 334, 335, 349
Dudley, R. L., 245
Due, L., 49, 104
Duelli-Klein, R., 223
Dugger, K., 24
Dujon, D., 139, 152
Dworkin, A., 235
Dye, N. S., 217, 218, 349

Eagly, A., 47
Ecker, M., 123
Edin, K., 139, 152
Ehrenreich, B., 109, 113, 196, 218, 221, 225, 252
Ehrenreich, J. H., 286
Ehrhardt, A. A., 26, 27
Eisenstein, Z., 325, 343, 344, 346, 352, 355, 362
Eitzen, D. S., 42, 108, 109, 153, 160, 179, 193
Elkins, L. E., 97
Ellis, H., 98
Emery, J. L., 51
Emmet, T., 70
Engels, F., 116, 334, 348, 350–351, 352, 353, 355–356, 357, 358, 372, 373, 374
England, P., 132, 346
English, D., 84, 109, 113, 158, 196, 218, 221, 225
Enloe, C., 305, 306, 308, 322
Epstein, A. M., 195
Epstein, C., 123, 295
Erkut, S., 135
Espin, O. M., 88
Evans, S., 36, 315, 316, 317, 318
Ex, C. T. G. M., 37

Falk, N., 234
Faludi, S., 319
Famighetti, R., 246

Farber, N., 187
Farkas, G., 132
Farnham, M., 333
Fausto-Sterling, A., 26, 28, 29, 30, 49, 89, 91, 92
Feagin, J., 57
Fee, E., 76
Feit, M., 180
Feldberg, R. L., 125
Fenstermaker, S., 18, 44
Ferazuti, F., 279
Ferree, M. M., 146, 314, 322
Feuerbach, L., 350
Ficarrotto, T., 197
Fidell, L. S., 207
Fields, J. P., 135
Figueroa, J. B., 189
Findlen, B., 49
Finklehor, D., 184
Finlay, B., 246
Firestein, B., 99
Firestone, J. M., 37, 132
Fischbach, R. L., 184
Fischer, I., 169
Flaks, D. K., 169
Flax, J., 352, 381
Flexner, E., 218, 311, 313
Flowers, R. B., 243, 248
Floyd, K., 96
Fonow, M. M., 278
Forbes, D., 19
Forcey, L. R., 170
Forten, C., 311, 330
Fortune, F. P., 286
Foucault, M., 157
Fox, M., 96
Fraga, M. T., 368
Francis, L. J., 243
Frankfurter, F., 203
Franklin, R., 75
Fraser, N., 380
Frazier, E. F., 175, 177, 247
Freedman, E. B., 81, 82
Freeman, J., 318
Freud, S., 83, 84
Frey, K., 92
Fried, A., 279
Friedan, B., 315
Friedl, E., 148, 281, 367
Friedman, E. B., 104
Frieze, I., 42, 45
Frieze, I. H., 184
Frohmann, L., 282
Frye, M., 6–7, 346
Fujimoto, T., 146
Fullerton, H. N., 119
Furnham, A., 35

Gagnon, J. H., 86, 100
Gagnon, J. T., 104
Gallup, G., 215

Gamson, J., 98
Garey, A. I., 193
Garfinkle, E. M., 32
Garnier, H., 36
Gasson, L., 35
Genovese, E., 107, 176, 240
Gerbner, G., 58, 60
Gerson, K., 33, 173
Gerstel, N., 167
Geschwender, J., 35, 129
Giallombardo, R., 286
Gibbons, S., 61, 63
Gibbs, M., 96
Gibson, D., 41
Gibson, R. C., 41, 50, 92
Giddens, A., 350, 351, 353
Gilkes, C. T., 247, 248, 309, 317, 331
Gill, G. K., 145
Gilliard, D. K., 285
Gilligan, C., 12–13, 302
Gilman, C. P., 349
Gingrich, N., 250
Glaser, R. D., 142
Glass, J., 146
Glenn, E. N., 109, 125, 170, 180
Gluckman, A., 101, 104
Goetting, A., 18
Goldman, E., 349
Goldstein, L., 213
Goleman, D., 169
Golub, S., 90
Gooding, S., 123
Goodman, M., 92
Gordon, L., 200, 212
Gordon, M. T., 276
Gordon, R., 235
Gornick, V., 73
Gorson, L., 216
Gough, K., 158
Gouldner, H., 96
Gourdine, R. M., 187
Gow, J., 52
Gramm, P., 250
Grant, J., 247, 248
Grant, L., 123, 226
Grasmuck, S., 119
Graves, S. B., 57
Gray, J., 55
Gray, V., 249, 250
Grebner, G., 59
Greene, B., 33
Greenfield, L. A., 275
Greif, G. L., 174
Grella, C. E., 166
Grimke, A., 311
Grisanti, C., 32
Gross, H., 168
Gross, J., 169
Groves, M. M., 168
Gutek, B. A., 125

Gutman, H., 176

Haft, M., 268, 283
Hagan, J., 124
Hahn, K., 370
Hall, E. R., 278
Hall, R. M., 72
Hamlin, N. R., 135
Hammer, D. H., 100
Hampton, R. L., 184
Handcock, M. S., 133
Hans, V. P., 283
Hansen, K. V., 193
Harding, S., 76, 79, 173, 341, 364, 378, 379, 388
Harford, T., 207
Hargrove, B., 233, 236, 244, 245, 255
Harlan, S. L., 187
Harland, M., 153
Harr, R. N., 285
Harris, R. J., 37, 132
Harrison, J., 25, 197
Harry, J., 32
Hart, K., 205
Hartmann, H., 108, 147, 186, 358, 366
Hartsock, N., 378
Haveman, H. A., 134
Hawkins, R. A., 29
Heath, J. A., 146
Hegel, G. W. F., 350
Helwig, A. A., 37
Henderson, J., 142
Henley, N., 15
Henning, K., 184
Herbert, B., 184
Herd, D., 206
Herman, J., 185, 186
Hernandez, J., 186
Hernstein, R. J., 263
Herring, F., 36
Herskovits, M., 175
Hess, B., 40, 91, 314
Hesse-Biber, S., 205
Heywood, L., 57
Hibbons, R., 145
Higginbotham, E., 133, 177
Higham, J., 113, 261
Hill, A., 294, 302
Hill, A. C., 202, 203
Hiller, D., 160
Hilts, P. J., 76
Himmelstein, J. L., 251, 252
Hine, D. C., 310
Hirschman, L., 185
Hochschild, A., 115, 143, 144, 152, 167, 168
Hoffman, T., 245
Hole, J., 237, 315
Holm, J., 305
Holt, J., 313

Hondagneu-Sotelo, P., 18, 34, 119, 129, 178, 179
hooks, b., 79, 375
Hooper, L. M., 130, 131, 137, 138, 165, 166
Horm-Wingerd, D. M., 168
Horowitz, R., 188
Horton, J. A., 3, 91, 198, 199, 200, 206, 208, 209, 222
Hosken, F. P., 22
Hossfeld, K. J., 126
Hotaling, G., 183
Howard, J. A., 278
Hoyenga, K., 25, 26, 29, 30
Hoyenga, K. B., 25, 26, 29, 30
Hu, N., 100
Hu, S., 100
Hubbard, R., 76
Hughes, H. S., 328
Hughes, J. O., 278
Hughes, M. E., 197
Hugick, L., 86
Hull, C. T., 35
Humez, J. M., 57, 79
Hummer, R. A., 278
Hunt, V. R., 203
Hurst, M., 200

Idle, T., 37
Illich, I., 158
Infante, P., 203
Ingram-Fogel, C., 286
Ireson, C., 189
Irvine, J. M., 104

Jackson, N. A., 169
Jacobs, J., 244
Jacobs, J. A., 149
Jacobs, J. L., 255
Jacobsen, R. B., 170
Jacobson, D., 22
Jaget, C., 268
Jaggar, A. M., 346, 352, 358
Janssens, M. A., 37
Janus, C. L., 100
Janus, S. S., 100
Jarett, R. L., 176
Jasinksi, J. L., 183, 194
Jelen, T. G., 245
Joe, K. A., 268, 269
Johnson, D. G., 123
Johnson, P., 42, 45
Johnson, V. E., 84
Jolin, A., 266
Jones, J., 107
Jones, S., 215
Jordan, W., 239
Joseph, G., 101, 169, 170
Joseph, H., 170
Jourard, S. M., 91
Julty, S., 83

Kalof, L., 278
Kamin, L. J., 263
Kanter, R. M., 17, 72, 125, 141
Kantor, G. K., 183
Kaplan, E., 187, 194
Kapp, Y., 351
Karraker, K. H., 35, 36
Katzman, D., 177
Kaufman, D. R., 257
Kaufman, M., 15, 18
Kaufman, S., 142
Kay, F. M., 124
Keller, E. F., 75
Keller, R. S., 238
Kelly, J., 170, 173
Kelly-Gadol, J., 12, 330, 342
Kendrick, P. L., 11
Kenny, M. E., 205
Kessler-Harris, A., 107, 110, 112
Kibria, N., 162
Kilbourne, B. S., 132
Killian, L. M., 311
Kimmel, M. S., 15
King, M. C., 142
Kinsey, A. C., 233
Kitzinger, C. A., 385
Klass, A., 207
Klatch, R., 250
Kleck, G., 282
Klein, D., 261, 262, 263
Kleinbaum, A. R., 331
Kluckhohn, C., 20
Knouse, S. B., 304
Kohlberg, L., 43
Kokopeli, B., 308
Kolata, G., 76, 86, 104
Komter, A., 168
Konradi, A., 283
Koopmans, L., 30
Kraditor, E., 112, 156
Kurz, D., 181, 184, 194

La Rossa, L., 173
La Rossa, R., 173
Ladner, J. A., 33, 176, 187, 188
LaFree, G., 283
Lai, T., 179
Lake, M. A., 36
Lakey, G., 308
Lambert, L. C., 132
Lamphere, L., 143, 367
Langhinrichsen-Rohling, J., 184
Lasch, C., 360
Laslett, B., 310
Laumann, E. O., 86, 100, 104
Lawrence, M., 204
Leacock, E., 116, 148, 363, 367, 370, 371
Lee, S. M., 137
Lehman, E. C., 246
Lein, L., 139, 152

Leitenberg, H., 184
Lemert, E., 266
Lennon, M. C., 145, 198
Lennon, R., 38
Leo, R., 32
Leonard, J., 86
Leong, R., 88, 102
Lerman, R. I., 174
Lerner, G., 12, 330, 345
Levi-Strauss, 363
Levine, E., 237, 313, 315
Lewin, M., 101
Lewinsky, M., 83, 290
Lewis, D., 280, 282
Lewis, K. G., 169
Lewis, R., 180
Lim, I. S., 119
Limbaugh, H. R., 3
Lincoln, C. E., 258
Lindsey, E. W., 37
Lips, H. M., 84, 97
Lipset, S. M., 334
Liss-Levinson, W., 173
Litoff, J. B., 218
Little, R. D., 306
Livson, F. B., 92
Lizotte, A., 283
Logio-Rau, K., 208
Lombroso, N., 261, 262
Long, M., 58
Longino, H., 77
Lopata, H. Z., 24, 145
Lorber, J., 18, 21, 123, 172, 173, 226
Loscocco, K. A., 197
Lott, B., 278, 283
Loucky, J., 36
Lowe, M., 30
Lucal, B., 117
Luckmann, T., 23
Lugalia, T. A., 164, 165, 169
Luker, K., 188, 250, 251, 252
Lummis, A. T., 245
Lundberg, F., 333
Lupton, M. J., 89
Luria, Z., 80
Lwein, E., 226
Lye, D., 169
Lynch, A. D., 32

MacCorquodale, P. L., 189
Machiavelli, 76
Machung, A., 125
MacKinnon, C., 294, 322, 364–365, 375
MacLeod, M., 54
Madriz, E., 276, 288
Magnuson, V., 100
Mahoney, P., 184, 185
Malbin-Glazer, N., 148
Malcolm, E. R., 300
Mamiya, L. H., 258

Manbegold, C. S., 303
Mandel, R., 302
Maney, A. C., 218
Mannheim, K., 66, 68–69, 372
Mansbridge, J., 322
Mansfield, P. K., 142
Mark, K., 63, 334
Markens, S., 89
Markson, E., 40, 91
Marshall, N. L., 146
Marsiglio, W., 174
Martin, D., 183
Martin, E., 300, 301
Martin, P. Y., 278, 283, 322
Martin, S. E., 141, 279
Martin, S. S., 208
Martineau, H., 333–335
Marx, K., 66–67, 116, 248, 348,
    350–351, 352, 353, 354,
    355–356, 357, 358, 372, 373,
    374
Marzolf, M. T., 59
Mason, S. M., 51
Massey, G., 370
Masterpasqua, F., 169
Masters, W. H., 84
Matthaei, J. A., 106, 108, 109, 151
Matthiasson, C., 367
Matza, D., 265, 266
Maume, D. J., 189
McCammon, H. J., 201
McCloskey, L. A., 19, 184
McCluskey, S. E., 51
McCormack, A. S., 141
McCrate, E., 138
McCreary, D. R., 31
McGuire, M. B., 239, 242, 244
McIntosh, M., 266
McIntosh, P., 11
McKinney, K., 142
McKinney, W., 242
McLanahan, S. S., 136
McMurray, C., 233
McQuiade, S., 285, 286
Mead, G. H., 36–37
Mead, M., 211–212
Meier, A., 107
Meigs, C. D., 70
Melendez, E., 189
Melosh, B., 143
Mendelsohn, E., 377
Mernissi, F., 235, 258
Mertz, E., 123
Messerschmidt, J., 273
Messing, K., 77
Messner, M. A., 15, 18, 24
Meyer, J., 101
Meyer, M. H., 210
Meyering, S. L., 375
Michael, R. T., 86, 100, 104
Micheals, S., 100

Middlebrook, D., 45
Mies, M., 375
Milkman, R., 46
Mill, H. T., 324, 331, 335–343, 345
Mill, J. S., 324, 328, 331, 335–343, 345
Miller, D., 19, 180
Miller, E., 259, 260, 272, 273, 288
Miller, J. B., 169, 237
Miller, S., 183, 289
Millman, M., 17, 204, 267, 268
Mills, C. W., 5–6, 74, 379
Mills, H. T., 349
Mills, J. S., 348, 349
Milner, J. S., 186
Minden, S., 223
Minnich, E. K., 13, 18
Mirandé, A., 175, 178, 180
Mitchell, J., 81, 358–360, 375
Mitchell, G., 36
Mize, J., 37
Modleski, T., 60
Mohr, J., 215–216, 274
Money, J., 26, 27, 98
Mongeau, B., 218
Monson, C. M., 184
Mooney, L. A., 38
Moore, D. W., 240
Moore, G., 135, 300
Moore, J., 178
Moraga, C., 386
Moran, E. G., 282, 288
Morash, M., 285
Morgan, M., 58
Morgan, S., 291, 310, 322
Morin, S. F., 32
Morris, L., 38
Morris, M., 133
Morton, W., 201
Moskos, C., 306
Mott, L., 312
Moulds, E. F., 282
Moynihan, D. P., 175
Mullin, K. R., 189
Murillo, N., 178
Myers, D., 119

Nadell, P. S., 246
Nadelson, C., 168
Nadelson, T., 168
Naff, K. C., 133
Naifeh, M., 137
Nanda, S., 21, 22, 49
Naples, N. A., 171, 309
Nardi, P. M., 104
Nason-Clark, N., 245
Nasrin, T., 8–9
Nathanson, C., 207
Nazzari, M., 367, 368
Nelson, A. 185
Nicholson, L., 380, 381, 382, 388
Niemi, R. G., 298

Nisbet, R., 328
Njogu, W., 123
Nock, S. L., 169
Novkov, J., 201

Oakey, R. E., 29
Oakley, A., 211, 212
Obradovich, S., 36
O'Brien, P., 281
O'Kelly, C. G., 116, 159, 369
Olesen, V., 226, 229
Oliver, P. 185
Ooms, T. J., 174
O'Toole, L. L., 194

Padavic, I., 2, 127, 152
Padula, A., 368
Palmer, P., 113
Parker, D., 207
Parker, E., 207
Parks, M. R., 96
Parsons, J., 42, 45
Pattatucci, A. M. L., 100
Patterson, C., 169
Paul, A., 313
Pavalko, E. K., 210
Pavett, L. A., 139
Payer, M., 23
Payne, D. M., 306
Pedraza, S., 119
Peres, Y., 169
Perkins, W. H., 146
Perlman, D., 97
Perstadlt, H., 296
Pesquera, B., 106
Pessar, P., 119
Petchesky, R., 211, 212, 217, 223
Peterson, C., 97
Peterson, R. D., 284
Peterson, R. R., 93, 138
Pettit, G. S., 37
Pharr, S., 32
Philliber, W. H., 161
Phillips, L., 39
Phillips, W. R. F., 296
Piaget, J., 43
Pierce, J. L., 42, 172
Piotrkowski, C. S., 93
Plaskow, J., 252, 253
Pleck, J., 32
Plummer, K., 99, 384
Pohli, C. V., 243
Pollak, O., 261, 262
Poston, C., 331
Pottieger, A., 266
Powell, R. M., 283
Powers, B. A., 96
Powers, M., 89
Press, E., 126
Press, J. E., 146
Presson, C. C., 208

Price, B., 289
Provenza, F. J., 35
Purcell, P., 38
Purifoy, F., 30
Pyke, K. D., 161

Raag, T., 37
Racliff, C. L., 37
Radway, J., 56
Raeburn, N. C., 100, 101
Rafter, N. H., 289
Ramirez, R., 368
Rapp, R., 159, 163
Reagon, B. J., 232
Redhorse, J. G., 180
Reed, B., 101, 104
Reilly, M. E., 278, 283
Reinhardt, J. S., 51
Reinharz, S., 222, 379
Reiter, R. R., 363
Reitz, R., 91, 92
Renzetti, C., 183, 184, 279
Repak, T. A., 119, 128
Repetti, R. L., 93
Reskin, B., 2, 12, 130, 131, 132,
      152
Reskin, G. F., 283
Resnick, J., 286
Reuther, R., 238, 253, 254
Rexroat, C. A., 198
Rhode, A. L., 59, 242
Rich, A., 5, 84, 170, 269
Rich, M. K., 53
Richardson, L., 278
Richie, B. E., 273, 289
Riger, S., 276
Risman, B., 174
Rist, D. Y., 100
Robbins, C., 206, 208
Roberts, C., 59
Roberts, H., 224
Robinson, B. E., 173
Rodriguez, C., 57, 79, 178
Roger, M., 29
Rojas, N. P., 368
Rollins, J., 128
Romero, M., 109, 116
Roof, W. C., 242
Roos, P. 132
Roosevelt, E., 315
Rorvik, 77
Rosaldo, M. Z., 366
Rosenau, P. M., 382
Rosenberg, J., 296
Rosenberg, R., 70
Rosenblum, B., 229
Rosenblum, K. E., 266, 267
Rosenfield, S., 198
Rosenman, R. H., 91
Ross, E., 159, 163

Rossi, A., 71–72, 76, 77, 90, 172, 173,
      222, 327, 332, 333, 335, 336,
      339, 340, 346, 349
Rossi, P., 90
Rossiter, M., 75
Rothblum, E. D., 33
Rothenberg, P. S., 346, 388
Rothenberg, S., 352, 358
Rothman, B. K., 221, 223, 229
Rothschild, M. A., 316
Rousseau, 331
Rubin, G., 363–364
Rubin, L. B., 104
Rubin, Z., 35
Ruble, D. N., 42, 45
Rucker, L., 285
Ruddick, S., 302
Rudwick, E., 107
Rupp, L., 314
Russell, D. E. H., 185
Rust, P., 99, 100
Rutter, V., 97, 104
Ruzek, S., 212, 226, 227, 229
Ryan, C., 33

Sacks, K., 110, 361, 363, 365
Sadker, D., 38, 39, 54
Sadker, M., 38, 39, 54
Saint-Simon, H., 328
Saiving, V., 254
Saltzman, L. E., 275, 277
Sanchez, L., 146
Sanchez-Ayendez, M., 96
Sanday, P., 281, 367
Sandler, B. R., 278
Sandmaier, M., 206, 207
Sargent, L., 375
Sarri, R. C., 283
Sattel, J., 54
Sayers, S. L., 32
Sayles, S., 282
Sayre, A., 75
Scanlan, A. R., 246
Schiffman, J. R., 194
Schlafly, P., 249
Schmid, J., 53
Schmidt, J. M., 233, 236, 244, 255
Schneider, B., 104, 142, 209, 210, 229
Scholler, R., 29
Scholten, C. M., 217, 219
Schorr, J. B., 143, 146
Schwartz, P., 97, 104
Scott, J. W., 106, 108, 110, 156
Scully, D., 280
Seccombe, K., 210
Segura, D., 42, 121, 172, 178
Seidman, G., 370, 383
Seidman, S., 99, 384
Sekulíc, D., 370
Seltzer, R., 86
Sen, G., 370

Shange, N., 254
Shappard, G. T., 245
Shehan, C. L., 198
Shelley, M., 218
Shelton, B. A., 2
Shepard, M., 102
Sherman, S. J., 208
Shilts, R., 322
Sielaff, A., 286
Sigelman, L., 302
Sigmundson, H. K., 27
Signorielli, N., 58
Silverstein, B., 32
Simmel, G., 73
Simon, R., 246, 271
Simonds, W., 79
Simpson, S., 273
Sims, J. M., 219, 220
Singer, A., 40
Skirboll, E., 168
Sklar, H., 135
Slevin, K. F., 40, 49
Smart, C., 262, 263, 295, 296
Smedley, A., 349
Smith, A., 339
Smith, B., 102
Smith, D., 18, 45, 67, 68, 73, 377, 378,
      379, 388
Smith, H., 134
Smith, H. L., 218
Smith, J., 138
Smith, J. P., 133
Smith, L. M., 368
Smith, L. S., 268
Smith, M. D., 281
Smith, S., 259
Smith-Rosenberg, C., 160
Snell, T. L., 285
Snipp, C. M., 199
Sokoloff, N., 351
Sorenson, A., 136
South, S. J., 146
Spain, D., 169
Speigel, D., 173
Spender, D., 54
Spitze, G., 93, 146, 197
Spretnak, C., 255, 258
Sprock, J., 32, 33
Stacey, J., 194, 368
Stack, C., 159, 177
Stanley, A., 11
Stanley, H. W., 298
Stanton, E. C., 231, 237, 312, 313
Staples, R., 175, 177, 178, 180
Steenland, S., 58
Steffensmeier, D., 272
Stein, A., 99, 384
Stein, D. K., 22
Steinberg, R., 149
Steingart, R. M., 195
Steinke, J., 58

Stellman, J. M., 202
Sterling, A., 49, 330, 334, 345
Stewart, L., 38
Stewart, M., 330
Stiehm, J. H., 322
Stohs, J. H., 146
Stoller, E. P., 41, 50, 92
Stoller, N., 209, 210, 229
Stone, V., 61, 62
Strong, M. S., 96
Strouse, J., 268
Stuck, M. F., 52
Sugarman, D., 183
Sullivan, D. A., 221, 223, 229
Sullivan, M., 169
Swatos, W. H., 258
Swerslow, A., 170
Szasz, T., 235

Takagi, D. Y., 102
Takaki, R., 95, 106, 179, 180
Tam, T., 132
Tannen, D., 55
Tanner, D. M., 169
Taylor, R., 168
Taylor, V., 100, 101, 169, 314
Tea, N. T., 29
Teachman, J. D., 169
Thomas, C., 294, 302
Thomas, S., 133
Thomas, W. I., 261, 262
Thompson, B., 50, 205, 230
Thompson, E. H., 32
Thompson, T. L., 38
Thomson, E., 146
Thorne, B., 24, 38, 50, 80, 81, 163
Thornton, A., 169, 242
Thornton, B., 32
Thorpe, J. S., 142
Tierney, A. M., 32
Tillich, P., 232
Tilly, L. A., 106, 108, 110, 156
Tipton, B., 44, 45
Titus-Dillon, P. Y., 123
Tocqueville, A. de, 328, 333–334
Tolman, D. L., 267
Toth, E., 89
Tovée, M. J., 51
Tovée, E. M., 51
Townsley, E., 146
Trent, K., 187
Tromberg, C., 36
Truman, H. S., 307
Truth, S., 312–313, 330
Tuan, Y. F., 88
Tuchman, G., 56, 57, 60, 61, 63, 64
Tucker, R., 67, 353, 354, 355

Turner, R., 311
Turner-Bowker, D. M., 38
Tyagi, S., 50

Ungs, T., 201

Van Den Daele, W., 377
Vance, C., 80
Vanek, J. A., 110, 147
Vanneman, R., 117
Veiel, H. O. F., 33
Verbrugge, L. M., 225
Vicary, J. R., 142
Vida, G., 170
Vidmar, N., 283
Vine, P., 170
Visher, C. A., 283
Vogel, D. A., 36

Waldron, I., 169, 197
Walker, R., 18
Walker, S., 95, 320
Wallace, R. A., 245, 246, 258
Wallen, J., 224, 225
Waller, K., 224
Wallerstein, I., 328
Walsh, M. R., 226
Walters, B., 59
Walters, S., 65, 79
Walzer, S., 173
Wardle, R. M., 333
Ware, M. C., 52
Warner, J. T., 306
Watson, D., 136
Watson, J., 75
Weber, L., 133, 177
Weber, M., 155
Webster, P., 363
Wechsler, H., 206
Weingart, P., 377
Weir, D., 132
Weisner, T., 36
Weiss, C. C., 197
Weitz, R., 221, 223, 229
Weitzman, L. J., 93, 138
Welch, S., 290, 297, 298, 302
Wells, I. B., 330
Welter, B., 236
Wemmerus, V. A., 278
Wermuth, L., 155
Wertz, D. C., 217, 218, 219, 221,
   222
Wertz, R. W., 217, 218, 219, 221,
   222
Weschler, H., 207
West, C., 44, 183, 184
Westkott, M., 73

Weston, K., 194
White, E. C., 230
White, R., 134
Whitely, R., 377
Whittier, N., 319, 320, 322
Wilcox, C., 243, 305, 306
Wilds, D. J., 71, 72
Wilkie, J. R., 146, 161, 167
Wilkinson, D., 177
Wilkinson, S., 385
Williams, C., 45, 152
Williams, D., 200, 208
Williams, K. R., 276
Williams, L., 184, 185, 194, 283
Williams, N., 249
Williams, P., 322
Willie, C. V., 177, 178
Wilson, J. Q., 263
Wilson, R., 71, 72, 123
Wingrove, C. R., 40, 49
Winokur, G., 91
Withorn, A., 139, 152
Wolak, J., 184
Wolfe, D., 161
Wolff, K. H., 73
Wolfgang, M., 279
Wollstonecraft, M., 218, 324, 331–333,
   335, 343, 345
Wolz, M., 207
Wong, A. K., 22
Woo, D., 179
Wood, E., 37
Wood, P. L., 282
Woodruff, J. T., 233
Woollacott, A., 305
Wright, M. J., 117, 202, 203
Wrong, D., 31
Wylie, M. L., 142

Yates, G. G., 254
Yoder, C. Y., 32, 33
Yoder, J. D., 140
Young, E. W., 142

Zambrana, R. E., 200
Zaretsky, E., 157, 233, 361
Zavella, P., 143, 178
Zeitlin, I., 349, 350
Zellman, G., 42, 45
Zerbinos, E., 38
Zihlman, A. L., 363
Zimmerman, D., 44
Zsembik, B. A., 40

❧ Subject Index

Abortion, 213–216
  and the church, 259–252
Academic knowledge of women,
  69–74
Acquaintance rape, 278–279
Acquired Immune Deficiency
  Syndrome (AIDS), 208–210
"Add-and-stir" approach to studying women, 11
Administrative support workers,
  124–125
Adult socialization, 39–41
Advancement in work organizations, 133–134
Advertisements and images, 51–53
Affirmative action, 149–150
African Americans:
  and crime, 273
  as faculty, 72
  and feminism movement,
    316–319
  households, 177–178
  labor and family-based economy,
    107
  labor and family-wage economy,
    108–109
  and occupational segregation,
    121
  portrayals of, on television, 57–58
  and religion, 232, 247–248
  and sexuality, 87–88
  slavery and, 175–176
  teen mothers, 187
Age of Enlightenment, 327–331
Aggression:
  and crime, 263
  and rape, 280
Aging process:
  physiological changes, 91–92
  and socialization, 39–41
Alcohol use and abuse, 206–207
Ambiguous sexual identities, 26–27
Androcentrism, 253
Antidiscrimination policies, 317–318
Antifeminism and religion, 249–252
Antimiscegenation laws, 180
Antislavery movement, 334
Arrests and women, 270–271

Artificial insemination, 223
Asian Americans, 179–180
  as faculty, 72
  labor and family-wage economy,
    109
Assembly-line work, 126
Attitudes:
  sexual, 83–87
  about women, 1–4
Authority, definition of, 292–293

Battering, 182–185
Beauty, cultural images of, 51–52
Biological determinism, 28–30
Biological differences and crime,
  261–262
Biological reductionism, 29
Biological sex differences, 20, 24–30,
  100
  ambiguous identities, 26–27
  nature/nurture debate, 27–28
Birth control, 82, 212–213
  and teens, 188
Birthing centers, 222
Bisexual relationships, 97–102
Blacks (see African Americans)
Blue-collar work, 125–127
Body image, 204
Bulimia, 204–205

Campaign financing, 300–301
Cancer mortality and occupation,
  201
Capitalism, 358–362
  and class (Marx), 352–354
  and the media, 63
  and patriarchy, 365–371
Chicana Americans:
  and gender identity, 42
  labor and family-based economy,
    107
  labor and family-wage economy,
    109
  and occupational segregation,
    121
Chicano American families, 178
  and gender identity, 42
Child care, 113, 189–192

  cost of, 189, 190
  as work, 12, 115
Child support, 191–192
Childbirth and pregnancy, 217–223
Childhood play and games, socialization process in, 36–38
Children's literature and gender
  stereotypes, 37–38
Children's television programming,
  58
Chinese immigrants and gender
  expectations, 34–35
Chinese women in socialist society,
  368–369
Civil rights movement, 292
  and feminism, 316–317
Class:
  and capitalism (Marx), 352–354
  consciousness of, 355
  and control, 117
  definition of, 116
  and gender and race, 13–15
  and intimate relationships, 95
  and sexuality, 82
  stratification, 116–117
Clergy, women as, 245–246
Clerical workers, 124–125
Cloning, 223
Cognitive-developmental theory and
  gender identity, 43
Cohabitation, 168
Collective consciousness of a society,
  definition of, 239
Color-blind hiring policies, 149–150
Combat roles in military, 304–306
Coming out, process of, 99–101, 142
Comparable worth, definition of,
  148–149
Compulsory heterosexuality, defini-
  tion of, 84
Constructionist approach and lan-
  guage use, 55
Content analysis, 56
Contingent workers, 135
Control and class, 117
Court environment for women, 296
Crime, 259–289
  deviance theory, 261–263

Crime, *cont.*
   sociological perspectives,
      263–269
   and women, 269–274
   women in criminal justice sys-
      tem, 282–287
   women as victims, 274–282
Crises in domestic life, 314–315
Cross-sex friendships, 96–97
Cuban women in socialist society,
   368
Cult of domesticity, 156
Cult of true womanhood, 111–112
Cultural attitudes:
   and menstruation, 90
   toward sexuality, 84
Cultural definitions:
   basis of gender, 21–22
   masculinity and femininity, 83
Cultural stereotypes and aging, 40
Cultural studies, 380–385
Cultural values and scientific facts,
   77
Culture:
   definition of, 20–21
   and gender (*see* Gender and
      culture)

Date rape, 278-279
Deadbeat dads, 191
Depression, 198
Deviance, definition of, 264–265
   (*see also* Crime)
Dialectical materialism, 351–352
Discontent, 314–315
Discrimination:
   definition of, 129
   experienced by gays and les-
      bians, 99–100, 101
Diverse life-styles and liberalism,
   329
Division of labor in housework,
   146–147
Divorce, 165–167
Doctor-patient relationships,
   224–225
"Doing gender" perspective of
   gender formation, 44–45
Domestic role of women, 156
Domestic violence, 161, 181–186
Domestic work, 128
Domesticity, cult of, 156
Dominance, definition of, 57
"Don't ask, don't tell" policy, 307
Donor insemination, 223
Double jeopardy, 14
Double-day work for women,
   143–144
Drug abuse, 207–208
Dual-earner couples, 167–168

Dual labor market theory, 132–133

Earnings and gender segregation,
   105, 117, 122, 129–133
Eating disorders, 204–205
Economic restructuring, 135–136
Economics and family systems,
   156, 161–162
Egalitarian societies, women's
   status in, 370–371
Either/or sexual identity, 98
Embezzlement and women, 271
Embryo transfer, 223
Emotional labor, 115
Emotional relationships within the
   family, 160
Employed mothers, 143–144
Employment and labor discrimina-
   tion, 315
Epistemology, definition of, 377
Equal Pay Act of 1963, 148
Equal pay for equal work, 105–117,
   148
Equal Rights Amendment (ERA),
   250
Equal rights for gays and lesbians,
   101–102
Essentialist position, 302–303
   and language use, 55
Ethnocentric, definition of, 342
Eugenics movement, 223
Evangelical women, 243
Expectations:
   of marital roles, 160–161
   of society, 30–33

Faith and spirituality, 237
   and feminism, 252–255
False consciousness (Marx), 67
Families, 153–194
   contemporary perspective,
      163–174
   defining, 153–154, 163
   and economy in capitalist society,
      358–362
   feminist perspective, 158–163
   headed by women, 3, 177–178
   historical perspectives, 154–158
   ideals, 153–154, 163
   and race and gender, 174–181
   and work, balancing, 113,
      143–144, 167–168
Familism, 42
Family:
   definition of, 164
   vs. work, 113, 143–144, 167–168
Family-based economy, 106–108
Family-consumer economy, 110–111
Family-friendly employment, 144
Family household, definition of, 164

Family-wage economy, 108
Fatherhood, 173–174
Faulty generalization, 13
Female-centered households, 3,
   177–178
Female sexuality, definition of, 83
Feminism:
   defining, 7–9
   and militarism, 308
   perspectives on deviance,
      267–269
   perspectives on families,
      158–163
   and postmodernism, 380–385
   and religion, 236–238
Feminist epistemology, 377–379
Feminist movement, 4
Feminist standpoint theory, 379
Feminist theory:
   frameworks of, 324–326
   purpose of, 325–326
   and sexuality, 383–385
   standpoint theory, 379
Feminization of poverty, 136
Fetal sex differentiation, 25–26
Financial strain and health, 197–198
Food and weight, 204–205
Friendship and gender, 96–97
Frigidity, 84

Gangs, 268–269
Gay, development of term, 98
Gay gene, 100
Gays, 97–102, 169–170
   in the military, 307–308
   and political movement, 384–385
   and work environment, 142
Gender-appropriate behavior, 31
Gender bending, 22
Gender bias:
   and the courts, 282–285
   in execution of laws, 296
   in media, 61–63
   in religious institutions, 233,
      240–243, 244
Gender and the courts, 282–285
Gender and culture, 51–79
   construction of knowledge, 65–69
   education, 51–74
   language, 53–56
   media and images, 56–65
   science, 74–77
Gender differences:
   in communication, 53–56
   and social learning, 337–339
Gender division of labor, 167–168,
   171–172
   housework, 146–147
Gender equity, policies for, 148
Gender expectations, 30–33

Gender and families, 174–181
Gender gap, 301–302
Gender and health care, 196–198
Gender identity, definition of, 30
Gender-neutral laws, 93
Gender and race and class, 13–15
Gender and religious beliefs, 240–243
Gender roles, definition of, 23
Gender segregation in labor force:
  blue-collar workers, 125–127
  clerical, 124–125
  farmers and migrant workers, 129
  professionals, 122, 124
  service workers, 127–128
Gender and sexuality, 82
Gender social construction (*see* Social construction of gender)
Gender socialization, 33–35
  as cause of rape, 280–281
Gender stereotyping learned in early childhood play, 37
Gender stratification, 115–116
Gendered institutions, definition of, 23
Genetic engineering, 223
Genotype, definition of, 27
Glass ceiling, 117–118, 133
Global assembly line, definition of, 126
Global restructuring, definition of, 126
Government positions, 297–303
Grass-roots politics, 309–310

Health insurance, 210, 211
Health issues:
  AIDS, 208–210
  alcohol, 206–207
  and gender roles, 196–198
  health care workers, 225–226
  insurance, 210, 211
  and race and class, 198–200
  smoking, 208–209
  substance abuse, 204, 207–208
  weight and food, 204–206
  women's health movement, 226–227
  in women's prisons, 286
  and work environment, 200–204
Hermaphroditism, 26
Heterosexism, definition of, 94
Heterosexuality, 84
  postmodernist perspective, 384
Higher education and women, 70–71
Hispanic Americans as faculty, 72
Historical materialism, 351–352
Homicide from family violence, 184
Homophobia, 101

definition of, 32, 94
Homosexuality (*see also* Gays; Lesbians):
  and crime, 269
  postmodernist perspective, 384
Hormonal sex differences, 29
Household:
  composition, 113, 165, 166
  definition of, 164
Householder, definition of, 164
Housewives, roles of, 145-146
Housework, 112–113, 115, 144–148
  as work, 12, 13–14
Human capital theory, 131
Humanitarian social change, 329
Hypertension, 196, 199

Identification theory and gender identity, 41–42
Ideology:
  and consciousness (Marx), 354–355
  definition of, 69
  and the family, 163
  and women's work, 111–113
Images:
  of reproduction in contemporary biology textbooks, 77
  of women in religion, 238–239
Immigration, rate of, 119
Imprisonment of women, 285 287
In vitro fertilization, 223
Incestuous abuse, 185–186
Inclusive thinking, 13
Income and gender segregation, 122
Industrialization and the economy, 108–109
Infancy, socialization during, 35–36
Infant mortality, 200
Institutional basis of gender, 22–23
Institutionalized power, 93
Intercourse, first, 85–86
Interdisciplinary scholarship on women, 7
Intermarriage, racial, 95
Internal gender segregation and occupations, 120–121
Intimate relationships (*see* Sexuality and intimate relationships)
Isolationism and motherhood, 171

Juvenile justice and gender, 284–285

Labeling and social deviance, 265–266
Labor force participation, 118–119
  and crime, 272
  of women, 106-113, 272
Laissez-faire economy, 339

Language and popular culture, 53–56
Latino American families, 178
  and religion, 248–249
Laws:
  and gender equity, 148–149
  and reproduction, 201–204
  and same-sex marriage, 101–102
  and sexual harassment, 141
  and women, 295–297
Lesbians, 97–102, 169-170
  and crime, 269
  in the military, 307–308
  and political movement, 384–385
  in women's prisons, 287
  and work environment, 142
Liberal feminism, 323–346, 385
  critique of, 343–344
  Martineau, Harriet, 333-335
  Mill, John Stuart and Harriet Taylor, 335-343
  vs. radical feminism, 371–373
  modern feminism, 326–327
  social-scientific thought, 327–330
  Wollstonecraft, Mary, 331–333
Liberalism:
  life-styles and, 329
  philosophical, 326
Life expectancy, 196–197
Life-styles and liberalism, 329
Love and intimate relationships, 92

Male sexuality, definition of, 83
Malleus Maleficarum, 234–235
Marital rape, 184
Marital status:
  of population, 164
  by race/ethnicity, 165
Marketing gender, 126
Marxist perspective of women's oppression, 350–357
Matriarchy, definition of, 175
Matrix of domination, 14
Media and culture, 51–53
Media and gendered images, 56–65
  capitalism, 63–64
  gender inequality within organizations, 61–63
  postmodernism, 64–65
  reflection hypothesis, 60
  role-learning theory, 60–61
Medicalization of childbirth, 221–223
Men helping at home, 167–168, 173
Men's studies, growth of, 15
Menopause, 91–92
Menstruation, 89
Mental health, 198
Meritocracy, definition of, 341

Mexican immigrants and gender expectations, 34
Midwives, 218–219, 221, 222
Migrant labor farming, 129
Military, 303–308
    and feminism, 308
    gays and lesbians, 307–308
    status of women, 304–306
Modernization and social change, 341–343
Morality:
    and abortion, 215
    and deviance, 267
    and sexuality, 82–83
Mortality rates, 197
Motherhood, 170–173
    and lesbians, 169–170
Music and sexism, 52

Native Americans, 180–181
    as faculty, 72
    labor and family-based economy, 108
Nature/nurture debate regarding behavior, 27–28
Nonmedical birth settings, 221–222
Nuclear family, definition of, 160
Nursing profession, 225

Object relations theory of gender identity, 41–42
Obstetric management of birth, 222
Occupation:
    and earnings, 111
    and status, 12
Occupational segregation, 119–120
"Old boy network," 123
Organizational theories of gender inequality, 61–63
Orgasms, 83
Overt discrimination, definition of, 129–130

Parenthood, 169–174
Patriarchal ideology of the culture, 76
Patriarchal institutions and power, 93
Patriarchal societies and men's power, 291–293
Patriarchal systems of religious thinking, 253
Patriarchy, 155–157
    and capitalism, 365–371
    definition of, 362
    and religious institutions, 244, 253
Phallocentric thinking, 83–84
Phenotype, definition of, 27
Physiological changes, 88–92

Pluralism model of the state, 293–294
Political activism, 309
Political campaigns, 300–301
Political-economic status of women and rape, 281–281
Political office, 297–303
Popular culture, definition of, 55–56
Pornography, 88
Position in society according to biology, 8
Postmodernist feminist theory:
    critique of, 382–383
    and the media, 64–65
Poverty, 136–138
    and crime, 272–273
Poverty line, definition of, 136
Power and deviance, 266–267
Power and families, 161, 168
Power and incest, 186
Power and politics, 290–322
    defining power, 291–293
    and feminism, 316–320
    and the law, 295–297
    women in government, 297–303
    women in the military, 303–308
    women's movement, 310-320
Power and relationships, 93
Power and sexuality, 87–88
Power and violence, 184
Power elite model of the state, 294
Powerlessness and victimization, 276
Pregnancy and childbirth, 217–223
Premarital sex, 86
Premenstrual syndrome (PMS), 89–90
Prison and women, 285–-87
Private sphere of women, 360–362
Prochoice vs. antiabortion, 250–252
Professional culture and women, 122–124
Promiscuous behavior, 83
Promotions, 133–134
Property crimes, 272
Prostitution, 266–267
Psychosomatic complaints, 224
Public assistance, 138–139
Public child care, 190–191
Public sphere of men, 360–362

Queer theory, 98–99

Race:
    and class, 13–15
    and intimate relationships, 95
    and occupational segregation, 121
    and sexuality, 82, 87–88

Race-ethnicity:
    and gender in television, 61–62
    and families, 174–181
    and health, 198–200
Racism:
    and discrimination in the labor force, 177
    and reproduction, 216–217
Radical feminism, 362–365, 386
    definition of, 347
    vs. liberal feminism, 371–373
    political context of, 348–349
    and sexuality, 364–365
    theology, 253–255
Rape, 276, 278–279
    law, 296
    trials, 282–283
Reflection hypothesis of women by the media, 60
Relationships:
    friendship, 96–97
    gay, lesbian, and bisexual, 97–102
    love and intimacy, 92–96
Religion, 231–258
    and antifeminism, 249–252
    faith and spirituality, 252–255
    and feminism, 236–238
    and gender, 240–243
    and images of women, 238–239
    and racism, 247–249
    and social control, 234–235
    sociological perspectives, 232–234
    women's status in religious institutions, 243–247
Religious belief and sexual behavior, 233, 241–242
Religious right, the, 249–250
Religious texts as interpretive documents, 239–240
Reproduction, 210–225
    abortion, 213–216
    birth control, 212–213
    childbirth, 217–223
    feminist perspectives, 210–217
    and protective legislation, 201–204
    and racism, 216–217
    technology, 223
Research studies and gender of researcher, 47
Resentment between men and women, sources of, 161–162
Retirement and stress, 40
Roe v. *Wade*, 213–215, 250
Role-learning theory and sexist racist images, 60–61
Russian women in socialist society, 369

Salary inequality:
  in the media, 63
  men's vs. women's, 105, 117
Same-sex violence, 183–184
Sanctions of society, 30–33
Schools and the socialization
    process, 38–39
Science/gender system, 75
Scientific knowledge and gender,
    74–77
Scientific method of study, 378
Second Great Awakening, 236
Secondary labor markets, 132
Service workers, 127–128
Sex, definition of, 20, 83
Sex chromosomes, 25–26
Sex discrimination, 46
Sex education, 188
Sex/gender system, 363–364
Sex reassignment, 26–27
Sexism:
  as ideology (Mannheim), 68–69
  in media (*see* Media and
      gendered images)
  popular culture, 51–53
Sexual abuse, 185
Sexual harassment, 141–142
Sexual liberation, movements of,
    82
Sexual orientation, 98
Sexual politics, definition of, 87
Sexual violence, 87
Sexuality and criminal behavior,
    262, 267–268
Sexuality and feminist theory,
    383–385
Sexuality and intimate relationships,
    80–104
  attitudes and behaviors, 83–87
  and bisexuals, 97–102
  development of, 88–92
  and friendship, 96–97
  and gays and lesbians, 97–102
  history of, 81–83
  and love, 92–96
  and power, 87–88
  and race, 87–88
Sexuality and radical feminism,
    364–365
Sexually dimorphic traits, 27–28
Single-father families, 174
Single-female heads of household,
    teens, 187
Single-parent African American
    households, 187
Slavery and labor, 107
Smoking, 208
Social construction of gender,
    19–50
  biological explanations, 24–30

institutional basis, 22–23
  during life course, 35–41
  limitations of, 46–47
  race and gender identity, 33–35
  sanctions and expectations of
      society, 30–33
  theories, 41–45
Social control ad religion, 234–235
Social deviance (*see* Crime)
Social expectations, 30–33
Social factors and position in
    society, 8
Social inequality, 115–117
Social learning and liberalism,
    337–339
Social learning theory and gender
    identity, 42–43
Social movements, definition of,
    311
Social problems and families,
    181–192
  child care, 189–192
  teen pregnancy, 186–189
  violence, 181–186
Social roles and expectations, 23
Social structure, definition of, 6–7
Socialist feminism, 357–358,
    385–386
  definition of, 347
Socialist societies, status of women
    in, 367–370
Socialization and gender identity,
    30–35
Sociological framework of study,
    16
Sociological imagination, 4–7
Sociology of knowledge, 65–69
Spousal abuse, 181–185
Standpoint theory of feminism, 379
State theory, 293–294
Status in families, measuring,
    164–165
Sterilization of women, 216
Stigma attached to gay identities,
    100
Stratification, definition of, 115
Stress:
  and home, 144
  patterns for men and women,
      33–34
  and work, 125, 144
Subculture of violence perspective,
    279
Subfamily, definition of, 164–165
Substance abuse, 206–208
Suffrage movement, 313
Symbolic annihilation of women by
    the media, 56
Symbolic interaction and gender
    identity, 44

Technology:
  and the economy, 110–111
  and housework, 147
Teen pregnancy, 186–189
Television and gender, 57
Temperance movement, 313
Testosterone levels, 29–30
Title VII of the Civil Rights Bill of
    1964, 148
Title IX of the Educational
    Amendments of 1972, 148
Tobacco use, 208–209
Tokenism, 140–141
Transnational families, 179

Underrepresentation of women:
  as military officers, 304
  in politics, 297–303
Unions, membership in, 126–127,
    130–131

Victims of crime, 274–282
Violence in the family, 181–186
Violent crime and victim-offender
    relationship, 275

Weight and food, 204–205
Welfare, 138–139
Wife abuse, 181–185
Wife battering, 182–185
Witchcraft, 234, 235
Woman's Bible, The, 237–238
Women:
  as blue-collar workers, 125–127
  as clergy, 245–246
  as clerical workers, 124–125
  as criminals, 269–274
  and education, 69–74
  as faculty, 70–71, 72
  as health care workers, 225–226
  as heart patients, 76
  as professionals, 122–124
  as service workers, 127–128
  status of, 1–4
"Women worthies" approach for
    recognizing women, 12

Women's health movement, 226–227
Women's liberation groups, 317–318
Women's movement, 310–320
  and civil rights movement,
      316–317
Women's prisons, 285–287
Women's studies, curriculum
    changes in, 10–13
Women's suffrage, 311–312
Women's work (*see* Work issues)
Work issues, 105–152
  class stratification, 116–117
  defining work, 114–115

Work issues, *cont.*
    environments, 139–143
    and the family, 143–148,
        167–168, 339–341 (*see
        also* Family, vs. work)
    gender equity, 115–116,
        148–150
    and health, 200–204

historical perspective on
    women's work, 106–113,
    156–157
poverty, 136–138
status of women, 117–136
stratification of genders,
    115–116, 148–150
studies of, 114–115

welfare, 138–139
Work life vs. family life, 113
Workfare, definition of, 138
Workplace culture, 143–143

Zimbabwe women in socialist
    society, 369